Museum of Anthropology, University of Michigan
Memoirs, Number 52

The Cherokees of Tuckaleechee Cove

by

Jon Marcoux

with contributions by

Kandace D. Hollenbach
Boyce Driskell
Jessica L. Vavrasek
Judith A. Sichler
Jeremy Sweat
Katherine McMillan
Stephen Carmody
Phyllis Rigney
Erik Johanson

Ann Arbor, Michigan
2012

Printed in the United States of America
ISBN 978-0-915703-79-1

Cover design by Katherine Clahassey

The University of Michigan Museum of Anthropology currently publishes two monograph series, Anthropological Papers and Memoirs, as well as an electronic series in CD-ROM form. For a complete catalog, write to Museum of Anthropology Publications, 4013 Museums Building, 1109 Geddes Avenue, Ann Arbor, MI 48109-1079, or see www.lsa.umich.edu/umma/.

Library of Congress Cataloging-in-Publication Data

Marcoux, Jon Bernard.
The Cherokees of Tuckaleechee cove / by Jon Marcoux ; with contributions by Kandace D. Hollenbach...[et.al.].
p. cm. -- (Museum of anthropology, University of Michigan memoirs ; number 52)
Includes bibliographical references.
ISBN 978-0-915703-79-1 (alk. paper)
1. Cherokee Indians--Tennessee--Townsend Region--Antiquities. 2. Cherokee Indians--Tennessee--Townsend Region--History. 3. Social archaeology--Tennessee--Townsend Region. 4. Excavations (Archaeology)--Tennessee--Townsend Region. 5. Townsend Region (Tenn.)--Antiquities. I. Hollenbach, Kandace D. II. Title.
E99.C5M3397 2012
975.004'97557--dc23
2012034199

The paper used in this publication meets the requirements of the ANSI Standard Z39.48-1984 (Permanence of Paper)

Contents

Figures

The authors sincerely regret omitting a number of important contributors to the Townsend Archaeological Project in our acknowledgments. The Tennessee Department of Transportation (TDOT) and Federal Highway Administration (FHWA) provided the funding for the project (Project No. 05006-1238-04). We thank Gerald Kline, manager of the TDOT Environmental Division, Archaeology Section, for his role in implementing the project. We also wish to thank the Tennessee State Historic Preservation Office (SHPO), the Tennessee Division of Archaeology (TDOA), and the Advisory Council on Historic Preservation (ACHP) for their efforts. Finally, we are indebted to the Eastern Band of Cherokee Indians and the Chickasaw Nation for their consultation.

Tables

Preface and Acknowledgments

This volume reports the analysis and interpretation of Cherokee remains that were recovered from the Townsend sites (40Bt89, 40Bt90 and 40Bt91) by archaeologists from the University of Tennessee between February 10, 1999, and December 31, 2001. Excavations at the sites were performed prior to the widening of Tennessee Highway 73 (U.S. Route 321) near Townsend, Tennessee. During this period, Charles (Chuck) Bentz initially served as Archaeologist in General Charge (Principal Investigator), but was replaced towards the conclusion of fieldwork by George (Nick) Fielder, then State Archaeologist and Director of the Tennessee Division of Archaeology.

Artifacts, samples and observations recovered during fieldwork come from site localities within an approximate 300-foot-wide construction right-of-way beginning at about mile 29.5 and extending eastward for about two miles along the route of Tennessee Highway 73 (U.S. Route 321) in Tuckaleechee Cove, an area of eastern Blount County, Tennessee, within the shadow of the Great Smoky Mountains National Park to the east. Nestled along the south bank of the Little River, Site 40Bt89 (Kinsel Springs Site) is to the west and separated from Site 40Bt90 (Apple Barn Site) by a small ridge spur extending almost to the southern bank of the river. Sites 40Bt90 and 40Bt91 (Pony Ride Site), to the east, are contiguous or nearly so, occupying parts of the same landform. These two sites are separated rather arbitrarily by a modern-day driveway.

Site 40Bt94 (Gas Company Site) is further to the east-southeast along the highway corridor, separated from the other sites by a rather broad hill spur that originally extended nearly to the southern bank of the river. While this site was part of the project, no Cherokee structures were located in this area. Although bisected by two hill spurs and certainly not homogeneous in content or distribution of archaeological materials, the four Townsend sites have been treated as a site complex for most purposes of analysis and reporting and are referenced generally as the "Townsend sites" for purposes of simplicity.

I took over the role of Archaeologist in General Charge (Principal Investigator) of the Townsend Project in April, 2002, during the very initial phases of laboratory processing. As director of the newly organized Archaeological Research Laboratory (ARL)—charged with the responsibility to process, analyze, and interpret the 1200 boxes (cubic feet) of artifacts; thousands of field maps and drawings; reams of field documents; and thousands of float, and other, samples—I organized teams to generate the necessary data and produce final reports.

The "database" team, led by Nick Herrmann, was responsible for developing a system to record, house, and organize the Townsend Project information. With the help of Rod Riley of IBM, a relational database was designed that allowed analysts to record artifact and other data directly into the database through a web-based interface available at each work station. Spatial data including thousands of field maps were geo-referenced and entered into an ArcGIS database.

As another part of its duties, the database team assessed and assigned a temporal/cultural designation (referred to as the TCA for temporal/cultural affiliation) for each provenience unit excavated and recorded at the Townsend sites.

Obviously, materials from well-preserved deposits that produced datable artifacts (ceramics, projectile points, beads, etc.) and/or dated samples were assigned TCAs reflecting placement into a cultural period. Others were assigned to more general categories such as "prehistoric" or "Archaic." Because of extensive plowing and other disturbances from 200 years of Euroamerican utilization of the Townsend sites, archaeological deposits were generally poorly preserved. Intact deposits were found only in a few small areas beneath the plow zone. Most of the intact deposits came from the

3395 features and thousands of postholes that were preserved in the otherwise mostly sterile deposits beneath the plow zone. For this reason, most of the analysis conducted on materials from the Townsend sites has focused on the contents and context of features like pits, postholes and houses.

After initial processing, so-called "period" teams began the arduous task of data analysis, interpretation, and writing in order to produce cultural-historical reports like this monograph. The Cherokee period team was led by Brett H. Riggs, Research Archaeologist at the Research Laboratories of Archaeology at the University of North Carolina, Chapel Hill, who along with Jon Marcoux, a PhD candidate at UNC, Chapel Hill, at that time, collaborated with the Archaeological Research Laboratory on the research and writing of this volume.

This archaeological report, penned primarily by Jon Marcoux, constitutes the first synthesis of archaeological data associated with late seventeenth- and early eighteenth-century Cherokee lifeways. It is also the first major work addressing Cherokee archaeology published since the 1980s. In the pages of this monograph, the reader will find a thorough discussion of the political, economic, and social landscape within which the Cherokees of Tuckaleechee Cove lived, as well as detailed descriptions and quantitative analyses of architecture, archaeological features, pottery, lithic artifacts, glass trade beads, and ethnobotantical and faunal remains. These data are combined to construct the most complete picture we have to date of what life was like for the members of late seventeenth- and early eighteenth-century Cherokee communities. The research into Townsend ceramics reported in this volume was greatly facilitated by the ARL ceramics team, led first by Todd Ahlman, then Scott Hammerstedt; the subsistence team led by Kandace Hollenbach; and the lithics team led by myself. Chapter 8 on stone tools and Chapter 10 on foodways were penned for this report by members of the lithics team and subsistence team, respectively.

The Townsend project, by any measure, was a huge undertaking involving hundreds of participants over the 11 years since its inception. I have tried to compile a list of participants (see Appendix A) that indicates their respective role/s in the project. All the participants in this project deserve our gratitude for their service, sometimes under trying circumstances. Please accept my apology if I have overlooked anyone.

Boyce Driskell, PhD, RPA
Principal Investigator

Chapter 1

Introduction

Individuals have been attempting to construct a comprehensive understanding of political, economic, and social life in Cherokee communities for over three hundred years. This has proven to be a formidable challenge given that Cherokee community "life" encompasses the dynamic histories of thousands of folk reaching across centuries from prehistory to today. In recent years, students in the disciplines of anthropology, archaeology, and history have made significant gains in this endeavor; however, there remains a conspicuous gap in our knowledge of Cherokee community life (e.g., Hatley 1995; Keel 1976; Perdue 1998; Riggs 1989; Rodning 2004; Schroedl 1986a, 1986b, 2000). The gap corresponds to the English Contact period of Cherokee history (ca. A.D. 1670–1740), a period of marked change that begins with the establishment of the Charles Town colony in A.D. 1670 and ends in the aftermath of a major smallpox epidemic that devastated Cherokee communities in A.D. 1738. The intervening years of this period witnessed increased interaction with European colonial governments, the emergence of the deerskin trade, and the Yamasee War among other events (Schroedl 2000:212). It is difficult for historians to address this period because written accounts of Cherokee communities are sparse until after A.D. 1715. Archaeology has great potential to address this period; however, the discipline is constrained by the task of identifying and excavating sites that were occupied in the late seventeenth and early eighteenth centuries. Presently, the number of such components is low in comparison to later eighteenth- and nineteenth-century occupations.

In this study, I address this gap by synthesizing extant data from surface collections and excavations of Cherokee settlements that were occupied during the English Contact period. Through the writings of historians, we have the general historic context of this period, but as historian John Phillip Reid (1976:117) admits, "We will never know the Cherokee until we hear from these lesser individuals: the nonheadman, the warriors, hunters, farmers, and traders [I would add women also] who did not negotiate or played secondary roles in negotiations with the Europeans." How would this period of history "read" in the words of these everyday folk living in Cherokee communities? How would these stories of life compare to the narratives written by historians?

I examine in greater detail a number of questions that address how this period was negotiated by the Cherokees through change and/or stability in the daily lives of community members. I use the household as the basic unit of my analysis because it represents the most fundamental and pervasive unit of economic and social production in the archaeological record (e.g., Blanton 1994; Hatch 1995; Lightfoot et al. 1998; Muller 1997; Riggs 1989, 1999; Schroedl 1989; Wilk and Netting 1984; Wilk and Rathje 1982). How were late seventeenth- and early eighteenth-century Cherokee communities organized socially, economically, and politically? What was the demographic composition of English Contact period Cherokee households? What were the similarities and differences in material culture among households in the same community? How were these reflective of identities of solidarity or separateness in the community? How did life in households during this period compare to that of households predating and postdating the establishment of sustained European contact?

I address these questions from the perspective of a particular Cherokee community located in the Little River Valley of eastern Tennessee, known to archaeologists as the Townsend sites (40Bt89, 40Bt90, 40Bt91, and 40Bt94). The community manifested at the Townsend sites was definitely not a major player in the colonial scene. In fact, its only appearance in the written record comes as an epitaph in Henry Timberlake's ([1762] 2001:118–19) journal, where he laments why anyone would abandon such a lovely valley. The mystery of the community's abandonment poses a deceptively simple research problem whose answer can only be found in an historical analysis of the playing out of the various strategies that constituted daily life in Cherokee households amid the sweeping social, political, and economic changes of the late seventeenth and early eighteenth centuries. The community's place in the regional landscape, its community history, the distribution of its households, its architecture, and its pottery were all crucial components of strategic actions taken by households within the community. In this way the members of the Townsend community were hardly passive recipients of history, but were active participants in it (Wesson 2008).

My study is presented in the ten chapters that follow this introductory chapter. Chapters 2 and 3 focus on establishing the historical, theoretical, and chronological frameworks that support this study. Chapter 2 provides a detailed examination of the historical context encompassing the English Contact period. In this chapter, I combine information from published secondary sources as well as primary sources to describe the social, political, and economic landscape inhabited by the Cherokees in the late seventeenth and early eighteenth centuries. In Chapter 3, I present a brief summary of archaeological research concerning Cherokee communities. In this chapter I also introduce an alternative theoretical framework for my study that is grounded in the concepts of agency and daily practice.

Chapter 4 introduces the case study for my research—the Townsend sites—within a broader discussion of Cherokee geography and settlement patterns. The next six chapters contain the results of the data analyses. Chapter 5 focuses on assessing the changes that occurred in Cherokee conceptions of domestic space and time during the English Contact period. This chapter includes my description and analysis of architecture, community organization, and subsurface pit features at Townsend and other Cherokee sites. Chapter 6 examines the features from Townsend and assesses their use while Chapter 7 discusses the household pottery assemblages from the Townsend sites. This discussion focuses on characterizing inter-household ceramic variability as a product of a collection of resident potters practicing distinct potting traditions. This hybridity in pottery assemblages leads me to argue that a significant number of individuals in the Townsend community were most likely immigrants from other Cherokee settlements.

In Chapter 8, stone implements found in Cherokee contexts at the Townsend sites are described and discussed by others working on this category of material culture. Chapter 9 includes my formulation of a chronological framework for English Contact period glass bead assemblages. This framework tackles a long-standing obstacle by providing researchers with a reliable way to identify English Contact period Cherokee occupational components. Chapter 10, authored by subsistence specialists, discusses Cherokee foodways as suggested by the data recovered from the Cherokee component at the Townsend sites.

In Chapter 11, I summarize the results of my analyses and discuss the strategies enacted by Cherokee households in their attempts to adapt to the social, political, and economic turmoil of the late seventeenth- and early eighteenth-century Southeast.

It is important to note that this work builds upon research that I presented in a previously published book, *Pox, Empire, Shackles, and Hides: The Townsend Site, 1670–1715* (Marcoux 2010). I am thankful to the University of Alabama Press for allowing me to use material from that book in the chapters covering historical context, architecture, and pottery. In this work, the reader will find additional data on these topics, as well as a number of new chapters covering archaeological features, stone tools, glass trade beads, and foodways.

Chapter 2

Pox, Empire, Shackles, and Hides

The English Contact Period in the Southeast 1670–1740

Differences in epistemology and methodology separate the many scholarly disciplines studying the past (e.g., literature, archaeology, history, paleontology); however, all are united by a shared concern with reconstructing the world in which their study objects once existed. Historians have done a great deal of this sort of contextual reconstruction in writing about the Cherokees in the late seventeenth and early eighteenth centuries (e.g., Hatley 1995; Corkran 1962; Crane [1929] 2004; Gallay 2002; Oatis 2004; Reid 1976). In this chapter, I outline the historical context for what I call the "English Contact period" in the Southeast beginning with the founding of Charleston in 1670 and ending with a smallpox epidemic that ravaged Cherokee communities in 1740.[1]

My discussion focuses primarily on the period leading up to the Yamasee War in 1715, for I believe that the historical processes operating during this period were crucial in setting the stage for the rest of the century. I outline three historical forces that I believe were instrumental in forging a dynamic, even chaotic, landscape across the Southeast during the period from 1670 to 1715. The interplay of these three forces—which included epidemic disease, European colonial competition, and trade in Indian slaves and deerskins—produced massive demographic and sociopolitical disruptions whose effects forever altered the histories of Indian groups and colonists (Bowne 2005; Ethridge 2006; Gallay 2002; Riggs, in press; Wood 1989). Ethnohistorian Robbie Ethridge's (2006, 2010) use of the "shatter zone" concept presents a particularly useful way to frame interpretations of this period. Originally defined by Eric Wolf (1982), the "shatter zone" describes a landscape that is rife with turmoil stemming from the incorporation of indigenous cultures into the transatlantic European trading economy. The Yamasee War in 1715 was in many ways the capstone of the English Contact period, marking the culmination of the chaos caused by the three historical forces. The war also was a catalyst for a number of dramatic changes that affected the social, political, and economic lives of both colonists and Indian groups across the Southeast (Crane [1929] 2004; Merrell 1989a; Oatis 2004; Ramsey 2003). I consider some of these postwar changes and their effects on Indian and colonial communities. The "English Contact period" was not a singular regional phenomenon; therefore, I argue that each case history should ultimately be viewed as the result of the complex, local, and highly contingent intersections of Indian and European colonial strategies. Consequently, in the conclusion of the chapter, I rely on historical syntheses and primary documents to explore the particular strategies that Cherokee groups appear to have enacted while negotiating this turbulent period.

The Shatter Zone: 1670–1740

Path to the Yamasee War: 1670–1715

Recently, the main historical processes that forged the southeastern shatter zone have been detailed by myself and others (e.g., Beck 2010; Jennings 2010; Ethridge 2006, 2010; Kelton 2002, 2010; see also Marcoux 2010 for a more detailed discussion). Here I offer a brief outline of what I argue are the three primary historical forces that acted in concert to cause such massive social, political, and economic disruption: (1) the spread of epidemic disease, (2) European colonial competition and conflict, and (3) trade in Indian slaves and deerskins.

Many researchers have reported on the devastating effects European diseases had upon native populations in North America (e.g., Dobyns 1983; Milner 1980; Smith 1987; Ward and Davis 1991, 2001). While it is difficult to quantify the losses suffered by Indian groups during the years leading up to the Yamasee War, Peter Wood's (1989) comprehensive compilation of historical population estimates for southeastern Indian groups offers a reliable estimate. Wood determined that between the years 1685 and 1715, the Indian population in the Southeast declined from 199,400 to 90,100, a reduction of nearly 55% (Wood 1989:90–91).

The economic and strategic ambitions associated with colonization naturally generated conflict among the fragile North American beachheads of England, Spain, and France (Gallay 2002:2). Spain and France were, after all, eternal rivals of England, and violent conflicts among the three colonial superpowers (or, more often, among their Indian allies) punctuated this period. The proprietors of the South Carolina colony were the most aggressive of the colonial powers. They implemented a proactive defensive strategy that deployed allied Indian groups to create a buffer zone protecting the colony from the Spanish and French and their Indian allies (Gallay 2002:96–97; Oatis 2004:38). Beginning in the 1680s, colonial officials set about encouraging allied Indian groups to settle along the Savannah River with the construction of a trading post at Savannah Town. By the first decade of the eighteenth century, the trading post had accomplished its mission by attracting numerous allied groups including the Savannah, Yamasee, Apalachicola, Yuchi, and Chickasaw (Gallay 2002:73).

The first fifteen years of the eighteenth century also witnessed the use of Indian allies in major colonist-led Indian military forays that cumulatively resulted in the deaths and enslavement of thousands of Indians. These forays included Colonel James Moore's invasions of Spanish Florida as part of Queen Anne's War, in 1702 and 1704. These operations, which resulted in the destruction of the Spanish-allied Apalachee Indians, included 370 Yamasee Indians and 1000 Muskogee-speaking Indians respectively (Crane [1929] 2004:79–81; Gallay 2002:136, 145; Oatis 2004:47, 50–51). Against French colonial interests, South Carolina traders and over 2000 allied Indians conducted attacks on French-allied Indians in 1705, 1709, and 1711 (Crane [1929] 2004:85–86; Gallay 2002:288–92). The buffer zone strategy and colonial raids resulted in the resettlement, enslavement, and/or death of thousands of Indians across the Southeast.

Sustained trade between southeastern Indian groups and the Spanish had existed for nearly a century when Charles Town was founded in 1670. The founding of English colonies in the Southeast, however, brought about major changes to the existing exchange system. Unlike Spanish colonies, the economic structures of South Carolina and Virginia were geared toward generating large profits by producing mass quantities of goods and resources for export. The sheer scale of slavery and deer hunting in this system produced profound sociopolitical disruptions that were variably felt by every Indian group across the Southeast. Based on transport records following major military campaigns (described above) and trader accounts, Gallay (2002:299), for example, estimated the total number of Indian slaves that were taken between 1670 and 1715 to be between 24,000 and 51,000 individuals.

The burgeoning trade in deerskins, which exported an average of 54,000 skins to England between 1699 and 1715, also resulted in significant changes to Indian communities on the regional and local levels. The effects were obviously variable from community to community, but a few general issues were widespread. First, the rather inelastic European demand for deerskins resulted in competition between colonies and gave certain Indian communities bargaining leverage in dealing with the colonies (Merrell 1989a). Second, entire Indian towns left their traditional territories in order to be closer to European trading posts. Finally, Indian communities themselves underwent fundamental changes as the growing participation in a commercial economy forced the reorganization of domestic life, as resident European traders clashed with local communities, and as families faced mounting debt.

The Yamasee War

The Yamasee War began on Good Friday, April 15, 1715 when a number of South Carolinian trade officials were murdered in the Yamasee town of Pocotaligo. These initial murders were quickly followed by major Yamasee attacks on plantations around Port Royal, south of Charleston, where the Yamasee managed to kill over 100 colonists and set the rest of the settlement's population to flight (Pennington 1931:253). In the following weeks, most of the English traders in the towns of the Tallapoosa, Abiehka, Alabama, Ochese, Coweta, Choctaw, Chicksaw, Catawba, and Cherokees had either been killed or chased off (Oatis 2004:128–32). Furthermore, the Catawba and a small group of Cherokees raided plantations north of Charleston and even managed to briefly capture a South Carolina militia garrison (Crane [1929] 2004:171–72).

South Carolina's military response to the Yamasee and Catawba raids was swift. Only a week after the murders at Pocotaligo, the governor of South Carolina personally led militia forces to decisive victories against the Yamasee towns, forcing them to retreat southward to the Altamaha River (Oatis 2004:144). Also, days after the assaults north of Charleston, South Carolina militia captain George Chicken managed to rout the invading Catawba force in an ambush that came to be known as the "Battle of the Ponds" (Crane [1929] 2004:172; Oatis 2004:145). While these were the only major military engagements, the Yamasee War officially carried on for almost two years (along with the anxiety and fear felt by the colonists in Charleston) until a peace with the Lower Creeks was brokered in 1717.

While historians have traditionally presented the Yamasee War as a united Indian revolt against the abuses of English traders, recent scholarship has taken a new direction, exploring the various motivations and strategies of the Indian groups that participated in the attacks (e.g., Gallay 2002; Merrell 1989a; Oatis 2004; Ramsey 2003). The authors of these works argue that while some of the Indian participants were in collusion, the Yamasee War was not a pan-Indian conspiracy carried out according to a "master plan" (Oatis 2004:123). Instead, they hold that each group acted toward its own goals. Some groups, like the Yamasee, had mounting pressure from debt, abuse by traders, and the fear of eventually being enslaved, as well as the encroachment of Europeans on their "treaty-protected" lands (Gallay 2002:330–31; Haan 1981; Ramsey 2003:46). For Muskogean, Cherokee, Chickasaw, and Choctaw groups, encroachment was not an issue during this period.

Renegotiating Diplomacy in the Post-Yamasee War Southeast: 1715–1740

As the confusion of the first violent weeks of the war settled down, it was obvious that the social, political, and economic landscape of the Southeast had changed dramatically and that Indian groups and colonial officials would have to renegotiate their diplomatic and trading relationships. For South Carolinians, in a matter of weeks the landscape had transformed from one of security, being surrounded by a protective buffer zone of Indian allies, to one of utter vulnerability (Oatis 2004:142). As for the instigators of the war, only weeks after their first successful raids, the Yamasee had lost a quarter of their number to death or slavery, and they were forced to move their towns south to seek protection from the Spanish (Oatis 2004:178). While not creating as perilous a situation as that experienced by the Yamasee, the chaos of war caused a temporary but crucial breach in the fundamental diplomatic and trading relationships among all southeastern Indian groups and South Carolina. In doing so, the war created a moment when everything was on the table and negotiable. Consequently, the twenty-five-year period following the war (ca. 1715–1740) included significant changes in diplomacy and trade that reflected the attempts of all groups to adjust to this new postwar landscape.

Postwar Diplomacy

The Yamasee War exposed a major flaw in South Carolina's diplomatic strategy and forced a change in the way colonial officials handled diplomacy with southeastern Indian groups. This flaw was exposed when the main southern and northern components of South Carolina's protective buffer zone, the Yamasee and the Catawba, unexpectedly became the colony's main adversaries in the war. The surprise nature of the attacks by presumed allies suggests that South Carolinians must have suffered from a complete diplomatic breakdown with their Indian neighbors. According to historian William Ramsey (2003), that is exactly what had occurred when an internal dispute consumed the regulatory board of trade (Commissioners of the Indian Trade) to the point where it ignored all business with Indian groups between November 1714 and the outbreak of the war in April 1715. Because trade formed the diplomatic "bonds of peace" between South Carolina and Indians, this "shut down" essentially severed all official contact with southeastern Indian groups and created "an abrupt and utter diplomatic vacuum everywhere" (Ramsey 2003:67–68). Because tensions over existing disputes were already at a boiling point in Yamasee and Muskogean communities when the diplomatic blackout began, Ramsey believes that South Carolina's attempt to negotiate in April 1715 came far too late.

In rebuilding diplomatic relations with Indian groups after the Yamasee War, South Carolina officials sought to avoid another disaster by making diplomatic relations with Indian groups as streamlined as possible. To do this, the government attempted to reduce the number of Indian entities with whom the colony negotiated by lumping politically independent Indian towns into composite groups called "nations" and assigning a single individual to "speak" for the entire group (Oatis 2004:193, 195, 212). This "nationalizing" strategy was evident, for example, in the designs of George Chicken's 1725 diplomatic mission to crown a "King" among the Cherokees (Chicken [1725] 1916:126–30) and Tobias Fitch's 1725 mission to appoint a "Comander in Chief" of the Creek nation (Fitch [1725] 1916:209). The overt attempt to create European-style national power structures among Indian groups was one-sided and quite ineffectual during this period. South Carolina's lesser mission to group Indian towns into collectivities, however, was much more successful because it tapped into a historical process that was already well underway among Indian groups by 1715 (Oatis 2004:242–43). This process, which was actually a strategic response of Indian towns trying to mitigate the disruptions of the shatter zone, included demographic consolidation carried out through the merging of Indian towns and the "adoption" of various refugee groups by more stable towns. It was likely the convergence of South Carolina's "nationalizing" strategy with the Indians' strategic response to population loss that resulted in the emergence of geographically bounded "ethnic" collectivities with identities like "Creek," "Cherokee," and "Catawba" (Knight 1994; Galloway 1995; Hudson 2002; Kowalewski 2006; Merrell 1989a; Rodning 2002).

One prominent feature of the southeastern landscape that did not change dramatically after the Yamasee War involved the violent conflicts that frequently erupted among Indian groups. Indeed, South Carolina officials spent much of the period from 1715 to 1740 attempting to "put out fires" by mediating these conflicts. During the post-Yamasee War period, conflicts among various southeastern groups revolved around a central war that was carried on between the Creek and Cherokees. The Creek-Cherokee War began in the midst of the Yamasee War when a Creek diplomatic delegation was murdered by a number of Cherokees in the Lower Cherokee town of Tugaloo.[2] Violent clashes between certain Creek and Cherokee groups had sporadically broken out in the years before the Yamasee War; this event, however, initiated a decade of violence that engulfed all Cherokee and Creek towns, destroyed entire towns, caused significant trade disruption, and eventually spread westward to the Choctaw and Chickasaw (Crane [1929] 2004:273–74; McDowell 1992:222; Oatis 2004:53, 235). In addition to the Creek-Cherokee War, the period included frequent raiding against Catawba and Cherokee towns by the Iroquois, Lower Creek raids against Yamasee refugee groups in Spanish Florida, and a little reported but apparently significant ongoing conflict between particular Upper Cherokee towns and French-allied Illinois Indian towns (Merrell 1989a:89, 97–98; Norton [1816] 1970:46, 82, 262–64; Oatis 2004:77, 132, 200, 210, 236, 246). South Carolinians were finally able to arrange a tenuous peace between the Creek and Cherokees in 1727; however, the colony never aspired to creating a lasting peace among all southeastern Indian groups, for they would always need belligerent Indian allies to fight against groups allied with the French or Spanish.

The complete breakdown of diplomacy and trade between South Carolina and Indian groups at the beginning of the Yamasee War provided an ideal opportunity for England's imperial rivals to reassert their colonial ambitions. By the first decade of the eighteenth century, Spanish colonial interests had suffered a string of defeats ending with South Carolina's raids on St. Augustine and their Apalachee missions. The Yamasee War briefly provided much needed succor to Spain's deflated imperial ambition in the form of Indian groups in search of alliance and trade. The resettlement of retreating Yamasee in Spanish Florida was taken as an optimistic sign, as were the diplomatic overtures of Creek headmen from the Tallapoosa and Coweta (Crane [1929] 2004:185). Having cut themselves off from English trade, these latter groups were in search of an alternative source for trade. By 1718, however, it was clear to the Spanish that they could not offer the Creek anywhere near the volume of trade that the English or even the French could, and that a long-term Creek alliance with Spain would probably never materialize (Oatis 2004:214–19).

During this period, France proved to be a more formidable colonial adversary for South Carolina. France's imperial ascendancy began in the Louisiana colony in 1717 with an influx of financial support from the mother country and a restructuring of the colonial economy that boosted plantation agriculture and Indian trading (Gallay 2002:339; Oatis 2004:213–14). That same year, the French were able to negotiate with Tallapoosa and Alabama Indian groups to build a fort and trading post, called Fort Toulouse, on territory at the confluence of the Coosa and Tallapoosa Rivers (Crane [1929] 2004:256). From this foothold deep within territory formerly dominated by South Carolinian traders, the French not only offered competition to South Carolina traders for the deerskin trade, they also harried English colonial ambitions by continually attempting to sway Creek and Cherokee groups to their influence. Like the Spanish, the French were ultimately never able to outpace South Carolina in the pursuit of Indian trade and alliances; however, their persistent presence as an alternative source of trade offered crucial diplomatic bargaining leverage to Chickasaw, Creek, and Cherokee groups between 1715 and 1740 (Martin 1994:314; Waselkov 1993, 1994).

Postwar Changes to Trade

The Yamasee War brought about two significant alterations to the existing trading system—the cessation of the trade in Indian slaves and South Carolina's attempt to reform the deerskin trade. The precipitous decline in the Indian slave trade likely came about as a result of decreases in both supply and demand (Gallay 2002:353–54; Oatis 2004:122, 152; Ramsey 2003:45). If Wood's (1989) demographic estimates for the previous period (ca. 1685–1715) are to be believed, then the combination of slave raids and disease reduced the southeastern Indian population by half in 1715. When population losses at this scale were combined with the accelerating rate of consolidation among surviving populations, the result was that the supply of potential slaves effectively dried up.

In regard to the demand for Indian slaves, the Yamasee War introduced South Carolinians to the real threat of Indian attacks on the colony. The war also brought to light the fact that when conflicts with Indians arose, there would be a large population of Indian slaves among the colonists that could easily turn on their masters. These fears likely influenced South Carolina planters to begin shifting their slave labor pool from Indians to Africans around 1715. The shift in preference to African slaves may also have been due to their long tenure as plantation labor in the Caribbean and the planters' belief that African slaves were more resistant to European disease (Martin 1994:313). Whatever the reason for this shift in demand, the result was a drastic and permanent decrease in the number of Indian slaves owned by South Carolina households. In a survey of South Carolina will transcripts, for example, Ramsey (2001:173) found that household ownership of Indian slaves declined from 26% in 1714 to just 2% by 1730.

The Yamasee War also brought about significant government reform in the deerskin trade. The disruptions caused in the first weeks of the war forced South Carolinians to restart the deerskin trade virtually from scratch, for in one year the colonists saw practically all the Indian groups involved in the trade become their enemies, they lost most of their experienced traders, and

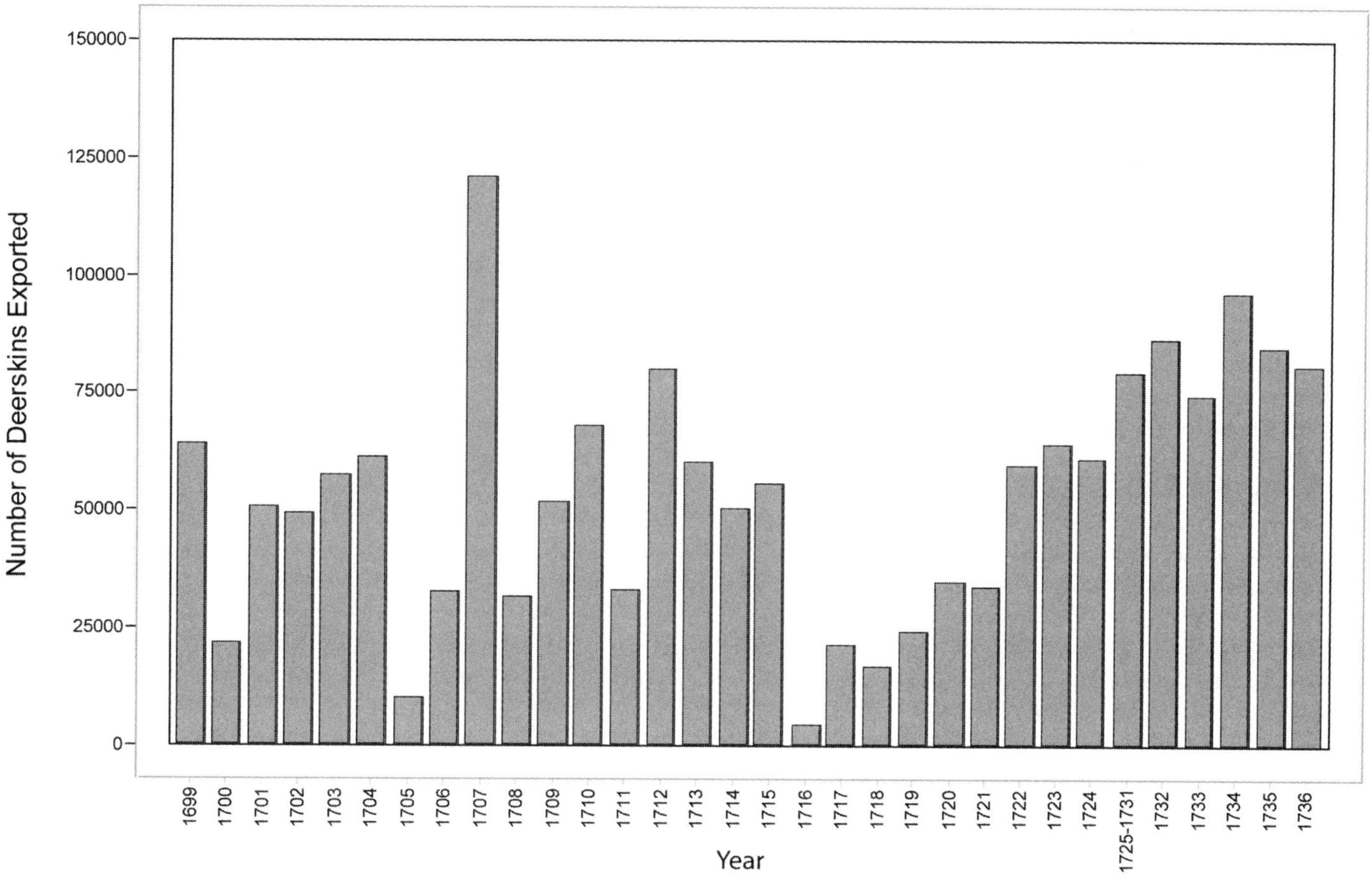

Figure 2.1. Annual deerskin exports from Charleston 1699–1736 (data taken from Crane [1929] 2004: Appendix A). Reproduced with permission from *Pox, Empire, Shackles, and Hides* (Marcoux 2010: Fig. 2.2), ©University of Alabama Press.

they witnessed their deerskin exports drop from 55,806 to just 4702 (Crane [1929] 2004: Appendix A; Oatis 2004:150) (Fig. 2.1). The colonial assembly began the recovery effort in June 1716 with the passage of An Act for the Better Regulation of the Indian Trade (McDowell 1992:325–29). The measures laid out in the act were drastic, and they reflected the urgency of the government's attempts to restore the deerskin trade while at the same time securing its frontiers.

At its core, the act established a complete governmental monopoly over the deerskin trade with three fundamental aims: (1) to restrict all deerskin trade to sanctioned "factories" staffed by governmental employees (called factors); (2) to curb the physical and credit abuses that occurred with private traders; and (3) to ensure the settlement of a peace between South Carolina and Indian groups like the Creek and Catawba who were, at the time, hostile toward the colony. The act initially authorized the construction of three factories—one located at Fort Moore along the Savannah River, one at a plantation garrison on the Black River, and one near the Congaree River. These original factories were purposefully placed *outside* Indian towns both for defense and to maintain a healthy "personal" distance between the factors and the Indians. The colonial assembly was also explicit in its desire to end the credit schemes and abuses of private traders and to increase the "morality" of the trade. To that end, the act of 1716 and the instructions given to factors forbade trading by any private individuals (including the factor himself), leveled substantial fines against any person who committed abuses against Indians, established specific price lists for goods traded to the Indians, totally abolished the use of credit, and severely restricted the sale of Indian slaves (McDowell 1992:85–87). The third aim of the monopoly was based on the colony's long-held axiom that trade formed the "bonds of peace" with Indian groups. Consequently, the trade act and official instructions to the factors stated that commerce was to be restricted to Indians "In Amity with this Government," and firearms were not to be sold to "any Indians that have not made Peace, or have not entered into Articles of mutual Friendship, with this Government" (McDowell 1992:85–86). This restriction played on the assembly's perception of the growing Indian "need" for European goods that would bring about the eventual acquiescence of hostile groups (Hahn 2002).

The public monopoly did not last very long. Suffering from complaints by merchants and Indian groups and from competition by "illegal" price-cutting Virginia traders, the Lords Proprietors began to allow private trading in 1719. By 1721, the trade reverted primarily to private interests (under government regulation) and the public factories were decommissioned (Crane [1929] 2004:197; Oatis 2004:154). The success of the monopoly has been debated by historians and in the end appears to have been mixed (e.g., Oatis 2004:152–53 contra Crane [1929] 2004:196–97). The principle of factories being "unaffiliated" vis-à-vis Indian towns was compromised rather quickly when a number of factories were established among various Cherokee towns following their refusal to continue carrying on trade at the distant Fort Moore factory (McDowell 1992:151–52, 188). This concession by South Carolina was a direct result of the significant bargaining leverage possessed by the Cherokees, who held a preeminent position in the deerskin trade. The monopoly did succeed in significantly reducing the number of complaints of Indian abuse, and although the commissioners eventually allowed the extension of credit to Indians, the debts never were allowed to grow to the astronomical levels attained just prior to the Yamasee War (Oatis 2004:153; Ramsey 2003:52–56). Also, during the tenure of the monopoly, South Carolina's two major Indian foes, the Catawbas and the Creeks, signed treaties to reopen trade (Merrell 1989a:79; Crane [1929] 2004:259). Taking these goals into account, it must be concluded that the monopoly was a success as an emergency stopgap measure that began the recovery of the deerskin trade (Crane [1929] 2004:211) (see Fig. 2.1).

The monopoly ultimately failed, however, because of growing opposition by both colonists and Indians and because of competition from Virginia traders. The colonists objected in principle to government monopolies of any kind because they took profit away from private pockets. Also, as bureaucratic institutions, government monopolies were often hamstrung by inflexibility and long time lags in reacting to market forces (Barker 1993:242–44). This exact problem was described in the memoir of a factor to the Cherokees who, writing sometime between 1716 and 1718, complained about his inability to compete with Virginia traders because he had to follow a government set price structure (e.g., Vassar 1961:411). Indian groups also increasingly mounted resistance to the commissions' insistence on using Indians as burdeners for the trade, ultimately choosing to trade with the Virginians because they used packhorses (Merrell 1989a:84; Vassar 1961).

The two decades following the nullification of the trade monopoly witnessed the growth of South Carolina's deerskin trade and the return of deerskin exports to prewar levels (Fig. 2.1). The largest source of growth doubtless came from the expansion of the trade to include for the first time substantial Cherokee participation (Crane [1929] 2004:194–97; Hatley 1995:23). The deerskin trade also grew in 1717, when a peace was reached and traders were once again sent west to Creek and Chickasaw towns (Crane [1929] 2004:259; McDowell 1992:238–41; Oatis 2004:211). The volume of trade increased after 1720 as Indian burdeners were gradually replaced by packhorses as the conveyors of the South Carolina deerskin trade. Human burdeners were less efficient and far more costly to the European traders because they could not carry as great a load, they were not keen on doing the job and increasingly required greater financial incentives to make the trip, and they sometimes absconded with a portion of the load (Barker 1993:112–15, 2001:152–55; Hatley 1995:37–38). The increase in the volume of trade was also due to the ending of the monopoly and the fact that South Carolinian traders were freed from governmental price restrictions. Without having to request changes from the commissioners, traders could more easily adjust their prices to compete with Virginian traders, while at the same time provide the amount of European goods demanded by Indian communities (Barker 1993:114; Hatley 1995:34–35; Merrell 1989a:84). The increased competition also benefited Indian communities who found much success in following their prewar strategies of diplomatically "playing off" the colonial powers.

Summary

All the historical and ethnohistorical sources indicate that the English Contact period (ca. 1670–1740) was an extremely turbulent time for both Indian groups and colonists in the Southeast. The first part of the period (ca. 1670–1715) featured the formation of a shatter zone—a landscape socially, economically, and politically disrupted by the increasing participation of Indian groups in the European capitalist economy. I argued that three historical forces largely influenced shatter zone development in the Southeast: epidemic disease, European colonial competition, and the trade in Indian slaves and deerskins. In discussing these forces, I emphasized the importance of considering the two-sided nature of interaction, particularly how the strategic decisions of Indian groups like the Westo or the Yamasee shaped the history of the Southeast. By 1715, the combination of epidemic disease, European colonial competition, and the trade in Indian slaves and deerskins had taken a devastating toll on most Indian groups. Indeed, there was no portion of the southeastern landscape left untouched by the effects of extensive depopulation, mass population movements, eruption of violent conflicts, growing debt, and fear of enslavement. The Yamasee War represented a sort of tipping point for southeastern Indian groups, a fait accompli whose beginning was engineered through the various strategies pursued by both the colonists and Indians since the beginning of the period. The war devastated South Carolina's economic and diplomatic ambitions as trading partners and valued Indian allies quickly turned against the colony. The complete breakdown caused by the Yamasee War offered colonial officials and Indian groups a brief respite during which they could reconsider and adjust their diplomatic and economic strategies to avoid reaping another whirlwind.

The years of the English Contact period following the Yamasee War (ca. 1715–1740) were generally a much more settled time in which Indian groups and colonists began to adjust to the disruptions and chaos of the previous forty-five years. While Indian groups continued to suffer from epidemics, increased disease resistance and decreased levels of slavery significantly reduced the rate of population loss affecting Indian towns. The postwar years also featured the abatement of frenetic population movements across the landscape as Indian populations consolidated and settled into particular areas such as the Chattahoochee River Valley, the Coosa and Tallapoosa River Valleys, the Catawba and Wateree River Valleys, and the Hiwassee and Little Tennessee River Valleys. As for the Europeans, South Carolina officials renewed diplomacy and trade with Indian groups amid a landscape inhabited by their reinvigorated European rivals. South Carolina's diplomatic strategies included numerous unsuccessful attempts to consolidate political power among Indian groups. Their strategies also included encouraging Indian conflicts that benefited England's imperial struggle against Spain and France (e.g., Creek vs. Spanish-allied Yamasee, Cherokees vs. French-allied Illinois) while discouraging conflicts that involved English-allied groups (e.g., Creek vs. Cherokees). Rather than settling down, the deerskin trade experienced a significant expansion during the postwar years of the English Contact period.

Thus far, I have attempted to reconstruct the general historical context of the English Contact period in the Southeast by describing a dynamic and even chaotic landscape—a shatter zone—in terms of historical forces that acted broadly across time and space. This type of discussion at a regional level has offered many important insights; however, I agree with Ethridge (2006:217) that our understandings of English Contact period Indian groups, like the Cherokees, can achieve even greater insight when we take into account the variable effects of *local* interaction between colonial and particular Indian groups.

Cherokee Communities in the Midst of the Shatter Zone: 1670–1740

Recent historical and ethnohistorical works mark a significant departure from traditional southeastern histories of the late seventeenth and early eighteenth centuries in that they place a greater analytical emphasis on the roles Indian groups played in making the history of the region. The narratives produced in these works are indeed richer as a result of framing history as the product of both strategic choice and necessity on the part of Indian groups rather than strictly the latter (e.g., Gallay 2002; Galloway 1995, 2002; Hatley 1995; Kowalewski 2006; Marcoux 2010; Merrell 1989a, 1989b; Oatis 2004; Waselkov 1993). In addition to demonstrating that history was a product of interaction between Indian groups and colonists, these works show that between 1715 and 1740 there was a tremendous amount of variability in the nature of interaction at the regional and even local level. Ramsey (2003:73), for example, argues that the search for general explanations for the Yamasee War is ultimately fruitless because each Indian group "faced a complex set of local considerations that defy generalization. Common elements shaped their decisions. . . . But the nature and value of those elements differed from region to region, and among them stretched a 'thousand threads' that wove them into the local reality."

The dynamic nature of the landscape during the English Contact period reflected the highly varied strategies enacted by Indian groups trying to negotiate a rapidly evolving dialectic with the European colonial powers. Even a cursory examination of current literature reveals that strategies varied from group to group and that the strategies practiced by a particular group changed through time. Some groups, like the Westo and the Savannah, engaged heavily in the Indian slave trade and moved their communities close to English trading posts (Bowne 2005, 2006; Ethridge 2006). Other groups, like the Kaskinampo and Yuchi, engaged in slavery, but moved about the periphery of European colonial territory in small groups (Bauxar 1957a, 1957b; Riggs, in press; Swanton 1930). Still other groups, like the Creek, Choctaw, and Catawba, formed large, sedentary, multiethnic confederacies around the nuclei of established Indian towns through the adoption of refugee groups (e.g., Galloway 1995; Knight 1994; Kowalewski 2006; Merrell 1989a). This "strategy of coalescence" (Kowalewski 2006) was a common response to the demographic disruptions of the shatter zone across the seventeenth- and eighteenth-century Southeast (e.g., Davis 2002; Drooker 2002; Hudson 2002; Perttula 2002; Rodning 2002). These brief examples indicate that the English Contact period was likely experienced and negotiated differently by different Indian groups. Consequently, current research needs to address variability by conducting analyses at the highest magnification possible given the restrictions of the data. In what follows, I use historic syntheses and primary sources to focus on the various strategies enacted by Cherokee groups as they navigated the social, political, and economic landscape outlined in the first part of the chapter.

1670–1715: "A people little conversant with whitemen"

The period spanning from the late seventeenth century to the early eighteenth century is one in which the Cherokees were transformed from "an ambiguous presence" in the mountains to a major focus of colonial trade and diplomacy (Hatley 1995:27). Indeed, the few European maps that date to this period suggest an extremely low level of knowledge about the Cherokees until after the Yamasee War (Fig. 2.2). Furthermore, it is clear from extant historic accounts that Cherokee participation in the deerskin and Indian slave trade was negligible until after the first decade of the eighteenth century (Crane [1929] 2004:41; Hatley 1995:32–33; Merrell 1989a). When compared to other large southeastern Indian groups (e.g., Creek, Chickasaw, Choctaw), the relative "invisibility" of the Cherokees is somewhat anomalous. I suggest that it is possible that the lack of Cherokee involvement in colonial affairs was a strategic response to the shatter zone—a

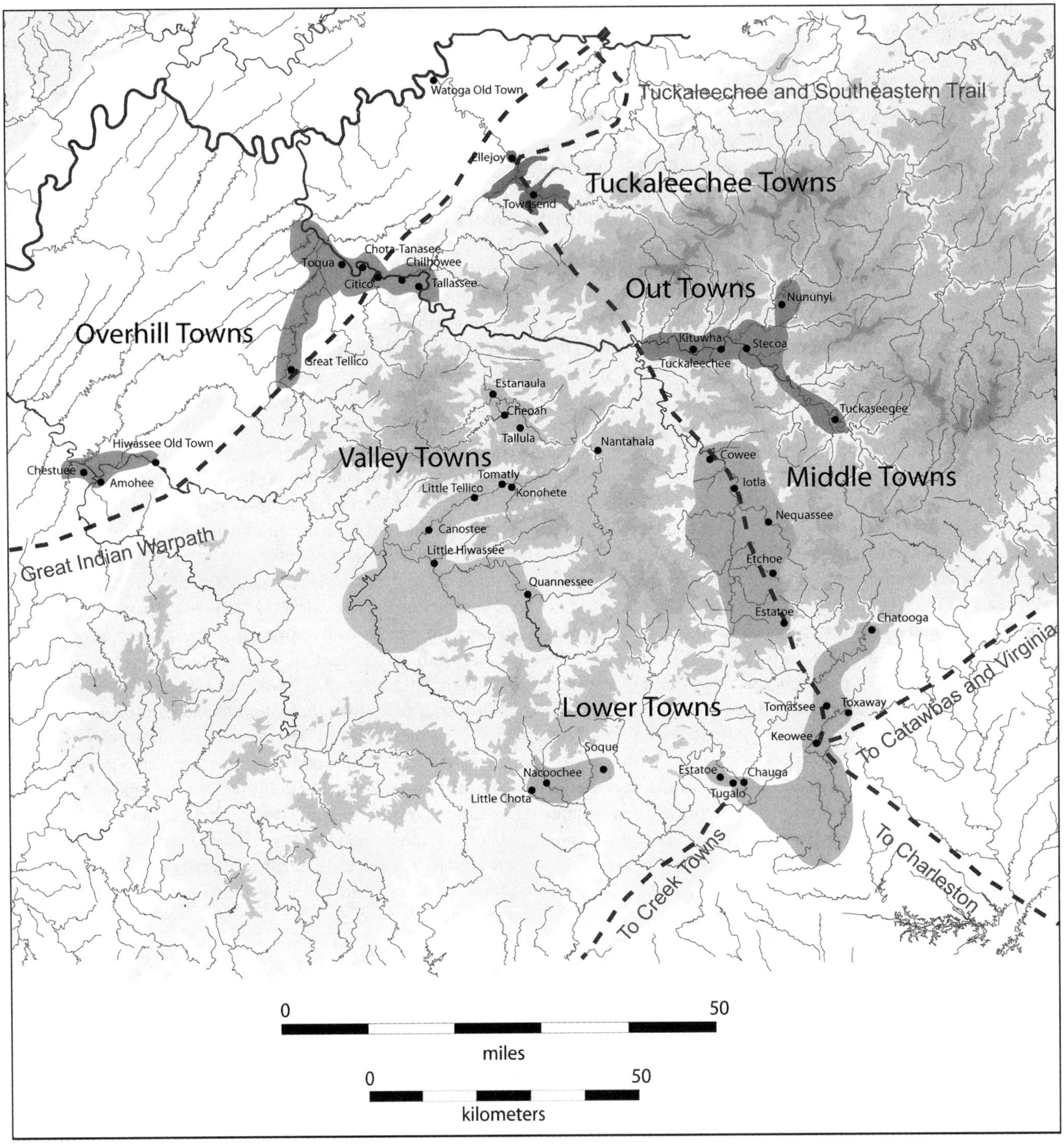

Figure 2.2. Cultural geography of Cherokee territory during the English Contact period (adapted from Duncan and Riggs 2003: Map 3). Reproduced with permission from *Pox, Empire, Shackles, and Hides* (Marcoux 2010: Fig. 3.2), ©University of Alabama Press.

way of avoiding the disruptions that inevitably befell those groups that developed intimate ties with Europeans (see Marcoux 2010 for a detailed discussion).

Late seventeenth- and early eighteenth-century maps of the interior Southeast offer a general picture of the degree of knowledge that Europeans had of the Cherokees during the first half of the English Contact period (Cumming 1998:20–27; Galloway 1995:205–9). While vague, French maps drafted in 1682 and 1701 from information provided by coureurs de bois appear to reference Cherokee settlements along the Tennessee and/or Hiwassee Rivers (Crane 1916; Swanton 1930). Three English maps of Cherokee settlements dating to this period are equally vague. Nairne's 1708 map, reproduced as an inset in the Edward Crisp (1711), depicts a single large cluster of "Cherecie" settlements among the Appalachian Mountains along with a population estimate of 3000 men (Cumming 1998: Plate 45). A later copy of trader Pryce Hughes's map of his 1713 voyage to the Mississippi River depicts Cherokee settlements with a single caption "The Cherokees. A great Nation inhabiting within & both sides of the Mountains consisting of 65 Towns" (Cumming 1998:23). An anonymous undated English map (ca. 1713–1715) features clusters of settlements that match the distribution of the Upper, Middle, and Lower settlements in their respective river valleys (Cumming 1998: Plate 46*A*). Taken together, these maps portray the poor but growing state of knowledge of the Cherokees that existed in the late seventeenth and early eighteenth centuries. Individual town names were not known, or at least were not printed, and the locations of settlements were poorly extrapolated from explorer and trader accounts. When viewed as a chronological series, however, the maps suggest that Europeans were coming to understand that the Cherokees represented a formidable population. As shown below, maps made just two decades later reflect an enormous leap in Europeans' knowledge of Cherokee settlements as they came to play a major role in southeastern history during the post-Yamasee War years.

Cherokee participation in the deerskin and Indian slave trade during this period was on a much smaller scale compared to other southeastern Indian groups. Cherokee communities were not strangers to European trade, however, with links to Virginians established during the first half of the seventeenth century (Smith 1987; Franklin 1932; Briceland 1987) and to the Spanish extending back to the late sixteenth century (Smith 1987; Waselkov 1989). In addition, South Carolinians opened trade with the Cherokees by 1690 (Rothrock 1929), and French coureurs de bois established contact with Cherokee communities by 1700 (Crane 1916, [1929] 2004:43–33). Aside from the accounts detailing the initial contacts between European traders and Cherokee communities, an overall dearth of written records between 1670 and 1715 suggests that the latter were largely forsaken by the former. Many historians have argued that the lack of Cherokee involvement in trade was the result of direct exchange being controlled by other Indian groups acting as middlemen. I have argued elsewhere that this explanation is unsatisfactory because it fails to account for the decades following the defeat of the middlemen groups by colonial militias, and it assumes that all Indian groups were actively seeking trade with Europeans (Marcoux 2010:40–41).

The evidence we do have lends weight to an alternative explanation, one in which there was a mutual distaste for trade on the part of Europeans and Cherokee groups. Indeed, numerous English trader accounts spanning from 1690 to 1713 demonstrate a certain level of contempt for what was perceived as a lack of interest in trade shown by the Cherokees. These accounts include James Moore's well-known initial foray to the Cherokees that ended in failure (Crane [1929] 2004:40–41; Oatis 2004:35–36). Fellow trader John Stewart ([1690] 1931:29–30) noted in a contemporary account that upon his return from the Cherokee voyage, James Moore petitioned the governor not for permission to return to the Cherokees, but instead for permission to trade with the "Tireagis," possibly a group of Yuchi who were settled in the middle Tennessee River Valley of northern Alabama (Bauxar 1957a, 1957b; Riggs, in press; Swanton 1930). Stewart's account also indicates that traders were more interested in the recent opening of direct trade with the towns of Coweta and Kasita and their migration to the Macon Plateau (see also Corkran 1967:50–51). A 1708 census compiled by Nathaniel Johnson, then governor of South Carolina, and his council mimicked the English perception that the Cherokees were apathetic toward trade (Johnson et al. 1708:209). He described the Cherokees as "Lazy," and the trade with them "Inconsiderable" (capitalization in the original document); as discussed below, he also stated that "they [were] but ordinary Hunters & less Warriors," suggesting that the Cherokees were not heavily involved in the Indian slave trade at the time. Finally, a letter from English trader and explorer Pryce Hughes (1713) highlighted the continued English ignorance of the Cherokees—even into the second decade of the eighteenth century. Numerous times in the letter, Hughes (1713) referred to the cultural isolation of the Cherokees from the English stating that they are "as a people little conversant with whitemen," and that "They live a great way off from any white Settlement & so are but little known to us."

Cherokee involvement in the Indian slave trade was minimal when compared to groups like the Westo, Savannah, Yamasee, Tallapoosa, and Chickasaw. In fact, it appears that before 1700 the Cherokees were typically the victims rather than the purveyors of slavery—particularly at the hands of the Savannah and Iroquois (Crane 1916:10*n*, [1929] 2004:40; Gallay 2002:94; Hatley 1995:33; Nairne [1708] 1988:76; Norton [1816] 1970:262). Indeed, in 1705, some Cherokees counseled South Carolina Governor Nathaniel Johnson to curtail the slave trade, imploring him to "trade for skins and furs" rather than "trade of Indians or slave making" (Martin 1994:313). This warning may have influenced the governor, who said of the Cherokees in the 1708 census, "Trade we have with them is Inconsiderable they being but ordinary Hunters & less Warriors" (Johnson et al. 1708:209). After 1700 there is evidence that some Cherokees were involved in incidents of slave raiding (e.g., Gallay 2002:220, 283; Oatis 2004:53, 89), including the well-known and oft-written about Chestowee raid of 1713, in which a group of Cherokees utterly routed the Yuchi town of Chestowee, killing or enslaving most of its inhabitants (Bauxar 1957a, 1957b; Lewis and Kneberg 1946; McDowell 1992:53–57).

The Yamasee and Creek Wars

The Yamasee War (or, more importantly, the related Creek-Cherokee War) was a watershed moment for the Cherokees because it marked South Carolina's recognition of the group's trading and military potential (Crane [1929] 2004:39–41; Hatley 1995:19–22; Oatis 2004:184–86). For the Cherokees, it also necessitated sustained social, economic, and political relations with South Carolina. After being drawn into the war on the side of South Carolina, the Cherokees were universally hailed by the English as the saviors of the colony. As I detail elsewhere (Marcoux 2010), however, the Cherokees did not eagerly join the fray as a single united nation, and the goal of their war was to destroy the Creek, not to help South Carolinians (see also Crane [1929] 2004:181–83; Hatley 1995:24–27; Oatis 2004:185–90).

The Creek-Cherokee War began during the Yamasee War in 1716 when a number of Cherokees murdered a Creek diplomatic delegation in the Lower Cherokee town of Tugaloo (Crane [1929] 2004:183–84; Hatley 1995:23–26). The details of the murders are not known, but historical records are clear that the Cherokees were not all motivated to join South Carolina in a military alliance against the Yamasee, Creek, and piedmont Indians. Indeed, for the South Carolinians involved in the diplomatic expedition to hold the Cherokees to their promise, this perception of a unified "nation" of Cherokees coming to the rescue was quickly and thoroughly shattered. The journal kept by Colonel George Chicken ([1715] 1894:313–54), one of the leaders of an expedition aimed at courting the Cherokees, documents a tenuous and fluid political structure among towns dominated by the autonomous and clashing dispositions of numerous Cherokee headmen. Indeed, Chicken encountered both hawkish and dovish factions among the various communities and along generational lines within individual communities. While trying to find a consensus among the various headmen, he received news of the murders, the fallout of which was that both pro- and anti-war factions of the Cherokees were drawn into a war with the Creek, and as an ancillary consequence they entered the Yamasee War on the side of South Carolina.

The opening of the Creek-Cherokee War has been the focus of much analysis by historians because it was a bona fide historical moment that marked a real turning point for South Carolina in the Yamasee War. Indeed, this moment has even been given various titles such as "The Incident at Tugaloo" (Reid 1976:61), "The Massacre at Tugaloo" (Crane [1929] 2004:183), and "Salvation at Tugaloo" (Hatley 1995:23). While the Cherokee entrance into a war with the Creek might have meant salvation to South Carolinians, it resulted in over ten years of retaliatory raiding for the Indian adversaries. The details of this war are largely missing in historical records, being confined to brief mentions and anecdotes. During the tenure of the war between 1716 and 1727, there were devastating Cherokee raids on the Creek towns of Abeihka, Okfuskee, and Tallapoosa and murders of a number of important Creek headmen including Ouletta, the son of the legendary Lower Creek headman Emperor Brims (Corkran 1967:73–77; Fitch [1725] 1916:181–90; McDowell 1992:140, 178; Piker 2004:22). These raids eventually forced Creek groups that had moved into central Georgia in the 1680s to move their settlements back to their original territory in the Lower Chattahoochee Valley (Corkran 1967:60).

Judging from historical records, the Cherokees appear to have been on the receiving end of more violence during the war. In the 1720s, reports indicated that Creek raiding parties were holding numerous Cherokee towns under siege. During a diplomatic mission through the Cherokee territory in 1725, it was reported that Creek war parties were hiding among the Upper and Middle settlements, "Continually within a mile of the Town[s] lurking about the Skirts thereof and very often Cut of [cut off] their People and make their Escape" (Chicken [1725] 1916:111–12). Period accounts also stated that Lower, Middle and Upper settlements were erecting fortifications to withstand these Creek attacks (Chicken [1725] 1916:111–12, 133, 143, 149–50; Fitch [1725] 1916:198). A more perilous fate befell the residents of the Lower Cherokee town of Nacoochee and the Valley town of Quanassee. These two towns were "cut off" (that is, utter destroyed) by the Creek, and the residents likely suffered a similar doom as the Yuchi of Chestowee (Chicken [1725] 1916:117; Vassar 1961:413). The situation was equally dire for other Cherokee settlements, for in addition to the threat of Creek raids, some towns were being raided by the Iroquois and some were engaged in back-and-forth raiding with French-allied Indians (Bonnefoy [1741] 1916; Chicken [1725] 1916:107, 121, 143; Fitch [1725] 1916:89; Herbert [1727] 1936:24).

South Carolinians found that bringing an end to the Creek-Cherokee War would require dealing with the same factionalism that plagued their efforts to begin the war (see below). In 1717, South Carolina made a peace agreement with the Lower Creek that effectively ended the Yamasee War, but at that time they could not manage to extend the peace to include the Creek-Cherokee War (Corkran 1967:66–67; Crane [1929] 2004:259; McDowell 1992:238–41; Oatis 2004:210–11, 246). Almost a decade later, two South Carolina diplomatic expeditions entered Creek and Cherokee towns with an agenda that included bringing an end to the war. Colonel George Chicken's expedition to the Cherokees began on a high note when he found that peace with the Creeks was at least considered a possibility by some Cherokees in Upper settlements. The Great Warrior of Great Tellico confided in Chicken, reasoning that his people "were hemmed in all round with their Enemies and if they were in Unity with the Southward Indians [Creek] they should have no Enemy then to look after but the French Indians" (Chicken [1725] 1916:114). In a meeting of most Cherokee headmen from across the region, however, the consensus reached was definitely not in favor of a peace. Rather, a spokesman for the Cherokee headmen argued "That the Creeks not only Abuse them [Cherokees], but also the

English (their brothers) . . . that the Creeks kill both their people [English] and Ours [Cherokees] (And what) must No Notice be taken of these abuses?" (Chicken [1725] 1916:127).

The attempt to bring the Creek to peace negotiations was no more successful. At the same time that Chicken was among the Cherokees, Captain Tobias Fitch carried his message to both Upper and Lower Creek towns. In the Upper towns, the headmen of the Abeihkas and Tallapoosas told Fitch they could not engage in a peace with the Cherokees, as they had recently killed some of their townspeople. But the headmen did hold out the possibility of a future peace with the Cherokees once they avenged those deaths saying, "As soon as our Corn is hard We Designe to be with them [attack the Cherokees] and after our Return if your King Will undertake To make a peace for us We will Readylie Except of it" (Fitch [1725] 1916:181). Emperor Brims of the Lower Creek was not as gracious, as he said that many of the men murdered at Tugaloo in 1715 were his kin and that the war "is not over with Me as yet, nor shall be While there is a Cawwataid [Lower Creek] Liveing" (Fitch [1725] 1916:181). In the end, while South Carolinians hailed the end of their war with the Indians in 1717, the violent chaos of the shatter zone continued for the Creek and Cherokees for another decade. Finally, in 1727 the governor of South Carolina managed to convene peace talks in Charleston between Cherokee and Creek representatives, who promised to cease their raids against one another and pledged their eternal "friendship" to the English (Oatis 2004:254). This tenuous peace held for the rest of the period, but another decade-long struggle erupted between the two ancient enemies in 1743.

The Yamasee War, or more specifically the Incident at Tugaloo, was in fact a major milestone in Cherokee history. From that moment onward, it is clear that the Cherokees could no longer maintain their identity as an "amibiguous presence" in the Appalachian Mountains. As South Carolinians reassessed their colonial strategies during and immediately after the Yamasee War, they recognized the profits they could reap from Cherokee alliance and trade. They subsequently enacted aggressive trading and diplomatic strategies that greatly increased interaction with the Cherokees. This change in colonial strategy was quite drastic considering that only a decade earlier they knew or cared little of the Cherokees. Whether or not the Cherokees actively sought out the attention of South Carolina, they quickly found themselves occupying a much more prominent position among the post-Yamasee War landscape, and they had to adjust their strategies accordingly.

1715–1740: A Most Potent Nation

The Cherokees' protracted war with the Creek and their role as an English ally in the Yamasee War intensified trade and diplomatic relations with South Carolina to a level they had never known before. Whereas in 1713 trader Pryce Hughes lamented that the Cherokees were "but little known to us," by 1721 the colony had produced a substantial body of knowledge regarding the Cherokees, including accurate and comprehensive maps depicting the locations of individual towns, town-based censuses, and numerous records related to the deerskin trade. Taken together, these documents outline the story of how, in less than a decade, Cherokee communities came to occupy a central position in the post-Yamasee War landscape of the Southeast during the latter half of the English Contact period (ca. 1715–1740). Two factors stand out as crucial to understanding how Cherokee communities were transformed from relatively isolated villages as late as 1713 to a primary focus of European trade and diplomacy by the 1720s: (1) the dramatic increase of Cherokee participation in the deerskin trade and (2) the growing importance of the Cherokees to England's colonial ambitions.

Period censuses and maps demonstrate better than any other type of documentary evidence the dramatic growth in South Carolina's knowledge of Cherokee demography. The 1708 census mentioned above contained only a brief description of "The Cherokee," a single population estimate (5000 men) and an estimate of the number of Cherokee towns (60) in their territory (Johnson et al. 1708:209). On the eve of the Yamasee War in 1715, a much more concerted effort was made by South Carolina to construct an accurate census of its Indian neighbors. John Barnwell synthesized the reports of a number of English traders and Indian agents, including Thomas Nairne, Pryce Hughes, and John Wright, and arrived at a much more accurate census than the one authored in 1708. This census, with the typically verbose eighteenth-century title *An Exact Account of ye number & Strength of all the Indian Nations that were Subject to the Government of South Carolina and Solely Traded with them in ye beginning of ye year 1715*, enumerated the Cherokee population using the classic tripartite division of settlements (i.e., Upper, Middle, and Lower)—the first time these divisions were featured in a colonial census (Barnwell 1719). Barnwell tallied the number of towns in each settlement division (he did not list the names of the towns), and for each division he listed the total number of men, women, boys, and girls. Barnwell's report estimated that in 1715 there were 19 towns with 2760 people in the Upper settlements, 30 towns with 6350 people in the Middle settlements, and 11 towns with 2100 people in the Lower settlements. He also commented on recent Cherokee population losses, saying that "by War Pestilence & Civll Warr Amongst themselves the Charokees may be computed reduced to ab[t] 10,000 Souls" (Barnwell 1719). Barnwell's census and accompanying map (discussed below) marked a definite improvement over the earlier 1708 census, and for the first time information regarding the Cherokees appears to have been on par with that of the Creek, Chickasaw, and other Indian groups.

In 1721 Francis Varnod ([1721] 1971:273), a missionary for the Society for the Propagation of the Gospel, completed another Cherokee census in preparation for his work in the mountains. The census was highly detailed, listing the number of men, women, and children in each of 53 towns. The name of each town was included, but he did not indicate to which of the three settlement divisions each town belonged. The overall demography calculated in Varnod's census is very similar to Barnwell's. The total Cherokee population he counted—10,379 in 53 towns—was very close to Barnwell's 1715 estimate of 11,530 in 60 towns. The increasing level of detail achieved in the 1708 census, the 1715 Barnwell census, and Varnod's 1721 census denotes South Carolina's growing desire for information regarding the Cherokees as they assessed how this group would fit into their colonial plans following the Yamasee War.

Maps dating to the period 1715–1740 also illustrate the dramatic increases in information about the Cherokees that flowed into Charleston just after the Yamasee War. The map of southeastern North America produced by John Barnwell in 1721 can be considered a magnum opus of eighteenth-century cartography. This map and its copy (known as the 1721 Barnwell-Hammerton map) were richly illustrated and annotated and included the accurate locations of Cherokee, Creek, Yamasee, Chickasaw, Chotaw, and other Indian towns, colonial forts, trading paths, and the routes taken in major military expeditions during Queen Anne's War and the Tuscarora War (Cumming 1998:218–19, Plate 48). Barnwell's map accurately portrayed the locations of 53 named Cherokee towns and gave population estimates (in terms of "fighting men") for each of the three settlement divisions. This map resulted from a major effort to compile and synthesize essentially all the extant knowledge of southeastern Indians at the time. With regard to the Cherokees, the Barnwell map represented a stellar improvement in detail and accuracy over maps drafted just a decade earlier. The level of detail achieved by the Barnwell map is attested to by the fact that it obviously served as the basis for maps of Cherokee territory made later in the period by Herbert in 1725 and Hunter in 1730 (Williams 1928:114). While maps and censuses stand as examples of the voracity with which South Carolina's colonial officials pursued relations with the Cherokees after 1715, documentary evidence from the deerskin trade suggests that at the same time many Cherokee communities began cultivating trading relationships with equal vigor.

The years immediately following the outbreak of the Yamasee War witnessed what can only be called an explosion of Cherokee participation in the southeastern deerskin economy. It was probably no coincidence that this explosion was concomitant with the outbreak of the Yamasee War and the Cherokee instigation of the Creek War. Furthermore, the rise of the Cherokees as a major player in the deerskin trade was greatly aided by the establishment of South Carolina's public trading monopoly in 1716. To South Carolina's profit-minded officials, the Yamasee War was devastating, for it brought the extirpation of the trade in Indian slaves and the loss of trade with the Creek and Yamasee, two of the colony's most prolific suppliers of deerskins. These losses created an economic vacuum that desperately needed to be filled in order to maintain deerskin exports to England. South Carolinians quickly tapped their new ally, the Cherokees, to fill this position, as they were the only friendly Indian group large enough to replace Creek and Yamasee trade (Hatley 1995:34–35). To the Cherokees, who participated little in the English deerskin trade in 1716, the material requirements of their burgeoning war with the Creek (namely, firearms and ammunition) were considerably greater than could be satisfied with trade at existing levels. Recognizing the Cherokees' shortfall and as repayment for joining the Yamasee War on their side, South Carolina's government began to provide "presents" of hundreds of guns to both Upper and Lower Cherokee settlements in 1716 (McDowell 1992:75). These diplomatic gifts could not, however, fulfill the Cherokees' long-term martial needs. Like earlier Indian groups that faced hostile well-armed foes, the Cherokees must have recognized that they could gain much by entering into the deerskin trade with South Carolina, and their entrance into the trade was made much easier with the support of South Carolina's new trading policies that heavily favored its new allies.

When South Carolina instituted the public monopoly over the deerskin trade in 1716, it was clear that officials planned on the Cherokees being major trading partners. As originally conceived, the monopoly legislation specifically restricted all Indian trading to three government-operated factories located far from any Indian town—the closest to the Cherokees being Fort Moore along the Savannah River. When actually implemented, however, the Cherokees alone were given their own factory in the Lower settlements at the town of Tugaloo along with a factor and two assistants (McDowell 1992:83). The factory was built in the Lower settlements for three reasons, all of which took advantage of geography: (1) the Lower settlements were located closest to Charleston near established trading paths to the Creek and Chickasaw; (2) Tugaloo's situation formed a natural gateway where trade could be funneled to and from the Middle and Upper Cherokee settlements; and (3) the Lower settlements were likely the earliest recipients of English trade and thus had the most stable and established trading relationships. A year later, the Cherokees' elevated position in the trade had earned them the bargaining leverage to demand and receive additional factories in the Lower settlement of Keeowee, the Middle settlements of Cowee and Quanassee, and the Upper settlement of Great Tellico (McDowell 1992:157, 188). In addition to the locations of the factories, the Cherokees also negotiated the prices of trade goods and the payment Cherokee burdeners would receive for carrying goods and deerskins between Cherokee towns and colonial entrepots (McDowell 1992:89; Reid 1976:74–87). The ability of the Cherokees to garner these concessions from South Carolina in just two years shows that they could no longer be considered "ordinary Hunters."

One of the benefits of South Carolina's public monopoly was that it produced prodigious records with which one can quantify Cherokee participation in the deerskin trade shortly after the Yamasee War. The records kept by the governmental board overseeing the monopoly between July 4, 1716 and August 29, 1718 are contained in the *Journals of the Commissioners of the Indian Trade* (McDowell 1992). The journals are replete with the kind of bureaucratic minutiae one would expect from such an endeavor—including reports of the number of deerskins periodically received from the various Indian trading factories as well as invoices for the trade goods that were sent to the factories (Tables 2.1, 2.2). These records signal the rapidity with which the Cherokees were able to dominate the southeastern deerskin trade. Between 1716 and 1718, the total number of deerskins received from Cherokee trading factories was greater than all of the other trading factories combined (Fig. 2.3). Also, invoices recording the value of trade goods sent to the factories showed that the Cherokees received over twice as many trade goods as other groups between 1716 and 1718 (Fig. 2.4). Indeed, if one excludes the trade goods sent to the Creek at the reopening of trade with that group in 1717, the total value of goods sent to the Cherokee factories would be more than all other trading factories combined. Certainly the reopening of South Carolina's trade with the Creek greatly reduced Cherokee dominance of the trade after 1717, but the Cherokees were able to maintain their position as a major trading partner for the rest of the eighteenth century (Hatley 1995:163–65). Unfortunately, the effects of Creek competition in the deerskin trade cannot be quantified due to a lack of comparable records after the dissolution of the public monopoly. Trade records are also lacking for the period before the monopoly (ca. 1670–1715); however, based on the historic accounts detailed above, the seemingly intentional lack of Cherokee participation in the deerskin trade suggests that trade prior to 1715 was "inconsiderable" (Johnson et al. 1708:209). Given this evidence, it is hard not to be awed by the meteoric rise of Cherokee communities who in 1713 were known "as a people little conversant with whitemen" and who by 1716 were the Southeast's foremost purveyors of deerskins.

The preeminent role of Cherokee hunters in the deerskin trade between 1715 and 1740 also afforded them significant opportunities to take advantage of the trade war that was being contested between South Carolina and Virginia. As discussed above, Virginia traders had been proverbial gadflies in South Carolina's trade relations with the Cherokees and piedmont groups since before the Yamasee War. Historic accounts of trade from the years immediately following the Yamasee War detail the growing influence of Virginia traders among the Cherokees—an influence that threatened South Carolina's existing monopoly (McDowell 1992:221, 290–91). One telling example happened in 1717 and 1718 when two large trading caravans, each consisting of some 200 packhorses laden with trade goods, made their way to Cherokee territory. These caravans were sponsored by the Virginian Indian Company, a publicly held entity that had been given monopoly power over Virginia's Indian trade and had as one of its major goals the establishment of sustained trade with the Cherokees (Franklin 1932:13).

The South Carolinian perspective on these trading expeditions was reported by William Hatton, trade factor to the Cherokees between 1717 and 1720 (Vassar 1961; see also McDowell 1992:290–91). Hatton (Vassar 1961:406) expressed his alarm at the eager reception given to the Virginian traders who "would Sell [trade goods] to them [Cherokees] much Cheaper then those from Carolina." The

Table 2.1. Deerskins sent to Charleston from trading factories between 1716 and 1718.

Month	Year	Number of Deerskins	Factory	Page Reference (McDowell 1992)
September	1716	252	Wineau	109
October	1716	2176	Cherokee	117
October	1716	29	Savano	117
November	1716	56	Wineau	132
December	1716	549	Wineau	142
January	1717	12	Wineau	149
January	1717	336	Cherokee	149
February	1717	640	Wineau	160
April	1717	672	Wineau	174
May	1717	50	Wineau	178
May	1717	1080	Catawba	178
May	1717	25	Wineau	184
June	1717	957	Cherokee	186
June	1717	65	Wineau	187
June	1717	730	Wineau	188
September	1717	54	Wineau	203
September	1717	378	Wineau	204
September	1717	90	Savano	204
September	1717	580	Catawba	211
October	1717	148	Cherokee	215
October	1717	150	Cherokee	219
October	1717	770	Cherokee	222
November	1717	55	Savano	228
November	1717	540	Wineau	232
November	1717	4800	Cherokee	232
January	1718	754	Savano	252
February	1718	708	Wineau	257
May	1718	500	Catawba	272
May	1718	282	Wineau	273
July	1718	704	Wineau	313

Table 2.2. Invoice value totals for trade goods sent to Indian factories.

Month	Year	Amount (£.s.d)	Factory	Page Reference (McDowell 1992)
July	1716	579.2.12	Cherokee	70
July	1716	239.28.6	Wineau	94
August	1716	1903.11.9	Savano	101
September	1716	86.15.3	Wineau	111
October	1716	35.7.9	Wineau	115
December	1716	62.11.1	Wineau	138
December	1716	119.15.6	Savano	143
January	1717	54.10.7	Wineau	144
January	1717	380.5.2	Catawba	156
January	1717	1437.14	Cherokee	157
February	1717	588.10.4	Savano	159
February	1717	913.8.1	Cherokee	159
February	1717	119.11	Wineau	163
April	1717	25.8.9	Savano	176
May	1717	307.2.11	Catawba	180
June	1717	398.18.12	Cherokee	190
June	1717	148.1.4	Wineau	191
September	1717	217.2.3	Wineau	210
September	1717	468.5.12	Catawba	212
October	1717	77.9.1	Cherokee	215
November	1717	191.1.5	Cherokee	223
November	1717	35.13.7	Catawba	230
December	1717	179.16.4	Wineau	236
December	1717	1849.8.8	Cherokee	239
January	1718	986.14.7	Creek	248
March	1718	202.12.3	Wineau	261
May	1718	129.8.5	Wineau	276
June	1718	241.15.4	Cherokee	290
June	1718	726.16.8	Catawba	292
July	1718	589.19.11	Cherokee	311
August	1718	72.16.11	Savano	318

Virginian traders also denounced South Carolina's burdener policy telling the Cherokees that the Carolina traders "made Horse [of] 'em to carrie Skins, but they [Virginians] had brought Horses abundance to eas them of that trouble" (Vassar 1961:406). Hatton's frustrations were multiplied by his inability to compete with the Virginians by lowering prices or renegotiating the burdener policy. As established in the monopoly legislation, these adjustments could only be made by the trade commissioners in Charleston. Hatton reported that South Carolina was in grave danger of losing trade with the Cherokees, who were eagerly building houses for the Virginians and were suddenly refusing to act as burdeners, leaving South Carolina's deerskins to rot in their towns (Vassar 1961:408). Even more alarming was the news that anti-Carolinian factions had broken into the factories at Quanassee and Tanasee and were threatening to kill the Carolina traders if they did not leave those towns (Vassar 1961:409, 419).

Hatton's account of this episode underscored the calculated nature of Cherokee trading strategies during the post-Yamasee War period. The Cherokees' enthusiastically warm reception of the Virginia traders was doubtless motivated by the desire to have an alternative source of trade, for they "thought it was good to have another string to their Bow" for bargaining leverage (Vassar 1961:407). Hatton also pointed out the Cherokees' shrewd business sense, recalling that they would often take the skins that had been refused by the Virginian traders to the South Carolina factor who was obliged to take them "as an article of Peace" (Vassar 1961:408). Judging by South Carolina's responses over the next three years, the Cherokee gambits appear to have worked—the commissioners agreed to lower the prices of trade goods, the burdener system was abolished and packhorses became the main mode of transportation, and by 1721 the public monopoly was nullified (Crane [1929] 2004:197; Hatley 1995:38–39; McDowell 1992:306; Oatis 2004:154; Reid 1976:123–29). With these reforms, South Carolina also managed to quell the initial onslaught by Virginia traders. Virginia trade was to remain a valuable bargaining chip for the Cherokees for the rest of the English Contact period, but the colony's traders ceased to be a serious threat to South Carolina after 1720. At that time, the monopoly powers of the Virginia Indian Company were revoked by the colonial legislature and the volume of trade entering the piedmont and Appalachian Mountains was cut in half (Franklin 1932:16; Merrell 1989a:84).

For better or worse, post-Yamasee War Cherokee diplomacy was inextricably linked to South Carolina's colonial strategies. This is not to say, however, that Cherokee strategies followed South Carolina policies lockstep. As will be shown, the autonomy of Cherokee towns, expressed in the contrary diplomatic dispositions of their headmen, caused much consternation to colonial officials. Rather, the "link" that bound these two parties was formed by the

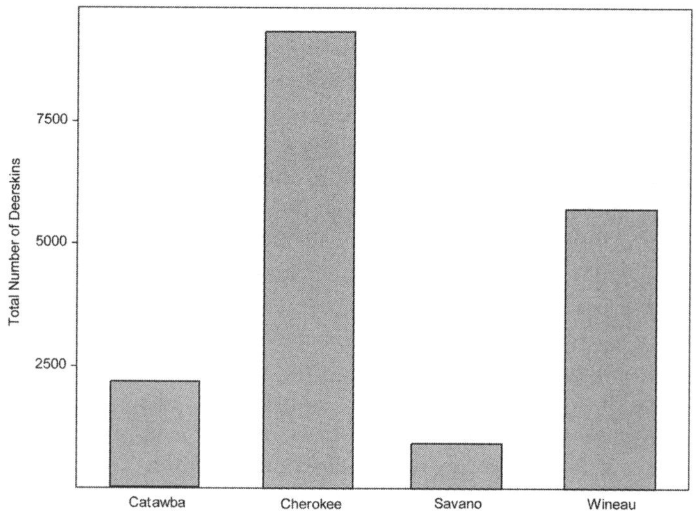

Figure 2.3. Total number of deerskins received from Indian factories between 1716 and 1718 (data taken from the *Journals of the Commissioners of the Indian Trade* [McDowell 1992]).

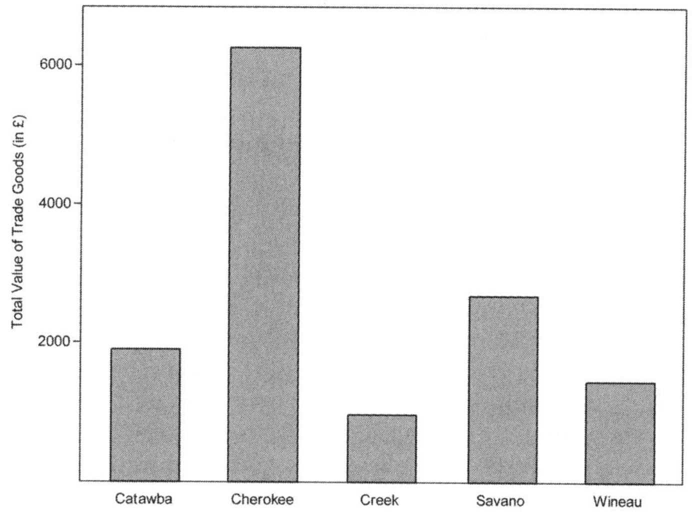

Figure 2.4. Total value of trade goods sent to Indian factories between 1716 and 1718 (data taken from the *Journals of the Commissioners of the Indian Trade* [McDowell 1992]).

fact that Cherokee diplomacy constantly came up against South Carolina's postwar agendas concerning its colonial rival France and its Indian neighbors. Between 1715 and 1740, the diplomatic challenges South Carolina imposed on Cherokee groups centered around three interrelated issues: erratic relations with the Creek, South Carolina's attempts to "nationalize" the Cherokees, and continuing Cherokee hostilities toward the French and their allied Indians. Records from two South Carolina diplomatic missions sent to resolve these issues provide a good deal of insight into the sovereignty of Cherokee communities and the factional political structure that loosely bound them together.

As discussed above, South Carolina's diplomatic missions to the Cherokees in 1715 and 1725 exposed a good deal of political factionalism among Cherokee communities, factionalism that ran along regional and generational lines (Chicken [1715] 1894, [1725] 1916).[3] In both these cases, South Carolina diplomat George Chicken was frustrated by the lack of consensus he found among the Cherokees at their regional townhouse meetings.

The records of these meetings give a brief glimpse into the decision-making process that likely took place in many Cherokee communities when faced with important issues. These regional-level meetings were marathon affairs held among various factions representing different sides of an issue. During the 1715 expedition, which sought to persuade the Cherokees to go to war with the Creek, Chicken recorded four major meetings involving pro-war and anti-war headmen from numerous Cherokee towns. These factions were led by two men, Caesar of Echota (pro-war) and Charitey Hagey (anti-war), whose frequent appearance in colonial records indicate that they were two of the most powerful Cherokee leaders at the time (Hatley 1995:67). The records of the townhouse meetings demonstrate that these men relied heavily on their oratory prowess to incite support for their position. From the reactions of the audience, it is certain that these men had amassed large contingents of loyalists and exerted a tremendous amount of regional influence over Cherokee communities. Indeed, the parity in the influence held by each headman caused a stalemate in reaching a consensus regarding the decision to go to war. In the end, Chicken's expedition was not able to break the impasse between the two factions, but the "massacre at Tugaloo" certainly resulted in dire consequences for all Cherokee communities. Seeing the Cherokees' political process in action and given the results of the meetings, South Carolina officials should have questioned whether ending factionalism among the Cherokees was an attainable goal (Gearing 1962:79–84). As a diplomatic expedition mounted by Chicken a decade later would show, however, South Carolina ultimately decided that they could indeed put an end to Cherokee factionalism by forcing them to "nationalize" under a single European-style government.

Chicken's diplomatic mission to the Cherokees in 1725 had a twofold agenda—to broker a peace between the Cherokees and the Creek and to ensure that the Cherokees were not being swayed by recent overtures from French envoys (Oatis 2004:238–52). While not an ostensive goal of the mission, it is obvious that Chicken was also trying to ensure that a newly instituted "national" government was operating up to English expectations. The failure of the mission to end the Creek-Cherokee War has already been discussed, and ensuring the continued Cherokee hostility toward the French was practically guaranteed; therefore, the most provocative aspect of the mission concerned the Cherokees' rejection of the new English-installed political structure.

The Cherokee political structure Chicken expected to deal with was supposed to be very different than the one he encountered on his 1715 mission. The two most powerful Cherokee headmen, Caesar of Echota and Charitey Hagey, the conjuror of Tugaloo, had died, and new headmen were vying for their positions of power. Whereas the earlier headmen had gained their status during the period of Cherokee isolation (i.e., prior to 1715), the new leading men among the Cherokees were "sanctioned" by South Carolina officials through an official system of commissions. In theory, the Cherokees were supposed to have been "a [single] people" governed by a hierarchically organized regional monarchy with elected regional "kings," representing each of the three settlement divisions, and an elected national "King," a headman named Crow, who ruled over all Cherokee towns (Chicken [1725] 1916:109, 130).

The accounts in Chicken's journal do not portray a unified and compliant Cherokee nation under a single monarch; instead, they reveal that the same regional and generational factionalism that dominated Cherokee politics a decade earlier persisted. Chicken spent the early weeks of his mission traveling through the settlements trying to set up a meeting of all the headmen in the entire Cherokee "nation" at Ellejoy in the Middle settlements. In his travels, Chicken repeatedly reminded the Cherokee headmen of their commitment to the new unified national government, saying "Crow was their King . . . made by them and Approved of by the English" (Chicken [1725] 1916:109, 111). He also admonished the Cherokee headmen "to keep their Young Men under them and make them obey them in every thing" (Chicken [1725] 1916:109).

For Chicken, the question of whether or not Cherokee communities would recognize the authority of this new government was answered at the national council held at Ellejoy. First, the council almost did not happen at all when—despite continued pleas from Chicken to arrive on time—the delegation from the Lower settlements kept the rest of the Cherokee headmen waiting a full week. The only explanation they offered for their tardiness was that they were told the wrong date by the king of the Lower settlements (Chicken [1725] 1916:125). Upon hearing this half-hearted excuse, Chicken wrote "I plainly perceive by all the lower people that [they] have not any regard for their King" ([1725] 1916:125). Second, after factionalism plagued the "national" council and the Cherokee headmen failed to reach a consensus regarding making peace with the Creek, Chicken repeated in a letter to the colonial government that the Cherokees "do not in the least harken to him [King Crow] and the reason of it is because he is a Man they can't rely on for truth" ([1725] 1916:136). Third, shortly after the council, King Crow admitted to Chicken that his monarchy essentially held no power, saying "that the people would work when they pleased and go to Warr when they pleased, notwithstanding his saying all he could to them" (Chicken [1725] 1916:153). Chicken concluded that King Crow was simply the wrong man for the position, being "more under the Comands of his Subjects than they [were] under him" (Chicken [1725] 1916:153). As a solution, Chicken suggested backing another Cherokee headman as king.

Chicken's conclusion showed an obvious lack of understanding that factionalism and personal charisma formed the axis mundi around which early eighteenth-century Cherokee politics revolved (Gearing 1962). It is clear from the experiences in his journal that the differing political agendas among Lower, Middle, and Upper Cherokee headmen were largely the result of substantive regional differences in the social, economic, and political situations of the towns they led—situations that had significant historical depth. If the Cherokees were ever to act as a single body, which had yet to happen, it would necessarily have to be a decision born out of consensus rather than edict. Given all of the experience Chicken had with Cherokee politics, the very notion that sovereign Cherokee communities would accept a European-style monarchy was arrogant if not utterly laughable.[4]

In 1727, another diplomatic mission headed by Colonel John Herbert ([1727] 1936) found no vestige of the Cherokee "monarchy" or King Crow; instead, like Chicken before him, Herbert had to deal with a regional political structure composed of different factions each vigorously pursuing their own strategies. Indeed, the only major change since 1715 was that the leading headmen Caesar and Charitey Hagey were gone, and the Cherokee political factions had new charismatic leaders with names like "Breakerface" and the "Long Warriour of Tanasee."

Summary and Implications

The historical accounts tell a story of dramatic change in Cherokee communities during the English Contact period (1670–1740). Furthermore, these sources demonstrate that this story was unique to the Cherokees and had no correlate among other southeastern Indian groups. During the first half of the period, from 1670 until 1715, the Cherokees were not well known to history. From what little was written, it is likely that they, like most southeastern Indian groups, were weathering the effects of disease, colonial wars, slave raiding, and the deerskin trade. It appears, however, that the Cherokees' relative isolation might have offered them an additional measure of refuge from the shatter zone that was not enjoyed by other Indian groups. I would go so far as to argue that Cherokee isolationism was an intentionally enacted strategy used to avoid the turmoil and chaos that wracked other Indian communities—turmoil that was invariably associated with interaction with Europeans.

The murder of the Creek peace delegation in 1716 and the Cherokees' entrance into the Yamasee and Creek Wars effectively ended any possibility of maintaining an isolationist strategy because these acts awakened both South Carolina's unyielding desire to bring the Cherokees under their aegis and the Cherokee communities' need for trade goods to prosecute their war. The resulting sea change in Cherokee strategies can be seen in their meteoric rise to dominate the deerskin trade. In 1708, trade with the Cherokees was described as "inconsiderable," yet a decade later the Cherokees received more trade goods and sent more deerskins to Charleston than all other Indian groups combined. Between 1715 and 1740, Cherokee diplomacy was aimed at reacting to South Carolina's colonial policies. The journals kept by South Carolina diplomats who visited the Cherokees describe a very fluid and factional consensus-based political structure that was divided along generational and regional lines. The stubborn endurance of this political structure in the face of South Carolina's attempts to enact a change to a monarchy suggests that it was a long-lived and deep-set institution among Cherokee communities. To be sure, the factional and autonomous character of Cherokee "national" politics was fiercely adhered to because it provided a strategic benefit on the community level. This benefit appears to have been flexibility, for often times the situations created by the chaos of the shatter zone required different Cherokee communities to act in different ways. Ultimately, during this period one gets the sense that Cherokee headmen reckoned their obligations to particular communities to be much more important than obligations to a political organization on the level of a "nation."

The end of the English Contact period was brought about by a lethal component of the shatter zone that had lain dormant for almost a half a century. In 1738, just when Cherokee communities appear to have been successfully adjusting to the shatter zone and their postwar political and economic roles, a smallpox epidemic ravaged their population. James Adair, a trader among the Cherokees beginning in the 1730s, wrote: "About the year 1738, the Cheerake received a most depopulating shock, by the smallpox, which reduced them almost one half, in about a year's time" ([1775] 1986:244).[5] For Cherokee communities, population losses at this level certainly dashed any semblance of order they had managed to achieve during the post-Yamasee War years. In the wake of this epidemic, the Cherokees had to formulate new social, political, and economic strategies in order to negotiate the next period of their history.

The implication of the historical research presented in this chapter is that historical narratives of the English Contact period need to recognize: (1) the historical contributions made by the strategic actions of Indian groups, and (2) the unique mix of strategies and external forces that made the period a unique phenomenon on the local level. Through the analysis of scores of documents, historians have constructed a detailed picture of the social, political, and economic landscape negotiated by members of Cherokee communities, but there are ways in which the picture can be improved. The perspective of the landscape created by historians is necessarily cast through the eyes of the European colonial powers that authored the documents. Even though historians have been able to filter through European ethnocentrism in period documents, their interpretations remain necessarily restricted by a "paper cage" (consider who *isn't* written about and what subjects *don't* appear in those texts).

I believe we need to relocate the focus of our research within English Contact period Cherokee communities themselves, for these places were the crucibles in which the shatter zone was forged and negotiated between 1715 and 1740. I further believe that archaeology can contribute a great deal to understanding the period at the community level in ways that history simply cannot, given the latter's reliance on documentary evidence. In the next chapter, I argue that an archaeological study of the English Contact period at the community level will benefit most from a nuanced approach using sensitive analytical concepts that can track culture change at the household level.

Notes

1. My use of the "English Contact period" (ca. 1670–1740) is different from the "Contact period" (ca. 1710–1745) as defined for Overhill Cherokee ethnohistory by Schroedl (1986a, 2000). It is obviously a difficult endeavor to "cut up" the continuous flow of time into discreet "chunks" that are objectively meaningful. I propose a new time range because I believe it incorporates two events (the founding of Charleston and a major smallpox epidemic) that marked significant disjunctures certainly affecting the Cherokees, if not most Indian groups across the Southeast.

2. As is discussed in greater detail later, this episode has been much analyzed by historians as an example of how factionalism among the Cherokees ultimately thwarted any attempt by South Carolinians at diplomatic control (Oatis 2004:186–90).

3. The opposition of Lower *versus* the Middle and Upper settlements appears to have had some time depth, for in the Chestowee raid the Lower towns appear to have been purposefully left out because the headmen from the Middle and Upper settlements did not want to share in the spoils (McDowell 1992:56).

4. Oddly enough, when eccentric traveler Alexander Cuming personally installed a Cherokee "emperor" just five years later in 1730, the act was portrayed in period accounts as an absurd escapade (Williams 1928).

5. Peter Wood (1989:64) doubts the mortality rate of this epidemic was as severe as 50%, arguing that Adair might have conflated this epidemic with the smallpox epidemic of 1697. Wood instead places Cherokee losses at around 10% or 1000 people. The actual mortality rate was somewhere in-between; however, given the corroborating testimony of other Cherokee traders who were present during the epidemic, I believe that the rate was more likely closer to Adair's estimate (Hatley 1995:81–82).

Chapter 3

A Brief Review of Contributions to the Archaeology of Seventeenth- and Eighteenth-Century Cherokee Communities

This chapter presents a brief summary of past archaeological research involving the Cherokees. This summary is meant only to introduce the reader to the various research projects conducted over the past century that have contributed to our growing understanding of Cherokee prehistory and history. In-depth discussions of contributions to particular subfields are presented in the chapters that follow. More exhaustive historical syntheses can be found in Schroedl (2000) and Rodning (2004).

Scholarly interest in the archaeology of the Cherokees began with a focus on their prehistoric ancestry. Some of the earliest excavations were carried out in western North Carolina by the Valentine Museum and the Smithsonian Institution's Division of Mound Exploration in the midst of the "moundbuilder" debate of the last decade of the nineteenth century (Dickens 1979; Keel 1976; Schroedl 2000; Thomas 1894). Later in the 1930s, Lewis and Kneberg (1946; Lewis et al. 1995) relied on data from the Hiwassee Island site and the Chickamauga Basin survey in eastern Tennessee to argue that the Cherokees were late prehistoric immigrants to the area who replaced existing Muskogee-speaking groups (Schroedl 1986b:123–24, 2000:209). While the interpretations of these early projects have largely fallen out of favor, their work nevertheless raised interesting questions about Cherokee origins that are still being worked out today.

The 1960s and 1970s can be described as a period of intense research focused on historically documented Cherokee communities. This period included the establishment of three large-scale university-sponsored research programs that provided a wealth of data and interpretations regarding Cherokee history and prehistory. The projects were undertaken by archaeologists from the University of North Carolina at Chapel Hill, the University of Georgia, and the University of Tennessee. Each university program focused on a specific region including the Middle, Out, and Valley towns (University of North Carolina at Chapel Hill), the Lower towns (University of Georgia), and the Overhill towns (University of Tennessee) (Baden 1983; Chapman and Newman 1979; Coe 1961; Dickens 1976; Egloff 1967; Guthe and Bistline 1981; Keel 1976; Kelly and de Baillou 1960; Kelly and Nietzel 1961; Polhemus 1987; Russ and Chapman 1983; Schroedl 1986a). While each project concentrated on a different subregion of the Cherokee territory, all had similar aims in regard to Cherokee archaeology: (1) determining the origins of historically known Cherokee groups; (2) describing the material culture of historic Cherokee groups in each subregion; and (3) exploring how changes in material culture signaled changes in the lifeways of resident groups (Keel 1976: v–vi; Schroedl 1986a:531–32, 2000:210–11). The results of these investigations comprise much of our knowledge of seventeenth- and eighteenth-century Cherokee communities. In the following discussion, I review this research and more recent complementary studies, paying particular attention to how analyses of pottery, floral and faunal remains, European-made objects, and architecture have resulted in our current ideas about the chronology, lifeways, and organization of seventeenth- and eighteenth-century Cherokee communities.

Cherokee Potting Traditions

One of the many benefits produced by the various Cherokee research programs was a better understanding of Cherokee ceramic chronology. Cherokee pottery can be divided into two ceramic series that are related to two different traditions of pottery making. One style or tradition, represented by the Overhill series, primarily consists of plain shell-tempered pottery in jar, simple and restricted orifice bowl, cazuela, and pan forms (Baden 1983:37–62; Bates 1986:289–305; King 1977; Schroedl 2000:215). A diagnostic attribute of this series is a pinched or notched rimstrip that is either modeled from the final vessel coil or applied as a separate coil just below the lip or on vessel shoulders. Minority surface treatments include check stamping, incising, complicated stamping, and cob marking or roughening.

The Overhill series was primarily defined using collections recovered from excavations at historically documented Overhill Cherokee towns in the Lower Little Tennessee Valley. These towns, including Citico, Chota-Tanassee, Mialoquo, Tomotley, Toqua, and Tuskegee, were excavated as part of the Tellico Archaeological Project (Baden 1983; Chapman and Newman 1979; Guthe and Bistline 1981; Polhemus 1987; Russ and Chapman 1983; Schroedl 1986a). Cherokee occupations at these towns predominately date to the mid-eighteenth century, as indicated by European artifacts. Consequently, the Overhill series is limited to pottery assemblages from the English Colonial and Revolutionary War periods (ca. 1746–1794). Presently, there is little known about Overhill Cherokee pottery assemblages dating to the English Contact period or before. In fact, the lack of recognized Overhill assemblages that predate 1700 has made it difficult to discern the relationship between the historic Cherokee Overhill phase and the late Mississippian Dallas phases in the Lower Little Tennessee Valley (Schroedl 1986a:533, 1986b).

The other Cherokee pottery-making tradition is represented by the Qualla series. Qualla series pottery is broadly characterized by a grit-tempered paste and incised, stamped, and/or burnished vessel surfaces (Keel 1976:63). Rectilinear and curvilinear complicated stamping is a much more common surface treatment in the Qualla series than the Overhill series. The ubiquity of plain, notched, and pinched rimstrips on Qualla series vessels is similar to the Overhill series. Vessel forms include jars, hemispherical bowls, and cazuelas.

Through forty years of research in western North Carolina, archaeologists have been able to demonstrate that the Qualla series represents a 500-year-long south Appalachian pottery tradition that is part of the Lamar pottery complex (Egloff 1967; Hally 1986a, 1994; Keel 1976; Riggs and Rodning 2002; Ward and Davis 1999). Using pottery assemblages recovered from securely dated contexts, the Qualla series has been divided into three ceramic phases based on variability in vessel form, rim form, surface treatment, and rimstrip attributes (Rodning 2004; Riggs and Rodning 2002; Ward and Davis 1999). Based on radiocarbon dates from features at the Coweeta Creek site, Rodning (2004:312) associates the following calendrical dates with these phases: Early Qualla phase (ca. A.D. 1300–1500), Middle Qualla phase (ca. A.D. 1500–1650), and Late Qualla phase (ca. A.D. 1650–1838). Middle and Late Qualla phase pottery is essentially identical to pottery associated with the Tugalo and Estatoe phases (seventeenth- and eighteenth-century occupations at Cherokee Lower towns) in northeast Georgia (Hally 1986a; Riggs and Rodning 2002:38). Until the mid-eighteenth century, the distribution of Qualla series pottery appears to be distinct from the Overhill series, being concentrated in the Middle, Valley, Out, and Lower towns (Schroedl 2000:230).

Cherokee Foodways

Pottery studies have value aside from time-space systematics, such as in exploring the connection between Cherokee pottery and lifeways. Functional studies of Qualla pottery from Coweeta Creek, a sixteenth- through early eighteenth-century Cherokee Middle town, have added to our knowledge of Cherokee lifeways by identifying the probable activities (for example, storage, processing, cooking, serving) associated with different vessel forms (Wilson and Rodning 2002).

Analyses of faunal and floral remains speak more directly to the foodways of seventeenth- and eighteenth-century Cherokee communities. Remains from Coweeta Creek, Chatooga (early eighteenth century), and Chota-Tanassee (mid-eighteenth century) indicate that pre-contact food resources (including the triumvirate of corn-beans-squash, wild plants, nuts, fish, deer and bear) dominated Cherokee diet while introduced European plants (e.g., peaches, apples) and animals (e.g., pigs, cattle, chickens) comprised a much smaller portion of the diet that increased during the latter half of the eighteenth century (Bogan et al. 1986; Schroedl 2000; VanDerwarker and Detwiler 2000, 2002; Walker 1995).

Cherokee Involvement in European Trade

European-made artifacts recovered from Native American sites are most often used by archaeologists as time markers in constructing chronologies and as indicators of changes in lifeways brought about by European interaction (e.g., Harmon 1986; Smith 1987; Waselkov 1989, 1993). Assemblages of European-made artifacts recovered from the seventeenth- and early eighteenth-century Cherokee occupations at Coweeta Creek, Chatooga, and Chota-Tanassee were relatively small and included such items as drawn glass beads, kaolin pipe fragments, ornaments and fragments of cut brass, buttons, gunflints, gun parts, iron wedges, iron blades, and bottle glass fragments (Harmon 1986; Newman 1986; Rodning 2004). But for the absence of perishables like cloth and blankets, these assemblages match what would be expected with the early deerskin trade—a time that preceded significant changes in Cherokee material culture associated with the adoption of European technologies (see Chapter 2; Crane [1929] 2004:116–17; Hatley 1995:46–47; Oatis 2004:190–91).

Cherokee Architecture and Community Organization

The large-scale excavations of the 1960s and 1970s also provided researchers with the opportunity to explore the architecture and community organization of seventeenth- and eighteenth-century Cherokee towns. Together with the contemporary European written descriptions of eighteenth-century Cherokee towns, the results of these excavations have provided researchers with a general view of Cherokee structural design and community planning (see Schroedl 1986a:219–28, 2000). Cherokee architecture is usually discussed in terms of a domestic/public dichotomy that corresponds to household and townhouse structures (e.g., Baden 1983; Howard 1997; Rodning 2004; Schroedl 1986a, 1994, 2000). Domestic structures at eighteenth-century sites often consisted of paired winter and summer houses and associated smaller buildings (Schroedl 2000). Winter houses, or *asi*, were substantially built round or octagonal structures averaging 7 meters in diameter with central hearths and bench-lined interior walls (Keel 1976:28–34; Schroedl 1986a:267, 2000; Shumate et al. 2005). Summer houses were more lightly built rectangular structures averaging 9 by 5.5 meters that were erected adjacent to the winter house (Schroedl 1986a:268, 2000; Shumate et al. 2005). These two structures and surrounding area apparently served as the nexus for the daily activities of the household.

Townhouses were large octagonal structures measuring 16 meters in diameter with prepared clay hearths and bench-lined interior walls (Schroedl 1986a:263–66, 2000). Adjoining "summer townhouses" or pavilions were rectangular structures that were similar to summer houses, only larger. Townhouses were surrounded by open plazas, which together provided the setting for public events and ceremonies. Surrounding the townhouse and plaza were domestic structures loosely spaced between 25 and 50 meters apart to accommodate household gardens (Schroedl 1986a:539). This extensive rather than intensive community pattern was replicated in the scattered individual households and small settlements of regional settlement patterns (Schroedl 2000:206).

Excavations at individual sites representing seventeenth- and eighteenth-century Cherokee communities have, in some cases, confirmed these general patterns, while in other cases, excavations indicated possible regional and/or temporal variability in architecture and layout. For example, the only structures associated with the late seventeenth- and early eighteenth-century occupation at the Coweeta Creek site were a townhouse and associated pavilion—the last of six superimposed structures that were built over some 200 years (Rodning 2004:365–68). The townhouse was not octagonal like most historically documented Cherokee townhouses; instead, the structure was square with rounded corners and had a corner wall trench entrance. A similar design was identified at the late seventeenth- and early eighteenth-century Lower Cherokee town of Chattooga where four superimposed square-with-rounded-corner townshouses were found (Howard 1997; Schroedl 1994). These townhouses were also different from the Coweeta Creek townhouse in that they lacked wall trench entrances. Excavations at the Overhill towns of Chota-Tanassee, Toqua, Tomotley, and Mialoquo also uncovered temporal and regional variability by documenting changes to the design of townhouses in the latter half of the eighteenth century, as well as the presence of domestic structures that were possibly associated with Lower Cherokee architectural styles (Baden 1983; Chapman and Newman 1979; Harmon 1986; Polhemus 1987; Schroedl 1986a, 2000).

Current Concerns and Research Questions

In this section, I have summarized the findings of past archaeological research dealing with the chronology, lifeways, and organization of seventeenth- and eighteenth-century Cherokee communities. In doing so, I focused on ceramic chronology, foodways, European artifact assemblages, and architecture. The review has documented the many contributions that researchers have made to our current understanding of Cherokee communities during this period. I now offer the following statements regarding three areas where I believe our current level of understanding can be improved through additional research:

(1) There is a disparity between the chronological resolution offered by the Qualla and Overhill ceramic series.

This disparity is a direct result of a lack of *recognized* Overhill pottery assemblages that predate the mid-eighteenth century. A plausible remedy to this problem is to search for sites containing temporally diagnostic European artifacts, especially glass beads, that predate the mid-eighteenth century and that evince relatively short-term occupations. Attribute-based analyses of pottery assemblages from several of these sites should have the potential to identify temporally sensitive traits such as those identified in the Qualla series. Then, we can begin to correlate Overhill and Qualla pottery and construct more refined ceramic phases for the Overhill Cherokee region. I believe this type of research will be necessary in resolving questions of Overhill Cherokee origins.

(2) There has yet to be a comprehensive definition of the material culture pattern associated with English Contact period Cherokee settlements (ca. A.D. 1671–1745).

One of the main research aims of the Tellico Archaeological Project in the Lower Little Tennessee Valley involved identifying and describing changes in Cherokee lifeways associated with contact and interaction with Europeans during the sixteenth through nineteenth centuries (Newman 1986:415; Schroedl 1986a:532). To facilitate this analysis, researchers attempted to define material culture assemblages that corresponded with historically significant periods of time (for example, Spanish Exploration [ca. A.D. 1540–1670], English Contact [ca. A.D. 1671–1745], and English Colonial [ca. A.D. 1745–1775]) (Schroedl 2000:222). The sites excavated during the Tellico project provided a wealth of information about Cherokee material culture patterns for the English Colonial and Revolutionary War periods, but contexts from the English Contact period were lacking. Synthesizing artifact, architecture, floral, and faunal data from English Contact period contexts at existing and recently excavated sites will provide the necessary comparative information for advancing the study of Cherokee culture change.

(3) Currently, we have a normative view of Cherokee community life that privileges information contained in written accounts and excavations at historically prominent towns.

The typological thinking associated with the construction of archaeological phases or material culture patterns (see above) necessarily involves some essentializing. Archaeologists should, however, regularly explore differences within these analytical categories in order to search for potentially important variation. I believe this needs to be done with the archaeological phases representing historic Cherokee communities. The current definition of the Overhill phase, for instance, is primarily based on excavations at the social, political, and economic centers of Cherokee life during a specific time period (ca. 1746–1794). As Riggs (pers. comm., 2004) argues, this may present a biased view of Cherokee lifeways and the changes associated with European contact. To avoid this bias, our definitions must also include data from communities and settlements outside these centers. Similarly, we must also examine variability within the phases that represent the Lower, Middle, Valley, and Out towns of the Cherokees. Only two phases are currently defined for these towns: the Estatoe phase in the Lower towns and the Qualla phase in the remaining towns. The refinement of these phases would better characterize Cherokee culture given that (1) the archaeological evidence discussed above points to temporal and regional variability both among and within current archaeological phases; and (2) we have historically and archaeologically documented evidence of differences among Cherokee towns in regard to the timing, degree, and nature of interaction with Europeans and each other (e.g., Crane [1929] 2004:40–41; Hatley 1995:32–33, 157, 220–26; Oatis 2004:78–79; Schroedl 2000:216).

The data obtained from excavations at the Townsend site are crucial for addressing these three areas of concern. In the following chapters, I address architecture, features, pottery, European artifacts and chronology, and foodways with the goal of answering the following research questions:

(1) How can we use material culture to recognize Cherokee settlements that date to the English Contact period (ca. A.D. 1671–1740)?

(2) Of what did the daily lives of householders in small English Contact period Cherokee settlements consist?

(3) What was the nature of economic, social, and political interaction among households in late seventeenth- and early eighteenth-century Cherokee communities?

(4) Can we define distinctions in the material culture among Overhill, Middle, Valley, and Lower Cherokee communities at this time?

(5) How did life in Cherokee households during the late seventeenth and early eighteenth centuries compare to that of households predating and postdating sustained European contact?

Chapter 4

The Setting and Archaeology of the Townsend Sites

Returning from a diplomatic mission to the Overhill Cherokee towns in 1762, a regiment of Virginia colonial infantry marched through the western reaches of the Appalachian Mountains along what is known as the Great Indian Warpath. Upon reaching the Little River near present-day Maryville, Tennessee, the expedition leader Lieutenant Henry Timberlake commented:

> At this place had formerly been an Indian Town, called Elajoy (Ellejoy); and I am surprised how the natives should ever abandon so beautiful and fertile a spot. Were it a more polished country, it would make the finest situation for a gentleman's seat I ever saw. [Timberlake (1762) 2001:118–19]

This statement could apply to untold numbers of Indian "old towns" and "old fields" that were encountered by European travelers during the eighteenth century. What makes it intriguing is that the town described by Timberlake is located outside the region usually attributed to Cherokee settlements. In fact, this is the only existing contemporary account of a Cherokee town north of the Little Tennessee River Valley. The statement provides a tantalizing clue that counters the common perception that few, if any, permanent Cherokee settlements were located outside the Lower Little Tennessee and Hiwassee River Valleys (Schroedl 1986b:131). Timberlake's description begs two questions. First, was there a significant Cherokee presence in the Little River Valley during the late seventeenth and early eighteenth centuries or was the town described by Timberlake an anomaly? Second, if there was a significant Cherokee occupation of the Little River Valley, why would the groups living in this region permanently abandon these communities?

My main goal in this chapter is answering the first of these two questions. In doing so, I characterize the physical and cultural geography surrounding the Little River Valley during the English Contact period. I also assess the ethnohistoric and archaeological evidence regarding Cherokee occupation in the Little River Valley. At the risk of presaging the answer to this first question, answering the second question reveals why the remains of the English Contact period Cherokee community at the Townsend sites (40Bt89, 40Bt90, 40Bt91) presents a particularly apt case study for examining how Cherokee households and communities dealt with the social, economic, and political disruptions of the southeastern shatter zone during the English Contact period (see Chapter 2).

Physical and Cultural Geography Surrounding the Little River Valley

Contemporary European accounts and archaeological evidence demonstrate that Cherokee communities were spread across three different physiographic provinces during the English Contact period, each corresponding to the settlement divisions recognized by the English traders, colonial diplomats, and the Cherokees themselves (i.e., Lower, Middle, and Upper settlements). These settlement divisions correspond to the Piedmont Province of northern South Carolina and Georgia, the Blue Ridge Province of eastern Tennessee and western North Carolina, and the Ridge and Valley Province of eastern Tennessee respectively.

Most of the Little River Valley is located in the Blue Ridge Province, which spreads across eastern Tennessee, western North Carolina, and extreme northern Georgia. This rugged mountainous region contains many peaks with elevations of 1500 m above mean sea level (amsl) or more (Southworth et al. 2005). The province can be divided into highland and foothills subregions based on general topography. The highland subregion lies at the center of the province and contains the tallest mountains in the southeastern United States (i.e., the Great Smoky Mountains), whose elevations reach over 2000 m amsl. The foothills subregion surrounds the highland subregion and possesses less extreme slopes with peaks ranging in elevation from 250 m to 1300 m amsl (Southworth et al. 2005). The major river systems in the Cherokee-occupied portions of the province include the Little Tennessee, the Savannah, the French Broad, and the Hiwassee. These rivers form broad alluvial valleys as they flow out of the Blue Ridge Province into the Piedmont and the Ridge and Valley Provinces, but within the province they are narrow and fast moving, offering few areas suitable for large-scale (i.e., greater than household level) agriculture (Dickens 1979, 1986).

There are isolated areas within the Blue Ridge Province that do not conform to this rugged, mountainous depiction. These areas, known as coves (i.e., Cades Cove, Miller Cove, Wear Cove, and Tuckaleechee Cove), were formed by the erosion of Blue Ridge rocks and the exposure of Ridge and Valley limestone (Southworth et al. 2005:49–51) (Fig. 4.1). The coves are in essence small pockets of Ridge and Valley landscape in the midst of the Appalachian Mountains, and they include long broad river valleys that are similar to those of the Ridge and Valley Province. These valleys not only possess great potential for agriculture, but they also host a diverse array of plant and animal resources (Bass 1977:7; Braun 1950:201).

There are very few extant records that map out the cultural geography of English Contact period Cherokee communities. Fortunately, one of the few examples is a detailed map drafted as part of the region-wide Indian census of 1715 (Cumming 1998: Plate 48*A–D*). We can reconstruct a sort of snapshot of the region's cultural geography from a version of this map, the Barnwell-Hammerton map drafted in 1721 (Cumming 1998; Schroedl 2000; Smith 1979). This map shows that the major English Contact period Cherokee towns were distributed in clusters. Annotations on the Barnwell-Hammerton map describe three settlement clusters: those on "this side of the mountains" (i.e., Lower towns), the "middle settlements" (i.e., the Middle, Valley, and Out towns), and those "beyond the mountains" (i.e., Overhill towns). These settlement clusters remained stable throughout the eighteenth and early nineteenth centuries (Smith 1979; Schroedl 2000).

Cherokee towns were tied together by a series of trails and by rivers, which also linked Cherokee communities to the wider English Contact period landscape (Dickens 1979; Myer 1928; Ramsey [1853] 1999; Schroedl 2000). Figure 2.2 shows that all Cherokee settlements were not equally connected to the outside world. The Lower towns had the most direct access to English traders via trails to the Catawba and the Savannah River, but they also were closest to hostile Muskogee-speaking groups—a position that made these communities preferred targets during the Creek-Cherokee War following the Massacre at Tugaloo in 1716 (see Chapter 2). The central location of the Middle, Valley, and Out towns insulated these communities from enemy raids, but this position also limited their contact with European traders vis-à-vis the other settlement divisions. Overhill towns, which had greater connections to points west through the Tennessee River and Cumberland trails, had easier access to French traders and diplomats as well as to enemy Indian groups like the Shawnee and Illinois. As I am defining them here, the Tuckaleechee towns formed the northernmost extent of dense Cherokee settlement. Because of this location, these communities were the least well positioned for European trade, but they were by no means isolated. Far from being backwater communities, the Tuckaleechee towns were located on a spur off the Great Indian Warpath, a major trail that connected Cherokee communities to points north, including the distant Cherokee nemeses, the Iroquois.

The Tuckaleechee Towns

The historical record is virtually mute when it comes to the "mystery" of the Cherokee community of Ellejoy described by Lieutenant Timberlake in 1762. Nineteenth-century historian James G. M. Ramsey ([1853] 1999:88) offers a mention of the town and eponymous creek (Allejay) in his discussion of the Great Indian Warpath. Although very brief, this discussion does provide some very insightful clues about Cherokee occupation of the Little River Valley. In his description of the route of the Great Indian Warpath, Ramsey speaks of a path that leads "to the Tuckalechee towns, and so on to the Over-hill villages of the Cherokees" ([1853] 1999:88). I believe that two important points are contained in this short quote: (1) the identification of a group of Cherokee settlements in the Little River Valley, and (2) the description of these towns as being separate from the Overhill towns. Unfortunately, with the current data, we cannot discern whether or not the Tuckaleechee towns were an autonomous settlement division. This will be a very important question for future researchers in this area. Also unfortunate is the fact that

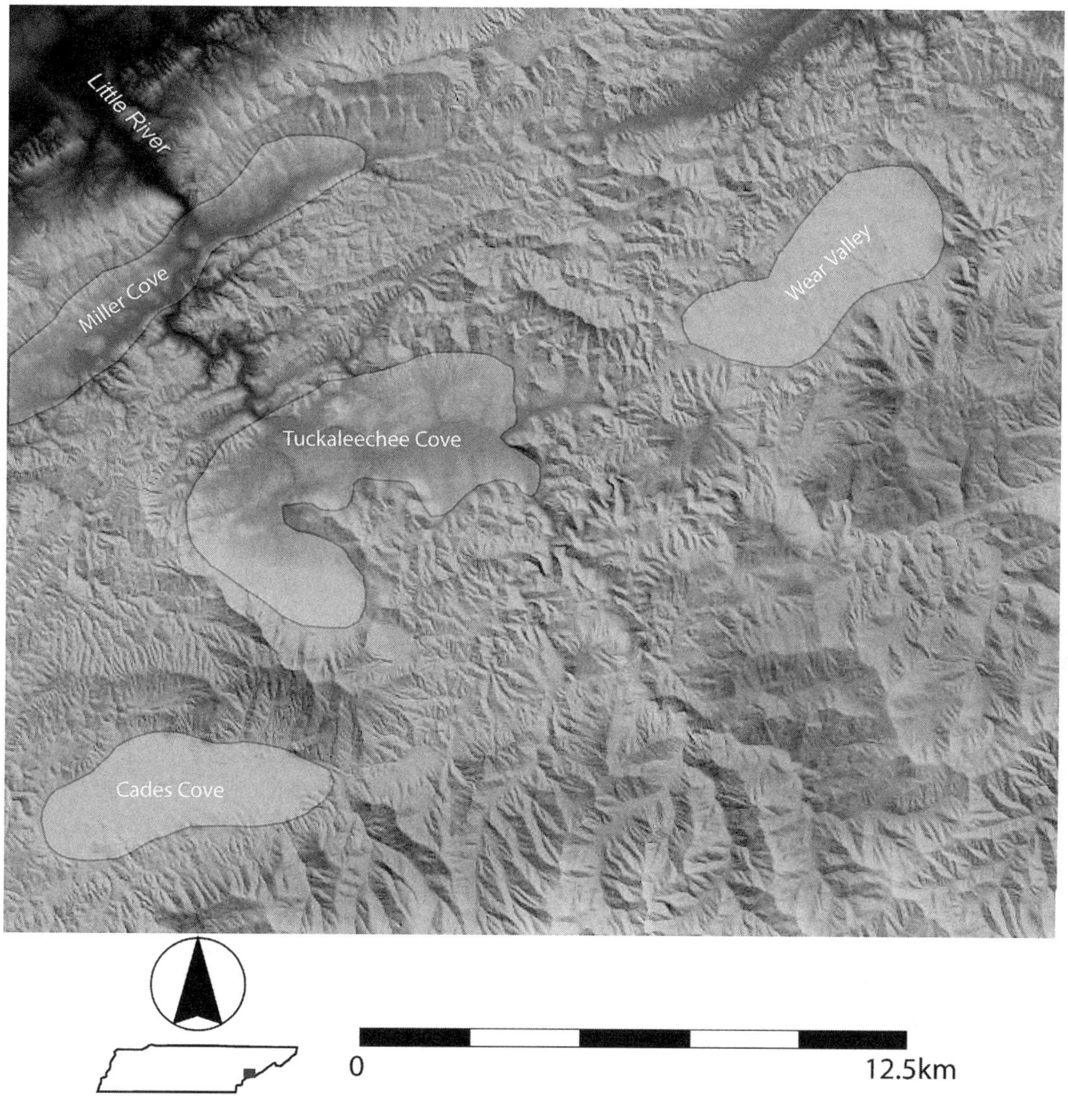

Figure 4.1 The physical geography of the western foothills subregion of the Blue Ridge Physiographic Province. Reproduced with permission from *Pox, Empire, Shackles, and Hides* (Marcoux 2010: Fig. 3.1), ©University of Alabama Press.

Ramsey is not clear about his sources and he does not reference any particular time period when offering this description. One is tempted to believe that Ramsey had access to the personal journal of Mr. Vaughn, a Virginia trader who proceeded down the Great Indian Warpath on a trading voyage around 1740 (Ramsey [1853] 1999:64).

Cherokee oral history suggests that Cherokee communities were found north of their eighteenth-century homeland at some point in the past. The early nineteenth-century journal of Major John Norton ([1816] 1970:46) records a voyage to his ancestral Cherokee homeland in 1813, where Cherokee elders relay that their "earliest traditions" place "original" Cherokee settlement at the head of the Tennessee River. Norton does not mention any specific towns or locations within this area, which lies further up the Tennessee River than the mouth of the Little River and the Tuckaleechee towns.

Nineteenth-century American actor, editor, and diplomat John Howard Payne (n.d.:88) argued that in earlier times the Cherokees lived near present-day Holston, Tennessee—closer to Virginia than the Tuckaleechee towns. In Payne's personal papers is a letter written to John Ross by Charles Hicks (1826), where the Cherokee chief relays a migration story that locates the earliest Cherokee settlements near the headwaters of the Clinch, Cumberland, and Holston Rivers in extreme northeastern Tennessee and southwestern Virginia. In this story, the Cherokees moved from this homeland to *Noh-nah-cloock-ungh* (*Na'na-tlu gun'*), Nolichucky or "Spruce-tree Place." Interestingly, there is archaeological evidence confirming the existence of early seventeenth-century-period Indian settlements located along the present-day Nolichucky River (Smith 1987, n.d.).

Perhaps the most detailed piece of ethnohistoric evidence for Cherokee settlement in or near the Little River Valley is contained in the Barnwell-Hammerton map of 1721 (Cumming 1998: Plate 48). Upriver from the confluence of the Little Tennessee River and Tennessee River, the cartographer placed the annotation "Deserted Settlem." (Fig. 4.2). The abbreviated form of the annotation makes it unclear as to whether the cartographer was referring to a single settlement or a group of settlements. Regardless, the map depicts the location of the deserted settlement(s), which lies between the "Canot" and "Agihqua" Rivers. These were the names given to the West Prong of the Little Pigeon River (Canot) and Pigeon River (Agihqua) during the eighteenth century (Ramsey [1853] 1999:87). Given the location, it is quite possible that this annotation refers to the "Tuckaleechee Towns" mentioned in Ramsey's ([1853] 1999) history.

The Barnwell-Hammerton map can never capture the dynamic nature of the period; however, that single annotation on the map does suggest that the Cherokees were in the process of shifting their settlement patterns during the early English Contact period. The Hunter Map of 1730 (Williams 1928:114) also shows that the

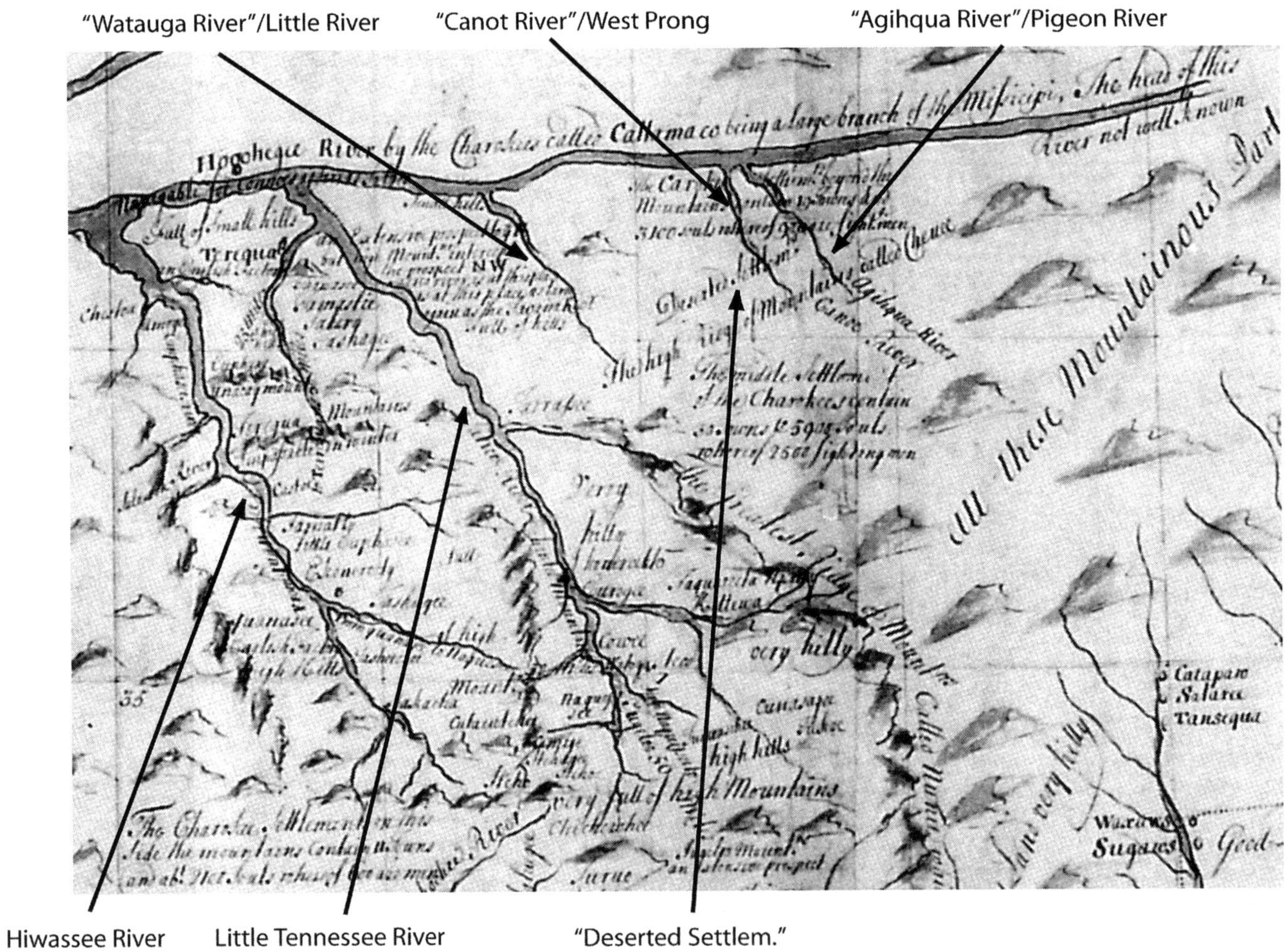

Figure 4.2. Magnified view of the 1721 Barnwell-Hammerton Map highlighting important landmarks for this study (ca. 1721: Map of part of North America from Cape Charles to the Mouth of the River Mississipi. Reproduced in Cumming [1998: Plate 48*A–D*]. Original at Yale Center for British Art). Reproduced with permission from *Pox, Empire, Shackles, and Hides* (Marcoux 2010: Fig. 3.3), ©University of Alabama Press.

northern settlements ("Tuckaleechee Towns") were abandoned by the time the map was drafted. Considering this together with the Barnwell-Hammerton Map, we can be reasonably confident that by the time of the Yamasee War in 1715 the Cherokees had largely abandoned their northern settlements, including those in the Little River Valley, and had concentrated their communities southward in the Little Tennessee and Hiwassee River Valleys.

Archaeology In and Near Tuckaleechee Cove and Excavations at the Townsend Sites

The Little River Valley and the surrounding coves area have seen little professional archaeological attention; however, what work has been done points to a significant English Contact period Cherokee occupation within Tuckaleechee Cove. An archaeological survey of the Great Smoky Mountains National Park identified two archaeological sites containing Qualla pottery (the diagnostic late prehistoric/historic Cherokee pottery series) (Bass 1977). One of these sites was located in Cade's Cove just south of Tuckaleechee Cove and the Little River Valley; the other site, which produced a whole simple stamped jar, was located near Cosby, Tennessee. Neither of these sites contained European artifacts, and it is difficult to assign the pottery to any archaeological phase based on what is published.

Except for these sites and the Townsend sites, current knowledge of the Cherokee occupation of the Little River Valley comes exclusively from a survey conducted by Mr. B. Kenneth Cornett, an avocational archaeologist and lifelong resident of Walland, Tennessee.[1] During the 1960s, Cornett surveyed plowed fields along the lower Little River Valley from Maryville to the entrance of the Great Smoky Mountains National Park east of Tuckaleechee Cove; he identified and made surface collections from 14 sites containing gravel-tempered complicated stamped and simple stamped pottery, plain shell-tempered pottery, and glass trade beads (Fig. 4.3). Based on its location at the confluence of Ellejoy Creek and the Little River, one of these sites is believed to be the Cherokee town of Ellejoy (40Bt11) described by Timberlake ([1762] 2001:118–19). During my interview with Mr. Cornett, he recalled giving the collections and records from the survey to the McClung Museum at the University of Tennessee. I was able to relocate the original USGS quadrangles that contained the site location information from Cornett's survey, but, unfortunately, I could not turn up any evidence of the artifact collections. In addition to the Townsend sites (described below), one other site identified by Cornett has been professionally excavated (40Bt47) (Bentz and Greene 1991). Virtually all the artifacts and features uncovered during the excavations were associated with an early Mississippian period settlement, but a single turquoise glass necklace bead was also found.

The Townsend sites (40Bt89, 40Bt90, and 40Bt91) are actually a single archaeological locality located in the western portion of Tuckaleechee Cove on a terrace south of the Little River near present-day Townsend, Tennessee (Fig. 4.4). The sites were formally recorded in 1999 as part of a cultural resources survey initiated by the widening of U.S. Highway 321 (Cornett's survey information was never incorporated into the Tennessee state site files). In addition to English Contact period Cherokee occupations, these sites contained evidence of occupations dating to the Late Archaic through Late Woodland periods (ca. 2500 B.C.–A.D. 900) and the Mississippian period (ca. A.D. 900–A.D. 1540). Later that year, archaeologists with the Transportation Center at the University of Tennessee-Knoxville conducted data recovery excavations at the sites. These excavations were truly monumental—on a scale that is rarely seen in post-Depression-era archaeology. Mitigation of the sites entailed the use of heavy machinery to strip plow-disturbed soil from the entire site in order to expose subsurface cultural features (pits, basins, hearths, postholes, burials, and so on) Over the course of the two-year field project, mechanical excavations uncovered over 100,000 m^2 of the sites, resulting in the identification of thousands of features and dozens of structures, including portions of two palisaded Mississippian villages, portions of multiple Woodland period villages, and the remains of six separate Cherokee households. The Cherokee occupational component at the Townsend sites is utterly dwarfed by the earlier occupations, especially those of the Woodland period. As the following chapters demonstrate, however, this small number of archaeological contexts provides a wealth of data regarding the daily lives of English Contact period Cherokee households in the Little River Valley.

The six Cherokee households at the Townsend sites form the core of my research. These households are composed of structures and pit features distributed widely over the length of the Townsend sites. Available evidence dating the household occupations indicates that they are generally contemporaneous (within 25 to 50 years or so of each other). Radiocarbon dating of samples from features provided spurious results, but archaeomagnetic dating of samples from the hearths of three of these households returned the same date range of approximately A.D. 1600–1740 (Lengyel 2004: Table 5.2). My analysis of beads and pottery from the site places the occupation between approximately A.D. 1650 and A.D. 1720 (see Chapter 9).

Conclusion

In this chapter, I introduced the thesis that the "Tuckaleechee Towns" were Cherokee settlements that were settled in the Little River Valley during the late seventeenth and early eighteenth centuries, and I provided supporting ethnohistoric and archaeological evidence. While much more work needs to be done identifying and synthesizing data from other sites in the Little River Valley, at this point we can indulge in some informed speculation regarding English Contact period Cherokee settlement patterns in this region. First, the physical and cultural geography surrounding the Tuckaleechee towns would have presented both advantages and disadvantages. The unique geology of the coves must have been attractive to Cherokee communities because they offered

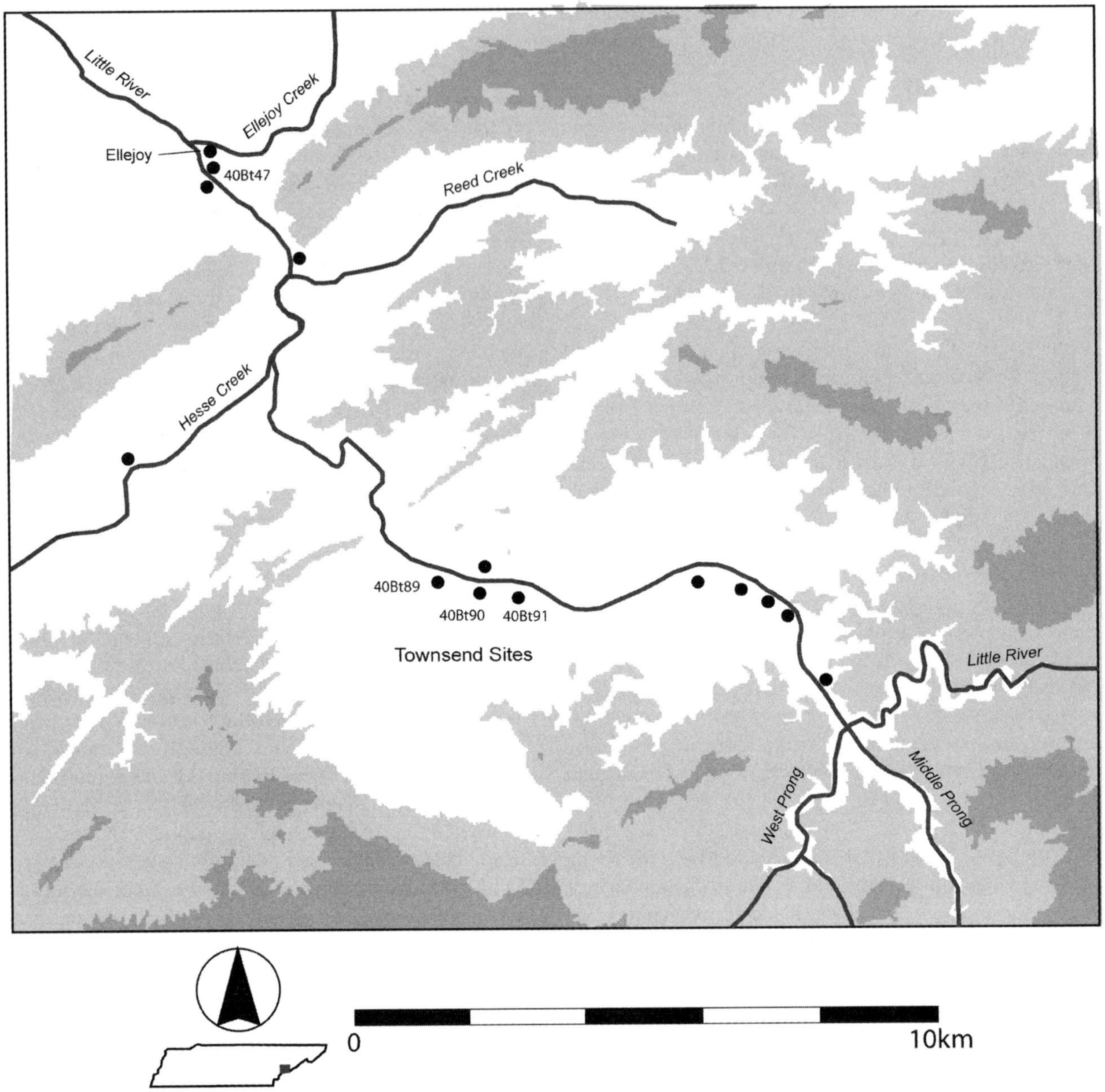

Figure 4.3. Map depicting the distribution of Cherokee sites in the Little River Valley (B. Kenneth Cornett, pers. comm., 2007).

the benefits of a broad alluvial landscape within a well-protected mountain refuge. Beginning in the early eighteenth century when Iroquois raiding parties began streaming southward, however, Tuckaleechee Cove would have become a dangerous location given its proximity to the Great Indian Warpath (Norton [1816] 1970:262). Indeed, these raids may have been a major contributing factor in the choice to abandon the area by approximately 1720.

If only historical sources were consulted, one would assume that Cherokee communities went largely unaffected by the disruptions of the shatter zone until they joined the fray of the Yamasee War in 1715 (see Chapter 2). This conclusion would be even easier to arrive at for the communities located in Tuckaleechee Cove. Fortunately, archaeology allows us to push beyond the dearth of maps and personal accounts that confines our historical understandings of the period to ask: What was life like for

Figure 4.4. Aerial photograph of excavations at the Townsend sites. Reproduced with permission from *Pox, Empire, Shackles, and Hides* (Marcoux 2010: Fig. 3.5), ©University of Alabama Press.

Cherokee families who chose to settle in Tuckaleechee Cove during the late seventeenth century? Were folks in this area spared the disruptions of the shatter zone, or were they instead, through their strategic actions, the very embodiment of the shatter zone? The household contexts at the Townsend sites present the perfect case study for analyses that attempt to answer these questions.

Note

1. Personal communication with Mr. B. Kenneth Cornett, Maryville, Tennessee, in 2007.

Chapter 5

Architecture

Excavations at the three Townsend sites uncovered post-hole patterns representing the remains of eight clearly defined structures and two to three poorly defined structure remnants associated with the historic Cherokee occupation. Based on size, shape, and construction technique, all of these structures correspond to ethnohistoric and archaeological descriptions of Cherokee domestic dwellings dating from the latter half of the seventeenth century to the early nineteenth century (e.g., Adair [1775] 1986:443; Bartram [1791] 1996:298–300; Norton [1816] 1970:54, 141; Schroedl 1986a:217–71, 2000; Shumate et al. 2005). In this chapter, I provide a brief review of seventeenth- through nineteenth-century Cherokee architecture based on ethnohistoric accounts and previous archaeological research. I then describe the architectural characteristics of the structures found at the Townsend sites, focusing on method of manufacture, structure function, household size, and occupation duration. I conclude the chapter by placing the Townsend structures within a temporal and geographic context through comparisons to structures from various protohistoric and historic Cherokee sites in eastern Tennessee and western North Carolina.

Ethnohistoric Descriptions of Eighteenth- and Early Nineteenth-Century Cherokee Architecture

Historic descriptions of Cherokee structures are commonly divided into a public/domestic architectural vernacular expressed in the opposition between large townhouse structures and smaller household dwellings. Mid-eighteenth- and early nineteenth-century descriptions of so called "winter townhouses" or "rotundas"—most notably those of Adair ([1775] 1986:453), Bartram ([1791] 1996:299–300), Norton ([1816] 1970:54), and Timberlake ([1762] 2001:59)—give the image of very large round or polygonal wooden structures that could house several hundred people. One of the main features of these substantially built structures were the central roof supports. These were massive wooden posts, 10–12 feet in length, which formed a square or ring at the center of the townhouse. The outer walls of the townhouse were made of interwoven cane or bark mats secured to upright posts and covered in clay daub. The roof was covered in bark and a layer of soil. Entrance to the building was gained through a very small doorway, which opened into an expansive inner chamber lined with benches for sitting. At the center of the townhouse was a formal hearth where a fire was kept alight constantly. Period descriptions sometimes mentioned a companion structure, known as a "summer townhouse," "ramada," or "pavilion." These appear to have been much less formal structures with open rectangular floor plans and open sides. These buildings were used for community rituals and meetings during warmer months.

Descriptions of Cherokee domestic architecture include paired winter and summer structures (Adair [1775] 1986:448–50; Bartram [1791] 1996:298–99; Norton [1816] 1970:141; Timberlake [1762] 2001:84). Winter domestic structures, sometimes called "hot houses" or *asi*, were essentially smaller versions of winter townhouses, built using the same architectural principles. The framework of these round or octagonal structures consisted of four large central roof support posts arranged in a square surrounded by an outer ring of upright posts forming the outer walls. Like townhouses, the walls of winter houses were described as being daubed and the roof was covered in a layer of soil. Also like the townhouses, these structures had a single small doorway, benches lining the walls, and a central hearth. Summer houses were described as smaller analogs to the townhouse ramada or pavilion. They were lighter built rectangular structures located within a few meters of the winter house. Summer houses contained a hearth and interior benches, they were sometimes divided into three compartments, and they sometimes featured at least one open side.

Archaeological Descriptions of Cherokee Architecture

Over the past few decades, there have been a number of archaeological projects that have included the excavation and analysis of a large number of prehistoric and historic Cherokee structures (e.g., Baden 1983; Chapman and Newman 1979; Coe 1961; Dickens 1976, 1979; Guthe and Bistline 1981; Keel 1976; Polhemus 1987; Rodning 2004, 2007; Riggs 1989; Russ and Chapman 1983; Schroedl 1986a, 1989). The temporal and geographic coverage of these projects is somewhat uneven; nevertheless, the results of this research have provided the foundations for developing a diachronic perspective on Cherokee architecture. The nascent architectural sequence emerging from this work not only lends additional insight to the ethnohistorical descriptions discussed above, but it allows researchers to explore relationships among architectural forms that existed before and after contact with Europeans (sensu Hally 2002). Furthermore, by shedding light on the use-histories of Cherokee structures, the results of this archaeological research allow interpretations to go beyond simply confirming or refuting the ethnohistoric descriptions.

Christopher Rodning's (2002, 2004) recent synthesis of University of North Carolina excavations at the Coweeta Creek site in western North Carolina has provided crucial descriptions of architecture in a Cherokee Middle settlement community occupied primarily during the sixteenth and seventeenth centuries. Rodning, like most other researchers discussed below, found that the architecture at the site could easily be divided into public and domestic types based on the size, location, and method of manufacture of the structures. Excavations of a low mound at the site uncovered the archaeological remains of at least six versions of a townhouse built sequentially on the same building footprint (Rodning 2002:12). The results of Rodning's (2004:329) analyses of European trade goods, pottery, and radiocarbon dating led him to date the first four townhouse stages to the Middle Qualla phase (ca. A.D. 1500–1650) and the last two stages to the first quarter of the Late Qualla phase (ca. A.D. 1650–1720). Over the course of its use-life, perhaps some two centuries, each incarnation of the townhouse was built according to a very consistent plan—a square edifice with rounded corners roughly measuring 14 m by 14 m that contained four large central roof support posts, a large central hearth, numerous small interior posts that likely supported benches, and a single entry marked by parallel wall trenches. Uncovered just next to the townhouse were posthole patterns representing multiple building episodes of a large ramada or summer townhouse. Numerous burials were placed in and around the townhouse during its use-life, a treatment that Rodning (2004:411) argued was largely restricted to adult male community leaders who excelled in diplomacy, warfare, and exchange—matters that were external to the community.

Rodning (2004:147–91) also identified fifteen domestic structures at the Coweeta Creek site. Along with the townhouse, these structures were tightly arranged around a central plaza. Like the townhouse, the remains of these domestic structures were materialized in the archaeological record as clustered palimpsests of postholes, hearths, and wall trench entries representing multiple rebuilding episodes on the same footprint. Rodning (2004:335–46, Tables 8.9, 8.10) was able to assign fourteen structures to occupational phases based on diagnostic pottery and radiocarbon dating. Of these, five structures were associated with the Early Qualla phase (ca. A.D. 1300–1500), eight were associated with the Middle Qualla phase (ca. A.D. 1500–1650), and one was associated with the early Late Qualla phase (ca. A.D. 1650–1720). Rodning (2004:187–89) found a distinction in the forms of domestic structures between the Early Qualla phase and Middle Qualla phase. Structures from both phases had four central roof support posts, central hearths, and wall trench entryways, and were rebuilt multiple times. Early Qualla phase structures, however, were larger than Middle Qualla phase houses (approximately 60 m^2 vs. 40 m^2 in floor area), were more round in shape, and, when rebuilt, their hearths were relocated and the structure was shifted slightly. Middle Qualla phase houses were shaped more like the townhouse (that is, square with round corners), and when they were rebuilt the hearths were remodeled in place and the location of the new building did not change. Neither form of domestic structure at Coweeta Creek appears to have had an adjoining summer house.

Rodning (2004:150) also pointed out that the Middle Qualla phase domestic structures at Coweeta Creek were more similar in shape and construction technique to domestic structures at contemporaneous protohistoric Mississippian sites in northern Georgia, western North Carolina, and southeastern Tennessee than to the historic Cherokee domestic structures featured in eighteenth-century descriptions (e.g., Blakely 1988; Hally 1988, 1994, 2002; Lewis et al. 1995; Polhemus 1987; Sullivan 1989). Hally (2002) has highlighted the widespread distribution of this particular house form across the Southeast during the protohistoric period, adding that at some sites these winter house forms were joined by rectangular structures that probably served as an earlier form of summer house. Both Hally (2002) and Waselkov (1990) have argued that the protohistoric house form was eventually abandoned at the beginning of the eighteenth century as southeastern Indian communities adjusted to the growing demands of the commercial deerskin trade by changing their community organization and mobility patterns.

The structures encountered at Cherokee sites dating to the English Contact period (ca. 1670–1740) evinced a continuation of the same basic architectural dichotomy of opposing public townhouses and domestic dwellings. There were also, however, some changes in the architectural form of both public and domestic structures. Three English Contact period townhouses were excavated by the Tellico Archaeological Project at the Overhill Cherokee settlements of Chota-Tanasee and Toqua (Polhemus 1987:342–45; Schroedl 1986a:263–66, 2000:214–15). The Chota-Tanasee townhouse differed somewhat from the Coweeta Creek townhouse in that it lacked wall trench entryways and was octagonal in shape rather than square with rounded corners. The Chota-Tanasee structure was similar in size to the Coweeta Creek townhouse, measuring 16 m in diameter, and it had four large central roof support posts, a large formal clay hearth, and bench-lined interior walls. The two townhouses excavated at the Toqua site were also octagonal (or, more accurately, square with truncated corners), lacked wall trench entryways, and measured roughly 15 m on a side. These structures also featured the other trademarks that defined Cherokee townhouse vernacular (that is, four large central roof support posts, a large formal clay hearth, and bench-lined interior walls). A very similar townhouse design was identified in excavations at the Lower settlement Cherokee town of Chattooga. At this site, four superimposed townhouses were uncovered that matched all the structural features of the Overhill townhouses except that they were square with rounded corners and had large ramadas like the townhouses associated with the Coweeta Creek site (Howard 1997; Schroedl 1994).

English contact period Cherokee domestic structures, like those found at the Townsend sites, appear to have undergone some degree of change from the preceding Middle Qualla phase (the results of a detailed quantitative comparison of domestic structures are reported below). Cherokee domestic structures dating to the English contact period have been identified at the Alarka and Tuckaseegee sites in western North Carolina, the Chattooga site in northern South Carolina, and the Chota-Tanasee site in eastern Tennessee (Howard 1997; Keel 1976; Schroedl 1986a, 1994; Shumate et al. 2005). The style of domestic architecture found across these sites was very similar and consisted primarily of paired winter and summer dwellings of the type described in European accounts. Winter houses, or *asi*, were no longer built in a square shape; instead, they were round or octagonal. The English Contact period form of winter house also lacked wall trench entryways. These structures were roughly the same size (approximately 40 m^2) as structures from the preceding period and had similar architectural features including four central roof support posts, central hearths, and bench-lined interior walls (Keel 1976:28–34; Schroedl 1986a:267, 2000; Shumate et al. 2005). Summer houses were very frequently found adjacent to winter houses. These rectangular structures were more lightly built with widely spaced posts, and averaged 9 m by 5.5 m (Schroedl 1986a:268, 2000; Shumate et al. 2005). Like the earlier phase, this style of domestic architecture appears to have been widely distributed across the Southeast. Similar forms of paired structures, for example, have been identified in excavations at the contemporaneous Creek sites of Fusihatchee and Tukabatchee (Hally 2002; Knight 1985:73–78; Waselkov 1990).

Throughout the remainder of the eighteenth century, Cherokee communities continued to employ the public/domestic dichotomy in their architecture. As with earlier periods, however, the styles of these buildings again underwent some degree of change. Excavations at the Overhill settlement towns of Chota-Tanasee, Tomotley, and Mialoquo demonstrated that the townhouses built in the later half of the eighteenth century retained the same shape, size, and basic configuration as townhouses of the English Contact period. In these later townhouses, however, the number of central roof supports was increased from four to eight posts (Schroedl 1986a:540). The same trend was evident in the townhouse sequence at the Lower settlement town of Chattooga, although the increase in interior roof supports took place before 1740 (Howard 1997; Schroedl 1994, 2000:214).[1]

Excavations at the Overhill settlements of Chota-Tanasee, Toqua, Mialoquo, and Tomotley, and the Lower settlement of Toxaway evinced much more variability in house form following the English Contact period (ca. post-1740) (Baden 1983; Harmon 1986; Polhemus 1987; Russ and Chapman 1983; Schroedl 1986a, 1989). At Chota-Tanasee and Toqua, paired winter and summer houses were still de rigueur during the later half of the eighteenth century, while at Mialoquo, Tomotley, and Toxaway these forms were largely abandoned in favor of single or clustered rectangular buildings built of vertical posts—a building style that Timberlake ([1762] 2001:84) described at Cherokee communities in the 1760s, and Bartram ([1791] 1996:564–66) attributed to the Creek in the 1780s. Some archaeologists have argued that rectangular dwellings were initially popular in Lower Cherokee towns and that this form of architecture spread to Overhill towns by refugees who fled the destruction of the Lower settlements during the Revolutionary War (Baden 1983). Early nineteenth-century architecture from Chota-Tanasee and the Bell Rattle Cabin site demonstrate that domestic house forms across many Cherokee communities began to undergo a further shift from native forms to single European-style horizontal log cabins by the turn of century (Riggs 1989; Schroedl 2000:225).

Cherokee Architecture at the Townsend Sites

The excavations at 40Bt89, 40Bt90, and 40Bt91 identified posthole patterns associated with eight clearly defined Cherokee structures and two poorly defined structure remnants. All but one of these structures were identified during the process of excavation based on size, shape, and diagnostic artifact associations. The remaining ambiguous structural remnant (Structure 27) was tentatively identified following excavations. Once identified, these structures were mapped and recorded in the field using standardized forms. Data recorded on these forms included north-south and east-west dimensions, the number of postholes comprising the structure, enumeration of associated features, and a general narrative of the structure's excavation. With the exception of Structure 27, all the postholes associated with each structure were bisected and excavated and a profile drawing of each posthole was made.

The architectural and artifact data from the entire project area were later linked with plan view maps and incorporated within a Geographic Information System (GIS) database. This allowed me to perform a check for the possible existence of additional Cherokee structures by exploring the distributions of diagnostic Cherokee pottery and glass trade beads and by searching for patterns in the configurations of postholes. Two additional locations of Cherokee occupation were identified through the presence of diagnostic pottery, but these occurrences were confined to a few postholes and isolated pits. While Cherokee structures could have been located in these areas, no additional evidence for structures could be found (see Chapter 6 for a discussion of these instances). The ten definitive Cherokee structures and associated Cherokee pit features were distributed across the Townsend sites in six discrete clusters, each representing a single household (Fig. 5.1). As discussed below, two of these households consisted of paired winter and summer dwellings; one household consisted of a winter dwelling, a summer dwelling, and a ramada; and two households consisted of single winter houses. The architectural form of the final household (Structure 27) could not be determined as confidently because the structures were not identified in the field and the postholes comprising the structures were not excavated. Consequently, the lack of any diagnostic Cherokee artifacts precluded the confident association of any posts with a Cherokee occupation.

Assessing the Method of Manufacture of Cherokee Structures at Townsend

As discussed above, ethnohistoric descriptions have provided archaeologists with detailed accounts regarding the method of manufacture of Cherokee winter and summer dwellings. The methods used to construct domestic structures were described most eloquently by James Adair in reference to "generic" summer and winter houses of southeastern Indians.

> For their summer houses, they generally fix strong posts of pitch-pine deep in the ground. . . . The posts are of equal height; and the wall plates are placed on top of these, in notches. They sink a large

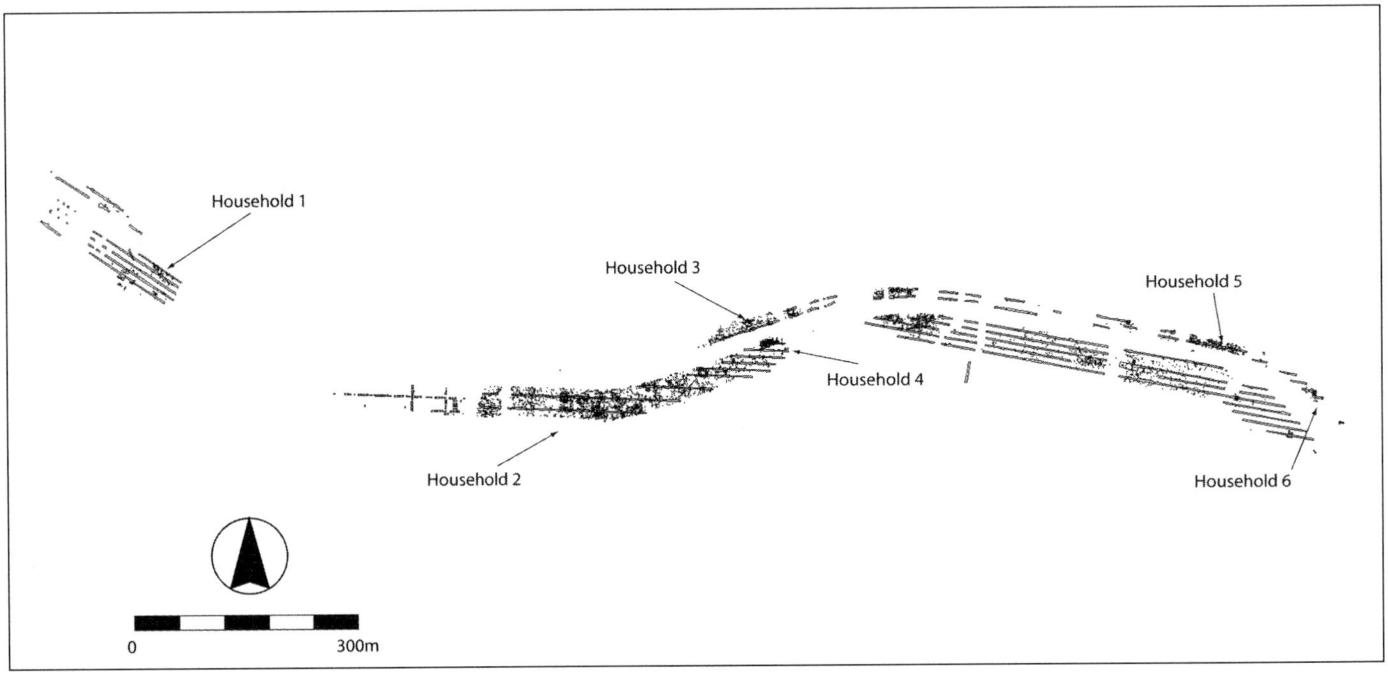

Figure 5.1. Map depicting the locations of the six Cherokee households identified during the Townsend project. Reproduced with permission from *Pox, Empire, Shackles, and Hides* (Marcoux 2010: Fig. 3.6), ©University of Alabama Press.

post in the center of each gable end, and another in the middle of the house where the partition is to be, in order to support the roof-tree [ridge pole]; to these they tie the rafters. . . . they cover the fabric with pine, or cypress clap-boards, which they can split readily; and crown the work with the bark of the same trees. . . . To raise these [winter houses], they fix deep in the ground, a sufficient number of strong forked posts, at a proportional distance, in a circular form, all of an equal height, about five or six feet above the surface of the ground: above these they tie very securely large pieces of the heart of white oak, which are of a tough flexible nature, interweaving this orbit, from top to bottom, with pieces of the same, or the like timber. Then, in the middle of the fabric they fix very deep in the ground, four large pine posts, in a quadrangular form, notched a-top, on which they lay a number of heavy logs, let into each other, and rounding generally to the top. Above this huge pile, to the very top, they lay a number of long dry poles, all properly notched, to keep strong hold of the under posts and wall-plate. Then they weave them thick with their split saplings, and daub them all over about six or seven inches thick with tough clay, well mixt with withered grass: when this cement is half dried, they thatch the house with the longest sort of dry grass, that their land produces. [Adair (1775) 1986:449–51]

Past archaeological research has confirmed these descriptions on a general level (e.g., Schroedl 1986a, 1989; Baden 1983; Polhemus 1987). However, these works lacked the kind of quantitative operationalization that allows for more objective intra- and inter-site comparisons of Cherokee house construction methods.

Elsewhere, I have offered a way to operationalize Cherokee house building practices in the attempt to better link our interpretations of Cherokee architecture to archaeological data (Marcoux 2010:111–17; see also Shumate et al. 2005).[2] This method is based on three important testable statements generated by Adair's description: (1) there should be different types of postholes comprising the posthole patterns of summer houses and winter houses—deep, large-diameter postholes that were dug to accept central roof supports and smaller diameter perimeter postholes that were dug for posts that supported wall plates; (2) in winter houses, the large deeply dug postholes representing the central roof supports should form a quadrangle in the center of a round pattern of postholes representing the structure walls; and (3) the large deeply dug postholes representing the central roof supports in summer houses should be arranged in a line down the center of a rectangular arrangement of postholes representing the structure walls.

The first expectation should be evident as multiple modes in the distribution of posthole depths, as well as significant differences in the median depths and/or diameters among those post types. Testing this expectation includes all excavated postholes associated with Cherokee structures at the Townsend sites with the exception of Structure 27, whose posts were not excavated ($n = 368$). The tri-modal distribution of posthole depths does indeed suggest the existence of separate types of postholes with modes at 11 cm, 21 cm, and 38 cm (Fig. 5.2). Three types are defined by these modes: exterior posts include postholes less than 15 cm deep, exterior support posts include postholes 16–30 cm deep, and central roof supports include posts greater than 30 cm deep (Fig. 5.3).

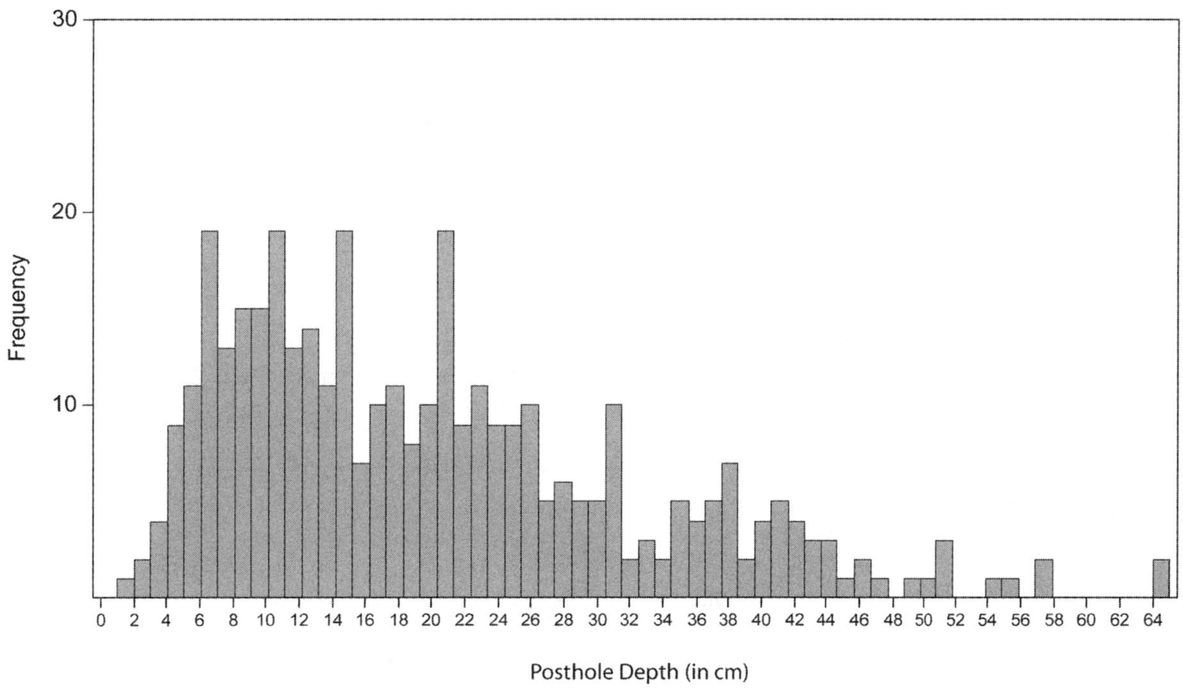

Figure 5.2. Histogram depicting the distribution of posthole depths for Cherokee structures at Townsend. Reproduced with permission from *Pox, Empire, Shackles, and Hides* (Marcoux 2010: Fig. 5.2), ©University of Alabama Press.

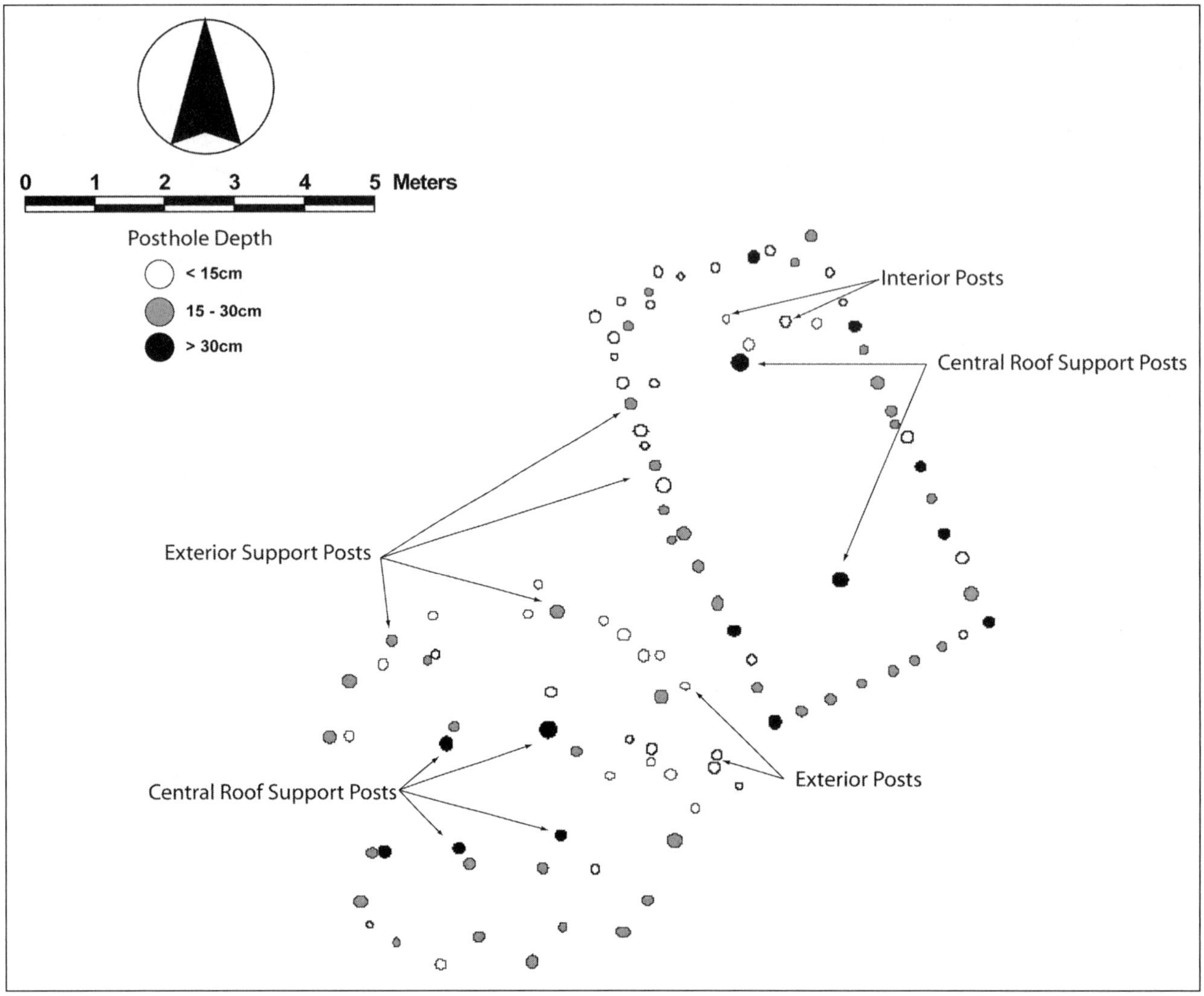

Figure 5.3. Hypothetical examples of post types based on posthole depth and location within structures. Reproduced with permission from *Pox, Empire, Shackles, and Hides* (Marcoux 2010: Fig. 5.3), ©University of Alabama Press.

Comparisons of median posthole depths and diameters can be used to test the likelihood that these posthole types represent, in some sense, real differences related to the choices made during the construction of Cherokee structures (Table 5.1).[3] Figure 5.4 depicts a comparison of the distributions of depths among the four posthole types. In the figure, the distributions of posthole depths are portrayed using a visual display known as a notched boxplot (McGill et al. 1978; Velleman and Hoaglin 1981:65–81). Boxplots graphically represent the spread of posthole depth values. The median is depicted as the center of the notch in each boxplot, and the length of the "box" represents the "H-spread" or the range within which the central 50% of the posthole depth values fall. The ends of this box are known as "hinges," whose values are essentially equivalent to the first and third quartiles of the distribution. The vertical lines extending from the box, known as "whiskers," mark posthole depth values that fall within 1.5 "H-spreads" of the hinges. Outliers in the distributions are marked as asterisks, and far outliers are marked by open circles. The notches within the boxes represent the 95% confidence intervals for each median value. In using boxplots to compare the median depths of the post types, if the notched intervals around any medians do not overlap, one can be confident that those post types are different at a 0.05 level of significance. The results depicted in Figure 5.4 indicate that there are significant differences in posthole depths among three of the four types. Central support posts have by far the largest depth values, followed by exterior support posts. Interior posts and exterior posts have median values that are significantly lower than the other two types

Table 5.1. Basic statistics for depth and diameter of Cherokee structure postholes.

Post Type	*n*	Mean Depth (cm)	Standard Deviation	Median Depth	Mean Diameter (cm)	Standard Deviation	Median Diameter
central roof support	33	41.60	1.42	37	23.36	0.82	22
exterior support	127	26.60	0.73	24	19.18	0.42	18
interior	113	14.61	0.78	12	16.70	0.44	16
exterior	95	9.40	0.86	10	17.02	0.48	17

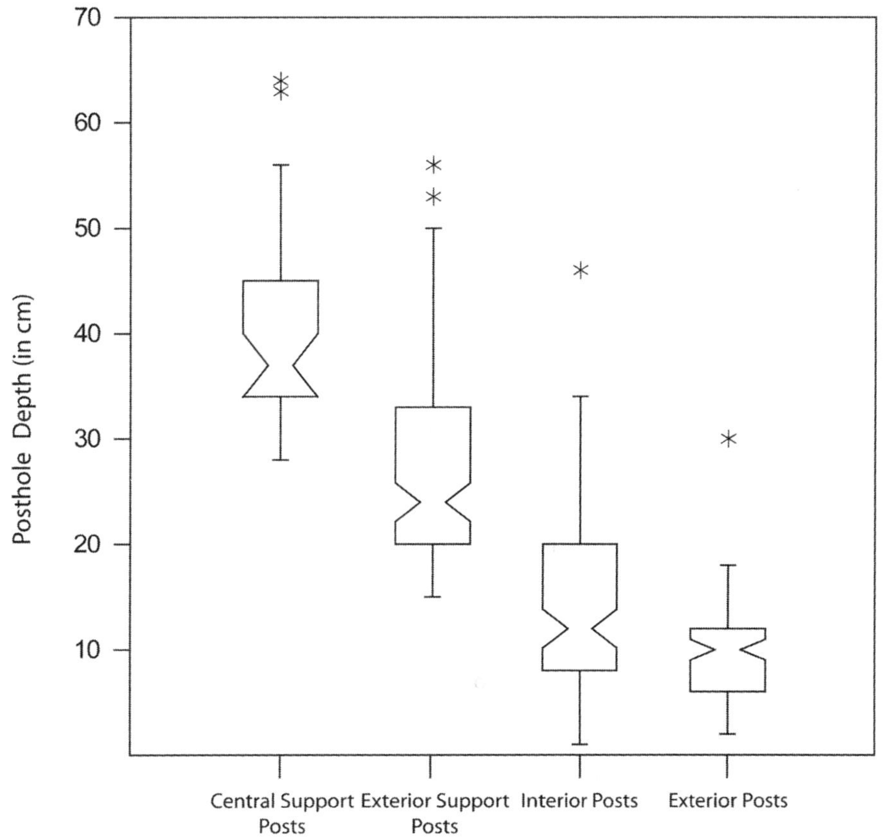

Figure 5.4. Boxplots comparing the distributions of posthole depth among post types.

but not significantly different from each other. A comparison of median posthole diameters indicates that central support posts are significantly larger than all other post types (Fig. 5.5). Taken together, these analyses suggest that Cherokee dwellings were constructed of posts of two different diameters, and that these posts were sunk to different depths depending on the role they played in the structural stability of the dwelling.

The second and third expectations regarding the arrangement of different post types in winter and summer houses can be tested by exploring the spatial distribution of the posthole types on plan view drawings of the structures. Figures 5.6–5.10 depict all the confirmed Cherokee structures at the Townsend sites with postholes shaded to represent the three depth types. Detailed descriptions of each structure are given later in this chapter, but to test the expectations regarding the arrangement of central support posts and other posts in Cherokee structures, these plan views will suffice. All the round to octagonal structures (i.e., Structures 1, 8, 12, 22, and 47), which presumably represent winter houses (see the discussion of structure function below), contain at least one set of four central postholes greater than 30

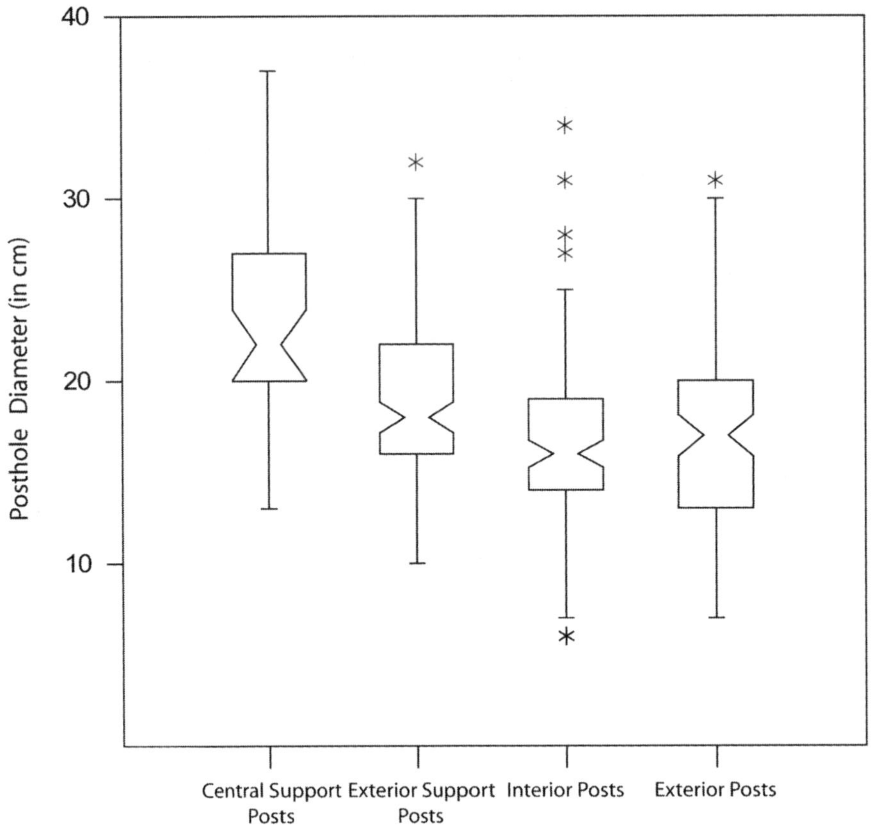

Figure 5.5. Boxplots comparing the distributions of posthole diameter among post types.

cm deep arranged roughly in a square and have a floor area of approximately 40 m^2 (Table 5.2). Two structures (Structures 22 and 47) feature widely spaced deep exterior postholes (exterior support posts) interspersed with more shallow exterior postholes (exterior posts). This posthole pattern, where deeper exterior postholes correspond to corner support posts linking wall segments, has been identified in the winter houses at the Chota-Tanasee site and at the Alarka site (Schroedl 1986a:267; Shumate et al. 2005:5.26, 5.27). Other Townsend winter houses evince exterior wall support posts that are more widely spaced and clustered in sets of two and three. Interior posts (those less than 30 cm deep and located more than 50 cm inside the structure walls) appear to have served as additional roof braces, as supports for sleeping benches, or as interior partitions.

Only Structure 41 among the summer houses (see the discussion of structure function below) (Structures 23, 41, 51, and 999) fits the expectations generated by Adair's description. Like the summer house identified by Shumate (Shumate et al. 2005) at the Alarka site, it has two large-diameter deep postholes located down the centerline of the structure (Fig. 5.9). The other summer houses do not show evidence of central roof support posts, and thus probably had single-faced slanted roofs supported by the exterior wall posts. The posthole patterns of Structure 51 and Structure 23, which are composed almost entirely of postholes over 15 cm in depth, are similar in form to the summer houses identified by Schroedl (1986a) at Chota-Tanasee. Except for Structure 41, which had a series of posts forming a possible entrance baffle in its northeast corner, Townsend summer houses did not have interior postholes.

The question of whether the Cherokee structures at Townsend had daubed walls cannot be adequately addressed because mechanical stripping removed the deposits that would have held the evidence. Only one structure (Structure 41), a summer house, was hand excavated, and the deposits of this house contained trace amounts of fired clay daub. This lack of fired clay does not mean, however, that the walls were not daubed, for none of the structures at Townsend appear to have been burned. In the absence of conditions that would vitrify the clay daub, one would not expect it to be preserved. It is worth noting that daub was found concentrated around the center of two burned winter houses at the Tuckaseegee and Alarka sites—a pattern consistent with the daubing of the smoke hole in the center of the structure roof rather than the structure walls (Keel 1976; Shumate et al. 2005).

Table 5.2. Architectural data for Cherokee structures.

Structure	Shape	Structure Type	Orientation[a]	Major Axis (m)	Minor Axis (m)	Area (m^2)	Total Posts	Post Spacing Circumference (m/posts)	Estimated Household Size (in persons)
1	circular	winter house	cardinal	8.05	7.50	44.31	22	1.85	7
8	octagonal	winter house	intercardinal	7.50	6.70	38.08	56	0.97	6
12	circular	winter house	intercardinal	8.10	7.00	44.29	75	0.68	7
22	octagonal w/ vestibule	winter house	intercardinal	8.20	7.50	45.31	58	0.85	8
23	rectangular	summer house	E-W	7.40	3.25	22.64	18	1.20	
27	undetermined	winter house?	n/a	n/a	n/a	n/a	32	n/a	n/a
41	rectangular	summer house	NW-SE	7.85	4.28	30.75	58	0.50	
47	octagonal	winter house	intercardinal	7.70	6.70	36.70	52	0.77	6
51	rectangular	summer house	NW-SE	7.60	4.50	28.81	18	1.37	
999	rectangular?	summer house?	E-W	7.00	4.00	22.90	15	n/a	

[a]Orientation was determined by the major axis of rectangular structures and by the locations of the four main roof supports of circular or octagonal structures.

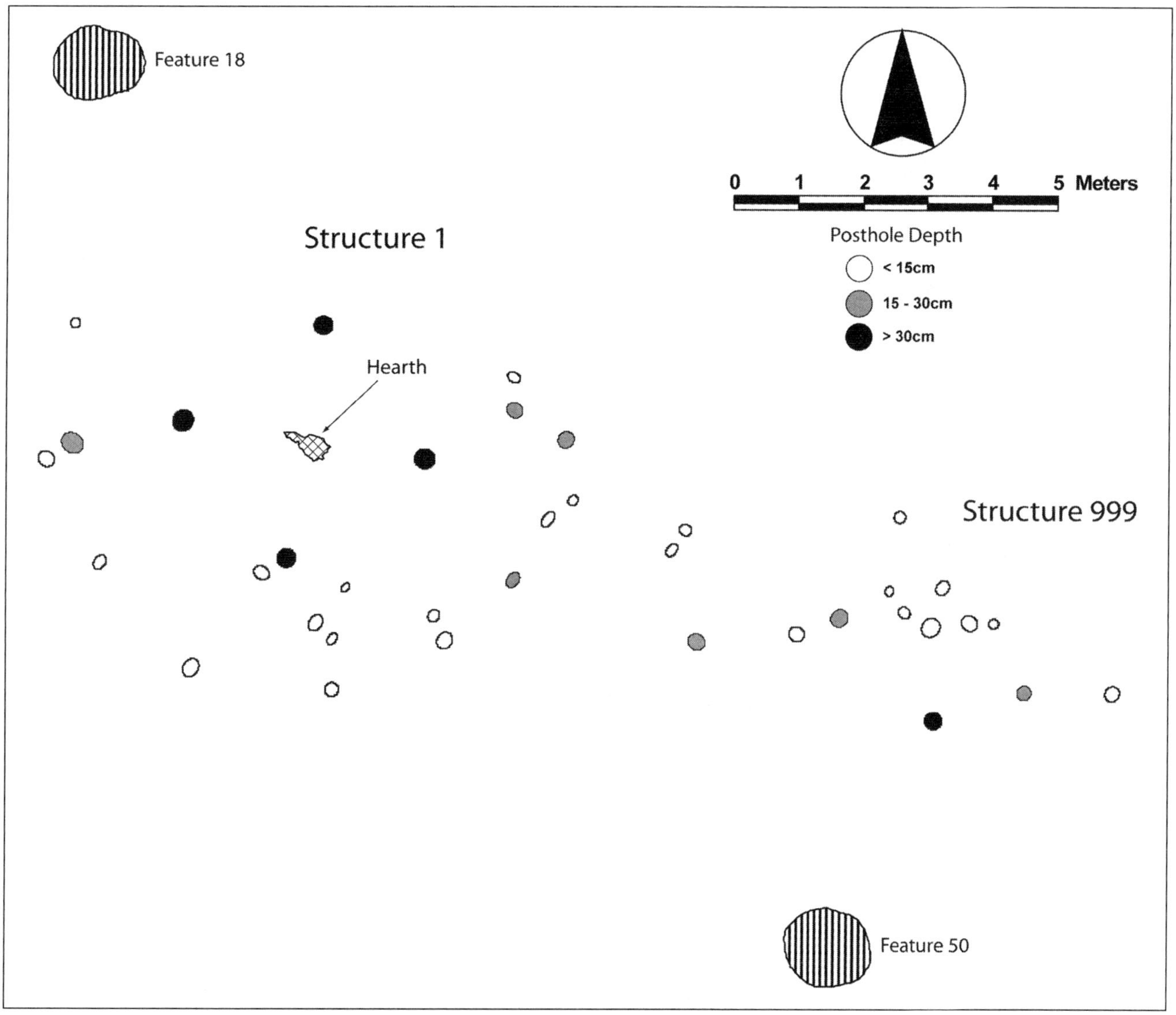

Figure 5.6. Posthole patterns of Household 1: Structure 1 and Structure 999. Posts are shaded to indicate posthole depth.

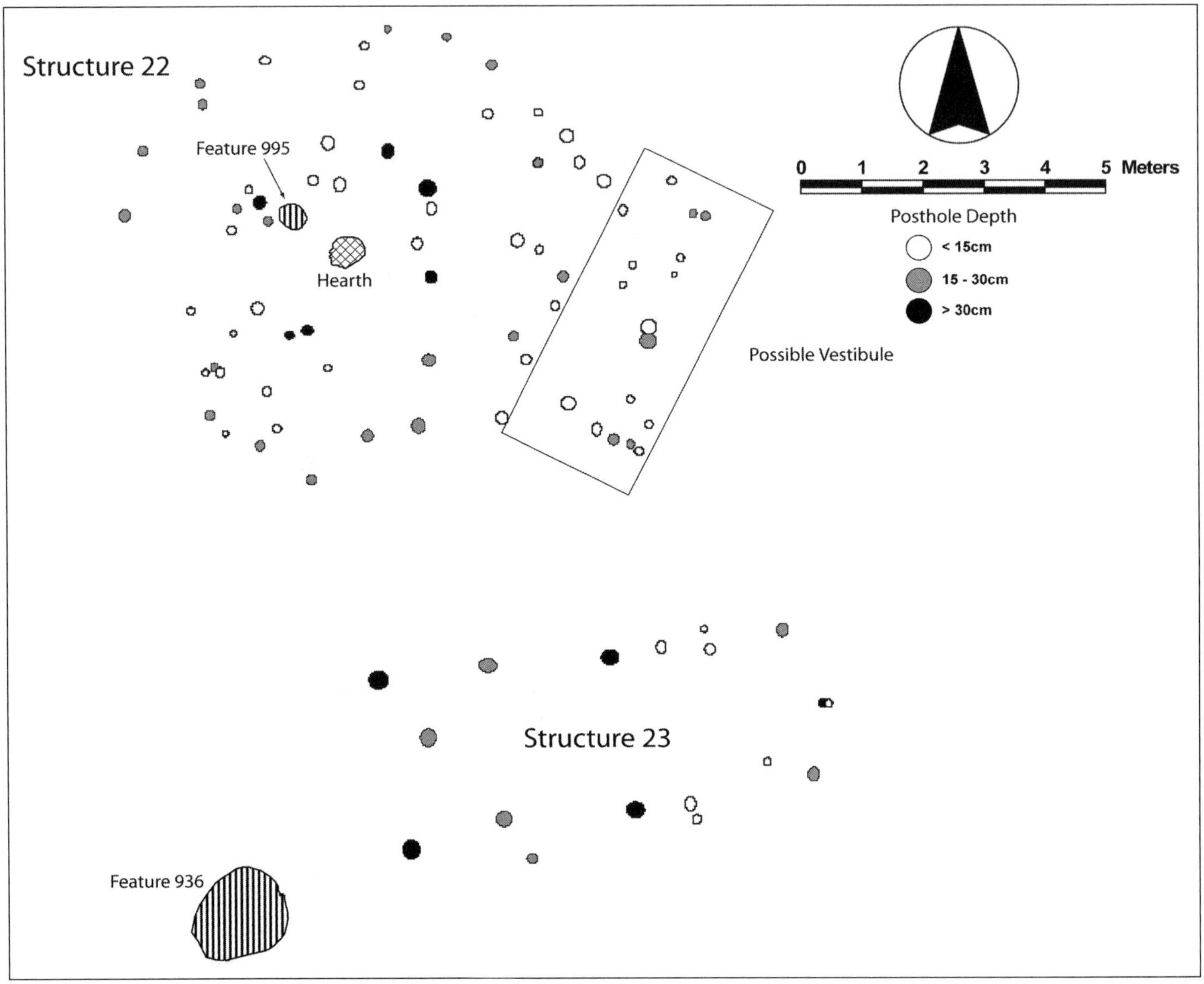

Figure 5.7. Posthole pattern of Household 2: Structure 22 and Structure 23. Posts are shaded to indicate posthole depth.

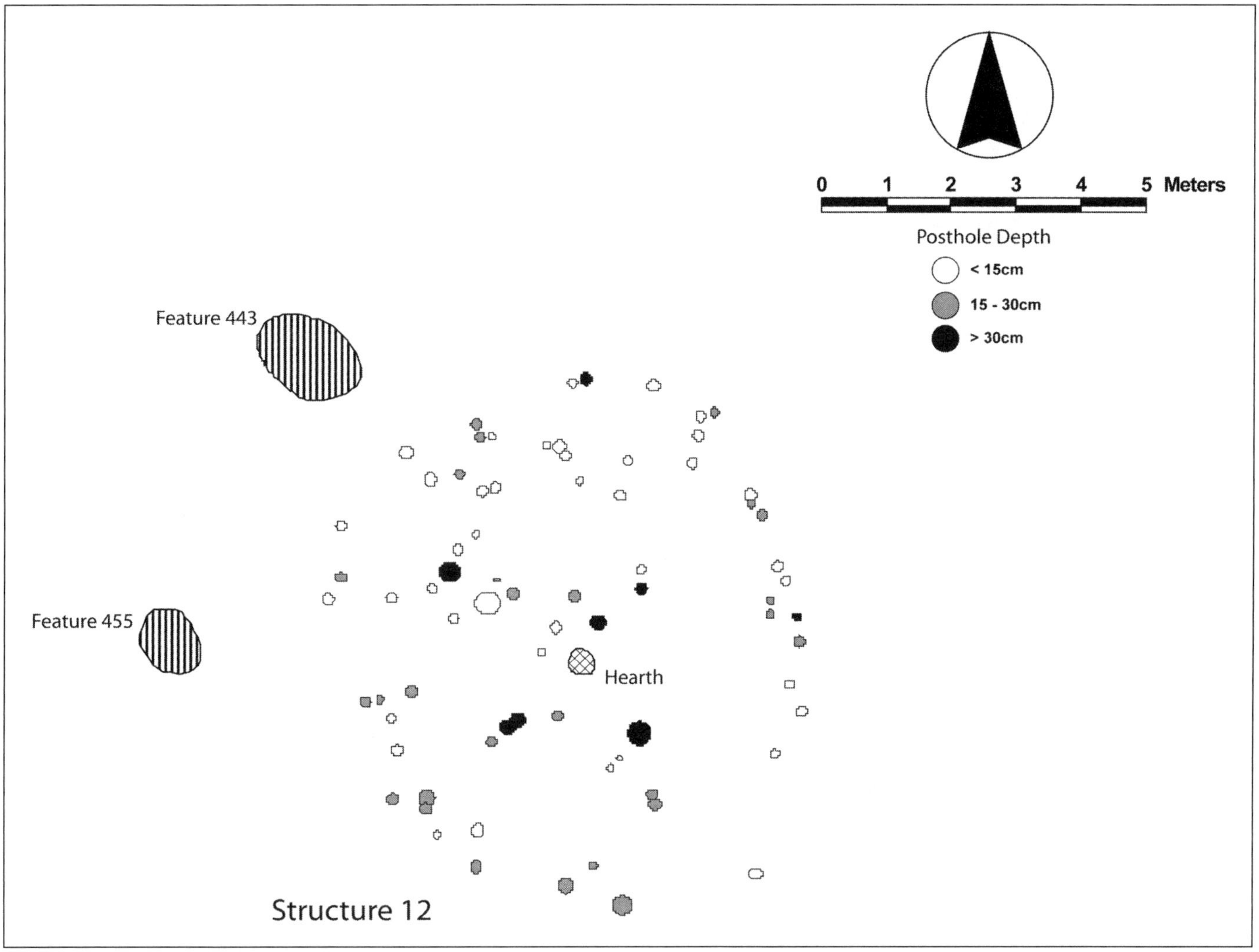

Figure 5.8. Posthole pattern of Household 3: Structure 12. Posts are shaded to indicate posthole depth.

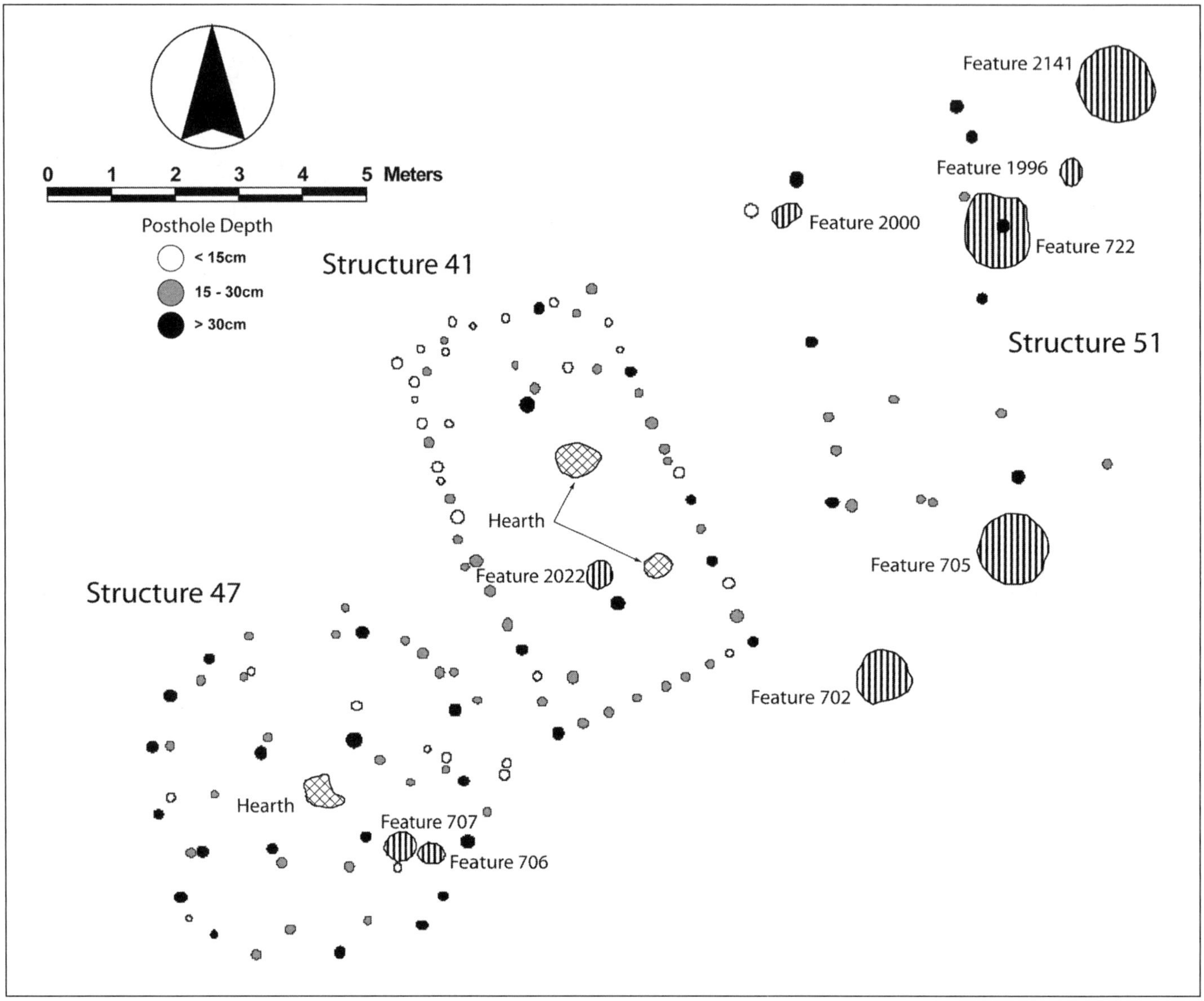

Figure 5.9. Posthole pattern of Household 4: Structure 41, Structure 47, and Structure 51. Posts are shaded to indicate posthole depth.

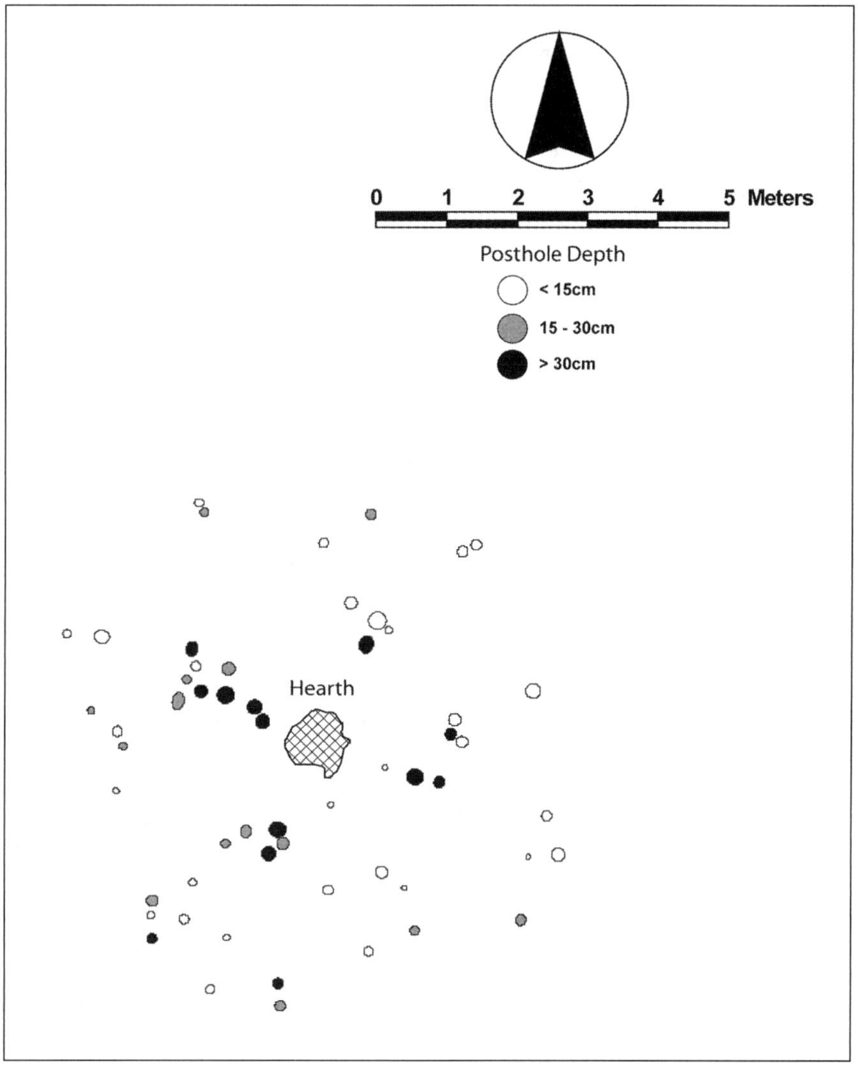

Figure 5.10. Posthole pattern of Household 6: Structure 8. Posts are shaded to indicate posthole depth.

Assessing the Function of Cherokee Structures at Townsend: Winter Houses and Summer Houses

The task of assessing the function of the Cherokee structures at the Townsend sites is relatively straightforward. As discussed above, the ethnohistoric descriptions are very clear that most eighteenth-century Cherokee households consisted of paired winter and summer dwellings, and these accounts give details regarding their form and construction. Archaeological excavations at eighteenth-century Cherokee sites have confirmed this distinction and have offered some important additional insights based on archaeological indicators. In his synthesis of excavations at various mid-eighteenth-century Overhill settlements, Schroedl (1986a:540–41, 1989:354) made a number of distinctions between winter houses and summer houses: (1) winter houses were round and summer houses were rectangular; (2) winter houses had clearly defined walls composed of closely spaced posts while summer houses had poorly defined walls composed of widely spaced posts (this led Schroedl to envision the latter as an open walled structure); (3) winter houses were very consistent in size, averaging 40 m^2, while summer structures displayed much more variability in size; (4) winter houses were marked by the presence of hearths, benches, and small pit features while summer houses generally lacked these features; and (5) burials were usually absent in winter houses yet were frequently encountered in summer house excavations. Data from the excavations of the Cherokee houses at the Townsend sites can be used to test these distinctions as well as provide additional information regarding the functions of winter houses and summer houses.

The first and second distinctions are based on differences in the methods used to construct the winter houses and summer houses. As detailed above, the Cherokee structures at the Townsend site can easily be divided into two groups based on structure shape, or, more accurately, based on the spatial arrangement of different post types. The five winter houses are circular or octagonal in shape with at least one set of four large-diameter deeply set posts. There are three clearly defined rectangular Cherokee structures at the Townsend sites, all of which are located within a few meters of Cherokee winter houses (Structures 23, 41, and 51) (Table 5.2). The shape of a fourth structure (Structure 999) is not clear, but it is likely that it too was rectangular.

The spacing of wall posts in the Townsend structures is determined by dividing the perimeter of each structure (measured in meters) by the number of posts making up the exterior walls. A comparison of the median and mean wall post spacing of winter and summer houses at Townsend results in a pattern similar to Schroedl's model of later Cherokee houses (Table 5.3). There is a difference of approximately 50 cm between the median wall post spacing of winter houses and that of summer houses. The difference would be even larger if Structure 41 were left out of the comparison. This was a substantially built Cherokee summer house that had the smallest wall post spacing value of all structures at Townsend and is very similar to the summer house excavated at the late seventeenth-century Alarka site (see Table 5.2) (Shumate et al. 2005). While it is certain that Structure 41 was a fully enclosed dwelling, it is not clear from the spacing of the wall posts in Structures 999, 23, and 51 whether these dwellings were open or enclosed.

The distribution of structure size, measured by the floor area of each structure, forms two mutually exclusive groups that represent winter houses and summer houses (Table 5.3). Winter houses at Townsend range in size from 36.5 m^2 to 45.31 m^2, while the substantially smaller summer houses range from 22.64 m^2 to 30.75 m^2. Not surprisingly, the largest summer house is Structure 41. This pattern is very different from that identified by Schroedl (1986a:540–41) for later mid-eighteenth-century Overhill Cherokee structures. While at Townsend there is consistency in floor area within structure types and a large difference in floor area between structure types, at the later Overhill sites winter and summer houses are very similar in size (see comparisons below).

With the exception of Structure 41, the data from the Townsend structures confirm distinctions between winter houses and summer houses based on the presence of hearths, benches, and small pit features in the former and their absence in the latter (Table 5.3). All five winter houses possess simple hearths dug into subsoil, while these are absent in all the summer houses except Structure 41 (which has two hearths). Based on the relative number of interior posts in the Townsend structures, benches are most likely present in all winter structures, while absent in all summer structures, including Structure 41. Also, small pit features are present in two of the five winter houses (Structures 22 and 47) and in a single summer house (Structure 41). The intrusion of a

Table 5.3. Comparison of Cherokee winter houses and summer houses.

	Structures	Median Post Spacing (m)	Mean Post Spacing (m)	Median Area (m^2)	Mean Area (m^2)	Hearths	Median Number of Interior Posts	Internal Pit Features	Burials
winter houses	1, 8, 12, 22, 47	0.85	1.03	44.29	41.74	5	23	3	0
summer houses	23, 41, 51, 999	1.28	1.33	25.85	26.28	2	4	1	0

posthole from Structure 51 into a pit feature suggests that this structure postdates the pit features in the area. Addressing the final distinction, no burials were encountered in either type of structure at the Townsend sites.

In sum, the Cherokee structures at the Townsend sites generally fit the expectations generated by Schroedl's (1986a, 1989) model for mid-eighteenth-century Overhill Cherokee winter and summer houses—with two important differences. First, the large disparity between the diminutively sized summer structures and the larger winter structures at the Townsend site is not duplicated among later Overhill Cherokee houses. Second, Structure 41 at Townsend represents a Cherokee architectural form that was not encountered in excavations at later eighteenth-century sites. This structure displays defining aspects of both Cherokee house types. It is rectangular in shape like the other summer houses at the site, but like winter houses it was substantially built with large central support posts and closely set wall posts. It lacks evidence for benches, yet like winter houses it boasts two hearths and a small interior pit feature. It may be that there were effectively two types of summer houses being built during the late seventeenth and early eighteenth centuries. One type, represented by Structure 41 and the summer house at the Alarka site (Shumate et al. 2005), was substantially built and had a peaked gabled roof. The other type, represented by Structures 999, 23, and 51, was built much more lightly with widely spaced wall posts and with a simple single-faced roof. Given its absence at the Overhill sites in Schroedl's model, perhaps the first type of summer house was no longer in use by the mid-eighteenth century. Other than these two exceptions, the general model of dual house types holds, as differences in shape, in method of manufacture, and in the presence of hearths, benches, and small pit features clearly separate the Cherokee structures at Townsend into two groups.

Assessing Household Size from Cherokee Structures at Townsend

Historians and ethnologists identify the nuclear and extended family household as the fundamental social unit in Cherokee communities stretching back at least to the eighteenth century (Gearing 1962:18–20; Gilbert 1943:202–3). While the fragmentary nature of the archaeological record precludes the reconstruction of the specific demographic makeup of each household, we can still estimate the number of individuals comprising each household. There are a number of examples in the literature that use estimation methods for household size based on the floor area of domestic structures (e.g., Casselberry 1974; Cook 1972; Hassan 1981; Scarry 1995; Smith 1995; Sullivan 1989, 1995). In a previous study I estimated household size for the Townsend structures using Casselberry's (1974) formula (household size [in persons] = 1/6 floor area [in m^2]) (Marcoux 2010: Table 5.1). I used this particular method to provide comparable results to Sullivan's (1989, 1995) early comparison of Cherokee and Mississippian households in eastern Tennessee. I did not include summer houses in the calculations because they were ancillary domestic structures. For the five households that possessed sufficient spatial integrity, the household size estimates ranged from 6 to 8 people per household (Table 5.2)—a range consistent with Sullivan's (1995: Table 3) estimates of household size at Chota-Tanasee.

Assessing the Occupation Duration and Abandonment of Cherokee Structures at Townsend

The occupation duration of domestic structures and the processes associated with the abandonment of these structures are two critical issues that have received little attention in southeastern archaeology (notable exceptions include Pauketat 1989, 2003; Smith 1995; Ward and Davis 1991; Wilson 2005). Indeed, the amount of time that structures and domestic spaces were occupied and the practices that were enacted upon the termination of occupation doubtless had significant effects upon the archaeological record of households. On a procedural level, issues associated with occupation duration and abandonment must be taken into consideration when attempting to make comparisons among archaeological contexts representing "households." On a more processual level, occupation duration itself becomes an extremely important piece of evidence in interpreting the changes that occurred in Cherokee households during the English Contact period.

Archaeological estimates for occupation duration are typically based on structure longevity and the processes of architectural deterioration as a result of moisture and insect infestation (e.g., McIntosh 1974; Moore and Gasco 1990; Warrick 1988).[4] These estimates are typically calculated by combining estimates of the use-lives of particular architectural materials in certain environments with archaeological evidence of remodeling and/or rebuilding. Because Cherokee structural repair involved individual post replacement rather than the replacement of entire wall sections (Wilson 2005:126–33), for the Townsend study I use Gary Warrick's (1988) wall post replacement estimation method developed for Iroquois longhouse structures (see also Marcoux 2010:118–23). The model assumes that the total number of postholes composing a structure represents the sum of the number of original wall posts and the number of posts used to replace deteriorated posts during the occupation span of the structure. Estimating occupation duration involves first determining the wall post density of the structure in terms of wall posts per linear meter by dividing the total number of exterior wall posts by the circumference of the structure. Second, this value is divided by the wall post density value representing the original number of posts (that is, the structure with the lowest wall post density in the sample). The resulting ratio measures the proportion of wall posts that have been added to the structure (for example, a value of 1.25 indicates that 25% of the wall posts have been replaced). Third, this ratio value is applied to use-life curves calculated for different types of wood in order to attain an estimate of elapsed time (Warrick 1988: Fig. 3). These curves are based on a number of related studies addressing the use-life of untreated fence posts (e.g., Blew and Kulp 1964; Krzyzewski et al. 1980; Purslow

Table 5.4. Average use-life of untreated fence posts made from southeastern trees.

Wood Type	Average Use-Life (years)
ash	10.43
white oak	9.69
hickory	3.55
southern yellow pine	2.59

1976) (Table 5.4). To adapt this method to the Townsend sample, I constructed new use-life curves for species commonly used in prehistoric southeastern architecture (namely ash, white oak, hickory, and southern yellow pine), using the average use-life estimates calculated solely from fence post studies conducted in southeastern environmental settings (Table 5.4) (Blew and Kulp 1964). There, use-life curves for southeastern wood types are created using a formula derived from a use-life study of over 50,000 railroad ties (MacLean 1926) (Figs. 5.11, 5.12).

Occupation duration estimates for the twenty-two Cherokee winter houses in the sample are given in Table 5.5. The sample used in this study includes data from four of the Townsend structures as well as eighteen clearly defined Cherokee winter houses uncovered at a number of other late seventeenth- and eighteenth-century Cherokee sites (Howard 1997; Keel 1976; Polhemus 1987; Russ and Chapman 1983; Schroedl 1986a, 1994). The Townsend houses all have similar duration estimates spanning from 2 to 12 years for various building materials. These results strongly suggest that most Cherokee winter houses were occupied for less than a decade. Most structures contain evidence for some degree of repair; however, with three exceptions, none of the structures were occupied long enough to replace all the wall posts. What is more, short occupations are indicated for houses across different types of communities—from isolated farmsteads like the household at the Alarka site, to the small hamlet-sized community represented by the Townsend sites, to households at large towns like Chota and Tanasee. The short occupation duration of Cherokee houses is likely related to changes in community organization that occurred as part

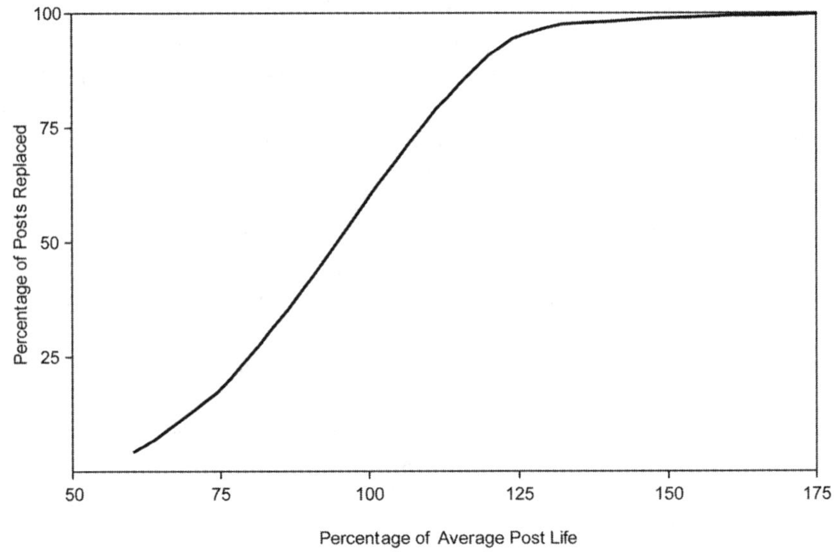

Figure 5.11. Curve describing the mathematical relationship between post replacement and average post life (adapted from MacLean 1926).

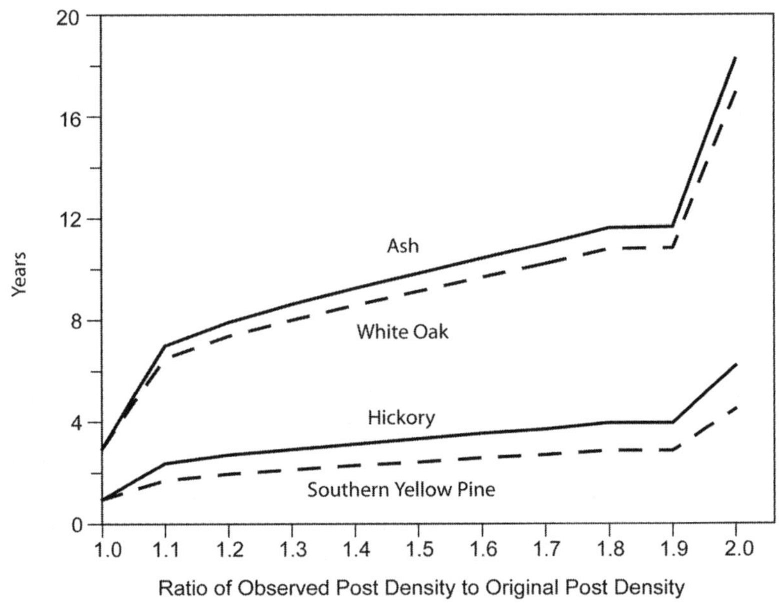

Figure 5.12. Use-life curves for untreated fence posts made from common southeastern trees (see also Warrick 1988 for use-life curves for fence posts made from northeastern trees). The *x* axis measures the proportion of wall posts that have been replaced in any given house. A value of 1 represents a house with no replaced wall posts, while a value of 2 represents a house with all of its wall posts replaced (calculated using use-life curve in MacLean [1926]). Reproduced with permission from *Pox, Empire, Shackles, and Hides* (Marcoux 2010: Fig. 5.4), ©University of Alabama Press.

Table 5.5. Estimated occupation duration for Cherokee winter houses.

Site	Structure	Circumference (m)	Linear Wall Post Density (posts/m)	Observed Wall Posts (density/original wall post density)	Estimated Occupational Duration (years)			
					ash	white oak	hickory	yellow pine
Townsend[a]	8	23.20	1.03	1.34	8–10	6–8	2–4	2–4
	12	25.29	1.46	1.90	10–12	10–12	4–6	2–4
	22	24.65	1.18	1.52	8–10	8–10	2–4	2–4
	47	22.54	1.29	1.67	10–12	8–10	2–4	2–4
Chattooga	1	23.56	1.06	1.37	8–10	8–10	2–4	2–4
	2	21.99	1.09	1.41	8–10	8–10	2–4	2–4
Alarka	1	23.20	1.25	1.62	10–12	8–10	2–4	2–4
Tuckaseegee	1	22.02	0.77[b]	1.00	2–4	2–4	0–2	0–2
Chota	6	20.10	1.94	2.51	> 20	18–20	8–10	6–8
	10	22.98	0.87	1.13	6–8	6–8	2–4	0–2
	12	22.02	0.95	1.24	8–10	6–8	2–4	2–4
	14	18.19	0.88	1.14	6–8	6–8	2–4	0–2
	15	21.06	0.81	1.05	4–6	4–6	0–2	0–2
	16	21.06	1.14	1.48	8–10	8–10	2–4	2–4
	18	22.59	1.06	1.38	8–10	8–10	2–4	2–4
	25	22.02	0.95	1.24	8–10	6–8	2–4	2–4
	27	21.06	1.04	1.35	8–10	8–10	2–4	2–4
Tanasee	3	21.06	1.28	1.66	10–12	8–10	2–4	2–4
	5	21.06	1.14	1.48	8–10	8–10	2–4	2–4
Mialoquo	1	22.50	1.29	1.67	10–12	8–10	2–4	2–4
Toqua	59	19.62	1.88	2.44	> 20	18–20	8–10	6–8
	104	19.15	2.19	2.64	> 20	18–20	8–10	6–8

[a]Structure 1 was not included in the sample because the northeastern portion of its posthole pattern was heavily disturbed.
[b]This wall post density value was used as a proxy for the original wall post density of Cherokee winter houses in the calculations of occupation duration.

of the formation of the shatter zone during the English Contact period (Marcoux 2010:130–36).

Any analysis of household data should also consider the circumstances and behaviors associated with the abandonment of domestic structures (e.g., Cameron 1991; Joyce and Johannessen 1993; Stevenson 1982; Stone 1993). Along with occupation duration, this issue is too often overlooked in southeastern archaeology. Unfortunately, the deposits that would contain evidence attributed to abandonment processes (e.g., floors or living surfaces) were heavily disturbed by plowing or were entirely removed by mechanical stripping during excavations. Based primarily on a lack of evidence for catastrophic abandonment (i.e., burning) or intentional post removal, it appears that the Townsend structures were left standing when they were abandoned. The one structure (Structure 41) that was hand excavated contained small vestiges of a floor around the central hearth and an approximately 30-cm-thick midden deposit. The deposit likely represents trash deposited after the structure was abandoned or it might be related to the collapsed roof, as soil was often placed on the roof as part of the construction process. In any event, post-depositional disturbances resulting from abandonment, historic agricultural activities, and excavation have removed the temptation to treat any of the Townsend households as "Pompeii-like" contexts.

Individual Structure Descriptions

I have thus far assessed the methods of manufacture, structure functions, occupation durations, and abandonment processes of Cherokee domestic structures by dealing with the Townsend data en masse. Now that I have identified and discussed the general patterns of Cherokee architecture, I move on to consider how this vernacular was manifest in individual domestic structures. The following section contains descriptions of each Cherokee structure identified during the Townsend project. The structure descriptions are organized by household, proceeding from west to east across the project area (Fig. 5.1). Table 5.2 presents the relevant architectural data for each structure including structure shape, structure function, orientation, dimensions, and floor area. Table 5.6 contains a breakdown of the various post types defining each of the structures.

Household 1: Structure 1 and Structure 999 (Figs. 5.6, 5.13, 5.14)

Structure 1 was a Cherokee winter house defined by a circular pattern of 22 postholes. The pattern consists of 4 central roof support posts, forming a quadrangle averaging 2.61 m on a side; 4 exterior support posts (> 15 cm in depth); 9 exterior posts (< 15 cm in depth); and 5 interior posts. One of the interior posts likely acted as a brace for a central roof support, and the rest may have formed an entrance baffle along the southern wall. The northeastern portion of the structure is poorly defined—any evidence of wall posts in this area was eradicated by activities related to the original construction of Highway 321. Indeed, the low number of posts defining this structure, compared to other structures at the site, is more a function of post abandonment disturbance than original design. The remains of a single hearth (Feature 56, see Fig. 5.6) were uncovered in the structure's center. This feature had been disturbed by plowing, but from what remained it appeared to be a simple shallow basin dug into subsoil. No interior pit features were found.

Structure 999 is a poorly defined remnant of a summer house located 1.75 m southeast of Structure 1. Most of the posthole pattern defining this structure was destroyed by the construction of Highway 321. Perhaps somewhat overly optimistic reconstruction of the structure indicates that it was rectangular in shape; lacked central roof support posts; and had 3 exterior support posts, 5 exterior posts, and 7 interior posts. If this classification of post types is correct, then this structure had many more interior posts than the other summer houses in the sample. No interior pits or hearths were found.

Table 5.6. Post types constituting Cherokee structures at the Townsend sites.

Structure	Total Posts	Central Support Posts	Mean Central Support Post Spacing (m)	Exterior Support Posts	Exterior Posts	Interior Posts
1	22	4	2.61	4	9	5
8	56	11	2.23	10	14	21
12	75	6	2.04	19	18	32
22	54	6	2.21	15	14	19
23	18	0	n/a	10	8	0
27	32	n/a	n/a	n/a	n/a	n/a
41	58	2	4.10	29	19	8
47	52	4	1.82	21	7	20
51	18	0	n/a	16	1	1
999	15	0	n/a	3	5	7

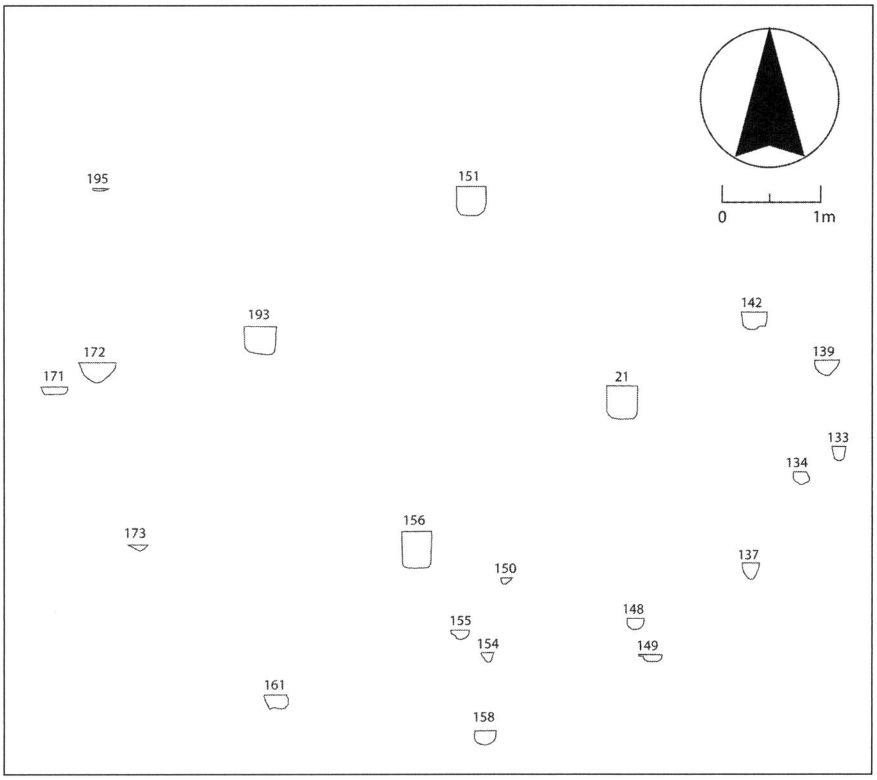

Figure 5.13. Schematic of posthole profiles for Structure 1. Note: Profiles were not available for all postholes. (Labels depict identification numbers assigned to individual postholes.)

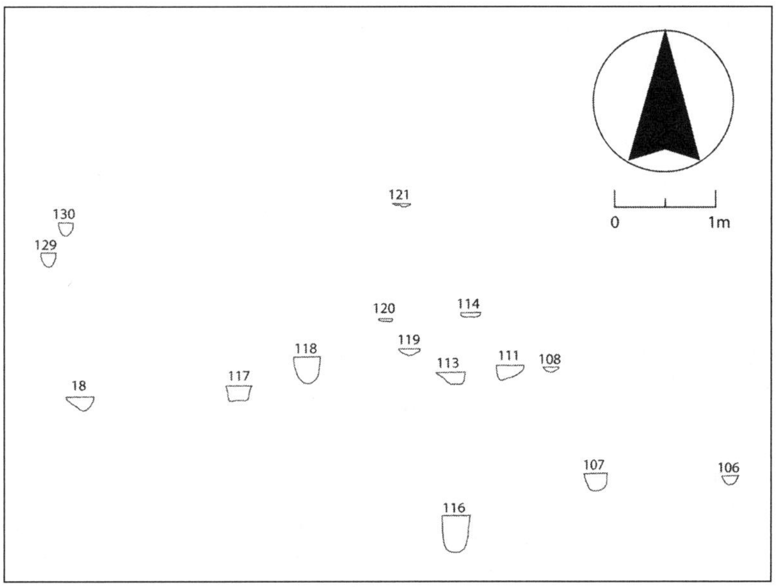

Figure 5.14. Schematic of posthole profiles for Structure 999. Note: Profiles were not available for all postholes. (Labels depict identification numbers assigned to individual postholes.)

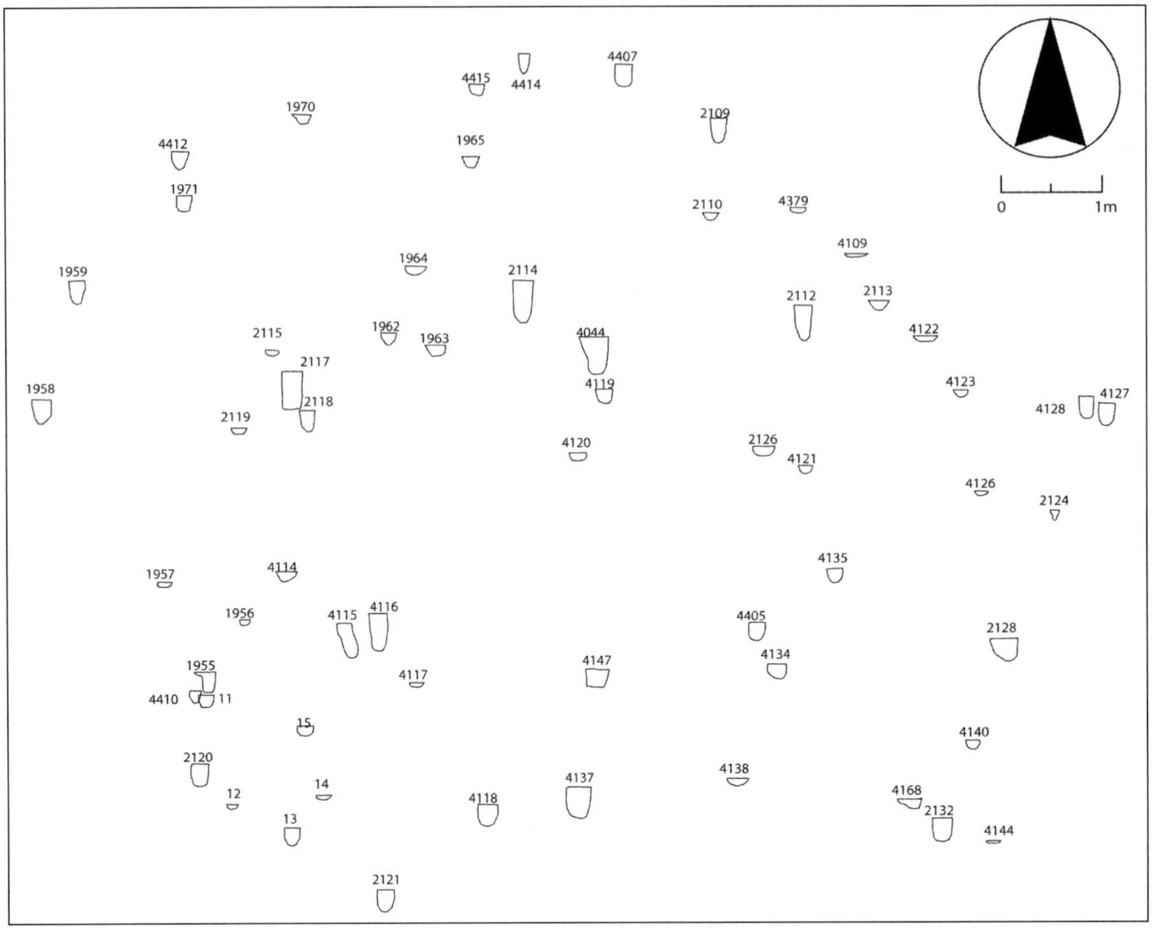

Figure 5.15. Schematic of posthole profiles for Structure 22. Note: Profiles were not available for all postholes. (Labels depict identification numbers assigned to individual postholes.)

Household 2: Structure 22 and Structure 23 (Figs. 5.7, 5.15, 5.16)

Structure 22 is identified as the remains of an octagonal Cherokee winter house consisting of a posthole pattern containing 58 posts. The structure had 6 central roof support posts with an average spacing of 2.21 m. Four of these posts were arranged in the typical quadrangle form, an additional post was paired with the post in the southwestern corner of the quadrangle, and another support post was located between the posts at the northeast and southeast corners. The 15 external support posts were arranged in sets of 3 at the northeast, northwest, and southwest corners of the structure and were likely arranged this way to provide structural support for the house. The wall posts defining the southeast perimeter of the house do not fit the shape of the typical Cherokee winter house. Inspection of Figure 5.7 suggests that 17 of the outermost posts in the southeast corner of the structure may represent the remains of a vestibule or attached ramada. If this interpretation is correct, then the large-diameter deeply set posts of the vestibule would have provided additional support along the southeastern wall of Structure 22. Based on their locations, the 14 exterior posts less than 15 cm in depth probably filled in the structure walls between the sets of exterior support posts or acted as post replacements. Of the 19 interior posts in the structure, the posts along the western and eastern walls likely supported benches, the posts clustered around the central roof supports probably acted as additional braces, and the posts in the southeast corner could have formed an entrance baffle coming in from the vestibule. Interior features include a hearth (Feature 996) and a small pit feature (Feature 995, Fig. 5.7). The hearth was largely destroyed by plowing, but it appears to be of a simple form like that located in Structure 1.

Structure 23 was a Cherokee summer house located 4 m south of Structure 22. The structure is defined by a rectangular pattern of postholes containing no central roof support or interior posts, 10 exterior support posts, and 8 exterior posts. The lack of interior posts, along with the large diameters and depths of the exterior posts, suggests that a ridgepole was not used and that the walls of this structure bore the entire weight of the roof. Furthermore, the lack of a ridgepole suggests that the roof was of the slanted single-faced variety rather than a peaked gabled affair. The interior of the structure lacked any evidence of benches, interior pits, or hearths.

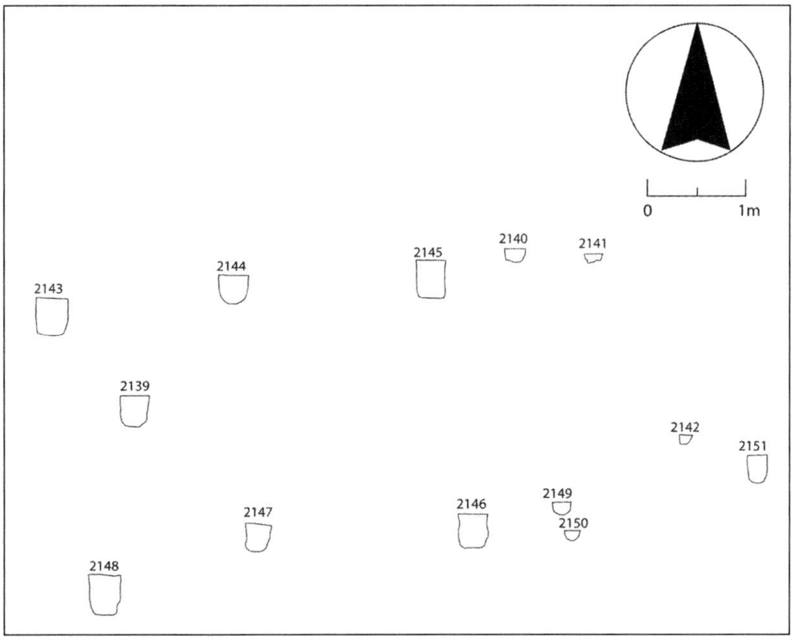

Figure 5.16. Schematic of posthole profiles for Structure 23. Note: Profiles were not available for all postholes. (Labels depict identification numbers assigned to individual postholes.)

Household 3: Structure 12 (Figs. 5.8, 5.17)

Structure 12 was a circular Cherokee winter house defined by a posthole pattern containing 75 posts. The structure had 6 central roof support posts forming a square that averaged 2.04 m per side. The fifth central roof support post was paired with the southwestern post of the quadrangle, and the sixth was located approximately 50 cm southwest of the northeastern support post. Based on the arrangement of the 19 exterior support posts and the 18 exterior posts, the walls of this house appear to have been supported by a series of relatively equally spaced sets of paired posts. This arrangement is similar to that of Structure 8. Structure 12 contained a large number of interior posts. Fifteen of the 32 interior posts were located in and around the central area of the house defined by the central support posts. These could have either been used as additional braces for roof support or to create interior partitions. The rest of the interior posts were located just inside the exterior walls and covered all but the southeastern quadrant of the structure. This suggests that benches lined most of the structure. The gap in the southeastern quadrant of the structure could indicate an entryway, but this is speculative as no baffle was identified. The scant remains of a simple hearth (Feature 1115, Fig. 5.8) were recorded in the center of the structure. No interior pit features were associated.

Despite efforts both in the field and in the preparation of this monograph, no posthole pattern representing an associated summer house could be identified. Attempts to identify a structure based on shape were confounded by the fact that the area around Structure 12 contained many rectangular posthole patterns associated with the Mississippian occupation of the site. Furthermore, since only those postholes associated with structures identified in the field were excavated, the artifactual evidence needed to support any post hoc structural identifications is missing. As excavations at Chota-Tanasee have demonstrated, Cherokee households consisting solely of winter dwellings are not unheard of (Schroedl 1986a).

Household 4: Structure 41, Structure 47, and Structure 51 (Figs. 5.9, 5.18, 5.19, 5.20)

Structure 41 represents the remains of a Cherokee summer house defined by a rectangular pattern of 58 postholes. This structure had 2 central support posts, spaced 4.10 m apart, located along the centerline of its northwest-southeast axis. The 29 exterior support posts and 19 exterior posts forming the walls of the structure are very closely spaced, approximately every 50 cm, which, along with the presence of central support posts, sets this structure apart from other known Cherokee summer houses. The structure had 8 interior posts. Four of these posts in the northeast corner of the structure form an L-shaped feature that may have been an entrance baffle or other kind of partition. Other interior posts against the west wall may represent bench supports. Alter-

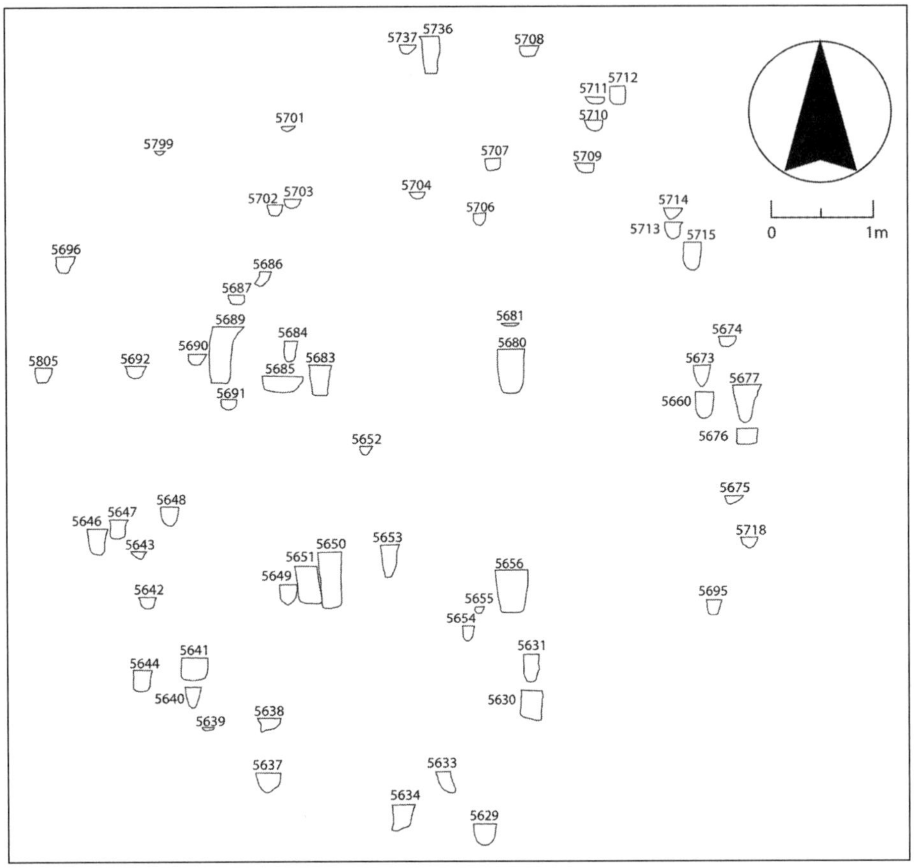

Figure 5.17.
Schematic of posthole profiles for Structure 12. Note: Profiles were not available for all postholes. (Labels depict identification numbers assigned to individual postholes.)

natively, given the possible entryway located along the eastern side of Structure 47, located just 1 m to the west, the interior post in the southwest corner of Structure 41 may represent an entryway that linked these two structures.

Unlike other Cherokee structures at Townsend, Structure 41 was excavated by hand. These excavations revealed that a sheet deposit of midden overlay the structure. Underneath this midden deposit and toward the center of the structure, these excavations encountered the possible remnants of a living surface and two hearths. One hearth located in the center of the structure (Feature 118) was heavily disturbed, and the other feature (Feature 703), located approximately 3 m to the south, appeared to be the result of surface fires. A small interior storage pit (Feature 2022) was also associated with the structure. As discussed above, Structure 41 is very different from the other summer houses at Townsend, as well as those described by Schroedl (1986a) at later mid-eighteenth-century Overhill sites. The configuration of its support posts, which certainly supported a ridgepole and a peaked gabled roof, and its closely spaced wall posts set this structure apart from other Cherokee summer houses. It is interesting, and likely significant, that a larger yet extremely similar form of summer house was recorded at the contemporaneous late seventeenth-century Alarka site.

Structure 47 was a Cherokee winter house identified by an octagonal posthole pattern of 52 posts. The structure had 4 central roof support posts arranged in a quadrangle measuring approximately 1.8 m per side. Like Structure 22, the walls of Structure 47 were supported by widely spaced deeply set exterior support posts interspersed with posts dug to lesser depths. As with the other winter structures at Townsend, some interior posts were used to brace the central roof supports and others, located along the western and southern walls, probably supported interior benches. As mentioned above, a linear cluster of interior posts near the eastern wall of the structure may be a baffle that shielded an entryway leading to Structure 41. The structure contained the remains of a heavily plow disturbed hearth (Feature 711) and two small interior pits (Features 706 and 707).

But for the presence of Structure 41 in this household, Structure 51 would certainly be classified as a Cherokee summer house. It was a rectangular structure that was similar in size to Structure 23, another well-defined summer house at Townsend. Structure 51 was also similar to Structure 23 in its lack of a hearth, interior pits, and central roof support posts, and in its deeply set, widely spaced exterior posts. Unlike other households, this structure appears to be superimposed over some exterior pit features. This leads to the interpretation that the construction of Structure 51 followed the use of these pits—perhaps after Structure 41 and 47 had been in use for some period of time. Consequently, I argue that this structure was more likely a more lightly built ramada that served a similar function as Structure 23.

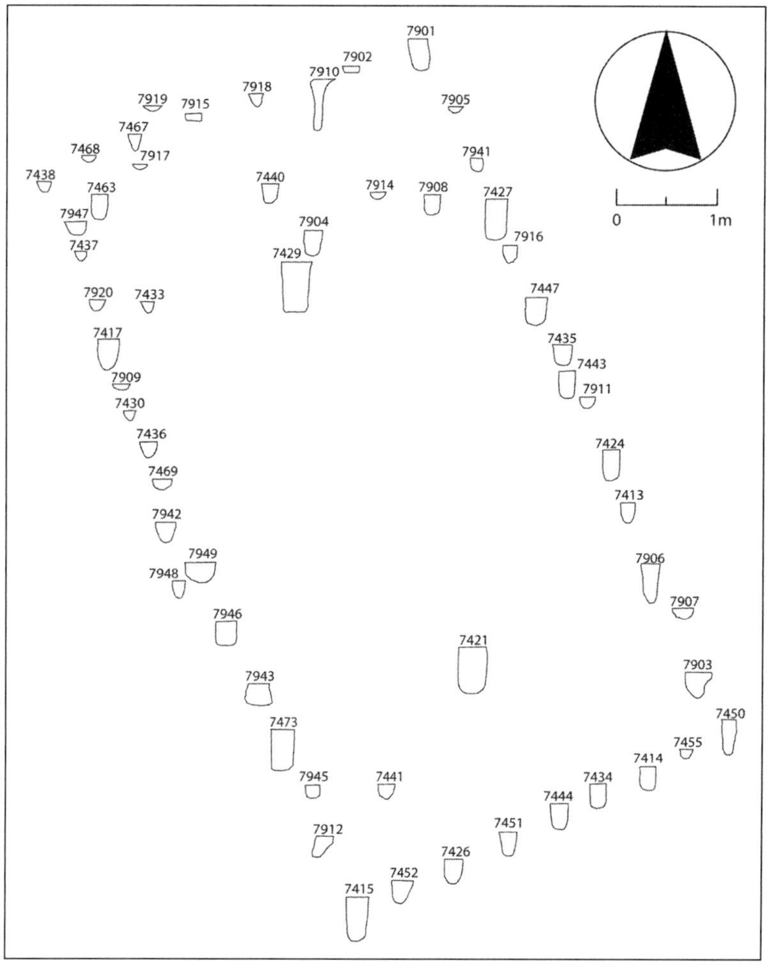

Figure 5.18.
Schematic of posthole profiles for Structure 41. Note: Profiles were not available for all postholes. (Labels depict identification numbers assigned to individual postholes.)

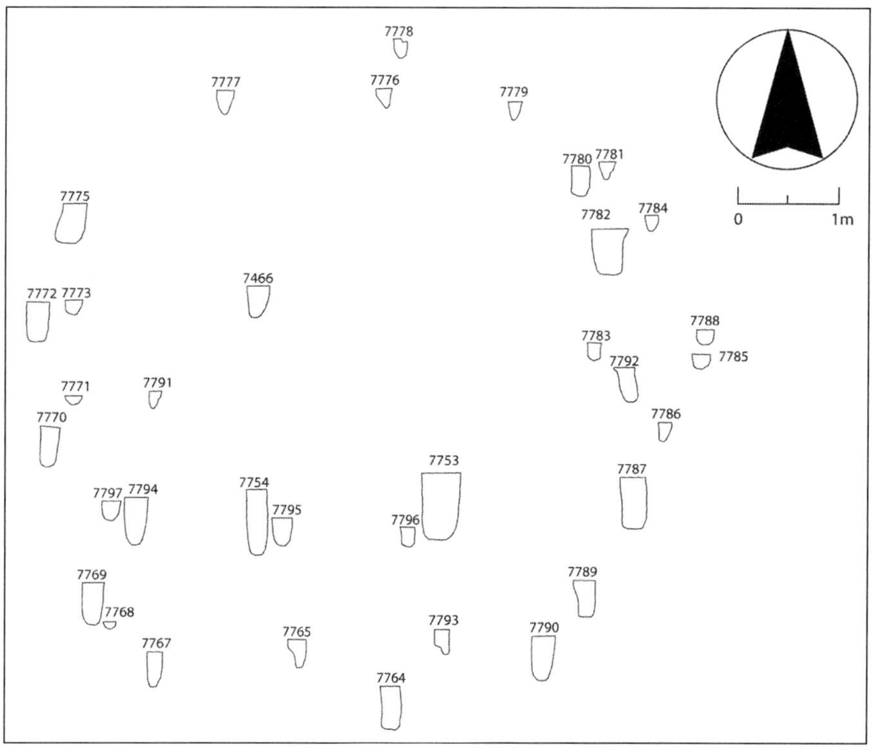

Figure 5.19.
Schematic of posthole profiles for Structure 47. Note: Profiles were not available for all postholes. (Labels depict identification numbers assigned to individual postholes.)

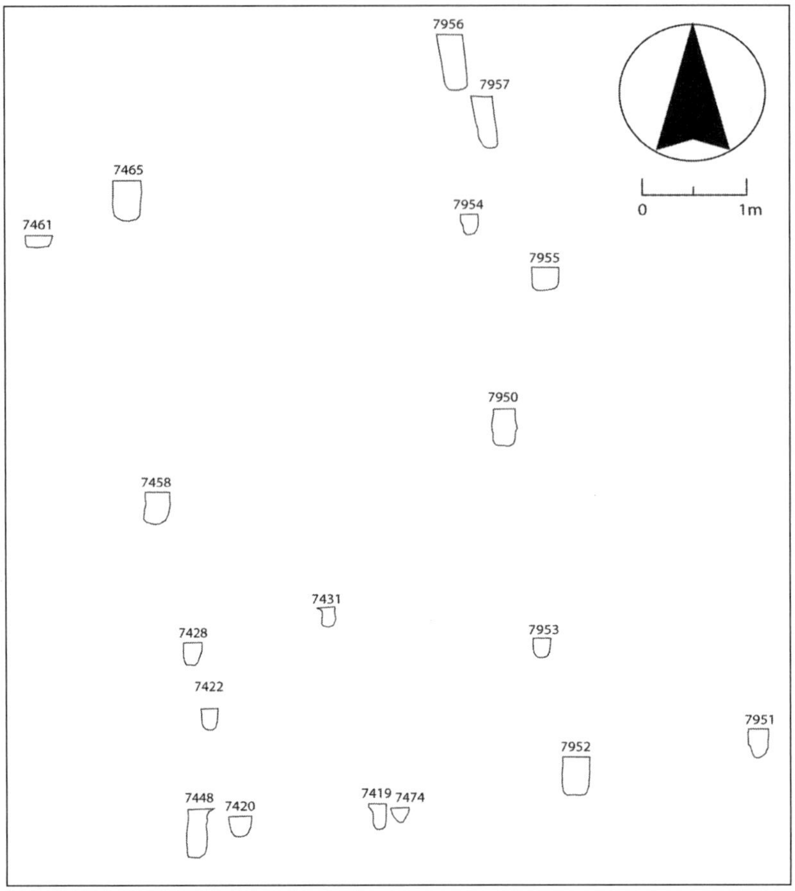

Figure 5.20. Schematic of posthole profiles for Structure 51. Note: Profiles were not available for all postholes. (Labels depict identification numbers assigned to individual postholes.)

Household 5: Structure 27 (Fig. 5.21)

Household 5 presents a vexingly ambiguous picture of Cherokee architecture. The source of frustration in this case results from the fact that this portion of the Townsend site received considerably less attention than other areas containing Cherokee structures. Structure 27, a vaguely circular pattern of posts surrounding a hearth, was first identified as a Cherokee structure based on its proximity to a pit containing Cherokee pottery (Feature 497) and the presence of a single glass bead recovered in test unit excavations in the area. In the last weeks of fieldwork, the posts comprising Structure 27 were probed rather than excavated. Consequently, it is impossible to confidently assign posts to the Cherokee occupation based on diagnostic material from the postholes. A number of months after fieldwork, Cameron Howell, Archaeological Research Laboratory researcher and crew member on the Townsend project, reconstructed Structure 27 as it appears in Figure 5.21. The only artifacts that can be associated with this structure come from the hearth (Feature 711). These include four Woodland period limestone-tempered sherds, and two shell-tempered plain sherds, which can be either Cherokee or Mississippian in origin.

In the massive palimpsest of postholes to the east of Structure 27, diagnostic Cherokee pottery was recovered from a few postholes that were excavated during the initial investigation of the area. These posts form a rectangular shape optimistically reminiscent of a Cherokee summer house. Considering all of this, I cautiously suspect that there was a Cherokee household in this area. If mine and Howell's extremely speculative and tentative reconstructions of Structure 27 and adjacent structure are correct, then this household consisted of a Cherokee winter and summer house.

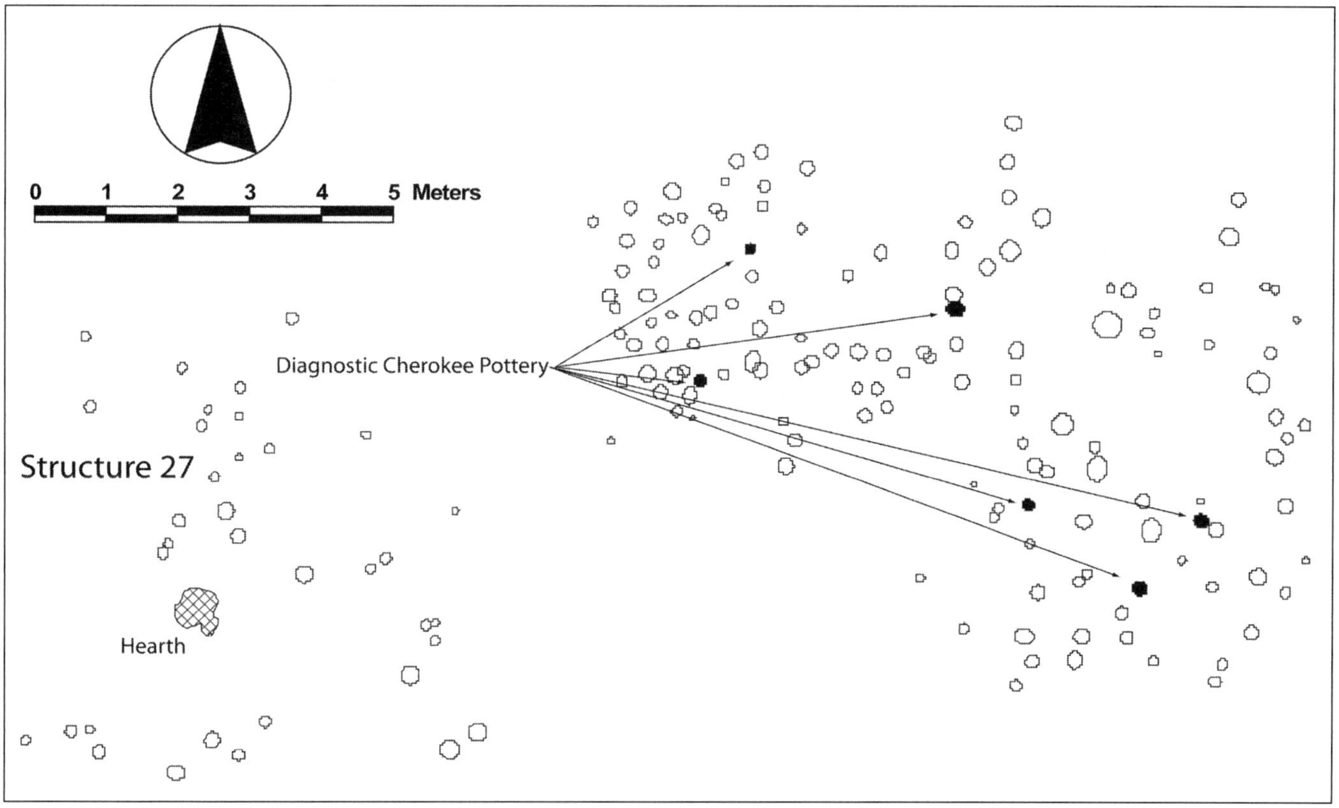

Figure 5.21. Plan view of the suspected location of Structure 27 and another possible Cherokee structure.

Household 6: Structure 8 (Figs. 5.10, 5.22)

Structure 8 was a Cherokee winter house manifest as an octagonal posthole pattern containing 56 posts. This structure contained a total of 11 central roof support posts forming a quadrangle averaging 2.23 m per side. Five posts were located in the northwest corner of this quadrangle, 2 posts were located in the southwest corner, 3 posts were placed in the southeast corner, and a single post was located in the northeast corner. This high number of central support posts, almost twice as many as other winter houses, suggests either that the house was occupied for a long period of time, or that the roof required an inordinate amount of bracing. The 24 exterior support posts and exterior posts were arranged in widely spaced clusters of 2 and 3—similar to the arrangement of wall posts in Structure 12. The shallow depths of many of these posts, if not due to post-depositional processes like plowing, suggest that the walls of Structure 8 would not have been as sturdy as other winter houses. If true, this may explain why so much additional bracing was required for the central roof supports. Of the 21 interior posts, 14 were located around the central support posts, and the rest were clustered along the southern wall and probably supported benches. The remains of a single hearth (Feature 394) were found. As with the hearths in other Cherokee houses, this one was truncated by plowing and backhoe excavation, but appeared to be a simple pit excavated into subsoil. No interior pits were identified in the structure.

Comparisons to Other Late Seventeenth- and Eighteenth-Century Cherokee Domestic Structures

The Cherokee houses identified at the Townsend sites are very similar to those excavated at Cherokee sites dating from the late seventeenth century to the late eighteenth century. Like at Townsend, the architecture at Cherokee sites predating 1740 (i.e., Alarka, Tuckaseegee, and Chattooga) consists entirely of octagonal or circular winter houses and rectangular summer houses (Table 5.7). These house types also appear at Cherokee sites with occupations postdating 1740, but the architecture of these later sites also includes an additional house type—the

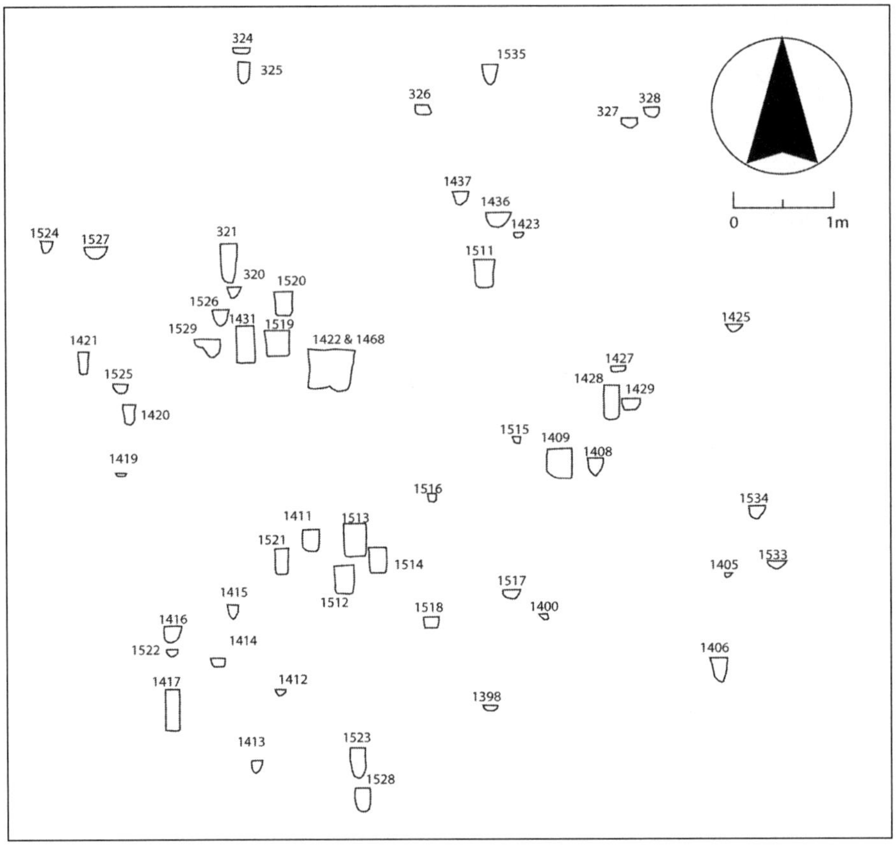

Figure 5.22. Schematic of posthole profiles for Structure 8. Note: Profiles were not available for all postholes. (Labels depict identification numbers assigned to individual postholes.)

Table 5.7. Architectural forms and house sizes among seventeenth- and eighteenth-century Cherokee sites.

Site	Occupation	Winter Houses	Summer Houses	Single Rectangular Houses	Mean Floor Area (m^2)	Median Floor Area (m^2)	Median Estimated Household Size (in persons)	Reference
Alarka	A.D. 1650–1700	1	1	0	42.5	42.5	7	Shumate et al. 2005
Tuckaseegee	A.D. 1650–1700	1	0	0	38.6	38.6	6	Keel 1976
Townsend	A.D. 1650–1715	5	4	0	34.87	36.7	7	
Chattooga	A.D. 1650–1740	2	1	0	45.13	45.13	7	Schroedl 1994
Chota-Tanasee	A.D. 1700–1820	14	9	2	40.62	38.55	6	Schroedl 1986a
Toqua	A.D. 1700–1820	2	1	2	33.30	29.45	5	Polhemus 1987
Tomotley	A.D. 1750–1776	0	0	9	46.49	50.79	8	Baden 1983
Mialoquo	A.D. 1760–1780	1	0	5	32.23	32.52	5	Russ and Chapman 1983

single rectangular house. As discussed above, this house type is argued by some to have been an architectural form brought to the Overhill settlements by refugee Cherokee groups from the Lower settlements (Baden 1983). The fact that the single rectangular house form was not found in excavations at the Lower settlement site of Chattooga, however, raises the possibility that this house type marks a temporal as well as a geographic difference.

The Cherokee winter and summer houses at Townsend evince essentially the same construction method as those at other Cherokee sites, but they differ in terms of size. Winter houses at all the sites were anchored by large central roof support posts forming a quadrangle that measured approximately 2 m per side, and their walls were formed of exterior posts arranged in an octagonal or circular shape. A comparison of median floor area suggests that winter houses dating to the late seventeenth and early eighteenth centuries were slightly larger than those occupied after 1740, but sample sizes are too small to attach statistical significance to this difference (Fig. 5.23). Furthermore, household size estimates, calculated using Casselberry's (1974) formula, are similar across Cherokee sites. These estimates, which ranged from 5 to 8 people per household, suggest that the nuclear family was the fundamental residential unit in Cherokee communities throughout the English Contact period and beyond (Table 5.7). The largest household size estimate, calculated for the late eighteenth-century Tomotley site, reflects the use of a larger single rectangular house form and may be related to an increase in the size of domestic groups as a result of taking in refugees (see above). Also, as discussed above, the occupation duration estimates of most Cherokee houses in the sample ranged from two to twelve years (Table 5.5). The three houses with substantially longer occupation duration estimates are located in Cherokee towns with occupations dating primarily to the later half of the eighteenth century.

The Cherokee summer houses at Townsend display a greater degree of difference. As discussed above, the presence of large central roof support posts and close wall post spacing demonstrate that Structure 41 at Townsend and the summer house at Alarka were built much more substantially than other known Cherokee summer houses. A sample size of two is hardly the foundation of a robust pattern, but given the contemporaneity of these sites, it is possible that this house form may be limited to the late seventeenth century. The other three summer houses identified at Townsend sites were similar to those at Chattooga, Chota-Tanasee and Toqua in their lack of central roof support posts and wider wall post spacing. As with the comparison of winter houses, the small sample size in this study precludes any statistically significant conclusions; however, it is interesting to note that summer houses dating to the late seventeenth and early eighteenth centuries (four out of six are located at Townsend) are much smaller than summer houses at Cherokee sites occupied during the later half of the eighteenth century (Fig. 5.24).

Comparison of Historic Cherokee Houses to Sixteenth- and Seventeenth-Century Southern Appalachian Mississippian Houses

As mentioned at the beginning of this chapter, researchers have recognized that domestic structures in the southern Appalachian region underwent a significant transformation during the seventeenth century (Hally 2002). My study aims to use quantitative comparisons between Mississippian and historic Cherokee structures to better characterize the dimensions along which this architectural change occurred (see also Marcoux 2010:130–36). The comparisons focus on three variables including (1) method of manufacture, (2) household size, and (3) occupation duration, and are conducted with published data from twenty-six late seventeenth- and eighteenth-century Cherokee winter houses as well as published data from twenty-three late sixteenth- and early seventeenth-century Mississippian structures at the King, Coweeta Creek, and Toqua sites (Table 5.8) (Hally 1988; Howard 1997; Keel 1976; Polhemus 1987; Rodning 2004; Russ and Chapman 1983; Schroedl 1986a, 1994).

The methods used to manufacture the domestic structures in the sample are assessed by considering structure shape and the configuration and number of posts. The most obvious difference between Mississippian structures and Cherokee structures is shape (Fig. 5.25). All but one of the Mississippian structures in the sample were square with rounded corners, while all the Cherokee winter houses were circular or octagonal. With regard to entryway design, Mississippian houses typically featured wall trench entryways while historic Cherokee winter houses employed a simple opening and wind baffle. The basic arrangement of posts in both Mississippian and Cherokee structures included large-diameter, deeply set central roof support posts, wall posts, and interior posts that presumably supported benches or formed interior partitions. The similar arrangement of posts suggests that both types of structures were based on the so-called "rigid-post" architectural vernacular. Structurally, this architectural style entails separate roof and wall components that were tied together at the wall plates. This style can be contrasted with the "flexed-pole" architectural style, which included domed houses constructed from long bent poles whose walls and roof formed a single structure. This style was popular during the twelfth and thirteenth centuries as is evident in Mississippian structures in Alabama and Tennessee (see also Lacquement 2004; Rodning 2004; Wilson 2005).

Another dimension of variability in construction methods is structural robustness—measured as a ratio of the total number of posts to floor area. The apparent vast differences in this ratio between Mississippian and Cherokee houses in terms of this value (Table 5.8) are actually the result of differences in rebuilding practices. Mississippian houses were frequently rebuilt in the same location while Cherokee house locations were often

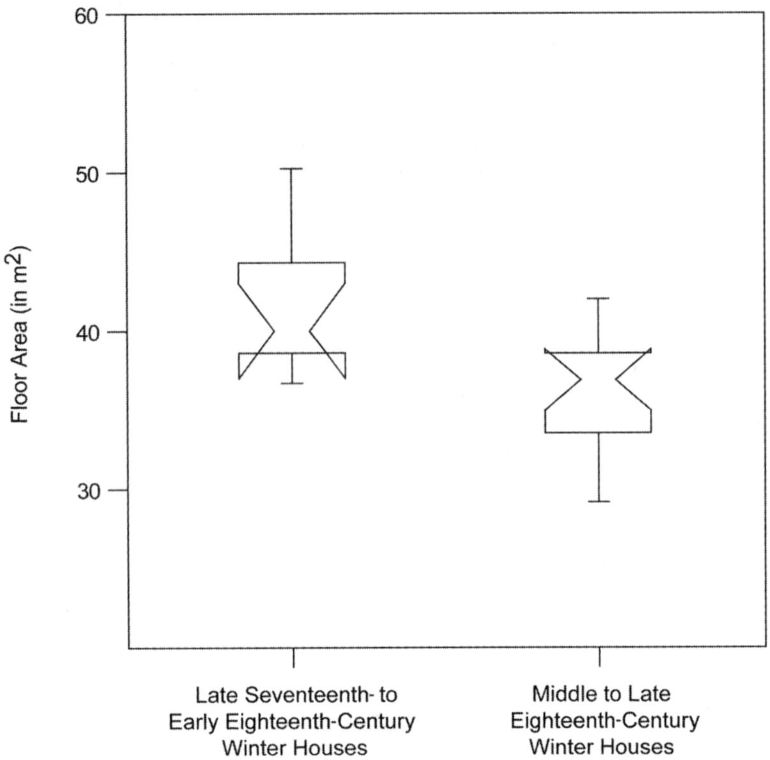

Figure 5.23.
Boxplots comparing the distribution of floor area between English Contact period (ca. A.D. 1670–1740) Cherokee winter houses and those occupied after A.D. 1740. Note: The "folded" appearance of the boxplots is due to small sample size and indicates that the 95% confidence interval of the median is greater than the H-spread.

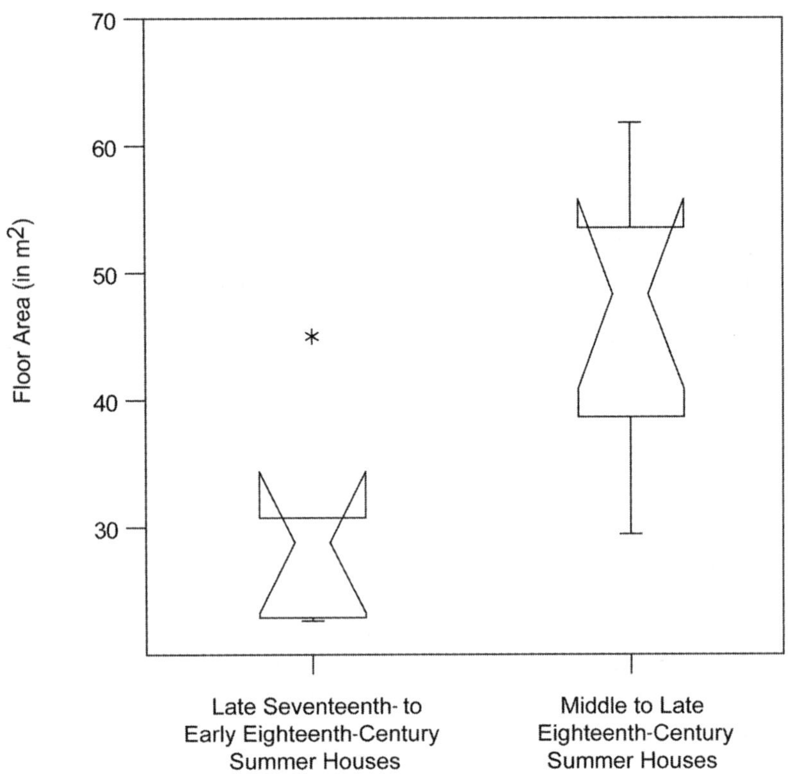

Figure 5.24.
Boxplots comparing the distribution of floor area between English Contact period (ca. A.D. 1670–1740) Cherokee summer houses and those occupied after A.D. 1740. Note: The "folded" appearance of the boxplots is due to small sample size and indicates that the 95% confidence interval of the median is greater than the H-spread.

Table 5.8. Architectural data for late seventeenth- and eighteenth-century Cherokee domestic structures and late sixteenth- and early seventeenth-century Mississippian domestic structures.

Site	Structure	Period	Structure Shape	Number of Hearths[a]	Total Posts	Floor Area (m^2)	Post Density (posts/m^2)	Standardized Post Density[c]
Alarka	Sw273-1	Historic	octagonal	1	98	40.00	2.45	1.60
Chattooga	Oc18-1	Historic	circular	1	54[b]	40.00	1.35	0.88
Chattooga	Oc18-2	Historic	circular	1	80[b]	50.25	1.59	1.04
Chota	Mr2-1	Historic	circular	1	40	36.88	1.08	0.71
Chota	Mr2-5	Historic	octagonal	1	33	38.55	0.86	0.56
Chota	Mr2-6	Historic	octagonal	1	57	32.14	1.77	1.16
Chota	Mr2-10	Historic	octagonal	0	57	41.99	1.36	0.89
Chota	Mr2-12	Historic	circular	0	48	38.55	1.24	0.81
Chota	Mr2-14	Historic	circular	0	26	33.54	0.78	0.51
Chota	Mr2-15	Historic	octagonal	0	45	35.30	1.27	0.83
Chota	Mr2-16	Historic	circular	1	69	35.77	1.93	1.26
Chota	Mr2-18	Historic	octagonal	0	77	40.60	1.90	1.24
Chota	Mr2-20	Historic	circular	0	22	29.17	0.75	0.49
Chota	Mr2-25	Historic	circular	0	36	38.55	0.93	0.61
Chota	Mr2-27	Historic	circular	0	35	35.30	0.99	0.65
Coweeta Creek	Ma34-3	Mississippian	square	3	441[b]	40.97	10.76	2.50
Coweeta Creek	Ma34-4	Mississippian	square	2	339[b]	30.10	11.26	2.61
Coweeta Creek	Ma34-5	Mississippian	square	5	343[b]	49.15	6.98	1.62
Coweeta Creek	Ma34-6	Mississippian	square	2	462[b]	37.16	12.43	2.88
Coweeta Creek	Ma34-7	Mississippian	circular	4	601[b]	61.32	9.80	2.27
Coweeta Creek	Ma34-8	Mississippian	square	3	266[b]	37.07	7.18	1.66
King	King-4	Mississippian	square	1	187[b]	29.73	6.29	1.46
Mialoquo	Mr3-1	Historic	circular	2	48	40.30	1.19	0.78
Tanasee	Mr62-3	Historic	circular	1	80	38.55	2.07	1.36
Tanasee	Mr62-5	Historic	circular	2	42	38.55	1.09	0.71
Toqua	Mr6-13	Mississippian	square	3	131	41.71	3.14	0.73
Toqua	Mr6-15	Mississippian	square	0	244	33.45	7.30	1.69
Toqua	Mr6-2	Mississippian	square	4	596	85.56	6.97	1.62
Toqua	Mr6-4	Mississippian	square	4	179	35.30	5.07	1.18
Toqua	Mr6-9	Mississippian	square	1	116	27.13	4.28	0.99
Toqua	Mr6-18	Mississippian	square	5	499	36.42	13.70	3.18
Toqua	Mr6-19	Mississippian	square	1	194	31.77	6.11	1.42
Toqua	Mr6-22	Mississippian	square	1	176	40.41	4.36	1.01
Toqua	Mr6-23	Mississippian	square	2	157	39.02	4.02	0.93
Toqua	Mr6-24	Mississippian	square	2	193	47.01	4.11	0.95
Toqua	Mr6-30	Mississippian	square	1	157	49.42	3.18	0.74
Toqua	Mr6-33	Mississippian	square	1	273	53.88	5.07	1.18
Toqua	Mr6-39	Mississippian	square	6	389	37.16	10.47	2.43
Toqua	Mr6-104	Historic	circular	1	69	29.17	2.37	1.55
Toqua	Mr6-118	Mississippian	square	2	193	62.80	3.07	0.71
Toqua	Mr6-57	Mississippian	square	1	73	18.58	3.93	0.91
Toqua	Mr6-58	Mississippian	square	1	75	18.58	4.04	0.94
Toqua	Mr6-59	Historic	circular	1	59	30.66	1.92	1.26
Townsend	Bt89-1	Historic	circular	1	22	44.31	0.50	0.32
Townsend	Bt91-8	Historic	octagonal	1	56	38.08	1.47	0.96
Townsend	Bt90-12	Historic	circular	1	75	44.29	1.69	1.18
Townsend	Bt90-22	Historic	octagonal	1	54	45.31	1.19	0.78
Townsend	Bt90-47	Historic	octagonal	1	53	36.70	1.44	0.94
Tuckaseegee	Jk12-1	Historic	octagonal	1	30[b]	38.60	0.78	0.51

[a]The lack of hearths in many structures is due to plow disturbance.
[b]These values were determined by the author by counting the posts in published scale drawings.
[c]Standardization involved dividing the post density values by the median post density of non-rebuilt houses (the median values are 4.1 for Mississippian houses and 1.53 for Cherokee houses).

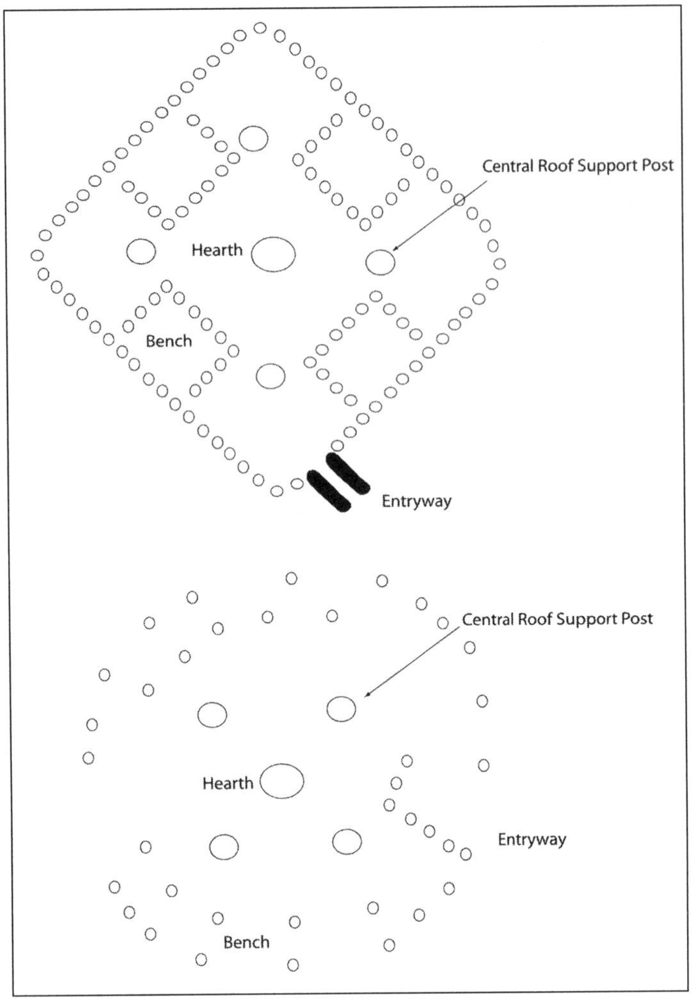

Figure 5.25. Schematic comparison of Mississippian house (*top*) and Cherokee winter house (*bottom*) (drawing of Mississippian house adapted from Rodning 2004: Fig. 5.2). Reproduced with permission from *Pox, Empire, Shackles, and Hides* (Marcoux 2010: Fig. 5.8), ©University of Alabama Press.

short-lived (see below). Controlling for this difference requires limiting the sample to structures with relatively short occupation spans. Based on previous studies of Mississippian structures in North Carolina and Alabama that linked occupation duration to the number of times a hearth is remodeled (Rodning 2004; Wilson 2005, 2008), I limit my sample to structures with a single hearth. The comparison of boxplots reveals that non-rebuilt Mississippian houses contained a significantly greater number of posts per square meter than non-rebuilt Cherokee winter houses (Fig. 5.26). Indeed, the median number of posts in Mississippian houses (median = 4.31 posts/m^2) was 2.78 posts/m^2 greater than that of Cherokee winter houses (median = 1.53 posts/m^2). Given that the structures from the two periods were built using the same basic architectural principles, this difference suggests that a good deal more material and energy were involved in constructing Mississippian houses.

A comparison of mean floor size between the two periods suggests that while the methods of manufacture of domestic structures changed from the late sixteenth to the late seventeenth centuries, structure household size remained stable. The mean floor area of Mississippian houses in the study sample is 41.03 m^2 while that of Cherokee winter houses is 38.12 m^2. Both Sullivan (1995:115) and Hally (2002:107) report similar floor area estimates for historic and prehistoric domestic structures, with an average household size of 7 individuals for the Mississippian period and 6 individuals for the historic period. Such a small difference in floor area is more likely related to the architectural differences between Mississippian and Cherokee houses rather than to actual differences in household size.

The most significant difference between Mississippian and Cherokee houses lies along the dimension of occupation duration. Quantifying this difference in a meaningful way, however, requires a different approach than Warrick's (1988) wall post replacement method. Even a cursory glance at the plan view drawings of houses at Mississippian period towns like Coweeta Creek and Cherokee towns like Chota reveals major differences in the density of posthole patterns (e.g., Rodning 2002: Fig. 2; Schroedl 1986a: Fig. 1.31). The differences doubtless result from differences in occupation duration, but they are also due in part to the use of two different rebuilding techniques. These techniques have been identified by Wilson (2005:124–25) in his study of Mississippian architecture at the Moundville site in Alabama. The first technique involves the complete *rebuilding* of the entire structure in situ, while the second technique involves the *repair* of particular architectural elements such as posts. The palimpsests of postholes at Mississippian sites across the southern Appalachian region suggest that most of these houses were entirely rebuilt in situ (Hally 1988, 2002; Polhemus 1987; Rodning 2004:152; Sullivan 1989, 1995). By contrast, the posthole patterns of Cherokee houses suggest that rebuilding occurred gradually through the repair of individual posts rather than complete rebuilding.

These differences in rebuilding technique call for a different way to compare occupation duration in Mississippian and Cherokee houses. One solution is to use a more general measure of post density as an alternative proxy for repair and rebuilding. Among the Cherokee winter houses listed in Table 5.5, this proxy, which is a simple ratio of total posts to the floor area of each structure (posts/m^2), has a relatively strong positive correlation with the linear wall post density measure used in Warrick's (1988) method (r = 0.67) (Fig. 5.27). The correlation suggests that the posts/m^2 post density variable can also be used as a relative measure of occupation duration. The comparison of occupation duration must also take into account structure robustness (that is, large differences in the initial number of posts used to construct Mis-

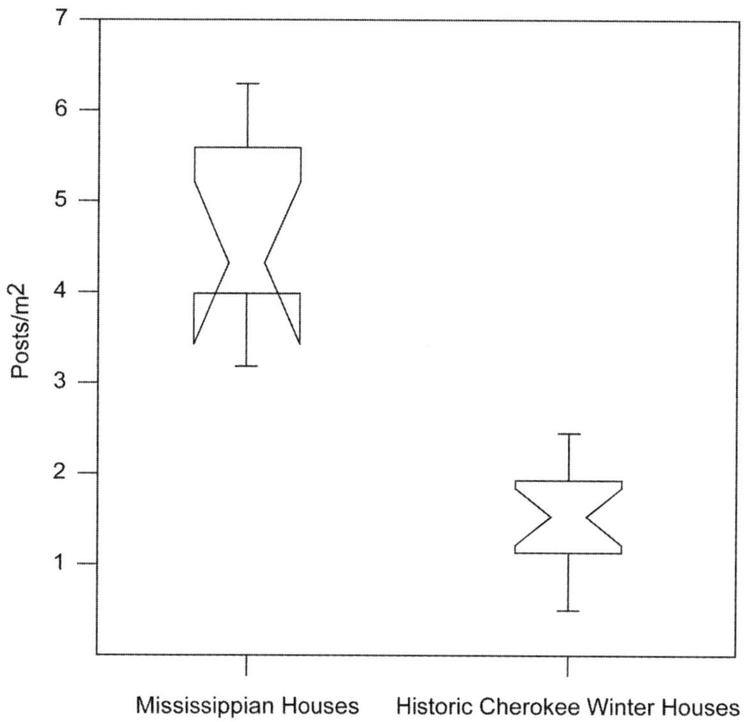

Figure 5.26.
Boxplots comparing post densities between non-rebuilt Mississippian houses and non-rebuilt historic Cherokee winter houses. Note: The "folded" appearance of the boxplot is due to small sample size and indicates that the 95% confidence interval of the median is greater than the H-spread. Reproduced with permission from *Pox, Empire, Shackles, and Hides* (Marcoux 2010: Fig. 5.9), ©University of Alabama Press.

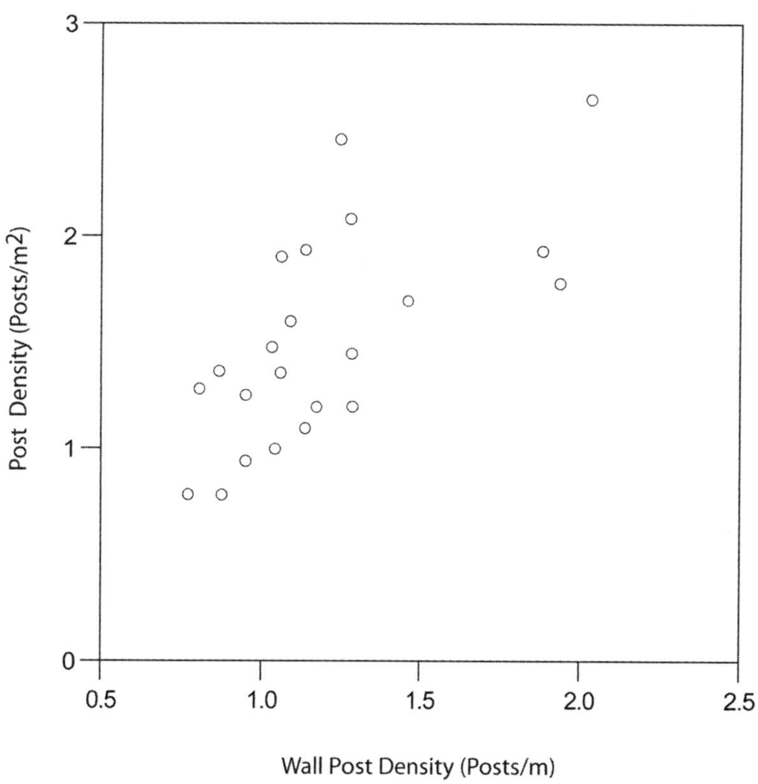

Figure 5.27. Scatterplot depicting the relationship between two post density measures ($r = 0.67$) for historic Cherokee winter houses. The x axis is a linear measure of post density using wall posts only, while the y axis measures post density using all structure posts and is expressed in terms of structure area.

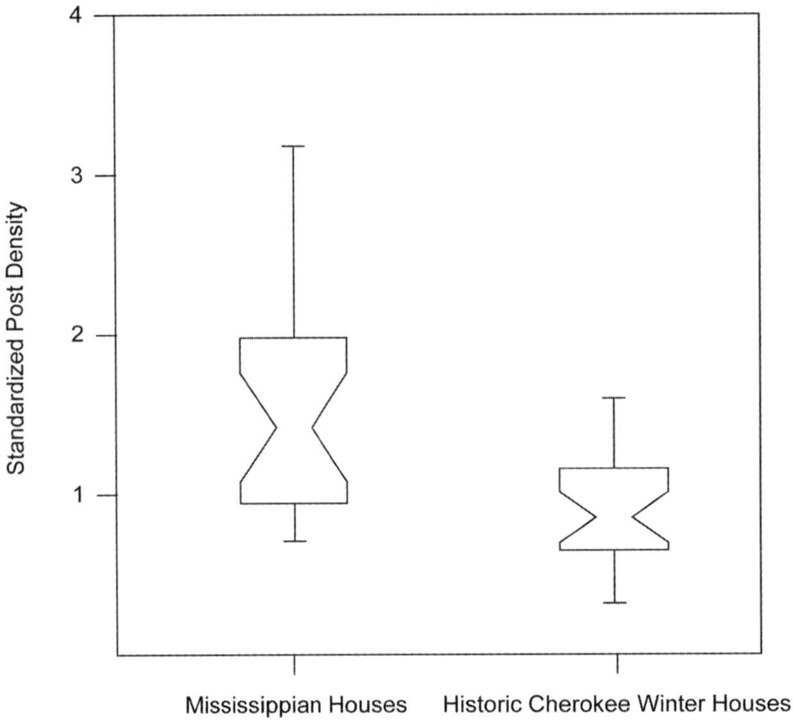

Figure 5.28. Boxplots comparing standardized post density measures between Mississippian houses and historic Cherokee winter houses. Standardization involved dividing the post density values of each Mississippian and Cherokee house by the median post density measures of non-rebuilt houses for each group. Reproduced with permission from *Pox, Empire, Shackles, and Hides* (Marcoux 2010: Fig.5.10), ©University of Alabama Press.

sissippian and Cherokee houses). I do this by standardizing the data—dividing the post density value of each house by the median post density value calculated for single building episodes of Mississippian (4.31 posts/m^2) and Cherokee (1.53 posts/m^2) houses. These median values were calculated above in the comparison of structural robustness.

Standardized post density values indicate that the occupation duration of Mississippian houses was significantly greater than that of Cherokee winter houses (Fig. 5.28). Indeed, the median value for Mississippian houses was nearly twice that of Cherokee houses. Unfortunately, unlike Warrick's (1988) method, this method does not result in occupation duration estimates expressed in actual years; however, the results still speak to large relative differences in occupation spans—the median values hinting that the occupation duration of Mississippian houses was twice that of Cherokee houses. Much longer occupation durations for Mississippian houses are further supported by evidence for multiple remodeling episodes of central hearths and entryways in Mississippian houses and the absence of this type of repair in Cherokee houses.

Summary and Implications

In this chapter I have sought to better characterize the Cherokee architecture uncovered during the Townsend project by introducing ways to operationalize concepts including method of manufacture, structure function, household size, and occupation duration. In accomplishing this task, I have referenced ethnohistoric descriptions and past archaeological research and have employed a number of different quantitative comparative methods. I believe that this study has resulted in identifying a number of data patterns associated with changes that occurred in the life of Cherokee households during the English Contact period (ca. A.D. 1670–1715).

This study found a good correspondence between the archaeological remains of houses at Townsend and ethnohistoric descriptions of Cherokee houses. Posthole data suggested that the Cherokees at Townsend built their houses according to a relatively prescribed architectural vernacular that resulted in robust patterns of posthole location and depth. The data also pointed to differences in shape, location, and wall post spacing that corresponded to the two types of domestic structures described in ethnohistoric accounts as "winter houses" and "summer houses." Floor area measurements across all Cherokee structures at Townsend were consistent with the interpretation that Cherokee household size approximated the nuclear family. Also, estimates of duration occupation indicated that the Townsend structures, and indeed most late seventeenth- and eighteenth-century Cherokee houses, were occupied for a decade or less.

Comparisons to houses at contemporaneous and later eighteenth-century Cherokee sites revealed a great deal of consistency. Winter house and summer house architectural forms were present at sites dating from the mid-seventeenth century to the late eighteenth century, although they were outnumbered by single rectangular dwellings at sites dating to the end of the period. Winter houses remained relatively the same size throughout the period, but earlier summer houses, particularly those found at Townsend, were much smaller than their later eighteenth-century counterparts. This may indicate that, with the exception of Structure 41, summer houses at Townsend largely served as auxiliary structures rather than true domiciles. Overall, the comparisons attest to a relative stability in Cherokee architectural practices at least between 1650 and 1776.

Extending the diachronic perspective back in time, on the other hand, reveals that significant changes in household architecture occurred between the late sixteenth century and the mid-seventeenth century. Cherokee houses and households were roughly the same size as during the preceding Mississippian period and they continued to be built using the architectural principles of rigid post architecture. There were, however, large differences in structure shape, in the types of entryways that were used, and in the overall structural robustness of structures dating to the two periods. Also, comparisons of post density measures attested to rather striking differences in rebuilding techniques and occupation duration between Mississippian and Cherokee houses. The architectural evidence suggested that Cherokee houses were gradually repaired during their occupation, which usually did not last long enough for all posts to be replaced. Mississippian houses, in contrast, were more often than not entirely rebuilt in situ and appear to have occupied the same structure footprint for at least twice the tenure of Cherokee houses. To sum up, the analysis suggested that sometime during the early to middle seventeenth century, folk began to construct houses that required much lower investments in materials and energy, and, furthermore, the household tenure of domestic space was shortened dramatically.

Notes

1. Schroedl (2000:220) has suggested that this form of townhouse likely reflected changes in village demography and the increasingly important role of clans in village life. The new townhouses would have contained seven partitioned benches, perhaps reflecting the seven matrilineal clans in Cherokee villages.

2. Recently, Shumate (Shumate et al. 2005:5.38, 5.39, 5.56–5.60) offered a very detailed discussion of the architecture of a single late seventeenth-century Cherokee winter and summer house pair in western North Carolina. In his analysis, Shumate made distinctions among a number of different post classes based partly on posthole depth and diameter and partly on his interpretation of Cherokee architectural vernacular. Shumate's identification of different post classes served as the inspiration for the analysis presented in this section.

3. For this and other statistical analyses, I emphasize measures and techniques associated with Exploratory Data Analysis (EDA) rather than traditional significance testing statistical methods. I choose to use EDA methods and measures primarily because they are better suited to the constraints of archaeological datasets. Exploratory data analysis—as set forth by its founders John Tukey (1977), Paul Velleman and David Hoaglin (1981)—is an inductive approach that aims to identify structure in datasets through relatively simple techniques and with minimal prior assumptions. The techniques are particularly well suited to archaeological datasets because they are nonparametric (i.e., they do not require assumptions of normally distributed data), they are resistant to the effects of outlier values, and they emphasize pattern recognition through simple visual display.

4. There have been some innovative attempts to calculate the occupation duration of households based on the accumulation rates of pottery (e.g., Pauketat 1989; Varien and Mills 1997; Varien and Potter 1997). Unfortunately, these methods work well only when one can be sure that the entire household ceramic assemblage has been collected, such as in the relatively undisturbed contexts in the southwestern United States. By comparison, it is almost impossible to fulfill this requirement in the plowed and often disturbed archaeological contexts of the Southeast.

Chapter 6

Features

Excavations at the Townsend sites identified 47 archaeological features associated with the late seventeenth- and early eighteenth-century Cherokee occupation. The features can be grouped into five basic types based on morphology and content: hearths, fired surfaces, refuse-filled depressions, refuse-filled basins, and refuse-filled pits. Following the convention set by previous studies of Cherokee features by Schroedl (1986a:46), basins are defined by smooth unbroken profiles while pits demonstrate sharp junctures between side walls and bottoms. Also following Schroedl (1986a:46), I admit that in many cases this distinction is largely an arbitrary one drawn by the analyst. In this chapter, I provide individual descriptions of each archaeological feature arranged by household. Following these descriptions, I discuss the results of a number of quantitative analyses aimed at (1) assessing the possible uses of the features, (2) identifying patterns in pottery refuse data associated with Cherokee discard behaviors and the abandonment of pit features, (3) characterizing household storage strategies through quantitative comparisons of pit volume among the six Townsend households, and (4) examining diachronic changes in Cherokee storage strategies that might have occurred during the eighteenth century.

Feature Descriptions

With the exception of the few features identified during Phase II hand excavations, the vast majority of the features identified during the Townsend project were uncovered by mechanized methods. Once uncovered, each feature was first cleaned, photographed, and mapped in plan view; then, each feature was bisected along its major axis and hand excavated as two halves. Excavation of each feature-half was carried out in arbitrary ten-centimeter levels except when excavators encountered changes in the soil color or texture. When this occurred, excavation by arbitrary levels ceased and provenience units were changed to represent breaks in natural stratigraphy. Field notes and data associated with the excavation of each feature were recorded on standardized forms. These data include: feature location, feature dimensions, depth, number of associated features, soil color and texture, types of material recovered, and narrative descriptions of the feature and its excavation. Excavators also produced measured profile drawings of each feature that portrayed its stratigraphy (or lack thereof). The feature descriptions and analysis presented in this chapter are based entirely on the information contained in these forms and in the profile drawings.

The following feature descriptions are organized by household (see Chapter 5). The locations of all the features are portrayed in a series of plan view maps, while summary data can be found in Table 6.1. In addition to metric data, Table 6.1 contains three proxy measures designed to better characterize the refuse deposits comprising the fill in each basin and pit. Schiffer (1972) makes important distinctions between three types of refuse that one encounters in archaeological contexts. The first type of refuse is de facto refuse, which Schiffer defines as "elements which reach archaeological context *without* the performance of discard activities" (Schiffer 1972:160, emphasis added). De facto refuse

Table 6.1. Summary data related to Cherokee archaeological features.

Site	Associated Household	Feature	Feature Type	Major Axis (cm)	Minor Axis (cm)	Depth (cm)	Estimated Pit Volume (liters)	Distance to Structure (m)	Number of Zones	Median Sherd Size (cm)	Sherd Size Range (cm)	Pottery Ubiquity (sherds/liter)
40Bt89	1	16	small basin	130	123	19	127.89	19.5	1	2	1–6	0.03
		18	medium basin	150	130	25	242.86	3.0	2	3	2–3	0.01
		21	large pit	174	170	38	489.22	6.5	1	2	< 1–6	0.29
		23	medium pit	158	148	37	228.38	7.5	2	3	1–11	0.44
		38	small basin	88	86	32	147.23	7.5	1	2	1–6	0.18
		44	small basin	114	112	18	98.38	15.0	2	2	1–8	0.66
		45	small pit	82	68	28	92.99	11.0	2	2	2	0.01
		48	medium bell-shaped pit	141	98	34	244.70	6.0	2	2.5	< 1–10	0.03
		50	medium pit	130	120	29	247.26	4.0	2	2	1–4	0.28
		55	small basin	109	100	25	98.53	4.0	1	2.5	1–15	0.89
		56	hearth	71	40	9	n/a	0.0	n/a	n/a	n/a	n/a
		59	fired surface	n/a	n/a	n/a	n/a	0.0	n/a	n/a	n/a	n/a
		143	burial	156	144	n/a	n/a	26.0	n/a	n/a	n/a	n/a
	unasso-ciated	24	small basin	118	107	22	121.40	n/a	1	3	3–7	0.02
40Bt90	2	936	medium basin	150	150	26	258.47	2.5	1	3	1–15	0.23
		995	small pit (interior)	46	43	26	14.23	0.0	1	2	1–4	0.42
		996	hearth	58	53	6	n/a	0.0	1	n/a	n/a	n/a
		1019	medium pit	133	133	40	309.15	8.0	1	2.5	1–14	1.05
		1020	small basin	121	114	17	110.11	10.0	1	3	2–5	0.08
	3	130	large pit	166	134	31	442.38	6.0	2	2	1–22	0.67
		135	medium pit	146	142	46	288.73	8.5	2	2	1–6	0.56
		438	depressed area	162	158	n/a	n/a	0.0	3	2	1–6	n/a
		443	small pit	147	127	25	111.57	1.5	1	2.5	2–4	0.05
		453	burial	80	60	n/a	n/a	5.0	n/a	n/a	n/a	n/a
		455	small pit	96	96	12	38.87	2.5	1	2	1–5	0.98
		1115	hearth	41	41	16	n/a	0.0	n/a	n/a	n/a	n/a
	4	118	hearth	192	102	43	n/a	0.0	n/a	n/a	n/a	n/a
		702	medium bell-shaped pit	96	90	46	183.48	2.5	4	2	1–6	0.16
		703	fired surface	n/a	n/a	n/a	n/a	0.0	n/a	n/a	n/a	n/a
		705	medium pit	132	124	40	306.43	5.5	3	3	1–11	0.96
		706	small pit (interior)	53	40	37	34.17	0.0	1	2	1–3	0.23
		707	small pit (interior)	62	58	27	55.57	0.0	3	4	1–5	0.05
		711	hearth	60	50	13	n/a	0.0	n/a	n/a	n/a	n/a
		722	depressed area	144	124	11	72.02	7.5	1	2	1–3	0.12
		1996	small pit	49	24	23	34.16	9.0	1	4	3–7	0.09
		2000	small pit (interior)	44	40	40	48.83	4.0	1	3	1–9	1.49

Table 6.1 cont.

Site	Associated Household	Feature	Feature Type	Major Axis (cm)	Minor Axis (cm)	Depth (cm)	Estimated Pit Volume (liters)	Distance to Structure (m)	Number of Zones	Median Sherd Size (cm)	Sherd Size Range (cm)	Pottery Ubiquity (sherds/ liter)
		2022	small pit (interior)	56	48	28	37.22	0.0	1	2	1–12	0.62
		2141	large pit	146	140	42	404.41	10.5	1	3	2–14	0.08
40Bt91	5	94	hearth	59	24	3	n/a	0.0	n/a	n/a	n/a	n/a
		497	small pit	110	105	21	236.53	5.0	3	2	1–11	0.42
		509	small pit	100	85	28	201.69	19.0	2	2	1–3	0.11
	6	390	small pit	104	96	20	68.69	7.5	1	2	1–4	0.22
		391	small pit	89	78	18	47.22	7.5	1	2	1–3	0.11
		392	small pit	99	87	22	97.22	7.0	1	1.5	1–2	0.02
		394	hearth	79	46	6	n/a	0.0	n/a	n/a	n/a	n/a
	unasso-ciated	438	large historic feature	438	142	42	n/a	n/a	2	2	1–6	n/a

would include all artifacts that were left in situ, such as a whole pot found on the floor of a catastrophically burned house or the contents of a storage pit whose location had been forgotten. Schiffer (1972:161–63) divides refuse that had been intentionally discarded into two types—primary refuse and secondary refuse. Primary refuse consists of material that was "discarded at its location of use" (Schiffer 1972:161). Obvious examples of primary refuse would include lithic debitage concentrations found near stone outcroppings or charcoal found in a hearth. This type of refuse is rare in Southeastern contexts where the degree of disturbance created by post-depositional processes is high. Schiffer defines secondary refuse as material that was discarded in a *different* location from where it was originally used. Given that the original function of refuse-filled basins and pits at Townsend was almost certainly not to act as trash receptacles, it is logical to assume that the material found in these features was not primary refuse. In addition to Schiffer's refuse typology, I consider a fourth type of refuse—tertiary refuse. I define tertiary refuse as material whose final location of discard was neither its location of use *nor* its location of initial discard. This material had been lying in a midden or on the ground surface for some period of time (an activity known as provisional discard) before it was deposited into a feature either incidentally through natural infilling or intentionally.

The last three measures in Table 6.1 (that is, the median size of the potsherds, the size range of potsherds, and the ubiquity of potsherds in the pit fill) are aimed at distinguishing between the different types of refuse—particularly secondary and tertiary refuse (the two types encountered at Townsend). I expect that secondary refuse will be indicated by a combination of the presence of large sherds (> 5 cm), a large median sherd size (> 2 cm), and a high pottery ubiquity measure (> 0.4 sherds/liter), while tertiary refuse will be associated with the absence of large sherds, a small median sherd size, and a low pottery ubiquity measure.

Household 1

Feature 16 (Figs. 6.1, 6.2)

Feature 16 was a broad shallow refuse-filled basin located approximately 19 m southwest of Structure 999. The fill of the pit consisted of homogeneous dark brown fine sandy silt loam with numerous charcoal flecks and contained only a few small potsherds. Nothing in the morphology or contents of the feature indicates a definitive use; therefore, following the interpretations of other Cherokee researchers (e.g., Baden 1983; Russ and Chapman 1983; Schroedl 1986a), I assume that Feature 16 was excavated to provide soil for winter house construction or for use as storage. Taken together with a lack of evidence for weathering of the basin walls, it appears that the pit was filled with tertiary refuse in a single episode relatively shortly after disuse.

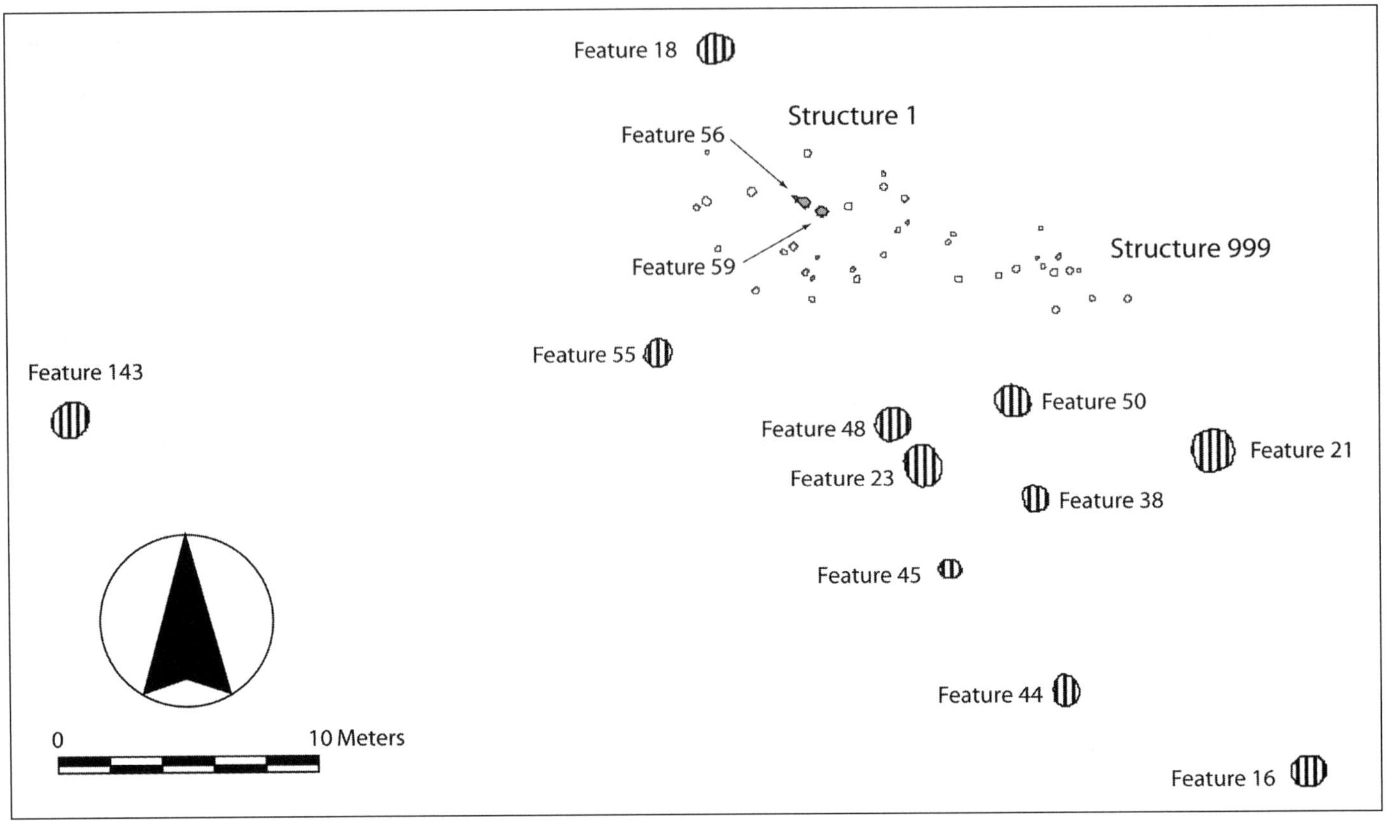

Figure 6.1. Cherokee features associated with Household 1.

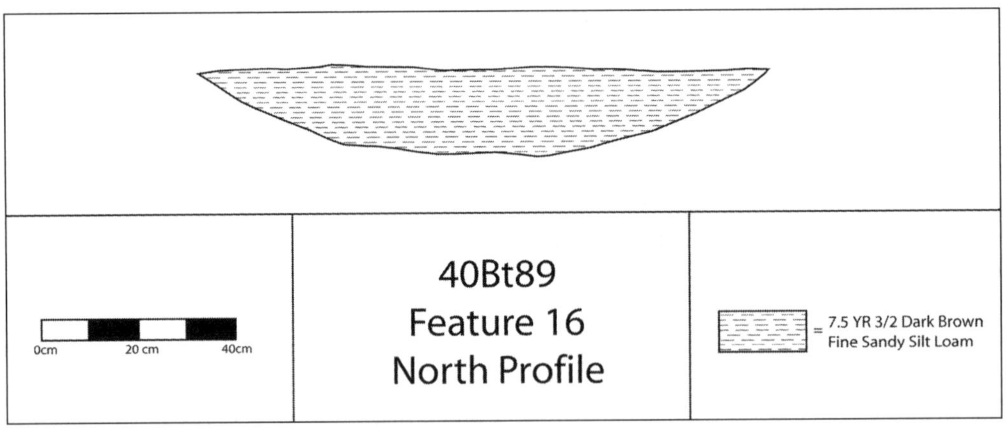

Figure 6.2. Profile of Feature 16.

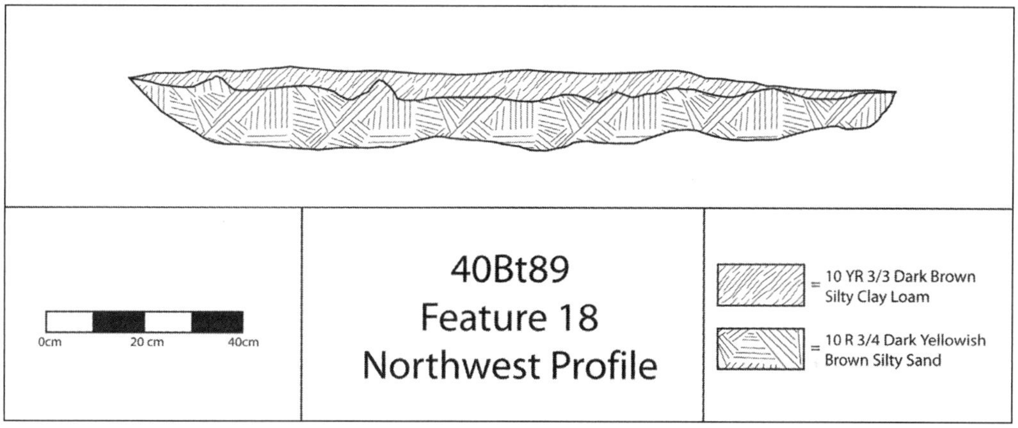

Figure 6.3. Profile of Feature 18.

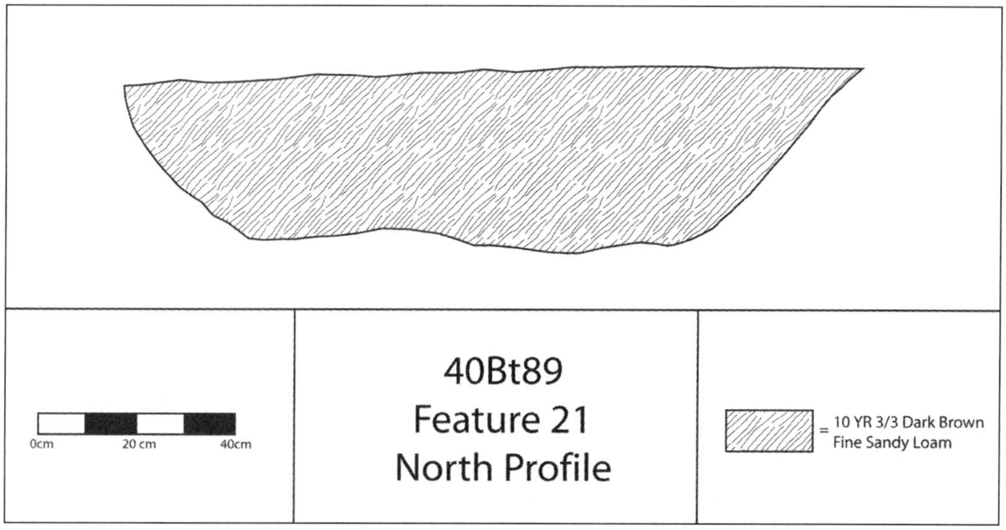

Figure 6.4. Profile of Feature 21.

Feature 18 (Figs. 6.1, 6.3)

Feature 18 was a broad, shallow basin located 3 m north of Structure 1. The fill was stratified, consisting of a zone of dark brown silty clay loam overlaying a zone of dark yellowish brown silty sand. The low value of the pottery ubiquity measure indicates that the basin was essentially devoid of pottery refuse (see Table 6.1). The shallow depth and irregularly shaped bottom of the feature suggests that more than likely it was excavated for soil rather than for storage. The evidence also indicates that the pit was filled quickly after disuse. Although the feature was stratified, the similarities in the colors and differences in the textures of the two soil zones could be the result of post-depositional processes acting on a single initial deposit.

Feature 21 (Figs. 6.1, 6.4)

Feature 21 was a large circular refuse-filled pit located 6.5 m southeast of Structure 999. It was the largest pit (in terms of volume) associated with the Cherokee occupation at the Townsend site. The homogeneous fill of Feature 21 consisted of dark brown fine sandy loam and contained over 100 small potsherds and 44 glass trade beads, likely a deposit of tertiary refuse. While the bottom of Feature 21 was somewhat irregular, its depth provides support for the interpretation that it originally functioned as a storage pit.

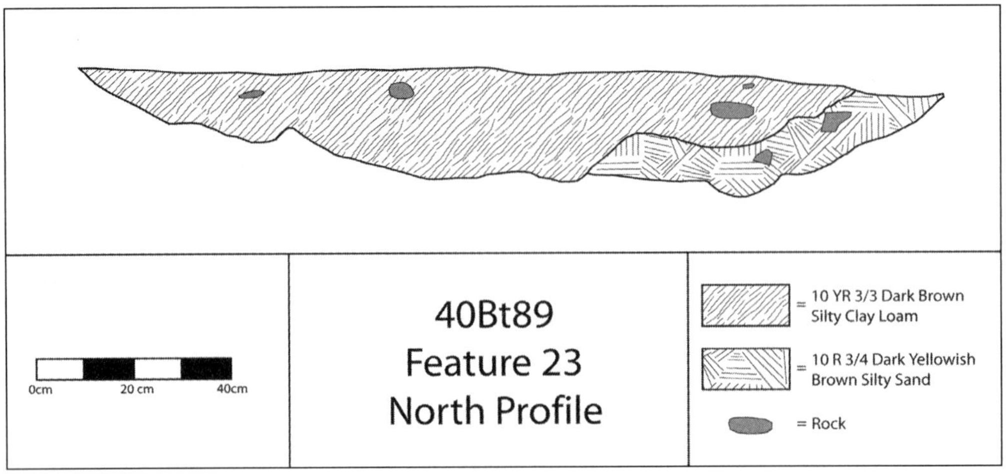

Figure 6.5. Profile of Feature 23.

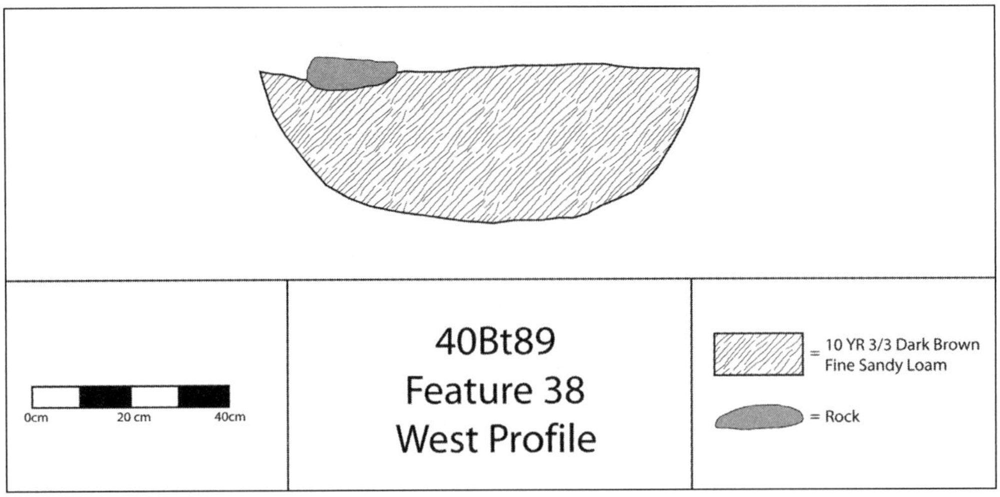

Figure 6.6. Profile of Feature 38.

Feature 23 (Figs. 6.1, 6.5)

Feature 23 was a large-diameter circular pit with an irregular bottom located 7.5 m south of Structure 1. The majority of the pit fill in Feature 23 consisted of dark brown silty clay loam with abundant charcoal flecks. The pit's profile evinced a single "slumping episode"—manifested in the mixed zone of pit fill and subsoil located along the east wall of the pit. This event occurred when part of the pit wall collapsed, which suggests that the pit remained unfilled for some length of time. The median size of potsherds and the pottery ubiquity measure for Feature 23 were relatively high compared to other features at the site, indicating that the refuse deposit in the fill of Feature 23 was secondary in nature. In addition to charcoal and about 100 potsherds, the pit contained a fair amount of fire-cracked rock (FCR) and 14 glass trade beads.

Feature 38 (Figs. 6.1, 6.6)

Feature 38 was a circular basin located 7.5 m south of Structure 999. The homogeneous fill of Feature 38 was likely tertiary refuse consisting of dark brown fine sandy loam with sparse charcoal flecks. The feature also contained a small amount of fire-cracked rock, 26 potsherds, and 2 glass trade beads.

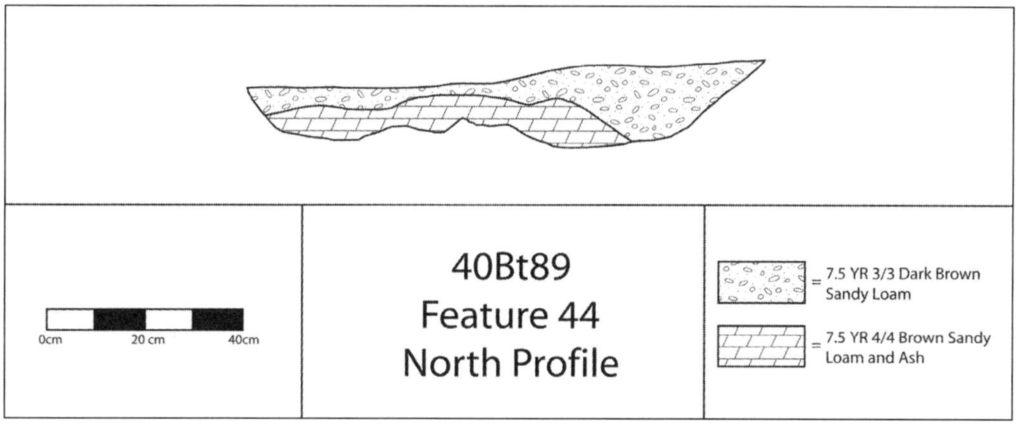

Figure 6.7. Profile of Feature 44.

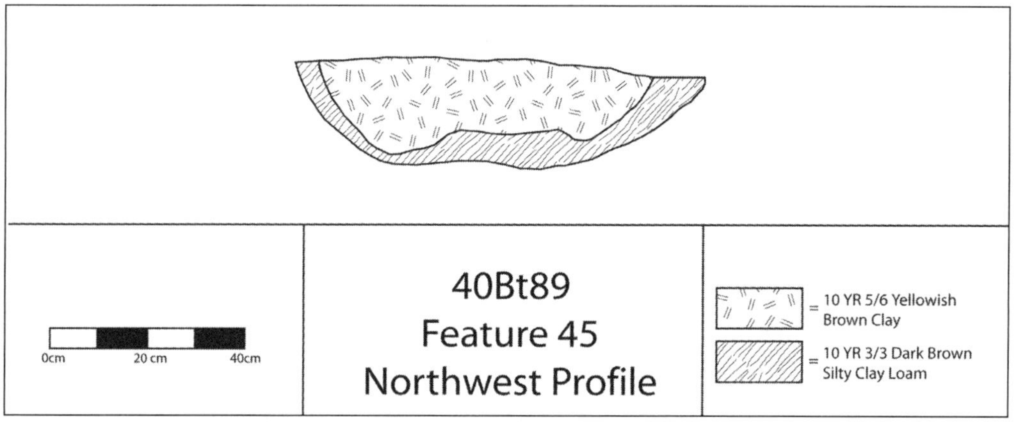

Figure 6.8. Profile of Feature 45.

Feature 44 (Figs. 6.1, 6.7)

Feature 44 was a broad circular shallow basin located 15 m south of Structure 1. The feature was separated into two stratigraphic zones including a zone of dark brown sandy loam and a zone of brown sandy loam mixed with ash. This stratigraphy could be the result of separate but closely timed fill episodes or the result of post-depositional settling. Feature 44 had 65 potsherds and a relatively high pottery ubiquity measure, and it contained 6 glass trade beads. Like most of the features at Townsend, the function of Feature 44 is not entirely clear, but the feature's lack of depth and its irregular bottom do not support a storage function.

Feature 45 (Figs. 6.1, 6.8)

Feature 45 was an oval pit located 11 m south of Structure 1. The fill of Feature 45 consisted of what was interpreted as a hard-packed yellowish brown clay "cap" covering a zone of dark brown silty clay loam with abundant charcoal flecks. Artifacts in the fill included a single potsherd and a single glass trade bead.

Feature 48 (Figs. 6.1, 6.9)

Feature 48 was a broad oval bell-shaped pit located 6 m south of Structure 1. The fill of the pit was composed of four distinct stratigraphic zones. The uppermost zone was dark brown fine sandy loam underlain by three zones of fine ashy loam, each probably representing an individual dumping episode. Based on its shape, the primary function of the pit was more than likely storage. The stratigraphy displayed by the pit suggests that it lay open for some time while the ash layers were deposited. Only 8 potsherds were recovered from the feature, resulting in a low pottery ubiquity value, but one of the potsherds was large (10–11 cm), making the assignment of the fill as secondary or tertiary refuse unclear. The pit also contained 3 glass trade beads. Given

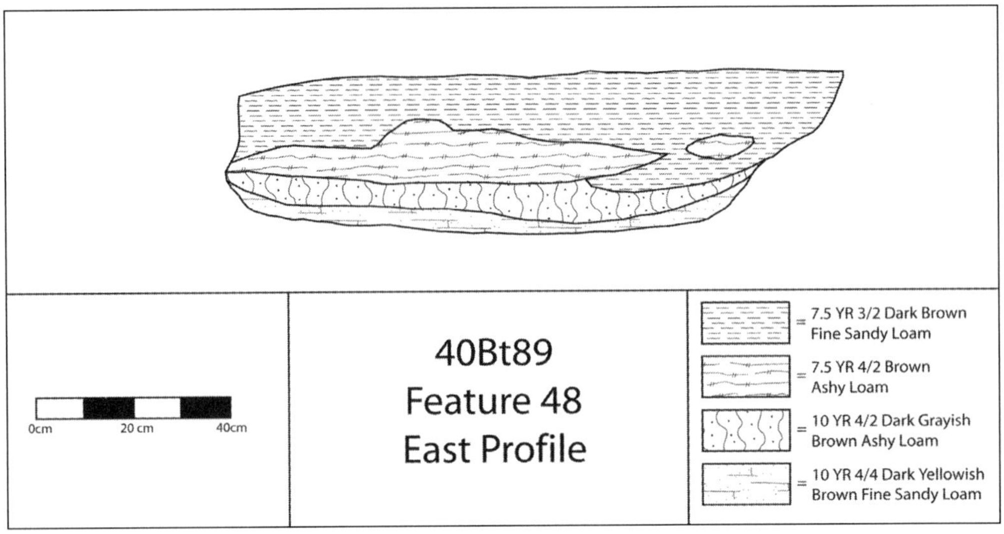

Figure 6.9. Profile of Feature 48.

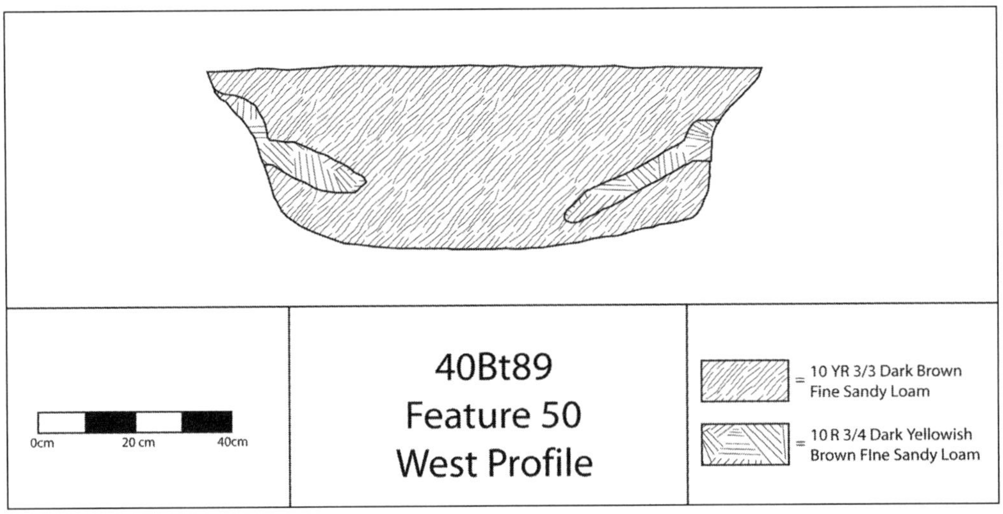

Figure 6.10. Profile of Feature 50.

the abundance of ash and the presence of a large potsherd in the pit fill, it is possible that the fill in Feature 48 was related to the periodic cleaning of the floor and hearth of Structure 1.

It is interesting to note that Feature 48 and Feature 702 (in Houshold 4) were the only bell-shaped pits associated with the Cherokee occupation. Bell-shaped pits are often associated with formal food storage practices (DeBoer 1988; Dickens 1985; Koldehoff and Galloy 2006; Ward 1985). As discussed below, the data suggest that subterranean food storage was a small-scale affair in late seventeenth- and early eighteenth-century Cherokee households and that formal large-scale subterranean food storage was not common until the later half of the eighteenth century.

Feature 50 (Figs. 6.1, 6.10)

Feature 50 was a large-diameter circular pit located 4 m south of Structure 999. The majority of the fill in Feature 50 consisted of dark brown fine sandy loam. The remainder of the fill in the pit consisted of two deposits of dark yellowish brown fine sandy loam that resulted from "slope wash"—a process in which waterborne sediments were carried into the pit while it lay open. The presence of these zones indicates that Feature 50 was filled over an extended period of time. The median sherd size and pottery ubiquity measures indicate that the pit fill contained tertiary refuse including 63 potsherds, fire-cracked rock, and 15 glass trade beads.

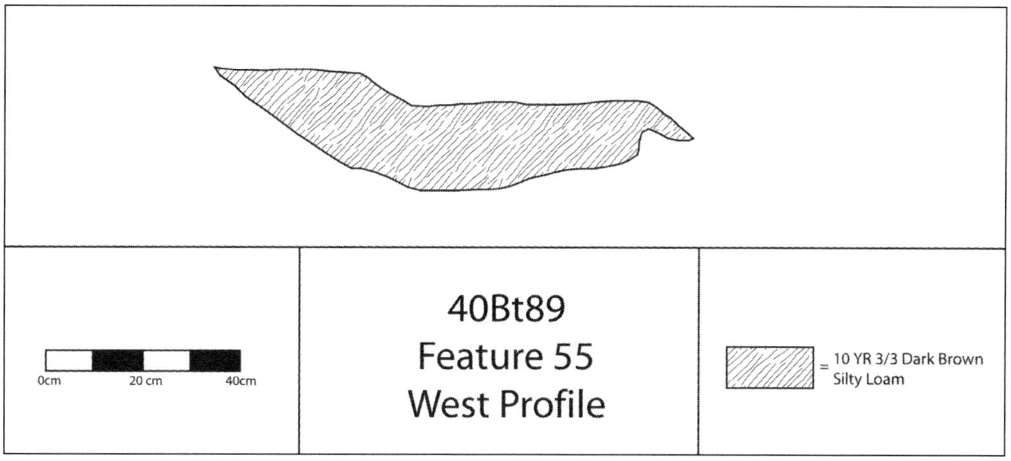

Figure 6.11. Profile of Feature 55.

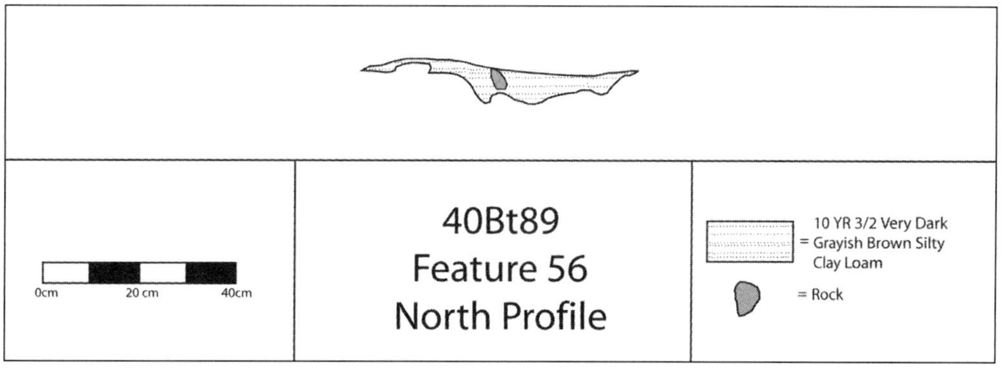

Figure 6.12. Profile of Feature 56.

Feature 55 (Figs. 6.1, 6.11)

Feature 55 was a large-diameter shallow basin located 4 m southwest of Structure 1. The soil comprising the fill of this feature was homogeneous dark brown silt loam with charcoal flecks. The profile drawing of Feature 50 indicates that the basin suffered some disturbance during the initial mechanized portion of excavations; however, the basic round-bottom shape of the feature is still clear. Feature 50, which contained 88 potsherds, has one of the higher values for the pottery ubiquity measure as well as a larger median sherd size and a few large sherds. Based on these measures, it is likely that the refuse deposited in Feature 50 was secondary rather than tertiary. Fifteen glass trade beads were also recovered from Feature 50.

Features 56 and 59 (Figs. 6.1, 6.12)

Features 56 and 59 represent a hearth and fired ground surface respectively. Both were located within Structure 1. Unlike the formal clay hearths found in the Cherokee winter houses at the Alarka (Shumate et al. 2005) and Tuckaseegee (Keel 1976) sites, the profile of Feature 56 shows that this was a simple hearth created by excavating a shallow pit into subsoil. The profile also demonstrates the high degree of historic plow disturbance that affected all the Cherokee hearths identified during the Townsend project. The hearth was filled with very dark grayish brown silt clay loam with abundant ash, charcoal, and fired clay pieces. No artifacts other than fire-cracked rock were recovered from this feature. Feature 59 was a designation given to a small patch of oxidized soil within the walls of Structure 1. This soil lens had virtually no depth and was likely the result of a small surface fire.

Feature 143 (Fig. 6.1)

Feature 143 was a burial. Excavation of the feature was guided by the suspicion that it was a burial based on its size, its shape, and the mottled nature of the fill. Human cranial elements were encountered at approximately 50 cm below the surface of the feature. When this occurred, excavation was halted and the remains were reburied.

The association of this burial with the Cherokee occupation rests solely on the excavator's noting the presence of Cherokee pottery in the feature fill.

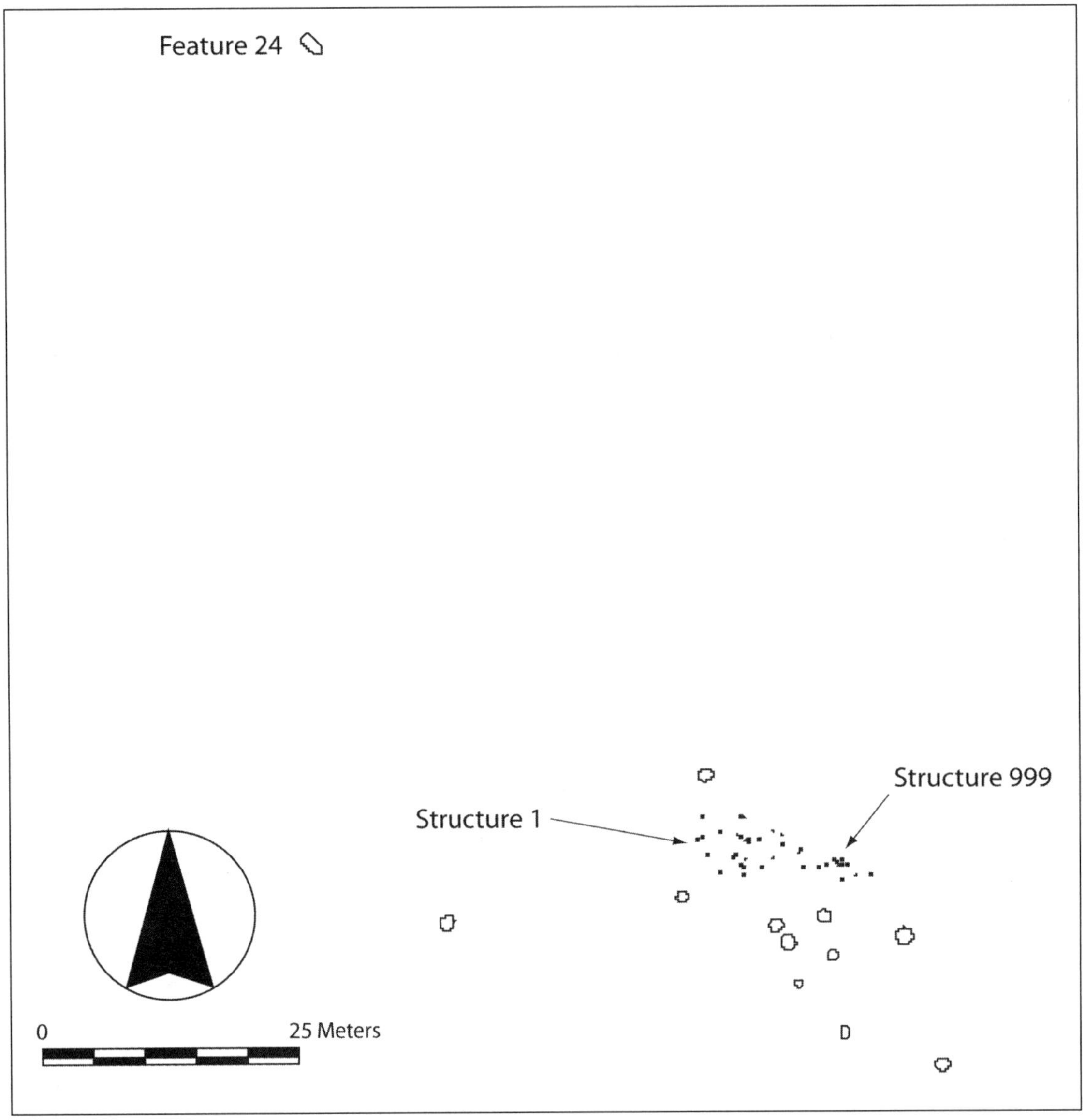

Figure 6.13. The location of Feature 24 in relation to Household 1

Unassociated Feature Near Household 1

Feature 24 (Figs. 6.13, 6.14)

Feature 24 was a circular, shallow basin located approximately 80 m northwest of Household 1. Given the isolated location of this feature, it is unlikely that it was associated with Household 1; instead, it is more probable that the basin was associated with another Cherokee household whose remains lie outside the excavation limits of the Townsend project. The fill of the basin consisted of homogeneous dark yellowish brown silty loam. The fill was generally lacking in artifacts, which consisted of a small amount of fire-cracked rock, a small number of potsherds, and a single glass trade bead. A large cobble with two worn depressions (i.e., a "nutting stone") was found at the interface between the plowzone and the surface of the feature. Given the typical association of this technology with Woodland period artifact assemblages, the association of this artifact with the Cherokee occupation is less than certain.

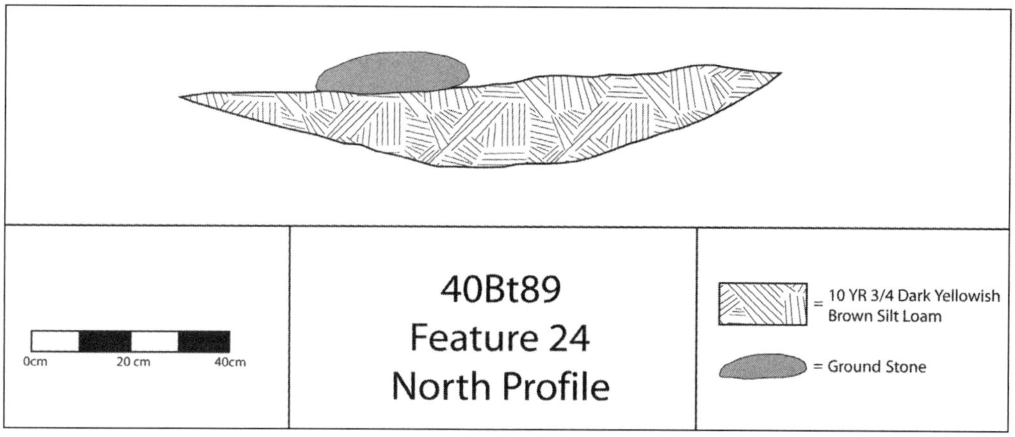

Figure 6.14. Profile of Feature 24.

Household 2

Feature 936 (Figs. 6.15, 6.16)

Feature 936 was a large-diameter circular basin located 3 m west of Structure 23. The soil filling the feature consisted of homogeneous very dark grayish brown silty loam with light densities of charcoal and moderate amounts of fire-cracked rock. Sixty potsherds representing a wide size range were present but were relatively sparse. The fill also contained 3 glass trade beads. Overall, the feature appears to have been filled quickly with soil containing a small amount of tertiary refuse.

Feature 995 (Figs. 6.15, 6.17)

Feature 995 was a relatively small flat-bottom pit located within Structure 22 approximately 1 m northwest of the hearth. The location of this feature inside a structure would indicate a probable storage function. The fill of the feature consisted of a single zone of very dark grayish brown loam with abundant charcoal specks and fired clay fragments. Six small potsherds were recovered in the fill along with 5 glass trade beads. It is likely that the pit was filled with tertiary refuse that was once lying on the house floor.

Feature 996 (Fig. 6.15)

Feature 996 was the hearth located in the center of the winter house of Household 2 (Structure 22). Field notes describe the feature as a "circular patch of burned earth" that was dissected by numerous plow scars. The hearth contained a single layer of what was described as very dark grayish brown clay—no ash was noted. The entire feature was excavated as a single provenience and no profile drawing was made. A single glass trade bead was recovered from the fill.

Feature 1019 (Figs. 6.15, 6.18)

Feature 1019 was a large-diameter circular pit located 8 m northeast of Structure 22. The majority of the pit fill in Feature 1019 consisted of dark brown silty loam with abundant charcoal flecks and fragments. The remnants of a slumping episode were apparent in the zone of mottled soil located along the west wall of the pit. With over 300 potsherds, the pottery ubiquity measure for Feature 1019 was among the highest in the sample. This value, along with the larger median sherd size and the presence of numerous large sherds, suggests that the feature was filled with secondary refuse. Numerous pieces of fire-cracked rock and 40 glass trade beads were also present in the fill.

Feature 1020 (Figs. 6.15, 6.19)

Feature 1020 was a broad circular, shallow basin located 10 m northeast of Structure 22. Feature fill consisted of a single zone of very dark gray silty loam with light densities of charcoal. The fill contained very little pottery (9 potsherds), 3 glass trade beads, and an abundance of fire-cracked rock. While the lack of artifacts points to tertiary refuse, the large amount of fire-cracked rock could indicate a deposit of secondary refuse that simply lacked pottery sherds.

Household 3

Feature 130 (Figs. 6.20, 6.21)

Feature 130 is a large-diameter oval-shaped pit with a relatively flat bottom located 6 m south of Structure 12. The soil filling the pit consisted primarily of very dark grayish brown silty loam with abundant charcoal flecks and fragments. A small concentrated zone of very dark brown mottled ashy loam was also located near the center of the pit. Potsherd size and density indicate that the pit was filled with secondary refuse that also contained a moderate amount of fire-cracked rock and 4 glass trade beads.

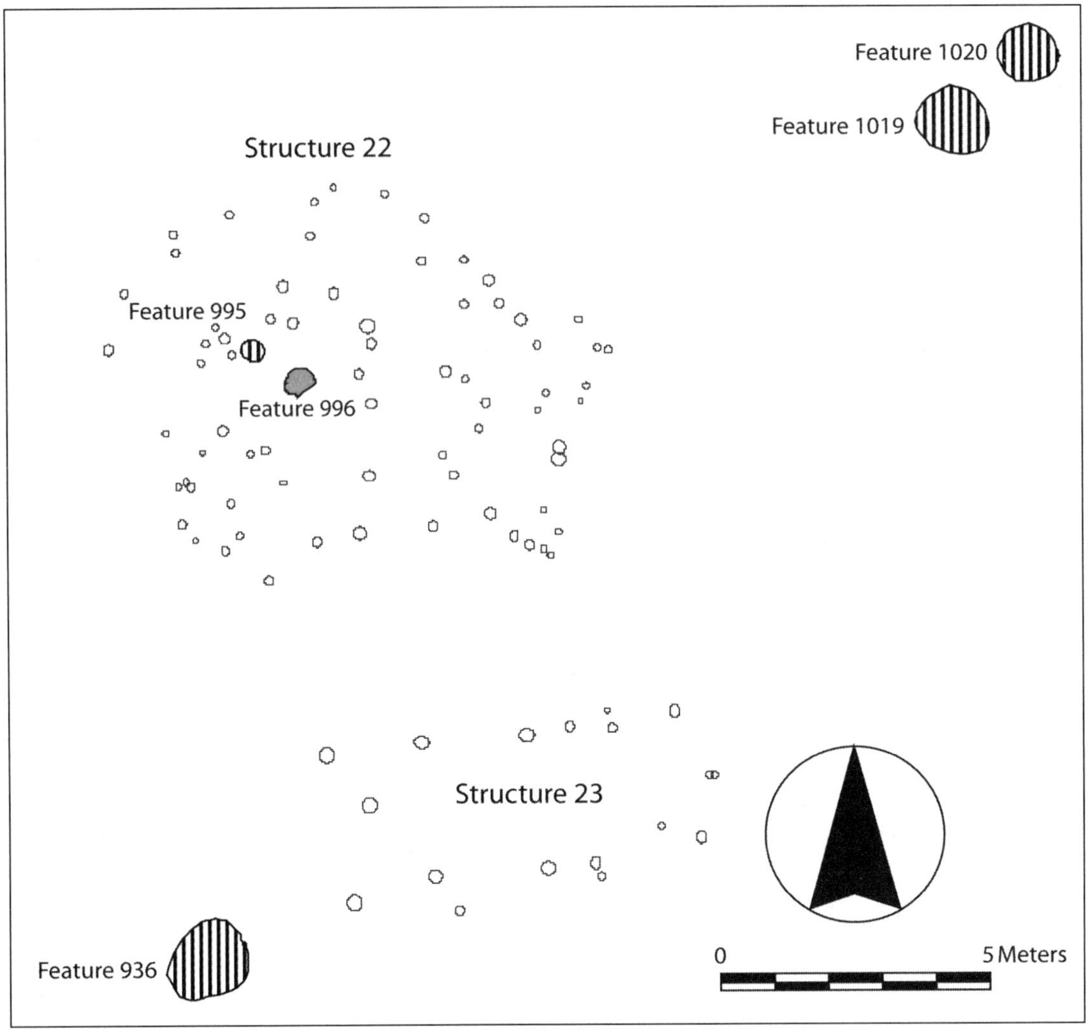

Figure 6.15. Cherokee features associated with Household 2.

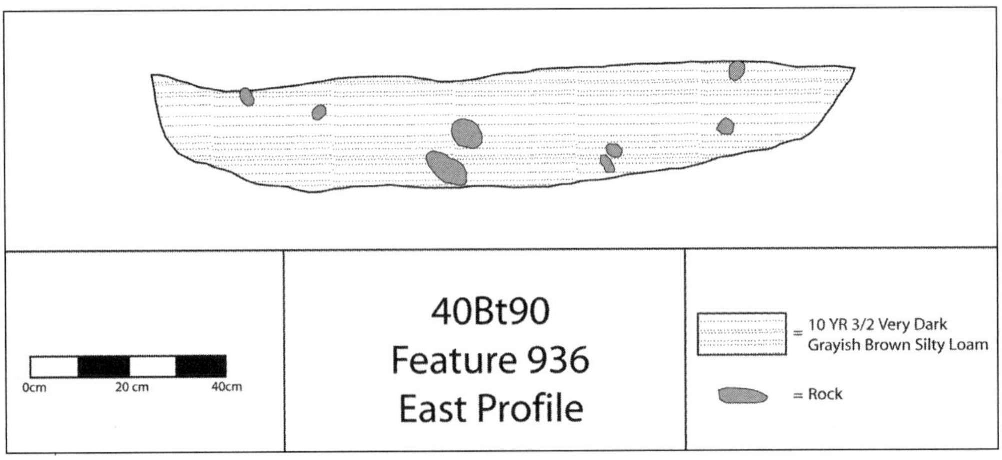

Figure 6.16. Profile of Feature 936.

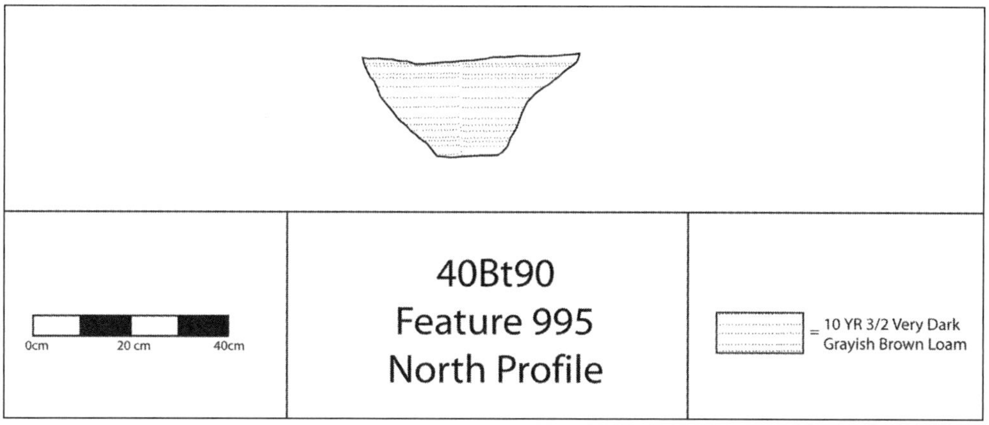

Figure 6.17. Profile of Feature 995.

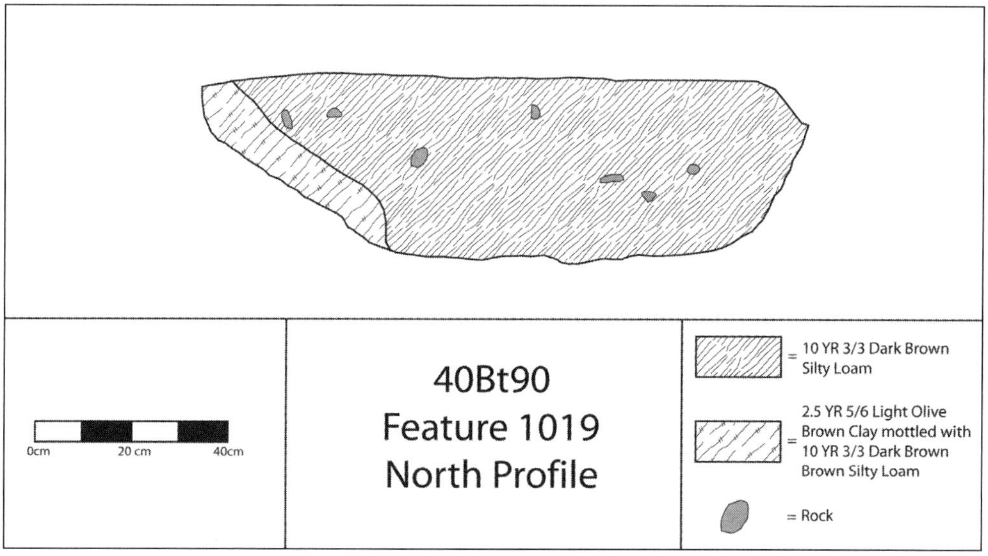

Figure 6.18. Profile of Feature 1019.

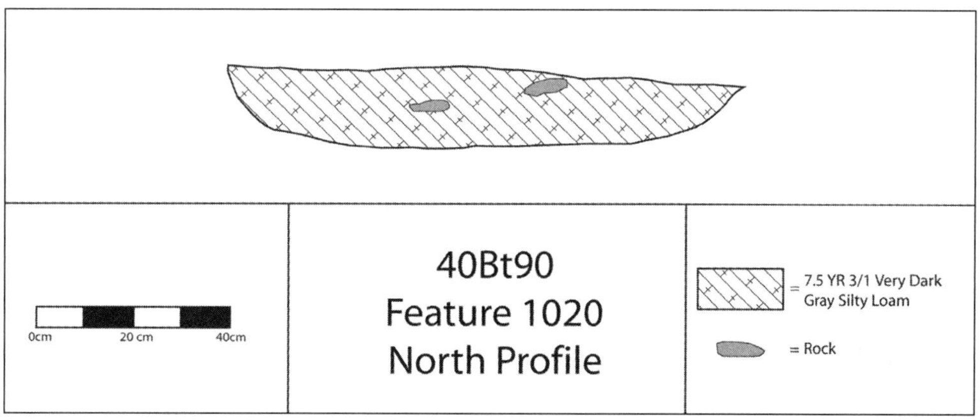

Figure 6.19. Profile of Feature 1020.

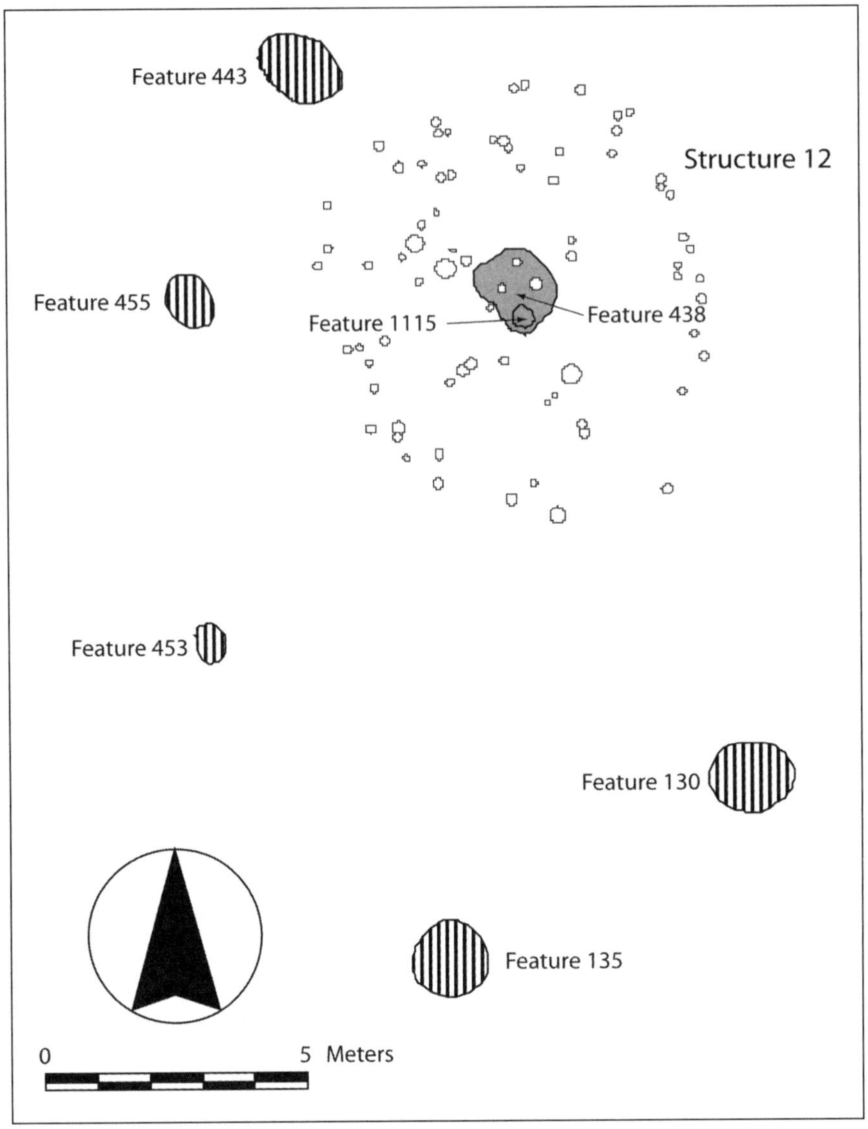

Figure 6.20. Cherokee features associated with Household 3.

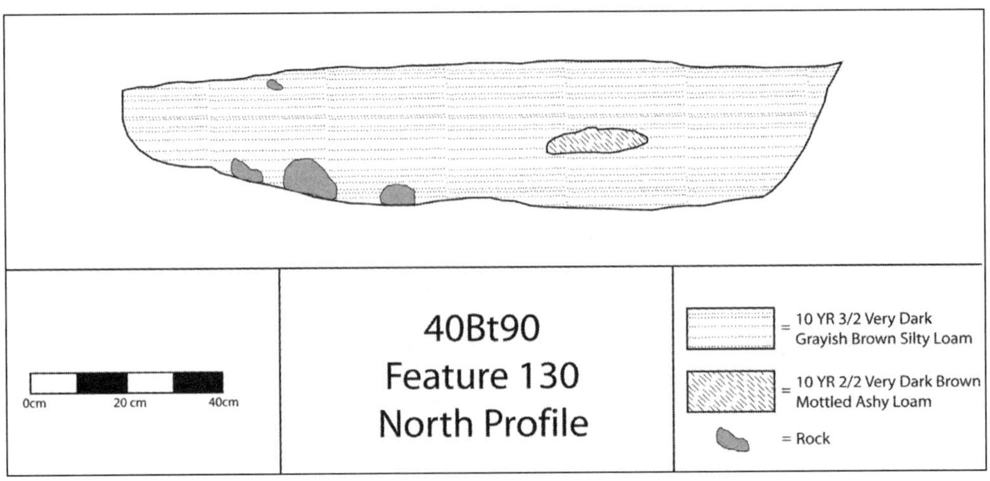

Figure 6.21. Profile of Feature 130.

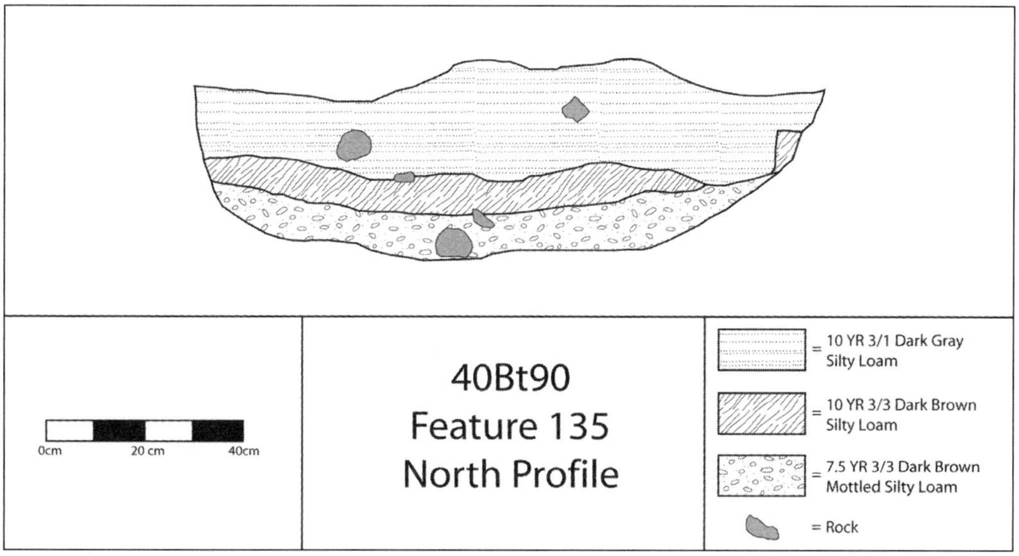

Figure 6.22. Profile of Feature 135.

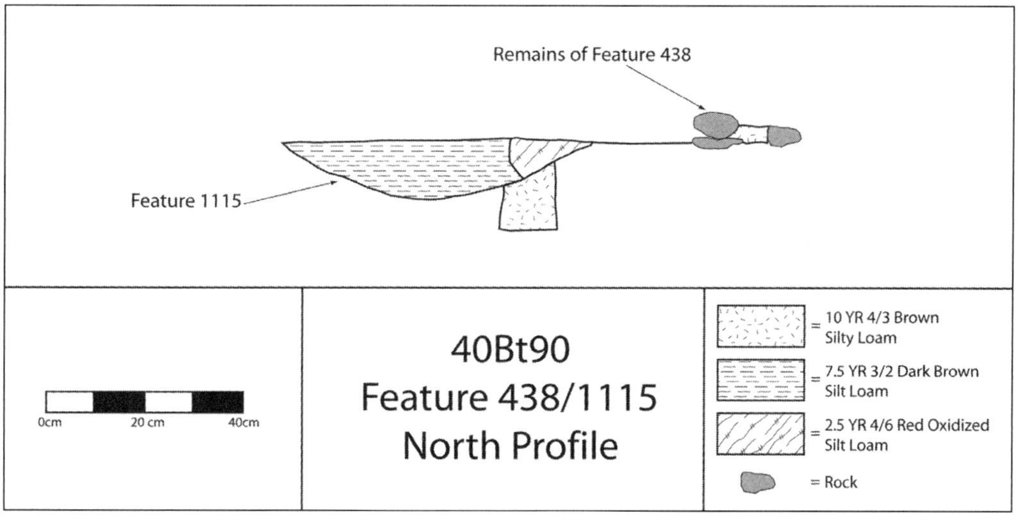

Figure 6.23. Profile of Feature 438 and Feature 1115.

Feature 135 (Figs. 6.20, 6.22)

Feature 135 was a broad circular pit located 8.5 m south of Structure 12. The pit exhibited stratigraphy composed of three zones. The topmost zone was a dark gray silty loam with heavy concentrations of charcoal flecks. This zone was underlain by a zone of dark brown silty loam with light densities of charcoal. The bottommost zone consisted of dark brown mottled silty loam with abundant charcoal. Nearly 300 potsherds were recovered from the feature, resulting in a high ubiquity measure. Fire-cracked rock was also moderately dense. Three glass trade beads were also recovered from the fill. The stratigraphy indicates that Feature 135 was filled incrementally, unlike most of the pits associated with Cherokee occupation, which were filled in a single episode.

Features 438 and 1115 (Figs. 6.20, 6.23)

Feature 438 represented a depressed area at the center of Structure 12 that surrounded Feature 1115—the remains of a hearth. When first encountered, the entire stain was treated as a single hearth feature; only after most of the depression (Feature 438) surrounding the hearth was excavated did excavators recognize that the hearth itself was much smaller in size. At this time, the hearth was given a separate feature designation. The fill of the depression consisted of a brown silty loam containing a moderate amount of medium-sized potsherds and 4 glass trade beads. Feature 1115 contained a zone of dark brown silty loam and a zone of reddish oxidized silt loam along its eastern edge. As can be seen in Figure 6.23, the hearth and depressed area intruded into an existing posthole.

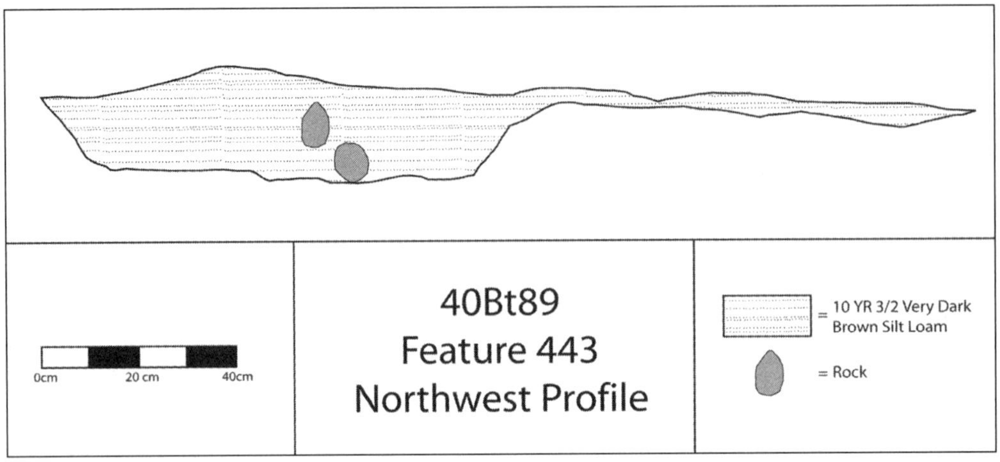

Figure 6.24. Profile of Feature 443.

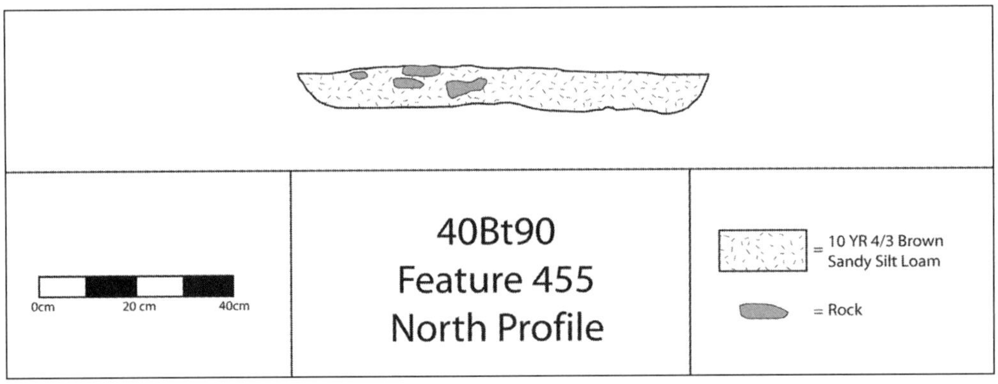

Figure 6.25. Profile of Feature 455.

Feature 443 (Figs. 6.20, 6.24)

Feature 443 is a shallow oval pit located 1.5 m northwest of Structure 12. Pit fill in Feature 443 consisted of homogeneous very dark brown silty loam with light densities of charcoal flecks. The pit was filled with soil containing some tertiary refuse, including a small amount of pottery and a moderate amount of fire-cracked rock.

Feature 453 (Fig. 6.20)

Feature 453 was determined to be a human burial located 5 m southwest of Structure 12. Given its small dimensions, the feature was not suspected to be a burial when first identified. Excavation of the feature was discontinued at approximately 30 cm below the surface when human teeth were identified in the fill. These remains and all associated artifacts were placed back in the pit and covered with fill. According to the excavation notes, the fill contained 13 glass trade beads, prompting its association with the Cherokee occupation.

Feature 455 (Figs. 6.20, 6.25)

Feature 455 was a broad, circular shallow pit located 2.5 m west of Structure 12. The fill of the pit consisted of a single zone of brown sandy silt loam with abundant charcoal fragments and specks. The field notes also indicated concentrations of ash in the fill, although these were not drawn in the profile. Potsherd density and size along with the proximity of the pit to Structure 12 suggest that the pit was filled with secondary refuse. Pit fill also contained moderate amounts of fire-cracked rock and a single glass trade bead.

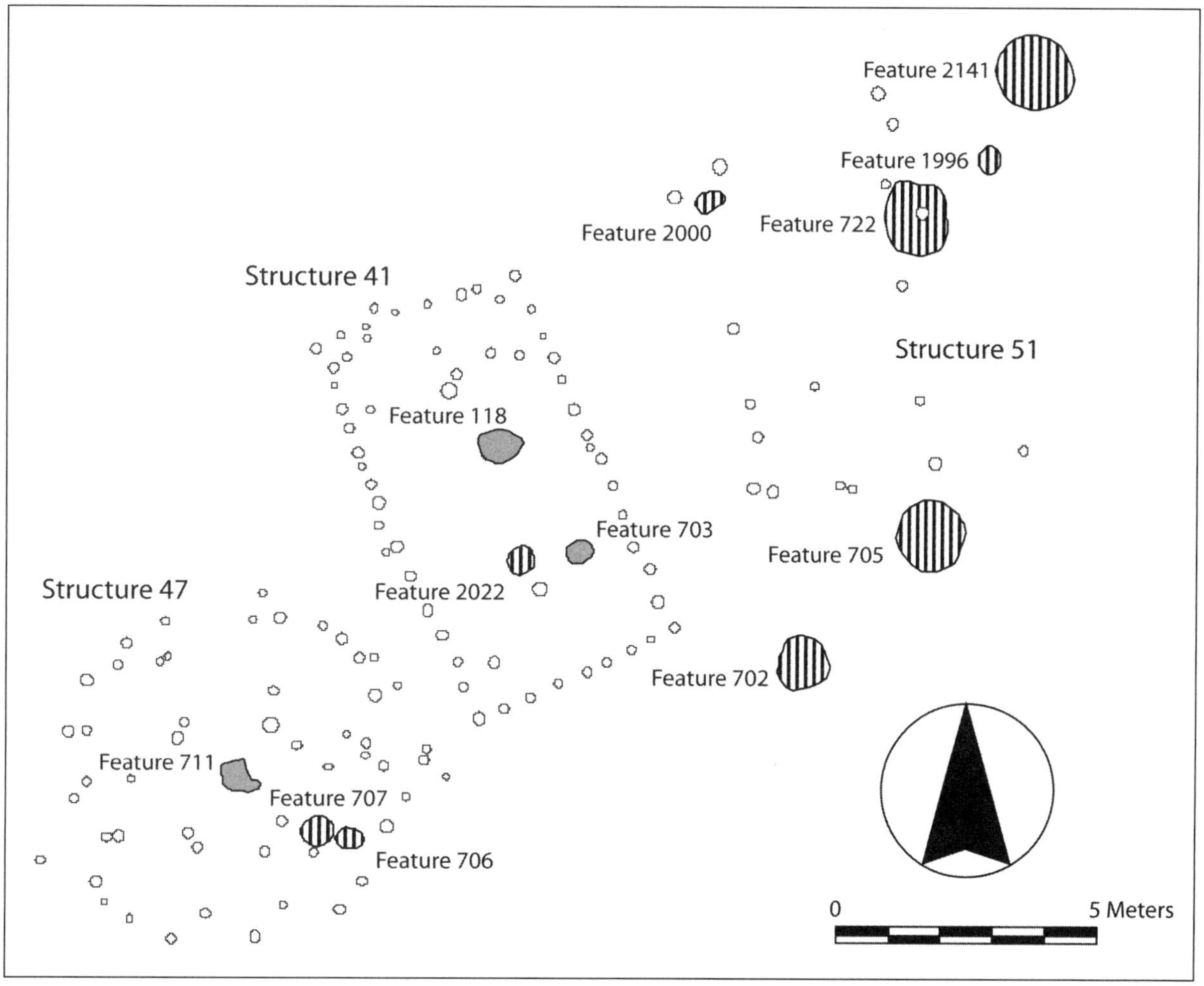

Figure 6.26. Cherokee features associated with Household 4.

Household 4

Feature 118 (Figs. 6.26, 6.27)

Feature 118 was a hearth located inside Structure 41, a Cherokee summer house. Post-depositional processes had severely affected the feature, resulting in a very mottled and amorphous profile. The hearth remains depicted in Figure 6.27 consisted of grayish brown ash, a mottled zone of dark brown fine ashy loam, and yellowish red oxidized loam. Overlaying this hearth deposit was a zone of very dark grayish brown fine silty loam. It is not clear from the field notes what processes might have led to the profile shape pictured in Figure 6.27. The field notes also described the presence of numerous "holes" around the perimeter of the hearth. These were interpreted as tree roots. Although there is no way to tell definitively, these holes alternatively may have been the remnants of a cane framework that was covered in clay in order to form a hearth. This style of hearth has been identified in the winter houses excavated at the Alarka and Tuckaseegee sites (Keel 1976; Shumate et al. 2005).

Feature 702 (Figs. 6.26, 6.28)

Feature 702 was a large-diameter, circular bell-shaped pit located 2.5 m southeast of Structure 41. The fill of Feature 702 consisted of four stratified zones. The uppermost zone, a brown heavily mottled sandy silt, likely resulted from sedimentation after the pit was filled. The second zone consisted of dark grayish brown silty loam with abundant charcoal fragments and flecks as well as fired clay fragments. Underlying this was a zone of concentrated dark grayish brown ashy loam that lacked charcoal. The remainder of the pit fill consisted of dark brown silty loam with sparse charcoal. Potsherds in the fill were small and relatively sparse. The stratification of the pit lends itself to the interpretation that the pit was filled in at least two episodes.

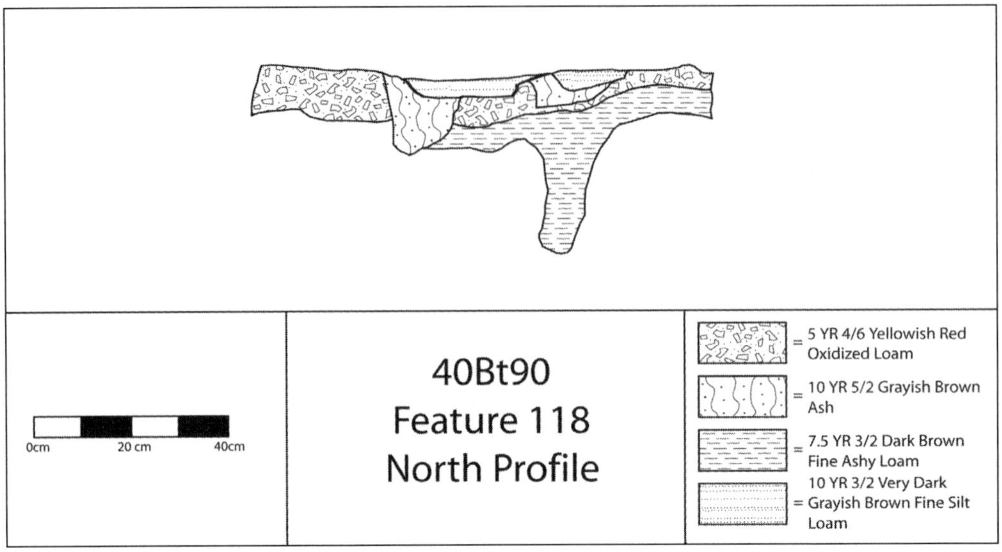

Figure 6.27. Profile of Feature 118.

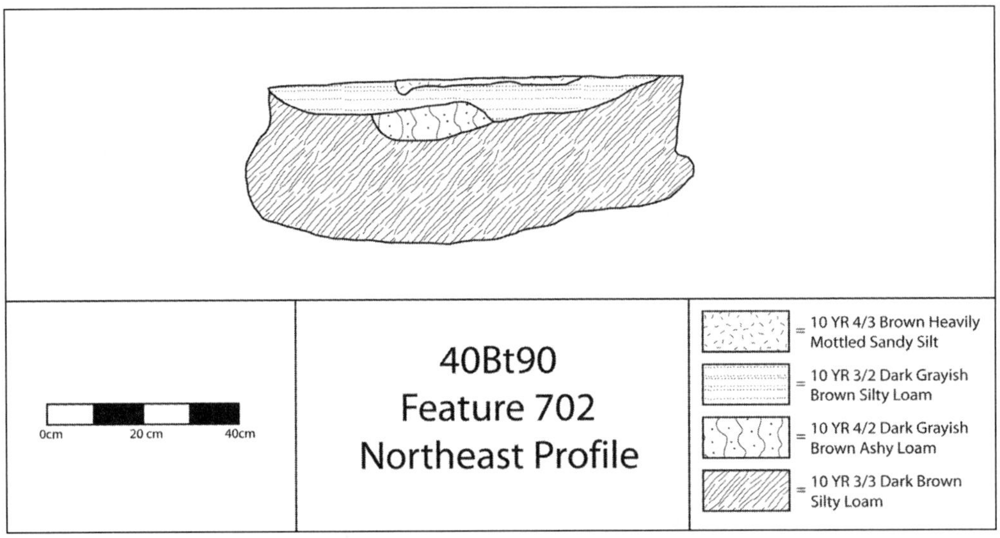

Figure 6.28. Profile of Feature 702.

Feature 703 (Fig. 6.26)

Feature 703 was described as a patch of oxidized soil located 3 m south of Feature 118 within Structure 41. No profile drawing of Feature 703 was made and excavators did not note the color or texture of the soil, but they did comment that the feature contained abundant charcoal flecks. Rather than being a formal hearth, Feature 703 more than likely resulted from a small surface fire.

Feature 705 (Figs. 6.26, 6.29)

Feature 705 was a large-diameter circular pit located 3 m east of Structure 41. The pit fill consisted of two zones including a central zone of dark brown fine silty loam with abundant charcoal flanked by a peripheral zone of brown loam with a high ash content. Nearly 300 potsherds were recovered from the pit. The pottery ubiquity measure and sherd size suggest that the fill was a secondary refuse deposit. The pit fill also included a fragment of iron (the only metal artifact definitively associated with the Cherokee occupation) and 2 glass trade beads.

Feature 706 (Figs. 6.26, 6.30)

Feature 706 was a small-diameter circular pit located inside Structure 47. The pit was filled with a single zone of homogeneous very dark grayish brown fine silty loam with abundant fragments of charcoal. Potsherds recovered from the fill were sparse and small, and likely were deposited into the pit from the house floor.

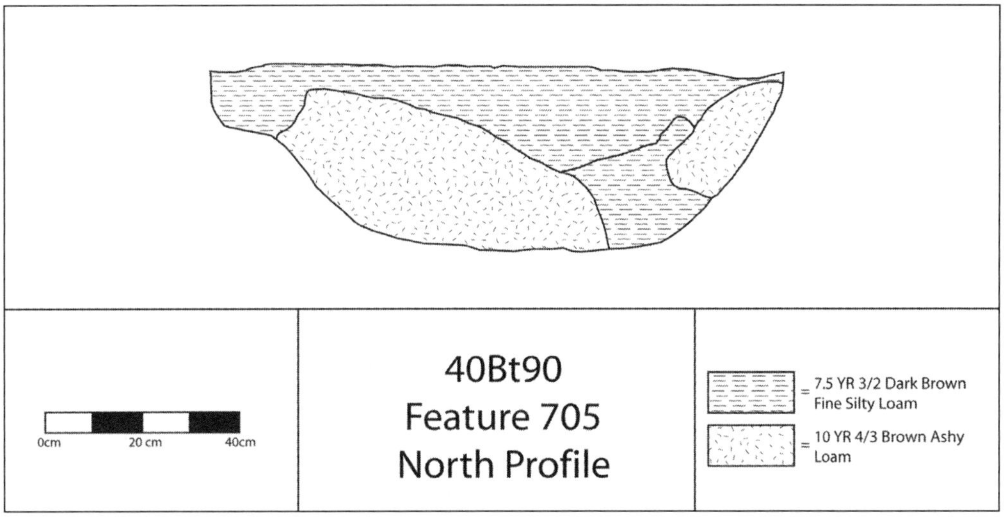

Figure 6.29. Profile of Feature 705.

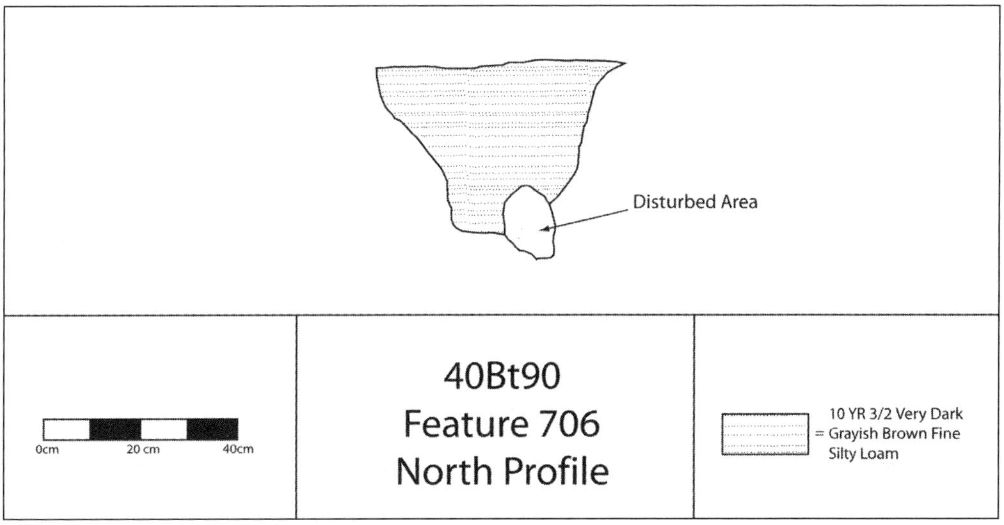

Figure 6.30. Profile of Feature 706.

Feature 707 (Figs. 6.26, 6.31)

Feature 707 was a small-diameter oval-shaped pit located adjacent to Feature 706 within Structure 47. The pit evinced three stratigraphic zones, which were composed of two different soil types. The top and bottom zones consisted of dark brown fine silty loam with abundant charcoal flecks and fragments. These zones surrounded a slope wash zone of brown silty clay loam that was carried (through natural deposition or sweeping) into the pit. The pit contained only a few small potsherds and a fragment of a carved stone pipe bowl.

Feature 711 (Figs. 6.26, 6.32)

Feature 711 was the central hearth of Structure 47. Much of this feature had been heavily disturbed as evidenced by multiple plow scars. The hearth consisted of a simple pit dug into subsoil, which was heavily oxidized, and its contents included brown fine sandy loam.

Feature 722 (Figs. 6.26, 6.33)

Feature 722 appears to have been a depressed area along the edge of Structure 51 into which a shallow lens of anthropogenic soil was deposited. The lens consisted of very dark brown silty clay with abundant moderately sized charcoal fragments. Potsherd size and density support the interpretation that this deposit contained tertiary refuse. Feature 722 overlaid a wall post associated with Structure 51.

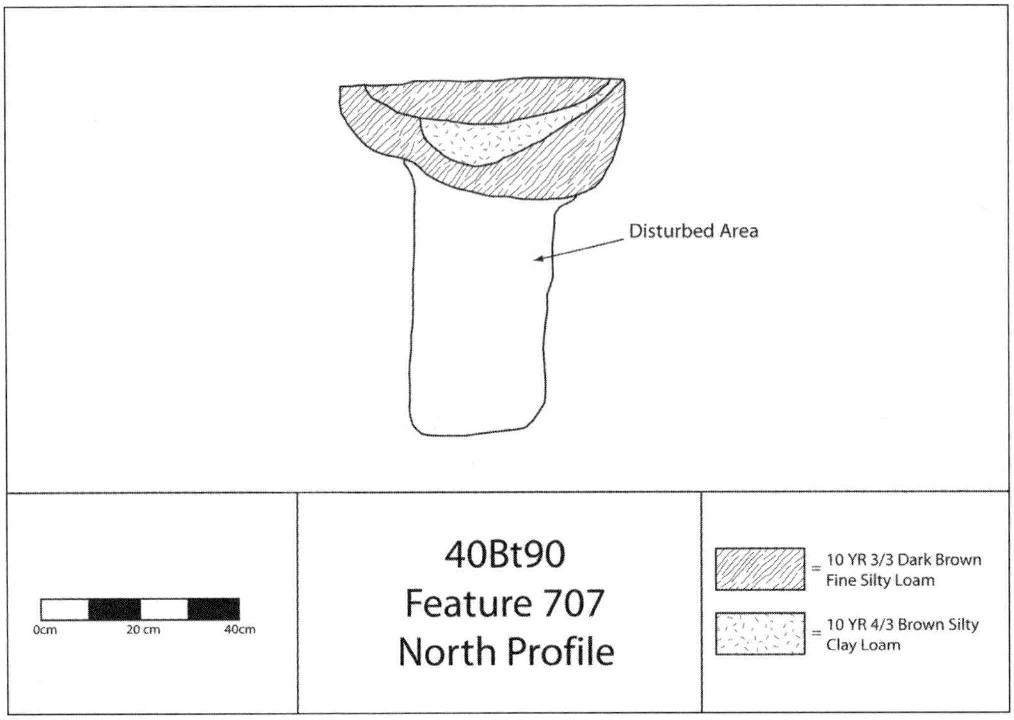

Figure 6.31. Profile of Feature 707.

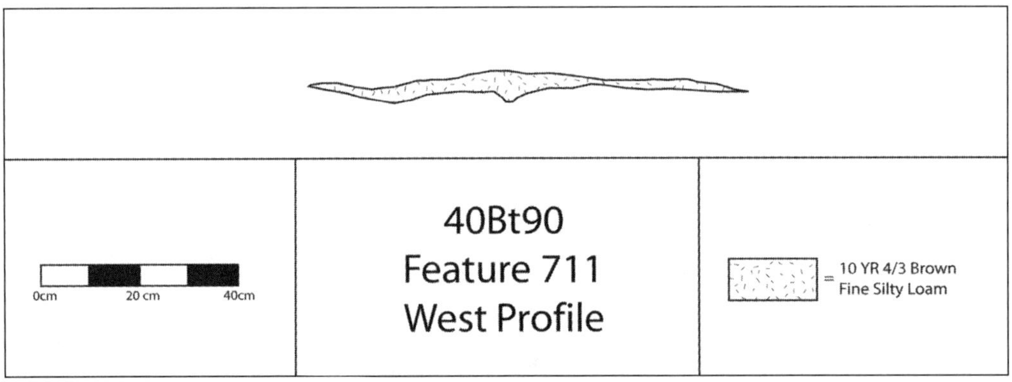

Figure 6.32. Profile of Feature 711.

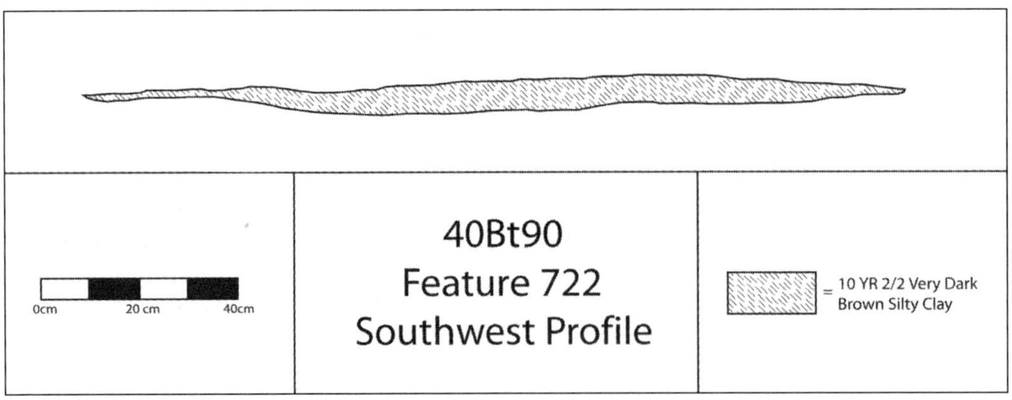

Figure 6.33. Profile of Feature 722.

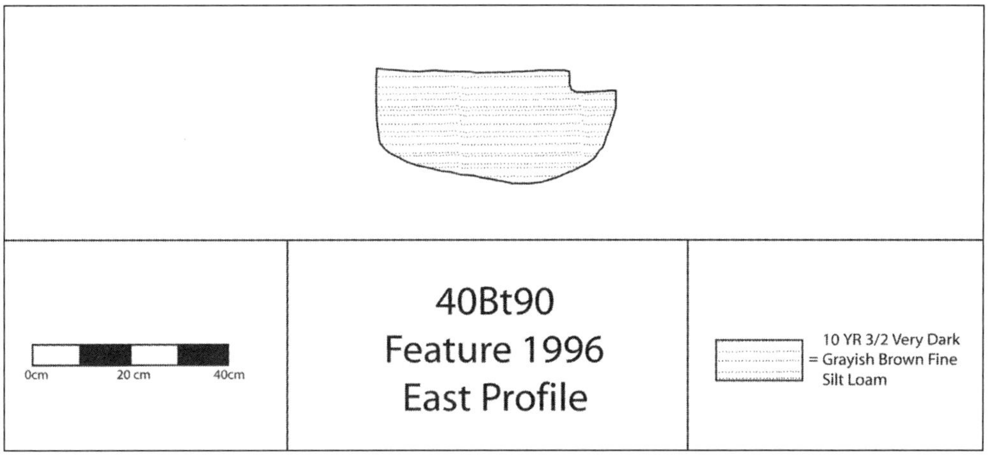

Figure 6.34. Profile of Feature 1996.

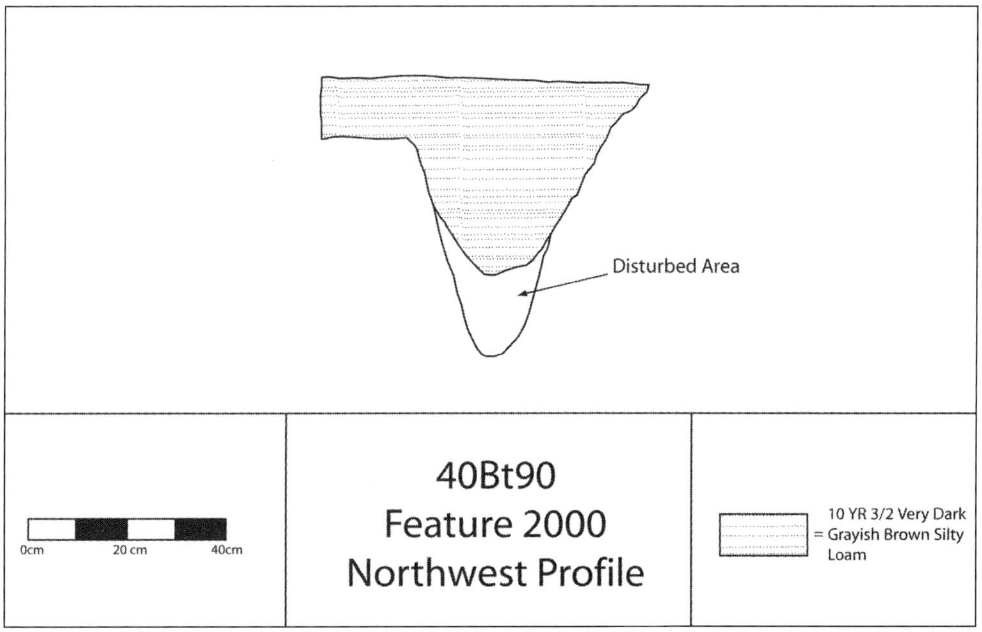

Figure 6.35. Profile of Feature 2000.

Feature 1996 (Figs. 6.26, 6.34)

Feature 1996 was a small-diameter oval-shaped pit located 9 m east of Structure 41. The pit was filled with a single zone of very dark grayish brown fine silty loam containing moderate charcoal inclusions. Three medium-sized potsherds were also recovered from the pit along with fire-cracked rock.

Feature 2000 (Figs. 6.26, 6.35)

Feature 2000 was a small-diameter circular pit located in the northwest corner of Structure 51. Feature 2000 was filled with a homogeneous zone of very dark grayish brown silty loam containing abundant charcoal. Seventy-three potsherds were recovered from the pit. Potsherd size and density suggest that the pit contained a secondary refuse deposit. Field notes stated that the bottom of the pit had been heavily disturbed by rodent burrowing.

Feature 2022 (Figs. 6.26, 6.36)

Feature 2022 was a small-diameter circular pit located near the center of Structure 41. The pit fill consisted of homogeneous dark brown silt loam with moderately dense charcoal fragments and flecks. Twenty-three medium-sized potsherds constituted a fairly dense fill, indicating a secondary refuse deposit.

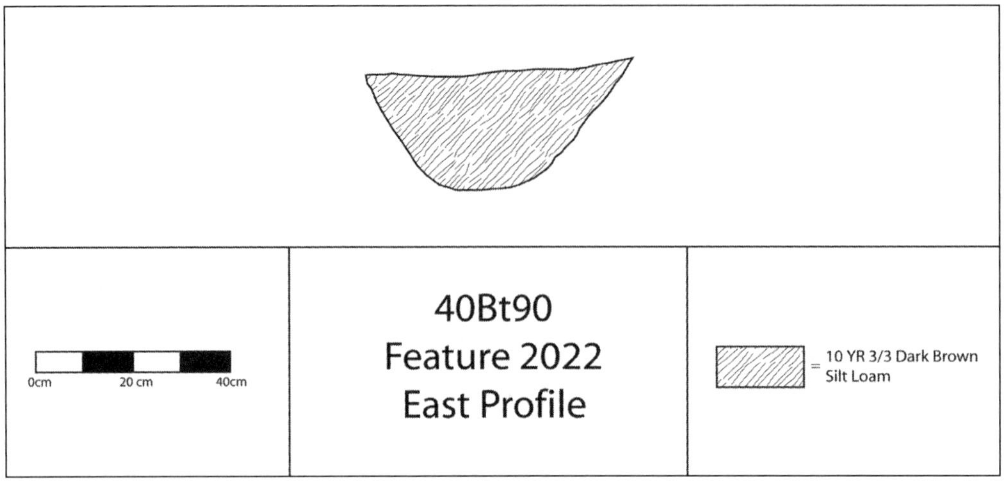

Figure 6.36. Profile of Feature 2022.

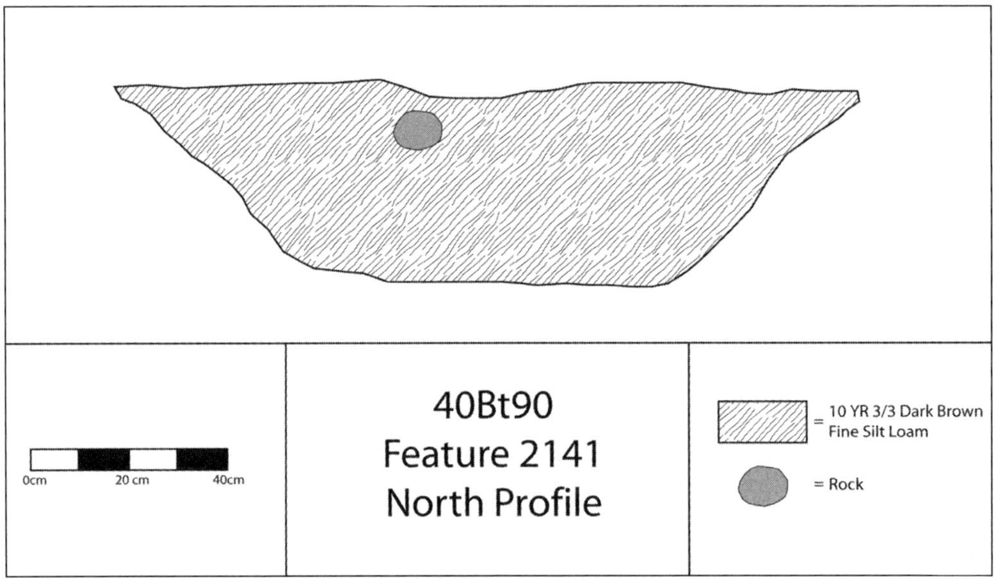

Figure 6.37. Profile of Feature 2141.

Feature 2141 (Figs. 6.26, 6.37)

Feature 2141 was a very broad, circular pit located 10.5 m northeast of Structure 41. It was among the largest Cherokee pits at the site, being one of only three pits in the sample whose volume exceeded 400 liters. The pit was filled with a single zone of dark brown fine silty loam. While 32 potsherds were relatively sparse in the fill, the size range of the sherds is more suggestive of a secondary than a tertiary refuse deposit.

Household 5

Feature 94 (Fig. 6.38)

Feature 94 represents the possible remains of a hearth at the center of a Cherokee winter house (Structure 27). As discussed in Chapter 5, unlike all the other structures associated with the Cherokee occupation of the site, none of the postholes comprising Structure 27 were excavated. Not

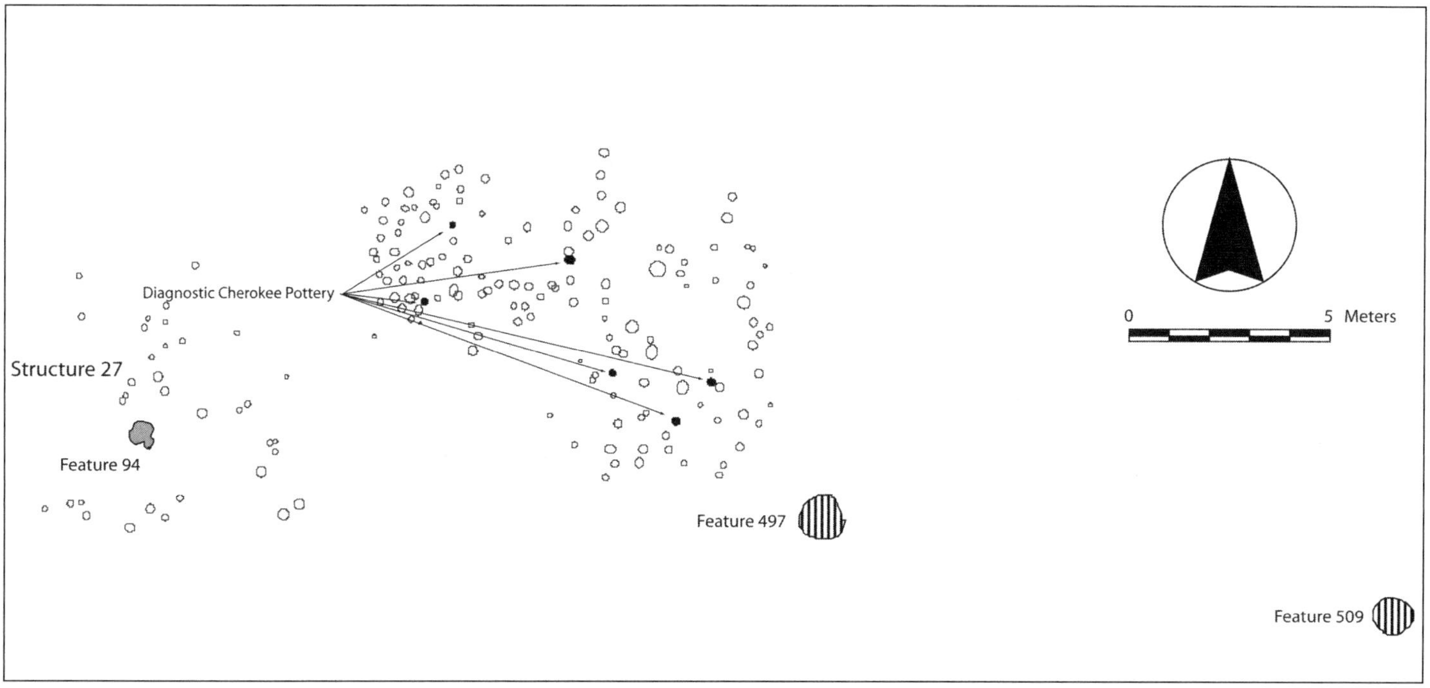

Figure 6.38. Cherokee features associated with Household 5.

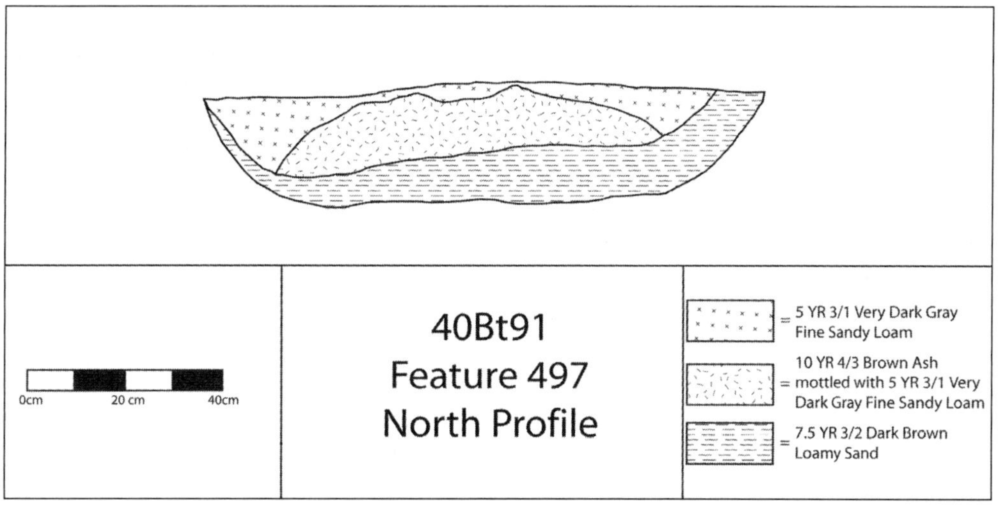

Figure 6.39. Profile of Feature 497.

having any diagnostic material from these postholes, it is impossible to confidently identify this structure as Cherokee. Feature 94 was described in the field notes as "a small reddish burnt area surrounding a 13 cm diameter dark brown/black stain." The center of the feature was very dark brown silt loam while the "burnt" periphery consisted of dusky red silt loam. No potsherds were recovered from the feature and no profile was drawn.

Feature 497 (Figs. 6.38, 6.39)

Feature 497 was a broad, shallow circular pit with a flat bottom located 5 m southeast of a possible Cherokee summer house. Three stratigraphic zones were noted in the pit profile. The top zone was a very dark gray fine sandy loam with abundant charcoal flecks. This zone was positioned above a mottled zone of brown ash and dark gray loam that contained masses of unfired clay. Beneath this mottled zone was dark brown loamy sand.

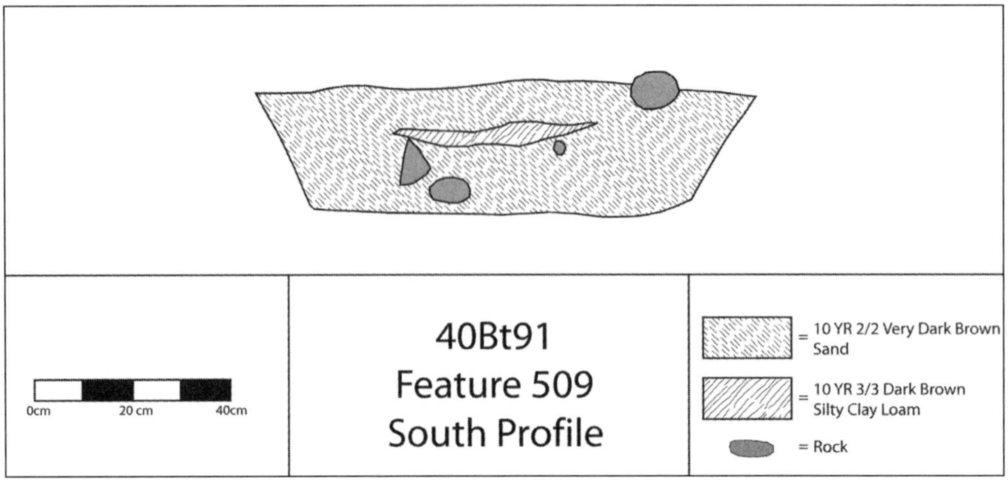

Figure 6.40. Profile of Feature 509.

Potsherd density and size values for the 100 potsherds recovered from the pit suggest it contained secondary refuse. Feature 497 also contained a single glass trade bead.

Feature 509 (Figs. 6.38, 6.40)

Feature 509 was a broad oval-shaped pit with a flat bottom located 19 m east of a possible Cherokee summer house. The fill of this feature consisted of very dark brown sand with a thin lens of dark brown silty clay loam running through the central portion. Charcoal flecks and fragments were noted in both zones. The pit contained a moderate amount of fire-cracked rock, 22 small potsherds, and 2 glass trade beads.

Household 6

Feature 390 (Figs. 6.41, 6.42)

Feature 390 was a broad, shallow circular pit located 7.5 m south of Structure 8. The fill consisted entirely of dark brown silty loam with very sparse charcoal inclusions. A small quantity of potsherds and a few pieces of fire-cracked rock, most likely tertiary refuse, were recovered from the fill.

Feature 391 (Figs. 6.41, 6.43)

Feature 391 was a pit located adjacent to Feature 390 and was nearly identical in size and shape. The fill of the pit was composed of dark brown sandy silt with very sparse charcoal flecks. The soil filling the pit contained 5 small sherds and a small amount of fire-cracked rock.

Feature 392 (Figs. 6.41, 6.44)

Feature 392 was a broad, shallow circular pit with an irregular bottom located 3 m west of Features 390 and 391. Like the other two features in this cluster, Feature 392 was filled with dark brown sandy silt. The feature fill was virtually free of potsherds and fire-cracked rock. Based on the shape and nature of the fill in Features 390, 391, and 392, it is possible that these three pits were dug in order to obtain soil, and were filled at roughly the same time.

Feature 394 (Figs. 6.41, 6.45)

Feature 394 was a hearth located in the center of Structure 8. Like the other hearths identified in Cherokee structures at Townsend, Feature 394 was a simple pit excavated into subsoil. The contents of the hearth included a mixture of dark reddish brown silty loam, yellowish red silty sand, and brown ash. A single potsherd and a fragment of a pottery pipe bowl were recovered from the fill.

Unassociated Feature in 40Bt91

Feature 438 (Figs. 6.46, 6.47)

Feature 438 is described in the field notes as a "large historic feature" associated with a nineteenth-century cabin located approximately 50 m southeast of Household 6 at the far eastern end of the project area. This large rectangular pit consisted of two stratified zones; the topmost was dark brown fine silty sand and the bottom zone was composed of a heavily oxidized yellowish

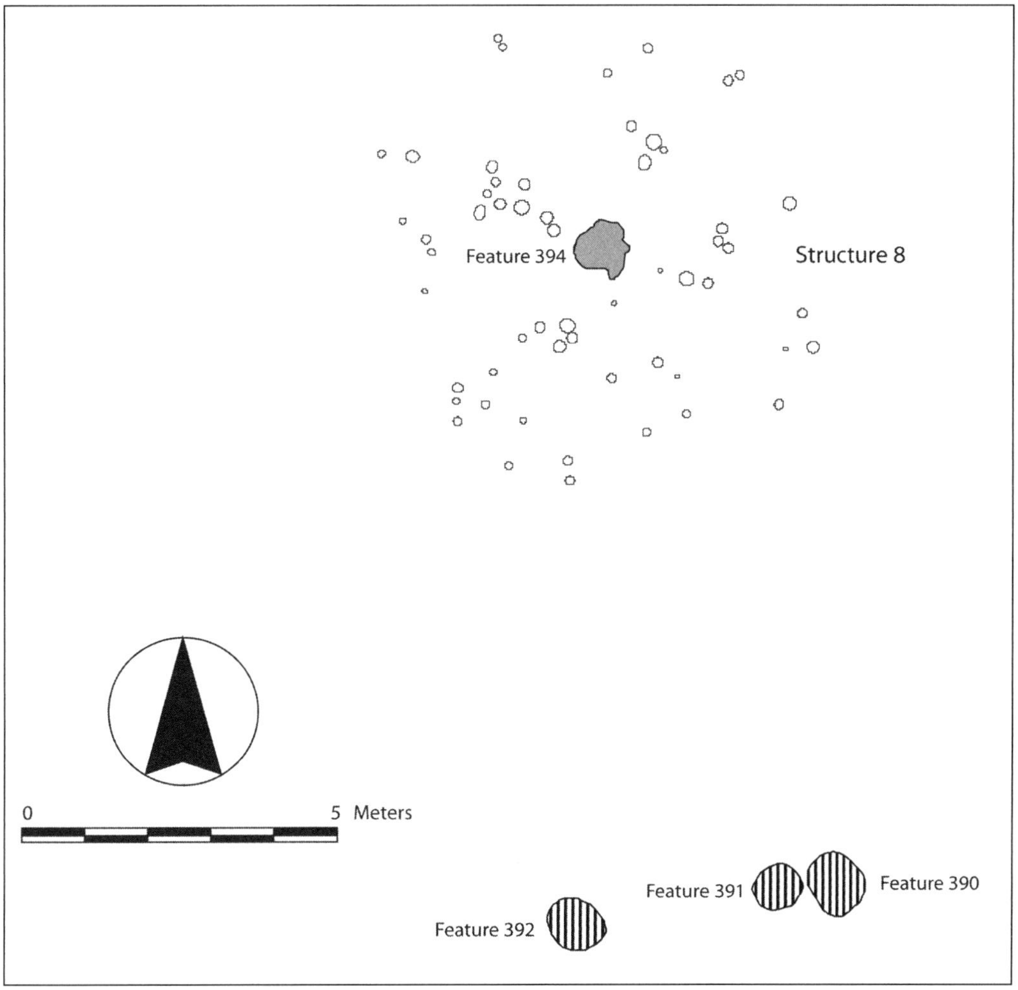

Figure 6.41. Cherokee features associated with Household 6.

brown fine silty sand. The pit contained a large quantity of burned limestone as well as cut nails, mortar, and 35 Cherokee potsherds and numerous potsherds associated with earlier Woodland period components. This mixture of artifacts suggests that Feature 438 was an intrusive feature that disturbed an existing Cherokee pit or basin associated with a household whose location was outside the limits of excavation.

Assessing Cherokee Pit Use and Abandonment at Townsend

Southeastern archaeologists working with data from sites spanning from the Archaic to the Historic periods have demonstrated that the detailed study of pit features is an extremely difficult yet rewarding endeavor for gaining an understanding of prehistoric lifeways (DeBoer 1988; Dickens 1985; Koldehoff and Galloy 2006; Ward 1985; Wesson 1999). Indeed, in many regions and time periods, pit features are by far the most common archaeological contexts encountered during excavations. As is the case with most archaeological contexts, however, ubiquity begets variability in form and artifact content, and with increased variability comes increased difficulty in assessing function. This situation has led to problems in characterizing the various uses of subterranean basins and pits among Cherokee contexts (Schroedl 1986a:85). The task is much more difficult than when dealing with features like hearths and burned surfaces that lack such variability and whose composition of heavily oxidized soils and locations inside structures render function self-evident. Logic dictates that the artifacts found in a given context should be the best indicators of behaviors that took place in that context; however, experience demonstrates time and again that the refuse found in Cherokee pits was associated with the abandonment and final filling of the pit rather than with its use-life. Making

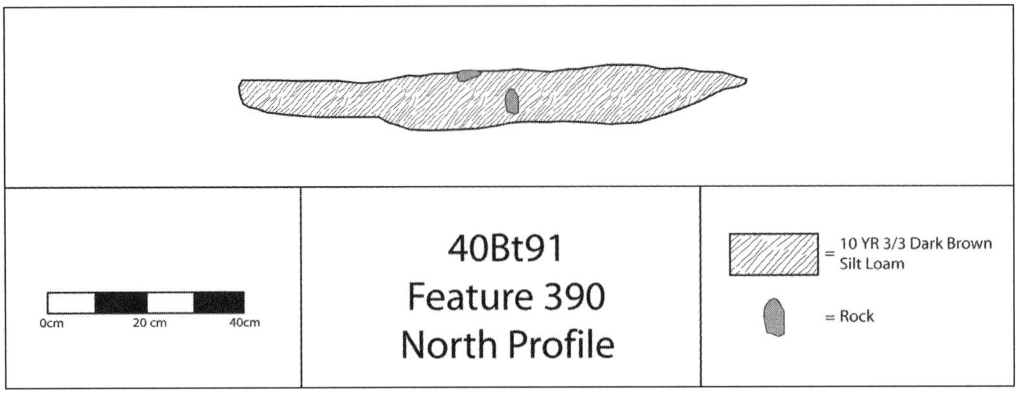

Figure 6.42. Profile of Feature 390.

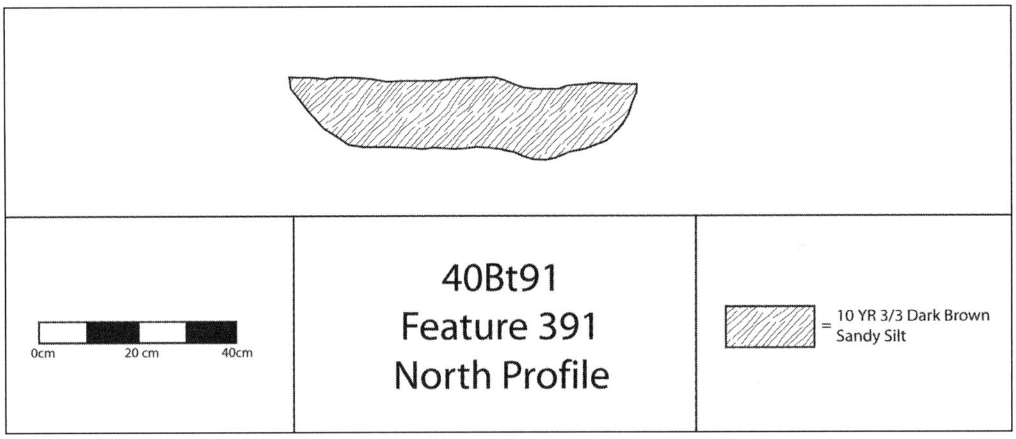

Figure 6.43. Profile of Feature 391.

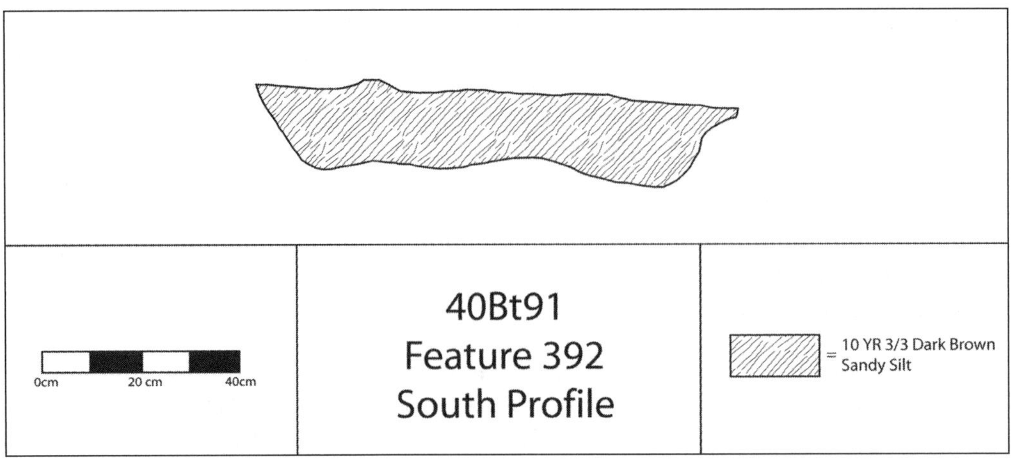

Figure 6.44. Profile of Feature 392.

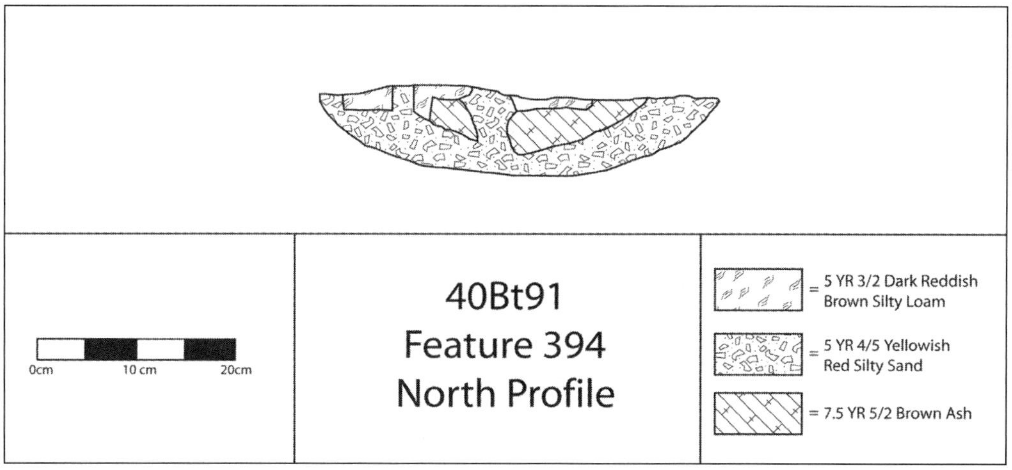

Figure 6.45. Profile of Feature 394.

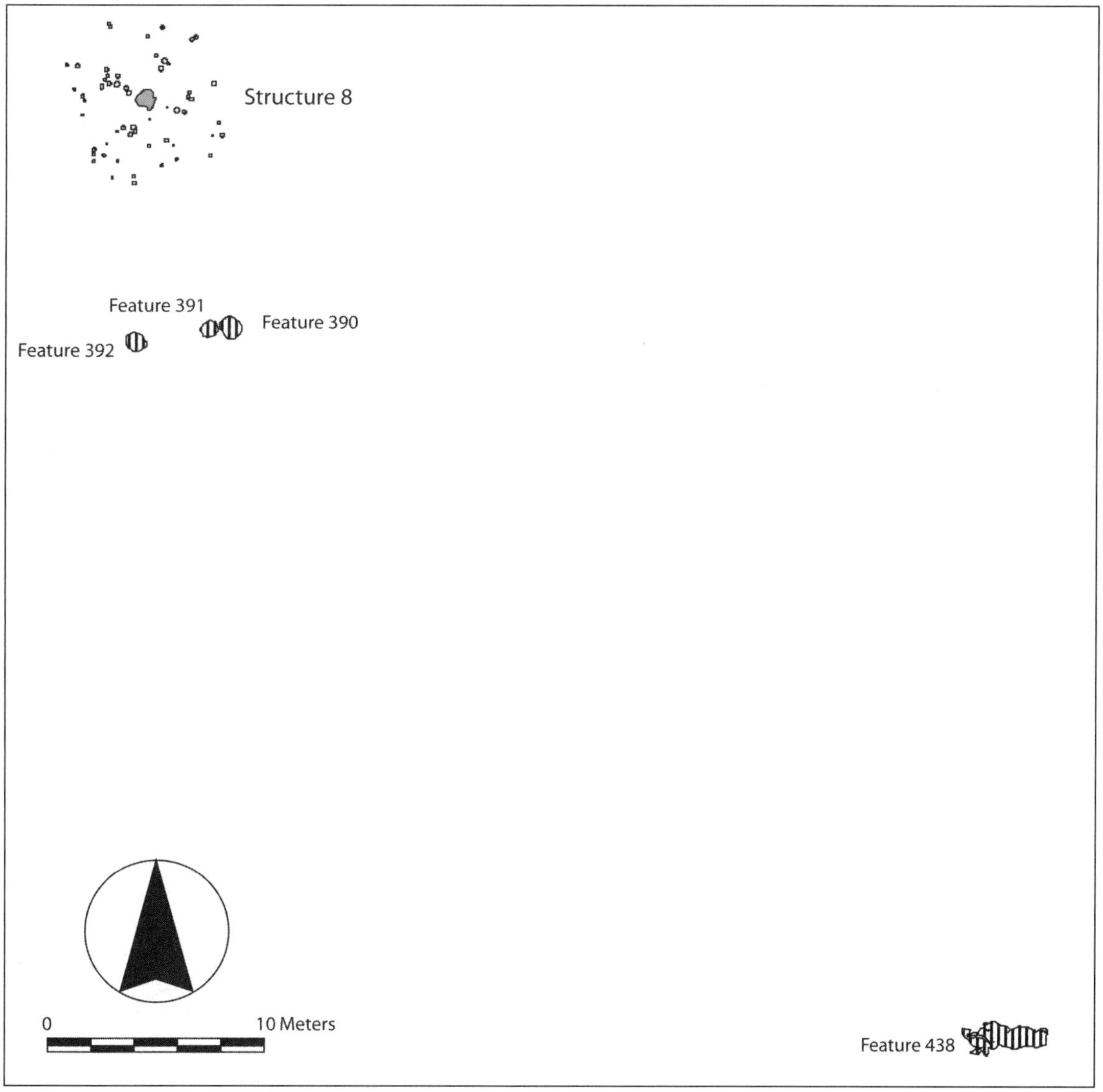

Figure 6.46. The location of Feature 438 in relation to Household 6.

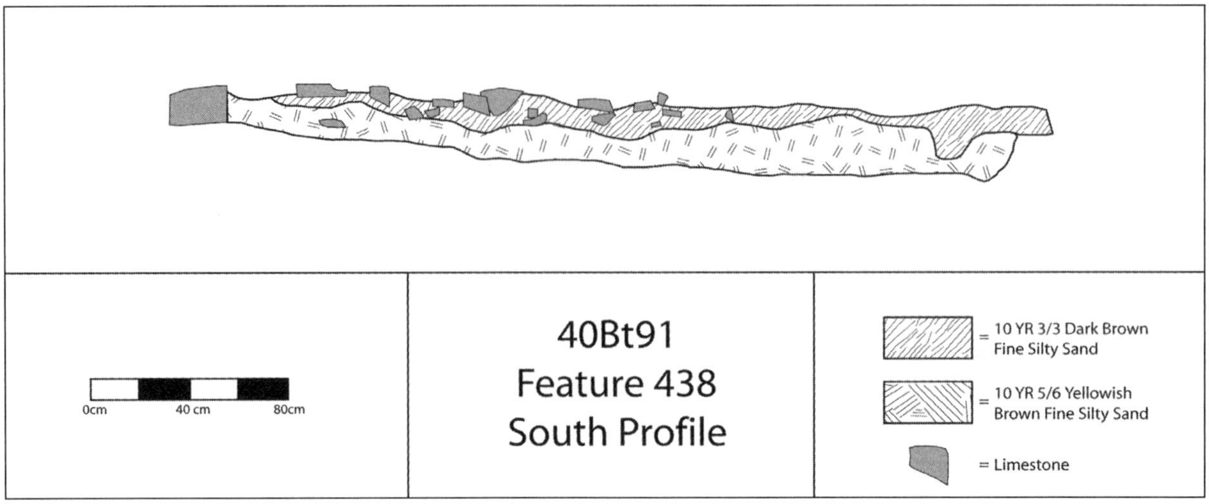

Figure 6.47. Profile of Feature 438.

the situation even less clear is the possibility that a Cherokee pit could have gone through a number of different use stages between its initial excavation and its final filling and abandonment (see Schroedl 1986a:85–97 for a detailed discussion). It is imperative, therefore, that the basin and pit features encountered in the archaeological record be viewed as the outcomes of drawn-out historical processes rather than as single instantaneous events—an admonishment we often hear but less often heed. In order to work within this conceptual constraint while attempting to gain any understanding of Cherokee basins and pits, I analytically separate use-life from abandonment. Consequently, in the following analyses I consider pit morphology and artifact content separately as reflecting pit use and abandonment respectively. I first examine morphological data from all the Cherokee pit features at Townsend (n = 33) to identify patterns in size and shape that might reflect pit use. I then address pottery refuse data to characterize the relationship between Cherokee discard behaviors and the abandonment of pit features.

The distributions of measures describing the shape and volume of Cherokee features at Townsend display patterning suggesting that most features were roughly circular in shape and that relatively well-defined size "classes" existed. The distribution of ratios measuring feature length to feature width (measured as the maximum diameter of a feature and its orthogonal complement) indicates that the vast majority of Cherokee features at Townsend are circular in shape (rather than oblong or square) (Fig. 6.48). As discussed below, during the later half of the eighteenth century, Cherokee households continued to use circular-shaped basins and pits, but they also began to employ basins and pits that were oblong and rectangular.

The distribution of feature volume reveals the existence of three separate size classes.[1] The histogram shown in Figure 6.49 depicts the volume estimates for all the basins and pits associated with the Cherokee occupation at Townsend. The distribution of these measures is clearly tri-modal with classes composed of (1) basins and pits with volumes less than 150 liters, (2) basins and pits with volumes between 175 liters and 325 liters, and (3) pits with volumes between 400 liters and 500 liters. A more detailed picture emerges when feature morphology is considered along with volume. A scatterplot diagram depicting maximum diameter and volume shows four clusters of values (Fig. 6.50). The cluster containing features with the smallest diameter and volume values (that is, those closest to the scatterplot's origin) is overwhelmingly composed of pits located inside Cherokee structures. Moving to the right, one encounters a group of small basins and pits that are similar in volume, but different in terms of shape. The five features forming the upper "branch" of the group are narrower and deeper than those of the lower "branch," which are broad and shallow. The lower branch may be the remnants of larger features that were truncated by historic plowing. Medium basins and pits form a relatively coherent cluster, and the location of large pits in the scatterplot clearly identifies them as a separate size class.

Patterning in the spatial distribution of Cherokee basins and pits is largely absent, with the exception of one feature class. A histogram depicting the distance of each feature from the closest Cherokee structure demonstrates that most features were located either inside structures or within 10 m of a structure (Fig. 6.51). What I call "interior pits" form a very cohesive spatial class that is also expressed in terms of morphology and size. The other size

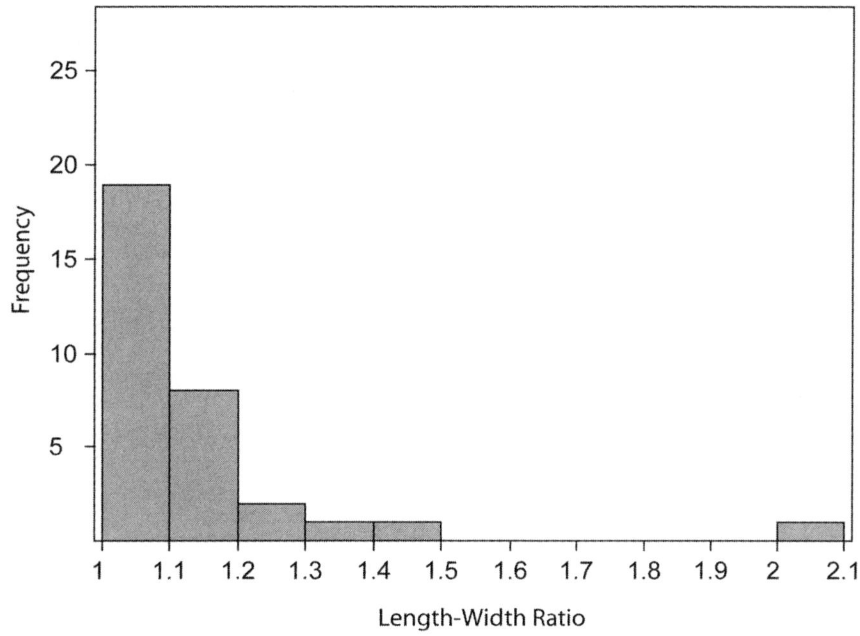

Figure 6.48. Histogram depicting the distribution of feature length to width ratios.

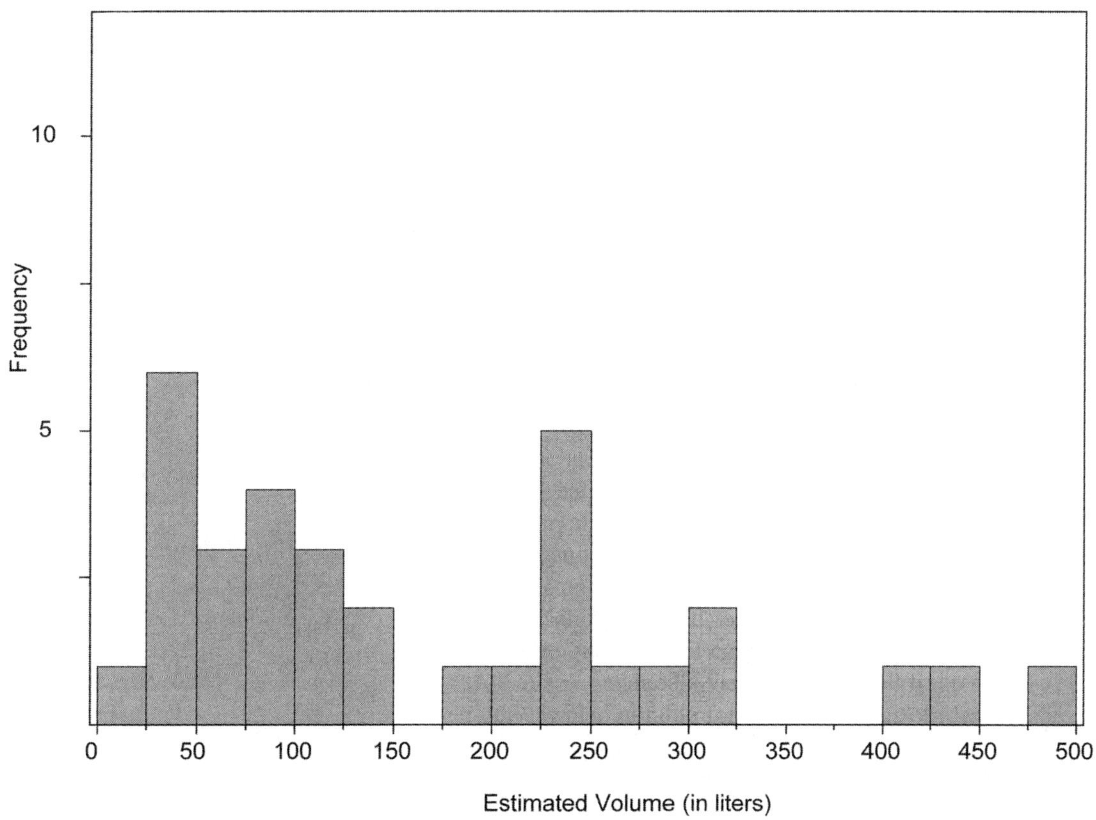

Figure 6.49. Histogram depicting the distribution of the volume among features associated with Townsend households. Reproduced with permission from *Pox, Empire, Shackles, and Hides* (Marcoux 2010: Fig. 5.6), ©University of Alabama Press.

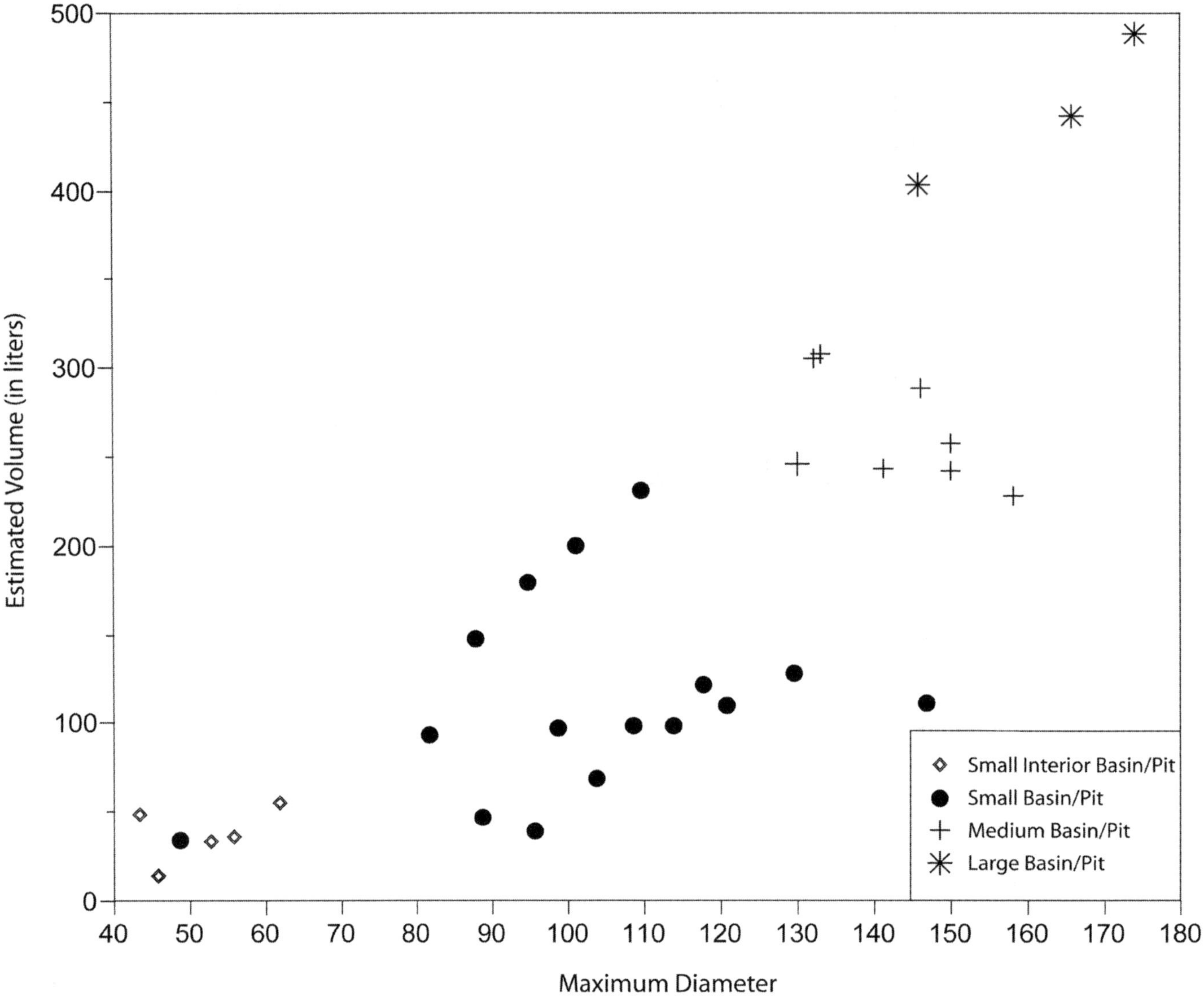

Figure 6.50. Scatterplot depicting the relationship between maximum feature diameter and estimated volume. Reproduced with permission from *Pox, Empire, Shackles, and Hides* (Marcoux 2010: Fig. 5.7), ©University of Alabama Press.

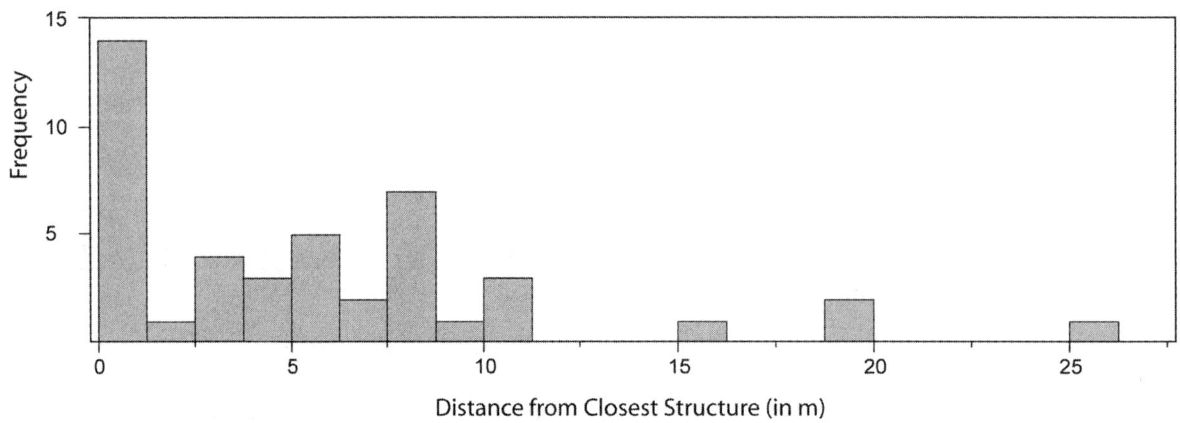

Figure 6.51. Histogram depicting the distribution of distance of features from the closest structure.

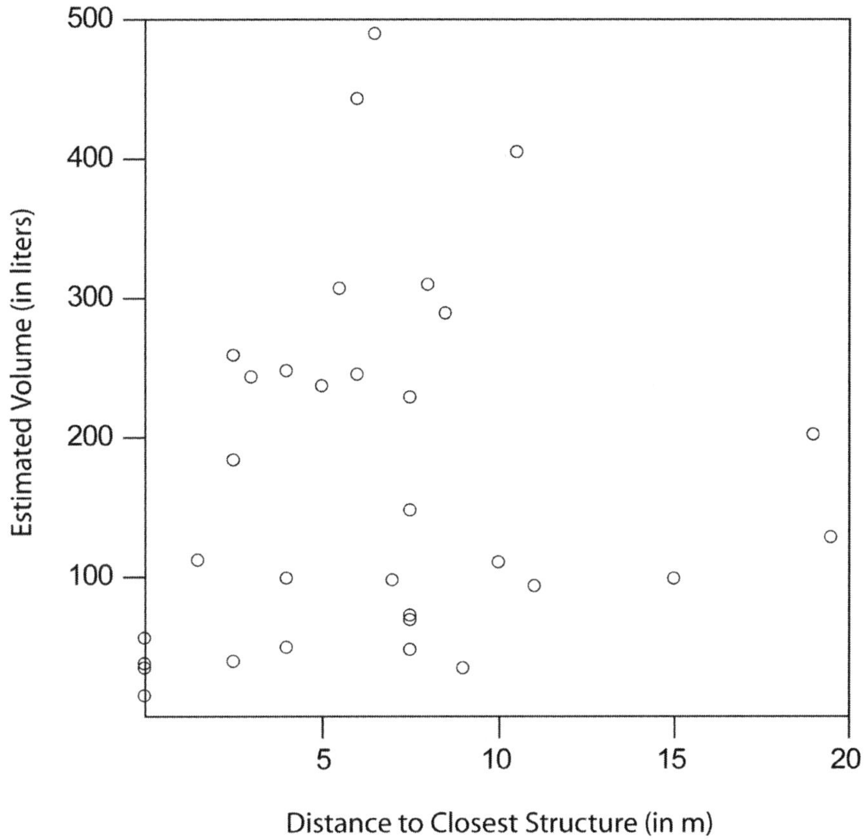

Figure 6.52. Scatterplot depicting the relationship between distance to closest structure and estimated volume ($r = 0.152$).

classes, however, do not share the same kind of cohesive patterning. Instead, the correlation between the estimated volume of features and their distance from structures is negligible ($r = 0.152$) (Fig. 6.52). Consequently, the only conclusion that can be reached with regard to spatial distribution is that while Cherokee households employed a specific "type" of feature within their houses, they dug basins and pits of various sizes within a 2- to 10-m area surrounding their houses.[2] This area likely represents each household's "yard," where most household activities took place.

A very rough relative estimate for the use-life of Cherokee basins and pits at Townsend can be arrived at using qualitative data. Researchers documenting the importance of subterranean storage to prehistoric and historic southeastern Indian communities have identified markers that can be used to assess the relative use-life of features based on their stratigraphy (DeBoer 1988:4; Koldehoff and Galloy 2006:285–86; Wesson 1999:151). Specifically, these researchers define a long use-life as (1) a feature being open (i.e., unfilled) for a relatively long period of time or (2) evidence of multiple uses over a long period of time. The correlate of the first part of the definition is seen archaeologically in a very distinct type of stratigraphy known as "slumping," caused by the erosion to the basin or pit wall, or "slope wash," resulting from sediments being carried into an open feature by wind, water, or human activity (e.g., Figs. 6.5, 6.10). The second part of the definition for long use-life is indicated by the presence of multiple stratigraphic zones indicating several filling episodes (artifact bearing soils) separated by periods of abandonment and inactivity (culturally sterile soils). Neither of these indicators of long use-life are particularly common at Townsend. Of the 33 features in the Townsend sample, 5 show evidence of slumping or slope wash. These are all single instances that occurred in 1 small interior pit and 4 medium-sized features.

Moreover, 28 of the 33 features contain only one or two stratigraphic zones, and no feature profile evinces the distinctive alternating pattern of filling and inactivity that is associated with a long use-life. Taken together, these patterns point to relatively short use-lives for most Cherokee basins and pits and support the interpretation that basins and pits were probably not used for any sort of long-term storage of food or any other material. Indeed, only 2 bell-shaped pits, a morphological form closely associated with food storage in ethnohistoric accounts and archaeological contexts (DeBoer 1988), were associated with the Cherokee occupation at Townsend. Both of these pits were smaller (i.e., less than 250 liters) than the average Woodland period bell-shaped pits (300–500 liters) cited by DeBoer (1988).

Turning to the artifact contents of the features, we must shift our focus from feature use to Cherokee discard behavior and abandonment. There are some cases when the contents of a basin or pit speak directly to its use—such is the case with burials, roasting pits, and storage pits whose contents were never retrieved. At Townsend, there were two Cherokee burials; neither was excavated. None of the Cherokee basins or pits displayed evidence of burning (i.e., oxidized walls) or contained large quantities of fire-cracked rock, and the perishable nature of non-carbonized food remains makes the identification of an undisturbed storage pit very difficult. What can be assessed using the contents of pit features at Townsend are Cherokee discard behaviors and the question of how households filled pits after disuse. In doing so, my analyses focus on distinctions between the different types of refuse discussed at the beginning of the chapter.

Three proxy measures are used to characterize the refuse deposits as secondary or tertiary (primary refuse was not present in the Townsend sample)—median sherd size, the range of sherd sizes, and the ubiquity of potsherds in the feature fill. In regard to the first measure, the overwhelming modal value for median sherd size in Cherokee features is 2 cm (Table 6.1). The highly fragmented nature of potsherds suggests that the fill of most Cherokee features consisted of secondary, and in most cases tertiary, refuse deposits. This interpretation is supported by the fact that the median sherd size for feature contexts is equal to that calculated for potsherds recovered from test unit excavations—proveniences that include sherds from sheet midden deposits and plowzone contexts (n = 1889, median = 2 cm). Together with median sherd size, the range of sherd sizes forms a reliable proxy measure for refuse type. Typically, those features that possess median sherd size values greater than 2 cm also contain numerous large sherds (> 5 cm). These values indicate a less fragmented refuse deposit that is more indicative of secondary refuse.

Overall, potsherd ubiquity values are quite low across all basins and pits in the sample (Fig. 6.53). The majority of the features contain less than .5 sherd per liter of fill and the highest recorded value is only 1.5 sherds per liter. Comparisons of potsherd ubiquity among the three feature size classes show no patterning in discard behavior (Fig. 6.54). While small features exhibit a lower median ubiquity ratio than medium and large features, the difference is not statistically significant. Instead, the ubiquity ratios suggest that features of all size classes contain similar amounts of pottery refuse.

Furthermore, no relationship exists between pottery ubiquity and distance from structures. A relationship between these two variables would be expected if Cherokee households intentionally discarded broken pots either in nearby basins and pits, for convenience's sake or for later recycling (i.e., provisional discard), or in distant basins or pits in order to avoid the hazards of sharp potsherds. The correlation between pottery ubiquity and distance from structures is negative, but very weak (r = -0.193), indicating no particular patterning in pottery refuse disposal (Fig. 6.55). The lack of correlation between pottery density and either feature size or distance from structures runs counter to the pattern found by Baden (1983:134) for the late eighteenth-century Cherokee site of Tomotley. There, artifact density measures indicated that larger features and features close to structures contained the most dense refuse deposits.

These analyses point to a number of general conclusions regarding Cherokee household use and abandonment of basins and pits at Townsend: (1) subsurface features fell into four distinct size classes including small interior pits, small exterior basins and pits, medium basins and pits, and large pits; (2) the spatial distribution of these features ranged from 2 to 10 m around houses, defining the space in which domestic activities took place; (3) no definitive function could be placed on any Cherokee basin or pit in the sample, but it is likely that interior pits and bell-shaped pits served as storage spaces and, for lack of better explanations, that the other features were used for storage or were created while extracting soil for winter house construction or repair; (4) basins and pits were not used for long periods of time and were filled relatively quickly after being excavated; (5) rather than being receptacles for newly generated refuse, the basins and pits were most often filled with secondary and tertiary refuse that had been provisionally discarded elsewhere; and (6) the fill used for the pits was not particularly rich in pottery refuse, suggesting that house sites were not occupied for sufficient time for surface middens to accumulate, that pots were highly curated and/or heavily recycled, or that pots were subject to provisional discard in distant locations (see Shumate et al. 2005 for a similar situation).

Comparisons of Cherokee Subterranean Food Storage Practices among Townsend Households and Beyond

A number of recent studies have addressed subterranean food storage practices in prehistoric and historic communities across the Eastern Woodlands of North America (DeBoer 1988; Dickens 1985; Koldehoff and Galloy 2006; Ward 1985; Wesson 1999). Many of these studies are derived from DeBoer's (1988) landmark synthesis of ethnohistoric and archaeological evidence related to subterranean food storage among eastern North American Indian communities. In this study, DeBoer (1988:14) concluded that subterranean food storage was most often associated with (1) seasonal abandonment of settlements and (2) resistance to the rise of inequality and hierarchical power relations. Despite the importance of the first conclusion in forming fundamental site-level interpretations, one rarely encounters it in southeastern archaeological literature (a notable exception being Koldehoff and Galloy 2006); instead, the latter conclusion has more often been seized upon and incorporated into political economy models of Mississippian and historic Creek communities (e.g., Emerson 1997; Wesson 1999). This section addresses DeBoer's (1988) conclusions through two quantitative

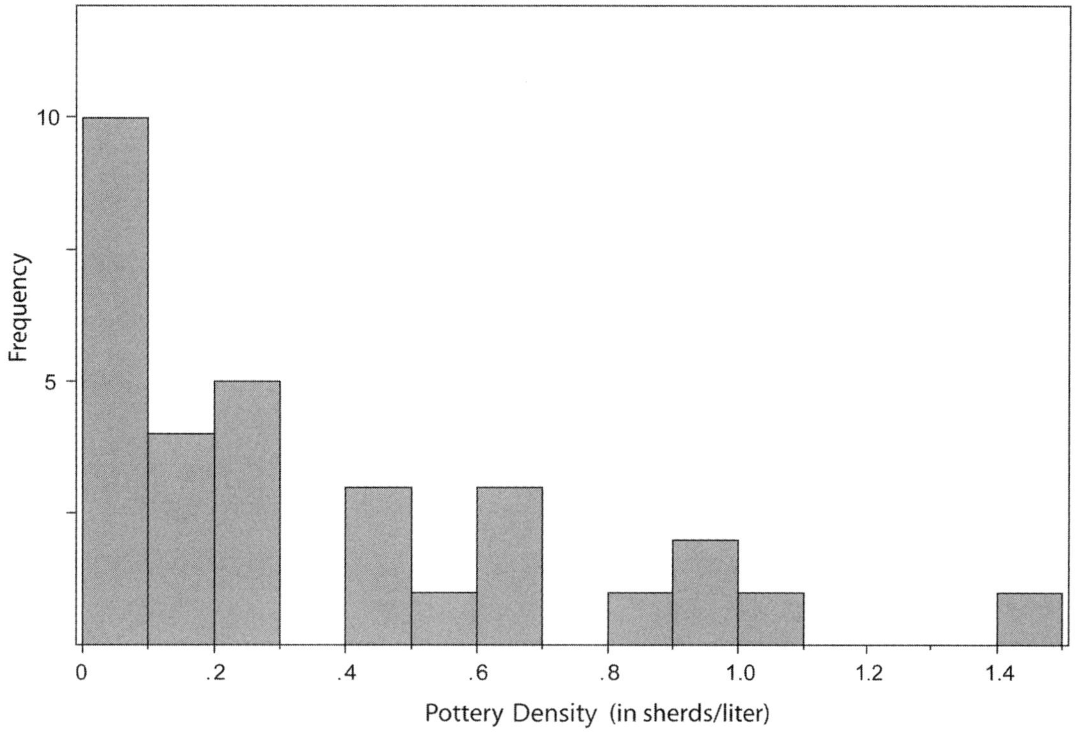

Figure 6.53. Histogram depicting the distribution of pottery density ratios.

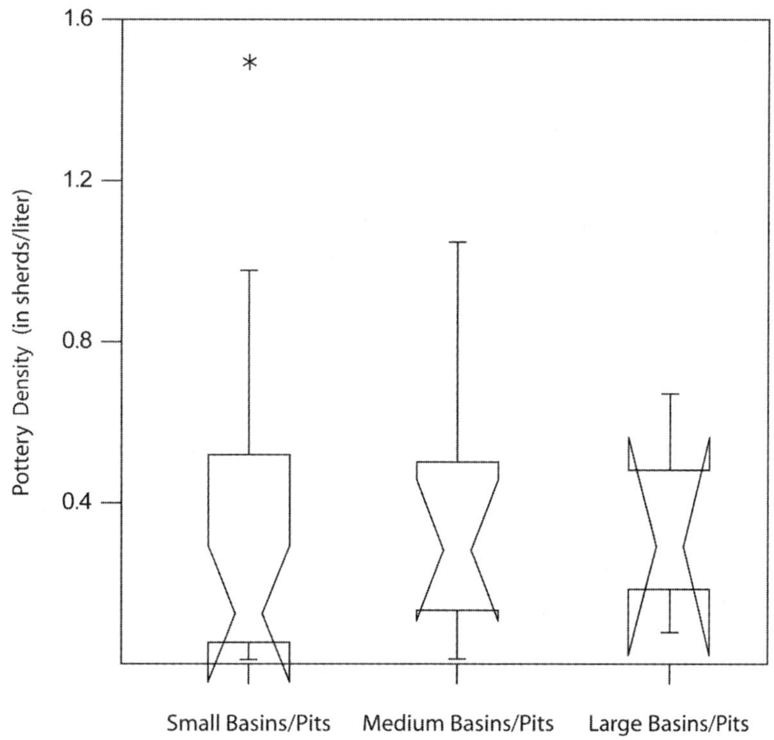

Feature 6.54. Boxplots depicting the distribution of pottery density ratios among feature size classes. Note: The "folded" appearance of the boxplots is due to the effect of small sample size where the confidence interval is greater than the h-spread.

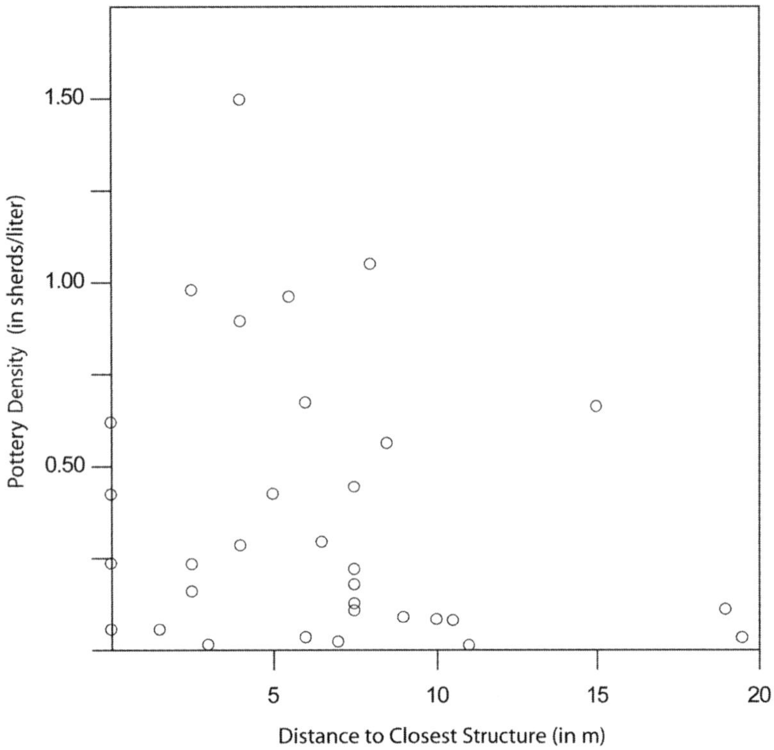

Figure 6.55. Scatterplot depicting the relationship between distance to closest structure and pottery density (r = -0.193).

comparisons related to Cherokee subterranean storage practices. First, the sizes of basins and pits are compared among the six Cherokee households at Townsend. This comparison is aimed at characterizing similarities and/or differences in storage practices at the household level. The second comparison includes data from subterranean features at other Cherokee sites and is intended to identify and characterize changes in Cherokee subterranean storage practices that occurred after the English Contact period (ca. A.D. 1670–1740).[3]

A comparison of basins and pits among the six Townsend households is presented in Table 6.2. The distribution of feature size classes among the households varies greatly. Medium and small features were common in all households, and three of the six households had large pits. Only two households had interior pits—all but one of these were associated with Household 4. Also, a great deal of variability is present in the number of features associated with each household and their combined volume. The most likely reasons for such variability include differences in household occupation duration and/or sample size differences due to historic disturbances and boundary issues associated with the excavation limits. Interestingly, the median and mean measures for feature volume evince much less variability across households. This suggests that while the composition of household storage facilities varied greatly in terms of size and number of individual basins and pits, the underlying storage capacity of each household was similar—and it was not particularly large (see comparison to later Cherokee storage pits below). Considering that all the Townsend houses were likely occupied for between 8 and 10 years, even the highest total household storage capacity (2000 liters for Household 1) would break down to 200–250 liters of subterranean storage capacity per year. If food storage capacity is an indicator of hierarchical status (that is, a fund of wealth that was used by individual households to achieve a social and political advantage), then the mean and median household storage capacity figures suggest that there were not pronounced differences in status among Townsend households. This conclusion is in accord with other archaeological and ethnohistoric studies that highlight the underlying egalitarian structure of Cherokee communities during the English Contact period (Gearing 1962; Rodning 2004; Schroedl 2000).

As is the case with domestic architecture (see Chapter 5), a better understanding of Cherokee subterranean food storage practices during the English Contact period can be produced by placing the Townsend data within a broader context through diachronic comparison. This can be achieved by comparing data from Townsend features with those from the contemporaneously occupied Alarka farmstead as well as four Overhill Cherokee communities occupied primarily during the latter half of the eighteenth century.[4] The results of the comparison (illustrated in Table 6.3 and Figs. 6.56, 6.57) indicate that subterranean storage became increasingly important in Cherokee communities after the mid-eighteenth century.

Table 6.2. Comparison of feature size classes and feature volume among Cherokee households at Townsend.

Household	Large Basins/Pits	Medium Basins/Pits	Small Basins/Pits	Small Interior Basins/ Pits	Combined Volume (liters)	Median Volume (liters)	Mean Volume (liters)
1	1	4	5	0	2017	187.81	201.75
2	0	2	1	1	692	184.30	173.00
3	1	1	2	0	882	200.15	220.39
4	1	1	2	4	1176	52.20	138.04
5	0	0	2	0	438	219.11	219.11
6	0	0	3	0	213	97.22	71.05

Table 6.3. Comparison of feature types and feature volume among late seventeenth- and eighteenth-century Cherokee communities.

Site	Occupation	Round and Oval Basins/Pits		Rectangular Basins/Pits		Pits with Posts		Median Estimated Volume (liters)	Mean Estimated Volume (liters)
		n	%	*n*	%	*n*	%		
Alarka	A.D. 1650–1700	5	100	0	0	0	0	60.00	75.83
Townsend	A.D. 1650–1715	33	100	0	0	0	0	124.65	170.88
Chota-Tanasee	A.D. 1700–1820	718	95	18	2	24	3	142.00	281.36
Toqua	A.D. 1700–1820	45	82	1	2	9	16	n/a	n/a
Tomotley	A.D. 1750–1776	59	94	0	0	4	6	345.70	526.95
Mialoquo	A.D. 1760–1780	32	80	2	5	6	15	213.80	362.48

One of the most important legacies of the Tellico Archaeological Project has been the massive corpus of published data regarding eighteenth-century Cherokee communities (Baden 1983; Polhemus 1987; Russ and Chapman 1983; Schroedl 1986a). Unfortunately, equivalent data from earlier late seventeenth- and early eighteenth-century Cherokee contexts is sorely lacking (except for those reported in Shumate et al. 2005). When extant morphological and size data are assembled and compared, some interesting diachronic patterns emerge. First, there is an increase in feature variability through time. Early feature assemblages consist entirely of simple round or oval basins and pits, while the feature assemblages at later sites also include rectangular pits and a significant number of what appear to be specialized storage features known as "pits with posts" (Table 6.3). As the name suggests, this form of feature consisted of a circular, oblong, or rectangular pit that contained two postholes located at the pit margins along the centerline of the major axis. These postholes represent the remains of posts used to support some sort of cover. While these curious features have been interpreted as "hot houses" or "sweat lodges," Schroedl (1986a:68–69) convincingly argues that their size, morphology, and location in relation to domestic structures made them most suitable for the household storage of foodstuffs like root crops. These facilities became increasingly common through time, comprising 15–16% of all features in the late eighteenth-century communities in the sample. More generally, a comparison of length to width ratios between English Contact period features and later Cherokee features indicates a shift in feature shape from circular to more oblong and rectangular during the later half of the eighteenth century (Fig. 6.56).

Along with the advent of new forms of subterranean storage and general changes in feature shape, large increases in feature volume through time are telling of a significant transformation that occurred in Cherokee storage practices following the English Contact period. Both median and mean measures of feature volume show an increasing trend during the eighteenth century (Table 6.3). Indeed, the mean volume of features at the Chota-Tanasee, Tomotley, and Mialoquo sites is two to three times greater than that of features at the Alarka site and Townsend. When feature volumes of these two groups are compared, the medians are significantly different (Fig. 6.57). These results may be partly because the three later contexts are nucleated towns whereas Alarka and Townsend represent outlying settlements. Given our findings in Chapter 5 (that is, that households at all of these Cherokee sites were generally the same size and that virtually all the Cherokee houses in the sample were occupied for approximately the same amount of time), however, we are left with the likelihood that Cherokee households enacted important changes to their food storage practices sometime during the later part of or after the English Contact period.

Analysis of metric data associated with the subterranean features at Townsend and the Alarka site thus indicates that English

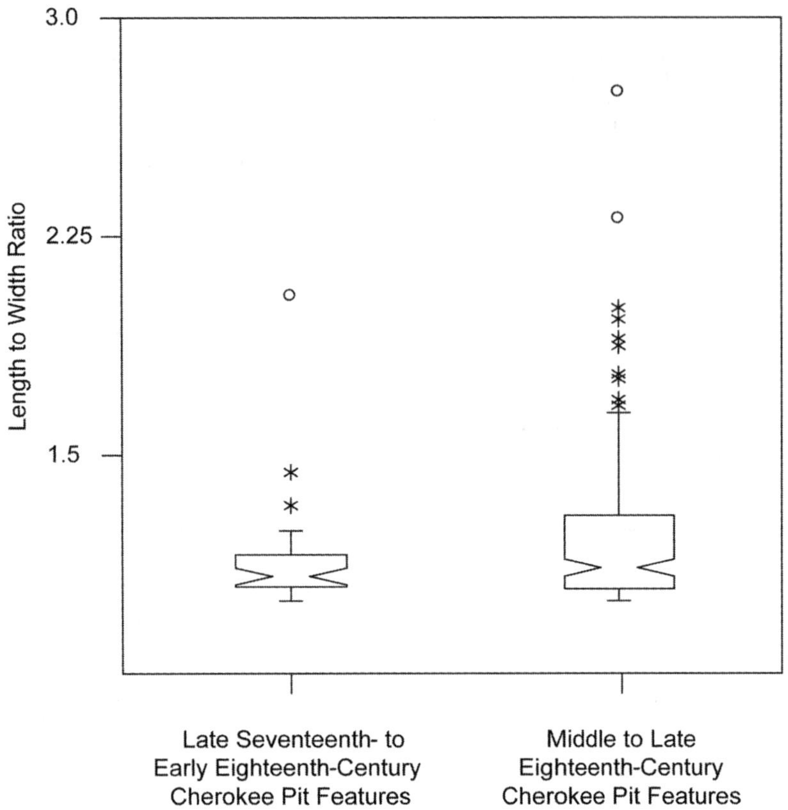

Feature 6.56. Boxplots depicting the distributions of feature length to width ratios at sites occupied during the English Contact period (ca. A.D. 1670–1715) and after.

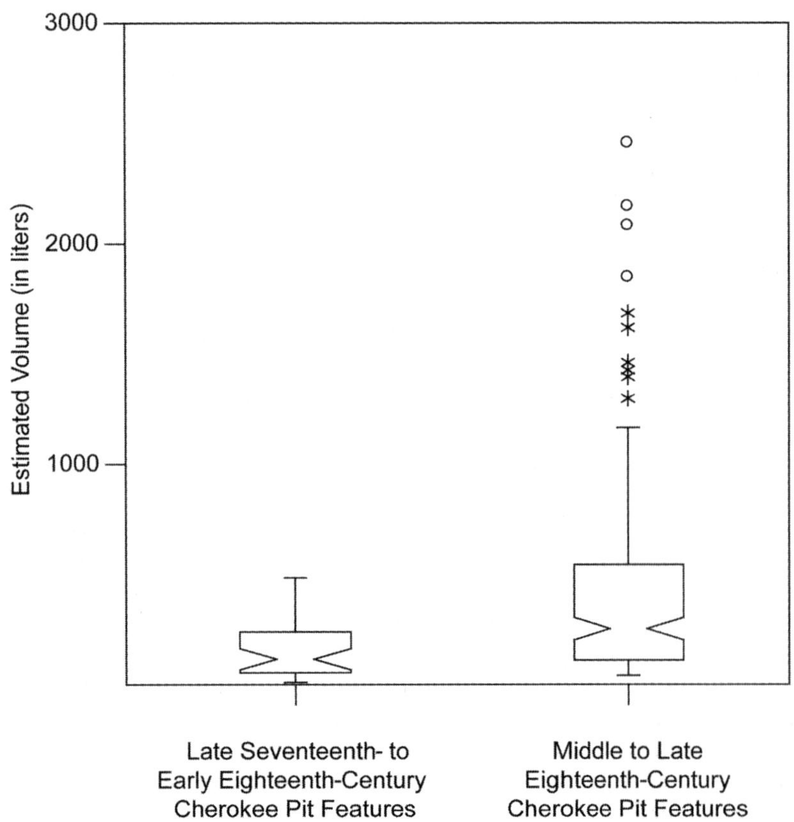

Feature 6.57. Boxplots depicting the distributions of feature volume estimates at sites occupied during the English Contact period (ca. A.D. 1670–1715) and after.

Contact period (ca. 1670–1740) Cherokee households did not employ subterranean storage facilities to any great extent; instead, these householders, like their Mississippian period counterparts, probably stored foodstuffs in above-ground facilities like corncribs or in their houses. Unfortunately, the ephemeral remains of corncribs are difficult to identify in the archaeological record. Excavations at the Alarka farm did identify a small cluster of posts that might have been a corncrib, but no further evidence of its function was recovered (Shumate et al. 2005:5.65). At Townsend, a number of small (1–2 m diameter) circular posthole patterns were identified, some near Cherokee structures; however, no artifact evidence was found to link these structures to the Cherokee occupation. The presence of large pottery jars in houses suggests that some of these vessels may have been used for storage as well as cooking (Hally 1986; Wilson and Rodning 2002). The feature data also seem to corroborate the household occupation duration estimates given in Chapter 5. While some households had more features than others, overall short household tenures are suggested by the lack of overlapping features at any household and by the short use-lives exhibited by most features.

If English Contact period Cherokee households did not employ subterranean food storage strategies, then what do the changes in feature morphology and increases in feature size in later Cherokee communities represent? The obvious answer is that subterranean storage becomes much more important to Cherokee households after the English Contact period. Similar increases in feature volume have been found among historic Upper Creek sites during roughly the same time period. Wesson (1999:151, 155) reports that features at the Upper Creek site of Fusihatchee shifted from shallow basins with an average volume of 170 liters to bell-shaped pits with an average volume of 590 liters after A.D. 1715. Wesson (1999) attributes the dramatic increase in subterranean household food storage to attempts by Upper Creek households to resist the increasing hegemony of Creek elites who were amassing power in a new landscape altered by European colonial interaction.

In consideration of the Townsend case, I wish to eschew a discussion of subterranean storage used as resistance to Cherokee elite hegemony. The ethnohistoric and archaeological evidence in the Cherokee case simply do not support the notion that social competition was at the forefront of Cherokee household strategies. Instead, I offer a more parsimonious interpretation of the patterns identified above based on DeBoer's (1988) first conclusion regarding subterranean storage—that increased subterranean food storage is indicative of the seasonal abandonment of settlements. As discussed in Chapter 2, the period following 1715 saw a dramatic increase in the participation of Cherokee (and Creek) groups in the deerskin trade. Involvement in the trade would have required large portions of Cherokee settlements to leave during the winter months. Subterranean storage offered Cherokee households a means for keeping foodstuffs safe from both animals and covetous neighbors. Indeed, prior to Wesson's work, Waselkov (1990:41) offered this same interpretation for the patterns identified at the Fusihatchee site.

A related explanation for the changes in storage facilities pertains to changes in the foods that were being stored. During the English Contact period, Cherokee households followed essentially the same foodways as their Mississippian ancestors, which featured storable foodstuffs like corn, beans, squash, and nuts. Given the wet environment of the southern Appalachian Mountain region, with the exception of nuts, none of these foodstuffs are particularly suited to subterranean storage. The dramatic increase in the size and form of subterranean storage facilities sometime during the mid-eighteenth century indicates that there was a shift to foodstuffs that were more suited to subterranean storage—most likely root crops like sweet potatoes (Riggs, pers. comm., 2007).[5] This explanation, while extremely provocative, requires further evidence. Perhaps this will come in the form of root crop starch grains or phytoliths that associate these foodstuffs with large late eighteenth-century Cherokee pit features.

Notes

1. Rather than using complicated mathematical equations (e.g., Baden 1983; Russ and Chapman 1983; Schroedl 1986a), I arrive at volume estimates by creating three-dimensional computer models of each pit feature using drafting design software (AutoCad2000). These models begin with individual profile drawings, which are bisected to provide what is essentially a quadrant profile. I use the design software to "revolve" the quadrant profile 360 degrees about an imaginary vertical axis, resulting in a geometric solid. The computer program then uses a rather advanced algorithm to calculate the volume of that solid. While this estimation method is restricted to circular features and essentially assumes (incorrectly in most cases) that pits are perfectly symmetrical, I believe it is still an improvement over older methods in terms of time and accuracy.

2. While not particularly riveting, this information is nevertheless valuable to future survey and excavation because it speaks to the likely spatial extent of occupation associated with individual Cherokee households (see also Shumate et al. 2005).

3. There are some important issues to consider when assessing the findings of this study. First, for the purposes of the study, I assume that all the basins and pits in the sample served storage functions. This probably was not the case, as some features doubtless served other functions. Second, six households is a rather small sample size. Consequently, it is impossible to determine with statistical certainty whether any similarities or differences among Townsend households are significant. Third, the shape of the excavated area at Townsend leads to significant boundary issues where the excavation limits do not incorporate all the archaeological contexts associated with all the households. Thus, it is likely that the study sample is missing basins and pits associated with households located near the limits of excavation. I conduct this comparison with the hope that future studies will incorporate these data and arrive at more robust conclusions.

4. Comparable subterranean feature data were not available for the preceding Mississippian period. In fact, the overall paucity of subterranean features at Mississippian period sites in the region has led some to argue that food storage was overwhelmingly practiced using above-ground granaries (Polhemus 1987; Scarry 1995).

5. Brett H. Riggs, University of North Carolina, Chapel Hill.

Chapter 7

Pottery Description and Analysis

Excavations of feature contexts and test units at the Townsend sites resulted in the recovery of 4711 potsherds (greater than 0.5 inch) associated with a late seventeenth- through early eighteenth-century Cherokee occupation. While not nearly as sizable as the Woodland period pottery sample recovered during the project, there are a number of reasons why the Townsend pottery sample is critically important to our understanding of English Contact period Cherokee (ca. A.D. 1670–1740) communities. First, the sample of Cherokee pottery recovered from the Townsend excavations represents the only relatively large and well-studied pottery assemblage from a Cherokee community located north of the Little Tennessee River Valley—a region where little research into Cherokee communities has been conducted (exceptions include the work of Bass [1977] and Cornette [pers. comm., 2007][1]). Second, the pottery sample from the Townsend site, together with a small sample from the Ocoee site in the Hiwassee River Valley, comprise the only Overhill Cherokee pottery assemblages thought to date to the late seventeenth and early eighteenth centuries. The overwhelming majority of what is currently known about Overhill Cherokee pottery has resulted from analyses of contexts dating to the latter half of the eighteenth century (e.g., Baden 1983; Bates 1986; Egloff 1967; King 1977; Russ and Chapman 1983). Third, the Townsend pottery sample is important because it differs dramatically from these later Overhill Cherokee assemblages. Indeed, the results of the analyses presented below suggest that three distinct potting styles were present in the Cherokee household pottery assemblages at Townsend. Analytically, two of these styles are related to previously defined ceramic series (Overhill and Qualla), but the third and most ubiquitous style expressed in the sample is a heretofore undefined phenomenon. This style, which I refer to as "Tuckaleechee," likely represents a late seventeenth- and early eighteenth-century manifestation of the Overhill series that was localized in the Cherokee settlements of Tuckaleechee, Cades, and other coves situated north of the Overhill Cherokee heartland.

I begin this chapter with a brief discussion of the historical development of Cherokee pottery taxonomy including the Overhill and Qualla ceramic series. Next, I present a detailed description of the Cherokee pottery sample recovered from the excavations at Townsend. In this description, I employ quantitative analyses of paste, surface treatment, rimstrip morphology, and vessel form to characterize variability in the pottery sample in terms of the three potting styles being practiced by Townsend households (i.e., Overhill, Qualla, and Tuckaleechee). Lastly, I attempt to place the Townsend pottery assemblage within a broader geographic and chronological context through comparisons to a number of other Cherokee pottery assemblages. Given the results of these analyses, I argue that the co-occurrence of three analytically distinct ceramic styles among the Cherokee households at Townsend represents the cohabitation of folks practicing three distinct potting traditions. Furthermore, I argue that such ceramic diversity supports the interpretation that the community at the Townsend sites was a "coalescent community" composed of households with different identities (sensu Kowalewski 2006; see also Marcoux 2010:65–107).

The Overhill and Qualla Pottery Series

The Overhill and Qualla pottery series are classification systems to characterize geographic and temporal variability among historic and prehistoric Cherokee pottery assemblages (Baden 1983; Bates 1986; Egloff 1967; Hally 1986; Keel 1976; Lewis and Kneberg 1946; Lewis et al. 1995; Riggs and Rodning 2002; Rodning 2004; Ward and Davis 1999; Wilson and Rodning 2002). The two fundamental differences between the series include the types of aplastic materials used as tempering agents and the types of surface treatments applied to vessel exteriors. Overhill series pottery features crushed mussel shell temper with smoothed or scraped exterior surfaces while Qualla series vessels were grit-tempered with carved wooden paddle stamped exterior surfaces. The repetition of this statement has resulted in the common belief that these series reflect clear differences in long-held traditions practiced by potters in Overhill Cherokee settlements, on the one hand, and by those in the Middle, Valley, and Lower settlements on the other (Dickens 1979; Egloff 1967; Schroedl 1986b).

The Overhill Ceramic Series

Overhill pottery was first described by Lewis and Kneberg in their works on the Hiwassee Island site excavations and the Chickamauga Basin survey (1946:98–99; Lewis et al. 1995:117). These initial descriptions of Overhill Cherokee pottery were significant for several reasons. First, Lewis and Kneberg's descriptions of Overhill pottery covered only pottery with check stamped and complicated stamped surfaces, and did not include shell-tempered sherds with smoothed surfaces (i.e., plain)—later known as a diagnostic hallmark of the Overhill series. This omission was most likely because the plain shell-tempered Overhill series body sherds were (and still are) indistinguishable from those associated with the earlier Mississippian period. Second, even though Lewis and Kneberg's descriptions of Overhill pottery appeared in the reports for Hiwassee Island and the Ocoee site, they were not based on the pottery assemblages recovered from these sites. Hiwassee Island's assemblage contained 3 possible Overhill sherds and the Ocoee site assemblage included approximately 30 rims with notched rimstrips and 30 complicated stamped body sherds. Instead, Lewis and Kneberg formulated their descriptions of Overhill pottery from samples excavated at the site of Fort Loudon, a mid-eighteenth-century English trading fort located in the lower Little Tennessee River Valley.

Brian Egloff's (1967) research was a major contribution to our understanding of the geographic distribution of historic Cherokee pottery. This study included samples from sites in each of the five historically documented Cherokee settlement divisions (that is, Overhill, Middle, Valley, Out, Lower); surface collections from the eastern Tennessee sites of Citico and Great Tellico comprised the Overhill Cherokee portion. While this study did not adequately consider time as a source of variability among pottery assemblages, it nevertheless succeeded in recognizing (1) that the majority of Overhill Cherokee pottery was shell-tempered with plain surfaces, and (2) that this pottery was largely restricted to sites located west of the Appalachian summit while occurring only in very small frequencies among the other Cherokee settlement divisions (Egloff 1967:43–44, 73).

The bulk of the development of the Overhill ceramic series resulted from the Tellico Archaeological Project (see Chapter 3), whose excavations expanded the corpus of Overhill pottery from a few thousand sherds to well over 500,000 sherds (King 1977:154–55). This large sample allowed for analyses at an unprecedented scale, including studies of Overhill vessel forms (King 1977) and more detailed descriptions of surface treatments and rimstrip morphology (Baden 1983; Bates 1986; Russ and Chapman 1983).

Since little research regarding the Overhill ceramic series has been conducted in recent years, in the following description I draw upon the primary sources of the Tellico Archaeological Project (Baden 1983:37–62; Bates 1986:289–305; King 1977; Russ and Chapman 1983:69–83). It is imperative to keep in mind that these sources report on Overhill pottery assemblages primarily associated with the English Colonial and Revolutionary War periods (ca. 1746–1794). As presented in these reports, the Overhill ceramic series was dominated by plain shell-tempered pottery with minority surface treatments including (in order of typical frequency) check stamping, simple stamping, complicated stamping, incising, cob marking or roughening, and cordmarking. In samples from Chota-Tanasee, Tomotley, and Mialoquo, plain shell-tempered sherds comprised 89%, 65%, and 33.5% of the total pottery sample respectively. Check stamping decorated between 0.5% and 11% of the Overhill sherds at these sites and exhibited considerable variation including square, rectangular, and diamond-shaped grids with individual checks ranging in size from two to six millimeters. Complicated stamped sherds comprised between 0.5% and 5% of the sample at these sites and included both curvilinear and rectilinear motifs, although the latter tended to be more common. Rectilinear motifs included concentric squares, triangles, and diamonds, and zigzag or herringbone patterns, while curvilinear motifs included concentric circles and wavy lines (Fig. 7.1). Incised motifs were predominately rectilinear and consisted of line-filled triangles (Fig. 7.2). Cordmarking made up the smallest minority in these Overhill assemblages, occurring in less than 1% of each site's pottery sample.

Unfortunately, vessel forms were not reported consistently in the various Tellico project publications. Neither Bates (1986) nor Russ and Chapman (1983) provide detailed discussions of Overhill vessel form or tallies of different vessel forms in their reports on the Chota-Tanasee and Mialoquo excavations. King (1977) collaborated with a number of contemporary Cherokee speakers and notable potter Amanda Swimmer in an innovative attempt to define vessel classes for the Tellico Archaeological Project Overhill pottery assemblages. Combining data recorded from whole vessels with suggestions provided by his collaborators, King (1977) came up with ten vessel classes for the Overhill series including: (1) small bowls, (2) medium bowls, (3) wide

Figure 7.1. Stamped motifs applied to Overhill series and Qualla series vessels. Reproduced with permission from *Pox, Empire, Shackles, and Hides* (Marcoux 2010: Fig. 4.2), ©University of Alabama Press.

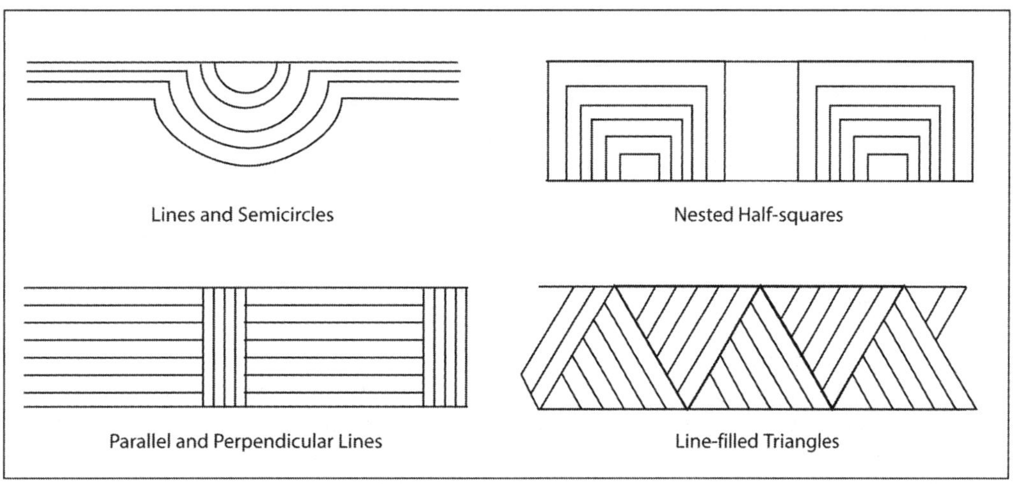

Figure 7.2. Incised motifs applied to Overhill series and Qualla series vessels. Reproduced with permission from *Pox, Empire, Shackles, and Hides* (Marcoux 2010: Fig. 4.3), ©University of Alabama Press.

shallow bowls with flaring rims, (4) wide, slightly deeper bowls with less flaring rims, (5) large cazuelas and hemispherical bowls, (6) small globular jars, (7) medium globular jars, (8) large globular jars, (9) very shallow flat-bottomed pans or plates, and (10) medium-sized flat-bottomed pans. At the site of Tomotley, Baden (1983:57) utilized a much less detailed vessel classification system, reporting that jars were by far the most abundant vessel form (n = 671), followed by hemispherical bowls (n = 148), flat-bottomed pans (n = 117), and cazuelas (n = 5).

Another diagnostic attribute of Overhill series vessels was a coil of clay that was added around the entire circumference of a vessel just below the lip or shoulder. These decorative additions, known collectively as "rimstrips," were typically either modeled from the final vessel coil by folding, or applied as a separate coil by a technique known as "filleting." Various decorative techniques were applied to rimstrips, including finger pinching, punctating, and notching with a sharp stylus. Such variability suggests that differences in rimstrip decoration may be associated with different vessel forms or that decorative techniques may be temporally sensitive. Like vessel form, there was little consistency in how rimstrip decoration was recorded in the various Tellico Archaeological Project reports, making the identification of patterning in particular rimstrip treatments impossible with the current dataset. The impression one gets from the reports, however, is that stylus notching was much more frequent than either pinching or punctating in the mid- to late eighteenth-century assemblages.

The Qualla Ceramic Series

Unlike the Overhill ceramic series, the Qualla ceramic series was constructed with data from regional surveys and excavations at both historic and prehistoric sites in western North Carolina. Consequently, it offers a much broader culture historical framework. Indeed, in forty years of research in western North Carolina, archaeologists have been able to demonstrate that the Qualla ceramic series represents a 500-year-long south Appalachian pottery tradition (Egloff 1967; Hally 1986b, 1994; Keel 1976; Riggs and Rodning 2002; Rodning 2004; Ward and Davis 1999; Wilson and Rodning 2002). Thorough histories of the development of this ceramic series can be found in other works (Riggs and Rodning 2002; Rodning 2004); therefore, here I offer a brief summary.

Egloff (1967) first defined Qualla series pottery, distinguishing it by grit tempering, surface treatments (including carved paddle stamping and bold incising), and folded and pinched rimstrips (Egloff 1967:34–35). Egloff found that Qualla series pottery was distributed primarily in the Middle, Valley, and Out town Cherokee settlement divisions and not in the Overhill and Lower settlement divisions. It would later be shown that the lack of Qualla series pottery in the Lower Cherokee settlement division was a spurious finding that resulted from sample bias. The bias resulted from Egloff's selection of excavation contexts from sites in the Lower Cherokee settlement division that were much earlier than samples from the other settlement divisions (Hally 1986b:109–10). A decade later, Keel's (1976) analysis of the pottery assemblage from the Tuckaseegee site (in the Out town area of western North Carolina) confirmed Egloff's definition of the Qualla series and expanded it to include brushed surface treatments.

After this initial period of establishing the definition of Qualla series pottery, research shifted focus to exploring how variability within this series might relate to the temporal dimension. Dickens (1979) took the first step in this endeavor by proposing a distinction between an early (ca. A.D. 1450–1650) and a late (ca. A.D. 1650–1838) subdivision of the Qualla archaeological phase. This separation reflected the distinction between pre- and post-contact time periods, but unfortunately Dickens never explained how this temporal split was materialized in the Qualla ceramic series. Some twenty years later, Ward and Davis (1999:180–83) established three subdivisions for the Qualla phase. They extended the beginning of the Qualla phase backward in time by conjecturing an unidentified early Qualla phase that predated A.D. 1450. They hypothesized that this subphase would include pottery styles similar to Early Lamar ceramic series like Wilbanks in northern Georgia and/or Dallas in eastern Tennessee. Later analyses by Riggs (et al. 1997) and Rodning (2004; Riggs and Rodning 2002) would confirm the existence of this provisional phase. The Middle Qualla phase (ca. A.D. 1450–1700) was characterized by carved paddle stamped jars with notched rimstrips and the appearance of incised cazuelas. The Late Qualla phase (ca. A.D. 1700–1838) ceramic assemblages were described as having very similar surface treatments to Middle Qualla phase assemblages; however, Ward and Davis (1999:181, 268) note that curvilinear motifs gradually replaced rectilinear motifs through time. Late Qualla phase assemblages were also characterized by the absence of the cazuela vessel form and the introduction of the "rolled" rim. As discussed below, recent work by Riggs (Shumate et al. 2005) and Rodning (2004; Riggs and Rodning 2002) has done much to further refine the Qualla ceramic series by identifying more fine-grained diachronic patterns of change involving surface treatment, vessel form, and rimstrip morphology.

After considering the radiocarbon dates calculated for features at the Coweeta Creek site in western North Carolina, Rodning (2004:312) made slight alterations to the calendrical date ranges assigned to the three Qualla phases by Ward and Davis (1999). Rodning's (2004:312) new phase ranges include: Early Qualla phase (ca. A.D. 1300–1500), Middle Qualla phase (ca. A.D. 1500–1650), and Late Qualla phase (ca. A.D. 1650–1838).[2] The portion of the ceramic series related to the Early Qualla phase is defined by assemblages recovered from the Cherokee Casino site and the Coweeta Creek site (Riggs et al. 1997; Rodning 2004). These assemblages contained both curvilinear and rectilinear complicated stamped surface treatments, with the latter tending to be more numerous. Less numerous but highly diagnostic Early Qualla phase surface treatments included diamond check stamping, redfilming, and wiping that resulted in the extrusion of temper particles to the vessel surface (called "coarse plain").

Sherds having a compact sandy paste, rimstrips with "saw-tooth" notching, and unmodified rims (i.e., lacking rimstrips) were also highly diagnostic of this subphase (Riggs and Rodning 2002:39; Rodning 2004:314). Early Qualla vessel assemblages contained everted-rim jars with and without rimstrips, tall-neck jars with unmodified rims (resembling late Savannah phase jars), and small redfilmed bowls with simple incised motifs. Incised cazuelas were rare.

Middle Qualla phase ceramic assemblages were dominated by curvilinear and rectilinear complicated stamped surface treatments. During this subphase, however, curvilinear motifs including scrolls (so-called figure "9" and figure "P"), concentric circles, keyholes, and wavy lines were much more frequent (Fig. 7.1). Minority surface treatments included cordmarking, smoothing (i.e., plain), and cob roughening, and Middle Qualla phase assemblages lacked the distinctive diamond check stamping of the previous subphase (Rodning 2004:314). Also, incising became a much more prevalent surface treatment during the Middle Qualla phase with both curvilinear and rectilinear motifs present (Riggs and Rodning 2002:43–44). The increase in incising as a surface treatment was due to a dramatic increase in the ubiquity of the cazuela vessel form in Middle Qualla phase assemblages. This vessel form had a sharply carinated profile featuring complicated stamping beneath the shoulder and incising above. Middle Qualla phase vessel assemblages also included jars with highly everted rims and pinched and flattened rimstrips, as well as small restricted orifice hemispherical bowls with folded and punctated rims (Shumate et al. 2005:6.10–6.11).

Rectilinear complicated stamping, particularly featuring barred diamond and line block motifs, and square check stamping became dominant surface treatments during the Late Qualla phase (Riggs and Rodning 2002:45). Incising was present in much diminished frequencies early in the subphase, but this surface treatment virtually disappeared from Qualla assemblages along with the cazuela form after the mid-eighteenth century (Rodning 2004:312). Jar forms during the Late Qualla subphase had excurvate rather than highly everted rims, and they featured much more prominent coronal rimstrips. These rimstrips were more often stylus notched than pinched and flattened as they were in Middle Qualla assemblages (Rodning 2004:312). By the late eighteenth century, Qualla vessel assemblages also included significant numbers of medium and large flat-bottomed pans (Riggs and Rodning 2002:45).

Riggs's (Shumate et al. 2005) study of a Qualla series pottery assemblage from the Alarka farmstead site provided a notable example of how small pottery assemblages recovered from household sites with short occupation spans (like those of the Townsend sites) can contribute greatly to increasing the temporal "resolution" of ceramic chronologies. The Alarka site consisted of the structural remains of a winter and summer house pair and a small number of subterranean pits. Little evidence for architectural repair suggested a relatively short (fewer than 10 years) occupation of the site by a single household (see Chapter 5). The pottery assemblage recovered from the site numbered just fewer than 1000 sherds and represented a minimum assemblage of 34 vessels. The assemblage exhibited diagnostic ceramic attributes dating primarily to the Middle Qualla phase, but the assemblage also included some attributes of the Late Qualla phase: (1) the majority of complicated stamped sherds featured curvilinear motifs; (2) jars with highly everted rims and pinched and flattened rimstrips (Middle Qualla) as well as jars with excurvate rims and prominent notched coronal rimstrips (Late Qualla) were present, with the former type predominating; and (3) a relatively large number of incised cazuelas were present in the vessel assemblage (Middle Qualla), but restricted orifice hemispherical bowls with folded and punctated rims were also present (Late Qualla). In regard to the Qualla ceramic series, Riggs concluded that this mixture of attributes represented what one would expect from a late Middle Qualla phase assemblage dating to the late seventeenth century.

Implications for the Present Study

With the exception of Egloff's (1967) research, the historical development of the Overhill and Qualla ceramic series has proceeded separately. These separate research histories have greatly impacted the way pottery has been related to the history and prehistory of Cherokee communities, especially Overhill communities. As a result of the isolated nature of Cherokee research, Middle, Valley, Out town, and Lower Cherokee settlement divisions currently appear as a coherent group whose deep regional histories are evinced in the half-millennium-long Qualla series (Riggs and Rodning 2002; Rodning 2004). Overhill communities, on the other hand, appear enigmatic because their style of potting is so different from Qualla (i.e., shell-tempered with plain surfaces) and because this style is not manifested in an unbroken regional ceramic sequence spanning multiple centuries. In terms of temper (i.e., shell), surface treatment (i.e., plain), and basic vessel form, Overhill assemblages are similar to the wares of the preceding Dallas and Mouse Creek phases in eastern Tennessee; however, the temporal distribution of these two prehistoric phases extends only into the late sixteenth century. This leaves an apparent gap in material culture assemblages spanning essentially the entire seventeenth century—a gap that has fueled the debates over the "origins" of the Overhill Cherokees in eastern Tennessee (Dickens 1979; Schroedl 1986a:533, 1986b).

What has not been considered, however, is the possibility that components of the Overhill ceramic series spanning this gap exist, but that these components were stylistically different from earlier sixteenth-century assemblages *and* later eighteenth-century assemblages. This would logically include entertaining the possibility that earlier Overhill series pottery assemblages were much more diverse than mid- to late eighteenth-century assemblages and that these earlier Overhill assemblages were in some ways similar to contemporaneous Qualla series assemblages. As shown below, the Townsend Cherokee pottery assemblage represents just such a scenario. Indeed, the analyses demonstrate that the potting styles practiced in these late seventeenth- and early eighteenth-century Overhill households were not nearly as homogeneous as they were in the mid-eighteenth century. The results also refute the implicit notion that the potting styles represented by the Overhill and Qualla series remained geographically isolated until the large-scale refugee migrations enacted during the American Revolutionary War (Baden 1983:148–49; Bates 1986:322; Russ and Chapman 1983:82–83).

Cherokee Pottery at Townsend

The Cherokee pottery sample from the Townsend excavations consisted of 4711 potsherds including 4343 body sherds and 329 rim sherds. To place the Townsend assemblage within a broader temporal and regional context, I also conducted analyses on an additional 1733 body sherds and 341 rim sherds from other Cherokee sites in eastern Tennessee and western North Carolina. These additions brought the total pottery sample in this study to 6746 sherds. This assemblage was obviously quite small when compared to the Overhill Cherokee pottery assemblage from Chota-Tanasee, which numbered over 100,000, and other Tellico Archaeological Project sites; however, the diminutive size of the Townsend assemblage made detailed attribute analyses possible at the individual sherd level. For every body sherd, I recorded data for 8 variables including the maximum diameter of the sherd (measured in one-centimeter classes, using a template of concentric circles), sherd thickness, sherd weight, temper, exterior surface treatment, decorative motif (if applicable), interior surface treatment, and temper particle size (see Appendix B). For every rim sherd, I recorded data for 26 attributes including the 8 used for body sherds plus 7 qualitative and 11 quantitative variables related to vessel form and rimstrip morphology (see Appendix C). The resulting database used in the study thus contained over 67,000 individual data points.

Pottery Ware

The foundations of three potting styles can be observed in three distinct pottery wares found among Townsend households.[3] Differences among these wares are evident in four attributes including: (1) the type of aplastic material used to temper the clay bodies of vessels, (2) the size of tempering agent particles, (3) the density of tempering agent used in the paste, and (4) the thickness of vessel walls.

The most readily observable difference among the three pottery wares involves the types of aplastic materials used as tempering agents in vessel construction. The most common tempering agent found in the Townsend pottery sample consists of a mixture of metaigneous and metamorphic rock types—primarily quartz, quartzite, feldspar, and muscovite-schist (n = 3579, 82.41%) (Table 7.1). The round shape of the particles in this ware group is reminiscent of water-worn gravel, suggesting that this tempering material was gathered from the nearby banks of the Little River (Fig. 7.3). The presence of a small amount of angular and/or subangular quartzite in some sherds raises the possibility that Townsend potters were also adding more formally prepared (i.e., crushed) rock as tempering.

Crushed mussel shell comprises the second most common tempering agent used in Cherokee pottery at Townsend (n = 510, 11.74%). In all but a few instances, the shell particles had leached out of the sherd, leaving a highly porous clay body (Fig. 7.3). Without the presence of the actual tempering agent, classification in these cases relies on the lenticular arrangement of the voids throughout the paste—an unmistakable hallmark of shell tempering.

A minority of sherds in the sample are tempered with various types of metaigneous particles—primarily quartz (n = 245, 5.64%) (Fig. 7.3). This tempering agent, known as grit, conforms to the typical definition of the Qualla series (see also Shumate et al. 2005:6.5). Grit differs from gravel in particle shape (angular, not round) as well as in lacking metamorphic rock types. The paste of this ware is also much more micaceous than the gravel-tempered or shell-tempered ware groups. The mica flecks contained in these sherds are probably natural inclusions and not intentional, suggesting that grit-tempered vessels were constructed using clay from source(s) other than those used in making gravel- and shell-tempered wares. Given the similarity of this ware to that of Qualla series sherds found among the Middle, Valley, and Out town settlement divisions to the east, it also raises the possibility that the grit-tempered sherds at Townsend may represent vessels made elsewhere. That these three tempering agents were the focus of "real" choices made by Townsend potters in creating three different pottery wares is attested to by the fact that only 9 sherds in the sample (0.21%) contain a mixture of tempers.

Townsend potters also appear to have made distinctions in the size of the temper particles they used in each of the three pottery wares. To quantify the size of temper particles, I essentially used the same method employed by Steponaitis (1983:33–34) in his study of Moundville pottery in which the diameter of the third largest temper particle visible in each sherd in the sample is measured—the third largest particle being more representative of overall paste composition. My method differed slightly from Steponaitis's in that I measured temper particles visible in the cross section of the sherd rather than the sherd surface. I did so because vessel surfaces were typically altered in some way before firing (usually by smoothing, scraping, or wiping); therefore, I thought that the cross section would offer an unaltered, and therefore more representative, "picture" of paste composition. A comparison of the temper particle size using notched boxplots reveals statistically significant differences among all three wares (Fig. 7.4). The shell-tempered ware has the largest temper particles (n = 510, median = 1.85 mm), followed by gravel-tempered ware (n = 3579, median = 1.40 mm) and grit-tempered ware (n = 245, median = 0.92 mm). Indeed, the differences among the ware groups are so great that the distributions of temper particle size barely overlap.

There are also appreciable differences among the three wares in regard to the density of temper particles in the clay

Table 7.1. Cherokee body sherd assemblage recovered from the Townsend excavations.

Temper	Exterior Surface Treatment	Count	Percent
gravel	plain	881	20.29
	indeterminate linear stamped	714	16.44
	indeterminate stamped	502	11.56
	coarse plain	476	10.96
	cordmarked	407	9.37
	eroded	259	5.96
	curvilinear complicated stamped	134	3.09
	scraped	56	1.29
	complicated stamped	48	1.11
	burnished	27	0.62
	simple stamped	26	0.60
	cob roughened	25	0.58
	incised	11	0.25
	brushed	10	0.23
	fingernail punctated	1	0.02
	stylus punctated	1	0.02
	rectilinear complicated stamped	1	0.02
	total	*3579*	*82.41*
shell	plain	360	8.29
	eroded	83	1.91
	scraped	54	1.24
	burnished	5	0.12
	cob roughened	3	0.07
	indeterminate linear stamped	2	0.05
	cordmarked	1	0.02
	fingernail punctated	1	0.02
	redfilmed	1	0.02
	total	*510*	*11.74*
grit	indeterminate linear stamped	92	2.12
	plain	55	1.27
	indeterminate stamped	28	0.64
	curvilinear complicated stamped	25	0.58
	complicated stamped	9	0.21
	eroded	9	0.21
	burnished	8	0.18
	coarse plain	6	0.14
	scraped	4	0.09
	cordmarked	3	0.07
	brushed	3	0.07
	check stamped	2	0.05
	incised	1	0.02
	total	*245*	*5.64*
shell and gravel	plain	3	0.07
	indeterminate stamped	2	0.05
	coarse	1	0.02
	cordmarked	1	0.02
	indeterminate linear stamped	1	0.02
	scraped	1	0.02
	total	*9*	*0.21*
	grand total	***4343***	***100.00***

Figure 7.3. Tempering material in the Townsend pottery assemblage: *top*, gravel; *center*, shell; *bottom*, grit. Reproduced with permission from *Pox, Empire, Shackles, and Hides* (Marcoux 2010: Fig. 4.4), ©University of Alabama Press.

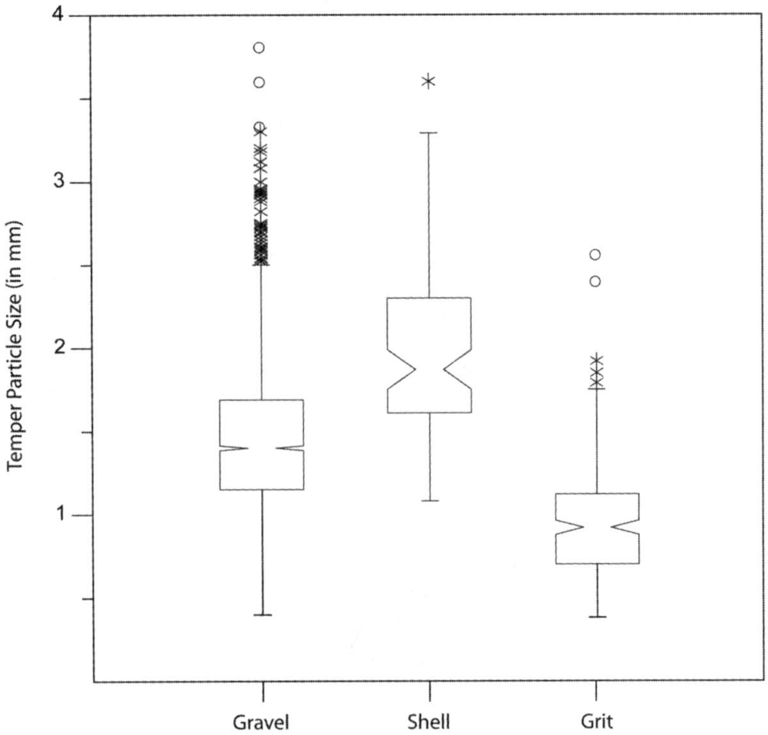

Figure 7.4. Boxplots comparing the distribution of temper particle size among the three Cherokee pottery ware groups. Reproduced with permission from *Pox, Empire, Shackles, and Hides* (Marcoux 2010: Fig. 4.5), ©University of Alabama Press.

body. The most accurate quantitative method for this type of comparison would involve point counting temper particles in thin section slides under a low power microscope—a method that neither time nor money would allow. As an alternative basis for comparison along this dimension, I employed published visual estimation charts of temper particle density (Mathew et al. 1997:215–63; Orton et al. 1993: Fig. A.4). While not as rigorous as petrologic analysis, I reasoned that visual estimation charts nevertheless provided a reasonably objective basis for comparison. The charts consist of a series of circles, each representing an equal area of a sherd cross section, containing various amounts of circular and angular temper particles. The charts are arranged according to different size ranges of temper particles (for example, 0.5 mm to 1.0 mm, 1.0 mm to 3.0 mm) and measure the percentage of temper particles in five-percent increments. To estimate the temper particle density of a sherd, one consults the chart with proper temper particle size range and compares the actual sherd to the various depictions on the chart. When a match is found, one then reads the percentage value on the chart's left-hand margin. In the Townsend pottery sample, gravel-tempered and shell-tempered sherds have similar density values ranging between 20% and 35%. The density values of grit-tempered sherds are significantly lower—10% to 20%. This last density value corresponds to that given by Riggs (Shumate et al. 2005) for the Qualla series ceramic assemblage recovered from the Alarka site.

Some degree of difference is also apparent among the ware groups in terms of vessel wall thickness. This measurement was taken along the midline of each body sherd in the sample. Sherds exhibiting spalling or significant erosion were not included in the analysis. The results of a comparison using notched boxplots indicate that the median sherd thickness of the gravel-tempered ware ($n = 3330$, median = 7.6 mm) was significantly greater than that of the shell-tempered ware ($n = 475$, median = 7.04 mm) and the grit-tempered ware ($n = 237$, median = 7.08 mm) (Fig. 7.5). The median sherd thickness measures of the latter two groups were essentially identical.

Exterior and Interior Surface Treatment

The Townsend pottery sample exhibits a number of different exterior and interior surface treatments (Fig. 7.6). The most common exterior surface treatment in the Townsend sample is "plain" (Table 7.1). Following the convention set by other researchers, in this study I make the distinction between three forms of plain surface treatment including "plain," "burnished," and "coarse plain" (Hally 1986, 1994; Marcoux 2010; Rodning 2004). Plain sherds have matte exterior surfaces and often feature very small striations resulting from the dragging of temper particles during the smoothing process (Fig. 7.6*a*). These striations suggest that smoothing took place while the vessel was still fairly wet rather than at a leather hard stage. Burnished sherds exhibit polished surfaces that had been rubbed with a very smooth-surfaced tool

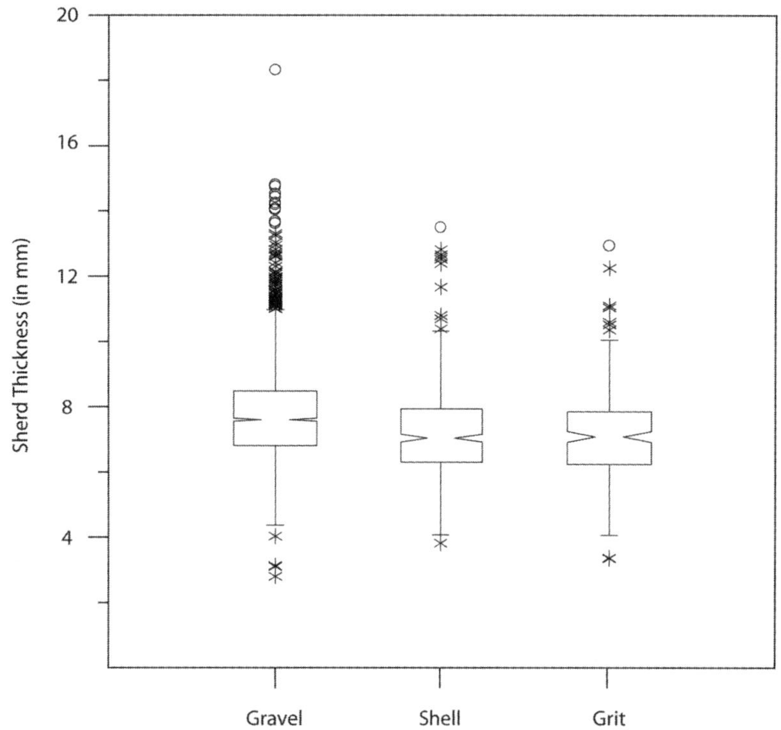

Figure 7.5. Boxplots comparing the distribution of sherd thickness among the three Cherokee pottery ware groups. Reproduced with permission from *Pox, Empire, Shackles, and Hides* (Marcoux 2010: Fig. 4.6), ©University of Alabama Press.

Figure 7.6. Exterior surface treatments and decorative rim modes in the Townsend pottery sample. *a*, plain globular jar with pinched rimstrip; *b*, coarse plain globular jar with smoothed rimstrip; *c*, indeterminate linear stamped globular jar with pinched and flattened rimstrip; *d*, curvilinear complicated stamped (wavy lines motif) globular jar with pinched and flattened rimstrip; *e*, cordmarked globular jar with stylus notched rimstrip; *f*, incised (line-filled triangles motif) cazuela with unmodified rim. Reproduced with permission from *Pox, Empire, Shackles, and Hides* (Marcoux 2010: Fig. 4.7), ©University of Alabama Press.

(such as a bone or river pebble) and wiped with a piece of cloth or hide when a vessel was leather hard. To be categorized as burnished, sherds must actually reflect light. Coarse plain is a surface treatment category that includes sherds with "bumpy" exterior surfaces that are "dotted with protruding temper particles" (Fig. 7.6*b*) (Hally 1986:108). Like burnishing, it appears that Townsend potters achieved this effect by wiping the vessel's exterior surface with a piece of cloth or hide. Unlike burnishing (where a potter wipes the exterior of a leather hard vessel, drawing fine clay particles to the surface in order to achieve a polished appearance), to create a coarse surface a potter wipes a wet vessel in order to *remove* clay particles from the exterior, leaving a rough or "coarse" surface studded with extruded temper particles. That this was an intentional practice is supported by the fact that the interior surfaces of many coarse plain sherds are smoothed or even burnished.

There has been little consistency in the way that carved paddle stamped pottery has been recorded and analyzed in Cherokee pottery assemblages. Because this surface treatment comprises such a large percentage of many Cherokee assemblages and because variability in this surface treatment appears to be temporally sensitive, these differences in classification method can potentially become a serious impediment to constructing a robust Cherokee ceramic chronology.

The major differences among current classification methods result from the way in which each method deals with the fact that the entire design field of a carved paddle is often not present on a single sherd. For example, how does one classify a sherd that features a stamped impression consisting solely of parallel lines? In one classification system, this sherd would be classified as "simple stamped" (e.g., Baden 1983:53; Bates 1986:300; Russ and Chapman 1983:80); in another system, it would be called "rectilinear complicated stamped" (Smith et al. 1988:54); and in yet another classification system, it would be called "linear stamped" (Rodning 2004:271). Given that the relative percentages of sherds bearing curvilinear complicated stamped motifs and rectilinear complicated stamped motifs change through time, these three classificatory schemas will likely give different chronological estimates to the same assemblage. Recognizing the promise of carved paddle stamped pottery to be a powerful component in constructing ceramic chronologies, I argue for a classificatory system that strives for the greatest specificity *while at the same time* acknowledges the fragmentary nature of potsherd samples.

Fortunately, this system has already been developed and employed by Riggs (Shumate et al. 2005) and Rodning (2004). With relatively minor differences, theirs is a hierarchical classification system for carved paddle stamped pottery that can be thought of as progressing from least to most specific given the size and surface conditions of each sherd. The least specific group in the system is called "Indeterminate Stamped." This group consists of sherds exhibiting evidence of being stamped with carved wooden paddles but whose surfaces had been smoothed over or were otherwise modified precluding the identification of any decorative pattern (e.g., check stamped, simple stamped, complicated stamped).

Moving up the hierarchy, the next group is called "Indeterminate Linear Stamped." Sherds belonging to this group bear the impressions of a series of straight parallel lines (2–5 mm in width) formed by the lands and groves of a carved wooden paddle. These lines could have been part of a paddle carved solely with a series of straight parallel lines (i.e., simple stamped), or they might represent a portion of a complex rectilinear or curvilinear motif (Fig. 7.6*c*). Because the fragmentary nature of the sherds makes distinguishing among these motifs impossible, analytically these sherds are all considered to be part of the same group. Along with plain sherds, indeterminate linear stamped sherds make up the vast majority of the Townsend pottery assemblage (see Table 7.1).

The next category, "Complicated Stamped," includes sherds that bear impressions of multiple adjoining lines whose junctures form distinct angles. In this case, the analyst knows that the potter used a paddle bearing a complex motif; however, the sherds in this category are too small to determine whether the complex motif was curvilinear or rectilinear.

The most specific analytical groups are "Curvilinear Complicated Stamped" and "Rectilinear Complicated Stamped." These groups include sherds featuring multiple parallel or intersecting curved lines in the case of the former, and multiple intersecting straight lines in the latter case. In most cases, the small size of sherds makes identifying any particular complex motif very difficult. Motifs in the Townsend assemblage include concentric circles, concentric squares, figure "9" and "P" scrolls, and wavy lines (Table 7.2; Fig. 7.6*d*). In most cases, however, a specific motif cannot be identified and the motif is classified as "indeterminate." In some cases, it is apparent that the motif is *either* a figure "9" *or* a figure "P," and in these cases I record the motif as "indeterminate scroll."

A number of other exterior surface treatments are also present in the Townsend pottery assemblage. Simple stamping is a rather difficult surface treatment to identify with certainty in samples dominated by small sherds (such as the Townsend sample). In keeping with the conservative structure of the hierarchical paddle stamped classification method, I only identify sherds as simple stamped when two abutting edges of a single paddle are visible. Consequently, it is likely that the "indeterminate linear stamped" category contains some simple stamped sherds and that simple stamped sherds are underestimated in this analysis.

Cordmarking, achieved by impressing the exterior surface of a wet vessel with a cord-wrapped paddle, is a rather common surface feature in the Townsend sample (Fig. 7.6*e*). The size of the cordage wrapped around the paddle ranges anywhere from 1 mm to 6 mm, suggesting different types of materials were used. In virtually all cases where the orientation of the sherd could be determined, the cordmarking is arranged vertically. In one case, a cord-wrapped paddle was applied in such a way as to create a complex line block motif.

Scraped sherds feature prominent striations that are different from those present on sherds with plain surfaces. Rather

Table 7.2. Relative frequencies of complicated stamped and incised motifs on Cherokee pottery at Townsend.

Motif	Frequency
complicated stamped	
concentric circles	3
concentric squares	1
figure "9" scroll	5
figure "P" scroll	1
indeterminate scroll	23
wavy lines	3
indeterminate	125
incised	
line-filled triangles	5
lines and semicircles	1
nested half-squares	1
indeterminate	21

than being caused by the dragging of temper particles across the vessel's surface during smoothing, the striations present on scraped sherds were caused by a planar tool (i.e., probably made of shell or wood) that was used to thin the vessel's walls. A small number of sherds exhibit surfaces that were battered or roughened with a corncob. This surface treatment is fairly easy to recognize even on small sherds given the distinct impressions left by the corn cupules.

Incised sherds feature straight or curved lines executed by dragging a pointed stylus across the exterior surface of a vessel. Most incised sherds in the Townsend sample are too small to identify a design motif; however, a few large sherds bear motifs including line-filled triangles (Fig. 7.6*f*), nested half-squares, and parallel lines with semicircles (Table 7.2).

Brushed surfaces evince a series of prominent striations that run in the same direction, usually perpendicular to the vessel lip. This surface treatment is distinguished from scraping by the depth of the striations and by the diagnostic ridges of clay that flank either side of each striation. These ridges represent the "wake" that results from dragging a bundle of twigs or some similar material across a wet vessel surface.

The remainder of the Townsend pottery sample is composed of exterior surface treatments that occur in very minor amounts. A few instances of body sherds bearing fingernail and stylus punctations are present, but the overwhelming majority of sherds bearing these modifications are rimstrips. The Townsend sample also includes two examples of large check stamping (> 3 mm) and a single example of exterior redfilming or slipping. Finally, while not necessarily a very small minority, the residual category, "eroded," includes sherds with surfaces that have been severely worn to the point where any decorative surface treatment is obliterated.

Interior surface treatments applied to the Townsend pottery assemblage evince much less variability than exterior surface treatments. Seven different interior surface treatments are present in the Townsend pottery sample—plain, plain and smudged, burnished, burnished and smudged, coarse plain, scraped, and redfilmed. The characteristics of the plain, burnished, coarse plain, and scraped interior surface treatments are identical to their exterior surface treatment counterparts. The blackened interior surfaces of smudged sherds result from a secondary firing procedure where already fired vessels are placed in a smoke rich, oxygen deprived (or reduced) atmosphere. This procedure allows carbon particles to permeate and fill voids in the vessel walls, making the vessels watertight. Redfilming is a rare interior surface treatment that also is aimed at making vessels watertight. This surface treatment is obtained by applying a red-tinted colloidal suspension or slip to the interior of vessels. Redfilming appears unique to the Townsend assemblage as it does not appear in any other published descriptions of Overhill or Qualla series pottery.

Distinctions among the three potting styles practiced by Townsend households are also manifested in exterior surface treatments. These distinctions are readily apparent when the relative percentages of exterior surface treatments are compared across the three Cherokee pottery wares in the Townsend sample. The most striking distinction involves the predominance of plain surface treatments among the shell-tempered ware and the ubiquity of paddle stamped surfaces (namely, indeterminate linear stamped, complicated stamped, curvilinear complicated stamped, simple stamped, cordmarked) among the gravel- and grit-tempered wares (Table 7.3; Fig. 7.7). Almost 99% of shell-tempered sherds evince plain, burnished, coarse plain, or scraped surfaces compared to 42.5% for the gravel-tempered ware and 31.2% for the grit-tempered ware. Conversely, only 0.7% of shell-tempered sherds bear paddle stamped surfaces, while these treatments comprise 38.5% of the gravel-tempered assemblage and 55.2% of the grit-tempered assemblage. Incising, while rare among gravel- and grit-tempered wares, is totally absent from the shell-tempered assemblage.

This major distinction involving plain and paddle stamped surface treatments sets the gravel-tempered and grit-tempered wares apart from the shell-tempered ware; however, a closer inspection of exterior surface treatments reveals that the two rock-tempered wares also differ in a number of ways. First, while the collective proportion of plain, burnished, and coarse plain are roughly similar in gravel- and grit-tempered wares, coarse plain is a much more prevalent exterior surface treatment among gravel-tempered sherds (Table 7.3; Fig. 7.7). Second, indeterminate linear stamped, complicated stamped, and curvilinear complicated stamped sherds are approximately twice as numerous in the grit-tempered assemblage than in the gravel-tempered assemblage. Third, although composing only a small minority of the total sample, simple stamping occurs only on the gravel-tempered ware. Lastly, the proportion of cordmarking in the gravel-tempered assemblage (12.3%) is significantly greater than in the grit-tempered assemblage (1.3%).

Table 7.3. Relative frequencies of exterior surface treatments among the three Cherokee temper groups at Townsend.[a]

Temper	Plain		Burnished		Coarse Plain		Indeterminate Stamped		Indeterminate Linear Stamped		Complicated Stamped		Curvilinear Complicated Stamped		Simple Stamped		Cord-marked		Scraped		Cob Roughened		Incised		Brushed	
	n	%[b]	*n*	%	*n*	%	*n*	%	*n*	%	*n*	%	*n*	%	*n*	%	*n*	%	*n*	%	*n*	%	*n*	%	*n*	%
gravel	881	25.6	27	0.8	476	14.4	502	15.1	714	19.9	48	1.5	134	4.0	26	0.8	407	12.3	56	1.7	25	0.8	11	0.3	10	0.3
shell	360	84.7	5	1.2	0	0.0	0	0.0	2	0.5	0	0.0	0	0.0	0	0.0	1	0.2	54	12.7	3	0.7	0	0.0	0	0.0
grit	55	23.5	8	3.4	6	2.6	28	12.0	92	39.3	9	3.9	25	10.7	0	0.0	3	1.3	4	1.7	0	0.0	1	0.4	3	1.3

[a]This comparison only includes surface treatments comprising more than 0.1% of the total pottery sample recovered from Townsend.

[b]Percentages are given for the ware group, not the total pottery sample. Thus, plain surfaces comprise 25.6% of the gravel-tempered ware, 84.7% of the shell-tempered ware, and 23.5% of the grit-tempered ware found at Townsend.

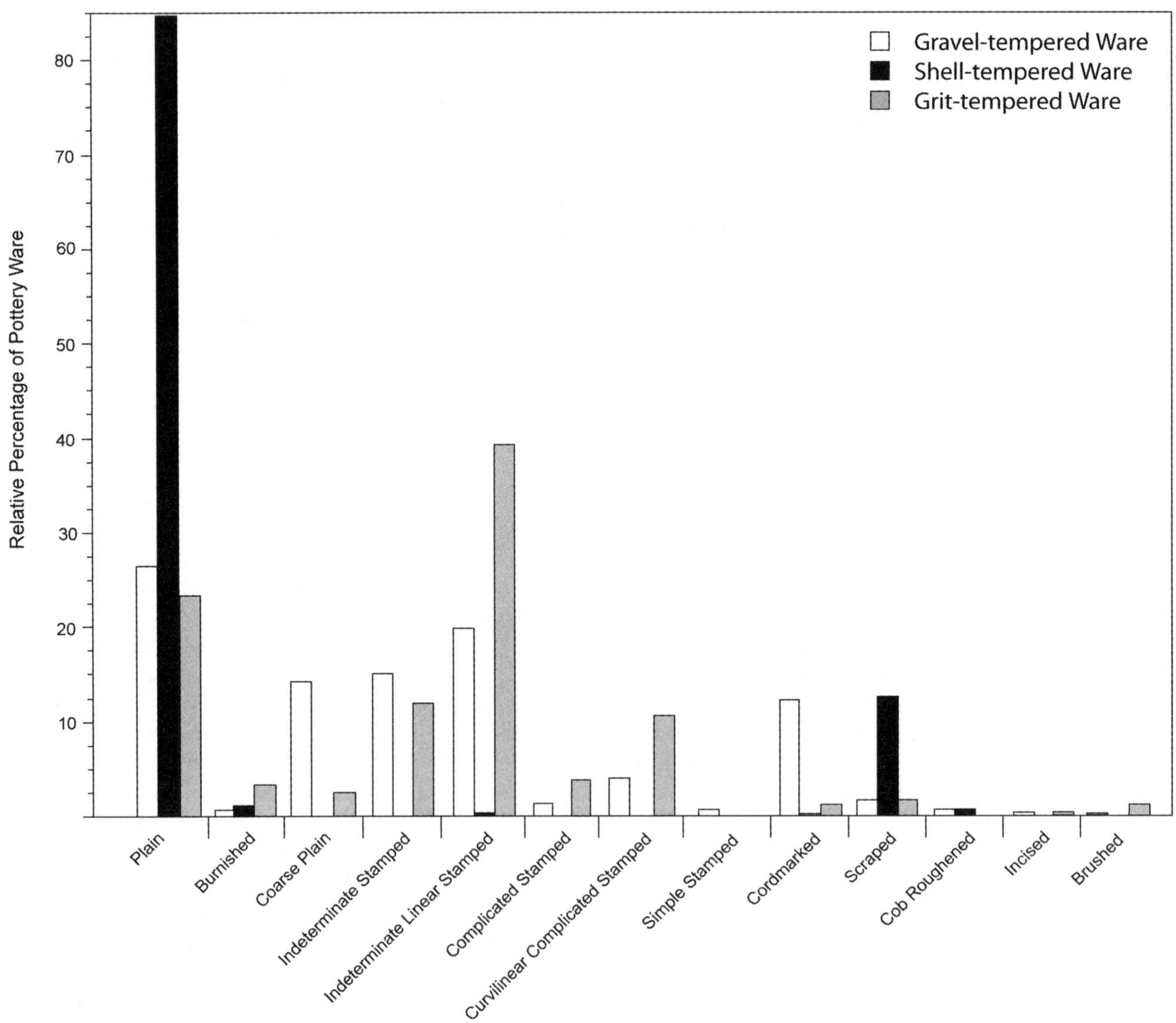

Figure 7.7. Relative percentages of exterior surface treatments among the three Cherokee temper groups at Townsend. This comparison only includes surface treatments comprising more than 0.1% of the total pottery sample recovered from Townsend. Reproduced with permission from *Pox, Empire, Shackles, and Hides* (Marcoux 2010: Fig. 4.8), ©University of Alabama Press.

Table 7.4. Relative frequencies of interior surface treatments among the three Cherokee temper groups at Townsend.

Temper	Plain		Plain/Smudged		Burnished		Burnished/ Smudged		Coarse Plain		Scraped		Redfilmed	
	n	%[a]	*n*	%	*n*	%	*n*	%	*n*	%	*n*	%	*n*	%
gravel	2303	69.0	547	16.4	152	4.6	204	6.1	101	3.0	9	0.3	23	0.7
shell	335	86.1	36	9.3	4	1.0	1	0.3	0	0.0	13	3.3	0	0.0
grit	159	68.2	22	9.4	21	9.0	26	11.2	1	0.4	0	0.0	4	1.7

[a]Percentages are given for the ware group, not the total pottery sample. Thus, plain interior surfaces comprise 69.0% of the gravel-tempered ware, 86.1% of the shell-tempered ware, and 68.2% of the grit-tempered ware found at Townsend.

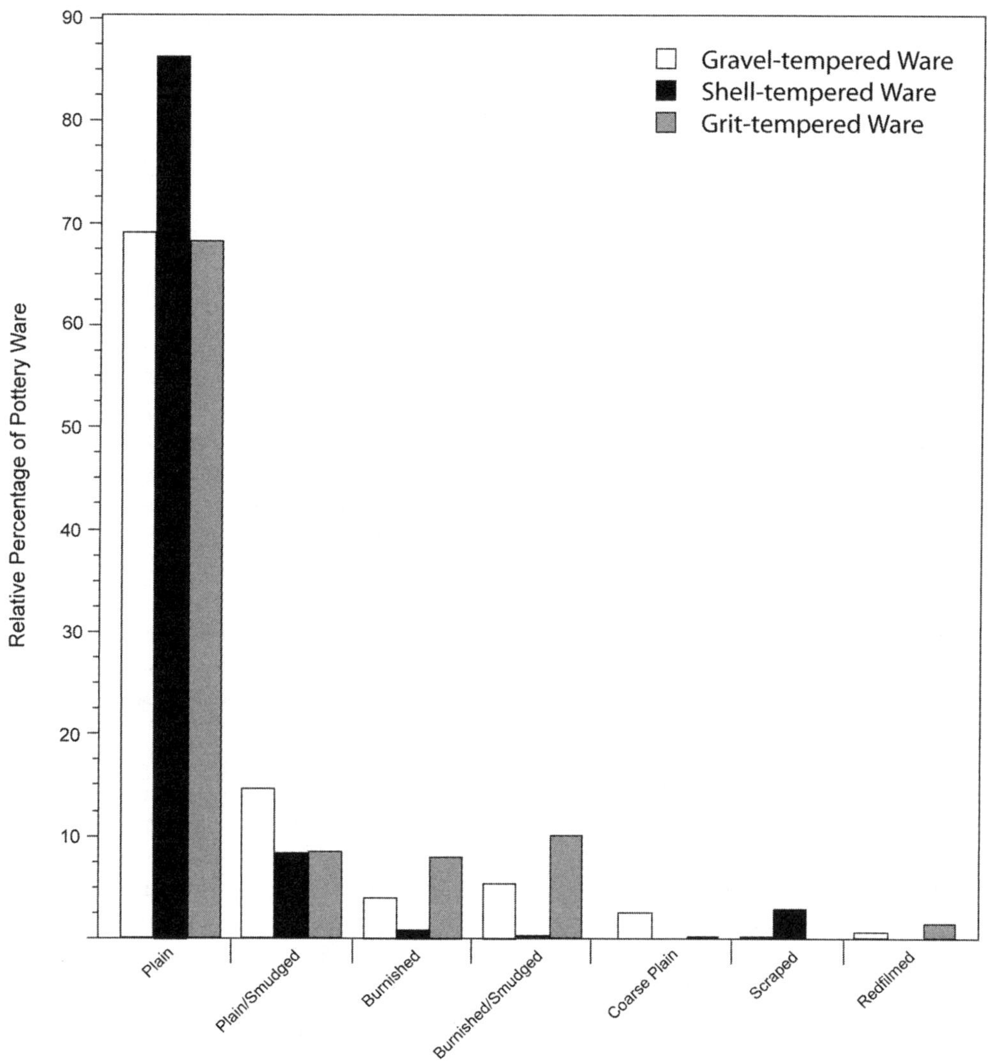

Figure 7.8. Relative percentages of interior surface treatments among the three Cherokee temper groups at Townsend.

There is much less ware-based variability among interior surface treatments in the sample. In this case, the distinction is largely between the shell-tempered ware on one hand and the gravel- and grit-tempered wares on the other. Plain, plain and smudged, and scraped interior surfaces dominate the shell-tempered assemblage, followed by very small amounts of burnished and burnished and smudged (Table 7.4; Fig. 7.8). The gravel-tempered and grit-tempered assemblages contain less plain interior surfaces than the shell-tempered ware. Conversely, sherds in these ware groups have relatively more burnished and burnished and smudged interiors than those in the shell-tempered assemblage. Redfilmed interiors comprise a small minority of the gravel-tempered and grit-tempered assemblages and are absent in the shell-tempered assemblage.

Vessel Form

Overhill and Qualla series pottery assemblages contain a number of different vessel forms (Bates 1986; Hally 1986b; King 1977; Riggs and Rodning 2002; Rodning 2004; Wilson and Rodning 2002). As discussed above, however, our understanding of variability in Qualla series vessel forms (especially temporal variability) is much more detailed than that of the Overhill series because the Overhill ceramic series is based on samples drawn primarily from Colonial, Revolutionary, and Federal period contexts (post-A.D. 1740). Because the pottery sample recovered from the Townsend sites represents an Overhill vessel assemblage associated with the preceding English Contact period (ca. A.D. 1670–1740), it provides crucial data needed to improve our understanding of temporal variability in Overhill vessel forms. The Townsend sample is especially suited to extending the Overhill ceramic chronology because it is composed of refuse from a number of short-term (probably less than a decade) single household occupations.

In this section, I define the major vessel classes present in the Townsend sample and explore variability both within these classes and among the three pottery wares. My definitions of vessel classes are based on the functional analyses of historic and prehistoric Overhill, Qualla, and Lamar series vessels conducted by King (1977), Hally (1986a), Wilson, and Rodning (Wilson and Rodning 2002). Collectively, these studies provide a very robust set of functional vessel classes based on vessel shape, use wear, ethnohistoric accounts, and interviews with contemporary potters. To provide a relatively unbiased basis for quantitative comparison, the analyses presented in this section are based on minimum number of vessel (MNV) estimates. Minimum number of vessel estimates have been derived using a number of methods, but I choose to base my MNV estimates solely on counts of unique rimsherds (see also Orton et al. 1993:169–71; Shapiro 1984; Wilson 2005). This method likely results in the most conservative vessel count estimates reflecting the composition of the vessel assemblages that were used and discarded by the Cherokee households at Townsend.

The Townsend pottery sample contains unique rim sherds representing a minimum of 329 vessels. These rim sherds can be sorted into four major vessel classes including globular jars (n = 129), simple bowls (n = 13), restricted orifice bowls (n = 34), and cazuelas (n = 17) (Table 7.5). The sample also includes a number of rimstrip fragments (n = 48) and rim sherds that were too small to confidently place into a vessel class. With the exception of cazuelas, the relative frequencies of the three pottery wares among vessels are essentially the same as the body sherd sample.

Table 7.5. Minimum number of vessel (MNV) counts in the Townsend study sample.

Basic Shape	*n*	%
globular jar		
gravel-tempered	105	31.9
shell-tempered	14	4.3
grit-tempered	10	3.0
total	*129*	*39.2*
simple bowl		
gravel-tempered	11	3.3
shell-tempered	2	0.7
grit-tempered	0	0.0
total	*13*	*4.0*
restricted orifice bowl		
gravel-tempered	30	9.1
shell-tempered	2	0.6
grit-tempered	2	0.6
total	*34*	*10.3*
cazuela		
gravel-tempered	16	4.9
shell-tempered	0	0.0
grit-tempered	1	0.3
total	*17*	*5.2*
indeterminate		
gravel-tempered	107	32.5
shell-tempered	17	5.2
grit-tempered	12	3.6
total	*136*	*41.3*
grand total	***329***	***100.0***

Globular Jars (Figs. 7.9–7.16). Globular jars are by far the most ubiquitous identifiable vessel class in the Townsend sample. This class includes vessels with recurvate profiles featuring rounded bases, restricted necks, and excurvate to highly everted rims (Hally 1986a:277; King 1977:160; Shapiro 1984:702). The distribution of orifice diameter estimates suggests that jars were produced in two sizes—small jars with orifice diameters ranging from 11 cm to 22 cm and large jars with orifice diameters ranging from 26 cm to 41 cm (Fig. 7.14). The existence of two size classes is supported by the identification of an identical distribution of orifice diameters among the jar assemblage from the Coweeta Creek site (Wilson and Rodning 2002:30). Small jars in the Townsend sample are further distinguished from large jars in that they possess unmodified rims (i.e., they lack rimstrips). Functional analyses and ethnohistoric accounts have demonstrated that large jars were most commonly used for preparing hominy, cooking, and storing large quantities of foodstuffs while small jars were used to cook or reheat small quantities of food (Hally 1986a:269, 285–86; Wilson and Rodning 2002:31–32). King (1977:162–63) adds that the largest Cherokee jars could have been used in the fermenting process of a form of corn beer or could have acted as serving pots for large communal meals.

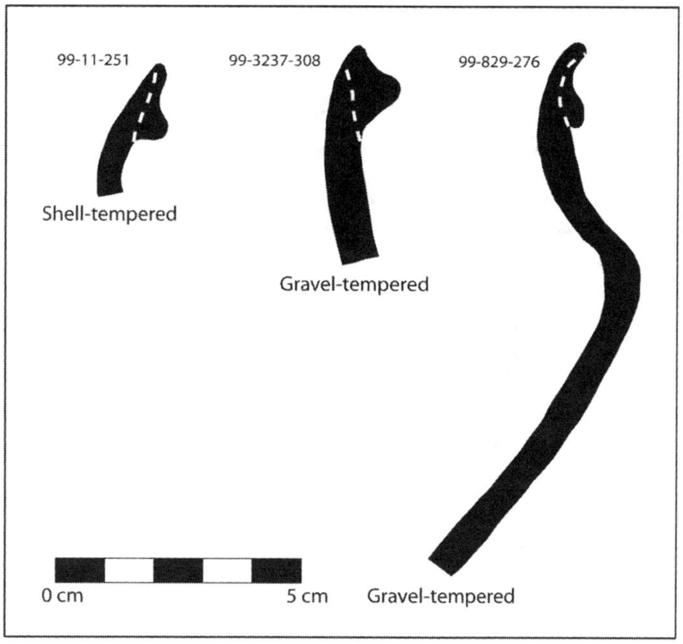

Figure 7.9. Large globular jars with pinched appliqué rimstrips.

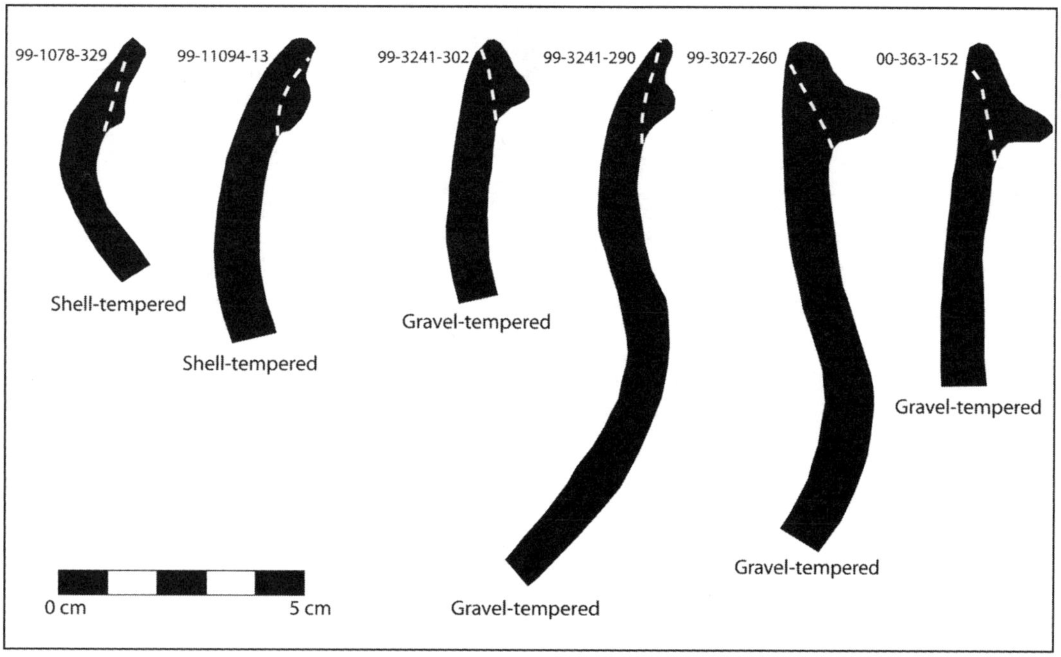

Figure 7.10. Large globular jars with stylus notched appliqué rimstrips.

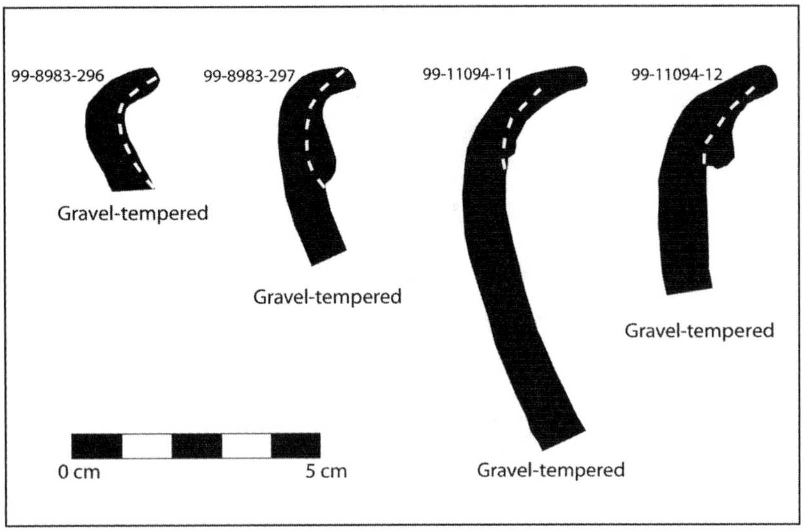

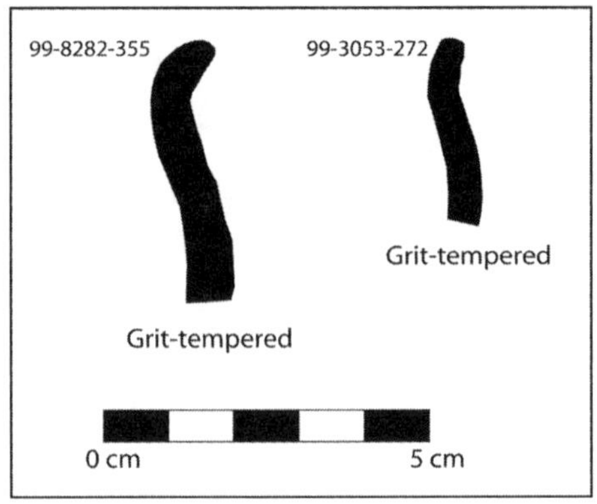

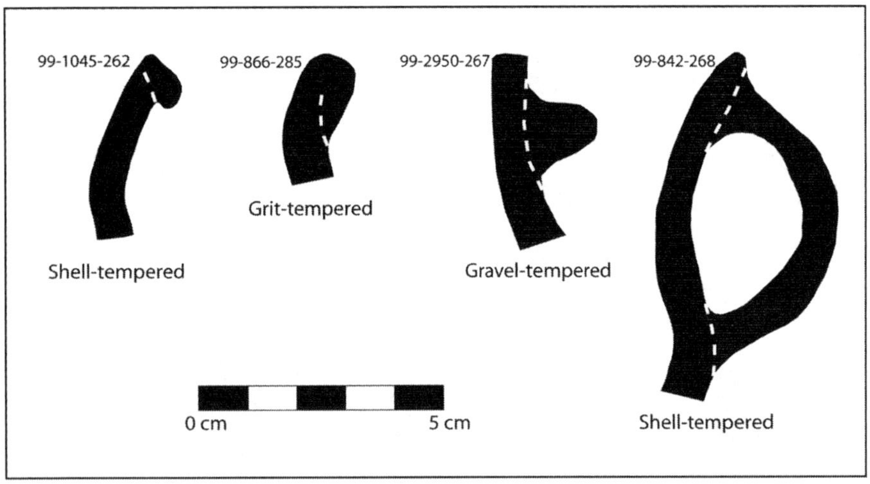

(*above left*) Figure 7.11. Large globular jars with pinched and flattened appliqué rimstrips.

(*above*) Figure 7.12. Small globular jars.

(*left*) Figure 7.13. Large jars with an L-shaped rim (*far left*), a rolled rim (*middle left*), a lug handle (*middle right*), and a strap handle (*far right*).

(*below*) Figure 7.14. Histogram depicting the distribution of orifice diameter estimates among globular jars. Reproduced with permission from *Pox, Empire, Shackles, and Hides* (Marcoux 2010: Fig. 4.10), ©University of Alabama Press.

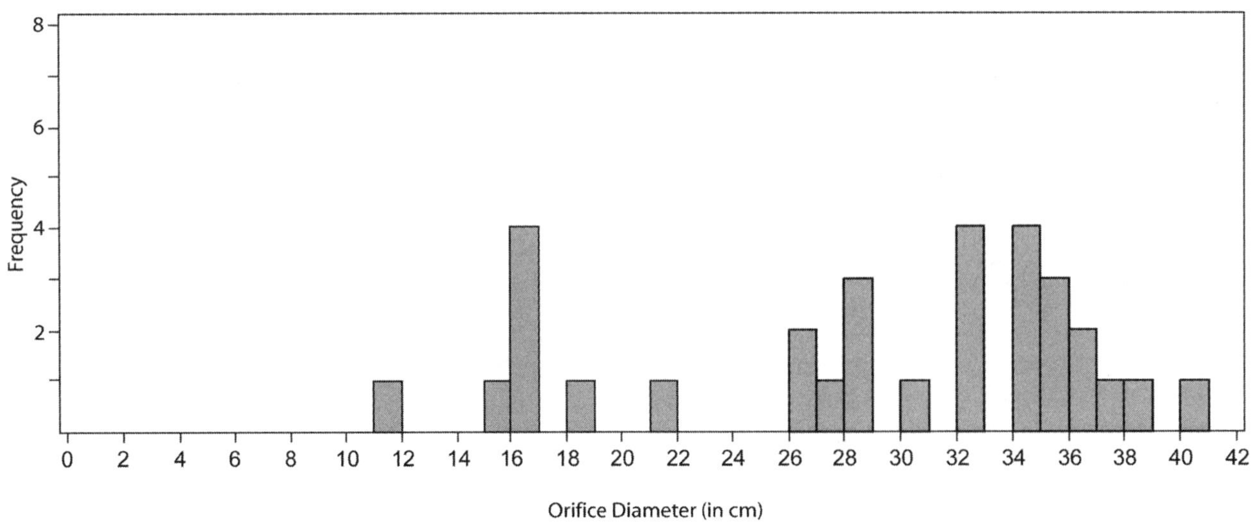

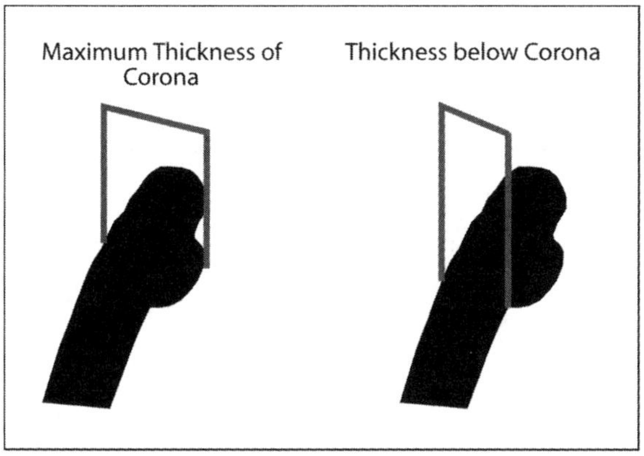

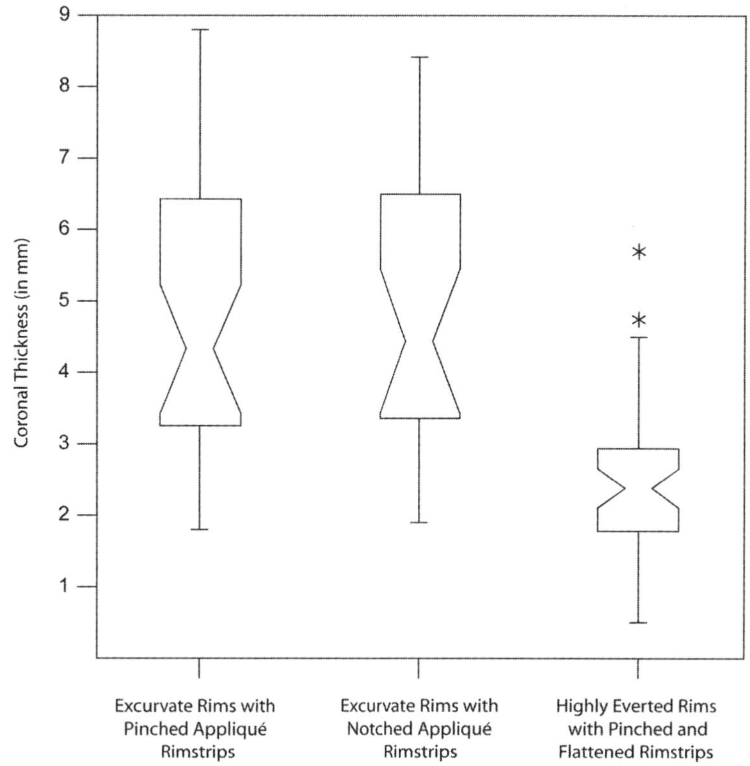

(*above*) Figure 7.15. Measuring coronal thickness.

(*right*) Figure 7.16. Boxplots comparing the distributions of coronal thickness among the three most common jar rim modes.

As with most Cherokee vessel assemblages, virtually all the large jars in the Townsend sample possess thickened rims achieved by the addition of a coil or strip of clay at or near the lip of the vessel (i.e., rimstrips). In past work, the term "pinched rim jar" has been applied broadly to many large jars found in Cherokee assemblages (Hally 1986b; Wilson and Rodning 2002). This naming practice, however, is confusing given that large jars in Cherokee assemblages typically exhibit a variety of different rimstrip elaborations, many of which are temporally diagnostic (e.g., Shumate et al. 2005; Riggs and Rodning 2002; Rodning 2004). Indeed, large jars in the Townsend sample can be divided into six groups based on distinct modes of rim elaboration (or lack thereof) (Table 7.6).

The three most common jar rim modes include excurvate rims with pinched appliqué rimstrips (Fig. 7.9), excurvate rims with stylus notched rimstrips (Fig. 7.10), and highly everted rims with pinched and flattened rimstrips (Fig. 7.11). Because of their pronounced thickness, the first two rim modes are commonly referred to as "filleted" rimstrips, while the latter is the rim mode for which the term "pinched rim" jar was originally coined (Smith et al. 1988; Hally 1986a). To empirically test this distinction between rim modes, I borrow a term coined by Riggs (Shumate et al. 2005:6.10) and employ a measure I call "coronal thickness." Coronal thickness is calculated by subtracting the thickness of the vessel just beneath the rimstrip corona from the maximum thickness of the rimstrip corona (Fig. 7.15). Comparing coronal thickness across the three main rim modes, there is a statistically significant difference between jars with excurvate rims and pinched appliqué rimstrips ($n = 31$, median = 4.33, mean = 4.81, SD = 2.00) and stylus notched appliqué rimstrips ($n = 23$, median = 4.40, mean = 4.98, SD = 1.86) on the one hand, and jars with highly everted rims and pinched and flattened rimstrips ($n = 55$, median = 2.19, mean = 2.07, SD = 1.40) on the other (Fig. 7.16). This result suggests that potters were intentionally choosing between three distinct styles of rim elaboration. Minority rim modes in the sample include 10 unmodified rims, a single "L-shaped" rim, and 3 "rolled" rims. A jar rim sherd with a single lug handle and another exhibiting a strap handle are also present in the sample (Fig. 7.13).

Exterior surface treatments do not exhibit much variability across the sample of large jars; however, the distribution of rim modes across the three pottery wares reveals some significant differences (Table 7.6). The three varieties of plain ware dominate the surface treatments of large jars, comprising over 82% of the assemblage. Among the gravel-tempered and grit-tempered wares, jars with highly everted rims and pinched and flattened rimstrips by far outnumber jars with pinched appliqué rimstrips and notched appliqué rimstrips. Conversely, in the shell-tempered ware group, jars with excurvate rims and pinched and notched appliqué rimstrips dominate, and jars with highly everted rims and pinched and flattened rimstrips are entirely absent.

Table 7.6. Exterior surface treatments and rim modes applied to large globular jars in the Townsend sample.

	Plain	Burnished	Coarse Plain	Indeterminate Stamped	Indeterminate Linear Stamped	Curvilinear Complicated Stamped	Cord-marked	Scraped	Eroded	Total
gravel-tempered jars										
excurvate rims with pinched appliqué rimstrips	18	0	4	0	1	0	0	0	0	23
excurvate rims with notched appliqué rimstrips	5	0	6	1	0	0	3	1	0	16
highly everted rims with pinched and flattened rimstrips	35	1	5	3	5	1	1	0	0	51
L-shaped rims	0	0	0	0	0	0	0	0	0	0
rolled rims	1	1	0	0	0	0	0	0	0	2
unmodified rims	5	0	0	0	1	0	1	1	0	8
shell-tempered jars										
excurvate rims with pinched appliqué rimstrips	5	0	0	0	0	0	0	0	1	6
excurvate rims with notched appliqué rimstrips	5	0	0	0	0	0	0	0	1	6
highly everted rims with pinched and flattened rimstrips	0	0	0	0	0	0	0	0	0	0
L-shaped rims	1	0	0	0	0	0	0	0	0	1
rolled rims	0	0	0	0	0	0	0	0	0	0
unmodified rims	0	0	0	0	0	0	0	0	0	0
grit-tempered jars										
excurvate rims with pinched appliqué rimstrips	2	0	0	0	0	0	0	0	0	2
excurvate rims with notched appliqué rimstrips	1	0	0	0	0	0	0	0	0	1
highly everted rims with pinched and flattened rimstrips	4	0	0	0	0	0	0	0	0	4
L-shaped rims	0	0	0	0	0	0	0	0	0	0
rolled rims	1	0	0	0	0	0	0	0	0	1
unmodified rims	1	0	0	0	1	0	0	0	0	2
total	*84*	*2*	*15*	*4*	*8*	*1*	*5*	*2*	*2*	*123*

Simple Bowls (Fig. 7.17). This vessel class is characterized by a hemispherical profile featuring a rounded base. This class includes vessels whose orifice diameter is also the maximum diameter of the vessel—vessels that lack shoulders. Only 2 rim sherds in the Townsend sample are large enough to obtain orifice diameter estimates, which are 22 cm and 24 cm. Both Hally (1986a:289) and King (1977:155) assign a serving function to simple bowls, pointing to the stability of this vessel form, the lack of evidence that it was used for cooking (i.e., exterior sooting and pitting), evidence of heavy use wear, and a large orifice diameter to depth ratio.

Of the 13 simple bowls in the Townsend sample, 11 were gravel tempered and 2 were shell tempered (Table 7.7). Ten of the 13 specimens were a form of plain ware, while surface treatments of the remaining 3 specimens included 1 indeterminate linear stamped, 1 complicated stamped, and 1 cordmarked. Stamping on these specimens covers the entire vessel. Although unmodified rims dominated the sample, 2 gravel-tempered specimens included pinched appliqué rimstrips and a single specimen of shell-tempered bowl had a notched appliqué rimstrip.

Table 7.7. Exterior surface treatments applied to simple bowls in the Townsend sample.

	Plain	Burnished	Coarse Plain	Indeterminate Linear Stamped	Complicated Stamped	Cordmarked	Total
gravel-tempered simple bowls	5	2	1	1	1	1	*11*
shell-tempered simple bowls	2	0	0	0	0	0	*2*
total	*7*	*2*	*1*	*1*	*1*	*1*	*13*

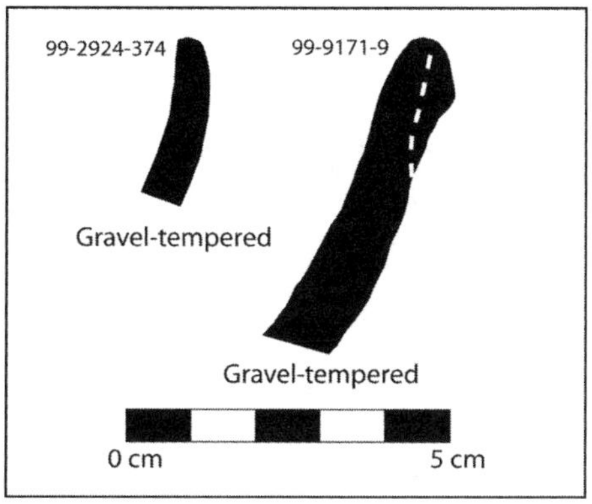

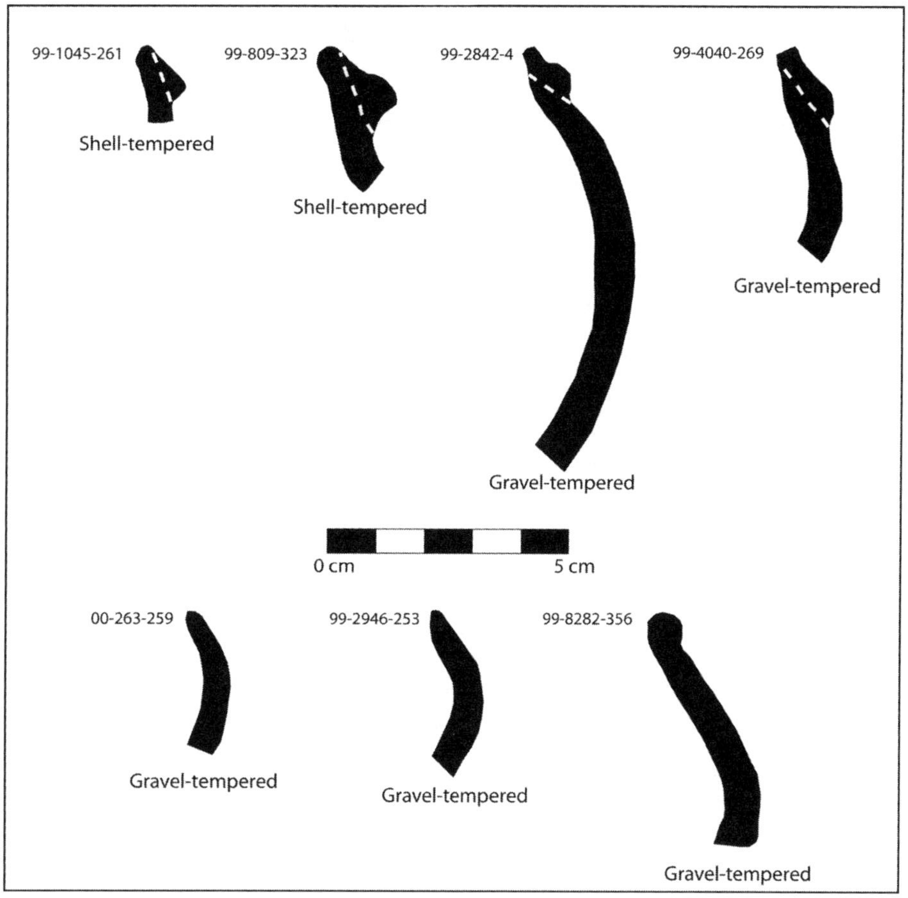

(*above*) Figure 7.17. Simple bowls.

(*right*) Figure 7.18. Restricted orifice bowls with folded rims (*top row*) and unmodified rims (*bottom row*).

Restricted Orifice Bowls (Figs. 7.18–7.20). Specimens belonging to this vessel class feature a hemispherical profile, yet as the name implies, they have inverted rather than vertical rims. Thus, unlike simple bowls, the maximum diameter of restricted rim bowls is located beneath the lip—it is a shouldered vessel. Restricted orifice bowls also differ in shape from cazuelas, another shouldered bowl form (see below), in that they lack sharply carinated shoulders. The range of orifice diameters among restricted orifice bowls in the Townsend sample (11 cm to 32 cm) is similar to that found by Wilson and Rodning (2002:32) for the same vessel class in the Coweeta Creek sample. Restricted rim bowls thus were made in a rather large range of sizes, but unlike globular jars, the sample size (n = 8) from Townsend is too small to distinguish any patterning indicative of size modes (Fig. 7.19). In their analysis of the Coweeta Creek assemblage, Wilson and Rodning (2002:32) assign a serving function to restricted orifice bowls based on their size, lack of sooting, and shape. In regard to shape, they argue that the restricted orifice would have allowed for easier movement of food contents with a lower risk of spillage than would a simple bowl form.

Table 7.8 presents a tabulation of rim modes and exterior surface treatments arranged by pottery ware. There are two major

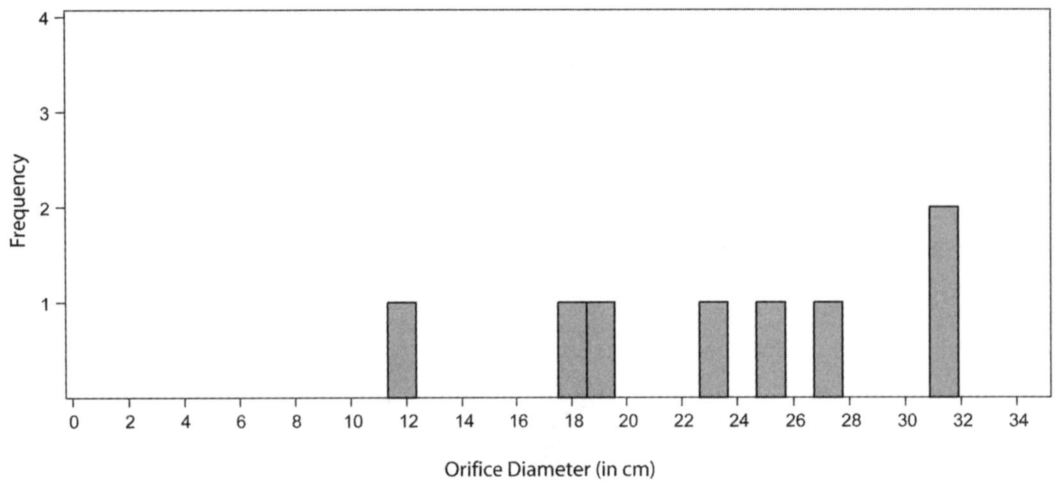

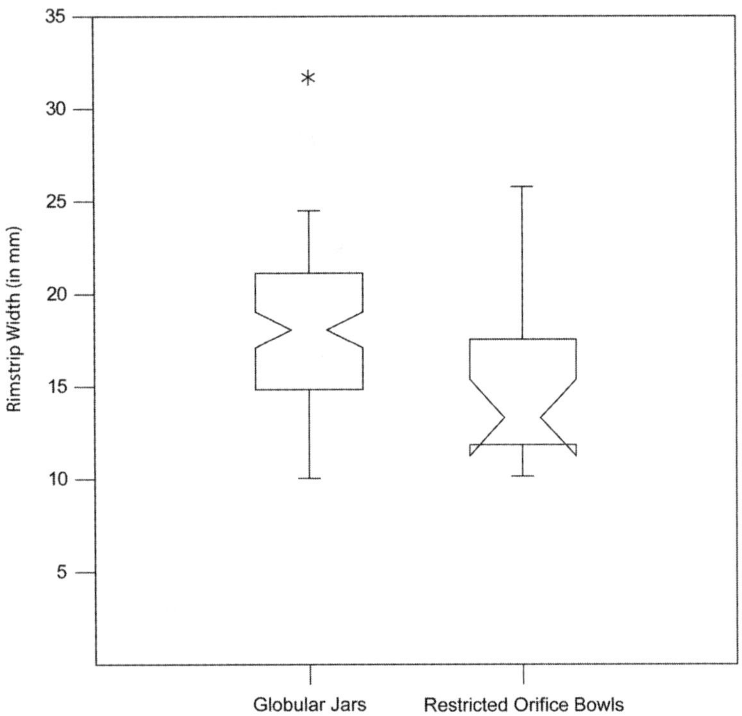

(*above left*) Figure 7.19. Histogram depicting the distribution of orifice diameter estimates among restricted orifice bowls.

(*left*) Figure 7.20. Boxplots comparing the distribution of rimstrip width between globular jars and restricted orifice bowls in the Townsend sample.

forms of restricted orifice bowl—those with thickened rims and those with unthickened (or unmodified) rims. The majority of restricted rim bowls in the Townsend sample possess thickened rims. The method used to thicken the rims of restricted rim bowls differs from jars in that most of the rimstrips appear to have been folded rather than applied as a single coil. Consequently, rimstrips on restricted orifice bowls tend to be narrower than those applied to globular jars as measured from the vessel lip to the bottom of the rimstrip (globular jars, n = 104, median = 18.08 mm; restricted orifice bowls, n = 19, median = 13.32 mm) (Fig. 7.20). Futhermore, while pinching and stylus notching are present, stylus punctating and smoothing are by far the most common forms of rimstrip embellishment occurring on restricted orifice bowls. The exterior surface treatments associated with this vessel class include plain, burnished, indeterminate stamped, indeterminate linear stamped, and cordmarked, with the first two treatments comprising over two-thirds of the sample. As with simple bowls, stamping and cordmarking is present across the entire surface of the vessel. Unfortunately, the small number of shell-tempered and grit-tempered specimens in the sample precludes the exploration of ware-based variability in rim mode or exterior surface treatment for this vessel class.

Table 7.8. Exterior surface treatments and rim modes applied to restricted orifice bowls in the Townsend sample.

	Plain	Burnished	Indeterminate Stamped	Indeterminate Linear Stamped	Cordmarked	Eroded	Total
gravel-tempered restricted orifice bowls							
folded and punctated rims	9	0	1	0	0	0	*10*
folded and smoothed rims	4	0	0	1	0	0	*5*
folded and pinched rims	3	0	0	0	1	0	*4*
folded and notched rims	2	0	0	0	0	0	*2*
indeterminate rims	0	0	1	0	1	1	*3*
unmodified rims	2	1	2	0	1	0	*6*
shell-tempered restricted orifice bowls							
folded and punctated rims	1	0	0	0	0	0	*1*
folded and smoothed rims	0	0	0	0	0	0	*0*
folded and pinched rims	0	0	0	0	0	0	*0*
folded and notched rims	1	0	0	0	0	0	*1*
indeterminate rims	0	0	0	0	0	0	*0*
unmodified rims	0	0	0	0	0	0	*0*
grit-tempered restricted orifice bowls							
folded and punctated rims	0	0	0	1	0	0	*1*
folded and smoothed rims	0	0	0	0	0	0	*0*
folded and pinched rims	0	0	0	0	0	0	*0*
folded and notched rims	0	0	0	0	0	0	*0*
indeterminate rims	0	0	0	0	0	0	*0*
unmodified rims	1	0	0	0	0	0	*1*
total	*23*	*1*	*4*	*2*	*3*	*1*	*34*

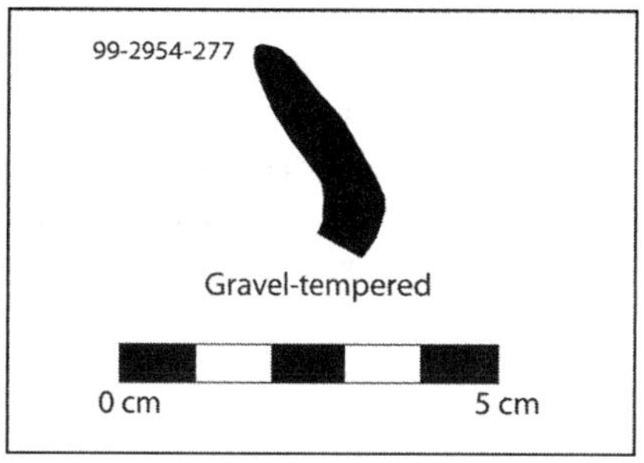

Figure 7.21. Cazuela.

Cazuelas (Fig. 7.21). Cazuelas, also known as carinated bowls, are vessels with inverted rims and sharply angled shoulders. Cazuelas possess either flat or round bases, although the latter form appears to be more common among historic period Cherokee assemblages. None of the rim sherds in the Townsend sample are large enough to provide a reliable estimate of orifice diameter. Wilson and Rodning (2002:33) report a size range of 9 cm to 30 cm for cazuelas in the Coweeta Creek sample, and it is likely that the Townsend cazuelas are similar in size to the other bowl forms. Shape, evidence of use wear, and the common presence of exterior sooting have led researchers to conclude that cazuelas were multipurpose vessels used in food preparation (i.e., mixing), cooking, and serving (Hally 1986a:288–89; King 1977:159; Shapiro 1984:707; Wilson and Rodning 2002:33).

Aside from their distinctive shape, cazuelas typically lack rim modification and evince incised decoration above the vessel shoulder (Shumate et al. 2005:6.11; Wilson and Rodning 2002:33). Rimstrips are usually absent from Overhill and Qualla series cazuelas, as they are in the Townsend sample; however, there are some known cazuela specimens, including 1 from the Townsend sample, that possess notched strips at the vessel shoulder (e.g., Egloff 1967:47; King 1977:159). All but 2 of the cazu-

Table 7.9. Exterior surface treatments applied to cazuelas in the Townsend sample.

	Incised (line-filled triangles)	**Incised** (nested half-squares)	**Incised** (lines and semicircles)	**Incised** (indeterminate motif)	**Plain**	**Total**
gravel-tempered cazuelas	4	1	0	9	2	*16*
shell-tempered cazuelas	0	0	0	0	0	*0*
grit-tempered cazuelas	0	0	1	0	0	*1*
total	*4*	*1*	*1*	*9*	*2*	*17*

Table 7.10. Decorative modes applied to rimstrip fragments in the Townsend sample.

	Pinched	**Notched**	**Pinched and Flattened**	**Smoothed**	**Indeterminate**	**Total**
gravel-tempered rimstrips	10	12	11	2	8	*43*
shell-tempered rimstrips	1	1	0	0	2	*4*
grit-tempered rimstrips	1	0	0	0	0	*1*
total	*12*	*13*	*11*	*2*	*10*	*48*

elas in the Townsend sample bear incised decorations between the vessel shoulder and lip (Table 7.9). Four of the specimens are decorated with line-filled triangle motifs, and single specimens bear nested half-square and lines and semicircles motifs. Most of the specimens bear one or two intersecting or parallel incised lines that are too incomplete to associate with a particular motif. In general, Qualla series cazuelas are complicated stamped beneath the vessel shoulders while Overhill series cazuelas are left plain. Only 1 of the Townsend cazuela sherds includes the area beneath the vessel shoulder and it is plain. Sixteen of the cazuelas in the Townsend sample are gravel-tempered and 1 is grit-tempered. The cazuela form is not represented among the shell-tempered ware.

Rimstrip Fragments. The pottery sample from Townsend contains 48 potsherds that represent fragments of rimstrips. These sherds cannot be identified as rims because they are missing the lip portion of the vessel. Table 7.10 presents a tabulation of these sherds arranged by pottery ware and rim mode. Most of these fragments are gravel-tempered, with pinched appliqué rimstrips, notched appliqué rimstrips, and pinched and flattened rimstrips occurring in roughly equal frequencies.

Summary

Taken together, the analyses presented above suggest that Overhill pottery assemblages dating to the English Contact period (ca. A.D. 1670–1740) were much more heterogeneous than those associated with later eighteenth-century contexts in the Little Tennessee River Valley. Indeed, differences in pottery ware, exterior surface treatment, and vessel form strongly indicate that the community of potters living at Townsend practiced three distinct styles of potting—two of which are recognized by archaeologists as belonging to the Overhill and Qualla pottery series. The third and most prominent potting style in the community appears to have been a geographically localized phenomenon that has only now been formally described.

Differences in four paste attributes (temper material, temper particle size, density of temper particles, and vessel wall thickness) indicate that the Cherokee households at Townsend were making pottery vessels of three different wares, each of which was intentionally created through the manipulation of paste composition. The most ubiquitous ware, comprising approximately 85% of the sample, was tempered with water-worn gravel and was by far the thickest and coarsest. This was most definitely a locally made ware. Another thinner, but equally coarse ware tempered with crushed shell was used by Townsend households. While much less common, it was nevertheless present in sufficient proportions (10%) to suggest that it was a local product. The least ubiquitous ware found at Townsend, comprising roughly 5% of the assemblage, was very similar in thickness and paste composition to Qualla series pottery. While not conclusive, the number of grit-tempered sherds ($n = 245$) is not out of line with the argument that this ware was produced locally, especially considering the high proportion of plain grit-tempered sherds in the Townsend sample compared with Qualla series samples from contemporaneous sites in North Carolina and South Carolina (see inter-site comparisons below).

Distinctions among the three pottery styles were also expressed as differences in surface treatment and vessel form. Virtually all the shell-tempered ware was plain surfaced, while the majority of both gravel-tempered and grit-tempered wares were paddle stamped. These latter two wares were also distinguished by the popularity of plain and cordmarked sherds among the gravel-tempered ware and the relatively high proportions of linear stamped and complicated stamped sherds among the grit-tempered ware. Ware-based variability in vessel form followed a similar pattern. Whereas the various vessel forms comprising the gravel-tempered and grit-tempered MNV assemblages were present in roughly similar proportions, jars with everted rims and pinched and flattened rimstrips and cazuelas were completely absent from the shell-tempered MNV assemblage.

Variability among Townsend Household Pottery Assemblages

Thus far, I believe I have demonstrated the existence of three distinct potting styles based on differences in pottery ware, exterior surface treatment, and vessel form. The last piece of evidence I marshal to support my argument involves the spatial distribution of these potting styles among Townsend households. Are the three potting styles present among each of the Townsend household pottery assemblages in equal proportions? If not, how do differences in the relative stylistic composition of household pottery assemblages spatially "map" onto the community? I answer these questions through quantitative comparisons of household pottery assemblages. First, I conduct a correspondence analysis in order to identify consistent associations of tempering agents and exterior surface treatments among household assemblages. Then, I compare the composition of household vessel assemblages using MNV.

As discussed in earlier chapters, the six Cherokee households identified during the Townsend excavations are widely spaced, making the association of archaeological contexts with particular households relatively clear-cut (see Fig. 5.1). Consequently, in the Townsend pottery sample, 4187 out of 4343 body sherds can be associated with a particular household. Table 7.11 presents the relative composition of each household pottery assemblage in regard to pottery ware and exterior surface treatment (exterior surface treatments that occurred only in very minor amounts are not included). A cursory glance at Table 7.11 reveals that the distribution of the three pottery wares among the six Townsend households is not uniform. Quite to the contrary, Household 1 and Household 2 contain much higher percentages of the shell-tempered ware than the other Townsend households. Moreover, the pottery assemblages from Households 3, 4, and 5 are all similarly dominated by the gravel-tempered ware, while the assemblage associated with Household 6 contains a greater relative amount of the grit-tempered ware.

Inspecting Table 7.11, it is difficult to discern any household-level patterning in the distribution of exterior surface treatments—there are simply too many variables. Fortunately, there are statistical methods that are specifically designed for use with such multivariate datasets. Correspondence analysis (CA) is one such method that excels at reducing the dimensionality of data matrices (such as Table 7.11) by measuring the associations among both cases (in this case, household pottery assemblages) and variables (in this case, exterior surface treatments and pottery ware) simultaneously (see Baxter 1994; Shennan 1997).

This seriation method, correspondence analysis (see Baxter 1994; Shennan 1997), is a powerful multivariate statistical technique that has been used widely for seriating artifact assemblages in European archaeology (e.g., Bech 1988; Madsen 1988). One rarely sees correspondence analysis, however, in the archaeological literature of North America (see Duff 1996 for a notable exception). The relative obscurity of correspondence analysis is curious given that (1) the technique is based on straightforward and fundamental statistical logic—essentially the same logic that underlies the chi-square test; (2) unlike other multivariate techniques, it requires no assumptions of the data and works directly on untransformed artifact frequencies (counts); and (3) like the chi-square test, it is resistant to differences in sample sizes.

One of the most useful results of this technique is a biplot that depicts the relative degree of association of household pottery assemblages, as well as that of the different combinations of pottery ware and exterior surface treatments (Fig. 7.22). In interpreting the biplot, one can infer: (1) that the pottery types located near one another in the biplot typically occur together in the same contexts; (2) that household assemblages (e.g., Household 1, Household 2) located near one another have similar pottery assemblages (and vice versa); and (3) that the pottery types located near each household assemblage in the biplot represent the dominant types in each of those assemblages. The distribution presented in the biplot (Fig. 7.22) accounts for 85.9% of variability in the data matrix, meaning that correspondence analysis is able to accurately portray the majority of the variability in the original twelve dimension data matrix (Table 7.11) using just two dimensions (the *x* and *y* axes in Fig. 7.22).

The biplot resulting from this correspondence analysis not only reveals the previously identified pattern in the distribution of the three pottery wares, but it also identifies significant patterning in the household-level distributions of surface treatments (Fig. 7.22). Clustering of the locations of the household-level pottery assemblages in the biplot (symbolized by open diamond symbols) suggests that the assemblages associated with Household 1 and Household 2 are similar and those associated with Household 4, Household 5, and Household 6 are similar. Furthermore, the locations of these clusters at opposite ends of the *x* axis indicate a large degree of difference between these pottery assemblages. The assemblage associated with Household 3 is different from both of these clusters. Considering the distributions of the pottery types, it is clear that the assemblages associated with Household 1 and Household 2 are dominated by shell-tempering and plain, burnished, and scraped exterior surface treatments. The assemblages associated with Households 4, 5, and, 6 are significantly

Table 7.11. Relative frequencies of pottery wares and exterior surface treatments among the six Cherokee household assemblages at Townsend.

	Plain		Burnished		Coarse Plain		Indeterminate Stamped		Indeterminate Linear Stamped		Complicated Stamped		Curvilinear Complicated Stamped		Simple Stamped		Cordmarked		Scraped		Incised		Brushed		Total	
	n	%	*n*	%	*n*	%	*n*	%	*n*	%	*n*	%	*n*	%	*n*	%	*n*	%	*n*	%	*n*	%	*n*	%	*n*	%
House 1																										
gravel	139	31	14	3	74	16	21	5	15	3	0	0	4	<1	0	0	14	3	5	1	0	0	0	0	*286*	*63*
shell	113	25	3	<1	0	0	0	0	0	0	0	0	0	0	0	0	0	0	32	7	0	0	0	0	*148*	*32*
grit	5	1	3	<1	4	<1	4	<1	5	1	0	0	0	0	0	0	0	0	0	0	0	0	0	0	*21*	*5*
total	*257*	*56*	*20*	*4*	*78*	*17*	*25*	*5*	*20*	*4*	*0*	*0*	*4*	*<1*	*0*	*0*	*14*	*3*	*37*	*8*	*0*	*0*	*0*	*0*	*455*	*100*
House 2																										
gravel	46	13	2	<1	52	15	20	6	18	5	2	<1	1	<1	2	<1	3	<1	9	3	0	0	3	<1	*158*	*45*
shell	166	47	2	<1	0	0	0	0	0	0	0	0	0	0	0	0	0	0	15	4	0	0	0	0	*183*	*52*
grit	1	<1	0	0	0	0	3	<1	1	<1	0	0	1	<1	0	0	1	<1	2	<1	0	0	0	0	*9*	*3*
total	*213*	*61*	*4*	*1*	*52*	*15*	*23*	*7*	*19*	*5*	*2*	*<1*	*2*	*<1*	*2*	*<1*	*4*	*1*	*26*	*7*	*0*	*0*	*3*	*<1*	*350*	*100*
House 3																										
gravel	206	43	1	<1	92	19	22	4	39	8	1	<1	14	3	2	<1	39	8	8	2	2	<1	1	<1	*427*	*90*
shell	25	5	0	0	0	0	0	0	0	0	0	0	0	0	0	0	0	0	1	<1	0	0	0	0	*26*	*5*
grit	17	4	4	<1	1	<1	1	<1	0	0	0	0	1	<1	0	0	0	0	0	0	0	0	0	0	*24*	*5*
total	*248*	*52*	*5*	*1*	*93*	*20*	*23*	*5*	*39*	*8*	*1*	*<1*	*15*	*3*	*2*	*<1*	*39*	*8*	*9*	*2*	*2*	*<1*	*1*	*<1*	*477*	*100*
House 4																										
gravel	402	18	9	<1	209	9	397	18	556	25	41	2	84	4	21	<1	297	13	29	1	6	<1	6	<1	*2057*	*92*
shell	39	2	0	0	0	0	0	0	0	0	0	0	0	0	0	0	0	0	2	<1	0	0	0	0	*41*	*2*
grit	26	1	1	<1	0	0	18	<1	70	3	7	<1	16	<1	0	0	2	<1	1	<1	0	0	0	0	*141*	*6*
total	*467*	*21*	*10*	*<1*	*209*	*9*	*415*	*19*	*626*	*28*	*48*	*2*	*100*	*4*	*21*	*<1*	*299*	*13*	*32*	*1*	*6*	*<1*	*6*	*<1*	*2239*	*100*
House 5																										
gravel	20	18	0	0	12	11	9	8	20	18	0	0	2	2	0	0	36	32	1	<1	3	3	0	0	*103*	*92*
shell	10	7	0	0	0	0	0	0	0	0	0	0	0	0	0	0	0	0	0	0	0	0	0	0	*10*	*7*
grit	0	0	0	0	0	0	0	0	0	0	1	<1	0	0	0	0	0	0	0	0	0	0	0	0	*1*	*<1*
total	*30*	*25*	*0*	*0*	*12*	*11*	*9*	*8*	*20*	*18*	*1*	*<1*	*2*	*2*	*0*	*0*	*36*	*32*	*1*	*<1*	*3*	*3*	*0*	*0*	*114*	*100*
House 6																										
gravel	25	17	0	0	1	<1	21	14	44	30	2	1	21	14	1	<1	8	5	1	<1	0	0	0	0	*124*	*85*
shell	1	<1	0	0	0	0	0	0	0	0	0	0	0	0	0	0	0	0	1	<1	0	0	0	0	*2*	*1*
grit	1	<1	0	0	0	0	2	1	13	9	0	0	5	3	0	0	0	0	0	0	0	0	0	0	*21*	*14*
total	*27*	*18*	*0*	*0*	*1*	*<1*	*23*	*15*	*57*	*39*	*2*	*1*	*26*	*17*	*1*	*<1*	*8*	*5*	*2*	*1*	*0*	*0*	*0*	*0*	*147*	*100*

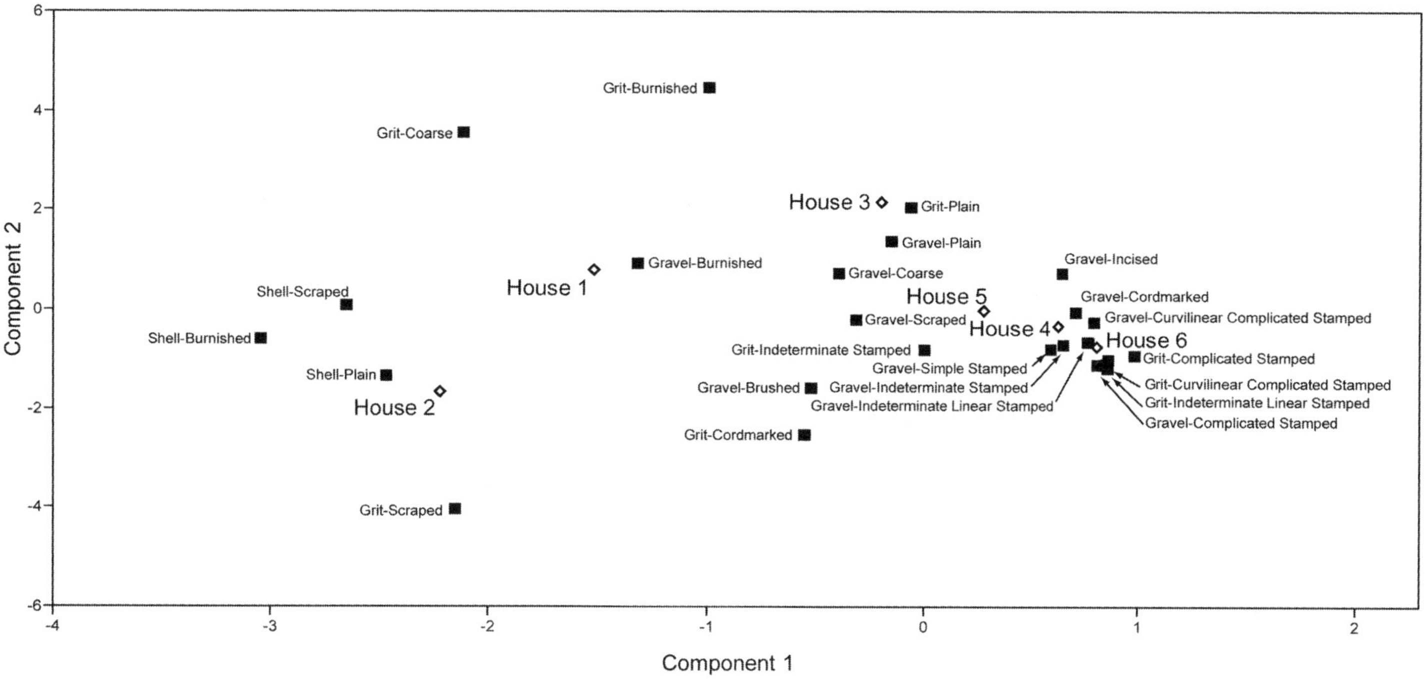

Figure 7.22. Biplot depicting the results of the correspondence analysis conducted on household pottery assemblages at Townsend. Reproduced with permission from *Pox, Empire, Shackles, and Hides* (Marcoux 2010: Fig. 4.11), ©University of Alabama Press.

different, being composed primarily of gravel-tempered and grit-tempered paddle stamped wares. The pottery assemblage associated with Household 3 differs from the other two clusters in its lack of shell-tempered ware and the predominance of plain, coarse plain, and burnished surface treatments. Also, the distribution of these three different pottery assemblage clusters is replicated in the actual spatial distribution of the Townsend households. Shell-tempered plain wares are concentrated in the two westernmost households while the pottery assemblages associated with the eastern households are dominated by gravel-tempered and grit-tempered paddle stamped pottery.[4]

The relative proportions of functional classes among household vessel assemblages are surprisingly similar considering the great variability in pottery ware and external surface treatment evinced by Townsend households. Ignoring differences in rim modes among globular jars, the vessel assemblages (measured using MNV) associated with Households 1, 2, 3, and 4 contain very similar proportions of globular jars, restricted orifice bowls, and simple bowls (Fig. 7.23). The vessel assemblages associated with Households 5 and 6 differ dramatically, but likely reflect bias because the former assemblage is dominated by sherds from a single pit feature and the latter assemblage only contains 2 unique vessel rims. When differences in rim modes among globular jars are considered, the vessel assemblage associated with Household 4 stands out because it includes a much higher proportion of jars with highly everted rims and pinched and flattened rimstrips (Table 7.12). In fact, this household includes 48 of the 52 instances of this rim mode in the Townsend sample. This difference is further emphasized by the significant presence of cazuelas in the Household 4 assemblage and their absence in non-biased assemblages associated with the other households (i.e., Households 1–3). It is possible that the differences in the Household 4 assemblage are associated with temporal differences in occupation given that the pinched and flattened jar rim mode and cazuelas are more typical of an earlier Middle Qualla phase assemblage (see above); however, the differences could equally be due to the much larger sample size associated with Household 4.

To summarize, the comparisons of household pottery assemblages identified two important patterns: (1) there was considerable stylistic variability among the potting practices of Townsend households—expressed as differences in pottery ware and in exterior surface treatments applied to vessels and manifested spatially among households in the community; and (2) in spite of these clear stylistic differences, household vessel assemblages were composed of similar proportions of functional vessel classes. Together, these patterns support the argument that household-level differences in pottery assemblages more than

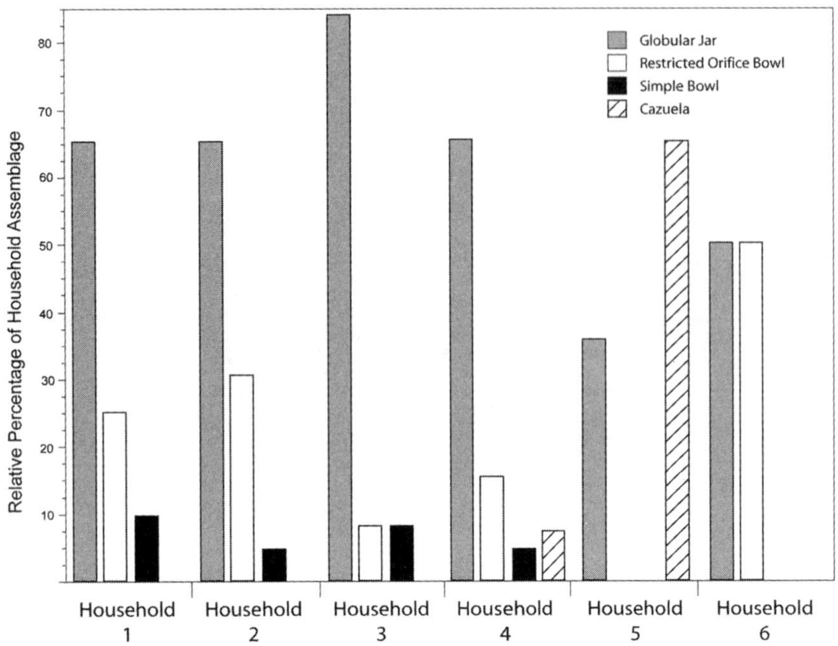

Figure 7.23. Comparison of vessel assemblages among Townsend households.

Table 7.12. Composition of household vessel assemblages (measured in MNV) at Townsend.

	Large Jars w/ Pinched Appliqué Rimstrips		Large Jars w/ Notched Appliqué Rimstrips		Large Jars w/ Pinched and Flattened Rimstrips		Other Large Jars		Restricted Orifice Bowls		Simple Bowls		Cazuelas		Total	
	n	%	*n*	%	*n*	%	*n*	%	*n*	%	*n*	%	*n*	%	*n*	%
Household 1	4	17	10	44	0	0	2	4	6	26	2	9	0	0	*24*	*100*
Household 2	4	20	8	40	1	5	0	0	6	30	1	5	0	0	*20*	*100*
Household 3	3	25	3	25	1	8	3	25	1	8	1	8	0	0	*12*	*100*
Household 4	19	17	1	<1	48	43	6	5	18	16	6	5	8	7	*106*	*95*[a]
Household 5	1	9	0	0	2	18	1	9	0	0	0	0	7	64	*11*	*100*
Household 6	0	0	0	0	0	0	1	50	1	50	0	0	0	0	*2*	*100*

[a]This total is less than 100% because the Household 4 vessel assemblage also includes six small jars—a vessel class that was not present in any other household context and thus was not included in this tally.

likely resulted from differences in the potting traditions that were being practiced by each household—traditions that were learned and passed on.

Contextualizing Townsend Pottery

To better locate the variability in the Townsend pottery sample within the larger geographic and temporal context of the English Contact period (ca. A.D. 1670–1740), it would be very profitable to make comparisons to pottery samples from a number of Cherokee contexts at other sites. The ideal collection of pottery samples for this comparison would represent sites from all five Cherokee settlement divisions (namely, Overhill, Middle, Valley, Out town, and Lower) and would include occupations dating throughout the period. As part of the Townsend project, I endeavored to undertake such a comparison by searching out published data and by conducting analyses on extant pottery collections. This research included inspecting a number of previously unanalyzed collections (including those from the Ocoee site, the Nacoochee mound, the Notla mound, and the Peachtree mound) as well as reanalyzing selected portions of the collections from the Tuckaseegee site (Keel 1976) and the Coweeta

Creek site (Rodning 2004). This study also benefited from data resulting from previous research with pottery collections from the Alarka farmstead (Schumate et al. 2005) and the Chattooga site. Unfortunately, I found that some of the collections had suffered extensively from the excavation and curation methods of the 1930s and 1940s. The collections from the Ocoee site, the Nacoochee mound, the Notla mound, and the Peachtree site in particular were severely "high-graded" (i.e., were highly biased toward large and decorated body sherds and rim sherds) and lacked detailed provenience information. Consequently, these collections had very limited value to the ceramic comparison and were only used to identify the *presence* of diagnostic pottery traits associated with particular chronological phases.

Comparisons to Other Overhill Pottery Samples

In this section, I compare the pottery data from Townsend with data from other Overhill Cherokee sites. Unfortunately, I could not identify a comparable dataset derived from a reliably dated English Contact period Overhill context. The closest candidate is the Ocoee site, which is located at the juncture of Ocoee and Hiwassee Rivers far to the south of the Townsend project area. Based on diagnostic European artifacts, the site—which was excavated in 1938 and reported in the Chickamauga Basin report (Lewis et al. 1995:562–88)—likely represents the remains of the late seventeenth- and early eighteenth-century Overhill Cherokee town of Amoyee. The site was excavated in two separate units located over 300 m apart. According to Lewis and colleagues (1995:565–66), the unit closest to the river (2Pk1) contained the remains of a stockaded Cherokee village, which they mistakenly identified as the late eighteenth-century village of Ocoee. This unit included ten burials interred with late seventeenth- and early eighteenth-century trade goods while the other excavation unit (1Pk1) contained occupations dated to the prehistoric Candy Creek and Mouse Creek phases. In their site report, Lewis and colleagues (1995: Table 30.4) combined the frequencies of potsherds from both excavation units, which is unfortunate as the plain shell-tempered Mouse Creek phase body sherds are indistinguishable from later Overhill body sherds.

Not knowing the relative frequency of shell-tempered plain potsherds associated with the Cherokee occupation of the site precludes a quantitative comparison to the Townsend sample. An admittedly rough impression of the Cherokee pottery assemblage at Ocoee, however, can still be gleaned from published data and from my recent inspection of collections housed at the McClung Museum at the University of Tennessee. Based on the frequency data presented by Lewis and colleagues (1995: Table 30.4), it appears that the Ocoee pottery sample was dominated by shell-tempered plain ware. Only 2 shell-tempered complicated stamped sherds were noted along with 30 rock-tempered complicated stamped sherds. My inspection of the surviving pottery collection from the site corroborates these proportions although I was only able to locate rim sherds and a small portion of the body sherd sample that resided in the museum's 1930s vintage type collection. I recorded 34 rim sherds from Unit 2Pk1 at the Ocoee site, 33 of which were shell-tempered and 1 of which was gravel-tempered like those from Townsend. I also identified 4 body sherds in the type collection that were grit-tempered and fit the description of Qualla series pottery. The shell-tempered sherds had surface treatments consisting of 32 plain sherds and 2 incised sherds (1 with lines and semicircles and 1 bearing parallel diagonal lines), the gravel-tempered sherd was plain, and the 4 grit-tempered sherds were curvilinear complicated stamped with indeterminate motifs. In regard to vessel forms, the Ocoee sample included 21 shell-tempered globular jars, 3 with pinched appliqué rimstrips and 18 with notched appliqué rimstrips; a single gravel-tempered globular jar with a notched appliqué rimstrip; 2 shell-tempered simple bowls both with notched appliqué rimstrips; and 3 shell-tempered restricted orifice bowls, 1 with a folded and punctated rim and 1 with a folded and notched rim (Table 7.13).

A cursory comparison of this sample with the Townsend sample reveals a number of things. First, the Ocoee site sample contains a much higher proportion of shell-tempered sherds than the Townsend sample; second, the Ocoee sample has a much higher proportion of plain ware than the Townsend sample; third, Ocoee vessel forms are by and large very similar to those found at Townsend (Fig. 7.24); and fourth, the absence of two vessel classes in the Ocoee sample (i.e., globular jars with highly everted rims and pinched and flattened rimstrips and cazuelas) is interesting in that these same vessel forms are missing in the shell-tempered ware found at Townsend. These patterns suggest that the potters of at least one Cherokee community were practicing a potting tradition centered around shell-tempered plain ware during the late seventeenth and early eighteenth century. Furthermore, this potting style appears to be related to the one practiced by some of the potters living at Townsend—especially Households 1 and 2.

All the other well-documented Overhill Cherokee pottery collections recovered from professional excavations are associated with contexts dating from the middle eighteenth century to the early nineteenth century—at least 50 years later than the estimated Overhill Cherokee occupation at Townsend. While these collections do little to improve our understanding of Overhill Cherokee potting traditions during the English Contact period, they are nevertheless important because they provide a diachronic dimension to the study of Overhill pottery. Comparing these collections to the Townsend sample, one can identify changes that occurred in Overhill potting practices between the time when Townsend was occupied (ca. 1650–1720) and later in the eighteenth century. In making this comparison, I consult published data associated with excavations at the Chota-Tanasee site (ca. A.D. 1700–1820) (Bates 1986:289–305), the Tomotley site (ca. A.D. 1750–1776) (Baden 1983:37–62), and the Mialoquo site (ca. A.D. 1760–1780) (Russ and Chapman 1983:69–83). I attempt to ameliorate as much as possible the differences in the classificatory schema used by myself and the other authors by limiting the comparison to the most ubiquitous exterior surface treatments found in the samples and by not including residual categories such as my "indeterminate linear stamped."

Table 7.13. Minimum number of vessel (MNV) counts in the Ocoee study sample.

Vessel Class	Exterior Surface Treatment	*n*
shell-tempered globular jars		
excurvate rims with pinched appliqué rimstrips	plain	3
excurvate rims with notched appliqué rimstrips	plain	18
gravel-tempered globular jars		
excurvate rims with notched appliqué rimstrips	plain	1
shell-tempered simple bowls		
notched appliqué rimstrips	plain	2
shell-tempered restricted orifice bowls		
folded and punctated rims	plain	1
folded and notched rims	incised (parallel diagonal lines)	1
unmodified rims	incised (lines and semicircles)	1
indeterminate	plain	7

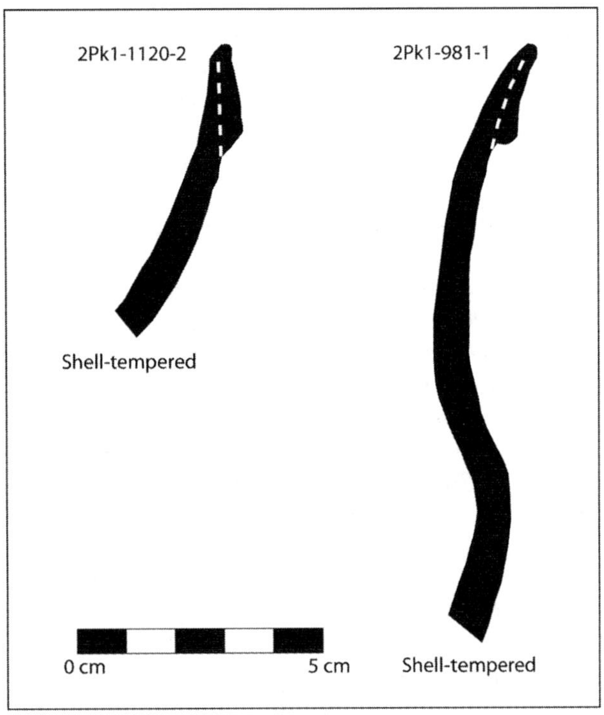

Figure 7.24. Simple bowl with a notched appliqué rimstrip (*left*) and globular jar with a notched appliqué rimstrip (*right*) from the Ocoee site.

This gross comparison of site-wide samples shows that Townsend pottery differs significantly from later eighteenth-century Overhill samples in regard to pottery ware and exterior surface treatments (Table 7.14). In the later Overhill samples, shell-tempered ware is by far the most common ware, making up 99% of the Chota-Tanasee sample, 98% of the Tomotley sample, and 81% of the Mialoquo sample. Unlike these samples, shell-tempered ware is a minority in the Townsend sample, comprising only 19% of the site sample, while gravel- and grit-tempered wares (combined and designated in Table 7.14 as "rock-tempered" wares) make up the remaining 81% of the sample. All the Overhill samples appear more similar when the relative frequencies of exterior surface treatments are considered. In all the samples, the majority of sherds have plain surfaces; however, plain sherds respectively comprise 97% and 86% of the Chota-Tanasee and Tomotley samples while totaling 68% and 72% of the samples from Townsend and Mialoquo. Popular minority surface treatments in the Tomotley and Mialoquo samples include check stamping and rectilinear complicated stamping, while cordmarking and curvilinear complicated stamping are more common in the Townsend sample. Thus, while the abundance of plain surfaced pottery in the Townsend sample is similar to that found in later Overhill contexts, the predominance of rock-tempered wares and much higher frequencies of cordmarking and paddle stamped surface treatments in the Townsend sample are strikingly different from the much more homogeneous Overhill samples from contexts dating to the later half of the eighteenth century.

Comparisons to Other Cherokee Pottery Samples

The differences that set the Townsend pottery sample apart from those associated with other Overhill Cherokee sites beg for comparisons to pottery samples recovered from Cherokee sites located further afield (i.e., Middle towns and Lower towns). The Townsend project afforded me the opportunity to compare a number of commensurate Cherokee pottery samples using a single analytical schema (the hierarchical classification system described above). Pottery samples used in this comparison include those from each of the six Townsend households as well as samples recovered from the following contexts: (1) a trash deposit located between the floor and the collapsed walls of a catastrophically burned winter house at the Tuckaseegee site (Keel 1976); (2) a large refuse filled pit (Feature 72) at the Coweeta Creek site (Rodning 2004); (3) all of the archaeological features and excavation units associated with the Alarka

Table 7.14. Frequency comparison of temper groups and major surface treatments including Townsend and later eighteenth-century Cherokee sites.

	Plain		Check Stamped		Simple Stamped		Curvilinear Complicated Stamped		Rectilinear Complicated Stamped		Incised		Cordmarked		Total	
	n	%	*n*	%	*n*	%	*n*	%	*n*	%	*n*	%	*n*	%	*n*	%
Townsend																
shell-tempered	360	19	0	0	0	0	0	0	0	0	0	0	1	<1	*361*	*19*
rock-tempered	936	49	2	<1	26	1	159	8	1	<1	12	<1	410	21	*1546*	*81*
total	*1296*	*68*	*2*	*<1*	*26*	*1*	*159*	*8*	*1*	*<1*	*12*	*<1*	*411*	*22*	*1907*	*100*
Chota-Tanasee																
shell-tempered	135,512	97	830	<1	129	<1	73	<1	242	<1	462	<1	254	<1	*137,502*	*99*
rock-tempered	1138	<1	177	<1	177	<1	10	<1	72	<1	107	<1	107	<1	*1788*	*1*
total	*136,650*	*97*	*1007*	*<1*	*306*	*<1*	*83*	*<1*	*314*	*<1*	*569*	*<1*	*361*	*<1*	*139,290*	*100*
Tomotley																
shell-tempered	9072	86	659	6	3	<1	26	<1	511	5	5	<1	14	<1	*10,290*	*98*
rock-tempered	50	<1	178	1	0	0	0	0	4	<1	0	0	9	<1	*241*	*2*
total	*9122*	*86*	*837*	*7*	*3*	*<1*	*26*	*<1*	*515*	*5*	*5*	*<1*	*23*	*<1*	*10,531*	*100*
Mialoquo																
shell-tempered	2750	59	659	16	40	<1	206	4	119	2	0	0	3	<1	*3777*	*81*
rock-tempered	618	13	162	3	8	<1	10	<1	106	2	0	0	0	0	*904*	*19*
total	*3368*	*72*	*821*	*19*	*48*	*1*	*216*	*4*	*225*	*4*	*0*	*0*	*3*	*<1*	*4681*	*100*

farmstead (Shumate et al. 2005); and (4) a trash deposit located around the central hearth of a winter house at the Chattooga site.[5] These contexts were chosen for quantitative comparison to the household pottery assemblages at Townsend because the samples drawn from them represent the pottery use and discard practices of single households over relatively brief periods of time (certainly less than a decade) spanning the English Contact period (ca. A.D. 1670–1740). This set of comparisons is in the same vein as those presented above and focuses primarily on pottery ware, surface treatment and vessel form.

Comparing pottery ware among the various samples, one sees a similar pattern of contrast to that seen in the comparison of pottery samples from Townsend and Ocoee. There is a sharp contrast between the diversity of pottery wares found in Townsend household assemblages, on the one hand, and a single grit-tempered pottery ware present in the assemblages from the other sites. Indeed, with the exception of a single shell-tempered body sherd from the Alarka site (Shumate et al. 2005:6.4), the pottery ware of all potsherds in the comparative assemblages conforms to the definition of the Qualla series (Egloff 1967; Hally 1986a, 1994; Keel 1976; Riggs and Rodning 2002; Rodning 2004; Ward and Davis 1999; Wilson and Rodning 2002).

Clear patterning emerges when variability in relative frequencies of surface treatments is considered—patterning that reflects both regional and temporal differences among the samples. Like the household-level analysis of Townsend pottery samples, the comparison of frequency data is greatly aided by correspondence analysis. Table 7.15 provides the frequency data for various surface treatments included in the correspondence analysis.[6] The results of the correspondence analysis, depicted graphically as a biplot (Fig. 7.25), indicate that the pottery samples are distributed in four discrete clusters. One cluster, which includes the samples from Townsend Households 1, 2, and 3, is dominated by plain and coarse plain surface treatments. The second cluster, containing pottery samples from Townsend Households 4, 5, and 6, is defined by lesser amounts of plain and coarse plain sherds and greater numbers of cordmarked and paddle stamped sherds. The third cluster includes the samples from the Tuckaseegee and Alarka sites, dominated by curvilinear complicated stamped pottery, and containing very little plain or coarse plain wares (less than ten percent). The fourth cluster includes pottery samples from the Coweeta Creek and Chattooga sites. These samples include plain, coarse plain, and indeterminate linear stamped sherds in similar proportions to the Tuckaseegee and

Table 7.15. Frequency comparison of major surface treatments including the Townsend household pottery assemblages and those of other selected Cherokee sites.

	Plain		Coarse Plain		Indeterminate Linear Stamped		Check Stamped		Curvilinear Complicated Stamped		Rectilinear Complicated Stamped		Cord-marked		Incised		Total	
	n	%	*n*	%	*n*	%	*n*	%	*n*	%	*n*	%	*n*	%	*n*	%	*n*	%
Townsend-1	262	64	79	19	45	11	2	<1	4	1	0	0	15	4	0	0	*407*	*100*
Townsend-2	209	68	51	17	40	13	0	0	2	<1	0	0	4	1	0	0	*306*	*100*
Townsend-3	248	54	93	20	63	14	0	0	15	3	0	0	39	9	2	<1	*460*	*100*
Townsend-4	468	22	209	10	1094	50	0	0	100	4	1	<1	300	13	7	<1	*2179*	*100*
Townsend-5	30	26	12	10	30	27	0	0	2	2	0	0	36	32	3	3	*113*	*100*
Townsend-6	28	21	10	8	62	46	0	0	26	19	0	0	8	6	0	0	*134*	*100*
Tuckaseegee	35	5	2	<1	318	49	18	3	223	35	32	5	19	3	0	0	*647*	*100*
Coweeta Creek	34	9	8	2	194	48	8	2	50	13	111	28	4	1	0	0	*409*	*100*
Alarka	58	7	1	<1	438	55	1	<1	274	35	8	1	6	<1	7	<1	*793*	*100*
Chattooga	0	0	0	0	32	36	0	0	26	29	30	33	2	2	0	0	*90*	*100*

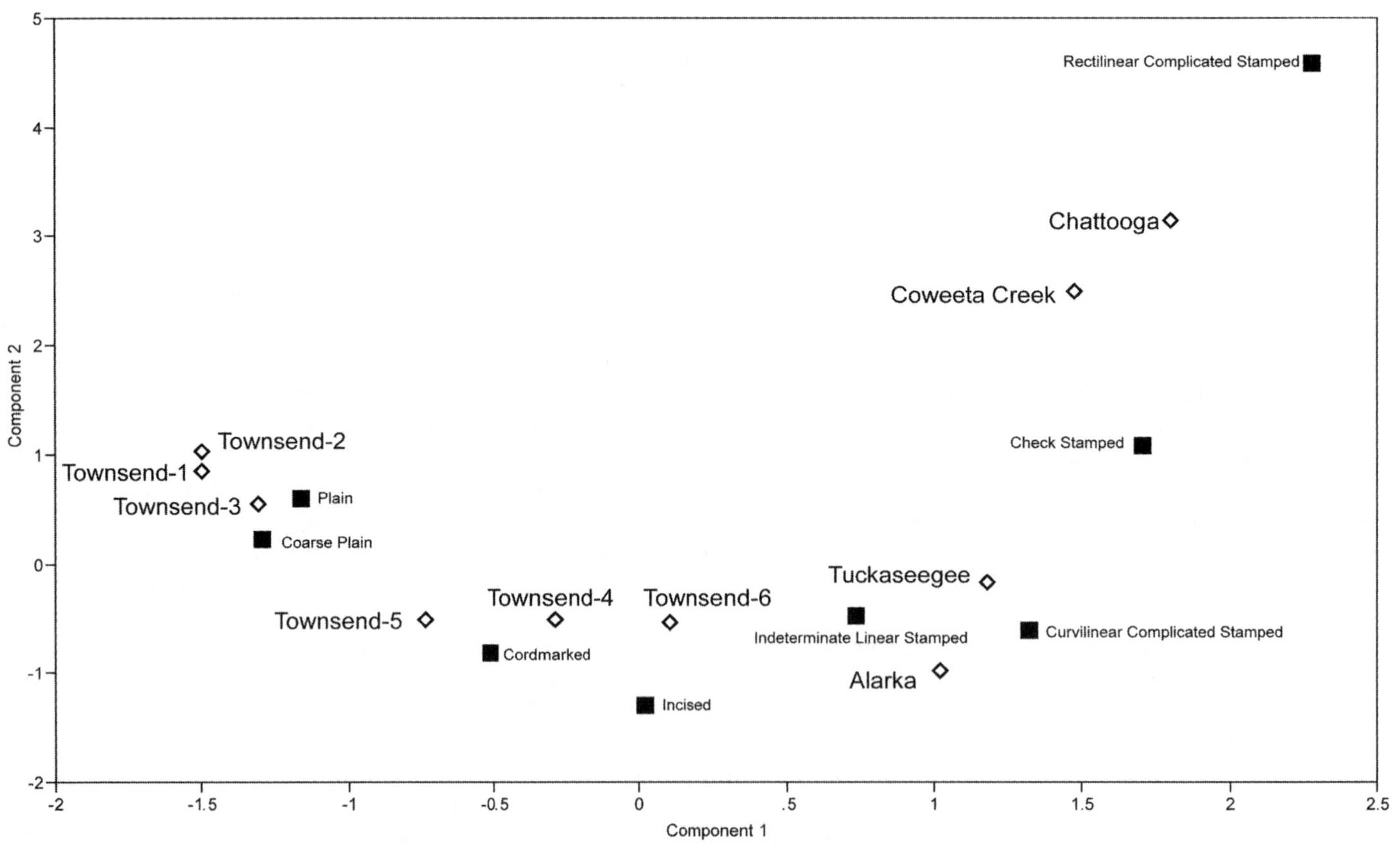

Figure 7.25. Biplot depicting the results of the correspondence analysis conducted pottery assemblages from the six Townsend households and other selected Cherokee sites. Reproduced with permission from *Pox, Empire, Shackles, and Hides* (Marcoux 2010: Fig. 4.13), ©University of Alabama Press.

Table 7.16. Composition of household vessel assemblages (measured in MNV) at Townsend and other selected Cherokee sites.

	Large Jars w/ Pinched Appliqué Rimstrips		Large Jars w/ Notched Appliqué Rimstrips		Large Jars w/ Pinched and Flattened Rimstrips		Large Jars w/ Rolled Rims		Large Jars w/ L-shaped Rims		Restricted Orifice Bowls		Simple Bowls		Cazuelas		Total	
	n	%	*n*	%	*n*	%	*n*	%	*n*	%	*n*	%	*n*	%	*n*	%	*n*	%
Townsend-1	4	17	10	44	0	0	1	2	1	2	6	26	2	9	0	0	*24*	*100*
Townsend-2	4	20	8	40	1	5	0	0	0	0	6	30	1	5	0	0	*20*	*100*
Townsend-4	19	17	1	<1	48	43	0	0	0	0	18	16	6	5	8	7	*106*	*95*[a]
Tuckaseegee	12	18	7	11	16	25	2	3	1	2	16	25	2	3	9	14	*65*	*100*
Alarka	3	10	1	3	14	47	0	0	0	0	5	17	0	0	7	23	*30*	*100*
Coweeta Creek	6	19	12	39	4	13	2	6	2	6	4	13	0	0	1	3	*31*	*100*

[a]This total is less than 100% because the Household 4 vessel assemblage also includes six small jars—a vessel class that was not included in this tally.

Alarka samples; however, rectilinear complicated stamped sherds comprise a much higher percentage of the Coweeta Creek and Chattooga samples.

Given that distance in the correspondence analysis biplot can be thought of as a measure of similarity among the samples, two conclusions can be drawn. First, the pottery samples from Townsend demonstrate a significant amount of inter-household variability with regard to surface treatment; however, when compared to "classic" Qualla series samples from Cherokee sites in other settlement divisions, the Townsend household assemblages form a geographically distinct potting "style" typified by plain, coarse plain, and cordmarked surface treatments. Second, the samples that are most similar to the Townsend households are those recovered from the Tuckaseegee and Alarka sites. Conversely, the composition of the pottery samples from the Coweeta Creek and Chattooga sites differs dramatically from the Townsend household samples with regard to surface treatment. According to the current ceramic chronology for Qualla series pottery, the Tuckaseegee and Alarka assemblages clearly date to the late Middle Qualla phase (ca. A.D. 1650–1700) while those of the Coweeta Creek and Chattooga sites are associated with the early Late Qualla phase (ca. A.D. 1700–1750) (Shumate et al. 2005; Riggs and Rodning 2002; Rodning 2004). The correspondence analysis thus strongly suggests that the Cherokee household occupations at Townsend all date to the period from roughly A.D. 1650 to 1715. The temporal placement of the Townsend household occupations in this period finds corroboration in the other dating measures considered in this monograph, particularly the robust glass bead chronology presented in Chapter 9.

The results of comparing vessel form using minimum number of vessel counts are far less provocative. Nevertheless, these findings are essential for placing the pottery assemblages of Townsend households within the larger context of English Contact period Cherokee potting practices. In the effort to reduce bias associated with sample size, only those sites with minimum number of vessel counts of 20 or greater are included in the comparison (Table 7.16). In regard to broad functional classes, the vessel assemblages are similar across all the sites in the study. The most common vessel form in the sample is the large jar, which comprises approximately 60% of the vessel assemblage at each site. Frequencies of restricted orifice bowls are second highest among the samples, ranging from 13% to 30% of assemblages. Simple bowls are a minority vessel form among the samples, being entirely absent in the Alarka and Coweeta Creek assemblages, and comprising less than 10% of the assemblages in the other sites. The relative abundance of cazuela forms varies among the sites. While they are completely absent from the vessel assemblages of Household 1 and Household 2 at the Townsend site, they constitute 7%, 14%, and 23% of the Townsend Household 4, Tuckaseegee, and Alarka assemblages respectively. These three assemblages are also differentiated by significantly higher frequencies of jars with highly everted rims and pinched and flattened appliqué rimstrips. As discussed above, past research has demonstrated that Cherokee jar rim modes are temporally sensitive. Pinched and flattened appliqué rimstrips are typically associated with the Middle Qualla phase while notched appliqué rimstrips typically dominate Late Qualla phase jar assemblages. When considered along with the concomitant pattern involving cazuelas, these results suggest that the Cherokee occupations of Household 4 at Townsend, Tuckaseegee, and Alarka are earlier than those of Townsend Households 1 and 2 and the Coweeta Creek site. However, other temporally sensitive artifacts at these sites indicate that the extent of the difference did not likely exceed 50 years.

Summary and Conclusions

My goals for this chapter were threefold. First, I wished to present the reader with an overview of past archaeological research concerning Cherokee potting practices. In doing so, I emphasized how the Overhill and Qualla ceramic series were (and continue to be) the historical products of very different research projects pursued by archaeologists affiliated with the University of Tennessee and the University of North Carolina at Chapel Hill. Second, I aimed to construct a detailed analytical description of the Cherokee pottery sample recovered during the Townsend project. My pottery description followed a traditional southeastern analytical schema focused on paste, surface treatment, and vessel form. I found a great deal of inter-household ceramic variability along these three dimensions—variability that I believe represents three distinct Cherokee potting styles. Finally, through quantitative comparisons to other Cherokee pottery assemblages, I strived to place the pottery assemblage recovered from Townsend households within the existing regional and temporal framework represented by the Overhill and Qualla ceramic series. I found that the Townsend pottery assemblages did not fit into either existing ceramic series; instead, I concluded that the Cherokee potters who lived at Townsend practiced a style of potting that has until now gone unrecognized by archaeologists.

I wish to emphasize four main conclusions drawn from my analyses and comparisons.

(1) Quantitative analysis clearly suggests that there were three distinct potting styles practiced by Townsend potters. These styles were based on three different pottery wares and involved significant differences in surface treatment and, to a lesser extent, vessel form.

(2) While not mutually exclusive, the spatial distributions of pottery wares and surface treatments strongly suggest that particular potting styles were associated with particular households. The pottery samples recovered from Households 1 and 2, for example, were overwhelmingly dominated by the shell-tempered plain potting style associated with the Overhill ceramic series. Samples from Households 3, 4, and 5, in contrast, contained large amounts of gravel-tempered plain surfaced and paddle stamped pottery. I refer to this heretofore undefined local Cherokee pottery style as "Tuckaleechee." While the sample from Household 6 was not very large, it did contain an unusual abundance of grit-tempered curvilinear complicated stamped pottery that is a hallmark of the Qualla ceramic series.

(3) The pottery assemblages recovered from Townsend households are very different from extant Overhill Cherokee pottery assemblages. Whereas Townsend pottery is defined by diversity in paste and surface treatment, pottery from the late seventeenth-century Overhill site of Ocoee and later eighteenth-century Overhill sites are largely homogeneous assemblages consisting of shell-tempered vessels with plain surfaces. Considering the predominance of rock tempering and paddle stamping at Townsend, one must conclude that these assemblages are more similar to contemporaneous Qualla series assemblages even though the Townsend site is located within what is historically thought of as Overhill Cherokee territory.

(4) When exterior surface treatment and vessel form are compared to English Contact period Cherokee assemblages from Middle town and Lower town sites, Townsend households form a distinct cluster; however, Townsend pottery assemblages are more closely related to late seventeenth-century Qualla assemblages (i.e., Alarka and Tuckaseegee) than to early eighteenth-century Qualla assemblages (Coweeta Creek, Chattooga). This comparison also suggests that the occupation of Household 4 may be slightly earlier than the other households at Townsend.

Notes

1. Personal communication with Mr. B. Kenneth Cornett, Maryville, Tennessee, in 2007.

2. Middle and Late Qualla phase pottery is essentially identical to pottery associated with the Tugalo and Estatoe phases (seventeenth- and eighteenth-century occupations at sites in the Lower Cherokee settlement division) in northeast Georgia (Hally 1986; Riggs and Rodning 2002:38).

3. I employ the concept of pottery ware following the tradition of researchers in the lower Southeast (e.g., Brain 1970; Jenkins 1981). Although not explicitly defined in these works, wares are defined primarily by paste characteristics.

4. The spatial patterning in the distribution of tempering agents was initially identified by Howell (2005) in his preliminary analysis of a sample of Townsend pottery.

5. While published data exist for the pottery samples from the Tuckaseegee and Coweeta Creek sites, I (re)analyzed these pottery samples using a slightly different analytical schema (outlined earlier in this chapter). The pottery samples from the Alarka and Chattooga sites were previously analyzed by other researchers using an identical schema, and I was graciously provided the resulting data by Brett Riggs and Gerald Schroedl.

6. To improve analytical clarity, surface treatments that comprise less than one percent of the total combined sample, such as scraping, burnishing, and brushing, are excluded from the analysis.

Chapter 8

Stone Implements from Cherokee Contexts at the Townsend Sites

Boyce Driskell, Jeremy Sweat, Katherine McMillan, Stephen Carmody, Phyllis Rigney, and Erik Johanson

While the Cherokees of the English Contact period (A.D. 1670–1715) lived in a changing social and economic environment increasingly influenced by European technology, Cherokees in Tuckaleechee Cove mostly made a living the old-fashioned way by employing stone tools to fashion ornaments, houses, other tools, and implements, and to dig pits, cultivate crops, and process vegetal and animal foods. With the exception of the glass beads discussed in Chapter 9, a single fragment of iron from the archaeological record reported here attests to adoption of European implements by the Cherokees of Tuckaleechee Cove. On the other hand, nearly 7000 pieces of worked stone from manufacture, use and discard of stone tools were recovered from Cherokee contexts at the Townsend sites.

The curious wording of this chapter's title belies the concern of analysts in dealing with this "assemblage" of Cherokee stone artifacts. Traditional methods and outcomes of stone toolmaking in Tuckaleechee Cove varied little through the four or five millennia of prehistoric utilization of the Townsend sites. Most artifact classes exhibit little functional or morphological change through the centuries or millennia, making assignment of cultural provenience based on time-sensitive stylistic characteristics difficult or impossible. Therefore, because stone is a durable material in most environments, including that of eastern Tennessee, and because the Cherokee households reported here made use of sites with long histories of previous, prehistoric occupation, it is not clear that most of the artifacts reported below are actually of Cherokee manufacture and use. While found in archaeological contexts such as features associated with or dated to the Cherokee occupation of the Townsend sites, some of the artifacts are very unlikely candidates for Cherokee provenience. Many others might be of Cherokee vintage, while a few of the artifacts discussed below are likely of Cherokee age.

This chapter first briefly discusses the rationale used to organize the analysis of lithic materials from the Townsend sites, and then describes the methods used to process, identify, and record stone artifacts. Next, the chapter describes the availability and acquisition of stone used by the prehistoric inhabitants of Tuckaleechee Cove. This discussion is followed by brief descriptions of artifacts by category found in contexts believed to be associated with the Cherokee occupation at the Townsend sites.

Rationale for Analysis of Stone Artifacts from the Townsend Sites

Every stone artifact is unique in some way, so that creating and understanding the meaning of types or categories of stone artifacts is a difficult task. In this study, stone artifact types are distinguished based on concern for several dimensions of artifact variability that can be labeled technology, morphology, and function.

Technology

Sometimes, the task of creating reasonable artifact types can be made a bit easier by taking into account the ways in which stone tools are manufactured since manufacturing methods and activities can account for many of the differences (both morphological variation in tools and other artifacts as well as relative proportions of artifact classes) we identify in our artifact assemblages. Beginning with a stone mass (objective piece) exceeding desired dimensions for the envisioned finished artifact, the prehistoric artisan shaped stone through removal of mass. Since this is a reductive process, and since stone is quite durable in most archaeological contexts, stone debris from the manufacturing process alone may (and often does) account for most of the artifacts recovered from an archaeological site.

Shaping was achieved in one or more of several methods. These methods include flaking, pulverizing, cutting, and grinding or polishing. Flaking, or knapping of stone, is possible when rocks "have very small or invisible grains, are all very hard and brittle, and fracture concoidally" (Andrefsky 2005:59). This was an important method of tool production worldwide and chipped stone tools have a very ancient pedigree. Most preindustrial peoples around the world had access to a source or sources of chippable tool stone, and they used this technology to produce most of their inventory of cutting, piercing, and scraping tools.

Otherwise, stones with visible grains can be reduced or shaped productively using another hard stone to pulverize (that is, detach grains from) the surface of the stone. This method is often used to roughly shape stone artifacts (which we categorize here as ground stone) such as axes, celts, pestles, and grinding stones before optionally finishing the artifact by grinding and polishing, often by using sand as an abrasive. Still other tools and ornaments are simply ground into shape by using another stone as an abrader and/or sand as an abrasive. Stone was also cut and snapped, incised or drilled with tools made of stone, or abrasive grits were applied with tools made from materials such as wood or cane in order to drill holes or otherwise shape or polish areas of a tool or ornament.

By recognizing that the manufacturing process alone, or primarily, can produce normative classes of artifacts, the search for artifact categories that might have been meaningful to the prehistoric inhabitants may be improved. Such classes have been segregated in this study, including the artifact classes of debitage, cores, modified flakes, flake tools, bifaces, projectile points, and ground stone tools. Artifacts in the assemblage that show evidence of errors in production (referred to here as knapping errors) or were likely broken during, or after, manufacture (recorded here as breakage types) also should be distinguished from specimens that appear to be intact so that potential tools and intended tool morphologies in the assemblage are more easily segregated.

Morphology

Obviously, most stone tool classification schemes are based primarily on morphology, that is, mostly on similar shapes of artifacts. Such is the case with the Townsend artifact classes in that specimens within each of the technological categories are assigned to types based mostly on some characteristic or characteristics of morphology such as outline, cross section, or edge confirmation. As with other tool classifications in the region, projectile points and other hafted tools are segregated into types based largely on the style of the hafting element, which is usually diagnostic of temporal placement of the tool. These stylistic types are also discussed in detail below.

Function

In many cases, tool classes identified within the lithic assemblage at the Townsend sites are labeled by terms suggestive of function, such as scraper, drill, or projectile point. While in common usage in the regional literature, functional designations should be viewed with a bit of skepticism. Accordingly, in selected cases, functional analysis of various sorts has been used to augment technological and morphological segregation of tool classes, and to test assumptions about the role of some stone artifacts in the prehistoric cultures represented by the archaeological sites at Townsend. Such studies include macroscopic examination of potentially utilized areas for edge damage, and microscopic examination of edges for use traces suggestive of the nature of work actions and work materials. Additionally, while the archaeological record is no doubt biased in favor of durable artifacts, functional analysis may provide evidence, direct and inferential, for manufacture and processing in other, less durable media. This type of analysis, often referred to as microscopic use wear analysis, has been conducted with a sample of the flake tools (Rigney 2009) and with the hafted scrapers and hafted bifacial drills (Carmody, pers. comm., 2010).[1]

Methods of Analysis of Stone Tools and Debris

In total, 57,945 records in the Townsend artifact database document the type, various attributes, and context of the 254,989 stone artifacts that were recovered during the Townsend project. These specimens include a large quantity of manufacturing debris such as chipped stone flakes, cores, or other categories of wastage. Other artifacts include pebbles or cobbles altered in various ways, chipped stone flakes showing edge damage suggestive of intentional retouch or use, bifacially worked tools of several types, and several types of ground stone implements.

Initial laboratory processing included cleaning each of these artifacts, then sorting them into general artifact categories such as fire-cracked rock, other stone artifacts, faunal specimens, ceramic sherds, historic artifacts, charcoal, or natural material (mostly unmodified gravels). Fire-cracked rock specimens were weighed, counted, entered into a separate database, and discarded. Other stone artifacts were sorted into general categories including debitage, chipped stone cores, flake tools, bifaces, projectile points, and ground stone.

Each stone artifact, or in the case of debitage, each lot of artifacts, was recorded in a relational database designed for the Townsend project. In addition to its provenience, the analyst entered data on each artifact or lot using a database interface that included lithic type and material type. Selection of a lithic type then allowed the analyst to record certain attributes. Table 8.1 lists the distribution of lithic types by cultural affiliation.

After all stone specimens were cleaned, sorted, cataloged and recorded in the project database, the lithics team (including the authors of this chapter) reviewed each artifact type and, in some cases, reassigned artifacts in the collection. After each artifact provenience was reviewed for its likely temporal and cultural association, the final list of artifacts assignable to each occupation at the Townsend sites was generated.

Procurement of Stone by the Inhabitants of Tuckaleechee Cove

A study of the location and availability of stone to the inhabitants of Tuckaleechee Cove was carried out by Jeremy Sweat, a graduate student at the University of Tennessee, Knoxville. His (2009) methodology for locating sources of tool stone involved systematic testing of cobbles in the Little River and its tributaries, and opportunistic survey of other areas in the region thought to produce useable stone. Geologic maps and local informants were quite helpful in selecting these survey areas.

Most (77.13%) of the chipped stone artifacts from the Townsend sites were made of Knox chert. Sweat found that while chert—particularly Knox chert from the Joneboro limestone—was widespread in local residuum and was found abundantly in the Little River drainage within the cove, "all the samples collected from Tuckaleechee Cove exhibited high amounts of fractures and inclusions that would have made this material a poor choice for the manufacture of most chipped stone tools" (2009:149). Obviously, in spite of its proximity to the Townsend sites, the Little River system upstream from, and within, Tuckaleechee Cove was not the source of most of the chipped stone artifacts recovered from the Townsend sites.

Sweat (2009:150) concludes that the "closest source of usable cryptocrystalline materials to Tuckaleechee Cove is the Shady Dolomite formation in Millers Cove, which is located approximately 12 kilometers northwest of Townsend by river." This formation is a source of chalcedony and jasper (red and yellow varieties); however, neither of these cherts is well represented in artifacts from the Townsend sites. Artifacts made of chalcedony at the Townsend sites represent only 3.16% of the total stone artifacts recovered; artifacts of jasper include about 1.72%.

Sweat (2009:152) thinks that the most likely source of most of the Knox tool stone was also outside the cove, several miles downstream (west) between the confluence of Ellejoy Creek and the Little River, and the confluence of Crooked Creek and the Little River. Here, along the terraces and hilly flanks of the river, Knox Black and Knox Banded cherts occur washing from

Table 8.1. Lithic artifact types from the Townsend sites by cultural affiliation.

Cultural Period	Debitage	Cores	Flake Tools	Bifaces	Projectile Points	Ground Stone	Total per Period
Archaic	130	5	1	0	1	1	*138*
Early/Middle Archaic	69	1	0	0	3	2	*75*
Late Archaic	13,460	105	62	270	82	47	*14,026*
Late Archaic/Early Woodland	9013	65	57	180	77	30	*9422*
Woodland	5270	62	40	114	41	82	*5609*
Early Woodland	10,173	69	48	174	63	115	*10,642*
Middle Woodland	42,500	684	238	659	232	1519	*45,832*
Late Woodland	555	3	6	15	2	13	*594*
Mississippian	3272	47	19	59	17	34	*3448*
Early Mississippian	6667	61	43	102	77	40	*6990*
Middle Mississippian	4439	42	32	68	37	32	*4650*
Historic/Cherokee	6595	66	30	95	38	16	*6840*
Unknown Prehistoric	137,144	1571	1246	3218	1387	2157	*146,723*
total all types	*239,287*	*2781*	*1822*	*4954*	*2057*	*4088*	*254,989*

the residuum and in shallow deposits that could have been easily reached by the prehistoric inhabitants.

A surprising number of artifacts (4607 specimens or 1.81% of stone artifacts) were made from nonlocal cherts, including those found in middle Tennessee and further to the west (St. Louis and Ft. Payne cherts mostly, but including Dover, Brassfield, and Monteagle cherts). Sweat (2009:154) notes that these artifacts of exotic material include unfinished forms such as crude bifaces as well as finished tools, suggesting import of blanks or performs into the cove.

Sweat (2009) found that the stream system draining Tuckaleechee Cove was a good source for cobbles made from sedimentary rocks such as limestone and sandstone, and cobbles made from granitic rocks such as quartzite. Thus, many of the ground stone tools described below were made of quartzite and similar materials that could have been found in the Little River adjacent to the sites.

Other stone artifacts, including ones made of steatite (soapstone) and mica, were found at the Townsend sites. The closest steatite sources are found to the east of Tuckaleechee Cove. Soapstone outcrops occur to the east of the Appalachian summit along the piedmont in Alabama through North Carolina (Wells 2006:2–3). The soapstone assemblage from the Townsend excavations (all from site 40BT90) consisted of 1359 vessel fragments and 20 ground stone objects, 4 of which were likely reworked from vessel fragments (Wells 2006:37). The vessels all seem to date to the terminal Archaic or Early Woodland. Ages of the objects may vary more widely; as noted below, a single fragmentary object, a pipe bowl fragment of soapstone, was found in Cherokee context.

Approximately 2951 fragments of mica, weighing a total of 338.6 g, were recovered from the Townsend sites. A few cut edges were noticed during excavation and processing but there were no recognizably shaped artifacts in the recovered pieces.

Sweat notes that the pattern of materials acquisition for Tuckaleechee Cove is in contrast to that of the Great Smoky Mountains National Park area and the Tellico Basin to the southwest. Bass (1977) found that most of the chipped stone tools from the prehistoric sites in the Great Smoky Mountains National Park, just a few miles to the south of the Townsend sites, were made of quartzite (Sweat 2009:150). In the Tellico Basin of the Little Tennessee River drainage just 35 miles to the southwest of the cove, lower proportions of nonlocal cherts were recorded (Kimball 1985), and few examples of cherts from as far away as the Cumberland Plateau or middle Tennessee were recovered (Sweat 2009:155). This suggests that occupants of the Townsend sites were somewhat less insular than their counterparts in the Little Tennessee Valley.

Cherokee Utilization of Stone in Tuckaleechee Cove

Stone artifacts from Cherokee contexts at the Townsend sites include 6840 specimens (listed by artifact class and material type in Table 8.2). Most of these stone artifacts are chipped stone (all but 16 artifacts), and most of these (all but 556 artifacts) were made from Knox chert (a material extensively available in the Valley and Ridge Province of east Tennessee, but in tool quality found closest to the Townsend sites about 20 km downriver to the northwest, eroding from Knox dolomites) (Sweat 2009:152). A few were made of chalcedony and jasper (also locally available downriver from the sites), and a few quartz and quartzite tools were chipped from the abundant and easily accessible sources near the Townsend sites.

Thus, local materials account for almost all the chipped stone tools, and all but a few artifacts that represent wastage (debitage) from making stone tools. Thirty-seven of the 38 projectile points that occur in Cherokee contexts were made from local materials (Knox, calcedony, and quartzite).

The few artifacts found in Cherokee contexts that were made of exotic (more distant) cherts—such as Brassfield, Dover, Fort Payne, Monteagle, and St. Louis—are from sources generally to be found to the west in middle Tennessee, southern Kentucky and northern Alabama. Because of the very low percentages of exotic cherts represented in apparent Cherokee contexts, caution should be exercised in any interpretations of Townsend Cherokee interaction with areas to the west based on these data alone. Because the Cherokee occupation is the latest in an approximate 5000-year history of use of this locale within Tuckaleechee Cove, these artifacts may be from earlier peoples, but secondarily included by chance in Cherokee contexts. That is certainly apparent with a number of the projectile points found in Cherokee contexts since their styles suggest earlier origins (see discussion below).

Ground stone artifacts are not well represented from Cherokee contexts. Of the artifacts recovered in this category, all were made from materials that were locally available in the Little River and its tributaries near the Townsend sites (Sweat 2009), with the exception of a steatite smoking pipe fragment. This material was available in areas of the piedmont east of the Appalachian summit (Wells 2006).

Debitage

Flakes and other chipped stone debris from each provenience unit were graded into five sizes by passing the mass through wire screens with square mesh sizes of 1 inch, ¾ inch, ½ inch, and ¼ inch. Each artifact in each of the four largest categories was examined for material type and evidence for thermal alteration. Each of the subsets (lots) of debitage for each provenience unit was then entered into the database by count and weight (in grams). Blocky shatter (included in Table 8.3) was similarly distinguished by material type and evidence for thermal alteration and each artifact lot (category by provenience) was recorded in the database by count and weight. Material types include those itemized in Table 8.3, which lists the counts of debitage by size grade, material type, and evidence for thermal alteration.

Debitage generally reflects the overall patterning of stone material use. The collection of debitage from Cherokee contexts

Table 8.2. Distribution of lithic artifacts by material and class from Cherokee contexts at the Townsend sites.

Material Type	Debitage	Cores	Flake Tools	Bifaces	Projectile Points	Ground Stone	Total Each Material
Brassfield chert	2	0	0	0	0	0	*2*
chalcedony	102	0	7	6	6	0	*121*
Dover chert	0	0	0	0	1	0	*1*
Fort Payne chert	22	1	1	2	0	0	*26*
indeterminate	9	0	0	0	0	0	*9*
jasper	11	0	0	0	0	0	*11*
Knox chert	6095	62	22	75	30	0	*6284*
limestone	1	0	0	1	0	0	*2*
Monteagle chert	0	1	0	0	0	0	*1*
quartz	252	2	0	7	0	2	*263*
quartz crystal	1	0	0	0	0	0	*1*
quartzite	12	0	0	0	1	7	*20*
sandstone	0	0	0	0	0	4	*4*
shale	2	0	0	0	0	0	*2*
siltstone	0	0	0	1	0	0	*1*
slate	82	0	0	3	0	1	*86*
St. Louis chert	4	0	0	0	0	0	*4*
steatite	0	0	0	0	0	1	*1*
transitional shale	0	0	0	0	0	1	*1*
total each type	*6595*	*66*	*30*	*95*	*38*	*16*	*6840*

Table 8.3. Debitage from Cherokee contexts by material, size, and thermal alteration.

Material	Debitage					Thermally Altered Debitage					Total Each Material
	<¼"	¼–½"	½–¾"	¾–1"	>1"	<¼"	¼–½"	½–¾"	¾–1"	>1"	
Brassfield chert		1					1				*2*
chalcedony	17	76	6	3							*102*
Fort Payne chert	2	16	1				2	1			*22*
indeterminate		8						1			*9*
jasper		9					2				*11*
Knox chert	743	4487	479	93	20	33	223	15	2		*6095*
limestone				1							*1*
quartz	23	165	35	15	5		6	2		1	*252*
quartz crystal			1								*1*
quartzite	1	5					3	3			*12*
shale		1	1								*2*
slate	18	56	3		1		2	2			*82*
St. Louis chert		3	1								*4*
total each size	*804*	*4827*	*527*	*112*	*26*	*33*	*239*	*24*	*2*	*1*	*6595*

at the Townsend sites is dominated by Knox chert (92.42% of the debitage). Minor additions of other local materials such as chalcedony, quartz, and slate account for most of the remainder of specimens. Patterns of exotic materials use are similar to those for the entire collection of stone artifacts from the Townsend sites. Thermally altered debitage (4.53% of the debitage collection) accounts for a small portion of the collection. Knox chert specimens comprise 94.65% of the thermally altered debitage, a proportion similar to the overall representation of Knox chert in the collection. Since proportions of Knox chert are nearly identical between unaltered and thermally altered debitage and since thermally altered debitage represents a minor portion of the debitage collection, incidental or accidental thermal alternation is indicated. It seems unlikely that thermal alteration was routinely employed by Cherokees in Tuckaleechee Cove as a pretreatment technique to enhance flakability of chipped stone. The similarity of the debitage assemblage from Cherokee contexts to the larger body of debitage recovered from the Townsend sites suggests that the Cherokees of Tuckaleechee Cove followed ancient traditions of toolmaking, or that much of the debitage found in Cherokee features was produced by their predecessors. Each proposition, or both, is very possible.

Cores

Additional categories of debitage include several types of cores (Table 8.4), which are chipped stone artifacts that served as objective pieces from which flakes (or blades) were detached. Attributes recorded for cores within the database include material type, thermal alteration, count, weight, length, width, and thickness. Multidirectional cores (*n* = 35), exhibiting opportunistic platforms where flakes were removed along multiple axes, dominate this class of artifacts from Cherokee contexts.

A category of unidirectional cores (*n* = 2) was defined in which flakes or blades were struck from a single opportune or prepared platform. Many of the nodules of Knox chert exhibit an existing facet as evidenced by a patinated surface, which served as a convenient platform to strike a series of flakes and blade-like flakes. In other cases, the nodule may be struck initially to produce a facet, which similarly served as the striking platform. These artifacts vary in size but tend to be small since the raw material (mostly Knox chert) is rarely found in unflawed large pieces. These cores are often conical in shape because flakes have been detached in the same orientation from a single platform. Some are flattened and thereby somewhat wedge-shaped, depending in large part on the shape of the original nodule or pebble. These cores vary from their bipolar counterparts (see below) mostly by lack of evidence for use of a stone anvil to support the objective piece during flake or blade production.

Bipolar cores were generally similar to the unidirectional cores but these objective pieces showed clear evidence that flakes (or blades) were detached by supporting the objective piece on an anvil stone when striking the top or opposite end with a percussor. These cores are usually quite small, no doubt necessitating this method of reduction. Normally, because of the technique used, cores are struck in the same axis to produce flakes or blade-like flakes. Telltale signs of bipolar production are seen on the distal end of the core (and detached flakes) in the form of damage from the anvil stone, such as shatter, crushing, or flake scars from flakes detached in the opposite direction to those from the platform. Three types of bipolar cores were recognized from the Townsend sites including Bipolar Cores I through III. Only Bipolar Core I and II types were found in Cherokee contexts.

Bipolar Core I specimens (*n* = 4), which otherwise show signs of use of an anvil stone, are technically similar to unidirectional cores (described above) in that a single striking platform is used, but there is no evidence for an opportune or prepared striking platform. Bipolar Core II specimens (*n* = 1), on the other hand, exhibit the single opportune or prepared striking platform like unidirectional cores, but also exhibit evidence for use of an anvil stone. Like Bipolar Core I specimens, Bipolar Core III specimens show signs of use of an anvil stone, and lack evidence for an opportune or prepared striking platform, but they show evidence for more than one axis of flake removal. Each axis (usually two nearly parallel axes) is represented by a proximal striking area and signs of anvil stone use. None of the Bipolar Core III specimens were associated with Cherokee contexts.

A number of artifacts were labeled as tested cobbles (*n* = 9) where, typically, one to several flakes had been removed (probably through use of a hammerstone in freehand percussion) from a water-worn cobble or nodule before disposal of the artifact. These cores were all made from Knox chert. Additionally, several blocky artifacts from Cherokee contexts, all of Knox chert, were cataloged as core fragments (*n* = 15).

Sizes of cores from Cherokee contexts vary considerably. Using a standardized measure of core size suggested by Andrefsky (2005:145), in which the total weight of each specimen is multiplied by its maximum dimension to calculate a core value, the 51 intact cores (Table 8.4) were sorted by categories of bipolar, unidirectional and multidirectional cores, and tested cobbles, then sorted by core value from smallest to largest value, and depicted in the graph shown in Figure 8.1. Bipolar (*n* = 5) and unidirectional (*n* = 2) were combined because of their low frequencies, but the two unidirectional core specimens exhibited larger values (plotted in Fig. 8.1 as values 6 and 7) than the five bipolar cores. Interestingly, values for the tested cobbles (*n* = 9) were all larger than those for bipolar and unidirectional cores. All of these artifacts were made from Knox chert, and while numbers of specimens are indeed small, it is tempting to see this set of values as an indication of a normative technological process of reduction. This continuum from larger (relatively speaking) cobbles with few flake removals, to midsized unidirectional cores, to smaller bipolar cores fits a pattern of utilization of this chert type seen in other occupations of the Townsend sites as well.

Alternatively, multidirectional cores recovered from Cherokee contexts range more broadly in size (core value), but this is mostly from the contribution of the two cores made of quartz, which constitute the last two entries (numbers 34 and 35) in Figure 8.1

with core values of over 5000. These two cores, weighing 87.4 and 86.8 grams, are more than twice as large (by weight) as any other multidirectional cores. Other multidirectional cores form a range of core values from about 60 to just over 1200, the lower half of this range corresponding to core values calculated for the bipolar and unidirectional cores. All but two of the remaining multidirectional cores are of Knox chert. A specimen made of Ft. Payne chert has a core value near the middle of the core values range; a second specimen made of Monteagle chert is near the upper end of the core value range for chert cores.

It seems likely that freehand reduction of larger objectile pieces (cores) was normal but when the original tool stone was too small, bipolar reduction techniques were employed. It is not clear how the roles of multidirectional and unidirectional/bipolar cores differed except that the latter were likely the sources of blades (discussed below).

Table 8.4. Cores from Cherokee contexts by type and material.

Material	Multi-Directional	Uni-Directional	Bipolar I	Bipolar II	Bipolar III	Tested Cobbles	Core Fragments	Total Each Material
Fort Payne chert	1							*1*
Knox chert	31	2	4	1		9	15	*62*
Monteagle chert	1							*1*
quartz	2							*2*
total each type	*35*	*2*	*4*	*1*	*0*	*9*	*15*	*66*

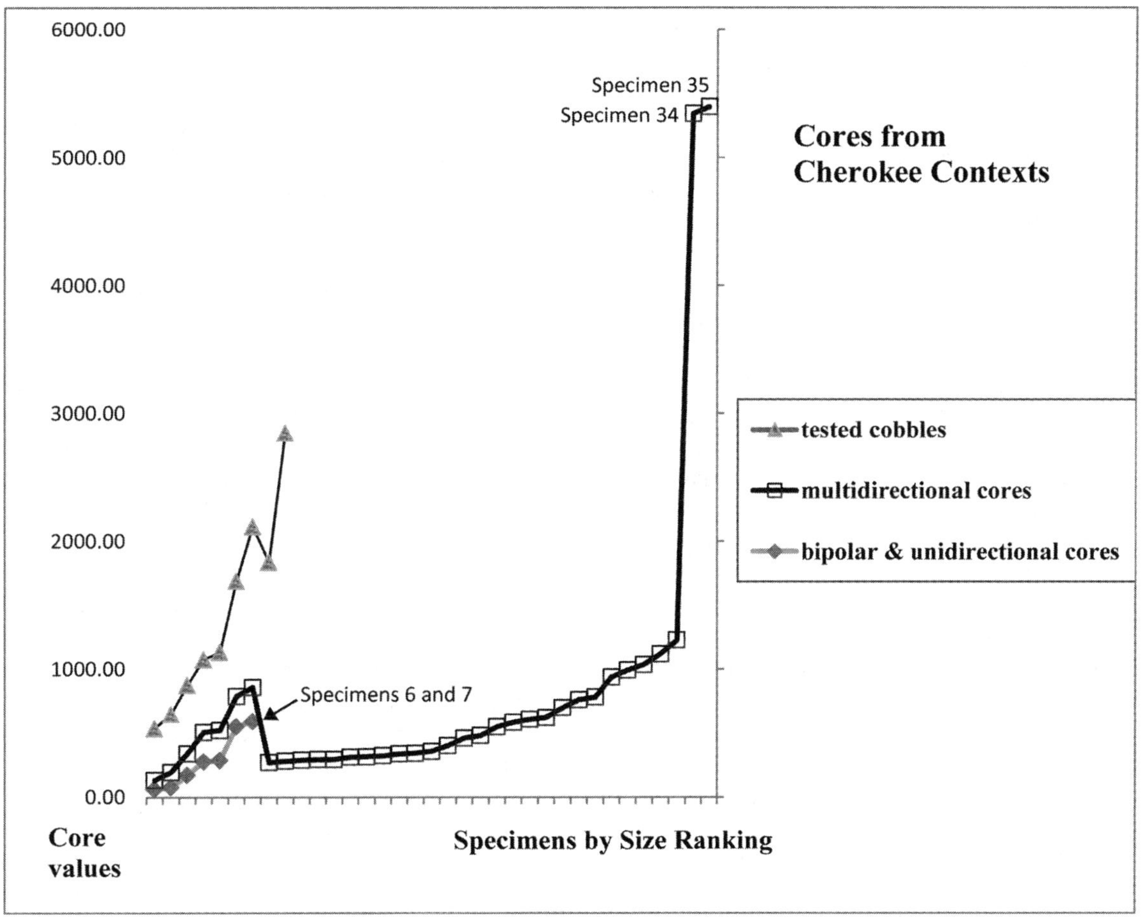

Figure 8.1. Size comparison of different core types from Cherokee contexts.

Flake Tools

Flake tools are provisional tools in that each exhibits an area or areas along an edge or edges that has been retouched or modified through edge damage. Edge damage may result from intentional retouch, from use, or by accident. Attributes recorded for flake tools included material type, thermal alteration, count, weight, length, width, thickness, damage, and manufacturing errors. Damage includes observations about the condition of the tool, such as seemingly intact, or obviously fragmentary. Manufacturing errors include observations concerning possible reasons for abandonment of the tool during manufacture, such as edge collapse, material flaw, and so on.

Included in this category of stone artifacts are modified flakes (n = 12 found in Cherokee contexts), which are flakes that show very limited retouch or damage to an edge. These artifacts may have been used but morphological evidence suggesting use is extremely limited. Other types of flake tools recognized from the Townsend sites include scrapers, incurvate scrapers, ovate scrapers, drills, humpbacked scrapers, wedges, gravers, and retouched blades. Only retouched blades and scrapers were found in Cherokee contexts (itemized in Table 8.5).

Flake scrapers (n = 14) are modified flakes that have been intentionally retouched, incidentally retouched, or modified through use on one or more edges of the specimen. Retouch is usually restricted to a single face of the flake and suggestive of movement against a work material in a scraping motion. Each of these artifacts exhibits a generalized shape, usually irregular, which does not fit into several more tightly defined categories of scrapers such as humpbacked, ovate, or incurvate scrapers.

Scrapers are one of the most common categories of flake tools collected at prehistoric sites in the region. More than half of the flake tools recognized from the Townsend sites were classified as scrapers (Rigney 2009:16). The majority of the literature on similar sites in the area divides the scraper category into "end scrapers" and "side scrapers." End scrapers are usually defined as those scrapers having retouch or modification to the distal end of the tool, while side scrapers are normally defined as having retouch or modification to one or more of the longer edges (sides) of the tool. These tools were recovered in relatively small quantities from the Tellico Reservoir project, yielding only 26 end scrapers and 17 side scrapers. Davis (1990:157–58) suggests that the end scrapers were most likely hafted and used to scrape hides. Investigators at both Toqua (Polhemus 1987:699), a late Mississippian site, and at Chota-Tanassee (Schroedl 1986a:361), an Overhill Cherokee site, differentiate between end scrapers and side scrapers using the same descriptions and criteria. Polhemus and Schroedl each suggests that these tools functioned as scraping implements, but more definite roles were not postulated. Several of these tools are described as exhibiting wear polish with either a hand lens or the naked eye. Scrapers and scraper fragments are also associated with other sites in the Ridge and Valley such as the Iddins and Bacon Bend sites (Chapman 1981), and the Phipps Bend site (Lafferty 1981).

In her thesis on the function of flake tools from the Townsend sites, Phillis Rigney (2009: 62) points out that the 39 scrapers examined for use wear exhibited use traces characteristic of use in a variety of activities including cutting and scraping, and on a number of materials including bone/antler, hide, plants, wood, and steatite.

Three specimens from Cherokee contexts were included in the microwear sample examined by Rigney. Specimen 89-99-1012-255 was interpreted as a flake used to cut plant material (Rigney 2009:65), specimen 89-99-1078-322 as an artifact used to scrape dry hide or leather (Rigney 2009:66), and specimen 90-99-381-319 as a flake used to scrape bone (Rigney 2009:65).

Four (n = 4) retouched blades were recovered from Cherokee contexts at the Townsend sites. Retouched blades are a category of flake tool that includes blades and blade-like flakes exhibiting intentionally retouched, incidentally retouched or use modified areas along edges. A few specimens lack obvious retouch but were placed in the category because of other shared characteristics of morphology. Some specimens are made on prismatic blades while others take advantage of elongated, blade-like flakes (length more than twice width). Thickness and other morphological characteristics of members of this type may vary considerably.

While the connection to the Townsend Cherokee occupation remains unclear, prismatic blades are a hallmark of the Middle Woodland Hopewell culture, which was centered in southwestern Ohio but whose influences are seen across the mid-South and southern Appalachian region. Hopewell blades are often made from Ohio Flint Ridge calcedony. As noted by Rigney (2009:18), a single prismatic blade from the Townsend excavations was made from nonlocal material, specifically Flint Ridge chalcedony. "It was recovered from Circle Midden 3, which has been dated to the Middle Woodland period, based on temporally diagnostic artifacts recovered from the midden" (Rigney 2009:18). The four blades from Cherokee contests are made from Knox chert (n = 3) and a local calcedony (n = 1).

At Tellico Reservoir, 261 blades were recovered from the twenty-six sites discussed by Davis (1990). None of these blades, however, are described as having been made from Flint Ridge calcedony. Blades were also recovered in low but varying quantities from the Iddins and Bacon Bend (Chapman 1981), Phipps Bend (Lafferty 1981), Toqua (Polhemis 1987), and Chota-Tanassee (Schroedl 1986a) sites. Interestingly, Chapman (1981:87) stated that the small number of blades recovered from the Iddins site suggests that the inhabitants lacked the need for such a form. While sparsely represented at most sites in east Tennessee, blades are much better represented in the Middle Woodland remains from the Icehouse Bottom site (Cridlebaugh 1981:70–78; Chapman 1973:91–97) in the adjacent Little Tennessee River drainage. Here, some 873 blades were recovered; 62 (or 7.1%) were made of Flint Ridge chalcedony (Cridlebaugh 1981:70). A much smaller number of blades (79 total) were recovered from the Garden Creek site in western North Carolina but a larger percentage (25%) of these are made of Flint Ridge chalcedony (Kimball 1992:2).

Table 8.5. Source material and metric attributes for flake tools found in Cherokee contexts.

Provenience	Specimen Number	Material	Weight (g)	Maximum Length (mm)	Maximum Width (mm)	Maximum Thickness (mm)
Retouched Blades						
Piece plot 21	89-99-1706-4	chalcedony	3.22	33.64	17.27	6.47
Feature 21	89-99-1045-255	Knox chert	1.18	22.84	10.97	3.74
Feature 936	90-99-3237-300	Knox chert	1.31	24	10.05	5.18
Feature 118	90-99-9089-282	Knox chert	2.19			
Flake Scrapers						
Feature 45	89-99-1012-255	chalcedony	3.4	32.7	30.2	4.0
Feature 23	89-99-1078-322	chalcedony	0.7	23.3	16.8	1.9
Feature 38	89-99-1023-266	Knox chert	1.0	21.9	13.3	3.0
Feature 48	89-99-1091-257	Knox chert	2.2	24.4	15.9	8.5
Feature 2141	90-99-11081-263	chalcedony	0.8	24.1	9.7	3.1
Feature 118	90-99-9112-271	Fort Payne chert	7.1	32.0	18.4	12.3
Feature 438	90-00-277-253	Knox chert	5.6	42.8	21.4	4.5
Feature 135	90-00-381-320	Knox chert	3.5	30.8	16.0	7.5
Feature 135	90-00-209-1	Knox chert	0.7	23.4	9.9	3.6
Feature 1996	90-99-8878-253	Knox chert	7.9	31.7	22.7	11.1
Feature 135	90-99-381-319	Knox chert	3.8	28.2	19.0	7.0
Feature 705	90-99-3045-267	Knox chert	17.1	38.9	32.2	14.7
Feature 995	90-99-5853-255	Knox chert	0.6	15.5	12.7	2.6
Feature 497	91-99-2171-252	Knox chert	6.8	43.5	24.7	4.7

Several different functions have been proposed for these artifacts, but there is still disagreement. Morrow (1987) suggested that Hopewell blades were representative of a regional identity of the Hopewell people, communicated through trade networks. Odell (1994) argues against this interpretation because these blade technologies were not produced solely by the Hopewell. Another very interesting interpretation was put forward by Grubb (1981) who proposed that blades from Ohio may have been used as razors for shaving one's head.

In the region and across the mid-South, blades sometimes served as blanks apparently produced with the intention of creating many other tools, such as burins, drills, end scrapers, spokeshaves, and knives, all of which occur on blades at several sites, including the Toqua (Polhemus 1987) and the Chota-Tanassee (Schroedl 1986a) sites in eastern Tennessee. Johnson (1987:204) agrees with this assessment and suggests that blades from the Southeast were created "to produce a large number of standard blanks for some specific functions."

Larry Kimball (1992) performed use wear analyses on the Icehouse Bottom and Garden Creek site blades using both a stereoscopic and an incident light microscope to determine the function of these tools. Kimball determined that 30% of these blades were used for more than one task, and he suggests that blades "were not special purpose tools" (Kimball 1992:2). The functions of these tools include primarily light butchery, hide cutting, bone and antler working, wood whittling and sawing, and the cutting and incising of soft stone, namely mica or soapstone. Overall, it seems that blades were used for varying functions in different areas of the Hopewell Interaction Sphere. Perhaps, once the Hopewell introduced this technology, groups of people in different regions used blades for whatever purpose was most needed and useful to their particular situation. In this way, blades most certainly represent the ultimate prehistoric multipurpose tool.

Although there has been very little research into the production and use of blades after the Middle Woodland period in east Tennessee, it is likely that blade technology persisted as a minor aspect of the lithic system. Two small blade cores of Knox chert (see the discussion on cores above) were recovered from Cherokee contexts in addition to the 4 blades discussed here. Recovery in such small numbers could mean that these artifacts are simply accidental inclusions from earlier occupations of the Townsend sites.

Two of the blades from Cherokee contexts were included in the microwear sample examined by Rigney. Specimen 89-99-1045-255 was interpreted as a blade used to scrape or cut dry hide while specimen 90-99-3237-300 was interpreted as an artifact used to cut or scrape fresh hide (Rigney 2009:69).

Chipped Stone Bifaces

Bifacially flaked stone tools from the project were divided into several categories of bifaces and formal tools (Table 8.6). The term "biface" was applied as a general category for artifacts including crude tabular bifaces, stage bifaces, and trimmed bifaces. Bifacially worked scrapers and drills/perforators (Table 8.7) recovered from Cherokee contexts are also discussed in this section (projectile points are discussed below). In addition to metric measurements—which included length, width, thickness, weight, haft length, haft width, and haft thickness—material type, thermal alteration, damage and manufacturing errors were recorded for these tool categories.

Most of the bifaces from Cherokee proveniences probably represent stages in the manufacture of bifacially worked formal tools and were not intended for use as tools. This is particularly likely with the bifaces exhibiting only early stage reduction. These artifacts are sometimes referred to in the literature as preforms, or blanks, but are referred to here as stage bifaces (n = 16). Crude biface fragments are likely fragmentary stage bifaces. All of these artifacts (stage bifaces and crude biface fragments) represent bifacial products produced early in the reductive sequence and are less likely to have functioned as finished tools.

Those products of a later stage of reduction that include some aspects of secondary trimming (Collins 1975:19–23) such as edge sharpening or straightening through retouch or other alterations like notching, serrating, or tip sharpening (trimmed biface or refined biface fragment) are more likely to have been used. The trimmed biface (n = 1) from the Cherokee component is the best candidate for a bifacial knife or cutting tool since it exhibits characteristics of shaping and sharpening of its edges through retouch. A group of biface fragments (n = 11) were labeled as "refined biface fragments and end breaks." All specimens were rounded end fragments detached from seemingly elongated bifacially worked blades with snap or transverse fractures suggestive of bending pressure applied to the edge. While candidates for end scraper bits, no use wear analysis has yet been conducted on these specimens.

Crude tabular bifaces (n = 2) are made of tabular stone, one of slate and one of limestone, of approximately 1 to 2 cm in thickness and roughly flaked into a rectangular outline. While shape and size varies somewhat, these artifacts are roughly of a size range that would allow them to function as digging implements or hoes. Each of the 2 specimens is fragmentary; in each case a portion of one end of the specimen is preserved (Fig. 8.2*A*, *B*). These artifacts are likely to have been digging or grubbing implements (Milner et al. 2010:103–13). Widely used in the eastern woodlands by prehistoric peoples, these chipped stone tools (hoes) are often made of chert in areas where it is easily found in large pieces.

Bifacial scrapers (n = 4) show at least limited evidence of secondary retouch along one or more edges. This may have been from the manufacturing process or, alternatively, from use of these artifacts in scraping or similar work activities. Two of these artifacts are illustrated in Figure 8.2*F*, *G*. Specimen 90-00-401-334 (Figure 8.2*F*) appears to be a triangular-shaped distal portion of a crudely shaped biface that has possibly been used as a scraper. Specimen 90-99-3021-318 (Fig. 8.2*G*) is an ovate scraper with retouch along one margin and a natural backing along the opposite margin. Both scrapers are made from Knox chert; microscopic use wear analysis has not been performed on either specimen.

Four bifacially worked drills or perforators (n = 4) were also found in Cherokee contexts. Three (specimens 90-99-3802-251, 90-99-3808-268, and 89-99-1090-263) are illustrated in Figure 8.2*C–E*. All made from Knox chert, each of the 3 illustrated specimens are distal fragments of drills or perforators. Their original length is unknown in each case.

Projectile Points

Thirty-eight projectile points (Table 8.8) were recovered from Cherokee contexts at the Townsend sites, but many of these projectile points date to earlier occupation of the sites. A single projectile point (specimen 91-99-2210-252) has been classified as a Robbins, a stemmed projectile point common during the Early Woodland (Justice 1987:187–89). The Broad Middle Woodland Triangular (specimen 90-99-3662-252), Copena (specimen 89-99-1785-1), Jacks Reef Pentagonal (specimens 89-99-1091-258 and 89-99-1775-1), and the Large Middle Woodland Triangular (specimen 89-99-1039-268) are also probably too early to be of Cherokee vintage (Justice 1987:201–20). Dating to earlier, Woodland periods, these projectile points are likely accidental inclusions in Cherokee contexts.

Two projectile points from Cherokee contexts (specimens 89-99-1062-274 and 90-99-4245-9) are classified as Late Woodland/Mississippian Triangular points. The first specimen is rather crudely shaped for a small late prehistoric triangular point and may be unfinished. It compares favorably with Justice's (1987:215–16) Unnotched Pentagonal Cluster dating to about A.D. 500 to A.D. 1000. The other specimen is an intact projectile point with apparent retouched blade margins giving it a pentagonal shape. This point may be a member of the Late Woodland pentagonal cluster but is more likely a Mississippian triangular point that has been retouched in the haft. It is unlikely that either of these projectile points date to the Cherokee period.

Two other projectile points from Cherokee contexts, classified as Hamilton Incurvate (specimens 89-99-1044-304 and 89-99-1082-254), are probably also too early to be of Cherokee vintage. If correctly classified, these 2 points date to a period from about A.D. 500 to A.D. 1000 (Justice 1987:229). Both specimens are fragmentary basal portions and the distinctions are slight

Table 8.6. Bifaces and formal tools from Cherokee contexts by type and material.

Material Type	Stage Bifaces	Crude Biface Fragments	Trimmed Bifaces	Refined Biface Fragments and End Breaks	Bifacial Scrapers	Crude Tabular Bifaces	Bifacial Drills/ Perforators	Projectile Points
chalcedony	2	4						6
Dover chert								1
Fort Payne chert		2						
Knox chert	9	47	1	10	4		4	30
limestone						1		
quartz	4	2		1				
quartzite								1
siltstone	1							
slate		2				1		
total all materials	*16*	*57*	*1*	*11*	*4*	*2*	*4*	*38*

Table 8.7. Source material and metric attributes for biface scrapers and drills/perforators found in Cherokee contexts.

Provenience	Specimen Number	Material	Weight (g)	Max. Length (mm)	Max. Width (mm)	Max. Thickness (mm)	Tool Type
Feature 705	90-99-3021-318	Knox chert	6.0	34.3	25.6	7.2	scraper
Feature 705	90-99-3021-319	Knox chert	1.2	27.9	12.2	4.0	scraper
Feature 118	90-99-10676-261	Knox chert	16.6	44.8	33.6	11.2	scraper
Feature 135	90-00-401-334	Knox chert	3.0	28.9	17.7	7.0	scraper
Feature 48	89-99-1090-263	Knox chert	0.3	14.0	10.4	2.6	drill/perforator
Feature 702	90-99-3808-265	Knox chert	4.3	27.3	24.0	9.1	drill/perforator
Feature 702	90-99-3808-268	Knox chert	1.0	23.2	9.7	4.5	drill/perforator
Feature 702	90-99-3802-251	Knox chert	0.8	21.9	9.7	4.3	drill/perforator

between these Late Woodland projectile points and Mississippian or Cherokee triangular projectile points.

Six artifacts classified as projectile points of indeterminate type were also recorded from Cherokee contexts. Three of these (specimens 91-99-2206-4, 90-00-363-16, and 90-99-11081-261) are small bifaces, generally trianguloid in shape, but larger and thicker than most late prehistoric triangular projectile points. These 3 specimens may represent unfinished artifacts, stage bifaces, or earlier, Woodland projectile points. Three other artifacts (specimens 91-99-2171-251, 90-99-3021-252, and 90-99-3245-364) are similarly rather thick in cross section for late prehistoric projectile points. Two of these 3 points, while fragmentary, exhibit evidence for a constricted or stemmed base while the third is a basal fragment with slight notches or an expanding base for a stemmed point. None of these 6 artifacts are good candidates as projectile points of Cherokee vintage.

The remaining 22 projectile points found in Cherokee contexts are considered to be of Mississippian or Cherokee manufacture and, as such, are more likely to represent projectile points manufactured, used and discarded by the Cherokee occupants of the Townsend sites. These projectile points, while quite similar to one another, have been classified into five types: Late Mississippian/Cherokee, Late Mississippian/Cherokee Elliptical, Late Mississippian/Cherokee Lanceolate, Late Mississippian/Cherokee Triangular, and Madison (Fig. 8.3).

Figure 8.2. Bifaces from Cherokee contexts. *A*, *B*, fragmentary crude tabular bifaces (hoes); *C–E*, drill/perforators; *F*, *G*, bifacial scrapers.

Table 8.8. Types, source material, and measurements of projectile points occurring in Cherokee contexts.

Provenience	Specimen Number	Material	Weight (g)	Max. Length (mm)	Max. Width (mm)	Max. Thick. (mm)	Haft Length (mm)	Haft Width (mm)	Haft Thick. (mm)
Broad Middle Woodland Triangular									
Feature 1020	90-99-3662-252	Knox chert	4.8	31.1	22.6	6.8	0.0	0.0	0.0
Copena									
Piece plot 38	89-99-1785-1	Knox chert	4.5	29.7	24.3	7.2	16.6	25.4	3.9
Hamilton Incurvate									
Feature 50	89-99-1044-304	Knox chert	0.6	12.9	14.6	2.9	5.7	18.5	2.4
Feature 21	89-99-1082-254	Knox chert	0.7	10.7	16.4	4.3	0.0	0.0	0.0
Indeterminate									
Feature 130	90-00-363-16	chalcedony	2.0	37.1	14.6	3.4	12.1	13.8	3.9
Feature 2141	90-99-11081-261	chalcedony	1.4	27.7	12.2	5.0	0.0	0.0	0.0
Feature 705	90-99-3021-252	Knox chert	5.7	43.0	19.9	6.9	0.0	0.0	0.0
Feature 1019	90-99-3245-364	Knox chert	1.5	10.9	19.8	5.9	0.0	19.8	5.9
Feature 497	91-99-2171-251	Knox chert	19.8	59.1	33.7	12.5	7.8	22.2	6.7
Feature 497	91-99-2206-4	Knox chert	2.9	33.7	13.5	7.1	13.4	12.5	5.4
Jacks Reef Pentagonal									
Feature 48	89-99-1091-258	Knox chert	1.2	23.0	14.3	4.3	7.8	11.5	2.6
Piece plot 16	89-99-1775-1	Knox chert	1.9	20.5	15.4	5.4	8.4	15.6	4.6
Large Middle Woodland Triangular									
Feature 38	89-99-1039-268	quartzite	10.1	44.1	21.9	10.3	0.0	0.0	
Late Mississippian/Cherokee									
Posthole 16	89-99-1259-255	Knox chert	0.8	23.6	10.8	3.6	0.0	0.0	0.0
Feature 21	89-99-1082-255	Knox chert	2.2	23.4	15.9	6.5	0.0	0.0	
Piece plot 18	89-99-1776-1	Knox chert	1.0	16.2	16.1	4.1	16.2	16.1	3.1
Feature 118	90-99-9095-256	chalcedony	1.1	25.8	12.9	3.6	0.0	0.0	
Late Mississippian/Cherokee Elliptical									
Feature 118	90-99-8901-251	chalcedony	0.9	25.4	9.9	3.3	8.9	7.0	2.5
Feature 705	90-99-3021-321	Knox chert	1.4	27.0	12.9	4.6	0.0	0.0	0.0
Feature 705	90-99-2956-256	Knox chert	1.0	17.9	13.5	3.8	0.0	0.0	0.0
Late Mississippian/Cherokee Lanceolate									
Feature 23	89-99-1657-11	Knox chert	2.2	22.9	17.0	5.5	0.0	0.0	0.0
Feature 130	90-00-363-17	chalcedony	2.0	19.9	18.3	3.9	0.0	0.0	0.0
Feature 2000	90-99-8983-254	Knox chert	1.7	29.5	13.4	4.6	0.0	0.0	0.0
Feature 135	90-00-381-254	Knox chert	2.2	24.1	17.8	4.1	10.2	14.3	3.5
Feature 130	90-00-334-254	Knox chert	1.0	25.7	11.2	3.2	0.0	0.0	0.0
Feature 705	90-99-2924-382	Knox chert	1.7	26.8	15.2	3.7	0.0	12.9	2.6
Feature 702	90-99-3808-267	Knox chert	1.1	24.5	11.9	3.7	0.0	0.0	0.0
Feature 706	90-99-3782-256	Knox chert	1.7	31.1	14.5	3.9	0.0	0.0	0.0
Late Mississippian/Cherokee Triangular									
Feature 130	90-00-334-253	chalcedony	1.4	25.1	11.8	4.1	0.0	0.0	0.0
Feature 130	90-00-334-252	Knox chert	1.9	31.0	16.0	4.0	0.0	0.0	0.0
Feature 135	90-00-381-257	Knox chert	1.8	29.1	13.1	4.5	0.0	0.0	0.0
Feature 135	90-00-210-1	Knox chert	0.8	22.2	11.8	3.1	0.0	0.0	0.0
Feature 50	89-99-1044-303	Knox chert	0.8	19.9	12.2	3.2	6.0	12.5	2.5

Table 8.8 cont.

Provenience	Specimen Number	Material	Weight (g)	Max. Length (mm)	Max. Width (mm)	Max. Thick. (mm)	Haft Length (mm)	Haft Width (mm)	Haft Thick. (mm)
Late Woodland/Mississippian Triangular									
Feature 21	89-99-1062-274	Knox chert	1.7	26.4	14.4	5.9	0.0	0.0	0.0
Feature 722	90-99-4245-9	Knox chert	1.3	23.5	17.9	3.5	0.0	0.0	0.0
Madison									
Piece plot 23	89-99-1778-1	Dover chert	2.8	23.9	18.0	5.9	14.3	23.7	5.1
Feature 1019	90-99-3254-253	Knox chert	2.7	28.9	18.2	5.7	0.0	0.0	0.0
Robbins									
Feature 509	91-99-2210-252	Knox chert	12.1	43.1	29.3	11.9	9.8	15.3	8.1

Figure 8.3. Chipped stone projectile points from Cherokee contexts at the Townsend sites. *A*, *B*, Late Mississippian/Cherokee projectile points; *C*, *D*, Late Mississippian/Cherokee Ellipical points; *E–G*, Late Mississippian/Cherokee Lanceolate points; *H–J*, Late Mississippian/Cherokee Triangular points; *K*, Madison point.

Late Mississippian/Cherokee Projectile Points (n = 4)

These 4 projectile points are late prehistoric or early historic artifacts exhibiting small, triangular outline similar to Dallas projectile points (Lewis and Kneberg 1946). Bases are straight to concave. These triangular points have straight to slightly excurvate blade edges, and appear to have been produced on flakes. Cross sections are flattened to mildly biconvex. Two specimens in this category (89-99-1082-255 and 90-99-9095-256) are complete (Fig. 8.3*A*, *B*), while the remaining 2 (89-99-1259-255 and 89-99-1776-1) are fragmentary. The first intact specimen is made of Knox chert; the second specimen is made of chalcedony.

Late Mississippian/Cherokee Elliptical Projectile Points (n = 3)

These small- to medium-sized elliptical points exhibit very excurvate blade margins that taper not only toward the tip, but also toward the base. The points described here are similar to the Mississippian-Protohistoric Nodena Elliptical type described by Chapman and Anderson (1955; see also Bell 1958). They bear some resemblance to Provisional Type 76 from the Westmoreland-Barber site, where Faulkner and Graham also suggest a Mississippian cultural affiliation (1966: 74, Plate XIX *F*). Two (specimens 90-99-8901-251 and 90-99-3021-321) of the 3 specimens are intact (Fig. 8.3*C*, *D*). The first specimen is of chalcedony; the other 2 specimens are of Knox chert.

Late Mississippian/Cherokee Lanceolate Projectile Points (n = 8)

These medium-sized points exhibit lanceolate, notchless, stemless blades with excurvate margins. Specimens resemble the Dallas Excurvate Triangular points recovered from Hiwassee Island (Lewis and Kneberg 1946:113, Fig. 24), and the Dallas or Mouse Creek Focus Excurvate Trianguloid type from Chickamauga (Lewis et al. 1995: Fig. 6.2*J*, *K*, *M*). It is important to note, though, that no Dallas component was recognized at Townsend, but these points still conform to other Late Mississippian or Protohistoric point types.

Similar forms have been noted from the Normandy Reservoir Project (Type 43; Faulkner and McCollough 1973:208, Plate XXV). Faulkner and McCollough (1973:88–90) note that these tools resemble both the Dallas type, and the Guntersville type defined by Cambron and Hulse (1964: A-59) from Alabama. These excurvate-bladed forms are also comparable to the Mississippian Nodena-Banks variety (Perino 1966:33–35; Justice 1987:230–32).

Specimens 90-99-8983-254 (Fig. 8.3*E*), 90-99-3782-256 (Fig. 8.3*F*), and 90-00-334-254 (Fig. 8.3*G*) are intact examples of this type. These 3 specimens are of Knox chert. The remaining 5 specimens (90-99-2924-382, 90-99-3808-267, 89-99-1657-11, 90-00-381-254, and 90-00-363-17) are all basal fragments. The last specimen is made of chalcedony; the other 5 specimens are of Knox chert.

Late Mississippian/Cherokee Triangular Projectile Points (n = 5)

The specimens in this category exhibit long, narrow, well-made triangular blades that are notchless and stemless. The projectile points described here resemble several Late Mississippian and early historic forms, including those associated with the Mississippian Dallas phase. Examples of these Dallas points occur at sites such as Toqua (Polhemis 1987; Roberts 1987:728–32) and Hiwassee Island (Lewis and Kneberg 1946:113–14, Plate 66*D*).

Similar projectile point forms are known from Pisgah phase sites and from other Cherokee contexts. The "Straight-Trianguloid" type from Chickamauga (Lewis et al. 1995: Fig. 6.2*G*, *H*) corresponds to these tools from Townsend. Lewis and colleagues (1995:134) note that this type "is almost always associated with Dallas or Mouse Creek components." Some of the larger Mississippian Triangular points from 40Mr20 (Gleeson 1970: Plate 76, row 3) also resemble these specimens. Specimens 90-00-210-1 (Fig. 8.3*H*), 90-00-381-257 (Fig. 8.3*I*), and 89-99-1044-303 (Fig. 8.3*J*) are intact examples in this category. These 3 specimens are made of Knox chert. Of the remaining 2 specimens, the first (specimen 90-00-334-253) is a basal/midsection fragment made of chalcedony and the second (specimen 90-00-334-252) is an almost complete specimen of Knox chert having sustained damage to the base. Some retouch is in evidence to rework one basal shoulder of the point, giving it a rounded corner. The other shoulder exhibits an unaltered break facet.

Madison Projectile Points (n = 2)

Two specimens were classified as Madison projectile points. Madison projectile points are generally thought to be of prehistoric vintage, but according to Justice (1987:224–27), these points, which are found in a large portion of the eastern U.S., may date as late as early historic times. The points are triangular in outline, generally straight-sided with a straight or slightly incurvate base. The maximum width of the point is always at the base.

Specimen 90-99-3254-253 (Fig. 8.3*K*) is an intact specimen made of Knox chert. The other specimen (89-99-1778-1) is a basal fragment with missing distal end. It is thought to have been made of Dover chert, a material that would have been imported from middle Tennessee.

Ground Stone Artifacts

Of the 1322 ground stone artifacts recovered from the Townsend sites, only 16 were found in Cherokee contexts. These artifacts are often naturally occurring stones showing signs of use or limited modification. To the extent that they are shaped, this generally was by roughing out the shape of the artifact through pecking with another hard stone, followed often by abrasive smoothing using another stone or an abrasive such as sand. In the case of the single artifact made from steatite, the method of manufacture probably involved carving into rough form using a chipped stone tool followed by abrasive polishing.

The classification of ground stone objects from the Townsend sites follows Sweat (2009:132–46), who organized the ground stone objects into twelve functional groupings, some of which follow Adams's (2002) classification. Those classifications that are represented in Cherokee contexts are discussed below and itemized in Table 8.9.

Abrading, Smoothing and Polishing Tools are considered by Sweat (2009:132) to include any tool "whose primary function is to modify the surface of an object." From a Cherokee context, this includes a single specimen (90-99-2924-19), made from shale. The artifact is made from a stream-smoothed, elongated, tabular piece of stone with additional, artificial smoothing along one edge. It is likely that the piece was discarded after a transverse break occurred across its short axis. Its function may have been as an abrading stone or it may be an unfinished artifact of unknown type.

Grinding and Pulverizing Tools include "any artifact used to grind or pulverize plant materials, pigments or other materials" (Sweat 2009:133). From Cherokee contexts, this category includes 5 specimens, all naturally occurring cobbles, that exhibit one or more areas of modification. Specimen 90-00-265-5 is fragmentary but appears to have been a flattened river cobble with at least two pecked depressions in one face. Similarly, specimen 90-00-334-2, a larger, fragmentary cobble, exhibits five depressions on one face (Fig. 8.4) and two on the reverse face. These artifacts are often referred to in the literature as "nutting stones" for their implied function as anvil stones for cracking walnuts or hickory nuts.

Specimen 90-00-255-6 is a nearly round river cobble showing minor impact and grinding damage on several facets. Specimen 89-99-10-319 is a larger, ovoid, flattened cobble (in several fragments) that also exhibits some impact damage and abrasive smoothing along one facet. These artifacts may have served as grinding stones.

The final specimen in this category, specimen 91-99-953-251, is a large, flat river cobble with minor damage along its periphery.

Table 8.9. Source material and metric attributes for ground stone implements found in Cherokee contexts.

Provenience	Specimen Number	Material	Weight (g)	Max. Length (mm)	Max. Width (mm)	Max. Thick. (mm)
Abrading Stone						
Feature 705	90-99-2924-19	shale	16.8	58.6	18.5	7.8
Grinding Tools						
Feature 455	90-00-265-5	quartzite	247.9	98.8	82.5	36.6
Feature 130	90-00-334-2	quartzite	2500.0	188.0	147.0	101.0
Feature 455	90-00-255-6	quartzite	174.8	54.0	47.1	47.0
Feature 21	89-99-10-319	siltstone	724.2	107.1	95.5	47.7
Feature 438	91-99-953-251	quartzite	9250.0	352.0	235.0	59.4
Percussion						
Feature 23	89-99-1078-321	quartz	237.1	68.0	63.7	43.3
Feature 1020	90-99-3662-10	quartzite	362.2	81.0	72.7	42.8
Feature 1508	90-99-9505-254	sandstone	297.1	99.5	69.6	34.9
Feature 705	90-99-2924-254	quartz	22.5	39.3	23.7	18.8
Hafted Percussion						
Feature 130	90-00-363-1	sandstone	577.2	147.1	104.5	34.5
Pipe Fragment						
Feature 995	90-99-5048-2	steatite	0.4	9.0	6.0	1.3
Discoidal						
Feature 391	91-99-890-6	slate	12.8	28.8	28.5	10.4
Indeterminate						
Feature 443	90-00-263-12	quartzite	89.8	56.9	45.5	22.1
Feature 55	89-99-829-274	quartzite	45.5	46.2	42.5	15.4
Feature 1508	90-99-9555-1	sandstone	815.8	126.6	98.1	45.9

This artifact may have been used as an anvil stone, although there are no obvious pecked depressions to confirm this function.

Stone Percussion tools "are used to remove unwanted portions of an object through the application of percussive force" (Sweat 2009:135). Four artifacts from Cherokee contexts were recovered. Three of these artifacts (specimens 89-99-1078-321, 90-99-3662-10, and 90-99-9505-254) are ovoid, somewhat flattened, river cobbles exhibiting some evidence for impact on margins of each tool. Specimen 90-99-2924-254 is a fragmentary example of this tool category. These artifacts were probably used as flintknapping hammerstones but could have also served for other percussion needs, or as pulverizing or grinding stones.

A Hafted Percussion Tool, according to Sweat's (2009:134) classification, is an artifact "whose primary function is to remove material from an object through percussion with a cutting edge." A single artifact, specimen 90-00-363-1, from a Cherokee context was recovered. This specimen, a grooved axe, is likely to have been used for heavy woodworking (Fig. 8.5*A*). The groove has been interpreted to stabilize the artifact within the haft, which was probably made of wood. This artifact is not likely of Cherokee vintage. The manufacture of grooved stone axes is normally associated with prehistoric cultures predating the historic Cherokees; these axes were produced by Middle Archaic through Middle Woodland cultures across the eastern Woodlands (Odell 1998:40), to be used mostly for woodworking. The "celt," a tapered, sharp-edged ground stone tool that was socketed into a wooden handle, replaced the grooved axe in most late prehistoric cultures in the mid-South.

According to Sweat (Sweat 2009:136), discoidals were likely used as gaming stones. A discoidal (specimen 91-99-890-6, Fig. 8.5*B*), roughly rounded from a tabular stone of about 28.5 mm in diameter and about 10 mm in thickness, was found in a Cherokee context. A similar artifact in size and shape is specimen 89-99-829-274 (Fig. 8.5*C*) (listed as an indeterminate ground stone artifact), which, although not definitively altered from its natural state, is of the size and shape to serve a similar function.

Figure 8.4. A nutting stone (specimen 90-00-334-2) is from a Cherokee context at the Townsend sites.

Figure 8.5. Other stone artifacts recovered from Cherokee contexts at the Townsend sites. *A*, grooved stone axe; *B*, *C*, discoidals or gaming pieces; *D*, steatite smoking pipe fragment; *E*, enlargement of specimen *D*.

A ground stone pipe fragment was also retrieved from a Cherokee feature. Sweat (2009:138) notes that most of the stone pipes recovered from the Townsend sites are made from sandstone. Made of steatite, the small fragment includes the lip of the bowl with a diamond incised design partially preserved (Fig. 8.5*D, E*).

Indeterminate ground stone ($n = 3$) included a flattened river cobble (specimen 90-99-9555-1) that may have been damaged slightly; a round, flattened, river cobble (specimen 89-99-829-274) that may have been shaped (see discoidal above and Fig. 8.5*C*); and a elongated river cobble (specimen 90-00-263-12) that has been damaged on each of its lateral margins. This latter specimen may be a fragment of a notched pebble, artifacts that were probably used as net weights. No other notched pebbles were recovered from Cherokee contexts.

Stone Tools in Cherokee Contexts

Even though the Cherokees of Tuckaleechee Cove existed in an era when Euroamerican tools and ornaments were available, few of these artifacts other than ornamental beads were a part of their material culture. Stone remained the primary medium for toolmaking. This stone tool inventory—as we know it through the artifacts recovered from the Townsend sites—was similar to the stone artifact inventories of Tuckaleechee Cove predecessors from Late Archaic foragers to Mississippian horticulturalists. That being the case, it is difficult to be sure that each artifact included in a Cherokee context was made and used by the Cherokees of Tuckaleechee Cove and was not a holdover from earlier times. Because of their normal durability, stone tools from any earlier vintage may be preserved as inclusions within Cherokee contexts.

Data relating to the distribution of lithic artifacts in Cherokee contexts were examined to help answer the question of whether, or to what extent, lithic artifacts found in Cherokee contexts suggested activities or functions not otherwise revealed by the presence of other artifact categories, or by areal associations of those contexts, one with another (see Chapter 6).

One activity that is often revealed by examining lithic distributions is stone tool manufacture. When lithic debitage density (feature volume/debitage count) for each feature associated with the six Cherokee households defined and described in Chapter 5 is calculated and compared, Features 16, 18, and 45 from Household 1 exhibit high lithic debitage concentrations. Feature 16, a small basin with a density of 9.14 specimens per liter, is ranked 30th among 33 features containing lithics. Feature 18 exhibits a density of 22.08 artifacts per liter, the highest density of any of the features. Similarly, Features 390, 391, and 392 from Household 6 contain high proportions of lithic debitage by volume. Feature 390 at 11.45 artifacts per liter is ranked 31st among the 33 features; Feature 391 at 6.75 artifacts per liter is 29th among the 33 features; and Feature 392 at 13.89 specimens per liter is ranked 32nd among the 33 features. These seven features are all small pits or basins with the exception of Feature 18, a medium-sized basin. Although high in debitage concentrations, lithic artifacts of likely Cherokee vintage (projectile points) are rare in these same features, suggesting that these debitage concentrations are not the result of Cherokee flintknapping, at least knapping episodes that involved working or refitting of projectile points. Interestingly, Marcoux (Chapter 6) found that each of these six features contained few Cherokee pottery sherds, and that each may have been a pit excavated for soil needed to repair structures. Pit fill likely represented a tertiary context in each case (see Marcoux's definition in Chapter 6)—that is, fill taken from a general midden or other mixed contexts in order to fill the holes.

On the other hand, Cherokee projectile points are concentrated in Features 130 and 135 of Household 3 and Feature 705 of Household 4. These features include a large pit and two medium pits. In Household 3, Feature 130, a large pit, exhibits a low lithic debitage concentration (0.79 artifacts per liter, ranked 9th among 33 features) but produced 16 cores, 9 stage bifaces, a crude tabular biface (hoe), the grooved axe discussed above (probably not Cherokee), a nutting stone (Fig. 8.4), and 5 projectile points, 4 likely of Cherokee vintage. Feature 135, also in Household 3, was a medium-sized pit containing a low concentration of debitage (0.38 artifacts per liter, ranked 6th of 33 features) but with 4 cores, 6 stage bifaces, 3 flake tools, a biface and 3 projectile points, all likely of Cherokee vintage. Similarly, Feature 705 in Household 4 is a medium-sized pit with a low debitage concentration (0.26 artifacts per liter, ranked 4th of 33 features) but containing 9 cores, 4 stage bifaces, a flake tool, 2 bifacial tools, and 4 projectile points, 3 likely of Cherokee origin. Seemingly, these features contain lithic assemblages that are the best candidates for features whose contents were produced by Cherokee inhabitants. In Marcoux's discussion of these pit features (Chapter 6), he notes that they seem to represent secondary contexts and exhibit high densities of Cherokee ceramics. Feature 705 produced a fragment of iron that reinforces the notion that its pit fill is of Cherokee origin.

Conclusions

The Cherokees and their predecessors employed two methods of stone tool manufacture—chipped stone and ground stone technology. Both are reductive in nature, meaning that the toolmaker must reduce a stone mass to produce the artifact shape desired. Chipped stone technology relies on the principle of flaking of suitable stone (materials that fracture concoidally) in order to reduce the mass. Most of the chipped stone tools were manufactured from local cherts, but as Sweat (2009) has convincingly demonstrated, suitable materials for most chipped stone tools are not available in Little River adjacent to the Townsend sites but rather probably come from about 20 km downstream outside the confines of Tuckaleechee Cove.

Chipped stone technology produces a large and usually quite durable byproduct—debitage. Debitage, or the detritus from stone reduction, includes flakes (detached pieces), cores (objective pieces), and other detritus such as blocky pieces and shatter.

Judging from the cores and flakes found in Cherokee contexts, tool stone (mostly Knox chert) was usually found in small nodules or small tabular pieces. While some freehand reduction is evident, much of the reduction was apparently accomplished through the bipolar method in which a piece of chert (objective piece) is held on an anvil stone, then hit with a hammerstone, producing flakes that may then be made into tools. Because raw materials were often quite small, most of the tools in the material inventory are small.

Importantly, many stone tools were made from flakes, or flakes were simply selected from the detritus for useful characteristics such as sharp edges or steep, strong break facets. Such tools in the Cherokee inventory include modified flakes and flake scrapers, expedient tools used for various cutting and scraping tasks such as animal butchery, skinning, and processing of hides and leather. While some of the more specialized flake tools such as gravers and perforator/drills are not represented in Cherokee contexts, these artifacts were probably made and used by Tuckaleechee Cove Cherokees in ways similar to their predecessors. Small, triangular or elliptical arrowheads were also mostly made from flakes (see Fig. 8.3).

Either a flake or core might be further reduced into a bifacial tool such as a scraper, knife, or drill. While most of the bifacial tools or fragments from Cherokee contexts were likely to have been preforms or blanks (artifacts that might have been unfinished tools), several appear to be bifacial scrapers and drills. Two artifacts were fragments of chipped stone hoes (see Fig. 8.2*A*, *B*), made from tabular, sedimentary stone.

Ground stone technology is based on the removal of particles of rock from the surface of a granitic material to shape the artifact. Several artifacts from Cherokee contexts loosely fit into this category including cobbles used as anvils, grinding stones, hammerstones, nutting stones, and, perhaps, gaming pieces. The grooved stone axe (see Fig. 8.5*A*), a likely woodworking tool, is also an excellent example of this approach to toolmaking, but this artifact probably predates the Cherokee occupation of the Townsend sites.

Together, while seeming to be an impoverished material inventory, the Cherokees of Tuckaleechee Cove employed these technologies and material resources to produce stone tools necessary for daily life. Remember that in addition to a rich ceramic technology, much of the material culture of the Tuckaleechee Cove Cherokees no doubt was produced in perishable materials such as wood, basketry, cane, animal skins, sinew and plant fibers.

Note

1. Personal communication with Stephen Carmody, 2010, concerning a use wear study (in progress) of drills and scrapers from the Townsend sites.

Chapter 9

Glass Trade Beads

The paucity of trade between Cherokee communities and English settlers during the early years of the English Contact period (ca. A.D. 1650–1715) (described in Chapter 2) is attested to by the small number of European artifacts recovered during the Townsend project. Indeed, the entire sample of European-made artifacts recovered from Cherokee occupational contexts consisted of 228 glass trade beads and a single small piece of iron. I begin this chapter with a formal description of the glass trade bead assemblage recovered from Townsend. I then provide an estimated date range for occupation of the site by incorporating the Townsend glass bead data into a regional glass bead chronology that I constructed for the Townsend project. This glass bead chronology—which is the result of a seriation of 106 burial assemblages containing a total of 37,866 glass trade beads from a number of seventeenth- and eighteenth-century sites across the Southeast—provides a robust chronological framework that can be used to estimate the occupation dates of sites, like Townsend, that produce small glass trade bead assemblages.

The Glass Trade Bead Assemblage from 40Bt89, 40Bt90, and 40Bt91

Following the traditional format for glass trade bead description (e.g., Deagan 1987; Karklins 1985; Kidd and Kidd 1970; Smith 1991, 1992, 2002b), the glass trade bead assemblages from 40Bt89, 40Bt90, and 40Bt91 were classified with respect to manufacturing technique, bead structure, and bead decoration.

Manufacturing Technique

There are two major methods of manufacture for glass trade beads. The first method is known as the drawn cane technique. In this method, a mass of molten glass is removed from the furnace, blown into a hollow globe, and extruded. When the desired diameter of the bead is achieved, this drawn-out "cane" of glass is set aside to cool. The cooled canes are then broken into short tubular sections that can be left as they are (that is, untumbled), or the beads can be tumbled in a heated barrel along with sand in order to produce a round or oval-shaped bead. The other manufacturing method, known as the "wire wound" or "mandrel wound" technique, involves winding a molten thread of glass around a metal mandrel until the desired diameter is achieved. Whereas beads are produced in batches using the drawn cane technique, they are individually manufactured using the mandrel wound technique. In most cases, these two manufacturing processes are readily distinguishable. Drawn cane beads are typically tubular, round, or oval in shape with a perceptible "grain" of air bubbles that runs parallel to the central perforation. Mandrel wound beads, on the other hand, are more regular in shape (round or oval) and have a "grain" that runs circumferentially around the central perforation.

Bead Structure

When applied to glass beads, the term "structure" refers to the composition of the bead body. Beads of simple construction consist of a single layer of glass, whereas beads of compound construction are made of multiple layers of glass, which in assemblages from the Southeast range from two to seven distinct layers. Compound bead structure is overwhelmingly associated with drawn beads rather than wound beads.

Bead Decoration

Bead decoration techniques include shaping, the addition of colored stripes, and, much less frequently, the addition of inlaid decorations. Shaping is typically done while the bead is still in a plastic state and is accomplished with a mold or, more commonly, by applying pressure with a smooth or carved paddle while the bead lies on a flat stone or iron surface. This latter technique is called "marvering." The most common shaped glass beads in southeastern assemblages are those with faceted sides, raspberry-shaped beads, and fluted or "melon"-shaped beads. Stripes are given to beads by applying canes of colored glass to the molten mass before it is extruded. Stripes can be of two types: simple and complex. Simple-striped beads have stripes of monochromatic glass. Beads with complex stripes have individual stripes that consist of two (or more) different colors with one color appearing to be bordered on both sides by another color. The bordered effect is achieved by placing a narrow cane of glass on top of another fatter cane of a different color. In the parlance of most classification systems a red stripe bordered by white stripes would be called a "red on white" stripe. Inlaid decoration is the rarest form of decoration in southeastern trade bead assemblages and typically occurs on wire wound specimens. Materials used in the inlaying process include colored glass and in some cases precious metal, such as gold or silver gilt.

The following description of the 228 glass trade beads recovered from Cherokee contexts at the Townsend sites (Table 9.1) is based upon the glass bead classification system pioneered by Kidd and Kidd (1970), as it is the most widely used and easily

Table 9.1. Glass trade beads recovered from Cherokee contexts.

Household	**Drawn Cane Necklace Beads**									**Drawn Cane Seed Beads**											**Total of all Beads**
	IIa40	IIa13	IIa44	IIa6	IIb'6	IIbb13	IIbb24	IIj	IVa5	Ia5	IIa40	IIa13	IIa44	IIa55	IIa28	IIa31	IIa46	IIa9	IIb18	IVa5	
1	5	7	0	0	0	0	1	0	3	0	56	16	3	3	2	5	1	1	3	3	109
2	5	0	1	1	1	1	0	1	1	1	30	10	0	15	2	2	0	0	0	2	73
3	1	0	0	1	0	0	0	0	0	0	6	2	0	2	0	1	0	0	0	0	13
4	5	0	0	0	0	0	0	0	0	0	14	0	2	0	0	7	0	0	0	0	28
5	1	1	0	0	0	0	0	0	0	0	1	0	0	1	0	0	0	0	0	0	4
6	0	0	0	0	0	0	0	0	0	0	1	0	0	0	0	0	0	0	0	0	1
total	*17*	*8*	*1*	*2*	*1*	*1*	*1*	*1*	*4*	*1*	*108*	*28*	*5*	*21*	*4*	*15*	*1*	*1*	*3*	*5*	*228*

understood system in the literature to date. This classificatory system first divides glass beads by manufacturing method, and then deploys beads into types based on bead structure, decoration, color, and diaphaneity (see individual descriptions). I make a further distinction by dividing the assemblage into two broad functional categories reflecting large necklace beads (larger than 4 mm) and small embroidery or "seed" beads (less than 4 mm).

Drawn Cane Necklace Beads

Type 1. Kidd Type: IIa40
Sample Size: 17
Diameter Range: 6.11–8.07 mm
Average Diameter: 6.51 mm

This bead type consists of monochromatic (simple construction) opaque turquoise or "robin's egg blue" tumbled necklace beads. They are round to oval in shape. This type is by far the most ubiquitous necklace bead found at seventeenth- and eighteenth-century southeastern and midwestern Indian sites. Its widespread distribution suggests that it was a major component of English, French, and Spanish trade (Brain 1979; Good 1972; Smith 1992; Stone 1974).

Type 2. Kidd Type: IIa13
Sample Size: 8
Diameter Range: 6.65–10.30 mm
Average Diameter: 7.80 mm

This type includes tumbled opaque white round and oval-shaped necklace beads of simple construction. Like Type 1, these beads were apparently traded widely across the Southeast.

Type 3. Kidd Type: IIa44
Sample Size: 1
Diameter: 6.03 mm

This specimen was a translucent medium blue tumbled round necklace bead of simple construction. Smith (1983, 1987, 1992) identifies this type with Contact and Colonial period Spanish sites spanning the late sixteenth to eighteenth centuries. I identified this bead type in late seventeenth-century burial assemblages from sites associated with English trade.

Type 4. Kidd Type: IIa6
Sample Size: 2
Diameter Range: 7.26–10.29 mm
Average Diameter: 8.78 mm

This type consists of translucent dark rose brown tumbled round necklace beads of simple construction. This particular bead type appears black until held up to light and is often classified as opaque black. Round and barrel-shaped versions of this bead have been found in Spanish and English trade contexts dating from the early seventeenth through eighteenth centuries (Smith 1992, 2001; Deagan 1987; Pluckhahn 1996).

Type 5. Kidd Type: IIb'6
Sample Size: 1
Diameter: 9.43 mm

This type includes a single specimen. It is an opaque white tumbled oval necklace bead of simple construction with six red spiral stripes. This bead type is present in mortuary assemblages at the late seventeenth-century Cherokee site of Ocoee and the eighteenth-century Cherokee town of Chota-Tanasee (Schroedl and Breitburg 1986), and at late seventeenth- and eighteenth-century Indian and colonial sites throughout the Gulf Coast and the Mississippi River Valley (Good 1972; Smith 2002b; Stone 1974).

Type 6. Kidd Type: IIbb13
Sample Size: 1
Diameter: 6.43 mm

This type consists of a single oval-shaped opaque white tumbled necklace bead of simple construction with three sets of complex navy blue on red stripes. While this bead type is never present in large frequencies, it does exhibit a wide geographic distribution across late seventeenth- and eighteenth-century Indian and colonial sites from the lower and upper Mississippi River Valley, across the Appalachian Mountains, to the piedmont of Georgia (e.g., Brain 1979; Fleming 1976; Good 1972; Stone 1974).

Type 7. Kidd Type: IIbb24
Sample Size: 1
Diameter: 7.43 mm

This type includes an opaque round turquoise tumbled necklace bead of simple construction featuring three sets of complex red on white stripes. As with Type 6, my research showed that this bead type has a widespread distribution across late seventeenth- and early eighteenth-century English and French colonial sites including Ocoee, Hiwassee Island, and Chota-Tanasee in Tennessee (Schroedl and Breitburg 1986), the Fredricks site in Piedmont North Carolina, and the Tarver sites in Piedmont Georgia (Pluckhahn 1996, 1997).

Type 8. Kidd Type: IIj
Sample Size: 1
Diameter: 13.07 mm

This type included a single translucent dark rose brown tumbled round necklace bead of simple construction with three inlaid white wavy stripes. This particular bead type appears black until held up to light and is often classified as opaque black. These distinctive beads, often referred to as "Roman" or "rattlesnake" beads, are very good temporal markers for the late seventeenth and early eighteenth centuries. I found them present in collections from Ocoee and Chota-Tanasee in Tennessee (Schroedl and Breitburg 1986), the Peachtree site in western North Carolina, the Fredricks site in Piedmont North Carolina, and the Tarver sites in Piedmont Georgia (Pluckhahn 1996, 1997).

Type 9. Kidd Type: IVa5
Sample Size: 4
Diameter Range: 5.9 mm–7.51 mm
Average Diameter: 6.54 mm

Type 9 includes tumbled beads of compound construction possessing an opaque red outer layer and a transparent green core. Beads in this type are usually referred to as Cornaline d'Aleppo beads. Tumbled and untumbled varieties of this bead type exhibit a wide geographic and temporal range, but appear to be most frequent during the eighteenth century (Brain 1979; Deagan 1987). Mortuary assemblages with large frequencies of round Cornaline d'Aleppo beads are found at the Tarver sites (Pluckhahn 1996, 1997) and the late seventeenth-century Indian sites in Piedmont North Carolina (Ward and Davis 1993).

Drawn Cane Seed Beads

Type 10. Kidd Type: Ia5
Sample Size: 1
Diameter: 2.87 mm

This type consists of a single small tubular untumbled opaque white seed bead of simple construction. Monochromatic untumbled seed beads like this specimen are typically found in glass trade bead assemblages spanning the second half of the eighteenth century (Baden 1983; Russ and Chapman 1983).

Type 11. Kidd Type: IIa40
Sample Size: 108
Diameter Range: 2.27 mm–3.77 mm
Average Diameter: 3.0 mm

This type includes small, circular and round tumbled opaque turquoise seed beads of simple construction. Monochromatic seed beads like these are quite frequent in glass trade bead assemblages spanning from the seventeenth to late eighteenth centuries, and thus are generally not good temporal markers.

Type 12. Kidd Type: IIa13
Sample Size: 28
Diameter Range: 2.36 mm–3.69 mm
Average Diameter: 3.0 mm

This type includes small, circular and round tumbled opaque white seed beads of simple construction.

Type 13. Kidd Type: IIa44
Sample Size: 5
Diameter Range: 3.06 mm–3.83 mm
Average Diameter: 3.43 mm

This type includes small, circular and round tumbled transparent medium blue seed beads of simple construction.

Type 14. Kidd Type: IIa55
Sample Size: 21
Diameter Range: 2.10 mm–3.89 mm
Average Diameter: 3.04 mm

This type includes small, circular and round tumbled transparent navy blue seed beads of simple construction.

Type 15. Kidd Type: IIa28
Sample Size: 4
Diameter Range: 2.71 mm–3.6 mm
Average Diameter: 3.03 mm

This type includes small, circular and round tumbled transparent green seed beads of simple construction.

Type 16. Kidd Type: IIa31
Sample Size: 15
Diameter Range: 2.43 mm–3.20 mm
Average Diameter: 3.04 mm

This type includes small, circular and round tumbled transparent turquoise seed beads of simple construction.

Type 17. Kidd Type: IIa46
Sample Size: 1
Diameter: 3.52 mm

This type includes small, circular and round tumbled opaque medium blue seed beads of simple construction.

Type 18. Kidd Type: IIa9
Sample Size: 1
Diameter: 3.20 mm

This type includes a single small round tumbled colorless seed bead of simple construction.

Type 19. Kidd Type: IIb18
Sample Size: 3
Diameter Range: 2.86 mm–3.54 mm
Average Diameter: 3.15 mm

This type consists of small round tumbled beads of simple construction. The beads are colorless (or light gray) with 10–12 thin white stripes. They are smaller versions of so-called "gooseberry" beads. The only known examples of this type are found in mortuary contexts at late seventeenth- and early eighteenth-century Cherokee sites in eastern Tennessee (Schroedl and Breitburg 1986). Given the small size of these beads, the stripes are very difficult to discern; therefore, it is possible that these beads do exist in earlier assemblages, but are misclassified.

Type 20. Kidd Type: IVa5
Sample Size: 5
Diameter Range: 3.19 mm–3.67 mm
Average Diameter: 3.41 mm

Type 20 includes small round and circular tumbled beads of compound construction possessing an opaque red outer layer and a transparent green core. Like Type 9 beads, the beads in this type are usually referred to as Cornaline d'Aleppo beads.

Chronology from Glass Beads: The English Period in the Southeast, circa A.D. 1607–1783

For Eastern Woodlands archaeologists, glass trade beads are among the small suite of artifacts that mark the watershed moment when Europeans first came into contact with native groups living in eastern North America. Indeed, it is widely known that glass beads accompanied Columbus on his first voyage to the New World and continued to be an integral part of Native American material culture assemblages well into the nineteenth century (Good 1983; Smith and Good 1982). For decades, research concerning glass beads has been pursued by archaeologists who see value in the ability of beads to aid in assigning precise occupation dates to historic sites. The alluring promise held by beads is understandable, for the combination of ubiquity in the archaeological record and celerity in style change is the stuff of robust artifact chronology. Research conducted over the last 50 years has gone a long way toward realizing the chronology-building potential of glass beads. This work can be summarized best geographically with regard to the three main regions of colonial eastern North America—the Northeast, the Midwest, and the Southeast.

The Northeast

In the Northeast, archaeological literature concerning glass trade bead chronologies has been dominated by seriations of bead assemblages recovered from sixteenth- through eighteenth-century colonial Dutch and English, Iroquois, and Huron contexts (e.g., Bennett 1983; Fenstermaker 1974; Huey 1983; Kent 1983; Kenyon and Kenyon 1983; Rumrill 1991; Wray 1983). The methods used in seriating the bead assemblages vary greatly among these researchers. On one end of the spectrum, there are quantitative seriations that emphasize changes in the relative percentages of different bead types through time (e.g., Huey 1983; Kent 1983). Kent (1983), for example, offered a frequency seriation of bead types (using the classification system developed by Kidd and Kidd [1970]) across numerous sites in the Susquehanna Valley whose occupation ranged from the 1570s to the 1760s. The results of his seriation evinced the classic "battleship-shaped" curves that indicated the monotonic increase and decrease in the popularity of particular bead styles through time. The seriation solution he offered highlighted a temporal trend from assemblages dominated by simple and compound tumbled beads in the late sixteenth and early seventeenth centuries, to those dominated by compound tubular beads in the early and mid-seventeenth century, to assemblages dominated by mandrel wound beads in the late seventeenth and eighteenth centuries.

On the other end of the spectrum of seriation techniques used in the Northeast are those that construct chronologies by marking the presence or absence of certain bead types at sites dating to different time periods (e.g., Bennett 1983; Fenstermaker 1974; Kenyon and Kenyon 1983; Rumrill 1991; Wray 1983). These chronologies, which comprise the majority of the published seriations in the Northeast, are more qualitative than quantitative. Researchers speak of the "average" assemblage that one finds on sites dating to a particular time period, or of a particular type of bead that is unique to a certain period, which can be used to date other sites.

Wray's (1983) study of Seneca trade bead assemblages offers a great example of this method. Wray presented a chronology of bead types (using Kidd and Kidd 1970) based on his reconstruction of the migration sequence of certain Seneca villages between 1550 and 1820 (Wray 1983). He divided the sequence into 15- to 20-year periods that roughly corresponded to the typical occupation span of a Seneca village. For each period, he provided a list of the "key" types of beads recovered from sites dating to this period. His method of seriation was especially adroit at identifying the introduction and "dropping out" dates of certain bead types through time.

Despite the difference between quantitative and qualitative methodologies, the chronologies of the Northeast share two premises. First, in all the chronologies, the archaeological site is used as the basic analytical unit. Thus, each assemblage of beads represents the entire occupation span of that site. Furthermore, the arraying of these site-level bead assemblages proceeds from known occupation dates, determined either by reference to historical documentation or by other temporally sensitive artifacts. Consequently, the chronological order of the assemblages is taken as a given, and the researcher's task is to look for the differences in the bead types among the assemblages.

The Midwest

In the Midwest, attempts at glass trade bead chronology are best exemplified by Good's (1972) analysis of glass beads from the Guebert site in Illinois and Stone's (1974) analysis of the assemblage from Fort Michilimackinac in Michigan. Respectively, these archaeological contexts represent a Kaskaskia Indian village occupied between 1719 and 1833 and a French-then-English occupied colonial fort dating to between 1715 and 1781. Because the main goal for each author was to produce an archaeological site report, their analyses were necessarily focused on issues of taxonomy for a single assemblage rather than the chronological ordering of a group of site-level assemblages. As a result, the authors used a very different methodology for building a chronology of glass trade beads. Most importantly, Good (1972:95–98) and Stone (1974:88–90) made bead *types* rather than bead *assemblages* the focus of their chronology. Although their typologies were somewhat different, the authors (and virtually all researchers since) relied upon attributes of shape, color, method of manufacture, and decoration in creating these types. Ultimately, the goals of this classification were to establish a range of dates for the circulation of each bead type and to identify its European trading source (that is, French or English). To fulfill these goals, they conducted comparative research by examining bead assemblages from other sites with established occupation dates and European colonial affiliations. From these comparisons, they were able to estimate a range of circulation dates and establish the likely trading sources for many bead types.

The Southeast

Researchers constructing glass bead chronologies in the Southeast have utilized a combination of seriation methods and type-based comparative methods (e.g., Brain 1979; Brown 1976; Deagan 1987; Polhemus 1983, 1987; Smith 1983, 1987). For his report on the Toqua site, Polhemus (1983, 1987) performed what he called a "sequential seriation" on glass bead assemblages recovered from individual burials at various historic period sites in east Tennessee. The method used by Polhemus was novel in that he made the individual burial assemblage the basic unit of analysis in his chronology rather than the site-level assemblage or bead type. He argued that burial assemblages were best for his seriation because burial contexts represented short-duration "closed" contexts where the co-occurrence of bead types almost certainly represented their contemporaneity. The exact seriation methods Polhemus used are not clear, but in the resulting chronology, he (1987:914) suggested that glass bead assemblages in east Tennessee dated either to the seventeenth or mid-eighteenth centuries.

Smith (1983) and Deagan (1987) each have offered glass bead chronologies that focus on the Spanish Colonial period in the Southeast (ca. A.D. 1500–1700). In both cases, the authors traced the presence or absence of particular bead types (which were similar in composition to Good [1972] and Stone [1974]) across a chronologically ordered series of sites whose occupation dates were to a large extent "known." These seriations resulted in estimated date ranges for the circulation of various bead types that are commonly found on Indian and Spanish colonial sites occupied between the late sixteenth and eighteenth centuries. As in the case of the Northeast, their identification of the introduction and "dropping out" dates of particular bead types has been a great aid in dating bead assemblages from undocumented sites. The so-called "flush eye" bead, for example, which was found to have a relatively short circulation period of 1575–1630, has become a good "index fossil" for dating assemblages to that time period (Smith 1982).

In the Lower Mississippi Valley, Brain's (1979) seminal typology and chronology of the large glass bead assemblage from the Trudeau site is very much in the same vein as the chronologies developed by Good (1972) and Stone (1974). Like these researchers, Brain was interested in establishing ranges of dates for the circulation of his bead types, as well as in identifying possible markers for particular European trading sources. Also, many of the bead types he identified from the mid-eighteenth-century Tunica village were the same as those likely traded by the French at the Guebert site and at Fort Michilimackinac. Brain (1979:114) assigned mean dates and date ranges for many of his bead types based on the occupation spans of numerous sites with comparative assemblages (see also Brown 1976 for a similar "bracketing technique" of dating assemblages). He also produced a series of regional maps depicting the geographical distribution of key bead types though time (Brain 1979:117–31). Today this typology and series of maps remain very important contributions to our knowledge of eighteenth-century beads, especially those beads traded by the French.

The preceding discussion is not meant to be exhaustive. There are indeed many additional reports in the literature, but the varied forums for their publication (including research manuscripts, regional journals, and cultural resource management reports) make them somewhat difficult to track down. In the Southeast, these reports often deal with assemblages from individual sites with relatively small sample sizes (e.g., Polhemus 1985; Smith 1991, 1992, 2001, 2002b). The methods used in these reports are similar to those followed by Good (1972), Stone (1974), and Brain (1979) and involve classification and comparison to other assemblages with the goal of placing the study assemblage within a chronological and cultural context. Many of these reports contain very important insights that contribute to our growing knowledge of glass bead chronology in the Southeast. A synthesis of these insights is desperately needed.

Our ability to use glass trade beads in dating historic occupations has progressed a great deal; however, there are some areas that require additional research. The particular area of my research interest involves glass trade bead assemblages associated with seventeenth- and eighteenth-century English-Indian trade in the Southeast. In the Southeast, the best chronological "resolution" established by current bead chronologies relates either to sixteenth- to the mid-seventeenth-century Spanish-traded bead assemblages or to mid-eighteenth-century French-traded bead assemblages (Deagan 1987; Brain 1979; Brown 1976; Smith 1983, 1987; Smith and Good 1982). While the Northeast contains many English-traded bead assemblages dating to the seventeenth and eighteenth centuries, many of the related diagnostic bead types are simply absent in southeastern assemblages (Smith 1983:151).

Additionally, small sample sizes impose two major limitations that reduce the temporal resolution of existing bead chronologies in the Southeast (Smith 1983:147–48). First, in most cases, bead assemblages from individual burials or features have had to be lumped together at the site level. In many cases, these sites were occupied for several decades or more. Second, because small samples preclude the possibility of seriating assemblages based on relative frequencies of bead types, researchers have been forced to rely solely on the presence or absence of particular diagnostic bead types at sites to assign occupation dates. The combination of using lumped site-level assemblages and presence/absence has resulted in chronologies with very large date ranges for many bead types (see mean dates and ranges for individual bead types in Brain [1979:114] for an example). I follow Smith (2002b:58) in arguing that we should strive to overcome these limitations and to construct bead chronologies that take into account the total bead assemblage from a context or site rather than the presence of a single bead type. I further argue that this can be accomplished by performing a quantitative seriation of relatively large glass bead assemblages from individual contexts whose chronological associations are certain—specifically, bead assemblages found in mortuary contexts.

Constructing a Glass Bead Chronology

This section addresses my attempt to perform a quantitative seriation (using a technique known as correspondence analysis) of numerous glass bead assemblages recovered from mortuary contexts at various seventeenth- and eighteenth-century sites across the Southeast (Fig. 9.1; Table 9.2). The seriation technique I am introducing orders mortuary assemblages by comparing the relative frequencies of various bead types found in each assemblage. This study will add to our current knowledge of glass bead chronology in the Southeast by synthesizing existing data as well as presenting new data. The seriation will also act as a robust quantitative test of current glass bead chronologies. Finally, the seriation method I introduce here can provide a more objective basis for regional and/or chronological comparison.

The Study Sample

This study focuses on a period that marks the English/British colonial presence in the Southeast bookended by the founding of Jamestown colony and by the end of the American Revolutionary War (ca. A.D. 1607–1783). I focus on this period for two principal reasons. First, I want to produce a bead chronology that complements, rather than duplicates, existing chronologies like Smith's (1983) important chronology of the preceding Spanish period or Brain's (1979) work with French-traded eighteenth-century Tunica bead assemblages. Second, as stated in this

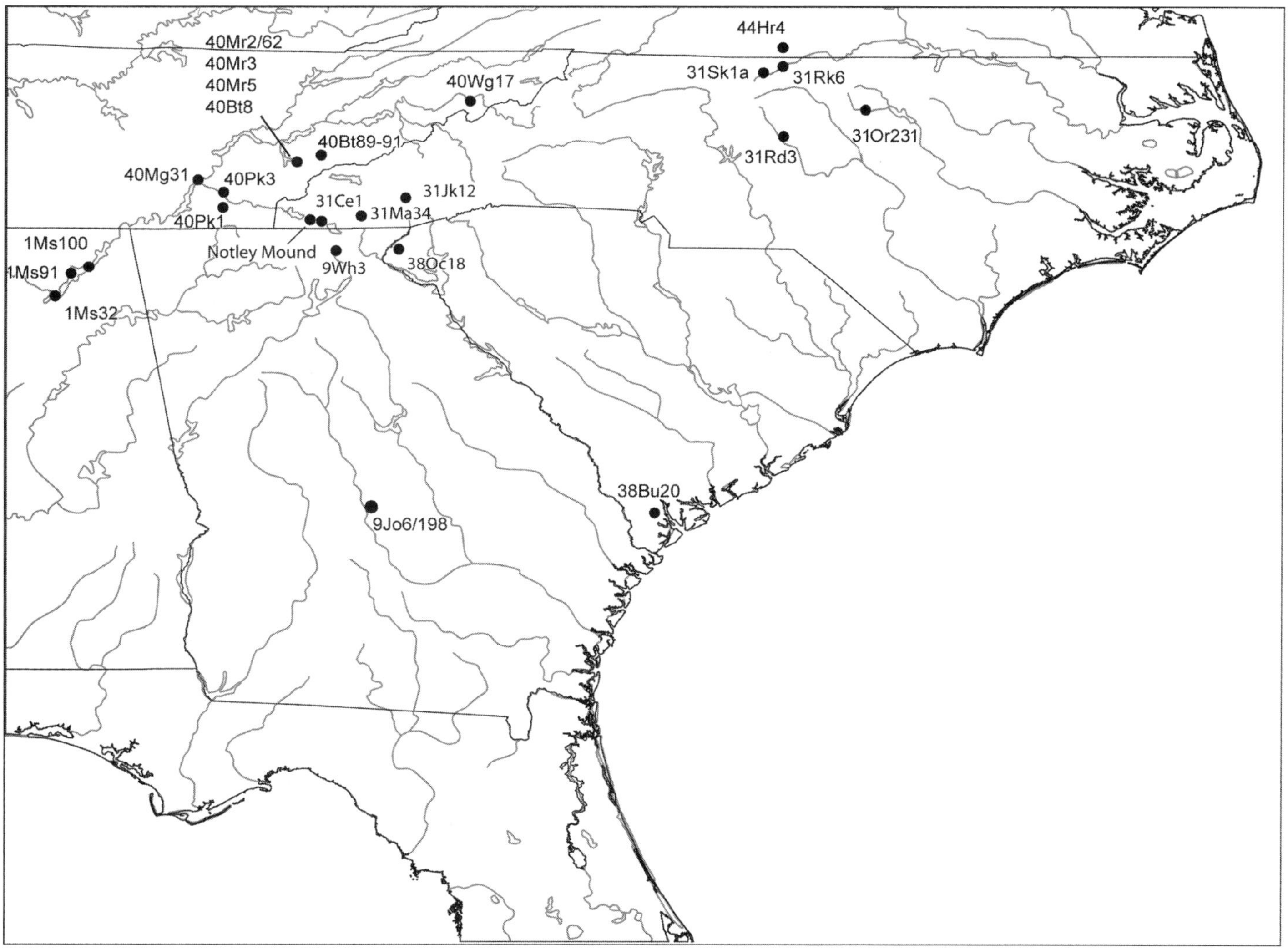

Figure 9.1. Locations of glass trade bead assemblages used in this study.

Table 9.2. Archaeological sites with glass bead assemblages used in the study.

Site	State	Occupation Range	References
Law's Site (1Ms100)	AL	1630–1690	Flemming 1976; Smith 1987
McKee Island (1Ms32)	AL	1630–1690	Flemming 1976; Smith 1987
Columbus City Landing (1Ms91)	AL	1630–1690	Flemming 1976; Smith 1987
Tarver and Little Tarver (9Jo6, 9Jo198)	GA	1695–1715	Pluckhahn 1996, 1997
Upper Saratown (31Sk1a)	NC	1650–1690	Eastman 1999; Ward and Davis 2001
Brickyard (31Rd3)	NC	unknown	Eastman RLA[a]
Fredricks (31Or231)	NC	1680–1710	Eastman RLA; Ward and Davis 1993
Madison (31Rk6)	NC	1607–1690	Eastman 1999; Ward and Davis 1993
Philpott (44Hr4)	VA	1620–1670	Eastman RLA; Ward and Davis 2001
Altamaha Town (38Bu20)	SC	1700–1715	Poplin, pers. comm., 2006
Plum Grove (40Wg17)	TN	1600–1700	Smith 1987, n.d.
Chota-Tanasee (40Mr2, 40Mr62)	TN	1700–1820	Newman 1986
Townsend (40Bt89-91)	TN	1650–1720	this monograph
Ocoee (40Pk1)	TN	1650–1700	Lewis et al. 1995; Smith 1987
Hiwassee Island (40Mg31)	TN	1650–1700	Lewis and Kneberg 1946; Waselkov 1989
Tallassee (40Bt8)	TN	1600–1780	Cornette 1976; Waselkov 1989
Mialoquo (40Mr3)	TN	1760–1780	Russ and Chapman 1983
Tomotley (40Mr5)	TN	1750–1776	Baden 1983
Hiwassee Old Town (40Pk3)	TN	1700–1760	Fenstermaker 1978
Notla Mound	NC	unknown	Turbyfill 1927
Peachtree Mound (31Ce1)	NC	1550–1780	Setzler and Jennings 1941; Skowronek 1991
Tuckaseegee (31Jk12)	NC	1650–1700	Keel 1976
Nacoochee Mound (9Wh3)	GA	1600–1700	Heye et al. 1918; Waselkov 1989
Chattooga	SC	1650–1740	Schroedl 1994
Coweeta Creek	NC	1300–1715	Rodning 2004

[a]The unpublished bead data from these sites are taken from analyses performed by Jane Eastman for the Research Laboratories of Archaeology, University of North Carolina at Chapel Hill.

chapter's opening, there is a significant gap in our knowledge of undocumented Indian communities in the interior Southeast that were occupied during this period.

I limit my sample to mortuary assemblages because they represent virtually instantaneous deposition events (Steponaitis 1983). The contemporaneity of bead assemblages from pit features, surface collections, and middens is much less certain; more likely, these contexts are the result of accumulation over a longer period of time. Thus, while there may be some time lag associated with the "heirlooming" of beads in some mortuary contexts, using these assemblages in a seriation will result in the best chronological clarity. It is hoped that bead assemblages from features or surface collections can be compared to the results of this study in order to estimate dates and/or the likelihood that an assemblage is chronologically mixed.

Seriation Method

The method used here to construct a glass bead chronology for the Southeast differs significantly from methods used in previous constructs (e.g., Brain 1979; Deagan 1987; Polhemus 1983; Smith 1983). First, the large study sample affords the opportunity to forgo lumping assemblages at the site level and allows individual mortuary assemblages to become the unit of analysis. Second, the chronology developed in this study uses a quantitative multidimensional seriation method based on the relative frequencies of different bead types. Third, the seriation technique used in this study does not proceed from "known" occupation dates for sites. Instead, this study uses an exploratory and nonparametric seriation technique that attempts to identify patterns in a dataset without any previous assumptions.

In the Southeast, material culture seriations have historically been associated with "Fordian" frequency seriations of ceramic assemblages. This method results in classic figures portraying the "battleship-shaped" frequency distributions of chronologically ordered ceramic assemblages (Dunnell 1970; Phillips, Ford, and Griffin 1951). Recently, authors have critiqued this traditional method of seriation, citing the largely intuitive nature of the procedure, inherent problems of "closure" when using percentages, and the inability of the method to portray variability in more than one dimension (e.g., Mainfort 2005; McNutt 2005). For these reasons, this study uses an alternative multidimensional method of seriating glass bead assemblages.

This seriation method, called correspondence analysis (CA) (see Baxter 1994; Shennan 1997), is a powerful multivariate statistical technique that has been used widely for seriating artifact assemblages in European archaeology (e.g., Bech 1988; Madsen 1988). One rarely sees correspondence analysis, however, in the archaeological literature of North America (see Duff 1996 for a notable exception). The relative obscurity of correspondence analysis is curious given that (1) the technique is based on straightforward and fundamental statistical logic—essentially the same logic that underlies the chi-square test; (2) unlike other multivariate techniques, it requires no assumptions of the data and works directly on untransformed artifact frequencies (counts); and (3) like the chi-square test, it is resistant to differences in sample sizes.

One of the largest obstacles to constructing a comprehensive glass bead chronology for the Southeast has been finding techniques that can simultaneously account for variability along dozens of dimensions represented by the different bead types. The dataset (data matrix) in this study, for example, consists of 98 mortuary assemblages (rows) and 46 separate bead types (columns) each representing a single dimension of variability (Table 9.3). It is impossible to ascertain any patterns simply by inspecting the data matrix alone, and while one could easily plot the mortuary assemblages in terms of the frequencies of 2 or perhaps 3 bead types in the same figure, one cannot simultaneously visualize the 46 dimensions that represent all the bead types. Correspondence analysis is an ordination technique that seeks to represent as accurately as possible the relationships between cases (i.e., individual mortuary assemblages) and between variables (i.e., glass bead types) using a small number of dimensions. Thus, correspondence analysis solves the dilemma by providing the analyst with a way to visually explore and present multivariate data by reducing the dimensionality of a data matrix. This technique is particularly suited to seriation because one of the major dimensions of variability among artifact assemblages tends to be temporal.

How correspondence analysis reduces the dimensionality of a data matrix is a bit involved, but a brief discussion should suffice to make it clearer (see Baxter 1994 and Shennan 1997 for in-depth discussions of CA). Correspondence analysis can be viewed as a more complex chi-square test that compares all the row and column profiles of a data matrix and computes the departure of each case and variable from an average profile. In this study, the average case profile would be a hypothetical mortuary assemblage consisting of the average proportions of each bead type, and the average column profile would simply be the average frequency of each bead type as calculated across all mortuary assemblages. In the biplot produced by correspondence analysis, the average profiles are represented by the intersection of the x and y axes. Using simple chi-square calculations, correspondence analysis measures both the degree and the direction of departure of each bead assemblage and bead type from the average profiles. In seriation applications of correspondence analysis, if the artifact types are temporally sensitive, the first dimension of variability (the x axis in the biplot) should represent relative time.

In this study, the correspondence analysis is carried out using the "Correspondence Analysis" module of the Bonn Archaeological Software Package (BASP). This program takes input in the form of a frequency matrix and returns output in the form of distributional biplots and diagnostic statistics. One of this program's benefits is that it depicts the distribution of individual mortuary assemblages and bead types together in a single biplot. In interpreting these combined biplots in the following discussion, one can infer that mortuary assemblages and bead types located near one another in the biplot are, in relative terms, temporally associated.

Results of the Seriation

The results of the correspondence analysis seriation are presented in Figures 9.2, 9.3, and 9.4. The seriation solution accounts for approximately 20% of the variability in the entire data matrix using two components. While this figure may seem unimpressive, it represents a significant amount of variability given that there are 98 cases and the number of dimensions is reduced from 46 to only 2. A biplot depicting the relationships among the individual glass bead mortuary assemblages (Fig. 9.2) reveals two important distributional patterns. First, the distribution of the glass bead assemblages has the classic parabola or "twisted one-dimensional object" shape that is the hallmark of chronological seriation using multidimensional techniques (Cowgill 1972; Kendall 1971; Steponaitis 1983). Second, the distribution of glass bead assemblages appears to form at least three and as many as six distinct clusters along the x axis—the axis that likely represents time. The same pattern describes the distribution of bead types (Fig. 9.3). When the distributions of individual assemblages and bead types are plotted together (Fig. 9.4), the redundancy of the patterns suggest that (1) there are "meta-assemblages" of glass beads marked by the consistent associations of particular bead types, and (2) these "meta-assemblages" are discretely distributed and are likely good chronological markers.

A k-means cluster analysis of the correspondence analysis component scores (the coordinates of each point in the biplot) provides a more objective means to identify and test the feasibility of these glass bead meta-assemblages. This is a nonhierarchical iterative clustering procedure that is particularly well suited to

Table 9.3. Glass trade bead assemblages used in this study.

Burial	IIIa1	IIa13	IIa24	IIa28	IIa31	IIa40	IIa44	IIa49	IIa55	IIa6	IIa61	IIb'3	IIb'6	IIb10	IIb1004	IIb1006	IIb18	IIb27	IIb32	IIb39	IIb56	IIb67	IIb990	IIbb13	IIbb15	IIbb24	IIbb27	IIga	IIgb	IIj	IVa11sd	IVa5	IVAa5sd	IVasd	IVb990	IVbsd	IVbb3	Ia15	Ia5	WIIc	WIId	WIIe	WIb	WIc	WIcb	IVk	Total
Jo6-31	0	161	0	0	0	2	0	0	3	53	0	0	0	0	0	0	0	0	0	0	0	0	0	0	0	0	0	0	0	0	0	13	0	0	0	0	0	0	0	0	0	0	0	0	0	0	232
Jo6-47	32	36	0	0	2	11	18	12	28	1	0	0	0	0	0	0	0	0	0	0	0	2	113	0	0	3	1	0	0	0	0	95	3	0	0	0	3	0	0	0	0	0	0	0	0	0	360
Jo6-49	0	375	0	0	0	0	0	0	0	1	0	0	0	0	0	0	0	0	0	0	0	0	0	0	0	0	0	0	0	0	0	0	0	0	0	0	0	0	0	1	0	0	0	0	0	0	377
Jo6-50	75	0	0	0	0	1	0	0	20	1	0	0	0	0	0	0	0	0	0	0	0	0	0	0	0	0	0	0	0	0	0	0	1610	0	0	0	0	0	0	0	0	0	0	0	0	0	1707
Jo6-53	0	51	0	0	0	0	137	0	22	2	0	0	0	0	0	0	0	0	0	0	0	0	4	1	0	4	0	0	0	0	0	0	4	0	0	0	1	0	0	0	0	0	0	0	0	0	226
Jo6-78c	0	2	0	0	0	220	0	0	5	0	0	0	0	0	0	0	0	0	0	0	0	0	0	0	0	2	1	0	0	0	0	3	0	0	0	0	0	0	0	0	0	0	0	0	0	0	233
Jo6-78d	0	467	0	0	1	2031	0	259	12	583	0	0	0	0	0	0	0	0	0	0	0	1	0	0	0	0	0	0	0	1	0	2	3	0	0	0	0	0	0	3	87	1	0	0	0	0	3451
Jo6-78f	0	41	0	0	0	14	0	0	1	1	0	0	0	0	0	0	0	0	0	0	0	0	0	0	0	0	0	0	0	0	0	0	0	0	0	0	0	0	0	0	0	0	0	0	0	0	57
Jo6-78g	0	1	0	0	0	1	0	0	0	0	0	0	0	0	0	0	0	0	0	0	0	0	0	0	0	0	0	0	0	0	0	587	45	0	0	0	0	0	0	0	0	0	0	0	0	0	634
Mr2-19	0	0	0	0	0	1	0	0	0	0	0	0	0	0	0	0	100	0	0	0	0	0	0	0	0	0	0	0	0	0	0	0	0	0	0	0	0	0	0	0	0	0	0	0	0	0	101
Mr2-2	0	17	0	0	0	7	0	0	0	0	0	0	0	0	0	0	0	0	0	3	0	0	0	0	0	0	0	0	0	1	0	7	0	0	0	0	0	0	0	14	1	0	1	0	0	0	51
Mr2-21	0	5	0	0	0	0	4	0	0	11	0	0	0	0	0	0	0	0	0	0	0	0	0	0	0	0	0	0	0	1	0	0	0	0	0	0	0	0	0	34	0	1	2	0	37	0	95
Mr2-29	0	0	0	0	0	0	0	0	0	0	0	0	0	0	0	0	0	0	0	0	0	0	0	0	0	0	0	0	0	0	0	1	0	0	0	0	0	20	0	0	0	0	0	22	0	0	43
Mr2-32	0	54	0	31	0	190	17	0	0	4	0	0	1	0	0	0	0	1	0	1	0	0	0	7	4	1	0	0	0	0	0	0	129	0	0	0	0	0	0	0	0	0	0	0	0	0	440
Mr2-38	0	43	0	0	0	104	3	0	0	4	0	0	0	0	0	0	0	0	1	1	0	0	0	6	0	0	0	0	0	0	0	47	0	0	0	0	0	0	0	0	0	0	0	0	0	0	209
Mr2-42	0	42	17	0	0	4	6	18	0	13	0	0	0	0	0	0	1428	0	1	1	0	0	0	0	0	0	0	0	0	0	0	0	0	0	0	0	0	77	64	14	0	0	21	25	0	0	1731
Mr2-43	0	0	0	0	0	0	0	0	0	0	0	0	0	0	0	0	0	0	0	0	0	0	0	0	0	0	0	0	0	0	0	0	0	0	0	0	0	0	75	0	0	0	22	0	0	0	97
Mr2-46	0	0	0	0	0	0	0	0	0	0	0	0	0	0	0	0	1	0	0	0	0	0	0	0	0	0	0	0	0	0	0	0	1	0	0	0	0	0	0	0	0	0	0	0	101	0	103
Mr2-52	0	0	0	0	0	0	0	0	0	0	0	0	0	0	0	0	0	0	0	0	0	0	0	0	0	0	0	0	0	11	0	0	0	0	0	0	0	0	0	12	0	0	11	0	0	0	34
Mr2-6	2	143	0	0	0	264	17	3	0	0	0	1	4	0	0	0	0	0	1	0	0	0	0	3	0	0	0	0	0	0	0	2	0	0	0	0	2	0	0	5	1	0	10	0	0	0	458
Mr2-65	0	34	0	0	0	888	0	0	0	0	0	0	4	0	0	0	0	0	0	10	0	0	0	4	1	0	0	0	0	0	0	0	0	0	0	0	0	0	0	0	0	0	0	43	0	0	984
Mr2-66	0	201	0	0	0	101	0	0	0	1	0	0	2	0	0	0	0	1	0	1	0	0	0	7	0	2	0	0	0	0	0	5	0	0	0	0	0	1	0	0	0	0	0	0	0	0	322
Mr2-7	0	78	0	0	0	0	0	8	0	0	0	0	0	0	0	0	0	0	0	0	0	0	0	0	0	0	0	0	0	31	0	0	0	0	0	0	0	0	0	23	0	0	12	0	0	0	152
Mr2-76	0	0	0	0	0	0	0	0	0	0	0	0	0	0	0	0	0	0	0	0	0	0	0	0	0	0	0	0	0	0	0	0	0	0	0	0	0	0	0	0	0	0	25	24	0	0	49
Mr2-80	0	0	0	0	0	0	0	0	0	0	0	0	0	0	0	0	0	0	0	0	0	0	0	0	0	0	0	0	0	0	0	0	0	0	0	0	0	0	0	28	0	0	19	0	0	0	47
Mr62-1	0	1	0	0	0	0	1	0	0	0	0	0	1	0	0	0	465	0	0	0	0	0	0	0	0	0	0	0	0	0	0	0	0	0	0	0	0	0	0	2	0	0	1	0	0	0	471
Mr62-10	0	3	0	0	0	0	0	0	0	0	0	0	0	0	0	0	0	0	0	0	0	0	0	0	0	0	0	0	0	1	0	0	0	0	0	0	0	0	0	44	0	0	0	32	0	0	80
Mr62-12	0	0	0	0	0	0	0	0	0	0	0	0	0	0	0	0	0	0	0	0	0	0	0	0	0	0	0	0	0	0	0	0	0	0	0	0	0	0	0	4	0	0	0	29	0	0	33
Mr62-2	0	0	0	0	0	0	3	0	0	0	0	0	0	0	0	0	1	0	0	0	0	0	0	0	0	0	0	0	0	0	0	34	2	0	0	0	0	0	0	2	0	0	6	11	0	0	59
Mr62-20	0	0	0	0	0	0	0	0	0	8	0	0	0	0	0	0	0	0	0	0	0	0	0	0	0	0	0	0	0	0	0	0	1	0	0	0	0	0	0	0	0	2	0	27	337	0	375
Mr62-4	0	0	0	0	0	0	0	0	0	0	0	0	0	0	0	0	0	0	0	0	0	0	0	0	0	0	0	0	0	0	0	4	77	0	0	0	0	0	0	0	0	0	0	0	0	0	81

Table 9.3. cont.

Burial	IIIa1	IIa13	IIa24	IIa28	IIa31	IIa40	IIa44	IIa49	IIa55	IIa6	IIa61	IIb'3	IIb'6	IIb10	IIb1004	IIb1006	IIb18	IIb27	IIb32	IIb39	IIb56	IIb67	IIb990	IIbb13	IIbb15	IIbb24	IIbb27	IIga	IIgb	IIj	IVa11sd	IVa5	IVAa5sd	IVasd	IVb990	IVbsd	IVbb3	Ia15	Ia5	WIIc	WIId	WIIe	WIb	WIc	WIcb	IVk	Total
Mr62-6	0	51	0	0	205	190	2	1	0	0	0	0	0	0	0	0	0	0	0	0	0	0	0	0	0	4	0	0	0	0	0	0	424	0	0	0	0	0	0	0	0	0	0	0	0	0	877
Mr62-7	0	0	0	0	0	0	0	0	8	19	0	3	0	0	0	0	0	0	0	0	0	0	0	0	0	0	1	0	0	6	0	0	2	0	0	0	2	0	0	2	0	0	0	0	0	0	43
Mr62-9	0	1	0	0	0	1	0	0	0	6	0	0	0	0	0	0	1	0	0	0	0	0	0	0	0	1	0	0	0	0	0	1	0	0	0	0	0	0	0	3	0	0	0	18	0	0	32
Ms100-13	0	2	0	0	0	3	0	0	334	0	0	0	0	0	0	0	0	0	0	0	0	0	0	0	0	0	0	0	0	0	0	0	0	0	0	0	0	0	0	0	0	0	0	0	0	0	339
Ms100-4	0	1	0	0	0	0	0	0	0	0	0	0	0	0	0	0	0	0	0	0	0	0	0	0	0	0	0	0	0	0	0	0	0	0	0	0	0	0	0	0	0	0	0	174	0	0	175
Ms100-56	0	89	0	0	0	0	0	0	0	0	0	0	0	0	0	0	0	0	0	0	0	0	0	0	0	0	0	0	0	0	0	172	0	0	0	0	0	0	0	0	0	0	0	0	0	0	261
Ms100-9	0	89	0	0	0	74	0	0	0	0	0	0	0	1	0	0	0	0	0	0	0	0	0	1	0	0	0	0	0	0	0	0	0	0	0	0	11	0	0	0	0	0	0	0	0	0	176
Ms32-13	0	0	0	0	0	216	0	0	4	0	0	0	0	0	0	0	0	0	0	0	0	1	0	0	0	0	0	0	0	0	0	0	0	0	0	0	0	0	0	0	0	0	2	0	0	0	223
Ms32-16	0	0	0	0	0	1283	0	0	0	3	0	0	0	0	0	0	0	0	0	0	0	1	0	0	0	0	0	0	0	0	0	0	0	0	0	0	0	0	0	0	0	0	0	0	0	0	1287
Ms32-22	0	0	0	0	0	30	0	0	10	1	0	0	0	0	0	0	0	0	0	0	0	0	0	0	0	0	0	0	0	0	0	0	0	0	0	0	0	0	0	0	0	0	0	0	0	0	41
Ms32-26	0	0	0	0	0	28	0	0	0	87	0	0	0	0	0	0	0	0	0	0	0	4	0	0	0	0	0	0	0	0	0	0	0	1	0	0	0	0	0	0	0	0	4	175	0	0	299
Ms32-27	0	0	0	0	0	309	0	0	2	0	0	0	0	0	0	0	0	0	0	0	0	0	0	0	0	0	0	0	0	0	0	0	0	0	0	0	0	0	0	0	0	0	0	0	0	0	311
Ms32-31	0	0	0	5	0	0	0	0	135	6	0	0	0	0	0	0	0	0	0	0	0	1	0	0	0	0	0	0	0	0	0	0	0	0	0	0	0	0	0	0	0	0	144	4	0	0	295
Ms32-42	0	0	0	1	0	31	0	0	0	3	0	0	0	0	0	0	0	0	0	0	0	3	0	0	0	0	0	0	0	0	0	0	0	0	0	0	0	0	0	0	0	0	0	0	0	0	38
Ms32-44	0	0	0	3	0	43	0	0	0	3	0	0	0	0	0	0	0	0	0	0	0	0	0	0	0	0	0	0	0	0	0	0	0	0	0	0	0	0	0	0	0	0	13	5	0	0	67
Ms32-48	0	0	0	0	0	245	0	0	0	0	0	0	0	0	0	0	0	0	0	0	0	0	0	0	0	0	0	0	0	0	0	0	0	0	0	0	0	0	0	0	0	0	1	0	0	0	246
Ms32-49	0	0	0	0	0	28	0	0	21	0	0	0	0	0	0	0	0	0	0	0	0	0	0	0	0	0	0	0	0	0	0	0	0	0	0	0	0	0	0	0	0	0	0	0	0	0	49
Ms32-68	0	0	0	2	0	109	0	0	0	3	0	0	0	0	0	0	0	0	0	0	0	1	0	0	0	0	0	0	0	0	0	0	0	0	0	0	0	0	0	0	0	0	42	0	0	0	157
Ms91-25	0	0	0	1	0	371	0	0	52	0	0	0	0	2	0	0	0	0	0	0	0	0	0	0	0	0	0	0	0	0	0	0	0	0	0	0	0	0	0	0	0	0	0	0	0	0	426
Ms91-44	0	0	0	0	0	199	0	0	0	0	0	0	0	0	0	0	0	0	0	0	0	0	0	0	0	0	0	0	0	0	0	0	0	0	0	0	0	0	0	0	0	0	1039	0	0	0	1238
Ms91-45	0	0	0	0	0	0	0	0	0	0	0	0	0	0	0	0	0	0	0	0	0	0	0	0	0	0	0	0	0	0	0	0	0	0	0	0	0	0	0	0	0	0	42	27	0	0	69
Ms91-5	0	0	0	1	0	839	0	0	0	1	0	0	0	0	0	0	0	0	0	0	0	1	0	0	0	0	0	0	0	0	0	0	0	0	0	0	0	0	0	0	0	0	0	4	0	0	846
Or231-1	0	0	0	0	0	1	0	0	2	0	16	0	0	0	0	0	0	0	0	0	0	0	0	0	0	0	0	0	0	10	0	1	0	0	0	0	0	0	0	0	0	0	0	0	0	0	30
Or231-10	0	45	0	0	0	5	0	0	1	0	1	0	0	0	0	0	0	0	0	0	0	0	0	0	0	0	0	0	0	0	0	70	0	0	0	0	0	0	0	0	0	0	0	0	0	0	122
Or231-11	0	0	0	0	0	0	0	0	0	0	1	0	0	0	0	0	0	0	0	0	0	0	0	0	0	0	0	0	0	0	0	232	0	0	0	0	0	0	0	0	0	0	0	0	0	0	233
Or231-2	0	25	0	0	2	16	0	0	0	0	0	0	0	0	0	0	0	0	0	0	0	0	0	0	0	1	0	0	0	0	0	0	96	0	0	0	0	0	0	0	0	0	0	0	0	0	140
Or231-6	0	0	0	0	0	3	0	0	1	0	1	0	0	0	0	0	0	0	0	0	0	0	0	0	0	0	0	0	0	0	0	17	0	0	0	0	0	0	0	0	0	0	0	0	0	0	22
Rd3-1	0	1	0	0	0	36	0	0	3	0	0	0	0	0	0	0	0	0	0	0	0	0	0	0	0	0	0	0	0	0	0	0	0	6	0	0	0	0	0	0	0	0	0	0	0	0	46
Rk6-112	0	0	0	0	0	92	0	0	0	0	0	0	0	0	0	0	0	0	0	0	0	0	0	0	0	0	0	0	0	0	0	0	0	1580	0	3	0	0	0	0	0	0	0	0	0	0	1675

Table 9.3. cont.

Burial	IIIa1	IIa13	IIa24	IIa28	IIa31	IIa40	IIa44	IIa49	IIa55	IIa6	IIa61	IIb'3	IIb'6	IIb10	IIb1004	IIb1006	IIb18	IIb27	IIb32	IIb39	IIb56	IIb67	IIb990	IIbb13	IIbb15	IIbb24	IIbb27	IIga	IIgb	IIj	IVa11sd	IVa5	IVAa5sd	IVasd	IVb990	IVbsd	IVbb3	Ia15	Ia5	WIIc	WIId	WIIe	WIb	WIc	WIcb	IVk	Total
Rk6-33	0	0	0	0	0	17	0	0	0	0	0	0	0	0	1	0	0	0	0	0	0	0	0	0	0	0	0	0	0	0	0	1	2	2190	0	440	0	0	0	0	0	0	0	0	0	0	2651
Rk6-65	0	0	0	0	5	81	0	1	0	0	0	0	0	0	1	0	0	0	0	0	1	0	0	0	0	0	0	0	1	0	0	0	0	783	0	12	0	0	0	0	0	0	0	0	0	0	885
Rk6-93	0	11	0	0	0	16	0	0	0	0	0	0	0	0	0	0	0	0	0	0	2	0	0	0	0	0	0	0	0	0	0	0	0	11	0	0	0	0	0	0	0	0	0	0	0	0	40
Sk1a-1	0	38	2	0	0	4	0	5	0	0	18	0	0	0	0	0	0	0	0	0	0	0	0	0	0	0	0	0	0	0	0	0	0	0	0	0	0	0	1	0	0	0	0	0	0	0	68
Sk1a-109	0	3	0	0	0	1	0	165	0	0	11	0	0	1	0	0	0	0	0	0	8	933	0	0	0	0	0	0	0	0	1	0	0	0	0	0	0	0	0	0	0	0	0	0	0	0	1123
Sk1a-13	0	1	0	0	0	0	0	0	0	0	0	0	0	0	0	0	0	0	0	0	0	0	0	0	0	0	0	29	0	0	0	0	0	1	0	0	0	0	0	0	0	0	0	0	0	0	31
Sk1a-19	0	0	0	0	0	0	0	0	0	0	0	0	0	0	0	0	0	0	0	0	0	0	0	0	0	0	0	0	0	0	86	0	0	1069	0	0	0	0	0	0	0	0	0	0	0	0	1155
Sk1a-22	0	0	0	1	3	12	8	0	4	0	0	0	0	0	0	0	0	0	0	0	0	0	0	0	0	0	0	0	0	0	0	0	0	0	0	0	0	0	0	0	0	0	0	0	0	0	28
Sk1a-24	0	84	0	0	0	11	0	0	0	0	0	0	0	0	0	0	0	0	0	0	0	0	0	0	0	0	0	0	0	0	0	0	0	0	2	0	0	0	0	0	0	0	0	0	0	0	97
Sk1a-35	0	1	0	0	0	0	0	0	0	0	0	0	0	0	0	0	0	0	0	0	0	0	0	0	0	0	0	0	0	0	0	0	0	1	23	0	0	0	0	0	0	0	0	0	0	0	25
Sk1a-36	0	0	0	0	0	2	0	0	0	0	0	0	0	0	0	0	0	0	0	0	0	0	0	0	0	0	0	0	0	0	1011	0	0	48	0	0	0	0	0	0	0	0	0	0	0	0	1061
Sk1a-38	0	205	0	0	0	173	0	18	6	0	15	0	0	0	0	0	0	0	0	0	0	3	0	0	0	0	0	2	0	0	0	0	0	0	4	1	0	0	0	0	0	0	0	0	0	0	427
Sk1a-39	0	1	0	0	0	0	1	0	0	0	0	0	0	0	0	0	0	0	0	0	0	0	0	0	0	0	0	0	0	0	14	0	4	2	0	0	0	0	0	0	0	0	0	0	0	0	22
Sk1a-43	0	0	0	0	0	30	1	42	0	0	0	0	0	0	0	0	0	0	0	0	0	0	0	0	0	0	0	0	0	0	1646	0	0	246	0	11	0	0	0	0	0	0	0	0	0	0	1976
Sk1a-48	0	133	1	0	0	179	0	0	0	0	43	0	0	2	0	0	0	0	0	0	0	205	0	0	0	0	0	0	0	0	0	0	0	1	0	0	0	0	0	0	0	0	0	0	0	0	564
Sk1a-50	0	0	5	0	0	15	0	7	0	0	18	0	0	0	0	0	0	0	0	0	0	0	0	0	0	0	0	1	0	0	0	0	0	0	0	0	0	0	0	0	0	0	0	0	0	0	46
Sk1a-51	0	0	0	0	0	1	0	0	2	0	0	0	0	0	0	0	0	0	0	0	0	0	0	0	0	0	0	0	0	0	0	0	0	0	0	38	0	0	0	0	0	0	0	0	0	0	41
Sk1a-55	0	29	0	0	0	8	0	0	0	0	0	0	0	0	0	0	0	0	0	0	0	0	0	0	0	0	0	0	0	0	0	0	0	3	0	0	0	0	0	0	0	0	0	0	0	0	40
Sk1a-6	0	1	0	0	0	142	0	69	3	0	0	0	0	0	0	0	0	0	0	0	0	0	0	0	0	0	0	0	0	0	0	0	0	0	0	0	0	0	0	0	0	0	0	0	0	0	215
Sk1a-64	0	52	1	0	0	135	0	0	0	0	0	0	0	0	0	0	0	0	0	0	0	0	0	0	0	0	0	0	0	0	0	0	0	0	0	0	0	0	0	0	0	0	0	0	0	0	188
Sk1a-65	0	13	0	0	2	165	0	8	0	0	0	0	0	0	0	0	0	0	0	0	0	0	1	0	0	0	0	0	0	0	0	0	0	0	0	0	0	0	0	0	0	0	0	0	0	0	189
Sk1a-68	0	51	0	0	0	0	0	0	0	0	4	0	0	0	0	0	0	0	0	0	0	0	0	0	0	0	0	0	0	0	0	0	0	0	0	0	0	0	0	0	0	0	0	0	0	0	55
Sk1a-76	0	2	0	0	0	0	0	0	0	0	0	0	0	0	0	0	0	0	0	0	0	0	0	0	0	0	0	0	0	0	0	0	0	75	0	0	0	0	0	0	0	0	0	0	0	0	77
Sk1a-84	0	1	0	0	1	40	0	0	0	0	0	0	0	0	0	0	0	0	0	0	0	0	0	0	0	0	0	0	0	0	0	0	0	224	0	0	0	0	0	0	0	0	0	0	0	0	266
Sk1a-9	0	1	0	0	0	194	0	12	0	0	0	0	0	0	0	0	0	0	0	0	0	0	0	0	0	0	0	0	0	0	0	0	0	0	0	0	0	0	0	0	0	0	0	0	0	0	207
Sk1a-95	0	65	0	0	0	0	0	0	0	0	4	0	0	0	0	0	0	0	0	0	0	1	0	0	0	0	0	2	0	0	0	0	1	6	0	0	0	0	0	0	0	0	0	0	0	0	79
Hr4-1	0	0	0	0	0	54	0	0	0	0	0	0	0	0	0	0	0	0	0	0	0	0	0	0	0	0	0	0	0	0	0	0	0	119	0	9	0	0	0	0	0	0	0	0	0	0	182
Wg17-14	0	0	0	2	0	15	36	0	2	0	0	0	0	0	0	1	0	0	0	0	0	0	0	0	0	0	0	0	0	0	0	0	0	0	0	0	0	0	0	0	0	0	0	0	0	0	56
Wg17-33	0	0	0	0	0	67	0	0	2	0	0	0	0	0	0	0	0	0	0	0	0	0	0	0	0	0	0	0	0	0	58	0	0	32	0	0	0	0	0	0	0	0	0	0	0	0	159

Table 9.3. cont.

Burial	IIIa1	IIa13	IIa24	IIa28	IIa31	IIa40	IIa44	IIa49	IIa55	IIa6	IIa61	IIb'3	IIb'6	IIb10	IIb1004	IIb1006	IIb18	IIb27	IIb32	IIb39	IIb56	IIb67	IIb990	IIbb13	IIbb15	IIbb24	IIbb27	IIga	IIgb	IIj	IVa11sd	IVa5	IVAa5sd	IVasd	IVb990	IVbsd	IVbb3	Ia15	Ia5	WIIc	WIId	WIIe	WIb	WIc	WIcb	IVk	Total
Mr2-10	0	8	0	0	0	1	0	0	0	0	0	0	0	0	0	0	0	0	0	0	0	0	0	0	0	0	0	0	0	0	0	0	0	0	0	0	0	0	62	0	0	0	0	0	0	0	71
Mg31-3-12	0	1	0	0	0	9	0	0	0	0	0	0	0	0	0	0	0	0	0	0	0	0	0	30	0	0	0	0	0	0	0	1	0	0	0	0	0	0	0	0	0	0	0	0	0	0	41
Mg31-6	0	0	0	0	0	0	0	0	0	42	0	0	0	0	0	0	0	0	0	0	0	0	0	0	0	0	0	0	0	0	0	0	298	0	0	0	0	0	0	0	0	0	0	0	0	0	340
Mg31-10	0	10	0	0	0	30	0	0	0	1	0	0	0	0	0	0	0	0	0	0	0	0	0	6	0	0	0	0	0	0	0	0	25	0	0	0	0	0	0	0	0	0	0	0	0	0	72
Bt8-90	0	0	0	0	0	2	11	0	10	0	0	0	0	0	0	0	0	0	0	0	0	1	0	0	0	0	0	1	0	0	0	0	0	0	0	0	0	0	0	0	0	0	0	0	0	0	25
Pk1-1	0	0	0	0	0	26	0	220	0	1	0	0	0	0	0	0	0	0	0	0	0	0	0	0	0	0	0	0	0	28	0	0	0	0	0	0	0	0	0	6	0	0	13	0	0	0	294
Pk1-7	0	1	0	0	0	9	0	0	0	0	0	0	0	0	0	0	0	0	0	0	0	0	0	0	0	0	0	0	0	0	0	0	0	0	0	0	0	0	0	26	0	0	0	0	0	0	36
Pk1-8	0	165	0	0	0	237	0	0	37	25	0	0	0	0	0	0	0	0	4	2	0	0	9	11	0	1	0	0	0	0	0	109	0	0	0	0	1	0	0	0	0	0	1	0	0	0	602
Pk1-11	0	0	0	0	0	1	0	0	0	0	0	0	0	0	0	0	0	0	0	0	0	0	0	0	0	0	0	0	0	2	0	0	445	0	0	0	0	0	0	52	0	0	380	12	0	0	892
total	*109*	*2936*	*26*	*47*	*221*	*9668*	*265*	*848*	*730*	*884*	*132*	*4*	*12*	*6*	*2*	*1*	*1996*	*2*	*7*	*19*	*11*	*1158*	*127*	*76*	*5*	*19*	*3*	*35*	*1*	*92*	*2816*	*1404*	*3172*	*6398*	*29*	*514*	*20*	*98*	*202*	*275*	*89*	*4*	*1811*	*632*	*475*	*0*	*37,381*

finding patterns in spatial distributions (Duff 1996; Kintigh and Ammerman 1982; Shennan 1997). The method begins with the analyst defining the number of clusters desired. The procedure then involves an iterative process of calculating the cluster centers and boundaries with the goal of minimizing dispersion within the clusters and maximizing dispersion between clusters. After numerous trials, it appears that a six-cluster solution of the k-means cluster analysis results in the best logical fit (Fig. 9.5).

Turning to the composition of the clusters or meta-assemblages, it is clear that the correspondence analysis seriation identified some substantive associations among bead types. Furthermore, beyond the parabolic distribution of these meta-assemblages, there is corroborating evidence indicating that the clusters are chronologically ordered. From this evidence, estimates of temporal ranges for these clusters can be suggested (Fig. 9.6, Tables 9.4, 9.5). These date ranges are based on the results of the current study, on published estimates of date ranges for the sites in the sample, on previous research regarding the chronology of various bead types, and on associations with other well-dated European artifact types (e.g., Deagan 1987; Smith 1982, 1983, 1987, 2002b). The date ranges that follow are estimates and should not be interpreted as absolute. Indeed, this seriation will only benefit from additional data, especially the rather loose ranges associated with the early seventeenth and late eighteenth centuries.

Cluster 1 (ca. A.D. 1600–1650) contains mortuary assemblages recovered from sites whose occupations are limited to the seventeenth century (Madison, Upper Saratown, Philpott, Plum Grove) (Eastman 1999; Smith n.d.; Ward and Davis 1993). These assemblages are dominated by seed beads composed of two and three layers with clear or light blue translucent cores and opaque outer surfaces (IVasd) (Fig. 9.7). Smith (1983) has found that seed beads with transparent cores and opaque outer layers are largely an early to middle seventeenth-century phenomenon.

Cluster 2 (ca. A.D. 1625–1675) contains glass bead assemblages with so-called "eye beads" (IIg) and translucent navy blue beads with 8–10 white stripes (IIb1004) (Fig. 9.7). The cluster contains assemblages from North Carolina Piedmont sites (Madison, Upper Saratown, Madison) whose occupations have been placed in the second half of the seventeenth century (Eastman 1999; Ward and Davis 1993). Smith (1982, 1983), however, has argued that "eye beads" typically occur in assemblages dating to the first half of the seventeenth century. The large distance between Cluster 1 and Cluster 2 on the correspondence analysis biplot demonstrates an important caveat about the seriation results—distance in the correspondence analysis biplot should *not* be interpreted on an absolute scale. Indeed, it is likely that the date ranges of these assemblages overlap quite a bit.

Cluster 3 (ca. A.D. 1650–1730) is by far the largest and most diverse meta-assemblage. It is composed primarily of monochrome and striped necklace beads of simple and complex construction (Fig. 9.7). This cluster also contains mandrel wound "raspberry"

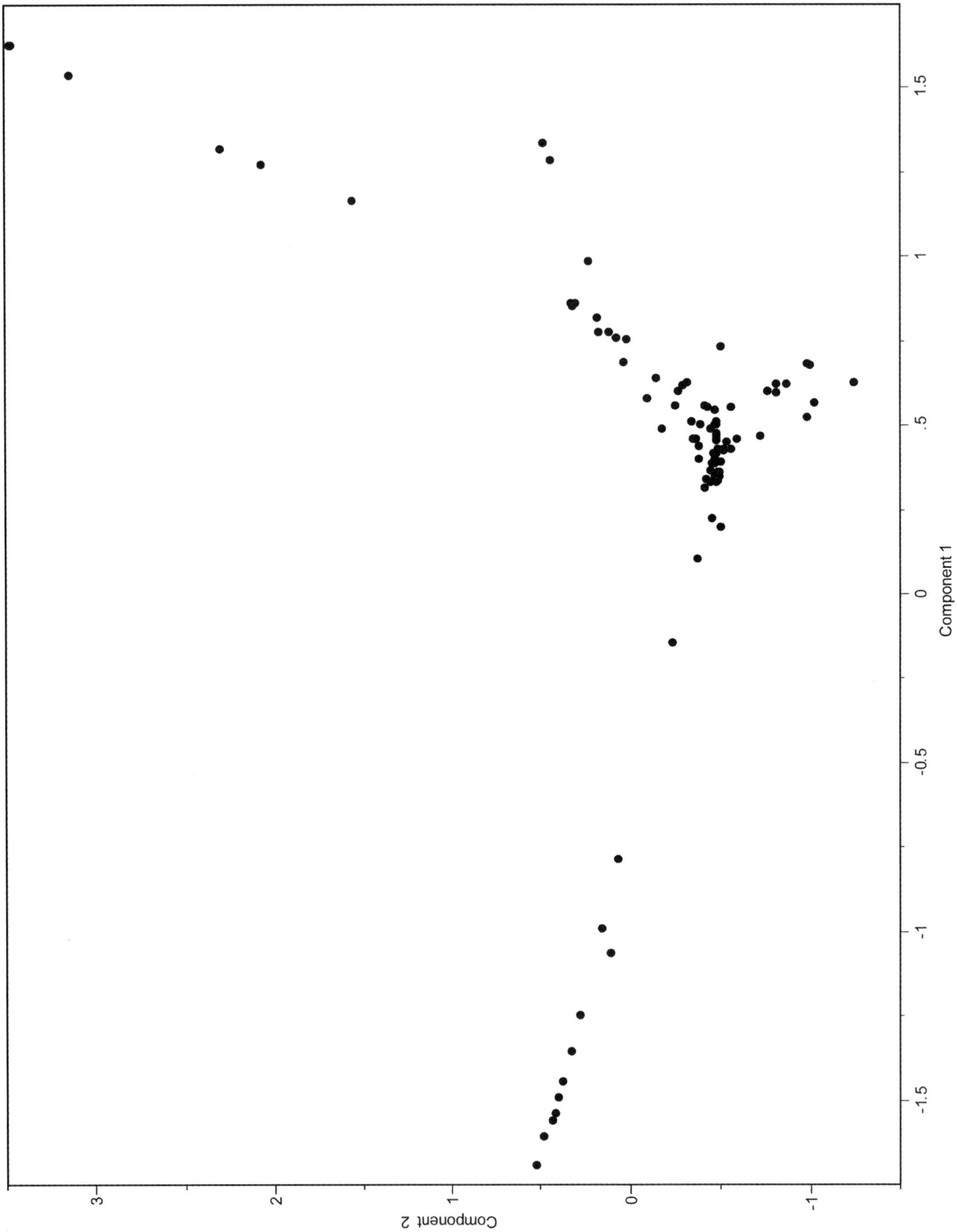

Figure 9.2. Biplot depicting the results of the correspondence analysis seriation of mortuary assemblages.

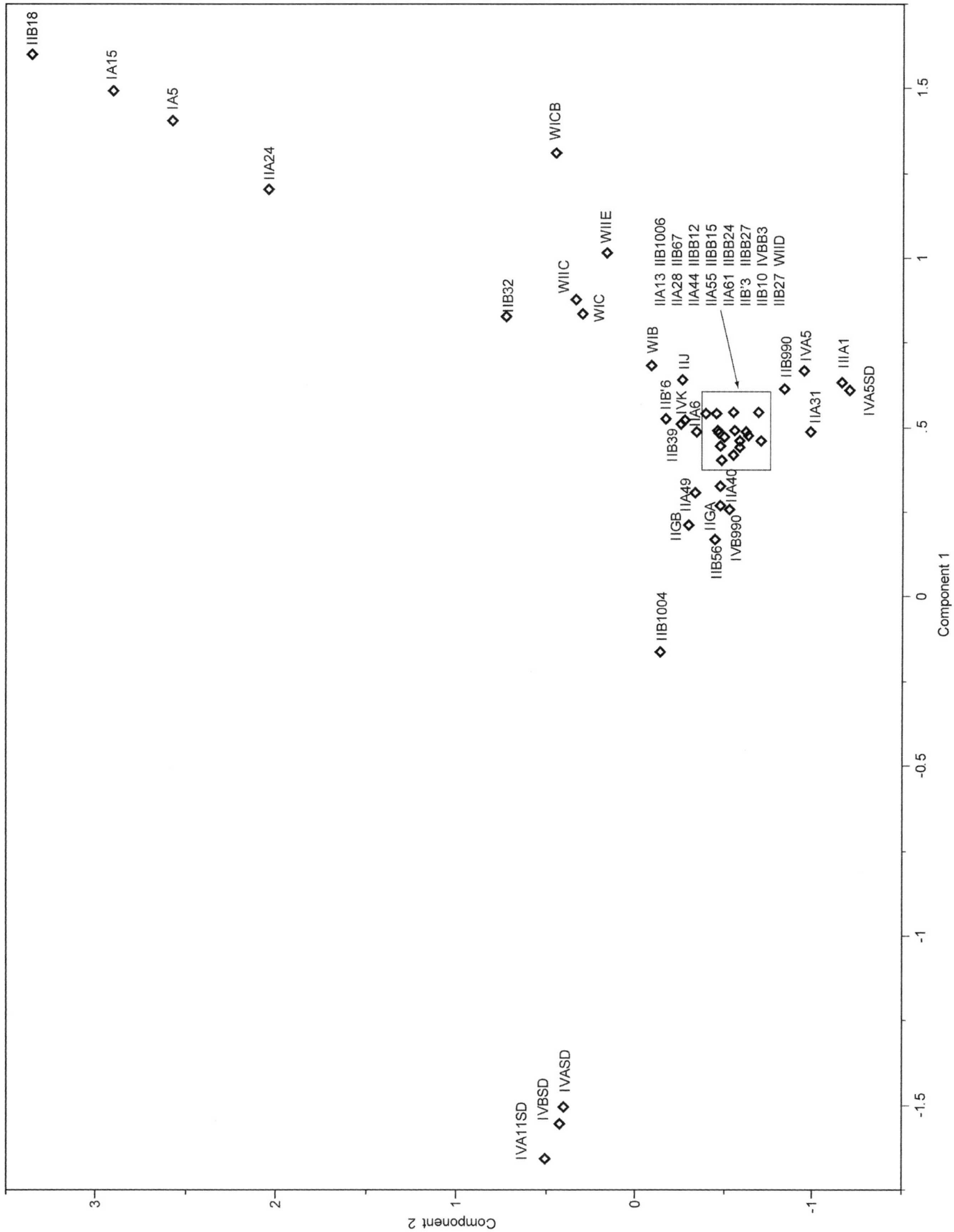

Figure 9.3. Biplot depicting the results of the correspondence analysis seriation of bead types.

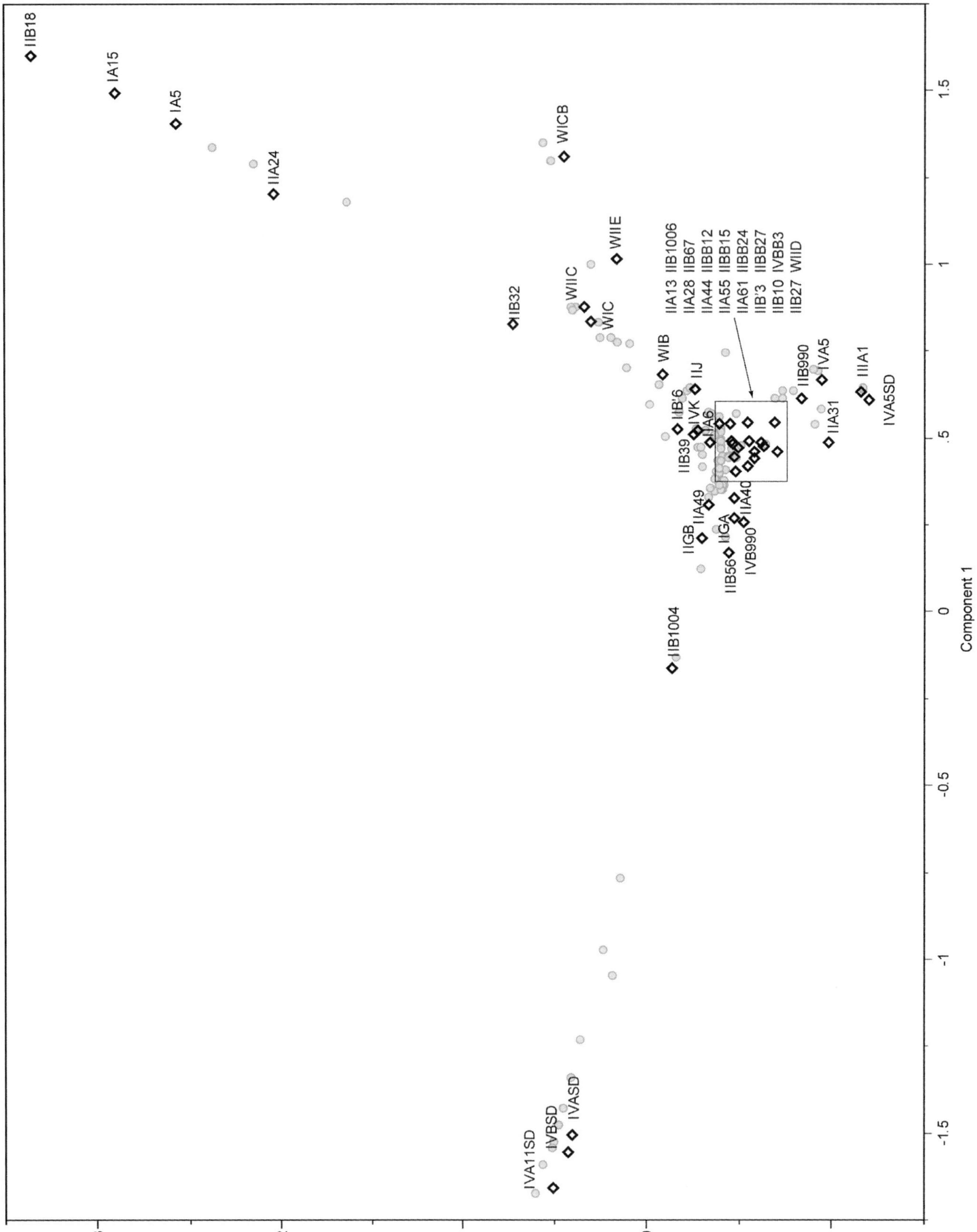

Figure 9.4. Combined biplot depicting the results of the correspondence analysis seriation of mortuary assemblages and bead types.

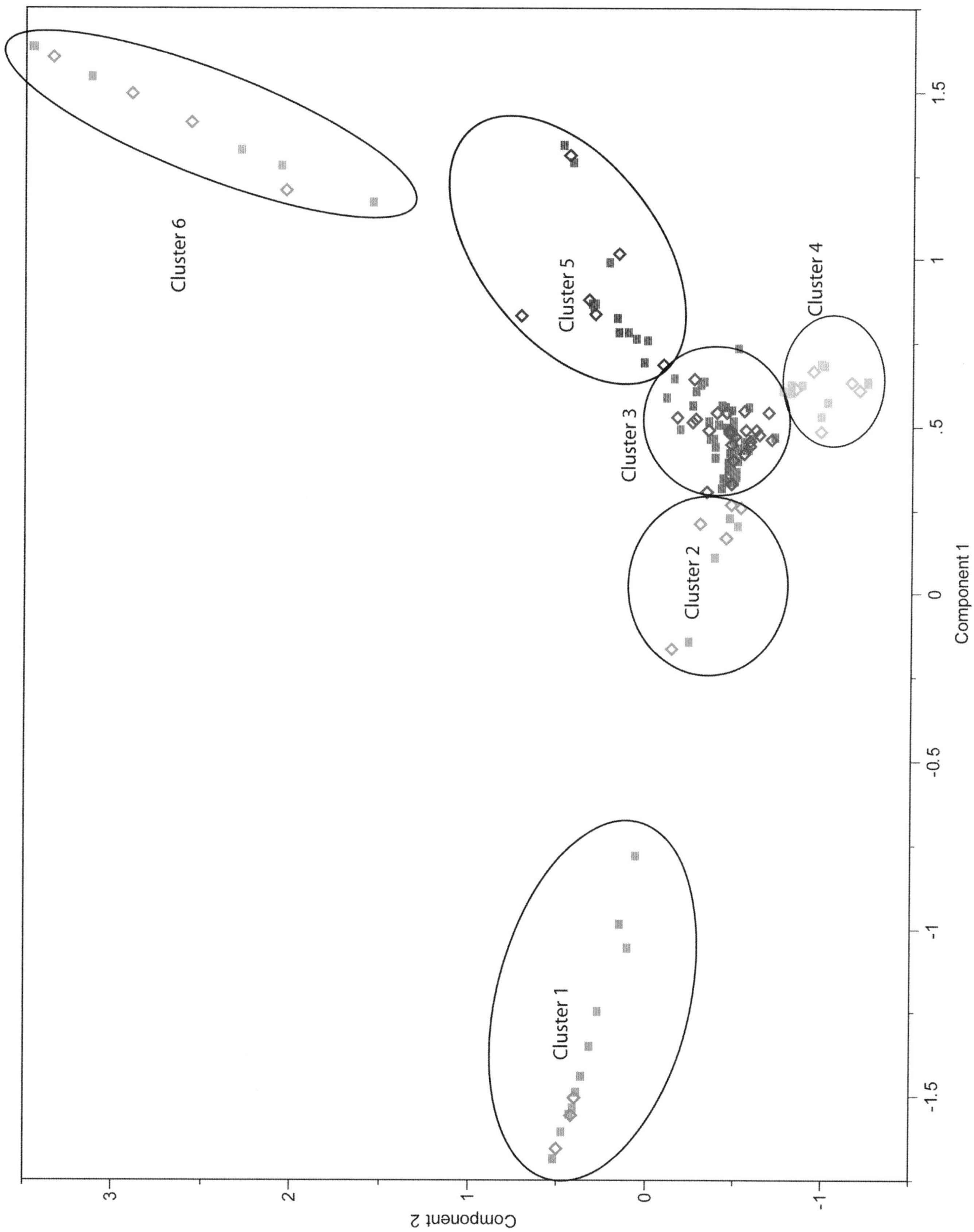

Figure 9.5. Biplot depicting the results of the k-mean cluster analysis.

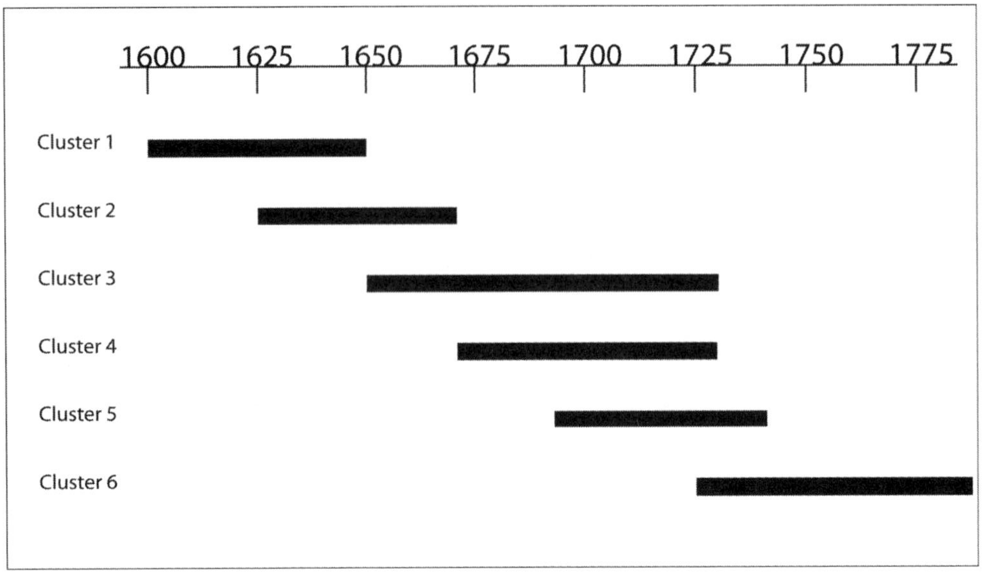

Figure 9.6. Estimated date ranges for glass bead "meta-assemblage" clusters.

beads (WIId). The majority of the mortuary assemblages in Cluster 3 were recovered from sites with occupations dating between 1630 and 1710. These include Upper Saratown and Fredricks in the Carolina Piedmont (Eastman 1999; Ward and Davis 1991, 1993, 2001); Columbus Landing, McKee Island and Law's Site in the middle Tennessee River Valley of northeast Alabama (Fleming 1976; Smith 1987); Tarver and Little Tarver in central Georgia (Pluckhahn 1996, 1997); and Plum Grove (Smith n.d.), Hiwassee Island (Lewis and Kneberg 1946), Ocoee (Lewis et al. 1995), Tallasee (Cornette 1976), and Chota-Tanasee (Newman 1986) in eastern Tennessee. Moreover, a number of mortuary assemblages in Cluster 3 burials include diagnostic seventeenth-century European-made items such as brass arm bands and cutout animal effigies (so-called ex-votos) (Waselkov 1989); cast bronze rumbler bells (crotals) (Butler 2000; Morris 1959); brass flush-loop bells (Brown 1979); doglock muskets (Brown 1980; Fithian 1985; Puype 1985; Shumway 1985); iron hoes and axes (Egloff 1980; Kauffman [1972] 1994); and lateen spoons (Price 1908; Noël Hume 1969; Victoria and Albert Museum 1927; see also Gibson 1980; Rubertone 2001; Simmons 1970; Turnbaugh 1984 for discussions of similar items among late seventeenth-century Narragansett burial assemblages in New England).

Cluster 4 (ca. A.D. 1670–1730) is primarily composed of so-called Cornaline d'Aleppo seed, tubular, and spherical beads (IVa5sd, IIIa1, IVa5) (Fig. 9.7). These compound beads with transparent green to almost black cores and opaque red outer layers are usually given a large date range typically spanning from the late sixteenth century to the mid-eighteenth century. In this study sample, however, the various varieties of the bead are consistently associated with each other and are limited to mortuary contexts at sites with occupations spanning from the last quarter of the seventeenth century to the first quarter of the eighteenth century. The sites in this cluster include Tarver and Little Tarver (Pluckhahn 1996, 1997), Law's Site (Fleming 1976), Fredricks (Ward and Davis 1993), Hiwassee Island (Lewis and Kneberg 1946), and Chota-Tanasee (Newman 1986).

Cluster 5 (ca. A.D. 1690–1740), a cluster made up of nearly all mandrel wound beads, contains assemblages that primarily date to the first half of the eighteenth century (Fig. 9.7). The earliest mortuary assemblages in this cluster—which are from Columbus Landing, McKee Island, the Law's Site in the Guntersville Basin, and the Ocoee in eastern Tennessee—may be a distinct phenomenon, however, in that all the mandrel wound beads in these assemblages are smaller (6–10 mm), are round, and are black, transparent brite blue or light gray. The rest of the mandrel wound beads in the cluster are larger (10–16 mm) and are from mortuary contexts at the Chota-Tanasee site. These probably date to the second and third decades of the eighteenth century given the lack of silver trade goods in these contexts (Newman 1986:427). Trade silver has long been thought to arrive among the upper Cherokees and other Indian groups after 1750. Marvin Smith (2002b:59) gives a similar date range for

Table 9.4. Bead types and mortuary assemblages included in seriation clusters.

Cluster	Bead Types		Mortuary Assemblages[a]		
1	IVa11sd	IVbsd	Rk6-33	Sk1a-36	Sk1a-76
	IVasd		Rk6-65	Sk1a-39	Sk1a-84
			Rk6-112	Sk1a-43	Vir199
			Sk1a-19	Sk1a-51	Wg17-33
2	IIb1004	IIgb	Rd3-1	Sk1a-13	
	IIb56	IVb990	Rk6-93		
	IIga				
3	IIa13	IIb1006	Jo6-31	Ms32-13	Sk1a-24
	IIa28	IIb27	Jo6-49	Ms32-16	Sk1a-38
	IIa40	IIb39	Jo6-53	Ms32-22	Sk1a-48
	IIa44	IIb67	Jo6-78c	Ms32-27	Sk1a-50
	IIa49	IIbb12	Jo6-78d	Ms32-31	Sk1a-55
	IIa55	IIbb15	Jo6-78f	Ms32-42	Sk1a-6
	IIa6	IIbb24	Mr2-2	Ms32-44	Sk1a-64
	IIa61	IIbb27	Mr2-32	Ms32-48	Sk1a-65
	IIb'3	IIj	Mr2-38	Ms32-49	Sk1a-68
	IIb'6	IVbb3	Mr2-6	Ms32-68	Sk1a-9
	IIb10	WIId	Mr2-65	Ms91-25	Sk1a-95
			Mr2-66	Ms91-44	Wg17-14
			Mr2-7	Ms91-5	Bt8-90
			Mr62-2	Or231-1	Mg31-3-12
			Mr62-7	Sk1a-1	Mg31-10
			Ms100-13	Sk1a-109	Pk1-1
			Ms100-9	Sk1a-22	Pk1-8
4	IIIa1	IVa5	Jo6-47	Mr62-4	Or231-11
	IIa31	IVa5sd	Jo6-50	Mr62-6	Or231-2
	IIb990		Jo6-78g	Ms100-56	Or231-6
			Mg31-6	Or231-10	
5	IIb32	WIb	Mr2-21	Mr62-10	Ms32-26
	WIIc	WIc	Mr2-46	Mr62-12	Ms91-45
	WIIe	WIcb	Mr2-52	Mr62-20	Pk1-7
			Mr2-76	Mr62-9	Pk1-11
			Mr2-80	Ms100-4	
6	IIa24	Ia15	Mr2-19	Mr2-42	Mr62-1
	IIb18	Ia5	Mr2-29	Mr2-43	Mr2-10

[a]Mortuary assemblages are coded as a combination of site number and burial number. See Table 9.2 for site names.

large mandrel wound beads in French colonial contexts. The inclusion of so-called "barleycorn" beads in Cluster 5 (WIcb) is probably spurious. These more appropriately belong later in the chronology as part of Cluster 6, as they are often associated with trade silver among Chota-Tanasee mortuary assemblages and are specifically mentioned in English trade records from 1758 until 1784 (Waselkov 1998:210).

Cluster 6 (ca. A.D. 1725–1783) represents the most recent meta-assemblage in the seriation. The cluster includes the mortuary assemblage associated with the burial of Chief Oconostota, whose funeral was recorded at Chota in 1783 (Schroedl and Breitburg 1986:136). While the dominance of small-diameter monochromatic tubular beads in this cluster certainly appears to be a good chronological marker for the late eighteenth century, the same cannot be said of the so-called "gooseberry" beads (IIb18) (Fig. 9.7). This bead type is known to have been in circulation much earlier in the period, with oval-shaped varieties dating as early as the sixteenth century (Deagan 1987; Smith 1983). It appears that the small sample size in this cluster combined with rather large frequencies of gooseberry beads in two late eighteenth-century burials resulted in the misplacement of this type in Cluster 6.

The Chronological Position of the Glass Trade Bead Assemblage from Townsend

The seriation solution presented above offers researchers a reasonably accurate method to aid in identifying and estimating the occupation dates for Contact period Indian communities, like Townsend, using small site-level glass bead assemblages. In this case, the method involves conducting another correspondence analysis seriation that depicts where the Townsend glass bead assemblage falls among the chronologically ordered glass bead clusters. To make the correspondence analysis seriation technique easier for others to replicate and the results easier to interpret, I modify the mortuary dataset used above by lumping together the bead assemblages at the level of the cluster. Combining the assemblages at this level has no effect on the overall seriation results, and the biplot is "cleaner" and much easier to interpret. The resulting seriation solution depicts how the Townsend glass trade bead assemblage falls within the chronology.

There are some important issues that should be considered when using this technique. First, there are major differences between bead assemblages recovered from mortuary contexts and those recovered from surface collections, feature contents, or general excavations. Consequently, one needs to be aware of the likelihood that assemblages from these contexts are chronologically mixed. This technique will place a bead assemblage in the seriation based on the relative frequencies of the bead types in the entire assemblage; therefore, the results may mask earlier or later occupations. One easy way of determining this is to see whether the assemblage contains bead types from different chronological clusters. For example, the presence of a few "eye" beads (Cluster 2) in a single site-level assemblage dominated by large mandrel

Table 9.5. Glass bead types included in the study.

Bead Types	Type Description
Ia5	Untumbled opaque white tubular necklace bead (4–10 mm) of simple construction.
Ia15	Untumbled translucent brite blue tubular necklace bead (4–10 mm) of simple construction.
IIa13	Tumbled opaque white spherical or oval necklace bead (4–12 mm) of simple construction.
IIa24	Tumbled opaque apple green spherical necklace bead (4–12 mm) of simple construction.
IIa28	Tumbled transparent emerald spherical necklace bead (4–12 mm) of simple construction.
IIa31	Tumbled transparent turquoise spherical necklace bead (4–12 mm) of simple construction.
IIa40	Tumbled opaque turquoise spherical or oval necklace bead (4–12 mm) of simple construction.
IIa44	Tumbled transparent cerulean blue spherical necklace bead (4–12 mm) of simple construction.
IIa49	Tumbled opaque dark shadow blue spherical necklace bead (4–12 mm) of simple construction.
IIa55	Tumbled transparent brite navy spherical necklace bead (4–12 mm) of simple construction.
IIa6	Tumbled opaque black round or barrel-shaped necklace bead (4–12 mm) of simple construction.
IIa61	Tumbled translucent burgundy spherical necklace bead (4–12 mm) of simple construction.
IIb10	Tumbled opaque black spherical or oval necklace bead (4–12 mm) of simple construction with 3 or 4 white stripes.
IIb1004	Tumbled translucent brite navy spherical necklace bead (4–12 mm) of simple construction with 8–10 thin white stripes.
IIb1006	Tumbled translucent medium blue spherical necklace bead (4–12 mm) of simple construction with alternating red and white stripes.
IIb18	Tumbled transparent light gray spherical necklace bead (4–12 mm) of simple construction with 12–15 white stripes.
IIb27	Tumbled opaque white spherical or oval necklace bead (4–12 mm) of simple construction with 3 sets of 3 blue stripes.
IIb'3	Tumbled opaque black spherical or oval necklace bead (4–12 mm) of simple construction with white spiraled stripes.
IIb32	Tumbled opaque white oval necklace bead (4–12 mm) of simple construction with alternating red and blue stripes.
IIb39	Tumbled opaque white spherical or oval necklace bead (4–12 mm) of simple construction with alternating red, green, and blue stripes.
IIb56	Tumbled opaque turquoise spherical or oval necklace bead (4–12 mm) of simple construction with 3 or 4 white stripes.
IIb'6	Tumbled opaque white oval necklace bead (4–12 mm) of simple construction with red spiraled stripes.
IIb67	Tumbled translucent to opaque brite navy spherical or oval necklace bead (4–12 mm) of simple construction with 3 or 4 white stripes.
IIb990	Tumbled translucent brite navy spherical necklace bead (4–12 mm) of simple construction with 2 white stripes.
IIbb12	Tumbled opaque white spherical or oval necklace bead (4–12 mm) of complex construction with 3 blue on red stripes.
IIbb15	Tumbled opaque white oval necklace bead (4–12 mm) of complex construction with 3 yellow on blue stripes.
IIbb24	Tumbled opaque turquoise spherical or oval necklace bead (4–12 mm) of complex construction with 3 red on white stripes.
IIbb27	Tumbled translucent brite navy spherical or oval necklace bead (4–12 mm) of complex construction with 3 red on white stripes.
IIga	Tumbled opaque white spherical or oval necklace bead (4–12 mm) of complex construction with dark blue inlaid "eyes."
IIgb	Tumbled opaque turquoise spherical or oval necklace bead (4–12 mm) of complex construction with inlaid red stars on white "eyes."
IIIa1	Untumbled tubular necklace bead (4–10 mm) of compound construction consisting of a transparent apple green inner layer and opaque red outer layer.
IIj	Tumbled opaque black spherical necklace bead (8–12 mm) of simple construction with white or yellow wavy stripes.
IVa11sd	Tumbled seed bead (1–4 mm) of compound construction consisting of a transparent light gray inner layer, an opaque white middle layer, and a transparent light gray outer layer.
IVa5	Tumbled spherical or oval necklace bead (4–10 mm) of compound construction consisting of a transparent apple green inner layer and opaque red outer layer.
IVa5sd	Tumbled seed bead (1–4 mm) of compound construction consisting of a transparent apple green inner layer and opaque red outer layer.
IVasd	Tumbled seed bead (1–4 mm) of compound construction consisting of a transparent light gray or aqua blue inner layer and an opaque white outer layer.
IVb990	Tumbled spherical or oval necklace bead (4–10 mm) of compound construction consisting of a transparent light gray inner layer and an opaque white outer layer with blue stripes.
IVbb3	Tumbled spherical necklace bead (4–10 mm) of compound and complex construction consisting of a transparent apple green inner layer and opaque red outer layer with black on white stripes.
IVbsd	Compound seed bead (1–4 mm) consisting of a transparent light gray inner layer, an opaque white middle layer, and a transparent light gray outer layer with 6 redwood stripes.
WIb	Large spherical mandrel wound necklace bead (8–16 mm) of various colors.
WIc	Large oval mandrel wound necklace bead (8–16 mm) of various colors.
WIcb	Small oval mandrel wound necklace bead (2–6 mm) of various colors. Also known as "barleycorn" or "rat turd" beads.
WIIc	Large mandrel wound marvered necklace beads (8–16 mm) of various colors with 8–10 pressed facets.
WIId	Large mandrel wound "raspberry" necklace beads (8–16 mm) of various colors.
WIIe	Large mandrel wound "melon-shaped" marvered necklace beads (8–16 mm) of various colors.

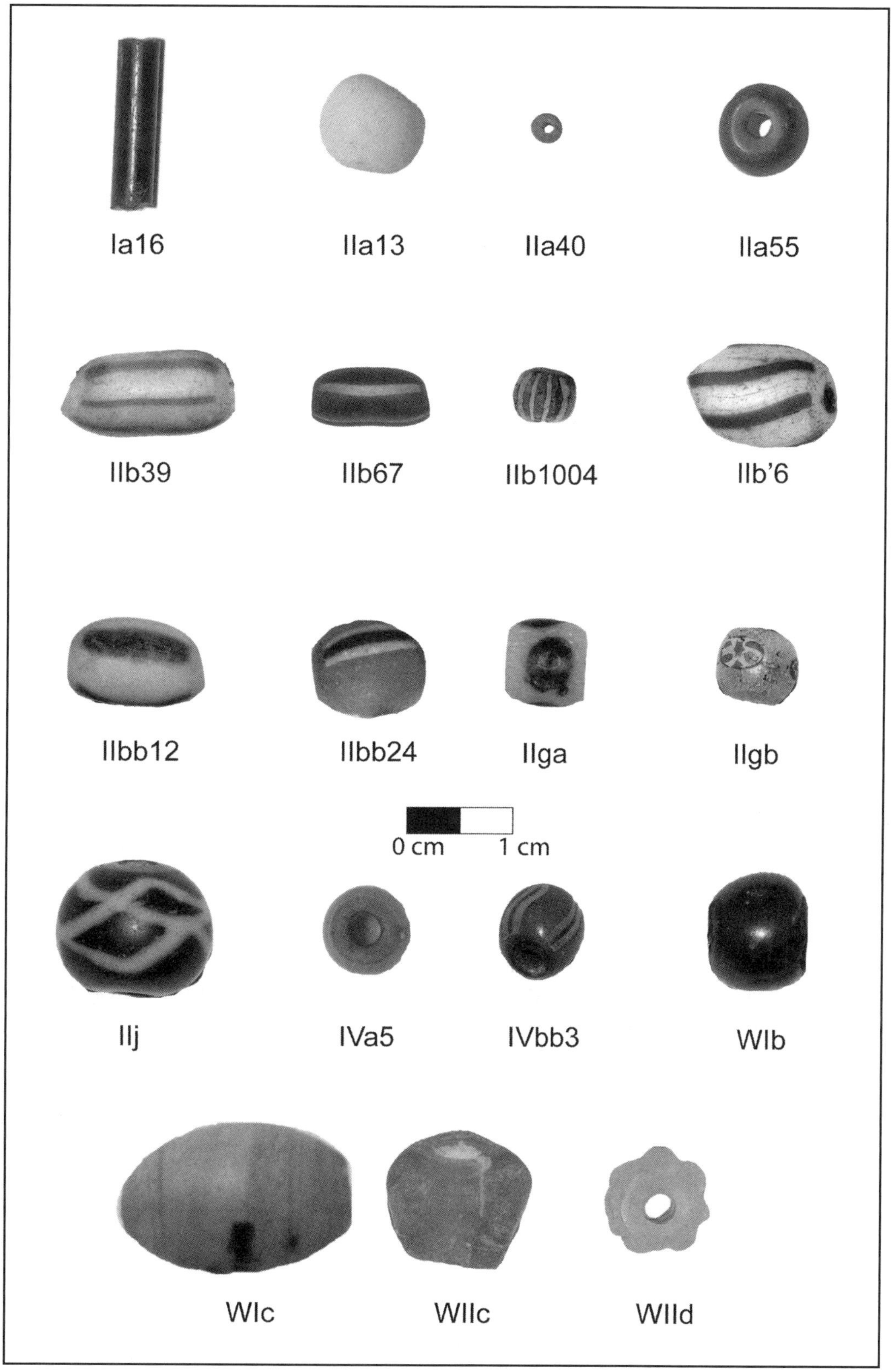

Figure 9.7. Bead types typically found in seventeenth- and eighteenth-century glass trade bead assemblages (bead types used in this study are based on the classification system pioneered by Kidd and Kidd [1970]).

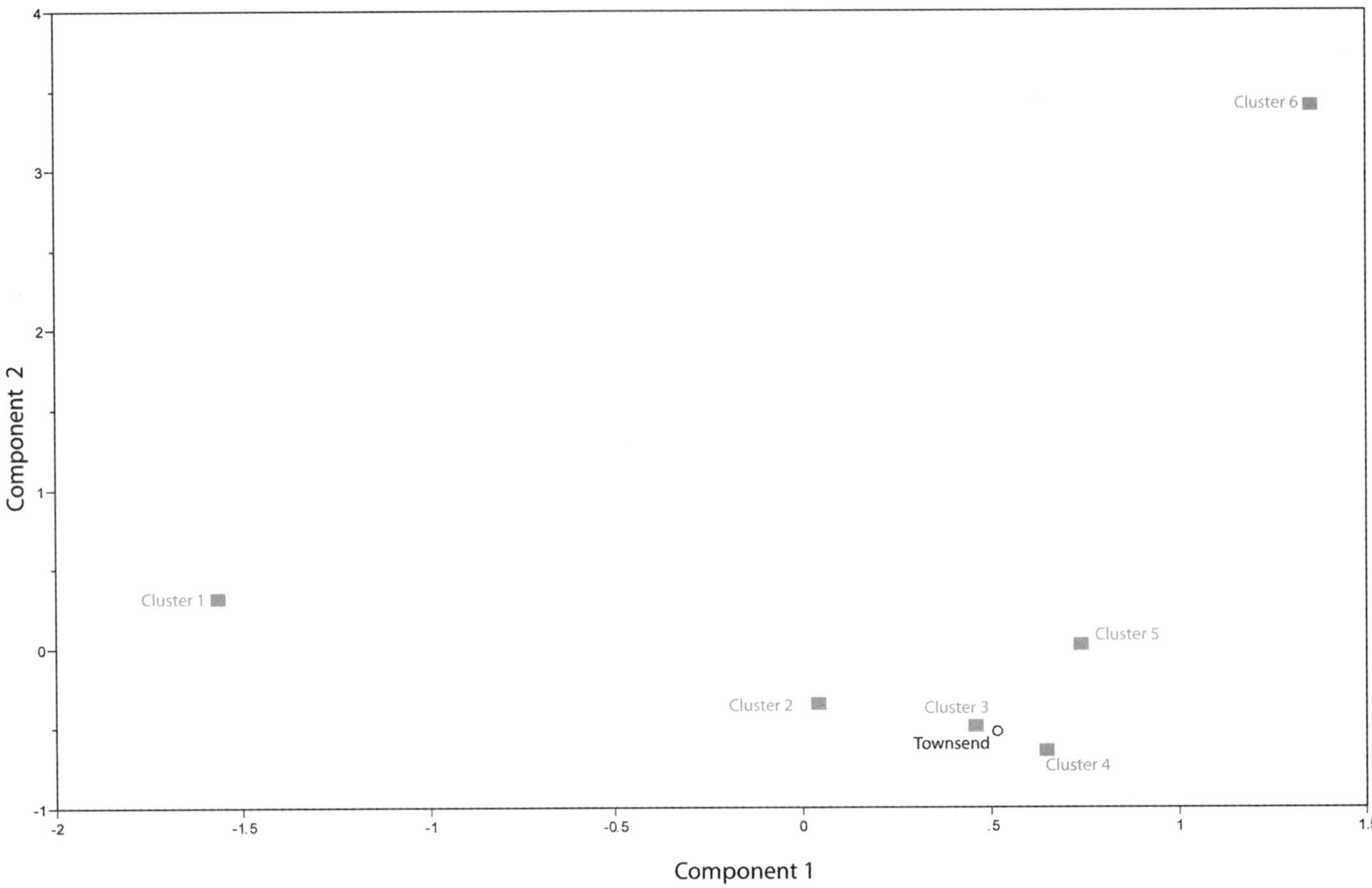

Figure 9.8. Biplot depicting the chronological position of the Townsend glass bead assemblage among the five seriation clusters.

wound necklace beads (Cluster 5) likely indicates either a long occupation span or two separate occupations at the site. Also, it is important to keep in mind that the seriation biplot *does not* measure absolute "time"; instead, distance is a factor of the degree of *relative* similarity between the sample bead assemblages and the clusters. Finally, one must remember that taxonomy is the axis around which this entire procedure revolves. As such, great care must be taken in analyzing glass bead assemblages to ensure that the classifications are consistent.

Figure 9.8 depicts the results of the correspondence analysis seriation. The results indicate (1) that the glass beads from Townsend represent a chronologically cohesive assemblage at the site level, and (2) that this assemblage is temporally closest to Cluster 3, which has an estimated time range of approximately A.D. 1650–1730. An even more precise date for the Townsend occupation can be achieved when the current ceramic chronology is considered along with the results of my glass trade bead seriation. Interestingly, it appears that major changes in the composition of both Cherokee pottery and glass bead assemblages accompany the shift from the pre- to post-Yamasee War era. "Early" English Contact period (ca. A.D. 1670–1715) pottery assemblages include a mixture of diagnostic attributes from the Middle and Late Qualla phases (see Chapter 7). Glass trade bead assemblages from this period consist of a wide variety of monochromatic and striped drawn and tumbled beads. "Late" English Contact period (ca. A.D. 1715–1740) pottery assemblages, on the other hand, evince primarily Late Qualla phase attributes (for example, check stamping, rectilinear complicated stamping, notched rimstrips). Also, glass trade bead assemblages from the post-Yamasee War years include significant numbers of large mandrel wound beads and small monochromatic tubular beads. These clear distinctions in material culture assemblages make the temporal assignment of "Early" and "Late" English Contact period Cherokee occupational components possible even with small artifact samples. Taken together with the ethnohistoric data presented in Chapter 4, these data suggest that an occupation estimate of approximately A.D. 1650–1720 for the Cherokee component at Townsend is in order.

Chapter 10

Cherokee Foodways in Tuckaleechee Cove

Kandace D. Hollenbach, Judith A. Sichler, and Jessica L. Vavrasek

The analysis of plant and animal remains is one avenue of research into a group's foodways—the procurement, production, preparation, consumption, display, storage, and discard of food. These practices vary by economic, social, and political situation, and thus give us an entry to study the cultural traditions of a group (Johannessen 1993). This chapter discusses samples analyzed, the method of analysis, and the results obtained. It is clear from this analysis that in foodways and in food choices, the Cherokees of Tuckaleechee Cove followed a traditional path little influenced by Euroamerican foods or foodways.

Plant Analysis

Plant remains from 38 floatation samples and 1 waterscreen sample were analyzed from Cherokee contexts at the three Townsend sites (Table 10.1). These represent 24 features that are associated with the six identified households. The one exception is Feature 24 from 40Bt89, a small basin that does not appear to be associated with Household 1. Marcoux (see Chapter 6) has identified several feature types, including pit, bell-shaped pit, basin, and hearth, and has further subdivided these by size into small, medium, and large categories.

Because uncarbonized plant materials are unlikely to be preserved in the moist, acidic soils of the Southeast, even from relatively recent historic contexts (Reitz and Scarry 1985:10; Yarnell 1982), only carbonized plant remains are considered here to be part of the archaeological record. Uncarbonized plant materials are assumed to be modern contaminants that reflect the present-day local habitat, and are therefore not reported or discussed.

Methods

The samples were processed in the field as well as in the laboratory using modified SMAP-type machines (Watson 1976). A cylindrical metal insert, fitted with a spout at the top and 1-mm mesh covering the base, was placed within a 43.7-liter (11.5-gallon) metal drum. The metal drum was plumbed through the base with a pipe through which water flowed, but the pipe was not fitted with a shower head; instead, samples were simply agitated by hand using a rubber spatula. Light fraction materials were collected in 0.25-mm geological sieves, and subsequently transferred to coffee filters. Heavy fraction materials were similarly transferred from the base of the cylindrical insert to trays lined with newspaper. Once dried, the light and heavy fractions of the samples were bagged and curated together.

The samples were analyzed using standard paleoethnobotanical procedures (Pearsall 2000). Once weighed, the light and heavy fractions were size-graded using nested geologic sieves. The portions greater than 2.00 mm in size were sorted into categories, including bone, shell, lithics, and plant materials. Using a stereoscopic microscope at 10 to 40 power magnification, plant remains were further sorted and identified to the lowest

Table 10.1. Analyzed Cherokee botanical samples from the Townsend sites.[a]

Feature	Associated Household	Feature Type	BCL	Sample Volume	Sample Weight	Subsample Weight	Contaminant Weight	Residue Weight	Plant Weight	Wood Weight
40Bt89										
16	1	small basin	99-910-1	10	15.48		1.82	7.13	5.01	0.43
18	1	medium basin	99-918-1	10	12.10		5.67	5.41	0.28	0.18
21	1	large pit	99-1080-2	10	34.15		5.17	10.57	16.61	8.02
21	1		99-1081-251	10	10.45		1.55	2.49	5.07	1.95
21	1		99-1085-1	10	3.17		1.56	0.50	0.42	0.23
21[b]	1		99-1642-1	10	5.92		0.02	4.06	1.67	1.28
23	1	medium pit	99-1070-2	10	64.96		80.20	330.40	17.10	5.85
24	unaffiliated	small basin	99-821-252	10	3.46		2.36	5.09	2.67	0.98
38	1	small basin	99-1041-1	10	31.83		8.31	22.25	0.38	0.29
44	1	small basin	99-840-252	10	20.91		6.18	9.58	2.99	2.30
44	1		99-843-251	10	39.92		9.93	21.15	4.82	4.19
45	1	small pit	99-1037-1	10	548.10		342.45	205.52	0.01	0.01
45	1		99-1043-3	10	13.61		7.40	4.34	0.17	0.12
48	1	medium bell-shaped pit	99-1099-258	10	609.10		375.23	126.84	76.07	47.32
50	1	medium pit	99-1049-4	10	25.94		4.66	10.43	4.80	3.08
55	1	small basin	99-817-4	–	65.77		22.25	25.06	13.08	11.63
55	1		99-825-252	–	10.23		4.26	5.47	0.95	0.56
40Bt90										
455	3	small pit	00-259-1	10	53.50		25.81	22.24	0.34	0.21
702	4	medium bell-shaped pit	99-3804-5	2	15.28		2.99	6.21	4.23	0.55
705	4	medium pit	99-3027-1	10	244.01		46.24	146.01	40.38	24.46
705	4		99-3052-1	15	286.37	179.84	34.65	47.96	82.59	58.18
706	4	small pit	99-3787-1	4	35.18		19.91	22.86	17.87	17.36
936	2	medium basin	99-3238-1	10	252.99		164.81	83.36	3.02	1.42
936	2		99-3240-251	10	168.37		98.41	66.26	1.43	0.94
1019	2	medium pit	99-3256-1	10	98.83		36.33	36.59	7.83	5.43
1019	2		99-3258-253	10	104.13	91.66	38.77	38.43	8.21	6.11
1020	2	small basin	99-3660-1	10	41.19		13.21	16.81	6.37	5.35
1996	4	small pit	99-8878-1	25	230.37		58.71	156.20	10.11	7.32
40Bt91										
94	5	hearth	99-2685-1	1	1.59		0.85	0.73	0.01	0.00
390	6	small pit	99-892-2	10	31.28		11.96	16.17	0.69	0.56
390[c]	6		99-893-3	NA	147.89		72.02	65.98	1.14	0.98
392	6	small pit	99-867-2	10	14.45		4.87	7.49	0.85	0.70
394	6	hearth	99-851-1	0.5	2.97		1.74	0.82	0.09	0.05
394	6		99-852-1	0.5	3.55		2.37	0.55	0.00	0.00
394	6		99-857-1	1	2.78		1.13	1.00	0.08	0.02
394	6		99-862-2		7.10		1.82	3.00	0.05	0.04
497	5	small pit	99-2204-251	10	109.02		12.42	49.96	39.89	36.23
497	5		99-2206-5	10	152.78		68.03	37.90	41.36	36.22

[a]Volumes are given in liters; weights are given in grams.
[b]Heavy fraction is missing; sample not included in quantitative analyses.
[c]Waterscreen sample, not included in quantitative analyses.

possible taxonomic level. Materials less than 2.00 mm in size were scanned for seeds and plant remains not represented in the larger size fraction. If present, acorn remains were pulled from the 1.40-mm sieve to mitigate biases against their preservation.

All materials were then counted (when feasible) and weighed. Identifications were made with reference to Martin and Barkley's (1961) *Seed Identification Manual* and the PLANTS database (U.S. Department of Agriculture, Natural Resources Conservation Service [USDA-NRCS] 2010), as well as modern comparative specimens housed at the Archaeological Research Laboratory and at the McClung Museum at the University of Tennessee-Knoxville.

Due to their large size, several samples (or portions of several samples) were subsampled using a riffle splitter (see Table 10.1). The raw numbers of the identified taxa are presented here; no effort has been made to extrapolate the total number of specimens in the complete sample.

Results

The 39 analyzed samples yielded 418.76 g of carbonized plant materials, 290.58 g of which are represented by wood. The non-wood taxa include a variety of nuts, wild fruits, crops, edible seeds, and miscellaneous taxa (Table 10.2).

Nuts

Among the nut taxa recovered from Cherokee contexts, hickory was the most abundant by count, with a total of 381 fragments of shell and 8 additional possible fragments. Black walnut, however, was the most abundant by weight and closely followed hickory in count, particularly if the specimens identified as black walnut/peach are included. Both peach pits and black walnut shells are dense and thick, and have highly contoured outer surfaces, making them difficult to distinguish when present as small fragments. Because no definitively identifiable peach pits were identified in the samples, these fragments most likely represent black walnut. Over 200 additional nutshell fragments could not be distinguished between hickory and black walnut and were identified as "walnut family." In addition to hickory and black walnut, over 70 fragments of acorn and at least 8 fragments of hazelnut were recovered.

The importance of nuts as a dietary staple is evidenced by their regular recovery from Cherokee contexts. Hickory nuts are nearly ubiquitous, being recovered from 31 of the 38 samples (Appendix D). Black walnut was recovered from 26 samples, and acorn from 19. It should be noted that acorn shell is much more fragile than hickory or walnut shell, and is therefore underrepresented at archaeological sites. Their consistent recovery from Cherokee contexts suggests that acorns were as important to the occupants' diets as hickory nuts and black walnuts.

Hickory nuts and acorns are frequently recovered from sites in the Southeast, as both were important staples in the diets of prehistoric peoples (Gardner 1997; Scarry 2003; Yarnell and Black 1985). Both would have been collected in autumn and could be stored and eaten through winter, until fresh plant foods became available again in spring. The two serve different dietary roles, however. While acorns are important sources of carbohydrates, hickory nuts are high in fats and proteins (Gardner 1997; Scarry 2003). Hickory nuts were often boiled down to make an oil or milk. The resulting liquid could be consumed as a beverage or used in stews or porridges (Carr 1895:171, 182–83; Fritz et al. 2001; Kavasch 1977:2; Kuhnlein and Turner 1991:209; Swanton 1946:265). Acorns, after being leached of tannins, were commonly ground into a meal and made into a mash or bread (Carr 1895:172; Densmore 1974:320; Kuhnlein and Turner 1991:200–201; Palmer 1871:409–10; Peterson 1977:204).

Black walnuts, however, are often recovered in low numbers from archaeological sites (Scarry 2003). Black walnuts grow as solitary trees, rather than in stands like hickories and oaks, making collection of large numbers of walnuts more difficult. In addition, black walnuts cannot be processed in bulk by boiling, as hickory nuts can. The bitter outer husk adheres to the shell and would release tannins into the water, making the resulting oil, milk, and nutmeats inedible (Gardner 1997; Talalay et al. 1984). The significant numbers of black walnuts recovered in Cherokee contexts at Townsend are thus quite notable. These flavorful nuts, which are high in fats and proteins like hickory nuts, must have been highly valued by the Cherokee occupants. Black walnut trees likely grew in the vicinity of Townsend, and the occupants may have encouraged their growth and productivity by clearing competitive trees, pruning, and the like.

The low recovery of hazelnuts in comparison to the other nut taxa is common to other sites in the region (Scarry 2003) and suggests that hazelnuts were used less frequently by the Cherokee occupants. Hazelnuts grow on shrubs and must be picked, similar to berries, requiring more time to collect than other nuts (Gardner 1997; Talalay et al. 1984). Furthermore, hazelnuts ripen as early as late summer (Schopmeyer 1974) and grow in thickets along forest margins, rather than in wooded stands like oaks, hickories, and walnuts (Radford et al. 1964). Use of hazelnuts thus requires gathering in slightly different settings and seasons than the other nuts. These differences may further contribute to the rarity of hazelnuts in the samples.

It is worth noting that chestnut was not recovered from the Townsend samples. Chestnuts, which have a papery outer shell that is quickly consumed in fires, were an important source of carbohydrates in the diets of historic Native Americans. According to one traveler to western North Carolina, entire Cherokee towns headed into "the mountains gathering chesnuts [sic] upon which many of them depend principally for a subsistence" (Benjamin F. Currey to Elbert Herring, letter, National Archives 1831:11:7:1). Chestnuts should have been abundant in the vicinity of Tuckaleechee Cove; their absence at Townsend is more likely related to their poor preservation potential than their lack of use.

Table 10.2. Plant remains recovered from Cherokee contexts at the Townsend sites.

Common Name	Taxonomic Name	Seasonality	Count	Weight (g)
Nuts				
acorn	*Quercus* sp.	fall	69	0.08
acorn cap	*Quercus* sp.	fall	1	0.00
acorn cap cf.	*Quercus* sp. cf.	fall	2	0.01
acorn cf.	*Quercus* sp. cf.	fall	9	0.00
acorn meat cf.	*Quercus* sp. cf.	fall	17	0.06
acorn meat/persimmon seed cf.		fall	3	0.01
acorn shell/meat	*Quercus* sp.	fall	1	0.01
black walnut	*Juglans nigra*	fall	278	8.66
black walnut cf.	*Juglans nigra* cf.	fall	4	0.03
black walnut/peach		fall	96	2.21
hazelnut	*Corylus* sp.	fall	8	0.03
hazelnut cf.	*Corylus* sp. cf.	fall	2	0.00
hickory	*Carya* sp.	fall	381	3.99
hickory cf.	*Carya* sp. cf.	fall	8	0.01
walnut family	Juglandaceae	fall	202	1.90
walnut family cf.	Juglandaceae cf.	fall	1	0.00
walnut family/peach			2	0.02
Fruits				
blackberry/raspberry	*Rubus* sp.	summer	8	0.00
blueberry	*Vaccinium* sp.	summer	2	0.00
blueberry cf.	*Vaccinium* sp. cf.	summer	1	0.00
elderberry cf.	*Sambucus* sp.		1	0.00
grape	*Vitis* sp.	summer	3	0.00
grape cf.	*Vitis* sp. cf.	summer	1	0.00
hackberry cf.	*Celtis* sp. cf.		4	0.00
honeylocust cf.	*Gleditsia triacanthos* cf.		2	0.00
maypop	*Passiflora incarnata*	summer	8	0.02
maypop cf.	*Passiflora incarnata* cf.	summer	3	0.00
persimmon seed cf.	*Diospyros virginiana* cf.	fall	6	0.00
persimmon seed coat cf.	*Diospyros virginiana* cf.	fall	5	0.00
persimmon/bean cf.	*Diospyros virginiana* cf.	fall	3	0.01
plum/cherry cf.	*Prunus* sp. cf.	spring/summer	6	0.00
Crops				
bean	*Phaseolus vulgaris*	late summer/fall	124	2.82
bean cf.	*Phaseolus vulgaris* cf.	late summer/fall	50	0.25
bean/legume			3	0.00
bean/persimmon cf.			1	0.01
bean/persimmon/acorn meat			8	0.05
corn cob	*Zea mays*	late summer/fall	1	0.24
corn cupule	*Zea mays*	late summer/fall	513	4.91
corn cupule cf.	*Zea mays* cf.	late summer/fall	91	0.36
corn embryo	*Zea mays*	late summer/fall	4	0.02
corn glume	*Zea mays*	late summer/fall	96	0.30
corn glume cf.	*Zea mays* cf.	late summer/fall	2	0.01
corn kernel	*Zea mays*	late summer/fall	326	2.43
corn kernel cf.	*Zea mays* cf.	late summer/fall	120	0.62
cucurbit rind	Cucurbitaceae	late summer/fall	82	0.28
cucurbit rind cf.	Cucurbitaceae cf.	late summer/fall	4	0.01

Table 10.2 cont.

Common Name	Taxonomic Name	Seasonality	Count	Weight (g)
Edible Seeds				
amaranth	*Amaranthus* sp.	late summer/fall	1	0.00
bearsfoot	*Polymnia uvedalia*		1	0.00
cheno/am	*Chenopodium/Amaranthus*	late summer/fall	5	0.00
chenopod	*Chenopodium* sp.	late summer/fall	13	0.00
chenopod cf.	*Chenopodium* sp. cf.	late summer/fall	7	0.00
chenopod embryo cf.	*Chenopodium* sp. cf.	late summer/fall	1	0.00
knotweed	*Polygonum* sp.		3	0.00
little barley	*Hordeum pusillum*	spring/early summer	45	0.01
little barley cf.	*Hordeum pusillum* cf.	spring/early summer	14	0.01
smartweed	*Polygonum* cf. *penslyvanicum*		1	0.00
sumpweed cf.	*Iva annua* cf.		2	0.00
weedy legume	Fabaceae	late summer/fall	1	0.00
Miscellaneous				
bark			213	2.35
bark cf.			6	0.05
bedstraw	*Galium* sp.		69	0.04
bedstraw cf.	*Galium* sp. cf.		6	0.00
bud			18	0.01
bud/achene?			1	0.00
bur			5	0.00
cane	*Arundinaria* sp.		356	3.70
cane cf.	*Arundinaria* sp. cf.		1	0.00
cane, partially carbonized	*Arundinaria* sp.		10	0.06
catkin		spring	2	0.00
false Solomon's seal cf.	*Smilacina* sp. cf.		5	0.00
grass family	Poaceae		303	0.08
monocot node/stem	Poaceae		10	0.02
morning-glory	*Ipomoea/Convolvulus*	summer/fall	1	0.00
pine cone	*Pinus* sp.		3000	12.16
pine cone cf.	*Pinus* sp. cf.		9	0.02
pine cone/bark	*Pinus* sp.		5	0.02
pine seed cf.	*Pinus* sp. cf.		1	0.01
pitch			4705	41.57
purslane	*Portulaca* sp.	summer/fall	11	0.00
sedge family cf.	Cyperaceae cf.		118	0.00
spurge family cf.	Euphorbiaceae cf.		23	0.00
stem			3	0.00
stem/catkin			1	0.01
thorn			1	0.00
tobacco cf.	*Nicotiana rustica* cf.		1	0.00
unidentifiable	unidentifiable		323	1.42
unidentifiable seed	unidentifiable		198	0.08
unidentified	unidentified		5	0.01
unidentified seeds	unidentified		85	0.00
wax myrtle cf.	*Myrica* sp. cf.		1	0.00
wood, partially carbonized			56	11.07

Fruits

A variety of fruits were represented in the Cherokee samples, including blackberry/raspberry, blueberry, grape, and maypop. Among the tentatively identified fruits are elderberry, hackberry, honeylocust, persimmon, and plum/cherry. Blackberry/raspberry and maypop seeds were the most frequently recovered, each with a count of 8 seeds or seed fragments, although 14 fragments were tentatively identified as persimmon. The remaining fruit taxa were recovered in low numbers.

The various fruits may be eaten fresh; cooked into bread, stews, or other dishes for flavor; made into preserves; or dried and stored for future use (Fernald and Kinsey 1943; Havard 1896; Kuhnlein and Turner 1991; Medsger 1972; Moerman 2004; Palmer 1871; Peterson 1977; Swanton 1946; Yanovsky 1936). Ripe persimmons apparently were consumed in "large quantities" (Palmer 1871:471) by some historic native groups. Persimmons were kept for winter use by fashioning the pulp into cakes and drying them (Swanton 1946) or making them into preserves (Palmer 1871:471). Maypops were generally used to make beverages. The pulp and seeds were scooped from the fruit and boiled to obtain a juice, which could be consumed or cooked with meal (Ulmer and Beck 1951:48, 58; U.S. Department of Agriculture, Natural Resources Conservation Service 2004). Honeylocust pods contain a sweet pulp that may be eaten raw (Moerman 2004; Yanovsky 1936:36) or used to sweeten medicines or children's dispositions (Moerman 2004). The pulp can also be used to make a beverage (Moerman 2004; Ulmer and Beck 1951:58) that may be fermented (Yanovsky 1936:36).

In addition to the fruits themselves, which served as good sources of vitamins, minerals, and flavor, other parts of the plants have useful properties. The spring shoots of blackberries/raspberries and grapes, for example, can be eaten as greens (Fernald and Kinsey 1943:236; Kuhnlein and Turner 1991:265; Medsger 1972:23; Peterson 1977:184, 198). The leaves, twigs, and roots also may be used to make tea, and often have medicinal properties (Medsger 1972; Moerman 2004; Yanovsky 1936).

The various fruits generally ripen in summer through early fall, with the exception of persimmons (Radford et al. 1964; Schopmeyer 1974). These fleshy fruits are not palatable until after the first frost of autumn. While grapes tend to prefer wooded habitats, most of the fruit taxa thrive in disturbed habitats, such as agricultural fields (Radford et al. 1964). Maypops in particular suggest the presence of fields. In fact, Yarnell (1993) argues that maypops were actively cultivated in prehistoric gardens. At the very least, the presence of these tasty fruits, along with peaches and persimmons, would certainly have been tolerated, if not encouraged.

As mentioned above, no definitive evidence for peaches was recovered from the Townsend sites. This lack is not likely due to preservation, as the dense, robust pit behaves similar to hickory and walnut shell. Although peaches are not native to North America, they are commonly found in protohistoric and historic contexts in the Southeast. Peaches may have first arrived in the New World as early as Columbus' second voyage, but were certainly propagated by the Spanish settlers of *La Florida* in the mid-sixteenth century. Peaches rapidly naturalized and spread throughout the region, as they were well suited to the climate and were likely encouraged and further disseminated by Native Americans (Gremillion 1993:16). Peach pits have been recovered at other Appalachian Cherokee sites such as Smokemont (31SW393; Carmody and Hollenbach 2008) and Coweeta Creek (31MA34; VanDerwarker and Detwiler 2000), as well as Cherokee sites in the Little Tennessee River Valley (Chapman and Shea 1981). Their absence at Townsend may speak to the timing of their spread in the region.

Crops

Crop taxa recovered from the Cherokee samples include the typical corn, beans, and squash, all three of which are well represented. These three crops formed the base of Eastern Woodland agriculture, with corn serving as a dietary staple (Smith and Cowan 2003). Corn remains include 1 cob fragment and over 600 cupules and glumes, inedible structures that secure the kernels to the cob. Over 300 fragments of corn kernels were identified, along with 124 beans and 82 cucurbit rind fragments. These quantities are substantial, given the fact that these are edible portions of the plant, unlike cobs, cupules, and glumes. As byproducts, the latter are often purposefully burned, either as a fuel or to reduce waste. In contrast, corn kernels, beans, squash seeds, and squash rinds are typically boiled, roasted, or dried, and eaten, and are therefore less likely to be preserved.

Cultivation of corn, beans, and squash requires preparation of fields, sowing, weeding, protecting crops from predators such as deer and birds, and harvesting (Smith and Cowan 2003). These activities were performed from spring through late summer or early autumn. Historic accounts relate that Native Americans intercropped their fields. Four to 8 kernels of corn were often planted in small mounds approximately half a meter in diameter, and spaced roughly a meter apart. Four beans were then planted around the base of the mound, so that the growing bean plants could use the corn stalks for support. Squash seeds were planted between the mounds, where they could spread their leafy vines, smothering weeds and keeping the ground moist and cool (Hudson 1976:292–94, 297; Wagner and Civitello 2000; Wilson 1917). It is likely that more than one variety of corn was grown, and that plantings were staggered. These strategies would reduce the risk of losing crops to late spring or early autumn frosts, late spring floods, or droughts (Hudson 1976:297; Scarry 1993:178–80; Smith and Cowan 2003).

Edible Seeds

In addition to crops, several taxa with edible seeds were recovered from the samples. The most important of these is little barley, with 45 positively identified specimens. In addition, 13 chenopod seeds were recovered, along with several knotweed, smartweed, amaranth, weedy legume, and possible sumpweed seeds.

Most of these starchy seeds are associated with a complex of native plants cultivated by peoples living in the Southeast beginning approximately 3500 years ago (Yarnell 1993). Relatively few of the native cultivated seeds display definitive morphological evidence of domestication, such as increasingly thin seed coats (e.g., chenopod, *Chenopodium berlandieri*) or an increase in seed size (e.g., sunflower, *Helianthus annuus*). Other seeds, including little barley, are repeatedly recovered from archaeological sites in association with these clearly domesticated species, however, suggesting that they were cultivated and harvested alongside each other. No attempt was made here to determine whether the recovered chenopod was the domesticated species, but 10 of the 13 seeds lacked a seed coat, suggesting that they were relatively thin. It is possible that the Cherokee occupants of Townsend cultivated native starchy and oily seed crops, but they may have simply tolerated the presence of these useful plants in fields and garden plots.

The edible seeds can be eaten raw or toasted, or boiled into porridge. The starchy seeds can also be ground into flour and subsequently used to make bread or mush (Kuhnlein and Turner 1991; Moerman 2004; Palmer 1871; Yanovsky 1936). In addition, the spring leaves and shoots, particularly of chenopod and amaranth, can be eaten as greens (Kuhnlein and Turner 1991; Palmer 1871; Yanovsky 1936).

The edible seed taxa thrive in disturbed settings, such as garden plots or agricultural fields. Chenopod and amaranth would have been planted in spring, with seeds ripening in late summer and early autumn (Radford et al. 1964). Little barley, however, typically requires planting in early winter and is harvested in May or June (Cowan 1994:267). All would have been planted by broadcasting the seeds, in contrast to the deliberate planting of each corn kernel, bean, or squash seed (Smith and Cowan 2003). However, it is perhaps more likely that the presence of these taxa was simply tolerated within corn fields, rather than purposefully cultivated.

Miscellaneous

The miscellaneous plant remains recovered from the site provide a general indication of the local habitat. For example, the recovery of numerous pine cone scales, as well as pitch among other vitrified material, suggests the presence of pine trees in the local forests. The numerous weedy taxa, including bedstraw, morning-glory, purslane, grass family seeds, and tentatively identified false Solomon's seal and members of the sedge and spurge families, indicate the presence of disturbed grounds, such as garden plots and domestic settings, in which these weedy species thrive (Radford et al. 1964). However, the stems of sedges can be woven into baskets and mats; in addition, the sedges, spurges, bedstraw, morning-glory, and purslane have a variety of medicinal uses (Gilmore 1932; Moerman 2004; Powers 1873–1874). As such, these weedy taxa may have been encouraged rather than weeded from gardens and fields.

In addition, a number of fragments of cane and monocot stem (both of which have a variety of utilitarian uses) were recovered from the samples. Fibers of monocot stems can be braided into cordage, as well as woven into a number of items. Cane was used in wattle-and-daub construction as webbing between larger posts; woven into baskets and mats; cut to make arrow shafts and blow guns; whittled into flutes; and burned as a fuel, notoriously in the form of torches (Moerman 2004; Watson and Yarnell 1966). Cane prefers to grow along riverbanks and in other wet grounds, but can be found in a number of settings (Radford et al. 1964).

One possible tobacco seed was recovered from Feature 50, associated with Household 1 on 40Bt89. Rather than being planted among food crops, tobacco plants were tended in separate garden plots, sometimes in relatively secluded areas (Hudson 1976:353; Wilson 1917). The leaves of tobacco may be applied to the skin as a poultice for a number of ailments. The dried blossoms, leaves, and stems may also be smoked, for both medicinal and ceremonial purposes (Hamel and Chiltoskey 1975; Knight 1975; Moerman 2004).

Comparison by Context

The Cherokee samples allow for both qualitative and quantitative comparisons among different contexts at Townsend, including by household and by feature type. Several of the features stand out based on the plant foods found in them (see Appendix D). For example, Feature 21, a large pit from Household 1, contained 117 of the 124 beans and nearly half of the black walnut fragments recovered from the samples. Two additional features from Household 1, Features 16 and 23, each contained over a hundred grass family seeds. Feature 1020, a small basin associated with Household 2, included 45 little barley, 18 bedstraw, 2 blueberry, and 24 unidentified seeds. Large quantities of corn remains were recovered from several features, including Features 705 and 1996, both pits associated with Household 4, and Feature 936, a medium basin associated with Household 2.

The distribution of plant remains among features can be further explored using quantitative methods. Boxplots readily display the distribution of data, facilitating comparisons of contexts (Velleman and Hoaglin 1981). For example, a boxplot of the density of plant remains (total weight [g] of carbonized plant remains in a sample divided by the sample volume [liters]) by feature type indicates that medium bell-shaped pits and large/medium pits tend to contain more plant materials than basins or hearths (Fig. 10.1). Small pits display a wide range of values, however.

Nut density (count of nutshell fragments divided by total plant weight in a sample) is largely similar among feature types (Fig. 10.2). Although hearths tend to contain greater densities of nut remains, this is largely due to the small quantities of plant remains recovered from hearth samples in general. Corn and crop densities (the latter includes corn, beans, and cucurbit rinds) are notably high among medium basins and low among bell-shaped

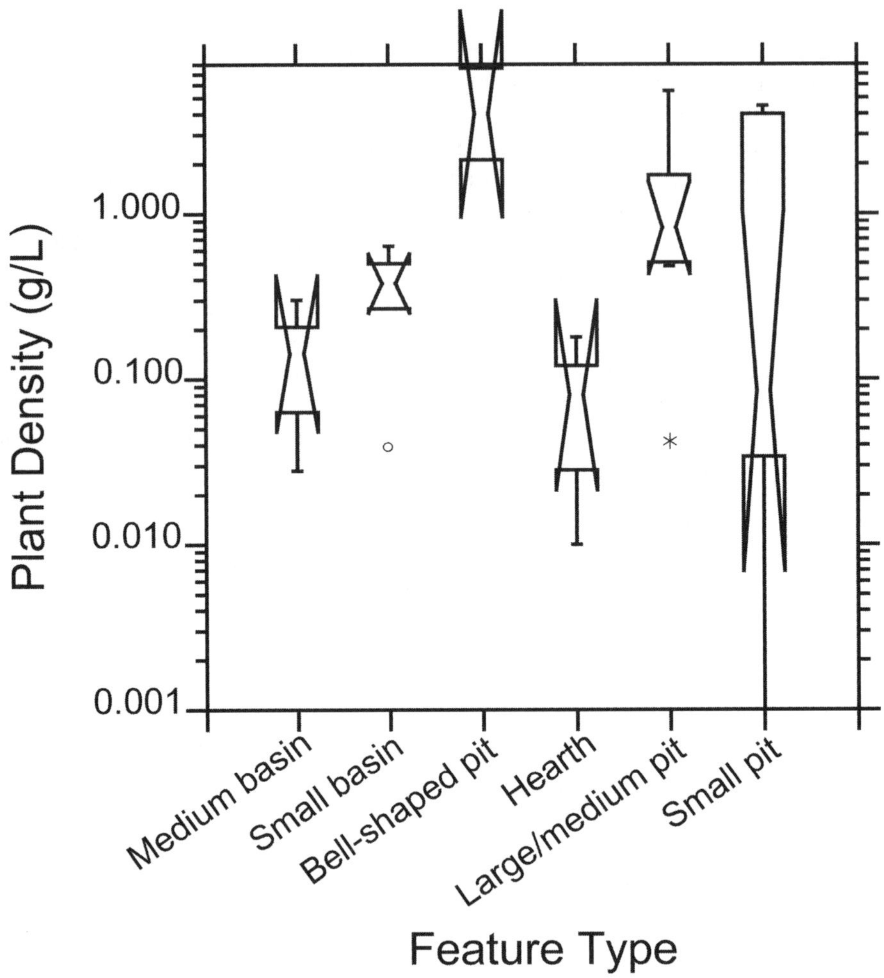

Figure 10.1. Boxplots comparing plant density (g/L) by feature type.

pits (Figs. 10.3, 10.4). Both of these categories are small: there are only 3 medium basins and 2 bell-shaped pits among the samples. However, as noted above, Feature 936, a medium basin with 149 kernels and 34 cupules and glumes, clearly stands out among the samples.

Comparisons between households indicate that the assemblages are largely dictated by the feature types associated with each. Plant density is high for Household 4, which includes a bell-shaped pit and 2 medium pit samples, both of which have higher plant densities (Fig. 10.5). Similarly, plant density is low for Household 6, which is predominantly represented by hearth samples. Little patterning is apparent for the densities of nuts, corn, and crops by household, however.

Faunal Analysis

Vertebrate faunal remains were recovered from 24 of the 45 designated Cherokee features at the Townsend sites. The majority of these are associated with Household 1, but each of the households is represented by at least two features (Table 10.3). The materials recovered from each household are discussed in turn after a review of the methods used for the analysis.

Methods

Vertebrate remains were recovered in the field from 1/4-inch and 1/16-inch waterscreens, and were identified at the Archaeo-

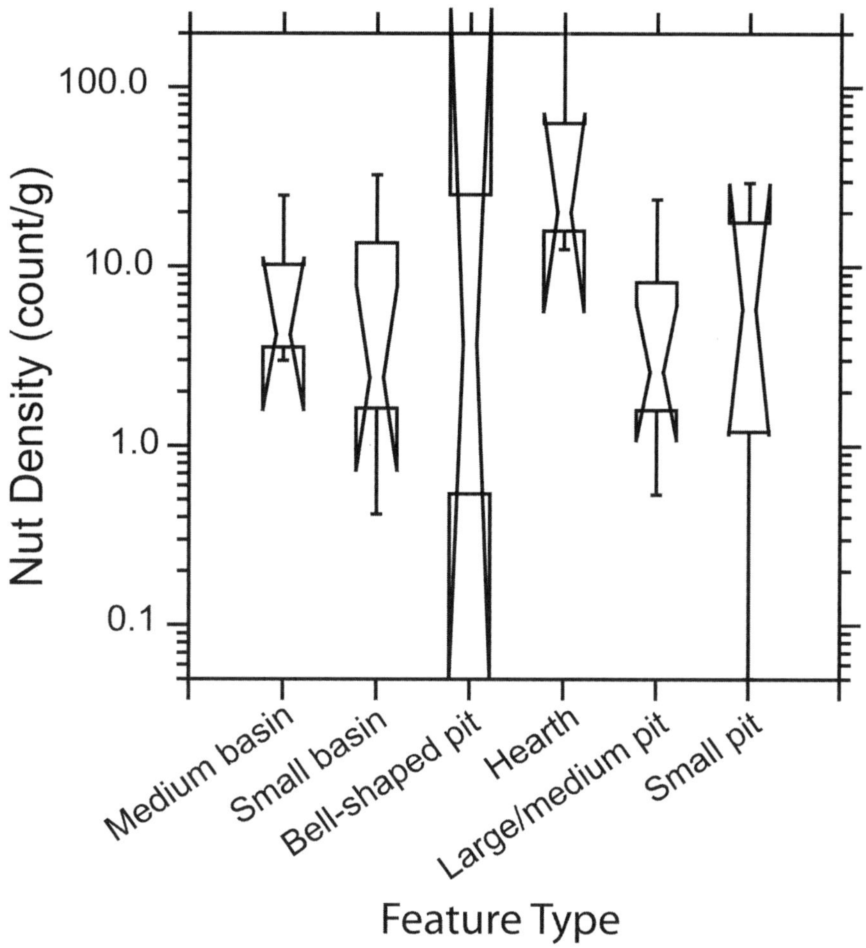

Figure 10.2. Boxplots comparing nutshell density (count/total plant weight) by feature type.

logical Research Laboratory (ARL) at the University of Tennessee using modern comparative collections. Initial sorting and classification of faunal remains was done to the most specific taxonomic level possible. The taxonomic nomenclature used for vertebrates follows the Peterson Field Guides (e.g., Burt and Grossenheider 1980; Conant and Collins 1991; Page and Burr 1991; Peterson 1980). Other information recorded includes element, side, portion, fusion, and whether any modification was noted on the bone.

When identification was limited to class, a size category was assigned when feasible. The Archaeological Research Laboratory faunal protocol for mammals is as follows. Large mammals are those represented by wild taxa such as white-tailed deer (*Odocoileus virginianus*) and black bear (*Ursus americanus*), and domestic taxa such as cow (*Bos taurus*) and pig (*Sus scrofa*). Representatives of the medium/large-sized category include animals referred to as canids (*Canis* spp.), primarily the coyote, wolf, and dog. The medium-sized mammal category includes wild taxa such as foxes (gray fox [*Urocyon cinereoargenteus*] and red fox [*Vulpes fulva*]), beaver (*Castor canadensis*), and raccoon (*Procyon lotor*). Medium-to-small mammals include wild taxa such as cottontail rabbit (*Sylvilagus floridanus*), opossum (*Didelphis marsupialis*), woodchuck (*Marmota monax*), and skunk (*Mephitis mephitis*). Examples of small-sized mammals include squirrels (*Sciurus* sp.) and Old World rats (*Rattus* sp.). Very small-sized mammals are represented by taxa such as mice,

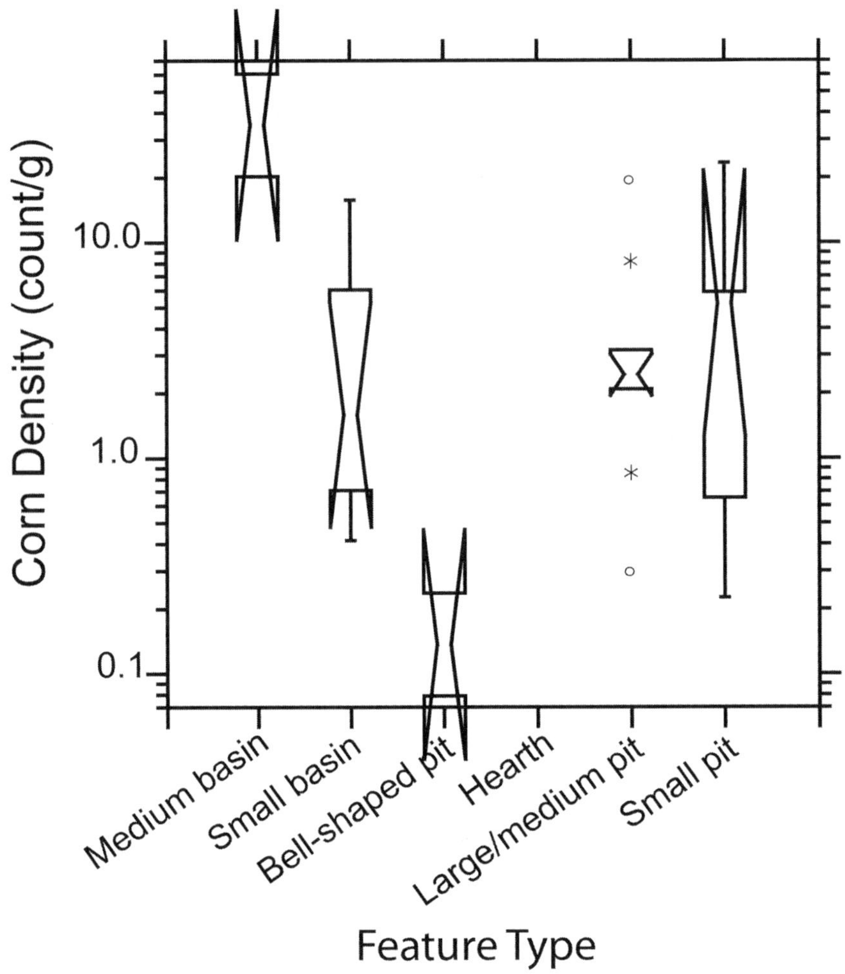

Figure 10.3. Boxplots comparing corn density (count/total plant weight) by feature type.

voles, and bats. Similar size classes are used when discussing bones attributable only to class Aves, the birds. Large-sized birds are represented by turkey (*Meleagris gallopavo*), large raptors (hawks and eagles), and large geese. Medium-sized birds include larger ducks and owls and the domestic chicken (*Gallus gallus*). Smaller-sized birds are represented by jays, warblers, and buntings, primarily the passerines or songbirds.

Minimum Numbers of Individuals (MNI) and Number of Identified Specimens (NISP) were calculated as a basic method of quantifying the assemblage. As stated by others, both MNI and NISP have their shortcomings (Breitburg 1991; Grayson 1979, 1984; Klein and Cruz-Uribe 1984; Ringrose 1993). MNI is calculated by looking at paired skeletal elements. First introduced by White (1953), it is done by separating the most abundant elements into their left and right sides and using the largest number as the unit of calculation. The measure can be further refined by assessing age and size variables (Grayson 1979). With MNI, the greatest problem deals with aggregation. The criteria used to aggregate a site affect the calculation of MNI. The more divisive the contexts, such as strata, arbitrary levels, time periods, or features, the closer the MNI values will approach NISP values (Grayson 1979, 1984; Reitz and Scarry 1985). However, if the contexts are not mixed and the aggregation units cannot be further divided, the MNI values may actually be more representative of actual individuals brought back to the site (Grayson 1984:67). Other problems with MNI include the assumption that the entire animal

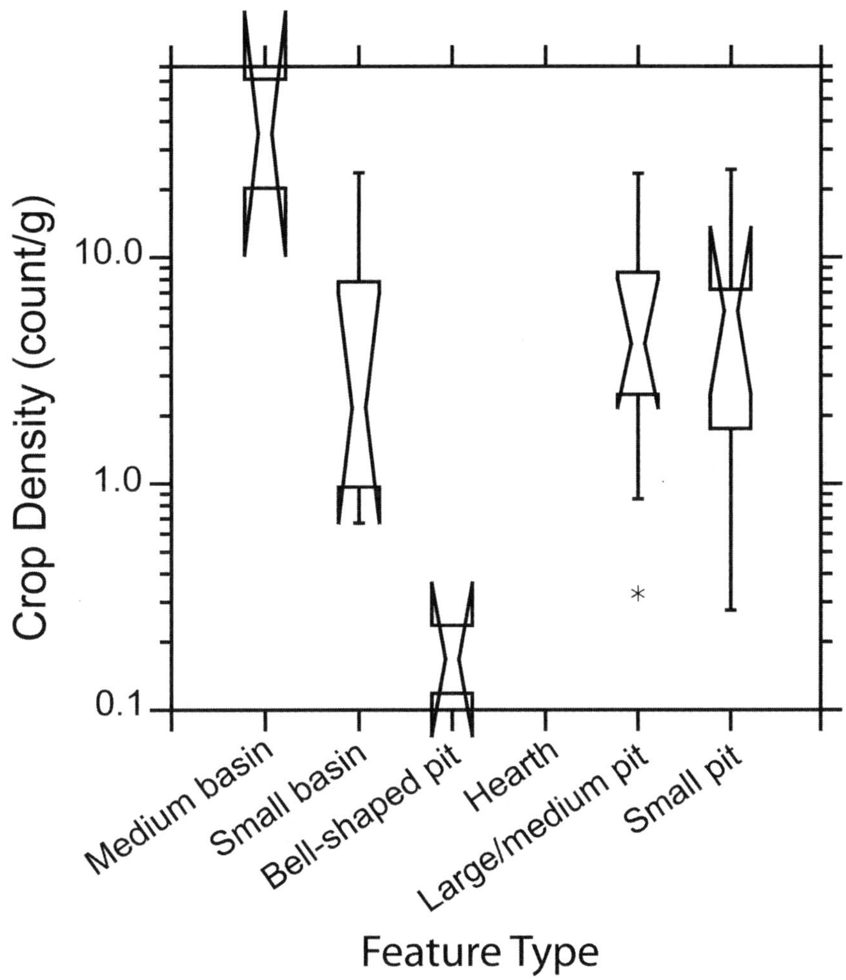

Figure10. 4. Boxplots comparing crop density (count/total plant weight) by feature type.

was consumed at the site, with the animal being represented by the identified element. This may or may not be the case, as indicated by butchery, exchange behaviors, or market evidence. By examining element distribution from the assemblage, the evidence can be evaluated. Another problem concerns the importance of smaller species in the diet. While smaller species, such as fish, may be identified at a site, their relative importance in the diet when compared to one identified deer is considerably less (Reitz and Scarry 1985).

NISP is obtained by an actual count of bone or tooth fragments assigned to a particular taxon. Criticisms exist for this measurement of taxonomic abundance in a faunal assemblage as well. First, the measure is affected by butchery and subsequent patterns thereof, and the subjective nature of species identification. Collection and taphonomic agents also affect the validity of the measurement. The greatest criticism deals with element interdependence (Grayson 1979, 1984). How do we know which elements and fragments come from different animals in the assemblage?

Despite the criticisms, MNI and NISP values were calculated for the Townsend Cherokee faunal materials. However, only NISP measures are used here when considering taxonomic abundance. While it is acknowledged that there is the problem of element interdependence, it is assumed to be less of a problem than site aggregation.

Other characteristics of the bones were noted as well. Taphonomic alteration of the bone in the form of burning (see Ben-

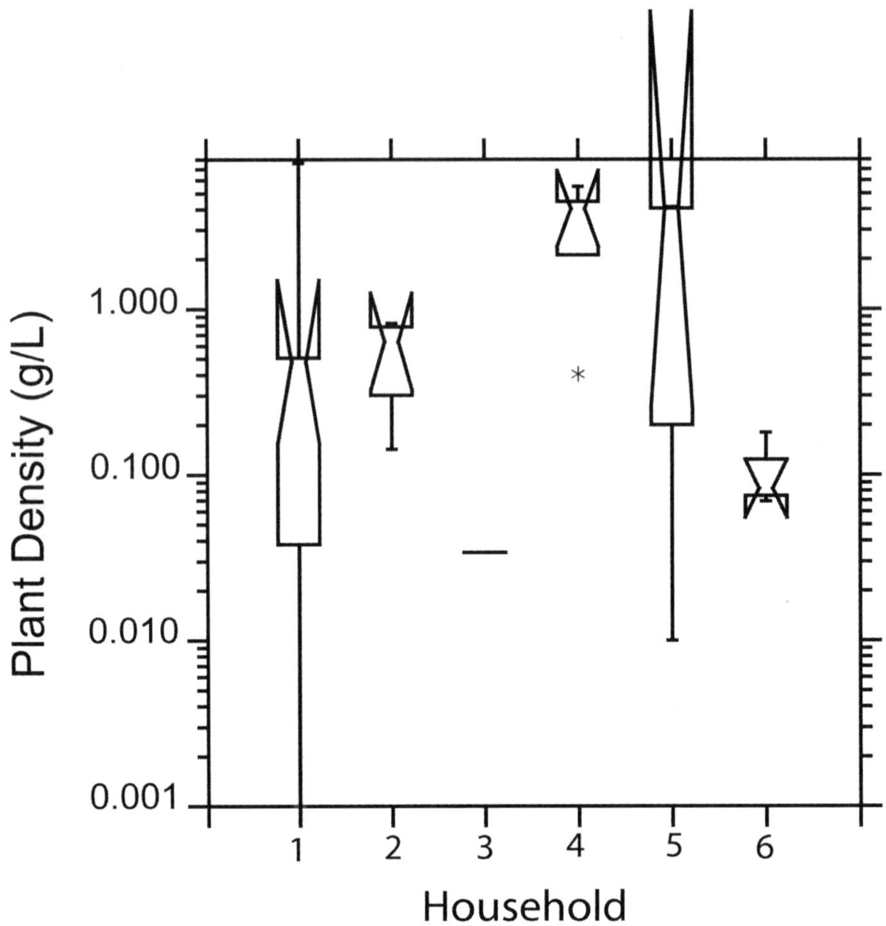

Figure 10.5. Boxplots comparing plant density (g/L) by household.

nett 1999; McCutcheon 1992), cut marks (Lyman 1994; Reitz and Wing 1999), and carnivore or rodent gnawing (Morey and Klippel 1991; Thornton and Fee 2001) were also recorded for the assemblage.

Results

A total of 1873 bones were recovered from Cherokee contexts; 731 of these were identifiable to class (Table 10.4). Unidentifiable (UID) specimens comprised the largest portion (61 percent) of the assemblage. Among identifiable materials, mammals are best represented, with an NISP of 365, followed by birds (NISP = 132), reptiles (NISP = 106), fish (NISP = 68), amphibians (NISP = 39), and mollusks (NISP = 20). Bullfrog was the most frequently recovered species, making up 1.12 percent of the assemblage. White-tailed deer was the second most represented identifiable species, comprising 1.01 percent of the assemblage. Approximately half ($n = 901$, 48.1 percent) of the bones exhibited modifications (Table 10.5). These modifications include burning, calcination, carnivore gnawing, rodent gnawing and worked bone. The most common modification is burning, and primarily calcined burning. Examples of rodent and carnivore gnawing are present, in addition to 1 worked bone recovered from Household 4.

Household 1

Thirteen features are associated with Household 1 situated on Site 40Bt89; seven of those features contained faunal remains. These include Features 21, 23, and 50, categorized as medium and large pits; Feature 48, a medium bell-shaped pit; and Features

Table 10.3. Townsend Cherokee contexts containing faunal remains.

Site	Household	Feature	Feature Type	NISP	Weight (g)
40Bt89	1	21	large pit	339	64.35
		23	medium pit	18	3.70
		38	small basin	9	6.84
		44	small basin	3	3.64
		48	medium bell-shaped pit	48	22.30
		50	medium pit	37	10.20
		55	small basin	69	80.62
40Bt90	2	936	medium basin	10	0.28
		995	small pit	8	0.68
		1019	medium pit	23	8.91
		1020	small basin	47	6.29
	3	130	large pit	175	18.09
		135	medium pit	32	4.87
		438	depressed area	9	9.13
	4	118	hearth	308	38.71
		702	medium bell-shaped pit	75	45.10
		705	medium pit	260	134.96
		722	depressed area	1	0.20
		2000	small pit	73	2.68
40Bt91	5	497	small pit	319	49.13
		509	small pit	28	2.52
	6	391	small pit	1	0.14
		394	hearth	7	1.30
	unassociated	438	historic feature	13	10.59

38, 44, and 55, which are small basins. Identified taxa included beaver, white-tailed deer and wild turkey (Table 10.6). Feature 48 stands out among these features, as it contained all of the identified bird and amphibian remains (see Appendix E).

Taphonomic alterations noted are predominantly varying degrees of burning (Table 10.7). One large mammal fragment exhibited carnivore gnawing. Burning was identified on white-tailed deer, rodent, reptile, and mammal bone. Unidentifiable bone made up 93.8 percent of the burned bone with the majority being calcined.

The remains from this household suggest that the occupants discarded faunal remains into a fire after consumption and then swept the debris into nearby pits, all of which were located outside the main structure. The non-burned remains could have been deposited into those pits during cleaning episodes after food processing. It is also possible that one or several amphibians or small mammals fell into one of the pits and were unable to climb out again.

Household 2

Household 2, located on Site 40Bt90, includes five features, four of which contained faunal remains. Features 936 and 1020 are medium and small basins, respectively. Feature 995 is a small interior pit, and Feature 1019 is a medium exterior pit. None of the specimens recovered from these features was identifiable to species (Table 10.8). Unidentifiable bone represents 86.4 percent of the remains associated with this household.

The only modification noted was calcination, observed on 54 (71 percent) of the unidentifiable bones. This high degree of

Table 10.4. Faunal remains recovered from Cherokee contexts at Townsend.

Taxon	Scientific Name	NISP	NISP (%)	MNI	MNI (%)	Weight (g)
Mammals						
white-tailed deer	*Odocoileus virginianus*	19	1.01	1	3.45	152.15
beaver	*Castor canadensis*	1	0.05	1	3.45	1.48
eastern fox squirrel	*Sciurus niger*	6	0.32	1	3.45	0.07
eastern gray squirrel	*Sciurus carolinensis*	3	0.16	1	3.45	0.74
eastern woodrat	*Neotoma floridana*	1	0.05	1	3.45	0.08
brown rat	*Rattus norvegicus*	1	0.05	1	3.45	0.07
squirrels	Sciuridae	1	0.05	1	3.45	0.01
tree squirrels	*Sciurus* sp.	2	0.11			0.25
rodents	Rodentia	7	0.37			0.11
gray fox	*Urocyon cinereoargenteus*	3	0.16	2	6.90	0.78
dogs, wolves, foxes	Canidae	1	0.05	1	3.45	1.59
black bear	*Ursus americanus*	1	0.05	1	3.45	0.74
domestic pig	*Sus scrofa*	1	0.05	1	3.45	8.78
small mammal		9	0.48			0.33
medium-large mammal		5	0.27			0.10
large mammal		50	2.67			110.69
indeterminate mammal		254	13.56			95.72
Birds						
wild turkey	*Meleagris gallopavo*	3	0.16	1	3.45	11.15
Perciformes	Perciformes	1	0.05			0.03
large bird		3	0.16			4.33
indeterminate bird		125	6.67			5.79
Reptiles						
musk turtle	*Sternotherus oderatus*	3	0.16	1	3.45	0.66
eastern box turtle	*Terrapenne carolina*	4	0.21	1	3.45	8.84
rat snake	*Elaphe obsolete*	3	0.16	1	3.45	0.09
timber rattlesnake	*Crotalus horridus*	5	0.27	1	3.45	0.23
turtles	Testudines	43	2.30	1	3.45	11.40
pond turtles	Emydidae	21	1.12			8.53
non-poisonous snakes	Colubridae	26	1.39			2.12
poisonous snakes	Viperidae	1	0.05	1	3.45	0.11
Amphibians						
bullfrog	*Rana catesbeiana*	21	1.12	1	3.45	0.47
frogs/toads	Anuran	10	0.53			0.82
toads	*Bufo* sp.	7	0.37	2	6.90	0.64
frogs	*Rana* sp.	1	0.05	1	3.45	0.05
Fish						
freshwater drum	*Aplodinotus grunniens*	2	0.11	1	3.45	0.13
rock bass	*Ambloplites rupestris*	1	0.05	1	3.45	0.03
suckers	Catostomidae	1	0.05			0.12
Centrarchidae	Centrarchidae	1	0.05	1	3.45	0.03
indeterminate fish		63	3.36			1.00
Mollusks						
gastropod	Gastropoda	2	0.11	1	3.45	1.55
bivalve	Bivalvia	1	0.05	1	3.45	2.92
indeterminate mollusk		17	0.91			5.77
Other						
mammal/bird		1	0.05	1	3.45	0.28
unidentifiable		1142	60.97			85.04
Total		*1873*	*100.00*	29	*100.05*	*525.82*

Table 10.5. Bone modifications in Cherokee contexts at Townsend.

Taxon	**Rodent Gnawed**	**Carnivore Gnawed**	**Burned Black**	**Burned Calcined**	**Burned Calcined/Black**	**Worked**	**Total**
Mammals							
white-tailed deer	1	3	1			1	*6*
rodents			1	3			*4*
medium mammal			1				*1*
large mammal		2	11				*13*
indeterminate mammal		2	17	64	13		*96*
Birds							
large bird		1					*1*
Reptiles							
eastern box turtle			3				*3*
turtles			9	3			*12*
pond turtles			18				*18*
non-poisonous snakes				1			*1*
indeterminate reptile			5		10		*15*
Amphibians							
frogs/toads			1		1		*2*
Fish							
indeterminate fish			1				*1*
Other							
unidentifiable			37	498	193		*728*
Total	*1*	*8*	*105*	*569*	*217*	*1*	*901*
Percent	*0.1*	*0.8*	*11.7*	*63.2*	*24.1*	*0.1*	*100*

Table 10.6. Household 1 faunal assemblage.

Taxon	NISP	NISP (%)	MNI	MNI (%)	Weight (g)
Mammals					
beaver	1	0.2	1	16.7	1.48
white-tailed deer	7	1.3	1	16.7	89.26
rodents	3	0.6			0.05
medium-large mammal	5	1.0			0.10
large mammal	21	4.1			48.09
indeterminate mammal	54	10.3			20.84
Birds					
wild turkey	2	0.4	1	16.7	4.81
indeterminate bird	10	1.8			2.94
Reptiles					
non-poisonous snakes	2	0.4			0
Amphibians					
frogs/toads	4	0.7			0.31
toads	5	1.0	2	33.2	0.55
Mollusks					
bivalve	1	0.2	1	16.7	2.92
Other					
unidentifiable	408	78.0			20.26
Total	523	100.0	6	100	191.61

Table 10.7. Household 1 bone modifications.

Taxon	Carnivore Gnawed	Burned Black	Burned Calcined	Burned Calcined/Black	Total
white-tailed deer		1			*1*
rodents			3		3
large mammal	1	7			*8*
indeterminate mammal			6	4	*10*
indeterminate reptile				2	*2*
unidentifiable		17	156	193	*366*
total	*1*	*25*	*165*	*199*	*390*
% of total bone in features	*0.2*	*4.8*	*31.5*	*38.0*	*74.6*

Table 10.8. Household 2 faunal assemblage.

Taxon	NISP	NISP (%)	MNI	MNI (%)	Weight (g)
indeterminate mammal	12	13.6			7.11
unidentifiable	76	86.4			9.05
total	*88*	*100.0*	*0*	*0.0*	*16.16*

burning suggests that faunal remains were discarded into fires and then later deposited in nearby pits.

Household 3

Seven features are associated with Household 3 on Site 40Bt90; three of these features contained faunal remains. These include Feature 130, a large pit; Feature 135, a medium pit; and Feature 438, a depressed area. Taxa identified include black bear, bullfrog, and freshwater drum (Table 10.9). The majority of the identifiable taxa were recovered from Feature 130, although the black bear specimen was from Feature 135. All of the unidentifiable bone was calcined (Table 10.10). One rodent bone and one large mammal bone fragment were burned black.

The majority of the faunal material from the household came from Feature 130, which is classified as a large pit located outside the structure. Because this feature contained a large amount of burned bone, it is likely that debris from hearth-clearing activities was deposited here.

Household 4

Household 4, located on Site 40Bt90, includes twelve features, five of which contained faunal remains. These five features include a hearth (Feature 118), a medium bell-shaped pit (Feature 702), a medium pit (Feature 705), a depressed area (Feature 722), and a small interior pit (Feature 2000). This household contained the most diverse set of animal taxa out of the six households. Taxa identified include eastern fox squirrel, eastern gray squirrel, eastern woodrat, brown rat, gray fox, white-tailed deer, musk turtle, eastern box turtle, bullfrog, and rock bass (Table 10.11). Features 118 and 705 contained the majority of the identifiable taxa. Most of the amphibian remains derive from Feature 118.

Burning was the most common modification noted (Table 10.12). Six bones had evidence of carnivore gnawing. These bones were not buried immediately and were exposed long enough for gnawing to occur.

A worked antler fragment was recovered from Feature 705, an exterior pit. This was the only worked bone, and also the only fragment of antler, found in any of the Cherokee contexts. This feature also contained all of the gnawed bones for Household 4.

Feature 118, an interior hearth, contained the majority of the burned bone associated with this household. This supports the idea that bones were tossed into fires after consumption and then swept into both interior and exterior pits during cleaning episodes.

Table 10.9. Household 3 faunal assemblage.

Taxon	NISP	NISP (%)	MNI	MNI (%)	Weight (g)
Mammals					
black bear	1	0.5	1	20	0.74
rodents	2	0.8			0.01
small mammal	1	0.5			0.04
large mammal	8	3.7			9.29
indeterminate mammal	7	3.3			3.40
Reptiles					
non-poisonous snakes	5	2.3			0.11
Amphibians					
bullfrog	7	3.3	1	20	0.12
Fish					
freshwater drum	2	0.8	1	20	0.13
suckers	1	0.5			0.12
Perciformes (perch-like)	1	0.5			0.03
indeterminate fish	7	3.3			0.06
Mollusks					
gastropod	1	0.5	1	20	0.95
indeterminate mollusks	2	0.8	1	20	3.19
Other					
unidentifiable	171	79.2			13.9
Total	*216*	*100*	*5*	*100*	*32.09*

Table 10.10. Household 3 bone modifications.

Taxon	Burned Black	Burned Calcined	Total
rodents	1		*1*
large mammal	1		*1*
unidentifiable		171	171
total	*2*	*171*	*173*
% of total bone in features	*0.9*	*79.2*	*80.1*

Table 10.11. Household 4 faunal assemblage.

Taxon	NISP	NISP (%)	MNI	MNI (%)	Weight (g)
Mammals					
eastern fox squirrel	6	0.9	1	5.6	0.07
eastern gray squirrel	3	0.4	1	5.6	0.74
eastern woodrat	1	0.2	1	5.6	0.08
brown rat	1	0.2	1	5.6	0.07
squirrels	1	0.2	1	5.6	0.01
tree squirrels	2	0.3			0.25
rodents	2	0.3			0.05
gray fox	3	0.4	2	10.4	0.78
dogs, wolves, foxes	1	0.2	1	5.6	1.59
white-tailed deer	10	1.5	1	5.6	53.79
small mammal	8	1.2			0.29
large mammal	14	2.1			41.53
indeterminate mammal	173	25.5			57.30
Birds					
large bird	3	0.4			4.33
indeterminate bird	23	3.4			1.43
Reptiles					
musk turtle	3	0.4	1	5.6	0.66
eastern box turtle	4	0.4	1	5.6	8.84
turtles	42	6.2			11.05
pond turtles	21	3.1			8.53
poisonous snakes	1	0.2	1	5.6	0.11
non-poisonous snakes	2	0.3			0.01
Amphibians					
bullfrog	13	1.9	1	5.6	0.34
frogs/toads	3	0.4			0.16
toads	1	0.2	1	5.6	0.03
frogs	1	0.2	1	5.6	0.05
Fish					
rock bass	1	0.2	1	5.6	0.03
indeterminate fish	9	1.3			0.41
Mollusks					
gastropod	1	0.2	1	5.6	0.60
Other					
mammal/bird	1	0.2	1	5.6	0.28
unidentifiable	325	47.9			28.24
Total	*679*	*100.0*	*18*	*100.0*	*221.65*

Table 10.12. Household 4 bone modifications.

Taxon	Carnivore Gnawed	Burned Black	Burned Calcined	Burned Calcined/Black	Worked	Total
Mammals						
white-tailed deer	2				1	*3*
medium mammal		1				*1*
large mammal	1	3				*4*
indeterminate mammal	2	17	58	9		*86*
Birds						
large bird	1					*1*
Reptiles						
eastern box turtle		3				*3*
turtles		9	3			*12*
pond turtles		18				*18*
non-poisonous snakes			1			1
indeterminate reptile				4		*4*
Amphibians						
frogs/toads		1		1		*2*
Fish						
indeterminate fish		1				*1*
Other						
unidentifiable		14	24			*38*
Total	*6*	*67*	*86*	*14*	*1*	*174*
% of total bone in features	*0.88*	*9.87*	*12.67*	*2.06*	*0.15*	*25.63*

Household 5

Household 5, on Site 40Bt91, consists of three features, and two contained faunal remains. Both features, 497 and 509, are classified as small pits. Taxa identified include white-tailed deer, wild turkey, rat snake, timber rattlesnake and bullfrog (Table 10.13). All of the identifiable taxa were recovered from Feature 497.

This household did not contain as large a percentage of burned bones as did the other households, with the exception of Household 4 (Table 10.14). One example of rodent and carnivore gnawing was noted on a white-tailed deer fragment.

Feature 497 contained a majority of the faunal material identified for Household 5. It contained all the identifiable specimens and a majority (n = 127, or 82 percent) of the unidentifiable specimens. The example of rodent and carnivore gnawing was also present in this feature.

Household 6

Located on Site 40Bt91, Household 6 consists of four features; two contained faunal remains. Feature 391, a small pit, and Feature 394, a hearth, contained only unidentifiable bone (Table 10.15). The majority of the bone (n = 6, or 86 percent) was calcined.

Unassociated

Feature 438 on Site 40Bt91 was designated as a large historic feature and was in close proximity to Household 6. The presence of the one domestic pig bone reinforces the interpretation that this was a historic feature (Table 10.16), probably associated with a nineteenth-century cabin site nearby.

Table 10.13. Household 5 faunal assemblage.

Taxon	NISP	NISP (%)	MNI	MNI (%)	Weight (g)
Mammals					
white-tailed deer	2	0.59	1	12.5	9.10
large mammal	7	2.03			11.78
indeterminate mammal	8	2.32			7.07
Birds					
wild turkey	1	0.25	1	12.5	6.34
indeterminate bird	92	26.52			1.42
Reptiles					
turtles	1	0.25	1	12.5	0.35
rat snake	3	0.88	1	12.5	0.09
timber rattlesnake	5	1.45	1	12.5	0.23
non-poisonous snakes	17	4.96			2.00
Amphibians					
bullfrog	1	0.25	1	12.5	0.01
toads	1	0.25	1	12.5	0.06
frogs/toads	3	0.88			0.35
Fish					
suckers	1	0.25	1	12.5	0.03
indeterminate fish	47	13.55			0.53
Mollusks					
indeterminate mollusk	3	0.88			0.77
Other					
unidentifiable	155	44.69			12.29
Total	*347*	*100.00*	*8*	*100*	*52.42*

Table 10.14. Household 5 bone modifications.

Taxon	Rodent Gnawed	Carnivore Gnawed	Burned Black	Burned Calcined	Total
white-tailed deer	1	1			2
indeterminate reptile			5	4	9
unidentifiable			6	87	93
total	*1*	*1*	*11*	*91*	*104*
% of total bone in features	*0.3*	*0.3*	*3.2*	*26.2*	*30.0*

Table 10.15. Household 6 faunal assemblage.

Taxon	NISP	NISP (%)	MNI	MNI (%)	Weight (g)
unidentifiable	7	100.0			1.3
total	*7*	*100.0*	*0*	*0.0*	*1.3*

Table 10.16. Feature 438 faunal assemblage.

Taxon	NISP	NISP (%)	MNI	MNI (%)	Weight (g)
domestic pig	1	7.7			8.78
indeterminate mollusk	12	92.3			1.81
total	*13*	*100.0*	*0*	*0.0*	*10.59*

Comparing Households

The distribution of faunal remains by class reveals some interesting differences among the households (Table 10.17). Most of the classes are represented in Households 1, 3, 4, and 5. In contrast, Households 2 and 6, as well as the Unassociated feature, contained very limited assemblages. This is, in part, due to a relatively low number of features associated with Households 2 and 6, although Household 5 also includes only three features. The sparse faunal assemblages may also be related to the use of the households. For example, they may have been occupied for a shorter duration than the other households, resulting in less accumulation of faunal remains.

The remaining four households are relatively similar to each other in the distribution of their faunal assemblages by class. Mammals comprise the greatest percentage of identifiable remains in all but Household 5. In this household, birds are best represented, followed by fish. However, it must be kept in mind that identifiable remains were recovered from only one feature associated with Household 5, and these more likely reflect the use of this small pit feature rather than the occupants' general use of faunal resources.

Households 4 and 5 are also notable for their relatively low percentage of unidentifiable remains. Both of these households also had markedly lower percentages of burned bone within their assembages. This suggests taphonomic differences between these two households and the remaining four, resulting from differences in discard patterns, in preservation of bone, or both.

Table 10.17. Comparison of animal class by household.

	Household						
	1	2	3	4	5	6	Unassociated
mammals	17.5	13.6	8.8	33.2	4.9		7.7
birds	2.2			3.8	26.8		
reptiles	0.4		2.3	10.6	7.5		
amphibians	1.7		3.3	2.7	1.4		
fish			5.1	1.5	13.8		
shell	0.2		1.3	0.2	0.9		92.3
mammal/bird				0.2			
unidentifiable	78.0	86.4	79.2	47.9	44.7	100	
% modified	*74.6*	*61.4*	*80.1*	*25.6*	*30.0*	*85.7*	

Discussion

The subsistence remains from Cherokee contexts at the Townsend site demonstrate that the occupants of Tuckaleechee Cove practiced full-fledged corn agriculture, intercropping beans and squash in their fields. They also appear to have cultivated little barley and perhaps chenopod, and may have encouraged or tolerated the growth of additional species that are edible and/or have medicinal properties.

These cultivated foods were supplemented by nuts and fruits, as well as animal resources. Important nuts include hickory nuts, black walnuts, and acorns. While no evidence of chestnuts was recovered, the occupants almost definitely took advantage of these nuts. Fruits include a variety of wild berries and grapes, as well as maypops, which were cultivated in gardens. Definitive evidence for peaches was not found in the samples, although peach pits are commonly recovered from Cherokee sites in eastern Tennessee and western North Carolina.

The faunal assemblage indicates that the occupants of Tuckaleechee Cove hunted white-tailed deer, squirrels, and turkeys; captured turtles and perhaps bullfrogs; fished; and collected mollusks. Deer and turkeys, which favor ecotone habitats, may have been hunted in agricultural fields, as part of a "garden hunting" strategy (Neusius 2007), or in the nearby uplands, where they would be attracted to autumn mast crops. The cove's occupants also took advantage of aquatic resources, such as fish, turtles, mollusks, and beaver, from the Little River.

Seasonal activities are suggested by the subsistence remains. Agricultural fields would have been prepared and sown in the spring, and tender leaves and shoots from various weedy plants could have been gathered. Most of the fruits ripen in summer. Fish, reptiles, and amphibians indicate warm season activities. Toward the end of summer, crops such as corn, squash, and beans would have been harvested. The various nuts and persimmons would have been collected in autumn. The various plant foods could have been dried and stored for use during winter, and the animal resources similarly smoked or preserved for future use. Terrestrial animals such as deer, turkeys, and squirrels could have been hunted through winter, although the meat they provide is much leaner in this season.

Qualitative and quantitative comparisons highlight several interesting contexts. Household 4 stands out in both faunal and plant analyses. Features associated with this household yielded relatively higher densities of plant remains, and relatively large quantities of corn cupules were recovered in Features 705 and 1996. Both also contained a variety of nutshell fragments and fruit seeds. This household was also notable for the diverse set of identifiable animal remains, which derive primarily from Features 118 and 705. Over a quarter of the bones recovered from Feature 118, a hearth, show evidence of burning. Approximately 12 percent of the bones from Feature 705 display modifications, which include carnivore gnawing and the single example of worked bone. As noted by Marcoux in Chapter 6, this feature appears to be a secondary refuse deposit, containing the byproducts of plant food processing (nutshell and corn cupules), as well as animal bones that had been exposed long enough to be gnawed by carnivores.

Feature 48 in Household 1 is also of interest. Large quantities of plant remains—primarily wood and pitch but also small quantities of nutshell and tentatively identified fruits—were recovered from this feature. It also contained 2 of the 3 turkey remains recovered from Cherokee contexts, as well as 9 frog/toad bones, and no other bones identifiable beyond the level of class. Eight of the 48 bones recovered were calcined. Based on the large quantities of wood and pitch in the sample, as well as the calcined bone, it is likely that this feature fill is related to the cleaning of the hearth and floor of the associated structure (see Chapter 6).

Several additional features associated with Household 1 yielded interesting plant assemblages, although faunal remains recovered from them are unremarkable or lacking. As noted above, Feature 21 contained 117 of the 124 beans recovered from Townsend. These may reflect the initial use of the feature as a storage pit (see Chapter 6). Over 100 grass family seeds were recovered from both Features 16 and 23, along with a wide variety of nuts, fruits, and weedy seeds.

Similarly, two features associated with Household 2 contained interesting plant assemblages. Feature 936 is notable for the range of plant remains recovered from it, but particularly for the large number of corn kernels identified. Over four times as many corn kernels were recovered as corn cupules and glumes, while most features have kernel to cupule ratios of less than one. This suggests that the refuse from this feature primarily reflects consumption rather than processing of plant foods. The relatively low recovery of nutshell, which also represents processing, further supports this. Feature 1020 may also reflect consumption: 45 little barley seeds, 2 blueberry seeds, and relatively few nutshell or corn cupule fragments were recovered from this feature.

In Household 5, Feature 497 stands out in terms of both the plant and animal remains recovered. It yielded all the identifiable faunal remains associated with Household 5, which includes deer, turkey, fish, frogs/toads, and snakes, including the only timber rattlesnake remains recovered from the site. The feature also yielded large quantities of plant remains, the majority of which are wood and pitch, although some nuts, corn, beans, and grape were also recovered.

Summary

The subsistence remains recovered from Cherokee contexts at Townsend are relatively similar to those found at other Cherokee sites in eastern Tennessee and western North Carolina (Bogan 1976, 1980; Chapman and Shea 1981; Guthe and Bistline 1981; VanDerwarker and Detwiler 2000). In Tuckaleechee Cove, Cherokee peoples practiced corn agriculture, intercropped with beans and squash, as well as native cultigens such as little barley, chenopod, and maypop. They also gathered nuts and wild fruits. Nuts likely served as a dietary staple, particularly in winter when the high fat content of hickory nuts and black walnuts would compensate for lean game.

The Cherokee occupants of the cove hunted deer and turkey, in addition to squirrel. They also took advantage of aquatic resources, including fish, turtles, and beaver, likely from the adjacent Little River. Frogs, toads, and snakes may be incidental to the site, although several of these remains do exhibit burning. In addition, a feature with over 6500 toad (*Bufo* sp.) bones, representing over 600 individuals, was excavated at the Coweeta Creek site in western North Carolina (VanDerwarker and Detwiler 2000). Although it is possible that these toads became trapped in this feature and died, it seems more likely that the large number of leg bones is attributable to human use. We would argue for the same at Townsend.

The Townsend subsistence assemblage is also interesting in what it lacks. Among faunal taxa, muskrat (*Ondatra zibethicus*) and raccoon (*Procyon lotor*) are notably absent. Bogan (1980) notes, with some surprise, that these species are poorly represented in Cherokee contexts among the Little Tennessee River Valley sites. Both would have provided some meat, but were likely more important for their pelts. It is possible that they were processed and discarded in a manner that did not favor preservation or recovery of these taxa.

Among plant foods, peaches were not identified at the site, which contrasts starkly with other Cherokee sites in the region. Another Spanish introduction, cowpea or black-eyed pea (*Vigna unguiculata*), was also not recovered at Townsend, although it was present among the Little Tennessee Valley sites (Chapman and Shea 1981). In addition, pig remains are notably scarce in the Cherokee faunal assemblage from Townsend, with only one specimen recovered from Feature 438, which appears to be a later, intrusive historic feature rather than a strictly Cherokee context (see Marcoux's discussion of the features, Chapter 6). The paucity or lack of peach, cowpea, and pig remains from Townsend, especially as compared to the regular recovery of these Old World resources at Overhill Cherokee sites in the Little Tennessee Valley (Bogan 1982:46; Chapman and Shea 1981), reflects the earlier occupation of Tuckaleechee Cove. This pattern may well date the timing of the introduction of Old World domesticates to eastern Tennessee, placing it after the A.D. 1650–1720 occupation of Townsend (see Chapter 9) but before the Colonial period (A.D. 1746–1775) occupation of the Little Tennessee Valley.

Chapter 11

Summary and Conclusions

Research Results

In Chapter 2, I recount a history of dramatic change in Cherokee communities during the English Contact period (ca. 1670–1740). The sources cited in this study demonstrate that this story was unique to the Cherokees and had no correlate among other southeastern Indian groups. During the first half of the period, from 1670 until 1715, the Cherokees were but little known to history. From what little was written, it is likely that they, like most southeastern Indian groups, were weathering the effects of disease, colonial wars, slave raiding, and the deerskin trade. It appears, however, that the relative isolation of the Cherokees might have offered them some additional measure of refuge from the shatter zone that was not enjoyed by other Indian groups.

The Cherokees' entrance into the Yamasee and Creek Wars effectively changed the situation forever and ended any possibility of their maintaining an isolationist strategy. Remaining "above the fray" became impossible because of South Carolina's unyielding desire to bring the Cherokees under their aegis, and because of Cherokee needs for trade goods to prosecute their war. These duel motivations resulted in the Cherokees' meteoric rise to dominate the deerskin trade.

The few early descriptions of the Cherokees describe a very fluid and factional consensus-based political structure that was divided along generational and regional lines. The stubborn endurance of this political structure in the face of South Carolina's attempts to impose a monarchy suggests that it was a long-lived and deep-set institution among Cherokee communities. This institution appears to have provided community-level flexibility, often at the expense of "national" politics, for often times the situations created by the chaos of the shatter zone required different Cherokee communities to act in different ways.

The end of the English contact period was brought about by a lethal component of the shatter zone that had lain dormant for almost a half a century. In 1738, just when Cherokee communities appear to have been successfully adjusting to the shatter zone and their postwar political and economic roles, a smallpox epidemic ravaged their population. For Cherokee communities, large population losses certainly dashed any semblance of order they had managed to achieve during the post-Yamasee War years. In the wake of this epidemic, the Cherokees had to formulate new social, political, and economic strategies in order to negotiate the next period of their history.

To answer questions about the ethnohistories of Cherokee communities, I have attempted to relocate the focus of research within English Contact period Cherokee communities themselves, for these places were the crucibles in which the shatter zone was forged and negotiated. In Chapter 3, I argue that an archaeological study of the English Contact period at the community level will benefit most from a nuanced approach using sensitive analytical concepts that can track culture change at the household level. In this chapter, I summarized the findings of past archaeological research dealing with the chronology, lifeways, and organization of seventeenth- and eighteenth-century Cherokee communities. I focused on ceramic chronology, foodways, European artifact assemblages, and architecture. While documenting the many contributions that researchers have made to our current understanding of Cherokee communities during this period, I conclude that our understanding of the Qualla and Overhill ceramic series is poor, that there is not a comprehensive definition of the material culture pattern associated with English Contact period Cherokee settlements, and that we have a normative view of Cherokee community life that is informed mostly from written accounts and excavations at historically prominent towns.

As I discuss in Chapter 4, the data obtained from excavations at the Townsend sites in Tuckaleechee Cove are crucial for addressing these three areas of concern. Ethnohistoric and archaeological evidence suggests that the "Tuckaleechee towns" were Cherokee settlements that were settled in the Little River Valley during the late seventeenth and early eighteenth centuries. What was life like for Cherokee families who chose to settle in Tuckaleechee Cove during the late seventeenth century? Were folks in this area spared the disruptions of the shatter zone, or were they instead, through their strategic actions, the very embodiment of the shatter zone? The household contexts at the Townsend sites present the perfect case study for analyses that attempt to answer these questions.

In Chapter 5, I have sought to better characterize the Cherokee architecture uncovered during the Townsend project by introducing ways to operationalize concepts including method of manufacture, structure function, household size, and occupation duration. In accomplishing this task, I have referenced ethnohistoric descriptions and past archaeological research and have employed a number of different quantitative comparative methods. I found a good correspondence between the archaeological remains of houses at Townsend and ethnohistoric descriptions of Cherokee houses. Posthole data suggested that the Cherokees at Townsend built their houses according to a relatively prescribed architectural vernacular that resulted in robust patterns of posthole location and depth. The data also pointed to differences in shape, location, and wall post spacing that corresponded to the two types of domestic structures described in ethnohistoric accounts as "winter houses" and "summer houses." Floor area measurements across all Cherokee structures at Townsend were consistent with the interpretation that Cherokee household size approximated the nuclear family. Also, estimates of duration occupation indicated that the Townsend structures, and indeed most late seventeenth- and eighteenth-century Cherokee houses, were occupied for a decade or less.

Comparisons to houses at contemporaneous and later eighteenth-century Cherokee sites revealed a great deal of consistency but some changes through time. While winter house and summer house architectural forms were present at sites dating from the mid-seventeenth century to the late eighteenth century, they were outnumbered by single rectangular dwellings at sites dating to the end of the period. Winter houses remained relatively the same size throughout the period, but earlier summer houses, particularly those found at Townsend, were much smaller than their later eighteenth-century counterparts. Overall, the comparisons attest to relative stability in Cherokee architectural practices at least between 1650 and 1776.

Extending the diachronic perspective back in time reveals significant changes in household architecture occurring between the late sixteenth century and the mid-seventeenth century. Cherokee houses were built using the architectural principles of rigid post architecture and households were roughly the same size as during the preceding Mississippian period. But Mississippian houses were more often entirely rebuilt in situ and appear to have occupied the same structure footprint for at least twice the tenure of Cherokee houses. In essence, sometime during the early to middle seventeenth century, folk began to construct houses that required much lower investments in materials and energy, and furthermore, the household tenure of domestic space was shortened dramatically.

What do the features associated with Cherokee households tell us about household organization? In Chapter 6, I report a comparison of basins and pits among the six Townsend households. The distribution of feature size-classes among the households varies greatly. Medium and small features were common in all households, and three of the six households had large pits. Only two households had interior pits; all but one of these were associated with Household 4. Also, a great deal of variability is present in the number of features associated with each household and their combined volume. The most likely reasons for such variability include differences in household occupation duration and/or sample size differences due to historic disturbances and boundary issues associated with the excavation limits. Interestingly, the median and mean measures for feature volume evince much less variability across households. This suggests that while the composition of household storage facilities varied greatly in terms of size and number of individual basins and pits, the underlying storage capacity of each household was similar and it was not particularly large. Considering that each of the Townsend houses was likely occupied between 8 and 10 years, even the highest total household storage capacity (2000 liters for Household 1) would break down to 200–250 liters of subterranean storage capacity per year. If food storage capacity is an indicator of hierarchical status, then household storage capacity figures suggest that there were not pronounced differences in status among Townsend households. This conclusion is in accord with other archaeological and ethnohistoric studies that highlight the underlying egalitarian structure of Cherokee communities during the English Contact period.

The results of a comparison of English Contact Cherokee households with later Cherokee households indicate that subterranean storage became increasingly important in Cherokee communities after the mid-eighteenth century. There is also an increase in feature variability through time. Early feature assemblages consist entirely of simple round or oval basins and pits, while the feature assemblages at later sites also include rectangular pits and a significant number of what appear to be specialized storage features known as "pits with posts." These facilities, which are likely root cellars, became increasingly common through time, comprising 15–16% of all features in the late eighteenth-century communities in the sample.

Along with the advent of new forms of subterranean storage and general changes in feature shape, large increases in feature volume through time are telling of a significant transformation that occurred in Cherokee storage practices following the English Contact period. Mean volume of features at Chota-Tanasee, Tomotley, and Mialoquo is two to three times greater than that of features at the Alarka site and the Townsend sites. These results may be partly due to the fact that the three later contexts are nucleated towns while Alarka and Townsend represent outlying settlements, but most likely, Cherokee households enacted important changes to their food storage practices sometime during the later part of or after the English Contact period.

In essence, Cherokee households of Tuckaleechee Cove did not employ subterranean storage facilities to any great extent; instead, these householders, like their Mississippian period counterparts, probably stored foodstuffs in above-ground facilities like corncribs or in their houses. Unfortunately, the ephemeral remains of corncribs are difficult to identify in the archaeological record. If English Contact period Cherokee households did not employ subterranean food storage strategies, then what do the changes in feature morphology and increases in feature size in later Cherokee communities represent? Involvement in the deer skin trade following 1715 would have required large numbers of individuals from each Cherokee settlement to leave during the winter months. Subterranean storage offered Cherokee households a means for keeping foodstuffs safe from both animals and covetous neighbors. Also, the dramatic increase in the size and form of subterranean storage facilities sometime during the mid-eighteenth century indicates that there was a shift to foodstuffs that were more suited to subterranean storage—most likely root crops like sweet potatoes.

Chapter 7, which discusses Cherokee ceramics from the Townsend sites, first presents an overview of past archaeological research concerning Cherokee potting practices. I emphasize how the Overhill and Qualla ceramic series were (and continue to be) the historical products of very different research projects pursued by archaeologists affiliated with the University of Tennessee and the University of North Carolina at Chapel Hill. I then construct a detailed analytical description of the Cherokee pottery sample recovered during the Townsend project. My pottery description followed a traditional southeastern analytical schema focused on paste, surface treatment, and vessel form. I found a great deal of inter-household ceramic variability along these three dimensions—variability that I believe represents three distinct Cherokee potting styles. Finally, through quantitative comparisons to other Cherokee pottery assemblages, I place the pottery assemblage recovered from Townsend households within the existing regional and temporal framework represented by the Overhill and Qualla ceramic series.

Quantitative analysis clearly suggests that there were three distinct potting styles practiced by Townsend potters. While not mutually exclusive, the spatial distributions of pottery wares and surface treatments strongly suggest that particular potting styles were associated with particular households. The pottery samples recovered from Households 1 and 2, for example, were overwhelmingly dominated by the shell-tempered plain potting style associated with the Overhill ceramic series. Samples from Households 3, 4, and 5, in contrast, contained large amounts of gravel-tempered plain surfaced and paddle stamped pottery. I refer to this heretofore undefined local Cherokee pottery style as "Tuckaleechee." While the sample from Household 6 was not very large, it did contain an unusual abundance of grit-tempered curvilinear complicated stamped pottery that is a hallmark of the Qualla ceramic series.

Results suggest that the Townsend community was an amalgam of households from different Cherokee settlements that, like many other Indian groups across the Southeast, formed a "coalescent community" as a strategy to negotiate the population loss and violence associated with the shatter zone between A.D. 1650 and 1715. Perhaps the isolation of the coves along the Little River afforded these households some measure of protection from the frequent raids that spread across the Southeast during the early decades of the English Contact period. By the third decade of the eighteenth century, the Cherokee settlements in this region appear to have been largely abandoned, and Overhill populations became concentrated in settlements along the lower Little Tennessee River Valley.

In Chapter 8, researchers from the Archaeological Research Laboratory's "lithics team" describe and discuss the stone artifacts found in Cherokee contexts from the Townsend sites. The Cherokees and their predecessors employed two methods of stone tool manufacture—chipped stone and ground stone technology. Chipped stone technology relies on the principle of flaking of suitable stone (materials that fracture concoidally) in order to reduce the mass. Most of the chipped stone tools were manufactured from local cherts (primarily Knox chert), but suitable materials for most chipped stone tools are not available in the Little River adjacent to the Townsend sites but rather probably come from downstream in Miller's Cove.

Because of the small size of available chert pieces, much of the reduction was apparently accomplished through the bipolar method in which a piece of chert (objective piece) is held on an anvil stone, then hit with a hammerstone, producing flakes that may then be made into tools. And, because raw materials were often quite small, most of the tools in the material inventory are small.

Importantly, many stone tools were made from flakes. Such tools in the Cherokee inventory include modified flakes and flake scrapers, expedient tools used for various cutting and scraping tasks such as animal butchery, skinning, and processing of hides and leather. While some of the more specialized flake tools such as gravers and perforator/drills are not represented in Cherokee contexts, these artifacts were probably made and used by Tuckaleechee Cove Cherokees in ways similar to their predecessors. Bifacially flaked artifacts including performs or blanks (artifacts that might have been unfinished tools), bifacial scrapers, and drills were also found. Two artifacts were fragments of chipped stone hoes (made from tabular, sedimentary stone) that were no doubt used in agriculture and other endeavors. Ground stone artifacts included cobbles used as anvils, grinding stones, hammerstones, nutting stones, and, perhaps, gaming pieces. A fragment of a smoking pipe, made from steatite, was also recovered.

Because these technologies and most of the resulting tools changed little in form, materials, or function over several millennia in Tuckaleechee Cove, it is not clear as to the vintage of particular artifacts found in Cherokee contexts. Five similar types of small, triangular or elliptical arrow points, mostly made from flakes of Knox chert, were likely of Cherokee manufacture and use. While a single piece of iron from a European-made tool was recovered from Cherokee pit fill, this traditional stone tool inventory attests to patterns of tool manufacture and use that were little influenced by Euroamerican artifacts or practices.

In Chapter 9, I develop a method to utilize glass trade beads to date the Cherokee households from Tuckaleechee Cove. Results indicate that the glass beads from Townsend represent a chronologically cohesive assemblage at the site level, and that this assemblage has an estimated time range of approximately A.D. 1650–1730. An even more precise date for the Townsend occupation can be achieved when the current ceramic chronology is considered along with the results of my glass trade bead seriation. Interestingly, it appears that major changes in the composition of both Cherokee pottery and glass bead assemblages accompany the shift from the pre- to post-Yamasee War era. "Early" English Contact period (ca. A.D. 1670–1715) pottery assemblages include a mixture of diagnostic attributes from the Middle and Late Qualla phases. Glass trade bead assemblages from this period consist of a wide variety of monochromatic and striped drawn and tumbled beads. "Late" English Contact period (ca. A.D. 1715–1740) pottery assemblages, on the other hand, evince primarily Late Qualla phase attributes (e.g., check stamping, rectilinear complicated stamping, notched rimstrips). Also, glass trade bead assemblages from the post-Yamasee War years include significant numbers of large mandrel wound beads and small monochromatic tubular beads. These clear distinctions in material culture assemblages make the temporal assignment of "Early" and "Late" English Contact period Cherokee occupational components possible even with small artifact samples. Taken together with the ethnohistoric data presented in Chapter 4, these data suggest that an occupation estimate of approximately A.D. 1650–1720 for the Cherokee component at Townsend is in order.

Members of the Archaeological Research Laboratory's "subsistence team" prepared Chapter 10 on the floral and faunal remains recovered from Cherokee contexts at the Townsend sites. The subsistence remains demonstrate that the occupants of Tuckaleechee Cove practiced full-fledged corn agriculture, intercropping beans and squash in their fields. They also appear to have cultivated little barley and perhaps chenopod, and may have encouraged or tolerated the growth of additional species that are edible and/or have medicinal properties.

These cultivated foods were supplemented by nuts and fruits, as well as animal resources. Important nuts include hickory nuts, black walnuts, and acorns. While no evidence of chestnuts was recovered, the occupants almost definitely took advantage of these nuts. Fruits include a variety of wild berries and grapes, as well as maypops, which were cultivated in gardens.

The faunal assemblage indicates that the occupants of Tuckaleechee Cove hunted white-tailed deer, squirrels, and turkeys; captured turtles and perhaps bullfrogs; fished; and collected mollusks. Deer and turkeys, which favor ecotone habitats, may have been hunted in agricultural fields, as part of a "garden hunting" strategy, or in the nearby uplands, where they would be attracted to autumn mast crops. The cove's occupants also took advantage of aquatic resources, such as fish, turtles, mollusks, and beaver, from the Little River.

Seasonal activities are suggested by the subsistence remains. Agricultural fields would have been prepared and sown in the spring, and tender leaves and shoots from various weedy plants could have been gathered. Most of the fruits ripen in summer. Fish, reptiles, and amphibians indicate warm season activities. Toward the end of summer, crops such as corn, squash, and beans would have been harvested. The various nuts and persimmons would have been collected in autumn. The various plant foods could have been dried and stored for use during winter, and the animal resources similarly smoked or preserved for future use. Terrestrial animals such as deer, turkeys, and squirrels could have been hunted through winter, although the meat they provide is much leaner in this season.

Several European species are notable for their absence at the Townsend sites. Peaches were not identified in the samples analyzed from the Townsend sites, which contrasts starkly with other Cherokee sites in the region. Another Spanish introduction, cowpea or black-eyed pea (*Vigna unguiculata*), was also not recovered at Townsend. And, pig bones were restricted to Feature 438, thought to be associated with a nineteenth-century cabin in the area. This pattern may well date the timing of the introduction of Old World domesticates to eastern Tennessee, placing it after the A.D. 1650–1720 occupation of Townsend but before the Colonial period (A.D. 1746–1775) occupation of the Little Tennessee Valley.

Conclusions

At its core, this study is about the impact of culture contact on southeastern Indian communities; however, from the outset I have attempted to approach the topic from a number of novel perspectives. Instead of using the traditional history of the Southeast during the English Contact period (ca. A.D. 1670–1740) (e.g., Crane [1929] 2004; Corkran 1967) as a backdrop for my research, I explored recent alternative historical narratives that introduced new theoretical concepts and critical analyses (e.g., Ethridge 2006; Gallay 2002; Oatis 2004). While traditional historians write in teleological language about passive Indian technological reliance and the inevitability of European dominance, these researchers stress the importance of local interactions, contingencies, and the active role of Indian groups in forging their histories (encapsulated in the shatter zone concept). I also chose to depart from past archaeological studies of Cherokee communities by avoiding the big topics of "O"rigins and "A"cculturation, choosing rather to frame my research with theories that stress the agency of small groups (i.e., Cherokee households and communities) and their ability to effect change (i.e., create their history) through the actions of daily life. To avoid the temptation of relying on acculturation as an explanatory frame, I chose as a case study a Cherokee community that had very little interaction with Europeans. My goal was to demonstrate, nevertheless, that significant changes could be identified in the daily lives of households in this community—sui generis changes that had little if no direct link to European trade.

I also took an alternative approach to data analysis in this study, one aimed at operationalizing the practices of daily life in Cherokee households. First, I employed a relatively novel multivariate statistical technique known as correspondence analysis to seriate a large sample of glass trade bead assemblages. I also employed the household as my basic unit of analysis. The well-defined archaeological household contexts at Townsend provided a solid basis for detailed comparisons of pottery, architecture, and subsurface pit features. In making these comparisons, I introduced new quantitative techniques including attribute analysis of pottery; empirical assessments of the construction methods, function, and occupation duration of Cherokee domestic structures; and function and use-life estimates of pit features.

The results of these alternative approaches, I believe, offer new insights into the ways that Cherokee households and communities dealt with the changes wrought by the southeastern shatter zone in the years leading up to the Yamasee War in A.D. 1715. To begin with, the location of the Townsend community likely resulted from a strategic choice made by Cherokee groups. The physical environment of Tuckaleechee Cove offered Cherokee communities a broad alluvial valley suitable for agriculture surrounded by an almost continuous wall of mountains. This protected location appears to have turned into a liability in the early eighteenth century, however, when Iroquois raiding parties made their way south along the nearby Great Indian Warpath.

The high degree of variability I recognized in my analysis of the pottery assemblages from households at Townsend strongly suggests that resident potters practiced distinct potting traditions. The technologically and stylistically heterogeneous assemblages found at Townsend are very different from the homogeneous assemblages found within contemporaneous Overhill, Middle, Out, and Lower town sites. This intra-site variability results from the choices made by individual potters at various stages of a pot's construction. The choices that Townsend potters made with respect to tempering material, external surface treatment, and vessel form were all informed by different "constellations of knowledge" or notions about the proper way that things are done (Sinclair 2000). These constellations of knowledge were passed on generationally through the repetitious act of making pots and teaching others to make pots. My analyses identified three separate potting traditions: one that resembled the Overhill series found at later eighteenth-century sites in the lower Little Tennessee and lower Hiwassee River Valleys; one that fit the definition of Qualla series pottery typically found at contemporaneous sites in the upper Little Tennessee and upper Hiwassee River Valleys; and a third tradition that represents a style that has not, until this study, been formally recognized. This tradition, which composed the majority of the pottery sample from Townsend, was defined by a unique tempering material (gravel) and a combination of plain (Overhill) and paddle stamped (Qualla) surface treatments. The spatial distribution of these three traditions among the Townsend households was not uniform, indicating that certain traditions were practiced by certain potters.

Based on these patterns, I argue that Townsend is an apt example of what Hudson (2002) and Kowalewski (2006) call a "coalescent society." As defined in these and other works, coalescent societies were formed by remnant or refugee groups as a strategic response to demographic collapse and other pressures associated with the southeastern shatter zone. Examples of coalescent societies abound during the English Contact period and include the Creek (Knight 1994), the Choctaw (Galloway 1995), the Catawba (Merrell 1989a), and Piedmont North Carolina groups (Davis 2002). Kowalewski (2006) extends the range of this concept to include colonial encounters across North America, Africa, and the Pacific Islands. He argues that coalescence is not a societal type, but a strategy that plays out in very different ways depending upon local historical contingencies (Kowalewski 2006:120–21).

In the case of Townsend, I believe that the households were pursuing a strategy of coalescence. These folks came together from different Cherokee communities to settle in a previously unoccupied area amidst the turmoil of the shatter zone. At the risk of partaking in the arcane cultural arithmetic of "pottery equals people," I believe that the results of the pottery analyses suggest some possibilities for where the Townsend potters could have originated. The potting traditions associated with the Overhill series and the Qualla series do have defined geographical distributions. Overhill series pottery has a local (i.e., eastern Tennessee) antecedent in the pottery of the Dallas phase, although a direct temporal link between these phases has yet to be established (Schroedl 1986b). Qualla pottery has a much better defined geographic distribution centered in the Cherokee Lower, Middle, and Out towns. The third, and most common, potting tradition represented in Townsend household assemblages has no known antecedent and combines aspects of both Overhill and Qualla series. More research is desperately needed, but at this point I will speculate that this tradition was either rooted in a potting tradition that existed formerly elsewhere, or it was a novel tradition that developed locally out of the negotiation of daily life by potters who lived together and shared their distinct constellations of knowledge.

The architecture and spatial organization of the Cherokee community at Townsend was very different from that of communities inhabiting eastern Tennessee and western North Carolina during the preceding Mississippian period. My analysis of architecture illustrated a number of changes: (1) houses in English Contact period Cherokee communities were constructed with a much lower investment in energy and materials than Mississippian houses; (2) English Contact period Cherokee houses were occupied for a much shorter duration than Mississippian houses, often less than a decade; (3) houses in English Contact period Cherokee communities were much more dispersed; and (4) space within English Contact period Cherokee communities was much less structured than Mississippian communities, lacking fortifications and prescribed areas with deep residential histories. My analysis of subsurface pit features confirmed the short tenure of most English Contact period Cherokee households.

These changes in domestic space and time, which continued into the Colonial period, reflect a major shift in the daily lives of Cherokee households and communities. Like the formation of a coalescent society, I believe that this sea change represents the strategic response of Cherokee communities to the many social, political, and economic changes that together constituted the southeastern shatter zone. The rapidly changing conditions of the shatter zone simply did not allow for the creation of strong sedimented community and household identities rooted in the *longue durée* of daily repetition, history, and memory (e.g., Rodning 2004, 2007; Wilson 2005). Quite the opposite, this environment favored strategies that were the very antitheses of those that constituted Mississippian identity—short-term strategies that emphasized flexibility and improvisation. In this sense, the Townsend community was the archetypal archaeological manifestation of habitus in a shatter zone community (Bourdieu 1977:78).

Directions for Future Research

This study represents a single effort within a long tradition of archaeological research addressing Cherokee communities. Indeed, this study rests firmly on past work whose contributions (in addition to data) include: the identification of the English Contact period as a crucial phase in Cherokee history (Schroedl 1986a, 1986b, 2000); a robust ceramic chronology (Egloff 1967; Keel 1976; Riggs and Rodning 2002; Rodning 2004); and an emphasis on the empirical analysis of data related to households and communities (Riggs 1989; Rodning 2007; Schroedl 1989). Now, I wish to provide a few directions that I believe will be important to future research into English Contact period Cherokee communities:

> We need additional research addressing how the Tuckaleechee towns and northern Cherokee settlements fit into Cherokee history. Specifically, we should ask whether these settlements represent what were essentially frontier Overhill towns, an autonomous settlement division, or the progenitors of what eventually became known as the Overhill towns.
>
> We need to conduct archaeological surveys in the Little River Valley that are focused on relocating, formally recording, and assessing the sites (including Ellejoy) that Kenneth Cornett identified during his 1960s survey. This effort should also include extending the survey area to nearby coves (Miller Cove, Wear Cove, Cades Cove, Pitman Center) in order to identify and characterize the Cherokee occupation of these areas.
>
> Future work can employ the glass trade bead and ceramic chronology constructed in this study in order to identify more English Contact period components and to isolate these components at sites with long occupational histories like Citico, Chota-Tanassee, Tallasee, and Chilhowee.
>
> Future research should be directed at Contact period sites located far to the north of Cherokee territory on the French Broad and Nolichucky Rivers, particularly the Plum Grove site. This site has been excavated, but the excavations and artifact analyses have never been published. European artifacts found in burials at the site date part of its occupation to approximately A.D. 1600–1670 (Smith 1987, n.d.). If we are to believe Cherokee oral history, this site may indeed hold important evidence related to the origin of the Tuckaleechee potting tradition and perhaps the Tuckaleechee towns themselves.

Appendix A

Participants in the Townsend Archaeological Project, 1999 to 2010

Name (alphabetically arranged)	**Position**
Abbott-Moore, Megan	Laboratory technician
Ahlman, Todd M.	Ceramics supervisor
Alvey, Richard (Rick) L.	Field supervisor, Analyst
Ammons, Jason D.	Field technician
Angst Michael G.	Field, Supervisor, Lithics supervisor
Archambault, Paul M.	Field technician
Avery-Quinn, Samual	Database entry
Avila-Mooney, O. Gabriel	Field technician
Ayer, Megan	Database entry
Baird, Sabrina R.	Field technician
Bajkiewicz, Stephen J.	Field GIS/technician
Baker, Jonathan	Database entry
Bales, Rodney A.	Field technician
Ballard, R. Renee	Field technician
Barkman, Molly L.	Field technician
Barry, Clayton	Database entry, Photography
Barton, Amanda	Database entry
Barton, James F.	Field technician
Bauguess, O. Jamie	Field technician
Bentz, Charles (Chuck)	Principal investigator
Berg, Christine A.	Field technician
Black, Rachel	Database entry, Photography
Borovy, Wayne	Database entry
Bowden, Heather L.	Field technician
Brock, Daniel	GIS technician
Brogan, Brian (Patrick)	Database entry
Brophy, Juliet	Database entry
Browder, Kimberly	Field crew chief
Brown, Christine	Field technician
Brown, Michael D.	Field technician
Broyles, Erin	Database entry
Cahill, Elizabeth	Database entry
Campbell, Leila C.	Field technician
Cannady, John	Field technician
Carmody, Stephen	Analysis, Database entry
Carroll, Mackenzie	Database entry
Caswell, Chad	IT supervisor, Field technician
Cleeton, Sarena	Database entry
Collins, Jennifer (Waybright)	Field technician
Compton, Anna	Database entry
Cook, Lisa	Database entry
Corley, Hugh S.	Field technician
Cox, Lauren	Database entry
Craven, Cynthia	Field technician
Creswell, Brad A.	Field supervisor, Ceramics supervisor
Crites, Gary, PhD	Analyst–wood charcoal
Cross, Vallie M.	Field technician
Cumming, James (Jater)	Backhoe operator
Daley, Diana J.	Field technician

Name	**Position**
Darby, Richard (Dale)	Database entry
Davis, D. Scott	Field technician
Dean, Jennifer J.	Field technician
DeCorse, Elizabeth Kellar	Historical archaeology supervisor
Devlin, Joanne L.	Specialist
Dickinson, William (Bill)	Database entry
Dixon, William T. (Bill)	Field technician
Donahue, David L.	Field technician
Driskell, Boyce, PhD	Principal investigator
Duey, Michael L.	Field technician
Duncan, Jessie	GIS technician
Dunn, Nicholas	GIS technician
Eckler, David	Database entry
Ellerbusch, Elijah C.	Field technician
Emlen, Katharine M.	Field technician
Esposito, Gina S.	Field technician
Fielder, Nick	State archaeologist, Principal investigator
Foss, John, PhD	Geoarchaeologist
Francisco, Richard G.	Field technician
Frankenberg, Susan	Curation design
Franklin, Jay D.	Field technician
Freeman, Mark	Laboratory technician
Gardner, Jason A.	Field technician
Garvin, Amanda	Field technician
Germaine, George J.	Field technician
Gibson, Tammy R.	Field technician
Giese, Ellen M.	Field technician
Gomez, Greta	Database entry
Greene, Theresa L.	Field technician
Griesmer, Laurie D.	Field technician
Guymon, Gail L.	Lab manager, Archivist
Haislip, Donna G.	Field technician
Hall, Amanda K.	Field technician
Hall, John	Field technician
Hamby, Erin Brooke	Field technician
Hammerstedt, Scott	Ceramics supervisor
Haney, Jennifer M.	Field crew chief
Hansen, Karla M. (Spear)	Field technician
Harle, Michaelyn S.	Field technician
Harris, Joshua S.	Field technician
Haun, Travis	Field technician
Haygood, Howard J.	Field technician
Helfrecht, Courtney E.	Field technician
Herrmann, Nicholas P.	GIS, Physical anthropologist
Highland, Steven	Field technician
Hill, William G.	Field technician
Hock, Andrew	Laboratory technician
Hodge, Wendy L.	Field technician
Hollenbach, Kandace D.	Subsistence team supervisor

Name	Position
Honsinger, Vivian M.	Field technician
Hoose, Brian	Field technician
Hoose, Tracy	Field technician
Howell, Cameron	Field crew chief, Ceramics specialist
Hoyt, J. Mick	Field technician
Huff, Jodie L.	Field technician
Jacobson, Jodi A.	Field technician
James, Dustin	Database entry
Johanson, Erik	Analysis
Johnson, Crystal (Brianne)	Database entry
Johnston, Kenneth (Kenny)	Site tour guide
Jones, Tonya	Database entry
Justice, Laura L.	Field technician
Kaplan, N. Cori	Field technician
Kekkonan, Sherry A.	Field technician
Ketteringham, Desiree	GIS technician
Kim, Yong W. (Willie)	Field director/supervisor
Kirkmeyer, Jennifer L.	Field crew chief
Koch, Christopher P.	Field technician
Kocis, James J.	Geoarchaeologist
Koener, Shannon	Laboratory technician
Kohan, Shari L.	Field technician
Koller, Brian M.	Field technician
Kvach, John	Laboratory technician
Lansdell, M. Brent	Field technician
Lavender, William (Will)	Database entry
Lawrence, William (Bill)	TDOA field supervisor
Lawrie, Gordon, B.	Field technician
Lecher, Sarah M.	Field technician
Linquist, Robert E.	Field technician
Loche, Andrew	Laboratory technician
Long, Matthew B.	Field technician
Longmire, C. Alan	Field technician
Loucks, Emily	Database entry
Lowe, Caroline A.	Field technician
Lowe, Sarah	Database entry
Malcolm, Adrienne	Database entry
Marcel, Dan L.	Field crew chief
March, Gregory H.	Field technician
Marcoux, Jon	Cherokee team supervisor
Martin, Steve A.	Field technician
Matchen Paul	Lithics supervisor
Mayberry, Neil	Field technician
McDonough, Jennifer L.	Curation supervisor, Photography
McKissick, Kathryn	Database entry
McMillan, Katherine	Analysis, Database entry
McNabb, Kelly	Field technician
Medina, Jowizza A.	Field technician
Meyers, Danielle F.	Field technician
Meyers, Spence C.	Field supervisor
Miller, Katherine	Database entry
Moore, Palmyra	Database entry
Morgan, Robert (Bob) D.	Field technician
Mucio, Michael A.	Field technician
Mullerud, Katy J.	Field crew chief
Murray, Sarah	GIS technician
Neff, Keil J.	Field technician
Nelson, Whitney L.	Field technician
Noe, Melanie	Database entry
Norrell, Robert	Database entry
Norton, Mark	TDOA field supervisor
Nurabas, Rico F.	Field technician
O'Donoughue, Jason	Database entry
Oliver, Elizabeth A.	Field technician

Name	Position
Oliver, Jonathan L.	Field technician
Omvig, Jeremy	Field technician
Owensby, Stehpanie D.	Field crew chief
Parker, Justin G.	On site observer
Perlin, Iwona	Field technician
Pickard, Jana	Field technician
Pidkowicz, Ryan	Database entry
Pironti, Paul M.	Field technician
Raisle, John	Field technician
Ramsey, Ann	Database entry
Randolph, Katherine M.	Field technician
Rich, James D.	Field technician
Richmond, Erin	Database entry
Riggs, Brett H.	Consultant
Rigney, Phyllis	Analysis, Database entry
Riley, Rod	IBM database specialist
Robbins, Ronnica J.	Field technician
Roberts, W. Nicholas	Field technician
Roup, Cynthia	Field technician
Savage, Ashley D.	Field technician
Savidant, Stacey	Report manager
Schneider, Patricia (Tricia) L.	Field technician
Schwartz, Joshua A.	Field technician
Sherwood, Sarah	Geoarchaeology team supervisor
Shular, S. Todd	Field technician
Sichler, Judith A.	Zooarchaeologist, Laboratory director
Silcos, Jocelyn	Database entry
Smith, Timothy J., III	Field technician
Snyder, Anna Marie Meador	Field technician
Spears, Anita K.	Database entry
Spence, Virginia	Database entry
Spinney, Brian R.	Field technician
Spradley, M. Katerine	Physical anthropologist
Stevenson, John A.	Field technician
Strickland, Glenn D.	Field technician
Stuart, L. Jaime	Field technician
Styer, Kenneth	Field technician
Suggs, Troy D.	Field technician
Sullivan, Lynn	Mississippian team supervisor
Susano, Charles D., III	Field crew chief
Sweat, Jeremy	Analysis, Database entry
Tate, Bryan	Database entry
Taylor, James J.	Field technician
Trook, Jason	Field technician
Turner-Herrmann, Sherri	Artifact photography
Vavrasek, Jessica	Zooarchaeologist, Curation
Vogel, Juliette	Database entry
Walker, Cassondra (Casey)	Field technician
Warner, D. M.	Field technician
Warren, J. Mitch	Field technician
Weaver, Matt	Field technician
Weidenhamer, Adrienne	Database entry
Weidman, Andrew	Database entry
Welborn, Heather	Database entry
Welch, Marcy K.	Field technician
Wells, Edward	Analysis, Database entry
Will, Bryan P.	Field technician
Williams, Hilary	Database entry
Wilson, Morgan	Database entry
Witcoski, Jonathan	GIS technician
Wood, Edward A.	Field technician
Wren, Kimberly	Database entry
Yerka, Stephen	GIS, IT manager
Young, Matthew	Database entry

Appendix B

Data Recorded for Body Sherds in the Ceramics Sample

KEY

br:	brushed	ind:	indeterminate
brn:	burnished	lin:	linear
col:	colander	ovrst:	overstamped
comp:	complicated	par:	parallel
conc:	concentric	punc:	punctated
cordm:	cordmarked	rgh:	roughened
CR:	crushed rock	S:	shell
curv:	curvilinear	scr:	scraped
fig:	figure	sm:	smoothed
fn:	fingernail	smdg:	smudged
G:	gravel	smpl:	simple
hrz:	horizontal	sqs:	squares
incs:	incised	st:	stamped

Provenience Code	Specimen Number	Size (cm)	Thickness (mm)	Weight (g)	Temper	Exterior Surface Treatment	Motif	Interior Surface Treatment	Temper Particle Size (mm)	Frequency	Comments
00-1470	3	5	7.06	9.8	G	coarse		sm	1.55	1	
00-1470	2	2	7.85	2.5	G	sm		sm	1.28	1	
00-236	251	2	7.2	2.3	G	sm		sm	1.5	1	
00-250	254	1	6.8	2.1	G	ind lin st		sm	1.32	1	
00-253	3	3	6.09	3.9	S	scr		sm	1.55	1	
00-253	2	2	6.81	3	G	ind lin st		sm/smdg	1.79	1	
00-254	254	2	7.75	3.8	G	ind lin st		sm	1.6	1	
00-255	272	3	3.13	5.4	G	sm		sm	1.86	1	
00-255	275	2	5.66	2.3	G	sm		sm	1.7	1	
00-255	280	3	5.74	5	G	sm		sm/smdg	1.07	1	
00-255	271	2	5.85	3.9	G	sm		sm	2.05	1	
00-255	278	1	6.16	2.2	G	coarse		brn	1.02	1	
00-255	279	2	6.27	3.1	G	coarse		sm	0.95	1	
00-255	269	1	6.33	6.9	G	sm		sm	1.4	1	
00-255	276	1	6.34	1.7	G	sm		sm/smdg	0.91	1	
00-255	274	2	6.44	2	G	sm		sm	1.19	1	
00-255	257	1	6.52	2	G	coarse		sm	1.42	1	
00-255	266	1	6.68	1	G	sm		sm	0.86	1	
00-255	270	3	6.71	4.6	G	cordm	sm over	sm/smdg	1.03	1	
00-255	263	2	6.74	2.6	G	sm		sm	2.06	1	
00-255	277	2	6.85	4.4	G	sm		brn	0.91	1	
00-255	273	4	6.98	11.9	G	scr		sm/smdg	1.44	1	
00-255	267	1	7.08	1.8	G	sm		sm/smdg	1.86	1	
00-255	264	2	7.15	5.3	G	coarse		sm	1.23	1	
00-255	258	2	7.23	3.2	G	sm		sm	1.22	1	
00-255	268	3	7.37	5.5	G	sm		sm	1.54	1	
00-255	262	1	7.81	1.5	G	sm		sm	1.36	1	
00-255	261	2	7.87	2.2	G	sm		sm	1.38	1	
00-255	255	5	8.12	15.6	G	curv comp st	wavy lines	sm	1.1	1	
00-257	258	2	5.01	3.2	G	coarse		sm	1.7	1	
00-257	257	2	5.88	4.1	G	ind lin st		sm/smdg	1.3	1	
00-259	253	2	6.5	4.1	G	sm		sm	1.5	1	
00-261	253	2	9.97	6.7	G	ind st		sm	1.98	1	
00-263	253	2	8.49	2.8	G	eroded		sm/smdg	2.29	1	
00-265	261	1	0	0.9	G	eroded		sm	1.12	1	
00-265	260	2	4.46	2.6	S	sm		sm	1.74	1	
00-265	256	2	4.86	2.2	S	sm		sm/smdg	1.1	1	
00-265	258	2	5.85	3.2	G	coarse		sm	1.53	1	
00-265	257	5	6.35	15	G	curv comp st	ind scroll	sm	2.03	1	
00-265	262	2	6.84	2.2	G	sm		sm	1.58	1	
00-265	254	5	7.13	19.1	G	br		sm	1.56	1	
00-265	259	2	7.55	5.5	G	coarse		coarse	1.74	1	
00-265	255	5	7.68	14	G	curv comp st	ind scroll	sm	2.02	1	
00-265	264	5	8.18	16.8	G	coarse		sm	1.52	1	
00-268	285	3	8.7	5.8	G	ind lin st		sm	1.33	1	
00-268	283	3	8.99	6.1	G	ind st		redfilmed	1.73	1	
00-268	286	4	9.95	15.2	G	sm		brn/smdg	1.45	1	
00-274	5	4	8.23	9.8	G	ind lin st	fine line	sm/smdg	1.46	1	
00-274	6	1	9.04	1.8	G	sm		sm	1.4	1	
00-280	3	2	7.48	2.5	G	cordm		sm	1.43	1	
00-280	1	1	8.64	1.8	G	cordm		sm	1.62	1	
00-280	2	2	9.59	2.9	G	cordm		sm	2.4	1	
00-281	256	2	7.47	2.7	G	sm		sm	1.91	1	
00-281	252	3	7.5	5.2	G	ind lin st	fine line	brn/smdg	1.66	1	
00-281	255	1	7.82	1	S	sm		sm	1.64	1	
00-281	251	6	7.96	24.9	G	ind lin st	fine line	sm	1.21	1	
00-281	253	5	8.07	20.7	G	ind lin st	fine line	brn	1.9	1	
00-281	254	2	8.12	2.2	S	sm		sm	2.19	1	
00-281	257	2	9.23	5.6	G	ind lin st	fine line	sm	1.3	1	
00-2837	253	3	5.09	4.3	grit	ind lin st		sm	0.67	1	
00-2837	252	4	6.56	6.6	S	sm		sm		1	
00-2890	253	2	6.14	2.9	G	sm		sm	1.39	1	
00-2890	256	2	6.23	2.8	G	ind lin st		sm/smdg	1.34	1	
00-290	252	2	5.74	2.7	G	sm		sm	1.92	1	
00-307	13	2	6.07	3.4	grit	sm		sm	0.76	1	
00-307	12	1	6.78	2.8	G	sm		sm	1.37	1	
00-332	252	3	4.06	3.6	grit	sm		sm	0.8	1	
00-334	290	2	0	2.3	G	eroded		brn/smdg	2.08	1	
00-334	282	2	0	2.9	G	eroded		sm	2.05	1	
00-334	317	2	5.18	2.3	S	sm		sm	1.43	1	
00-334	365	2	5.2	3.1	G	sm		sm	0.79	1	
00-334	352	2	5.24	2.6	grit	curv comp st	ind	sm	1.04	1	
00-334	348	2	5.25	2.2	G	sm		sm	1.06	1	
00-334	358	2	5.39	3.4	G	coarse		sm	1.14	1	
00-334	330	3	5.45	5	G	sm		sm	0.99	1	
00-334	349	2	5.45	3.4	G	sm		sm	0.83	1	
00-334	322	3	5.57	4.9	G	comp st	ind	sm	0.97	1	
00-334	356	2	5.6	2.5	G	sm		sm	1.26	1	
00-334	324	1	5.63	1.7	G	coarse		sm/smdg	1.47	1	
00-334	300	3	5.85	6.4	G	sm		sm	0.66	1	
00-334	325	3	5.88	4.6	grit	sm		sm/smdg	0.42	1	
00-334	350	1	5.96	2.4	G	sm		sm	0.87	1	
00-334	331	4	5.97	5.7	G	curv comp st	wavy lines	brn	0.94	1	
00-334	357	1	5.99	2	G	sm		sm	1.25	1	
00-334	298	2	6.05	3.7	G	sm		sm	1.2	1	
00-334	309	2	6.08	2.9	G	sm		brn/smdg	1.25	1	
00-334	314	2	6.17	4.1	G	sm		sm	1.89	1	
00-334	364	1	6.26	2.1	G	coarse		sm	1.56	1	
00-334	342	2	6.29	3.5	G	sm		brn/smdg	1.29	1	
00-334	305	1	6.3	1.5	G	sm		sm	1.11	1	
00-334	270	2	6.33	4	G	sm		sm/smdg	1	1	sooted
00-334	329	2	6.34	2.6	G	sm		brn/smdg	0.96	1	
00-334	272	2	6.34	3.8	G	scr		sm	1.6	1	
00-334	320	3	6.36	5.1	grit	sm		sm	0.94	1	
00-334	326	2	6.36	2.5	G	sm		sm	0.65	1	
00-334	288	3	6.41	4.4	G	coarse		coarse	1.64	1	
00-334	303	1	6.45	2.4	G	sm		sm	0.78	1	
00-334	269	2	6.45	3.6	G	eroded		sm/smdg	1.61	1	
00-334	319	1	6.5	2.3	G	sm		sm	1.39	1	
00-334	302	1	6.57	1.7	grit	sm		sm	1.03	1	
00-334	263	5	6.58	18.8	G	cordm		sm	1.49	1	
00-334	363	4	6.61	6.9	G	sm		sm	1.07	1	
00-334	343	2	6.64	3	G	coarse		sm	1.45	1	
00-334	370	3	6.65	6.6	G	coarse		brn/smdg	0.74	1	
00-334	292	2	6.69	5.4	G	sm		sm	2.15	1	
00-334	381	1	6.72	2.1	G	sm		sm	0.58	1	

00-334	385	9	6.73	41.3	G	coarse		sm/smdg	1.83	1	
00-334	339	3	6.75	5.2	G	scr		sm	0.92	1	
00-334	276	3	6.76	7.3	G	sm		sm	1.21	1	
00-334	301	3	6.77	6.4	G	sm		sm	1.08	1	
00-334	295	2	6.81	3.1	G	coarse		sm	0.84	1	
00-334	360	2	6.82	3.5	S	sm		brn/smdg	1.87	1	
00-334	345	3	6.83	5.8	G	coarse		sm	1.2	1	
00-334	355	3	6.85	5.7	G	sm		sm	0.95	1	
00-334	313	2	6.9	2.3	G	sm		eroded	1.53	1	
00-334	334	2	6.92	2.3	G	ind lin st		sm	1.13	1	
00-334	341	2	6.95	2.7	G	sm		sm	1.49	1	
00-334	306	2	6.99	3.9	S	sm		brn	2.22	1	
00-334	299	3	6.99	5.6	G	sm		brn	1.01	1	
00-334	366	1	7	1.8	S	sm		sm/smdg	1.19	1	
00-334	277	3	7.08	4.9	G	curv comp st	ind	sm	1.5	1	
00-334	286	2	7.08	2	G	sm		sm	1.35	1	
00-334	304	2	7.08	2.8	G	sm		brn/smdg	1.31	1	
00-334	368	4	7.11	13.3	G	sm		sm	1.16	1	
00-334	274	2	7.12	2.5	G	cordm		sm	1.3	1	
00-334	359	2	7.15	3.1	G	ind st		sm	1.29	1	
00-334	372	3	7.17	6.6	G	coarse		sm	1.7	1	
00-334	283	2	7.17	3.5	G	coarse		sm	0.97	1	
00-334	271	3	7.19	7.3	G	coarse		sm	1.72	1	
00-334	382	4	7.25	4.2	G	ind lin st	sm over	sm	1.25	1	
00-334	285	4	7.27	10.3	G	sm		sm	1.17	1	
00-334	362	3	7.28	4.6	G	sm		sm	1.87	1	
00-334	346	3	7.3	7.1	G	ind lin st		sm	1.57	1	
00-334	287	4	7.31	10.6	G	sm		sm	1.56	1	
00-334	278	2	7.32	4.1	G	sm		sm	1.9	1	
00-334	367	4	7.32	9.8	G	sm		sm	1.69	1	
00-334	262	5	7.37	19	G	curv comp st	ind	sm	1.46	1	
00-334	267	5	7.38	19.7	G	sm		sm	1.86	1	
00-334	257	6	7.45	26.3	G	coarse		sm	1.7	1	
00-334	323	2	7.46	2.2	G	sm		brn/smdg	1.46	1	
00-334	321	2	7.47	2.5	G	coarse		sm	1.15	1	
00-334	280	2	7.47	4.7	G	sm		sm	1.14	1	
00-334	374	2	7.48	2.7	G	sm		sm	1.99	1	
00-334	340	2	7.54	5.6	grit	sm		sm	1.48	1	
00-334	376	3	7.55	8.7	G	sm		sm/smdg	1.04	1	
00-334	335	3	7.58	4	G	sm		brn	1.6	1	
00-334	312	2	7.62	5.8	G	coarse		sm	1.72	1	
00-334	353	2	7.64	2.9	G	coarse		sm	1.53	1	
00-334	266	5	7.69	17.9	G	sm		sm	1.78	1	
00-334	289	2	7.71	2.8	G	sm		sm	1.35	1	
00-334	344	2	7.72	3.1	G	ind st		sm	1.69	1	
00-334	354	2	7.73	5	G	ind st		sm	1.97	1	
00-334	260	6	7.78	21.7	G	coarse		sm/smdg	2	1	
00-334	347	3	7.79	4.2	G	sm		sm/smdg	1.42	1	
00-334	373	2	7.79	5.7	G	sm		sm/smdg	1.41	1	
00-334	332	2	7.8	3.7	G	sm		sm	1.67	1	
00-334	337	2	7.86	4.4	G	sm		sm	1.72	1	
00-334	291	4	7.87	12.2	G	ind st		sm	1.7	1	
00-334	328	3	7.9	9.6	G	coarse		sm	1.67	1	carinated shoulder
00-334	268	2	7.9	3.7	G	sm		sm	1.06	1	
00-334	336	4	7.95	13.9	G	sm		brn	1.76	1	
00-334	294	1	7.96	2.1	G	sm		sm	1.58	1	
00-334	318	1	8.03	2	G	sm		brn/smdg	0.84	1	
00-334	409	2	8.04	3.3	G	sm		sm	2.12	1	
00-334	327	4	8.15	13.6	G	sm		sm	0.83	1	
00-334	316	2	8.18	4.7	G	sm		sm	1.73	1	
00-334	361	3	8.22	7.4	G	coarse		sm/smdg	2.37	1	
00-334	351	2	8.24	1.9	S	sm		eroded	1.37	1	
00-334	383	2	8.28	3.7	G	coarse		sm	1.07	1	
00-334	256	6	8.31	23.2	G	coarse		sm	1.21	1	
00-334	275	2	8.4	3.6	G	eroded		sm/smdg	1.35	1	
00-334	264	5	8.49	24.2	G	coarse		sm/smdg	1.52	1	
00-334	293	4	8.49	9.6	G	coarse		sm	1.73	1	
00-334	261	4	8.51	19.9	G	scr		sm	1.55	1	
00-334	281	2	8.52	4.5	G	coarse		sm	1.92	1	
00-334	296	3	8.56	9.9	G	sm		sm/smdg	2.28	1	
00-334	375	3	8.57	5.9	G	sm		sm/smdg	2.36	1	
00-334	333	2	8.62	3.6	G	scr		sm	1.32	1	
00-334	258	6	8.68	26.9	G	coarse		sm	1.72	1	
00-334	371	2	8.74	3	G	sm		sm	1.09	1	
00-334	307	1	8.78	2.4	G	ind st		sm	1.56	1	
00-334	310	1	8.8	3.1	G	sm		brn/smdg	1.93	1	
00-334	273	1	8.87	2.3	G	sm		sm	1.7	1	
00-334	284	3	9.02	6.7	S	sm		sm	2.69	1	
00-334	384	2	9.07	4.6	G	sm		sm	0.98	1	
00-334	308	2	9.08	6.7	grit	sm		sm	1.15	1	
00-334	265	6	9.23	23.6	G	sm		sm	1.74	1	
00-334	315	3	9.41	10.2	grit	sm		sm	1	1	
00-334	2580	6	9.42	22.5	S	sm		sm	2.38	1	
00-334	297	3	9.43	8.4	G	coarse		coarse	2.28	1	
00-334	338	2	9.66	4.4	grit	sm		sm	1.13	1	
00-334	311	3	9.66	9.4	G	sm		sm	1.65	1	
00-334	2860	7	10.05	65.3	grit	sm		brn	1.02	1	
00-334	380	3	10.6	9.9	grit	sm		sm	1.07	1	
00-339	255	3	6.47	7.3	G	sm		brn/smdg	1.71	1	
00-339	252	3	6.64	5	G	ind st		sm/smdg	2.09	1	
00-339	251	2	6.81	3.4	G	coarse		sm/smdg	0.96	1	
00-339	254	1	8.22	2.9	G	sm		brn	1.58	1	
00-339	256	2	8.92	5.3	G	sm		sm	1.43	1	
00-339	257	4	11.04	18.1	grit	brn		brn	1	1	
00-340	270	2	0	2	G	eroded		sm	1.56	1	
00-340	273	3	6.57	4.7	G	sm		sm	1.38	1	
00-340	282	2	7.84	2.5	G	ind lin st		sm	1.69	1	
00-340	272	3	8.58	4.8	G	ind lin st		brn	1.59	1	
00-340	283	6	9	28	G	smpl st		sm	1.56	1	comp design made with a smpl paddle?
00-340	284	2	9.13	2.9	G	sm		brn	1.13	1	
00-354	14	2	6.46	4.1	G	coarse		redfilmed	1.09	1	
00-354	15	2	7.4	3.6	G	sm		brn	1.33	1	
00-354	18	6	8.07	31.4	G	smpl st		sm	1.72	1	comp design made with a smpl paddle?
00-354	16	5	8.54	20.2	G	ind st		redfilmed	1.42	1	
00-354	12	3	8.73	10.3	G	ind lin st		redfilmed	1.73	1	
00-354	13	5	10.13	18.9	G	sm		sm	1.67	1	
00-356	257	1	5.49	1.7	G	sm		sm	1.2	1	
00-356	253	3	5.86	4.4	G	sm		sm/smdg	1.3	1	
00-356	256	1	5.89	2.2	G	sm		sm	1.35	1	
00-356	252	3	9.18	7.4	grit	sm		sm	1.25	1	
00-356	254	2	10.03	7.7	G	sm		sm	1.56	1	
00-356	258	4	10.52	17.8	grit	ind st		brn	0.69	1	
00-356	255	3	12.07	14.6	G	sm		sm	2.3	1	
00-357	258	2	0	2.6	G	sm		eroded	1.46	1	
00-357	251	4	6.25	7.5	G	ind lin st		sm	1.22	1	
00-357	253	4	6.63	10.6	G	coarse		sm/smdg	1.09	1	
00-357	260	4	7.18	12.5	G	brn		sm/smdg	1.12	1	
00-357	256	3	7.33	8.9	G	sm		brn	1.1	1	
00-357	252	6	7.85	14.9	G	coarse		coarse	1.64	1	
00-357	261	2	7.99	2	G	coarse		sm	1.92	1	
00-357	259	1	8.14	2.2	G	sm		brn/smdg	1.22	1	
00-357	255	4	8.17	7.2	grit	sm		sm	0.86	1	
00-357	265	3	8.27	6.3	G	ind st		sm/smdg	0.83	1	
00-357	262	3	8.34	5.9	S	sm		sm	2.65	1	
00-357	254	3	8.4	7.8	G	coarse		sm/smdg	1.3	1	
00-357	257	4	9.02	11.4	G	sm		sm	1.7	1	

00-357	264	4	9.35	13	G	ind lin st		sm	1.15	1
00-357	263	3	9.63	9.2	G	ind lin st		redfilmed	1.18	1
00-363	48	2	0	2.2	G	eroded		sm	1.59	1
00-363	125	2	5.17	2	G	sm		sm	1.29	1
00-363	37	2	5.5	2.8	G	sm		sm	1.57	1
00-363	60	2	5.6	2.7	G	ind lin st		sm	1.45	1
00-363	112	3	5.68	5.7	G	sm		sm	0.86	1
00-363	116	2	5.69	1.7	S	sm		sm	1.47	1
00-363	54	1	5.71	1.8	S	sm		sm	1.34	1
00-363	44	22	5.73	2.1	grit	sm		sm	0.49	1
00-363	67	2	5.8	2.6	G	sm		sm	1.53	1
00-363	108	2	5.94	3.1	G	sm		brn	1.02	1
00-363	69	2	5.99	2.6	G	sm		brn/smdg	1.04	1
00-363	131	2	6.02	2.3	grit	sm		sm	0.82	1
00-363	36	3	6.08	5.5	G	sm		brn/smdg	0.67	1
00-363	65	2	6.12	2.9	G	sm		sm/smdg	1.09	1
00-363	88	2	6.15	2.4	G	curv comp st	ind	sm	1.6	1
00-363	33	2	6.18	3.8	G	sm		sm	1.3	1
00-363	50	3	6.2	4.2	G	sm		sm/smdg	1.59	1
00-363	127	2	6.3	2.7	grit	coarse		sm/smdg	1.16	1
00-363	35	3	6.3	7.3	grit	brn		sm	0.38	1
00-363	39	2	6.32	3	G	coarse		sm/smdg	1.05	1
00-363	56	1	6.32	1.4	G	sm		sm	1.23	1
00-363	61	1	6.36	1.7	G	sm		sm	1.26	1
00-363	129	1	6.36	2.2	G	sm		sm	2.22	1
00-363	45	3	6.43	4.5	G	coarse		sm	0.96	1
00-363	47	1	6.48	2.1	G	ind lin st		sm	1.21	1
00-363	121	2	6.52	2.7	G	sm		brn	1.17	1
00-363	62	2	6.55	2.8	S	sm		sm	2.33	1
00-363	74	2	6.58	4.9	grit	sm		sm	1.75	1
00-363	66	2	6.63	3	G	sm		sm	0.92	1
00-363	72	1	6.66	2.4	G	sm		sm	1.49	1
00-363	84	5	6.76	17.8	G	coarse		sm	1.03	1
00-363	106	4	6.79	9.7	G	coarse		sm	1.16	1
00-363	118	1	6.79	1.9	G	coarse		sm	1.07	1
00-363	124	2	6.8	1.9	grit	sm		sm	0.83	1
00-363	46	2	6.8	3.3	G	ind st		sm/smdg	1.03	1
00-363	82	7	6.85	21	G	coarse		sm	1.4	1
00-363	49	2	6.93	3.1	G	curv comp st	ind	brn/smdg	0.79	1
00-363	91	1	6.95	1.9	G	sm		sm	1.37	1
00-363	38	2	6.99	4.9	G	ind st		sm/smdg	1.35	1
00-363	128	1	7.03	1.6	G	sm		coarse	0.98	1
00-363	55	1	7.09	2	G	ind st		sm	1.65	1
00-363	97	2	7.09	3.2	G	sm		redfilmed	1.15	1
00-363	119	2	7.12	2.5	G	sm		sm	1.12	1
00-363	93	3	7.12	7.7	G	coarse		brn/smdg	1.67	1
00-363	27	5	7.18	16.7	G	sm		sm	1.05	1
00-363	30	5	7.26	13.7	G	sm		sm	1.13	1
00-363	105	3	7.27	7.9	G	ind lin st		sm	1.56	1
00-363	130	2	7.34	2.9	G	coarse		sm	1.6	1
00-363	123	1	7.37	2.5	G	sm		sm	1.1	1
00-363	90	4	7.45	8.4	G	sm		sm	1.67	1
00-363	115	3	7.48	9.8	G	ind lin st		sm	2.2	1
00-363	52	3	7.49	5.7	G	coarse		sm	1.27	1
00-363	43	2	7.5	3.6	G	sm		sm	1.58	1
00-363	122	1	7.5	2	G	sm		sm	1.29	1
00-363	87	3	7.54	7.8	G	sm		brn	1.1	1
00-363	99	2	7.58	3.6	G	cordm	sm over	sm	0.97	1
00-363	75	6	7.6	21.8	G	coarse		sm	1.44	1
00-363	59	2	7.64	3.8	G	ind st		sm	0.92	1
00-363	24	4	7.64	13.3	G	coarse		brn	1.46	1
00-363	53	3	7.67	5.7	G	coarse		sm/smdg	1.57	1
00-363	51	2	7.73	4.6	G	ind lin st		sm/smdg	1.01	1
00-363	86	7	7.74	39.7	G	sm		sm	1.33	1
00-363	73	2	7.81	5.2	G	sm		sm	1.2	1
00-363	25	4	7.87	12.1	G	coarse		sm/smdg	1.26	1
00-363	136	5	7.9	18.1	G	coarse		sm	1.25	1
00-363	42	3	7.91	5.2	G	curv comp st	ind	sm	0.96	1
00-363	29	3	7.93	8.2	G	sm		sm	2.01	1
00-363	32	1	7.96	2.5	G	coarse		sm	1.03	1
00-363	26	3	8	7.6	G	coarse		sm	1.6	1
00-363	70	2	8.01	3.3	G	ind lin st		sm	1.38	1
00-363	83	7	8.08	35.2	G	coarse		sm	1.61	1
00-363	40	4	8.14	13.5	G	coarse		sm	1.01	1
00-363	102	4	8.15	14.2	G	ind lin st		sm	1.26	1
00-363	31	1	8.23	2.5	G	sm		sm	2.15	1
00-363	103	2	8.23	5.5	G	sm		sm	2.25	1
00-363	23	4	8.24	14.2	G	curv comp st	ind	sm	1.06	1
00-363	34	3	8.26	6.3	G	coarse		sm	1.2	1
00-363	81	6	8.27	28	G	coarse		sm	1.69	1
00-363	132	2	8.28	3.6	G	sm		coarse	1.71	1
00-363	117	1	8.3	2	G	sm		sm	2.58	1
00-363	113	3	8.31	7.5	G	cordm		sm	0.98	1
00-363	57	2	8.32	5.3	G	sm		sm/smdg	1.72	1
00-363	96	1	8.32	2.9	G	ind st		redfilmed	2.3	1
00-363	111	3	8.34	6.9	G	coarse		sm/smdg	1.12	1
00-363	92	3	8.37	6.8	G	sm		sm	1.54	1
00-363	21	5	8.44	28	G	ind lin st		sm	1.23	1
00-363	107	3	8.62	4.3	G	sm		sm	1.18	1
00-363	120	2	8.62	4.2	G	sm		sm	1.32	1
00-363	98	2	8.69	3.6	G	coarse		sm	1.18	1
00-363	41	2	8.82	5	S	sm		sm	2.8	1
00-363	94	1	8.83	1.7	G	coarse		sm	1.3	1
00-363	89	2	8.86	5.4	grit	brn		brn	0.64	1
00-363	110	5	8.96	13	G	ind lin st		sm	1.4	1
00-363	100	2	8.98	3.2	G	ind lin st		sm	1.93	1
00-363	126	2	9.02	4.7	G	eroded		sm	1.48	1
00-363	114	3	9.14	9.1	G	ind st		sm	1.21	1
00-363	109	5	9.28	15.3	G	coarse		sm	1.48	1
00-363	63	1	9.28	3.6	G	ind lin st		sm	1.95	1
00-363	77	6	9.3	29.5	G	sm		sm	1.26	1
00-363	95	2	9.31	5.1	G	ind lin st		sm	1.07	1
00-363	22	5	9.31	13.2	G	ind lin st		sm	1.45	1
00-363	68	2	9.46	4.4	grit	brn		sm	0.96	1
00-363	76	7	9.79	58.5	G	curv comp st	ind	sm	1.25	1
00-363	104	3	9.79	14.4	G	sm		sm	2.17	1
00-363	101	3	9.96	7.2	G	sm		sm	1.28	1
00-363	80	6	10.15	32.2	G	curv comp st	ind	sm	1.26	1
00-363	64	1	10.24	2.5	G	sm		eroded	1.58	1
00-363	28	2	10.29	7.2	S	sm		sm	2.09	1
00-363	78	6	10.48	33.9	G	sm		sm	1.8	1
00-363	79	6	11.47	30.4	G	sm		sm	1.81	1
00-363	58	2	12.3	5.1	G	coarse		brn/smdg	1.92	1
00-365	254	3	8.26	10	G	ind st		sm	1.05	1
00-365	252	3	8.89	11.3	G	ind lin st		sm	1.42	1
00-381	261	3	0	4.1	G	eroded		sm	2.4	1
00-381	291	2	0	2.1	G	eroded		sm/smdg	1.4	1
00-381	293	2	0	1.7	S	sm		sm	1.52	1
00-381	301	2	5.8	3.4	G	cordm		sm	1.53	1
00-381	311	3	5.83	6.3	G	sm		brn/smdg	1.3	1
00-381	312	3	5.93	4.7	G	cordm		sm	1.56	1
00-381	277	3	5.94	4.5	G	coarse		sm	1.73	1
00-381	281	2	6.05	3.6	G	coarse		sm	1.68	1
00-381	273	4	6.15	7.2	G	cordm	ovrst	sm	1.31	1
00-381	296	2	6.19	3.6	G	ind lin st		brn/smdg	1.46	1
00-381	270	2	6.31	3.3	G	coarse		sm	1.61	1
00-381	263	2	6.34	3.5	G	cordm		sm	1.23	1
00-381	286	2	6.53	3.5	G	sm		sm/smdg	1.44	1

00-381	271	4	6.56	6.1	G	cordm		sm	1.56	1	
00-381	304	2	6.66	2.9	G	cordm		sm	1.14	1	
00-381	272	2	6.74	2.7	G	sm		sm	0.77	1	
00-381	308	1	6.77	1.9	G	sm		sm/smdg	1.36	1	
00-381	288	2	6.88	3.5	G	cordm		sm/smdg	1.94	1	
00-381	283	2	6.89	4.7	G	sm		sm/smdg	1.67	1	
00-381	302	1	6.95	2	G	sm		sm	1.24	1	
00-381	289	1	6.95	2.1	G	cordm		sm/smdg	1.62	1	
00-381	303	2	6.96	2.6	G	sm		sm	0.93	1	
00-381	266	2	7	3.1	G	incs	ind	sm/smdg	2.26	1	
00-381	274	2	7	2.6	G	cordm		sm	1.82	1	
00-381	269	3	7.03	5.5	G	scr		sm/smdg	1.86	1	
00-381	284	2	7.09	3.6	G	coarse		sm	2.2	1	
00-381	264	1	7.21	1.9	G	sm		sm	1.39	1	
00-381	299	4	7.27	10.7	G	cordm		sm/smdg	1.05	1	
00-381	268	2	7.32	3.5	G	sm		sm	1.5	1	
00-381	287	1	7.36	2.5	G	sm		sm	1.91	1	
00-381	290	2	7.38	3.7	G	coarse		sm	1.35	1	
00-381	292	3	7.4	7.3	G	coarse		eroded	1.24	1	
00-381	297	2	7.42	2.9	G	coarse		sm	2.07	1	
00-381	275	2	7.5	3.3	G	sm		sm	1.02	1	
00-381	278	3	7.6	6.5	G	cordm	lineblock	sm	1.5	1	
00-381	260	2	7.62	3.1	G	sm		sm/smdg	1.67	1	
00-381	294	2	7.76	5	G	sm		sm	1.54	1	
00-381	262	5	7.8	15.9	G	coarse		sm/smdg	2.63	1	
00-381	280	2	7.83	2.4	S	sm		sm	2.94	1	
00-381	310	3	8.22	8.2	G	cordm		sm/smdg	1.89	1	
00-381	279	5	8.31	16	G	sm		sm	0.94	1	
00-381	265	3	8.46	5.3	G	coarse		sm	1.13	1	
00-381	307	2	8.5	3.1	G	sm		eroded	2.2	1	
00-381	285	2	9.04	3.7	G	cordm	sm over	sm	2.25	1	
00-381	300	3	9.25	3.8	G	ind lin st		sm/smdg	1.74	1	
00-381	306	2	9.98	4.5	G	sm		sm/smdg	1.37	1	
00-381	309	3	10	8.4	G	eroded		sm	1.59	1	
00-381	305	3	10.34	7.8	G	sm		sm	1.48	1	
00-381	298	2	10.79	4.3	G	cordm		sm	1.67	1	
00-381	267	2	11.08	6.8	G	coarse		sm	1.92	1	
00-381	282	3	11.1	2.1	G	sm		sm	1.84	1	
00-382	254	2	5.07	1.5	S	sm		sm	2.08	1	
00-382	2	5	6.11	12.2	S	sm		sm/smdg	1.73	1	
00-382	1	1	6.35	2	G	sm		sm/smdg	1.76	1	
00-382	252	2	6.57	1.9	S	sm		sm	1.94	1	
00-385	259	2	5.26	2	G	coarse		coarse	1.2	1	
00-385	252	2	6.36	1.4	G	coarse		sm	1.37	1	
00-385	260	3	6.36	4.2	G	cordm		sm	1.49	1	
00-385	254	1	6.65	2.3	G	ind lin st		sm/smdg	1.2	1	
00-385	256	2	6.98	3.1	G	sm		sm	1.12	1	
00-385	255	2	7.03	3.4	G	sm		sm/smdg	1.04	1	
00-385	266	2	7.07	3	G	sm		sm	1.38	1	
00-385	262	1	7.5	2	G	sm		sm	1.24	1	
00-385	264	2	7.51	2.2	G	sm		sm/smdg	1.34	1	
00-385	257	1	7.63	2.8	G	sm		sm	1.43	1	
00-385	265	2	7.75	3.2	G	coarse		sm	1.24	1	
00-385	253	3	7.93	7	G	coarse		sm	1.4	1	
00-385	258	3	8.18	7.5	G	sm		sm	1.41	1	
00-385	263	1	8.7	3.3	G	sm		sm/smdg	1.17	1	
00-385	251	3	9.47	7.4	G	curv comp st	ind	sm	1.48	1	
00-385	261	2	11.57	6.8	G	ind st		sm	1.5	1	
00-401	269	2	0	1.6	G	eroded		brn/smdg	1.37	1	
00-401	259	2	4.47	2.7	G	sm		sm	2	1	
00-401	303	2	5.28	2	G	cordm		sm/smdg	1.43	1	
00-401	325	3	5.3	3	S	sm		sm	1.87	1	
00-401	317	2	5.49	2.1	G	sm		sm	1.26	1	
00-401	288	2	5.64	2.1	G	sm		sm	1.07	1	
00-401	272	1	5.73	1.7	G	sm		sm	1.31	1	
00-401	284	2	5.82	2.4	G	cordm		sm	1.36	1	
00-401	333	2	5.96	3.2	G	ind st		sm	1.68	1	
00-401	295	2	6.14	2	G	cordm		sm	1.3	1	
00-401	291	1	6.2	2.2	G	sm		sm	1.27	1	
00-401	322	3	6.29	7.2	G	cordm		sm/smdg	1.4	1	
00-401	319	2	6.41	2.8	G	cordm		sm	0.78	1	
00-401	274	2	6.43	4.2	G	sm		sm	1.7	1	
00-401	316	2	6.51	3	G	sm		sm	1.5	1	
00-401	285	2	6.56	3.8	G	ind lin st		sm	1.65	1	
00-401	286	2	6.62	2.4	G	sm		sm	1.37	1	
00-401	282	2	6.74	1.9	S	sm		sm	1.77	1	
00-401	278	1	6.74	2.4	G	incs	ind	sm/smdg	0.98	1	
00-401	2720	2	6.83	4.6	G	sm		sm	1.73	1	
00-401	267	2	6.84	3.3	G	cordm		sm/smdg	1.37	1	
00-401	265	1	6.89	2.6	G	sm		sm	2.05	1	
00-401	260	2	6.89	3.8	G	ind st		brn/smdg	1.64	1	
00-401	262	3	6.97	4.8	G	cordm		sm/smdg	1.53	1	
00-401	275	1	7.05	2.7	G	sm		sm	1.59	1	
00-401	289	1	7.07	1.9	G	sm		sm/smdg	1.32	1	
00-401	287	2	7.07	2.9	G	cordm		sm	1.37	1	
00-401	261	1	7.16	2.2	G	sm		sm/smdg	1.45	1	
00-401	283	2	7.18	3.1	G	sm		brn/smdg	1.31	1	
00-401	323	4	7.19	14	G	coarse		sm	1.45	1	
00-401	270	2	7.2	4.2	G	coarse		sm/smdg	1.28	1	
00-401	301	2	7.23	2.5	G	cordm		sm	1.37	1	
00-401	298	3	7.25	6.6	G	sm		sm	1.66	1	
00-401	321	3	7.26	5.3	G	ind st		sm/smdg	1.59	1	
00-401	327	3	7.26	4.1	G	sm		sm	0.94	1	
00-401	300	1	7.28	2.5	G	sm		sm	2.05	1	
00-401	263	2	7.31	3.8	G	coarse		sm	1.54	1	
00-401	293	3	7.35	9	G	sm		sm	1.24	1	
00-401	277	1	7.37	2.2	G	sm		sm	1.99	1	
00-401	329	2	7.48	3.3	G	sm		brn/smdg	1.27	1	
00-401	314	4	7.55	6.6	S	sm		sm	1.99	1	
00-401	294	2	7.56	4	G	coarse		sm	1.25	1	
00-401	255	6	7.73	29.4	G	coarse		sm	1.62	1	
00-401	299	2	7.76	2.5	G	cordm		sm	1.37	1	
00-401	312	3	7.83	4.7	G	sm		sm	1	1	
00-401	296	2	7.86	2.8	G	sm		sm	1.12	1	
00-401	271	1	7.87	2.2	G	sm		sm/smdg	1.97	1	
00-401	318	2	8.03	4.6	G	sm		sm	1.54	1	
00-401	326	2	8.08	3.5	G	sm		sm	1.04	1	
00-401	308	1	8.12	2.4	G	cordm	sm over	sm/smdg	2.29	1	
00-401	311	1	8.12	2.3	G	sm		sm/smdg	1.5	1	
00-401	324	1	8.16	2.3	G	coarse		sm	1.61	1	
00-401	315	2	8.17	4	G	sm		sm/smdg	2.24	1	
00-401	258	2	8.34	2.6	G	eroded		sm	1.68	1	
00-401	307	2	8.35	4.7	G	coarse		sm/smdg	1.65	1	
00-401	281	2	8.37	3.4	G	rgh		sm/smdg	1.14	1	corn cob
00-401	331	1	8.43	2.4	G	ind st		sm/smdg	1.08	1	carinated shoulder
00-401	266	3	8.44	9.9	G	rgh		sm	1.35	1	corn cob
00-401	320	3	8.57	10.4	G	sm		sm	0.92	1	
00-401	276	2	8.63	8.1	G	rgh		sm/smdg	1.98	1	corn cob
00-401	268	2	8.72	6.4	G	sm		sm/smdg	1.58	1	
00-401	302	3	8.73	8.1	G	sm		sm/smdg	1.12	1	
00-401	256	6	8.77	28.6	G	scr		sm	1.38	1	
00-401	309	2	8.91	3.1	G	cordm		sm/smdg	1.72	1	
00-401	280	2	8.97	5.5	G	cordm	sm over	sm	1.56	1	
00-401	328	4	9.04	12	G	rgh		sm	1.8	1	corn cob
00-401	209	2	9.04	5.6	G	coarse		sm/smdg	1.45	1	
00-401	330	2	9.11	3.9	G	sm		sm/smdg	1.92	1	
00-401	306	3	9.15	9	G	rgh		sm	1.84	1	corn cob
00-401	297	3	9.27	9.9	G	coarse		sm/smdg	1.16	1	

00-401	264	1	9.4	3.2	G	rgh		sm/smdg	1.62	1	corn cob
00-401	310	2	9.52	4.1	G	sm		sm/smdg	1.5	1	
00-401	292	3	9.62	6.4	G	cordm	sm over	sm	1.09	1	
00-401	305	3	10.42	9.3	G	coarse		sm	1.92	1	
00-401	257	4	11.32	25.1	G	cordm		sm/smdg	1.8	1	base fragment
00-401	304	2	11.74	6.5	G	coarse		sm/smdg	1.34	1	
00-401	273	1	11.79	2.1	G	cordm		brn/smdg	1.52	1	
00-516	257	2	6	7.6	G	ind lin st		sm	1.33	1	
00-516	255	4	6.94	11.6	G	curv comp st	ind	sm	1.8	1	
00-516	256	2	8.17	5.5	G	coarse		sm	1.52	1	
99-1	523	3	7.51	5.2	G	coarse		sm	1.12	1	
99-1	520	3	8.31	8.5	G	coarse		sm	1.23	1	
99-1	510	2	8.87	6.3	G	ind lin st		sm	1.41	1	
99-10	316	1	0	1.2	G	coarse		eroded	1.13	1	
99-10	317	1	0	1.2	S	eroded		eroded		1	
99-10	304	3	0	2.9	S	sm		eroded		1	
99-10	299	2	0	2.3	G	eroded		sm		1	
99-10	268	3	3.37	4.5	grit	ind lin st		sm	0.82	1	
99-10	262	3	4.66	4.6	S	sm		eroded		1	
99-10	285	2	5.13	1.9	G	cordm	sm over	sm	1.48	1	
99-10	300	2	5.4	3.2	G	coarse		sm	1.43	1	
99-10	269	2	5.44	2	S	cordm		eroded		1	
99-10	301	2	5.56	4.6	grit	ind lin st		sm	0.7	1	micaceous paste
99-10	290	4	5.91	6.2	S	sm		eroded		1	
99-10	278	4	5.91	11.6	G	coarse		brn	1.41	1	
99-10	282	4	5.94	5.5	S	sm		sm		1	
99-10	260	3	5.97	4.2	S	sm		eroded		1	
99-10	309	1	6.06	2.8	grit	ind st		sm	1.05	1	
99-10	289	2	6.14	3	S	sm		sm		1	
99-10	257	4	6.2	8.3	S	sm		sm		1	
99-10	294	2	6.21	3.2	S	eroded		sm		1	
99-10	318	3	6.26	12.4	G	brn		brn	1.07	1	
99-10	252	3	6.28	5.2	S	sm		eroded		1	
99-10	295	3	6.33	4.1	S	sm		sm		1	
99-10	307	2	6.36	3	grit	check st	>3mm	sm	0.78	1	
99-10	270	3	6.52	4.7	G	coarse		brn	1.62	1	
99-10	291	2	6.54	2.9	G	sm		sm	1.33	1	
99-10	296	1	6.58	1.8	G	sm		brn	0.79	1	
99-10	279	3	6.58	5.4	grit	brn		brn/smdg	0.85	1	
99-10	314	2	6.65	3.1	S/CR	sm		brn/smdg	1.9	1	
99-10	312	1	6.69	1.8	S	sm		sm		1	
99-10	287	2	6.76	2	S	sm		eroded		1	
99-10	272	4	6.83	11.2	G	coarse		brn	1.34	1	
99-10	273	3	6.9	4.4	S	eroded		sm		1	
99-10	293	2	6.91	3.3	G	brn		sm	1.37	1	
99-10	311	2	7.17	2.6	S	eroded		eroded		1	
99-10	288	2	7.2	3.1	G	coarse		sm	1.75	1	
99-10	308	1	7.21	2.2	G	sm		brn	1.96	1	
99-10	261	2	7.22	1.9	S	eroded		sm		1	
99-10	258	1	7.24	1.5	grit	ind st		brn/smdg	0.5	1	
99-10	267	1	7.27	2	G	ind st		sm	2.05	1	
99-10	310	1	7.38	1.7	S	sm		sm		1	
99-10	271	4	7.47	15.3	G	sm		brn	1.59	1	
99-10	303	3	7.55	4.9	S	brn		sm		1	
99-10	298	4	7.68	7.2	S	eroded		sm		1	
99-10	313	2	7.82	2.8	S	eroded		sm		1	
99-10	305	1	7.93	1.5	G	coarse		brn	1.47	1	
99-10	266	3	7.95	2.4	S	sm		sm		1	
99-10	284	2	7.95	3.7	G	coarse		brn	1.5	1	
99-10	281	3	7.97	3.7	S	eroded		sm		1	
99-10	276	2	8.03	3.6	G	sm		sm	0.9	1	
99-10	274	5	8.05	19.8	G	coarse		coarse	1.76	1	
99-10	292	2	8.11	1.6	S	sm		eroded		1	
99-10	302	2	8.12	4.1	G	coarse		sm	1.4	1	
99-10	306	3	8.31	4.3	S	sm		sm		1	
99-10	315	2	8.43	4.1	G	coarse		sm	1.62	1	
99-10	259	2	8.53	4.9	G	coarse		sm	1.75	1	
99-10	264	1	8.55	2.2	G	coarse		sm		1	
99-10	254	4	9	12.3	G	coarse		sm	1.83	1	
99-10	275	2	9.68	7.3	G	coarse		coarse	2.17	1	
99-10	297	3	10.11	6.8	S	scr		sm		1	
99-10015	254	2	5.86	0	G	ind lin st		sm/smdg	1.13	1	
99-10015	256	3	7.25	0	G	cordm		sm	1.25	1	
99-10015	255	3	7.5	0	G	cordm		sm	1.35	1	
99-10034	252	3	7.92	8.1	G	ind lin st		sm	2.31	1	
99-10036	251	2	7.73	4.9	G	cordm		sm	1.82	1	
99-10037	253	2	8.45	4.7	G	coarse		sm/smdg	3.32	1	
99-10037	252	2	8.54	4.3	G	coarse		sm	1.7	1	
99-10037	254	4	8.56	17.7	G	ind lin st	ovrst	sm	1.92	1	
99-10039	263	2	7.14	4.8	G	sm		eroded	1.34	1	
99-10039	256	2	7.3	4.3	G	ind st	sm over	sm	1.26	1	
99-10039	259	3	7.77	5.7	G	sm		sm	1.53	1	
99-10039	255	2	7.95	2.8	G	ind lin st		sm	1.12	1	
99-10039	262	4	8.42	10.9	G	cordm		sm	1.63	1	
99-10039	258	2	8.46	4.2	G	ind st		sm	1.26	1	
99-10039	257	3	8.47	10.2	G	ind lin st	sm over	sm	1.5	1	
99-10039	264	2	8.48	1.9	S	sm		sm		1	
99-10039	260	3	8.72	5.7	G	eroded		scr	2.1	1	
99-10039	261	2	9.25	6.2	grit	ind lin st	sm over	sm	0.8	1	
99-10044	251	2	0	2.4	G	eroded		brn	1.5	1	
99-10044	252	2	5.02	2.3	G	coarse		brn	1.4	1	
99-10045	254	2	6.47	2	G	ind lin st		sm	0.89	1	
99-10045	253	3	7.64	5.1	G	ind st		sm	1.16	1	
99-10045	256	1	8.36	1.9	G	ind st		sm	1.55	1	
99-10045	252	1	9.1	2.3	G	ind st		brn	0.95	1	
99-10046	7	2	5.86	2.7	G	ind st		sm	1.24	1	
99-10046	3	2	6.27	2.5	G	ind lin st		sm	1.49	1	
99-10046	1	3	8.36	6.1	G	sm		brn	1.3	1	
99-10046	5	2	9.1	4.8	G	ind st		brn	1.3	1	
99-10046	2	2	9.27	3.5	G	sm		brn/smdg	1.3	1	
99-10046	6	2	9.44	4.8	G	cordm		brn/smdg	1.44	1	
99-10047	252	1	0	1.3	G	eroded		sm	2.5	1	
99-10047	254	2	0	1.7	G	ind lin st		eroded	1.7	1	
99-10047	253	1	7.69	1.7	G	sm		sm	2.06	1	
99-10048	6	2	0	2.1	G	ind lin st		eroded	1.12	1	
99-10048	7	2	0	1.8	G	eroded		eroded	0.92	1	
99-10048	8	12	7.2	103.1	G	ind st	sm over	brn/smdg	1.77	1	
99-10048	4	3	8.93	7.3	G	sm		sm/smdg	1.01	1	
99-10048	5	2	9.26	7	G	sm		sm	1.38	1	
99-10049	256	2	7.25	0.9	G	ind st		sm	1.25	1	
99-10049	252	2	7.59	4	G	curv comp st	ind	sm	1.72	1	
99-10049	254	3	9.15	4.3	G	sm		sm	1.35	1	
99-10049	255	1	9.5	1.8	G	eroded		sm	1.52	1	
99-10049	253	1	12.41	3.3	G	sm		sm	1.36	1	
99-10052	257	2	6.38	4.8	G	ind lin st	sm over	sm	2.37	1	
99-10052	258	3	6.91	5.8	grit	ind st	sm over	sm	0.7	1	
99-10052	256	2	9.48	3.9	G	ind lin st		sm/smdg	3.18	1	
99-10052	254	3	9.56	9.3	G	curv comp st	ind	sm/smdg	1.38	1	
99-10052	255	2	9.97	7.4	G	ind st		sm/smdg	1.99	1	
99-10056	252	4	7.78	15.6	G	curv comp st	conc circles	coarse	2.02	1	
99-10056	253	2	7.85	5.7	G	ind lin st		sm	1.12	1	
99-10067	253	3	6.7	9.1	G	ind st	sm over	sm	1.08	1	
99-10067	255	2	6.83	2.3	G	ind lin st		sm	1.4	1	
99-10067	254	3	7.52	8.4	S	sm		sm/smdg	1.73	1	
99-10070	255	2	6.07	3.7	G	cordm		sm	0.99	1	
99-10070	254	1	9.59	2.2	G	eroded		sm	1.56	1	
99-10075	1	5	9.4	12.9	S	sm		sm/smdg		1	
99-10075	2	3	9.51	3.9	S	sm		sm/smdg		1	

99-10082	253	3	8.18	7.8	G	coarse		sm	2.88	1	
99-10084	255	2	7.35	5.1	G	ind lin st		sm	2.43	1	
99-10085	254	1	0	1.1	G	eroded		sm/smdg	1.62	1	
99-10087	261	2	7.74	3.1	G	sm		sm	1.23	1	
99-10087	260	2	8.22	2.7	G	ind lin st		sm	1.09	1	
99-10087	259	1	9.38	2.2	G	sm		sm	1.68	1	
99-10088	251	2	0	1.8	G	eroded		sm/smdg	1.15	1	
99-10092	256	1	7.59	2.1	G	sm		sm	0.68	1	
99-10092	255	3	8.04	6	G	coarse		sm/smdg	2.31	1	
99-10093	10	2	6.14	3.3	G	cordm		sm	2.48	1	
99-10093	11	3	6.52	7.8	G	cordm		coarse	2.08	1	
99-10093	13	6	8.02	31.2	G	ind lin st		scr	1.21	1	
99-10093	9	3	9.02	7.5	G	ind lin st		eroded	2.82	1	
99-10093	12	5	10.09	24.4	G	ind st	sm over	brn/smdg	1.63	1	
99-10094	255	1	5.97	1.7	G	cordm		sm	1.56	1	
99-10095	256	2	0	1.7	G	eroded		sm	1.38	1	
99-10095	255	2	5.72	2.6	G	scr		sm	1.44	1	
99-10095	257	2	10.36	4	grit	sm		sm	0.98	1	
99-10096	10	3	5.44	5.2	G	coarse		sm	1.32	1	
99-10096	8	2	6.46	6.3	grit	ind lin st	sm over	brn/smdg	0.78	1	
99-10096	11	3	6.89	4.7	G	ind lin st	sm over	sm	1.62	1	
99-10096	7	3	7.62	8.2	G	ind st	sm over	eroded	1.61	1	
99-10096	9	3	7.71	6.8	G	sm		sm	1.6	1	
99-10096	6	2	8.49	6.9	G	ind lin st	sm over	sm	1.35	1	
99-1012	252	2	7.6	3.3	G	sm		sm	1.65	1	
99-1023	262	1	6	1.1	S	sm		sm	0	1	
99-1023	259	2	6.06	2.4	G	ind st		eroded	1.83	1	
99-1023	255	4	6.7	10	G	coarse		sm	1.08	1	
99-1023	257	2	7.1	2.9	G	sm		brn/smdg	1.47	1	
99-1023	260	2	7.7	2.9	G	ind st		sm	1.33	1	
99-1023	263	1	7.76	2.3	G	ind lin st		sm	1.32	1	
99-1023	256	3	7.8	11.3	G	coarse		sm	1.25	1	
99-1023	258	2	8.28	4	G	sm		sm	1.5	1	
99-1023	264	1	9.14	3.7	G	sm		brn/smdg	1.34	1	
99-1023	261	2	9.5	3.7	G	sm		sm	1.46	1	
99-1039	256	1	0	1.3	G	sm		eroded	1.67	1	
99-1039	251	2	0	3	G	sm		eroded	1.96	1	
99-1039	262	2	5	2.5	G	sm		sm	1.12	1	
99-1039	263	3	6.02	4	S	sm		sm	0	1	
99-1039	254	1	6.18	1.5	G	sm		sm	1.52	1	
99-1039	264	3	6.42	9.6	G	coarse		brn	1.72	1	
99-1039	259	4	6.94	9.8	G	coarse		brn	1.06	1	
99-1039	266	3	7	2.5	S	sm		sm	0	1	
99-1039	255	1	7.4	2.4	G	sm		sm/smdg	2.28	1	
99-1039	267	3	7.8	6.6	G	sm		sm	1.8	1	
99-1039	253	1	7.8	1.6	G	cordm		sm	1.5	1	
99-1039	265	5	8.22	10.2	S	sm		sm	0	1	
99-1039	260	6	8.32	31.9	G	coarse		sm	1.22	1	
99-1039	261	2	9.5	7	G	sm		sm	1.74	1	
99-1040	252	2	8.27	2.6	G	cordm		sm/smdg	1.3	1	
99-1044	293	2	0	1.7	S	eroded		sm		1	
99-1044	297	1	0	1.5	S	eroded		eroded		1	
99-1044	302	2	0	2.9	grit	eroded		eroded	0.7	1	
99-1044	294	2	5.04	2.2	S	sm		brn		1	
99-1044	299	1	5.23	0.8	S	sm		sm		1	
99-1044	283	2	5.33	2.2	grit	ind lin st		brn	1.12	1	
99-1044	269	2	5.5	2.4	grit	coarse		sm	0.6	1	
99-1044	266	2	6.08	2.8	G	coarse		brn	1.04	1	
99-1044	273	1	6.17	2.4	G	ind lin st		sm	1.42	1	
99-1044	277	2	6.24	5	G	coarse		sm	1.6	1	
99-1044	292	1	6.32	1.2	S	eroded		eroded		1	
99-1044	282	2	6.34	2.2	G	sm		brn	0.89	1	
99-1044	287	1	6.63	2	G	scr		sm	0.92	1	
99-1044	280	2	6.75	2.5	G	brn		brn	1.6	1	
99-1044	298	2	6.77	1.6	S	sm		sm		1	
99-1044	271	2	6.91	5.1	G	ind lin st		sm	1.43	1	
99-1044	296	1	6.95	1.3	S	sm		sm		1	
99-1044	281	3	7.02	6.3	G	coarse		sm	1.07	1	sooted
99-1044	264	1	7.02	1.5	G	ind st		brn/smdg	1.63	1	
99-1044	284	2	7.14	2.8	grit	coarse		eroded	0.96	1	
99-1044	257	2	7.15	5.1	G	brn		brn/smdg	0.77	1	
99-1044	295	2	7.22	2.4	S	sm		sm		1	
99-1044	275	2	7.3	4.4	G	ind st		sm	1.62	1	
99-1044	301	2	7.5	5.3	grit	brn		coarse	0.56	1	
99-1044	285	1	7.53	2.6	G	ind lin st		brn	1.35	1	
99-1044	256	2	7.55	4.1	grit	coarse		sm	0.66	1	
99-1044	262	4	7.82	8	G	sm		sm	1.05	1	
99-1044	263	3	7.99	4	S	eroded		sm		1	
99-1044	289	1	8	1.9	G	brn		eroded	1.13	1	
99-1044	255	3	8.03	4.7	G	sm		brn	0.99	1	
99-1044	270	2	8.07	4.6	G	sm		sm	2.12	1	
99-1044	288	2	8.08	3.1	G	ind st		brn	2.05	1	
99-1044	276	1	8.19	2.9	G	ind st		coarse	1.31	1	
99-1044	278	2	8.23	2.9	S	sm		sm		1	
99-1044	279	2	8.34	4.1	G	coarse		eroded	1.39	1	
99-1044	267	1	8.58	1.5	S	fn punc		sm		1	
99-1044	286	1	8.93	2.1	G	eroded		eroded	2.07	1	
99-1044	290	4	9.18	19.1	grit	sm		brn/smdg	0.95	1	
99-1044	272	2	9.19	4.6	G	coarse		sm	0.73	1	
99-1044	268	1	9.5	2.1	S	sm		sm		1	
99-1045	7	2	0	0.9	S	eroded		eroded		1	
99-1045	6	2	0	1.3	S	sm		eroded		1	
99-1045	38	0	0	0.4	S	eroded		eroded		1	
99-1045	37	0	0	0.6	S	eroded		eroded		1	
99-1045	34	2	5.5	2.9	S	sm		sm		1	
99-1045	36	2	5.5	2.9	S	sm		sm		1	
99-1045	14	3	5.69	4.2	S	sm		sm		1	
99-1045	31	2	5.87	2.5	G	coarse		brn		1	
99-1045	8	2	5.91	1.1	S	sm		sm		1	
99-1045	11	4	5.98	8.4	S	scr		sm		1	
99-1045	9	1	6.05	1.3	S	sm		sm		1	
99-1045	15	3	6.17	4.3	S	sm		sm		1	
99-1045	16	3	6.58	4.2	S	scr		eroded		1	
99-1045	13	5	7	10.9	S	scr		sm		1	
99-1045	33	2	7.21	2	S	brn		sm		1	
99-1045	32	2	7.22	1.7	S	sm		eroded		1	
99-1045	35	2	7.29	3	S	scr		eroded		1	
99-1045	3	1	7.32	1.4	G	brn		brn		1	
99-1045	28	2	7.34	2.9	G	coarse		sm		1	
99-1045	29	2	7.67	3.5	G	coarse		sm		1	
99-1045	18	2	7.72	4.4	S	scr		eroded		1	
99-1045	30	2	7.84	2.8	G	sm		sm		1	
99-1045	12	2	7.85	6.1	grit	check st	>3mm	brn		1	
99-1045	2	1	8.18	1.5	grit	brn		brn/smdg		1	
99-1045	19	1	8.55	1.4	S	sm		sm		1	
99-1048	265	3	5.17	5.1	G	coarse		brn/smdg	1.35	1	base fragment
99-1048	258	3	5.3	5.1	G	ind st	sm over	sm/smdg	1.47	1	
99-1048	259	2	6.06	3	G	coarse		brn/smdg	1.28	1	
99-1048	256	2	6.74	3.9	G	sm		sm/smdg	1.59	1	
99-1048	261	2	8.12	5.8	G	ind st	sm over	sm	1.47	1	
99-1048	255	3	8.52	4.9	G	sm		sm/smdg	1.58	1	
99-1048	252	3	9.22	8.9	G	coarse		sm	1.68	1	
99-1048	268	1	9.4	1.8	G	sm		sm	1.38	1	
99-1050	251	1	8.09	2.1	grit	sm		sm	1.14	1	
99-1062	9	2	0	1.9	S	eroded		eroded		1	
99-1062	270	1	0	1	S	eroded		sm		1	
99-1062	267	2	0	1	S	sm		eroded		1	
99-1062	8	2	0	1.7	S	eroded		sm		1	

99-1062	7	2	3.82	1.6	S	sm		sm		1	fine shell
99-1062	283	2	5.56	2.7	G	eroded		coarse	1.7	1	
99-1062	6	3	5.68	7.6	S	brn		brn		1	
99-1062	15	2	5.95	1.8	S	sm		sm		1	
99-1062	254	2	6.08	1.8	G	eroded		coarse	1.68	1	
99-1062	252	2	6.74	2.3	G	sm		brn	1.72	1	
99-1062	255	3	6.86	4.8	G	sm		sm	2.07	1	
99-1062	266	2	6.9	2	S	sm		sm		1	
99-1062	268	2	7.07	3.3	G	rgh		sm	0.85	1	corn cob
99-1062	251	1	7.65	1.6	S	sm		sm		1	
99-1062	12	4	7.7	3.9	S	scr		eroded		1	
99-1062	262	3	7.82	9.4	G	coarse		sm	2	1	
99-1062	261	2	7.95	4	S	sm		sm		1	
99-1062	1	3	8.15	8.9	G	rgh		sm	1.24	1	corn cob
99-1062	10	2	8.29	2.9	S	sm		sm		1	
99-1062	13	4	8.44	8.9	S	scr		eroded		1	
99-1062	258	3	8.66	6.8	G	cordm	sm over	sm	2.56	1	
99-1062	14	2	10.3	4.4	S	sm		sm		1	
99-1064	251	2	5.75	2.3	grit	ind lin st		brn	0.81	1	
99-1065	2	4	6	8	G	cordm	sm over	sm	1.71	1	
99-10676	260	2	8.65	2.5	G	ind lin st		sm	1.22	1	
99-10678	1	2	6.78	3.4	G	ind lin st		sm	1.91	1	
99-10680	251	2	18.31	9.2	G	sm		sm	1.18	1	base fragment
99-1070	254	2	5.98	2.3	S	scr		sm	0	1	
99-1070	256	3	6.58	2.9	S	sm		sm/smdg	0	1	
99-1070	251	2	6.9	5	G	ind lin st		sm	0.98	1	
99-1070	260	2	7.12	3	S	scr		sm/smdg	0	1	
99-1070	253	3	7.38	4.8	G	sm		brn	1.22	1	
99-1070	258	2	7.8	3.8	G	sm		sm	1.72	1	
99-1070	255	1	7.94	2.1	G	sm		sm	1.45	1	
99-1070	259	3	8.32	6.5	G	sm		sm	1.52	1	
99-1070	257	4	8.73	7.5	G	sm		sm	1.74	1	
99-1070	252	2	8.9	2.6	S	sm		sm/smdg	0	1	
99-1071	3	1	6.89	2.7	G	ind lin st		brn/smdg	1.58	1	sooted
99-1073	272	2	0	4.5	G	eroded		eroded	2.65	1	
99-1073	278	1	0	2.8	G	eroded		brn	1.08	1	
99-1073	264	2	6.06	2.3	S	scr		sm		1	
99-1073	268	1	6.12	2.1	G	ind lin st		brn	1.17	1	
99-1073	271	1	6.17	2	G	sm		brn	0.92	1	
99-1073	273	1	6.17	2.1	G	coarse		brn	1.97	1	
99-1073	263	4	6.55	7.5	grit	sm		brn	1.05	1	base fragment
99-1073	262	2	6.76	2.8	G	coarse		coarse	1.4	1	
99-1073	270	2	6.84	2.6	G	sm		brn	0.95	1	
99-1073	258	2	7.16	3.6	G	brn		brn	1.83	1	
99-1073	261	4	7.53	8.4	grit	ind st		sm	1.42	1	
99-1073	259	2	7.83	3	G	sm		sm	1.55	1	
99-1073	277	2	8.36	6.1	G	ind st		brn	1.09	1	
99-1073	252	2	8.51	1.8	S	sm		sm		1	
99-1073	276	1	8.53	3.4	G	sm		coarse	1.52	1	
99-1073	274	1	8.95	1.9	G	coarse		brn	1.42	1	
99-1073	256	4	8.97	15.7	G	sm		coarse	1.14	1	
99-1073	257	3	9.33	12.3	G	sm		brn	0.97	1	
99-1073	275	1	9.36	2.8	G	coarse		sm	1.49	1	
99-1073	254	1	9.45	1.9	G	sm		brn	1.69	1	
99-1073	269	3	9.85	6.9	G	sm		sm	1.65	1	
99-1078	307	1	0	1.2	G	sm		eroded	1.1	1	
99-1078	274	3	0	6.7	G	eroded		sm	1.87	1	
99-1078	286	2	0	1.9	S	eroded		eroded	0	1	
99-1078	253	3	5.08	1.4	S	sm		sm	1.64	1	
99-1078	277	3	5.97	3	S	eroded		eroded	0	1	
99-1078	288	3	6.04	5.1	G	coarse		sm	1.75	1	
99-1078	279	4	6.07	5.8	S	scr		sm/smdg	0	1	
99-1078	297	1	6.28	1.7	S	scr		sm	0	1	
99-1078	308	1	6.34	1.7	S	sm		sm	0	1	
99-1078	280	3	6.36	2.7	S	eroded		eroded	0	1	
99-1078	311	2	6.42	2	S	scr		sm	0	1	
99-1078	315	2	6.48	4.5	G	ind st	sm over	sm	1.74	1	
99-1078	309	2	6.5	1.8	S	sm		sm/smdg	0	1	
99-1078	278	3	6.52	4.2	S	scr		sm/smdg	0	1	
99-1078	284	4	6.72	12.3	G	ind lin st		sm	1.94	1	
99-1078	303	3	6.86	5.7	G	sm		sm/smdg	1.89	1	
99-1078	262	2	6.92	3.6	G	sm		sm	1.18	1	
99-1078	287	2	6.94	3.8	G	brn		sm	1.09	1	
99-1078	270	2	6.96	3.4	G	coarse		sm	1.37	1	
99-1078	316	3	6.98	6.9	G	cordm		eroded	2.09	1	
99-1078	298	2	6.98	4.7	G	eroded		sm	0.96	1	
99-1078	264	2	7.02	1.8	S	scr		sm	0	1	
99-1078	281	2	7.12	2.1	S	scr		sm/smdg	0	1	
99-1078	301	5	7.14	12	G	coarse		sm/smdg	1.07	1	
99-1078	276	3	7.2	3.7	S	sm		sm	0	1	
99-1078	254	5	7.22	10.4	S	sm		sm	0	1	
99-1078	306	1	7.25	1.6	S	sm		sm/smdg	0	1	
99-1078	273	2	7.28	3.8	S	scr		sm	0	1	
99-1078	314	2	7.3	3.1	G	sm		sm	1.32	1	
99-1078	265	3	7.34	10.6	G	sm		sm/smdg	1.18	1	sooted
99-1078	305	3	7.35	4.8	S	sm		sm	0	1	
99-1078	252	4	7.7	4.1	S	scr		sm	0	1	
99-1078	283	6	7.8	19.7	S	sm		scr	0	1	sooted
99-1078	320	2	7.8	5.6	G	curv comp st	ind	sm/smdg	1.56	1	
99-1078	325	4	7.8	8.6	S	sm		sm	0	1	
99-1078	272	1	7.92	1.9	G	sm		eroded	1.89	1	
99-1078	269	2	7.92	2.6	G	sm		sm	2.31	1	
99-1078	256	3	7.94	6.8	G	ind lin st		sm/smdg	1.02	1	
99-1078	312	2	7.96	1.6	G	sm		sm	1.52	1	
99-1078	263	2	7.99	3.7	G	coarse		sm	1.32	1	
99-1078	282	4	8.04	19.6	G	sm		sm	1.32	1	
99-1078	299	3	8.1	7.8	G	sm		sm/smdg	1.7	1	
99-1078	257	3	8.12	8.5	G	sm		sm	1.07	1	
99-1078	260	3	8.18	9.5	G	scr		brn/smdg	1.25	1	
99-1078	251	4	8.28	12.5	G	sm		sm/smdg	1.64	1	
99-1078	294	2	8.42	3.8	G	sm		sm/smdg	1.44	1	
99-1078	275	3	8.58	8.9	G	sm		sm	1.35	1	
99-1078	293	1	8.62	2.6	G	coarse		sm	1.72	1	
99-1078	289	5	8.8	15.9	G	sm		sm	1.15	1	
99-1078	255	3	8.87	10.5	G	sm		sm	1.62	1	
99-1078	258	2	8.94	6	G	sm		sm	1.22	1	
99-1078	268	3	9.1	11.7	G	ind st	sm over	sm	2.07	1	
99-1078	285	5	9.1	15.8	G	coarse		sm	1.1	1	
99-1078	267	3	9.42	8.9	G	sm		sm	1.96	1	
99-1078	295	4	12.95	15.7	G	sm		sm	2	1	
99-1082	38	3	0	3.9	S	sm		eroded		1	
99-1082	24	1	0	3.1	G	eroded		sm		1	
99-1082	20	2	0	2.3	G	eroded		brn		1	
99-1082	16	2	5.88	3.2	grit	ind st		brn/smdg		1	
99-1082	34	3	6.08	6.5	S	scr		sm		1	
99-1082	19	3	6.26	3.1	S/CR	coarse		sm		1	
99-1082	9	3	6.26	4.9	G	cordm	sm over	sm		1	
99-1082	21	2	6.3	4	G	brn		brn		1	
99-1082	36	3	6.53	5.4	G	sm		sm		1	
99-1082	10	3	6.65	4.1	G	cordm	sm over	sm		1	
99-1082	35	3	6.89	9.4	G	coarse		brn		1	
99-1082	2	1	6.99	1.3	S	eroded		eroded		1	
99-1082	37	3	7.16	9.6	G	coarse		brn/smdg		1	
99-1082	29	2	7.2	2.9	S	sm		sm		1	
99-1082	22	2	7.23	5.8	G	coarse		coarse		1	
99-1082	1	2	7.28	2	S	sm		eroded		1	
99-1082	39	2	7.39	2.7	S	sm		eroded		1	
99-1082	32	4	7.45	9.9	S	sm		eroded		1	

99-1082	15	3	7.67	4.9	S	eroded		eroded		1	
99-1082	33	4	7.73	13.9	G	coarse		brn		1	
99-1082	27	3	7.89	4.7	S	sm		sm		1	
99-1082	40	1	7.92	1.5	G	sm		sm		1	
99-1082	13	3	8.17	3.2	S	eroded		eroded		1	
99-1082	11	3	8.17	6	S	sm		sm		1	
99-1082	30	5	8.19	11.4	S	sm		eroded		1	
99-1082	41	2	8.2	3.6	G	sm		sm		1	
99-1082	23	3	9.19	5.3	S	sm		eroded		1	
99-1090	257	2	5.82	1.8	G	cordm		sm/smdg	1.12	1	
99-1091	254	2	6.5	3	grit	sm		sm	1.05	1	
99-1098	258	1	7.8	1.9	G	cordm		sm	1.07	1	
99-1098	257	2	10.02	7.2	G	curv comp st	ind	sm/smdg	2.12	1	
99-1099	253	3	7.14	4.8	S	sm		sm	0	1	
99-11	254	1	0	1.4	G	eroded		eroded	0.55	1	
99-11	252	2	0	1.4	G	eroded		brn	0.9	1	
99-11	251	2	6.63	2.3	G	ind lin st		sm	2.44	1	
99-11	253	2	8.74	2.2	G	ind lin st		sm	1.57	1	
99-11081	254	2	6.53	2.1	S	sm		sm	3.22	1	
99-11081	259	4	7.1	14.5	G	comp st	ind	sm	1.7	1	
99-11081	257	2	7.43	2.4	G	sm		sm	1.68	1	
99-11081	256	3	8.09	7.3	G	sm		sm	1.31	1	
99-11081	258	2	9.35	5	G	ind st		sm	2.08	1	
99-11082	7	4	6.75	8.6	G	sm		brn/smdg	1.47	1	
99-11082	3	3	6.87	8.7	G	ind st	sm over	sm	1.93	1	
99-11082	4	3	7.7	5.1	G	coarse		sm	1.12	1	
99-11082	6	3	8.6	8.4	G	sm		sm	1.67	1	
99-11082	5	3	8.78	8.9	G	ind st		sm	1.72	1	
99-11082	2	3	9.51	8.2	G	coarse		sm	1.42	1	
99-11087	19	2	6.1	3.5	S	sm		sm	1.79	1	
99-11087	14	4	6.49	14	G	coarse		coarse	1.64	1	
99-11087	18	2	7.21	2.3	S	sm		sm	1.39	1	
99-11087	17	3	7.5	7.2	G	ind st		sm	1.94	1	
99-11087	15	5	7.92	14.2	G	smpl st	ovrst	sm	1.82	1	comp design made with a smpl paddle?
99-11087	20	5	8.06	21.2	G	curv comp st	ind	sm	1.92	1	
99-11087	16	2	9.31	4.3	G	coarse		sm	1.95	1	
99-11090	4	2	6.68	2.7	S	sm		sm/smdg	1.67	1	
99-11094	3	4	5.96	13.2	G	coarse		sm	1.56	1	
99-11094	8	6	6.92	22	G	coarse		sm	2.13	1	
99-11094	6	5	7.29	11.8	S	sm		sm	2.51	1	
99-11094	10	6	7.68	21.2	G	smpl st	ovrst	sm	1.15	1	comp design made with a smpl paddle?
99-11094	2	3	7.73	5.5	S	sm		sm/smdg	2.47	1	
99-11094	9	6	8.4	21.5	G	cordm		sm	1.7	1	
99-11094	5	7	8.68	26.8	G	ind lin st		sm	1.97	1	
99-11094	7	5	8.69	20.1	G	ind lin st		sm	1.8	1	wide grooves
99-11094	4	3	9.45	11	G	ind lin st		sm	1.46	1	
99-11418	258	2	0	2.8	G	eroded		eroded	1.32	1	
99-11418	256	1	5.45	2.5	grit	incs	ind par hrz lines	sm	0.86	1	
99-11418	260	2	6.7	2.8	G	sm		sm	0.6	1	
99-11418	257	2	7.02	5.6	G	curv comp st	ind	sm	1.08	1	
99-11418	254	4	7.45	15.8	G	cordm		sm	1.48	1	
99-11418	253	2	7.8	4.3	grit	ind lin st		sm	0.87	1	
99-11418	255	2	8.25	4.6	G	cordm		sm	1.1	1	
99-11418	259	3	8.25	10.1	G	coarse		sm	1.52	1	
99-11429	1336	3	6.68	5.3	G	scr		sm	1.1	1	
99-11429	1223	3	7.53	7.7	G	ind st		sm	1.47	1	
99-11429	1237	4	11.15	14.7	G	sm		sm	1.38	1	carinated shoulder
99-11430	398	2	7.75	3.5	G	sm		sm	1.4	1	
99-11430	334	3	8.81	8.2	G	sm		sm	1.05	1	
99-11431	385	3	6.65	8.2	grit	ind lin st		sm	0.57	1	
99-11441	391	2	6.5	3	G	coarse		sm/smdg	1.7	1	
99-11441	411	2	6.52	3.9	G	sm		sm	1.15	1	
99-11441	328	3	7.42	5.8	G	curv comp st	ind	sm	1.64	1	
99-11441	415	2	7.5	3.2	G	sm		sm	0.67	1	
99-11441	319	3	8.08	6.5	G	sm		sm	0.89	1	
99-11452	262	1	0	1.4	G	eroded		coarse	1.9	1	
99-11452	265	2	5.78	1.8	G	sm		eroded	1.78	1	
99-11452	271	2	6.42	3.5	G	sm		sm	0.98	1	
99-11452	264	2	6.68	2.8	G	sm		sm	1.96	1	
99-11452	273	2	6.72	3.8	G	ind st		sm	1.45	1	
99-11452	272	2	6.72	2.2	G	coarse		eroded	0.57	1	
99-11452	274	2	6.75	4.5	G	ind st		sm	1.54	1	
99-11452	266	4	6.96	10.6	G	ind lin st		sm	1.92	1	
99-11452	268	2	7	4.5	G	sm		sm	1.58	1	
99-11452	259	2	7.02	2.8	G	ind st		sm	1.08	1	
99-11452	263	2	7.05	2.1	G	ind lin st		sm	1.28	1	
99-11452	270	3	7.14	5.8	G	ind lin st		sm	0.98	1	
99-11452	261	3	7.18	3	G	coarse		sm	1.25	1	
99-11452	260	2	7.32	1.8	G	sm		sm	1.53	1	
99-11452	276	3	7.34	6	G	ind lin st		sm	1.04	1	
99-11452	257	5	7.48	18.3	G	sm		sm	1.18	1	
99-11452	275	2	8.12	4	G	comp st	ind	sm	1.18	1	
99-11452	258	3	8.89	6.6	G	sm		sm	1.32	1	
99-11452	267	2	9.54	2.4	G	sm		sm	1.32	1	
99-11531	1	2	8.39	4.8	G	scr		sm	1.3	1	
99-11620	239	3	8.05	5.7	G	ind lin st		sm	1.37	1	
99-11629	73	2	0	3.5	S	sm		eroded		1	
99-11629	111	2	0	3.1	S	eroded		eroded		1	
99-11629	118	2	0	2.5	S	eroded		eroded		1	
99-11629	39	3	4.82	8.4	G	br		sm/smdg	1.82	1	
99-11629	77	2	4.94	2.6	S	sm		sm		1	
99-11629	132	6	5.17	13.7	S	sm		sm		1	
99-11629	88	3	5.82	7.6	G	coarse		sm/smdg	1.49	1	
99-11629	34	3	5.88	2.8	S	sm		sm		1	
99-11629	67	3	5.99	5.8	S	sm		sm		1	
99-11629	152	3	6	3.3	S	sm		sm		1	
99-11629	157	2	6.08	3.9	grit	scr		brn/smdg	1.08	1	
99-11629	145	3	6.11	3.4	S	scr		sm		1	
99-11629	10	6	6.12	12.7	S	scr		sm		1	
99-11629	66	3	6.14	5.3	S	eroded		eroded/ smdg		1	
99-11629	144	2	6.15	3.6	S	sm		sm		1	
99-11629	102	3	6.2	4	S	scr		sm/smdg		1	
99-11629	151	2	6.22	2.7	S	sm		sm/smdg		1	
99-11629	121	2	6.28	1.7	S	eroded		eroded		1	
99-11629	134	3	6.3	6.8	grit	sm		sm	1.18	1	
99-11629	109	2	6.31	2.4	S	sm		sm		1	
99-11629	76	3	6.31	4.8	S	sm		sm		1	
99-11629	147	2	6.32	3.3	S	sm		sm		1	
99-11629	60	3	6.36	5.1	S	sm		sm		1	sooted
99-11629	65	4	6.4	7.5	S	sm		sm		1	
99-11629	46	3	6.41	7.9	S	sm		sm		1	
99-11629	136	2	6.42	3.1	S	sm		sm		1	
99-11629	138	3	6.42	3.2	S	sm		sm		1	
99-11629	27	3	6.44	4.6	S	sm		sm		1	
99-11629	122	1	6.46	1.5	S	eroded		sm		1	
99-11629	62	4	6.48	7.3	S	sm		sm		1	sooted
99-11629	137	2	6.5	2.6	S	sm		sm		1	
99-11629	93	3	6.5	4.7	S	sm		sm		1	
99-11629	54	3	6.52	4	S	scr		scr		1	
99-11629	19	5	6.56	17.6	S	scr		scr		1	
99-11629	141	2	6.58	3	S	scr		eroded		1	
99-11629	125	3	6.6	5.5	S	sm		sm		1	
99-11629	107	2	6.6	2	S	eroded		sm		1	
99-11629	140	3	6.64	3.4	S	sm		sm		1	

99-11629	112	2	6.65	3.6	S	brn		sm		1	
99-11629	30	3	6.67	4.4	S	sm		sm		1	
99-11629	69	5	6.68	12.2	S	sm		sm		1	
99-11629	49	4	6.68	7	S	sm		sm/smdg		1	
99-11629	42	4	6.72	6.6	S	sm		sm		1	
99-11629	79	2	6.76	2.6	S	sm		sm		1	
99-11629	150	2	6.78	2.8	S	sm		sm		1	
99-11629	142	2	6.82	2.9	S	sm		sm		1	
99-11629	3	5	6.87	23.2	S	sm		sm		1	
99-11629	117	2	6.87	2.8	S	sm		sm		1	
99-11629	99	3	6.89	4.9	S	sm		sm		1	
99-11629	105	2	6.89	4.2	G	coarse		brn/smdg	1.28	1	
99-11629	149	2	6.91	2.6	S	sm		sm		1	
99-11629	8	5	6.93	12.7	S	sm		sm		1	
99-11629	38	3	6.94	6.8	G	ind st	sm over	brn/smdg	1.56	1	
99-11629	51	4	6.94	8.2	S	sm		sm		1	
99-11629	43	3	6.98	5	S	sm		sm		1	
99-11629	98	2	7.01	3.8	S	sm		sm/smdg		1	
99-11629	57	3	7.01	6.2	S	sm		sm		1	
99-11629	56	3	7.02	5.1	S	sm		sm		1	
99-11629	85	2	7.07	3	S	eroded		eroded		1	
99-11629	100	3	7.07	4.6	S	sm		scr		1	
99-11629	139	2	7.08	3.8	S	sm		sm		1	
99-11629	120	2	7.09	3.7	grit	ind st	sm over	brn/smdg	0.7	1	
99-11629	78	1	7.1	1.8	S	sm		sm		1	
99-11629	31	3	7.13	3.4	S	sm		sm		1	
99-11629	7	7	7.17	17.2	S	sm		sm		1	
99-11629	4	6	7.18	17.8	S	sm		sm		1	
99-11629	81	3	7.2	3.5	S	sm		sm		1	
99-11629	59	3	7.27	6.2	S	sm		sm		1	
99-11629	156	2	7.28	3.5	grit	scr		brn/smdg	1.21	1	
99-11629	113	2	7.28	2.8	S	sm		eroded		1	
99-11629	16	3	7.32	9.4	S	sm		sm		1	
99-11629	123	1	7.38	2.9	grit	ind st	sm over	brn/smdg	1	1	
99-11629	58	5	7.44	8.8	S	eroded		eroded		1	
99-11629	89	3	7.44	8	grit	curv comp st	ind sm over	sm	1.12	1	
99-11629	29	2	7.46	5.4	G	scr		brn/smdg	1.94	1	
99-11629	82	2	7.46	2.5	G	ind lin st		brn/smdg	1.23	1	
99-11629	146	2	7.52	3.6	S	sm		sm		1	
99-11629	119	2	7.6	2.1	S	brn		eroded		1	
99-11629	41	4	7.66	8	S	sm		sm		1	
99-11629	32	3	7.68	5	S	sm		sm		1	
99-11629	74	2	7.68	4.1	S	sm		sm		1	
99-11629	80	2	7.68	3.1	G	sm		brn/smdg	1.28	1	
99-11629	87	3	7.76	10.9	G	sm		sm	1.76	1	
99-11629	72	2	7.82	3.5	S	sm		sm		1	
99-11629	95	3	7.85	4.3	S	sm		sm		1	
99-11629	84	3	7.86	6	S	sm		sm		1	
99-11629	61	4	7.87	13	G	coarse		brn/smdg	1.1	1	
99-11629	92	3	7.88	4.6	S	sm		eroded/ smdg		1	
99-11629	47	4	7.94	12.5	G	scr		sm	1.83	1	
99-11629	75	2	7.99	3.5	S	sm		sm.		1	
99-11629	143	3	8	3.5	S	sm		sm		1	
99-11629	153	2	8.06	2.4	S	eroded		eroded		1	
99-11629	71	2	8.08	3.8	G	sm		sm/smdg	0.92	1	
99-11629	97	2	8.12	3.6	S	sm		sm		1	
99-11629	104	2	8.22	4.3	S	sm		eroded		1	
99-11629	96	3	8.23	5.6	S	sm		eroded		1	
99-11629	63	4	8.24	10.1	S	sm		sm		1	
99-11629	108	2	8.27	4.2	S	sm		sm		1	
99-11629	53	3	8.38	6.4	S	sm		sm		1	
99-11629	115	2	8.44	2	S	sm		sm		1	
99-11629	40	5	8.46	19.6	S	sm		sm		1	
99-11629	17	4	8.49	11.9	S	sm		sm		1	
99-11629	114	2	8.52	2.6	S	sm		sm		1	
99-11629	68	5	8.58	11.3	S	sm		sm		1	
99-11629	20	4	8.65	14.2	G	sm		coarse	1.4	1	
99-11629	155	2	8.71	3.4	S	sm		sm		1	
99-11629	131	2	8.76	6.1	G	ind lin st		sm	1.5	1	
99-11629	126	3	8.78	8.4	G	coarse		sm	1.67	1	
99-11629	55	3	8.89	6.9	S	sm		sm/smdg		1	
99-11629	154	3	8.95	3	S	sm		sm		1	
99-11629	148	2	9.01	4.8	S	sm		sm/smdg		1	
99-11629	45	3	9.04	6.9	S	scr		sm		1	
99-11629	70	3	9.11	9.2	G	ind lin st		sm	1.76	1	
99-11629	110	2	9.3	5.7	G	sm		brn/smdg	1.68	1	
99-11629	129	4	9.31	10.1	G	sm		coarse	2.25	1	
99-11629	48	5	9.5	21.6	G	coarse		coarse	2.22	1	
99-11629	94	3	9.5	5.9	S	sm		sm		1	
99-11629	22	4	9.52	22.4	G	coarse		coarse	1.68	1	
99-11629	6	7	9.52	55.1	G	coarse		coarse/ smdg	2.6	1	
99-11629	18	4	9.68	13.5	G	coarse		coarse	2.28	1	
99-11629	44	4	9.92	12.2	G	coarse		coarse	1.78	1	
99-11629	52	5	9.97	17.7	G	curv comp st	ind ovrst	sm	2.2	1	
99-11629	9	6	9.99	21.8	S	sm		sm		1	
99-11629	25	3	10.02	7.5	S	sm		sm		1	
99-11629	33	2	10.17	4.2	G	coarse		eroded	1.3	1	
99-11629	130	2	10.24	8.1	G	coarse		sm	2.07	1	
99-11629	86	3	10.26	6.8	G	coarse		coarse	1.62	1	
99-11629	23	4	10.34	14.9	G	coarse		coarse	1.99	1	
99-11629	128	3	10.48	9.8	G	coarse		sm	1.88	1	
99-11629	5	6	10.51	59.2	G	coarse		sm	1.82	1	
99-11629	90	2	10.6	6.4	G	coarse		coarse	1.65	1	
99-11629	24	4	10.8	13.1	S	sm		sm		1	
99-11629	28	4	10.94	20.7	G	coarse		sm/smdg	1.66	1	
99-11629	11	6	11.67	29.4	S	sm		sm		1	
99-11629	36	3	11.68	10.4	G	sm		sm	1.52	1	
99-11629	2	12	12.39	156.2	S	sm		sm		1	
99-11629	12	8	12.52	44.9	S	sm		sm		1	
99-11629	26	2	12.59	5	S	sm		sm		1	
99-11629	37	4	12.63	24.7	G	sm		sm	2.31	1	base fragment
99-11629	13	10	12.66	102.8	S	sm		sm		1	
99-11629	21	3	12.73	18.2	G	sm		sm	1.32	1	
99-11629	50	3	12.81	9.6	S	sm		sm		1	
99-1222	276	2	7.1	3.4	G	rgh		sm	2.04	1	
99-1257	7	2	6.9	2.8	G	ind st	sm over	sm/smdg	1.44	1	
99-1257	5	5	6.96	19.5	G	ind st	sm over	sm/smdg	1.52	1	sooted
99-1257	4	3	7.06	6.4	G	sm		sm/smdg	0.86	1	
99-1257	6	2	7.07	2.3	G	ind st	sm over	sm/smdg	2.4	1	
99-1294	251	3	9	9.6	G	sm		sm	1.57	1	
99-1295	252	3	8.06	7.7	G	coarse		sm	1.04	1	
99-1295	251	2	8.84	3.2	G	coarse		sm	1.08	1	
99-13	255	3	8.45	4.9	G	cordm		brn/smdg	0.97	1	
99-1304	3	2	8.12	3	G	brn		brn	1.26	1	
99-1304	1	2	8.9	4.1	G	coarse		brn/smdg	1	1	sooted
99-1304	2	4	14.06	24	G	ind st		sm	2.2	1	base fragment
99-1306	251	1	6.02	1.6	G	sm		sm	1.02	1	
99-1307	257	2	7.15	4.7	G	sm		sm	1.22	1	
99-1312	252	2	6.52	4	G	sm		sm	0.95	1	
99-1312	253	1	7.46	1.5	G	sm		sm	1.15	1	
99-1314	252	2	9.86	3.1	G	sm		sm	1.85	1	
99-15	1	2	7.47	2.9	G	ind lin st		sm	1	1	
99-1505	9	7	7.6	14	S	sm		sm	2.82	1	
99-1657	8	2	6.7	2.7	S	sm		sm	0	1	
99-1657	9	4	6.82	8.9	S	scr		sm	0	1	
99-1657	2	7	7.04	22.5	S	sm		sm/smdg	0	1	

99-1657	7	5	7.42	10	S	sm		sm/smdg	0	1	
99-1657	10	2	7.68	2.2	G	ind st		brn	1.15	1	
99-1657	4	6	7.72	16.3	S	sm		sm/smdg	0	1	
99-1657	3	11	7.96	37.9	S	sm		sm	0	1	
99-1657	5	5	8.32	13.2	S	sm		sm/smdg	0	1	
99-1657	6	2	9.18	4.1	G	sm		sm	1.48	1	
99-1663	253	2	6.02	3.1	S	sm		sm	0	1	
99-1702	253	8	6.45	38.7	G	scr		scr	1.29	1	
99-1702	251	7	7.98	36	G	coarse		sm	1.59	1	
99-1702	252	6	9.04	13.7	S	sm		sm		1	
99-1720	1	3	9.92	10.7	G	sm		sm	1.89	1	
99-1731	1	4	8.74	18.9	G	ind st		sm/smdg	2.48	1	
99-1739	336	2	5.63	2.7	G	sm		brn/smdg	1.08	1	
99-1739	421	4	8.27	9.8	G	coarse		brn	2.08	1	
99-1740	287	2	5.29	2.7	G	ind lin st		sm	1.33	1	
99-1a	470	4	9.44	13.6	G	coarse		sm	1.63	1	
99-1b	439	3	6.12	5.3	G	sm		sm/smdg	1.39	1	
99-1b	414	2	6.54	2.4	G	ind lin st		sm	1.06	1	
99-1b	394	1	6.7	2	G	sm		sm	0.76	1	
99-1b	432	3	7.2	5.7	G	sm		sm	1.57	1	
99-1b	458	1	7.2	2.5	G	sm		sm	1.21	1	
99-1b	433	2	7.45	1.9	G	ind st		sm	1.2	1	
99-1b	434	2	7.72	5.5	G	sm		sm	0.88	1	
99-1b	460	2	7.76	3.1	G	sm		sm	1.39	1	
99-1b	325	2	7.83	4	grit	comp st	ind	sm/smdg	0.85	1	
99-1b	332	4	7.99	12.1	G	sm		sm	1.3	1	
99-1b	372	2	8.1	5.5	G	sm		sm	1.21	1	
99-1b	450	2	8.13	5.6	G	coarse		sm	1.22	1	
99-1b	461	2	9.3	4.7	G	sm		sm	2.72	1	
99-1b	321	2	10.08	5.2	G	cordm		sm	2.95	1	
99-20	267	2	6.81	4.7	G	cordm		sm	0.95	1	
99-20	266	2	7	3.6	G	sm		sm	1.42	1	
99-20	270	3	7.96	4.9	G	ind st		sm	1.17	1	
99-202	252	1	5.5	1.3	S	rgh		sm	0	1	
99-204	257	2	5.36	2.5	grit	ind lin st		sm	1.08	1	
99-204	252	2	6.54	2.8	G	sm		sm/smdg	2.01	1	
99-204	254	2	6.84	2.6	G	ind lin st		sm/smdg	1.76	1	
99-204	253	2	7.17	4.2	G	ind st		sm/smdg	0.87	1	
99-2121	261	6	7.71	24.5	G	ind st	sm over	sm/smdg	1.32	1	
99-2168	252	2	7.52	2.9	G	coarse		sm	1.72	1	
99-2171	281	2	5.62	1.7	G	cordm		sm	1.8	1	
99-2171	280	2	6.15	2.5	G	ind lin st		sm	1.01	1	
99-2171	274	3	6.15	5.1	G	cordm		sm	1.38	1	
99-2171	268	3	6.26	5	G	cordm		brn	1.49	1	
99-2171	260	3	6.54	6.2	G	cordm		brn	1.97	1	
99-2171	264	3	6.59	7.1	G	cordm		brn	1.08	1	
99-2171	267	3	6.62	6.3	G	cordm		sm	1.59	1	
99-2171	262	5	6.84	11	G	cordm		brn	1.88	1	
99-2171	279	2	7	3.8	G	cordm		sm	1.06	1	
99-2171	266	4	7.07	13.6	G	cordm		brn	1.32	1	
99-2171	270	3	7.12	4.2	G	sm		sm	1.38	1	
99-2171	288	1	7.35	1.8	G	cordm		sm	1.41	1	
99-2171	273	2	7.47	4.8	G	cordm		brn	0.95	1	
99-2171	263	3	7.72	8.2	G	cordm		brn	1.93	1	
99-2171	255	4	7.8	14.5	G	curv comp st	ind	sm	1.16	1	
99-2171	265	3	7.83	7.4	G	sm		sm	1.96	1	
99-2171	286	1	7.94	2.6	G	ind st		sm	1.4	1	
99-2171	258	3	7.98	5.1	G	ind lin st		sm	1.72	1	
99-2171	282	2	8.02	2.4	G	sm		sm	1.26	1	
99-2171	276	2	8.23	3.3	G	cordm		sm/smdg	2.03	1	
99-2171	283	2	8.36	2.7	G	coarse		scr	1.64	1	
99-2171	269	3	8.39	5	G	incs	ind par hrz lines	sm/smdg	1.16	1	
99-2171	275	2	9.21	6.5	G	sm		sm	1.26	1	
99-2180	269	2	4.3	1.5	S	sm		sm	1.08	1	
99-2180	271	2	5.05	2	G	ind st		sm	0.94	1	
99-2180	259	3	5.86	7.6	G	cordm		sm	1.14	1	
99-2180	253	2	6.58	1.7	G	coarse		redfilmed	1.21	1	
99-2180	272	1	6.8	1.8	G	sm		sm	0.94	1	
99-2180	263	3	6.84	5.4	G	cordm		sm	0.65	1	
99-2180	257	5	7	18.5	G	cordm		sm	1.63	1	
99-2180	261	3	7.18	6.5	G	cordm		sm	1.01	1	
99-2180	270	2	7.56	3.2	G	coarse		sm	1.64	1	
99-2180	262	3	7.71	7.2	G	coarse		sm	1.56	1	
99-2180	265	1	8.19	2.2	G	ind lin st		sm	1.19	1	
99-2180	268	1	8.44	1.4	S	eroded		eroded	2.12	1	
99-2180	266	2	8.52	2.8	G	coarse		sm	1.56	1	
99-2180	267	1	8.61	1.6	G	incs	ind	sm/smdg	1.43	1	
99-2180	258	4	8.68	11.7	G	cordm		sm	1.11	1	
99-2180	256	4	8.69	15.5	G	cordm		coarse	2.05	1	
99-2180	251	2	9.2	6.4	G	ind st		sm	1.2	1	
99-2184	273	7	3.1	6.2	G	sm		sm	1.29	1	
99-2184	279	1	4.03	1	G	coarse		sm	1.54	1	
99-2184	269	3	5.94	3.3	G	ind lin st		brn/smdg	1.34	1	
99-2184	267	3	6.01	5.4	G	cordm		sm	1.14	1	
99-2184	265	3	6.03	6.9	G	ind lin st		sm	1.03	1	
99-2184	268	2	6.09	3.4	G	eroded		sm	3.59	1	
99-2184	261	5	6.15	12.3	G	cordm		sm	2.53	1	
99-2184	277	2	6.16	2.7	G	cordm		sm	2.09	1	
99-2184	264	4	6.27	7.7	G	cordm		sm	1.37	1	
99-2184	260	7	6.3	22.5	G	cordm		brn/smdg	1.37	1	
99-2184	275	2	6.31	2	G	sm		sm	1.25	1	
99-2184	276	2	6.38	2	G	cordm		sm	1.35	1	
99-2184	270	3	6.48	4.7	G	cordm		sm	1.59	1	
99-2184	254	4	6.74	13.7	G	ind lin st		sm	1.15	1	
99-2184	253	6	7.21	17.1	G	cordm		sm	1.36	1	
99-2184	266	5	7.27	13.1	G	ind lin st		sm/smdg	1.2	1	
99-2184	256	2	7.31	4.2	G	ind st		sm/smdg	1.75	1	
99-2184	272	3	7.31	3.9	G	sm		sm	1.93	1	
99-2184	255	2	7.7	6.1	G	incs	ind par hrz lines	sm/smdg	1.66	1	
99-2184	263	4	8.07	9.2	G	ind st		sm	1.37	1	
99-2184	271	2	8.13	3.7	G	sm		sm	1.92	1	
99-2184	262	4	8.31	9.1	G	ind lin st		sm	1.66	1	
99-2184	257	7	8.42	38.6	G	coarse		sm	1.67	1	
99-2184	274	2	9.49	4.2	G	sm		sm	2.15	1	
99-2202	280	2	4.84	1.4	G	sm		sm/smdg	1.33	1	
99-2202	275	2	4.85	1.5	G	sm		sm	1.33	1	
99-2202	271	2	5.66	3.3	G	ind lin st		sm	1.88	1	
99-2202	273	1	5.77	1.7	G	ind lin st		sm	1.16	1	
99-2202	258	4	6.07	7.3	G	cordm		sm	1.68	1	
99-2202	268	2	6.17	2.1	G	ind st		sm	1.31	1	
99-2202	277	2	6.32	3.4	G	ind lin st		sm	2.12	1	
99-2202	261	3	6.47	6.4	G	ind lin st		sm	1.52	1	
99-2202	267	2	6.58	2.5	G	cordm		brn	1.52	1	
99-2202	260	4	6.69	8.9	G	cordm		sm	1.29	1	
99-2202	264	3	6.72	4.5	G	cordm		sm	0.81	1	
99-2202	252	5	6.89	15	G	cordm		sm	1.96	1	
99-2202	272	2	6.94	3.5	G	sm		brn	0.5	1	carinated shoulder
99-2202	278	1	7.01	2.1	G	coarse		sm	1.56	1	
99-2202	265	3	7.07	4.5	G	scr		sm	1.27	1	
99-2202	263	3	7.09	5	G	coarse		sm	1.56	1	
99-2202	259	3	7.28	6.9	G	cordm		sm	1.63	1	
99-2202	279	1	7.73	2	G	sm		sm	1.47	1	
99-2202	266	3	7.9	5.5	G	rgh		sm	1.67	1	corn cob
99-2202	256	11	8.75	86.3	G	cordm		sm	1.41	1	
99-2205	253	2	7.47	3.1	G	sm		sm	1.9	1	
99-2210	262	2	6.14	3	G	ind lin st		brn	0.92	1	

99-2210	264	2	6.79	2.8	G	ind lin st		brn	1.62	1
99-2210	263	2	6.84	3.8	S	sm		sm	2.67	1
99-2233	262	3	0	3.5	S	sm		sm	1.15	1
99-2233	274	2	4.5	1.7	S	sm		sm	1.7	1
99-2233	269	2	5.42	3	G	ind lin st		sm	0.9	1
99-2233	268	2	5.73	3.3	grit	comp st	ind	sm	0.87	1
99-2233	258	2	6.12	2.9	S	sm		sm	1.72	1
99-2233	270	2	6.14	2.5	S	sm		sm	2.87	1
99-2233	254	3	6.16	8.1	G	sm		sm/smdg	1.61	1
99-2233	256	3	6.23	5	S	sm		sm	3.29	1
99-2233	273	2	6.46	1.9	S	sm		sm	2.4	1
99-2233	265	2	6.68	3	S	sm		sm	2.06	1
99-2233	266	2	6.94	4	G	ind lin st		sm	0.94	1
99-2233	261	3	6.95	7.1	G	ind lin st		sm	1.53	1
99-2233	275	1	7.01	1.7	G	sm		sm	0.96	1
99-2233	272	2	7.02	2.8	G	ind st		brn/smdg	1.7	1
99-2233	260	2	7.03	4.1	G	curv comp st	ind	sm/smdg	1.45	1
99-2233	257	3	7.33	5	S	sm		sm	2.6	1
99-2233	276	2	7.59	2.2	G	sm		sm	1.74	1
99-2233	263	2	7.76	7.8	G	coarse		sm	1.59	1
99-2233	264	2	8.31	5.3	G	sm		brn/smdg	1.54	1
99-2396	255	3	5.4	3	G	eroded		sm	1.16	1
99-2396	256	3	5.93	4.8	G	coarse		sm	1.01	1
99-2403	254	2	7.25	2	G	coarse		sm/smdg	1.11	1
99-2483	251	4	7.05	0	G	ind lin st		sm/smdg	1.71	1
99-261	324	3	9.23	4.6	G	sm		sm	1.77	1
99-2662	251	2	5.4	2.1	G	sm		sm	1.21	1
99-272	268	2	6.95	2.8	G	brn		sm		1
99-2842	3	3	6.09	3.8	G	cordm		sm	1.64	1
99-2842	1	2	7.23	2.1	G	coarse		sm	1.75	1
99-2842	2	4	7.68	9.1	G	ind lin st		sm	1.48	1
99-2870	252	3	5.99	3.4	G	coarse		sm	1.85	1
99-2884	254	2	0	2.7	G	eroded		sm	1	1
99-2884	252	2	0	2.8	G	eroded		sm	1.32	1
99-2884	258	3	7	5.4	G	ind lin st		sm/smdg	1.56	1
99-2884	255	2	7.08	2.9	G	cordm		sm	1.27	1
99-2884	253	1	7.44	3.1	G	cordm		sm	1.21	1
99-2884	257	2	8.05	2	G	ind st		sm	1.22	1
99-2884	251	2	9.14	2.5	G	ind lin st		brn/smdg	1.45	1
99-2885	251	2	0	2.6	G	eroded		sm	2.26	1
99-2885	253	2	0	3.3	G	eroded		sm	1.04	1
99-2885	259	2	6.12	2.5	G	ind lin st		brn/smdg	1.72	1
99-2885	257	2	6.46	3.8	G	eroded		sm	0.98	1
99-2885	261	2	6.53	1.9	S	eroded		eroded	1.08	1
99-2885	255	1	6.94	1.3	G	ind lin st		sm	1.82	1
99-2885	256	2	7.12	2.4	G	ind lin st		sm	1	1
99-2885	252	3	7.22	5.7	G	coarse		sm/smdg	1.06	1
99-2885	260	1	7.5	1.9	G	sm		sm	1.51	1
99-2885	258	2	7.58	2.2	G	coarse		brn/smdg	0.96	1
99-2885	254	2	9.03	4.7	G	sm		sm	1.86	1
99-2888	251	2	0	1.9	G	eroded		sm	0.87	1
99-2889	7	2	0	2.3	G	ind st		eroded	1.08	1
99-2889	6	2	7.43	3.6	G	sm		sm	0.67	1
99-2890	255	2	7.77	2.8	G	coarse		sm	1.76	1
99-2891	254	1	5.75	5.8	G	sm		sm/smdg	1.1	1
99-2891	253	2	7.06	3.2	G	comp st	ind	sm	1.58	1
99-2891	255	1	7.28	1.9	G	sm		sm	0.89	1
99-2892	256	1	6.8	2.3	G	sm		sm/smdg	0.62	1
99-2892	265	2	7.04	4.2	G	coarse		sm	1.24	1
99-2892	257	2	7.2	3.6	G	ind st		sm	1.28	1
99-2892	258	2	7.3	3	G	sm		sm	1.61	1
99-2892	259	2	7.3	4.8	grit	ind lin st		sm	0.54	1
99-2892	254	3	7.76	7.6	G	sm		sm	1.25	1
99-2892	263	2	8.7	3.5	G	cordm		sm	1.24	1
99-2892	260	3	8.75	7.5	G	ind lin st		sm	1.44	1
99-2892	262	2	9.13	3.5	G	ind lin st		sm/smdg	0.92	1
99-2892	264	2	9.13	2.2	G	ind lin st		sm/smdg	1.64	1
99-2892	261	3	10.46	6.4	G	ind lin st		sm	1.52	1
99-2892	255	2	11.02	4.9	G	sm		sm	1	1
99-2895	19	2	0	2.6	G	eroded		sm	1.86	1
99-2895	16	2	6.03	3.8	G	ind lin st		sm	1.72	1
99-2895	21	2	6.56	2.9	G	sm		sm	0.82	1
99-2895	27	2	6.96	3.8	G	cordm		sm	1.65	1
99-2895	22	2	8.25	3.7	G	ind lin st		sm	0.4	1
99-2895	20	2	8.28	2.3	G	cordm		sm	0.62	1
99-2895	23	2	8.79	4.2	G	brn		eroded	0.87	1
99-2896	251	2	9.85	2.6	G	sm		sm	1.68	1
99-2897	251	1	0	1.7	G	eroded		eroded	1.36	1
99-2897	252	3	7.31	6.2	G	cordm		sm	1.15	1
99-2899	260	1	0	2.1	G	eroded		sm	2.1	1
99-2899	261	1	0	2.5	G	eroded		eroded	1.74	1
99-2899	256	2	5.78	2.5	G	ind st		sm	1.22	1
99-2899	266	2	5.82	1.9	G	ind lin st		sm	0.82	1
99-2899	255	2	6.1	2.9	G	ind st	sm over	sm	1.48	1
99-2899	267	2	6.18	2.6	G	ind st		sm	1.08	1
99-2899	268	2	6.38	2	G	ind lin st		sm	1.28	1
99-2899	262	2	6.5	3.7	G	ind st		sm	1.44	1
99-2899	259	1	6.8	2.7	G	ind st		sm/smdg	1.9	1
99-2899	253	2	7.14	4.1	G	cordm		sm	1.65	1
99-2899	254	2	7.16	3	G	cordm	sm over	sm/smdg	1.22	1
99-2899	258	2	7.22	3.3	G	sm		sm	1	1
99-2899	257	2	7.25	4.6	G	ind st		sm/smdg	1.15	1
99-2899	264	2	8.4	2.5	G	eroded		sm	1.65	1
99-2899	263	2	8.41	1.5	G	eroded		sm/smdg	1.06	1
99-2901	252	2	5.38	2.1	G	ind st		coarse	1.07	1
99-2910	254	2	7.8	3.2	G	sm		sm	1.88	1
99-2911	4	3	6.12	4.6	G	ind lin st		sm/smdg	1.68	1
99-2915	258	2	9.06	3.8	grit	ind lin st		sm	1	1
99-2916	253	1	8.72	2.3	G	ind st		sm	1.45	1
99-2922	252	2	0	2.1	G	eroded		sm	1.07	1
99-2922	253	2	6.06	3.2	G	cordm		sm	0.74	1
99-2922	254	2	8.63	4.4	G	ind st		brn/smdg	1.96	1
99-2923	282	3	0	6.5	G	eroded		brn/smdg	1.23	1
99-2923	316	2	0	2.4	G	coarse		eroded	1.05	1
99-2923	318	2	0	2.6	G	coarse		eroded	0.98	1
99-2923	327	2	0	2.6	G	sm		sm/smdg	1.25	1
99-2923	323	2	0	1.9	G	sm		eroded	0.98	1
99-2923	321	2	0	2.9	G	eroded		sm	0.94	1
99-2923	320	2	0	3.5	G	sm		sm	1.13	1
99-2923	273	2	0	2.3	S/CR	ind lin st		sm/smdg	1.07	1
99-2923	289	1	0	1.9	G	eroded		sm	1.29	1
99-2923	331	2	0	1.8	G	eroded		brn/smdg	0.94	1
99-2923	306	1	0	2.1	G	ind st		eroded	1.3	1
99-2923	302	2	0	2.5	G	coarse		eroded	1.44	1
99-2923	334	2	0	2.6	G	eroded		brn/smdg	1.46	1
99-2923	336	1	0	1.5	G	eroded		eroded	1.63	1
99-2923	335	2	0	2.6	G	eroded		eroded	1.16	1
99-2923	341	3	5.36	7	grit	eroded		eroded	0.55	1
99-2923	262	3	5.53	3.4	G	ind lin st		sm	0.89	1
99-2923	294	2	5.86	2	G	ind lin st		sm	1.24	1
99-2923	338	2	5.98	1.9	S	sm		sm		1
99-2923	279	2	6.02	3.5	G	ind lin st		sm	0.85	1
99-2923	299	2	6.04	2.4	G	sm		sm	0.92	1
99-2923	268	2	6.13	3	G	cordm		sm	1.21	1
99-2923	266	2	6.16	3.9	G	ind lin st		sm	1.3	1
99-2923	312	2	6.16	2	G	coarse		sm	1.46	1
99-2923	286	2	6.28	2.7	G	sm		sm	0.68	1
99-2923	301	2	6.28	3.2	G	ind st		sm	1.18	1

99-2923	297	1	6.5	1.7	G	sm		sm	0.72	1	
99-2923	263	3	6.6	8	G	ind lin st		sm	1.9	1	
99-2923	259	3	6.63	11.8	G	cordm		sm	1.64	1	
99-2923	261	2	6.63	3.3	G	ind st		sm	1.06	1	
99-2923	317	2	6.82	2.4	G	ind st		sm	1	1	
99-2923	324	2	6.84	2.8	G	ind lin st		sm	1.13	1	
99-2923	296	2	6.87	2.3	G	ind st		sm	0.95	1	
99-2923	3190	3	6.89	4.9	G	coarse		brn/smdg	1.46	1	
99-2923	307	2	6.89	2.7	G	coarse		sm	1.58	1	
99-2923	272	3	6.96	6	G	cordm		sm	1.78	1	
99-2923	255	10	6.98	82.2	G	smpl st		sm	1.38	1	same vessel complex motif w/ smpl stamping; photograph
99-2923	337	2	7.01	4	G	ind st		sm	1.76	1	
99-2923	290	2	7.22	2.4	G	coarse		brn/smdg	0.9	1	
99-2923	264	3	7.3	9.6	G	ind lin st		sm	1.72	1	
99-2923	265	3	7.38	7.7	G	ind lin st		sm	1.69	1	
99-2923	267	2	7.42	5.3	G	cordm		eroded	1.48	1	
99-2923	276	3	7.44	4.5	G	comp st	ind	sm	1.1	1	
99-2923	277	3	7.44	5.9	G	ind lin st		sm	1.88	1	
99-2923	330	2	7.47	3.5	grit	eroded		sm	0.65	1	
99-2923	275	2	7.5	1.8	G	ind lin st		sm	1.28	1	
99-2923	291	2	7.55	3.7	grit	sm		sm	0.68	1	
99-2923	287	3	7.6	5.3	G	sm		sm	0.72	1	
99-2923	310	4	7.64	14.4	G	ind lin st		sm/smdg	1.56	1	
99-2923	308	2	7.64	2.4	G	eroded		sm/smdg	1.12	1	
99-2923	326	1	7.72	2.9	G	ind st		eroded	2.4	1	
99-2923	309	3	7.94	3.8	grit	sm		brn/smdg	0.96	1	
99-2923	311	3	7.98	8	G	ind st		sm	1.65	1	
99-2923	293	2	8	4.4	grit	ind st		sm	0.92	1	
99-2923	278	2	8.03	5	G	ind lin st		brn/smdg	1.42	1	
99-2923	280	3	8.05	10.8	G	sm		sm	1.06	1	
99-2923	288	3	8.05	4.3	G	ind st		sm	0.98	1	
99-2923	313	4	8.06	8.8	G	coarse		brn/smdg	1.59	1	
99-2923	340	2	8.12	3.5	G	ind st		eroded	1.26	1	
99-2923	333	3	8.17	3.4	G	ind st		brn/smdg	1.07	1	
99-2923	298	1	8.24	2.8	grit	ind st		sm/smdg	0.64	1	
99-2923	339	2	8.3	2.3	G	coarse		sm/smdg	1.2	1	
99-2923	314	1	8.37	1.9	G	ind st		sm	0.84	1	
99-2923	303	2	8.4	5	G	coarse		brn/smdg	1.24	1	
99-2923	295	2	8.47	2.4	G	ind st		sm/smdg	0.96	1	
99-2923	269	2	8.53	5.2	G	ind lin st		sm	0.78	1	
99-2923	329	1	8.62	1.8	G	ind st		sm	1.14	1	
99-2923	271	2	8.62	3.9	G	cordm		sm	1.3	1	
99-2923	304	1	8.74	3.2	G	ind st		sm	1.84	1	
99-2923	260	2	8.76	5.4	G	ind lin st		brn/smdg	1.86	1	
99-2923	256	6	9.15	28.4	G	smpl st		sm	2.08	1	same vessel complex motif w/ smpl stamping; photograph
99-2923	322	1	9.16	2.4	S/CR	sm		sm	1.64	1	
99-2923	300	1	9.18	2.7	G	ind st		sm/smdg	0.96	1	
99-2923	284	3	9.24	6.6	grit	sm		sm	1.04	1	
99-2923	270	3	9.28	9.5	G	ind lin st		coarse	1.8	1	
99-2923	283	3	9.28	7.6	G	ind st		sm	1.08	1	
99-2923	257	6	9.42	49.7	G	sm		brn	2.22	1	same vessel complex motif w/ smpl stamping; photograph
99-2923	319	2	9.52	3.8	G	coarse		sm/smdg	1.46	1	
99-2923	328	1	9.62	2.6	G	sm		brn/smdg	0.7	1	
99-2923	325	2	9.62	2.9	G	ind st		sm/smdg	1.3	1	
99-2923	258	3	9.62	10.9	G	br		sm	1.2	1	
99-2923	285	2	9.77	6.9	G	sm		sm/smdg	0.98	1	
99-2923	332	2	10.15	2.8	G	eroded		sm/smdg	1.51	1	
99-2923	274	2	10.18	6.6	G	cordm	sm over	eroded	1.12	1	
99-2923	292	2	10.44	3.9	G	scr		sm	1.25	1	
99-2923	281	3	11.26	8.3	G	coarse		eroded	1.27	1	
99-2923	305	2	11.52	6.2	G	coarse		brn/smdg	1.76	1	
99-2924	345	2	0	2.2	G	eroded		eroded	1.44	1	
99-2924	350	2	0	2.7	G	ind lin st		eroded	1.12	1	
99-2924	339	2	0	2.7	G	ind lin st		eroded	1.65	1	
99-2924	328	2	0	1.1	G	sm		eroded	1.65	1	
99-2924	321	2	0	1.6	G	eroded		eroded	1.52	1	
99-2924	332	2	0	2.2	G	eroded		sm	1.72	1	
99-2924	330	2	0	1.2	G	eroded		eroded	1.02	1	
99-2924	334	2	5.18	2.1	G	ind st		sm	1.35	1	
99-2924	280	2	5.25	2.7	G	ind st		sm	1.08	1	
99-2924	298	3	5.6	4.3	G	ind lin st		sm	0.98	1	
99-2924	311	3	5.68	5.4	S	sm		sm	2.05	1	
99-2924	318	3	5.9	3.7	G	sm		brn/smdg	1.4	1	
99-2924	353	1	5.98	2.5	G	ind st		sm	1.12	1	
99-2924	272	4	6.06	6.9	G	ind st		brn	1.82	1	
99-2924	303	2	6.1	3.9	G	ind lin st		sm	1.8	1	
99-2924	316	2	6.14	3.7	G	coarse		sm	1.04	1	
99-2924	327	1	6.21	2	G	ind lin st		sm	1.4	1	
99-2924	335	2	6.22	3.2	G	ind lin st		sm/smdg	1.15	1	
99-2924	310	1	6.24	3.2	grit	ind lin st		sm	0.78	1	
99-2924	269	4	6.32	10.1	G	smpl st	ovrst	sm	1.8	1	comp design made with a smpl paddle?
99-2924	276	4	6.34	8.6	G	ind lin st	ovrst	sm/smdg	1.45	1	
99-2924	288	3	6.38	7.4	G	ind lin st		sm/smdg	1.28	1	
99-2924	319	2	6.38	3.5	G	ind st		sm	1.45	1	
99-2924	257	7	6.4	30.9	G	ind lin st		sm/smdg	1.54	1	
99-2924	279	2	6.48	4.3	G	cordm		brn/smdg	1.14	1	
99-2924	302	4	6.5	8.9	G	ind lin st		sm	1.02	1	
99-2924	305	2	6.52	2.8	G	scr		sm	1.4	1	
99-2924	275	2	6.64	3.4	G	cordm		brn/smdg	2.21	1	
99-2924	267	4	6.68	9.7	G	comp st	ind	sm/smdg	0.89	1	
99-2924	258	7	6.7	35.7	G	ind lin st	ovrst	coarse	1.87	1	
99-2924	317	2	6.72	2.7	G	cordm		sm	0.98	1	
99-2924	354	2	6.78	3.4	G	coarse		coarse	1.82	1	
99-2924	300	3	6.8	4.8	G	ind lin st		sm	1.15	1	
99-2924	292	3	6.85	6.1	G	ind lin st		sm	1.98	1	
99-2924	263	4	6.9	11.9	G	curv comp st	ind	sm	2.3	1	carinated shoulder
99-2924	333	3	6.9	4.1	G	sm		eroded	1.6	1	
99-2924	307	2	7	3.9	G	ind lin st		sm/smdg	1.45	1	
99-2924	324	1	7.02	1.9	G	ind st		sm	1.72	1	
99-2924	336	2	7.02	2.6	G	ind lin st	sm over	eroded	1.62	1	
99-2924	343	1	7.02	2.5	G	coarse		sm	1.2	1	
99-2924	320	2	7.04	2.8	G	sm		eroded	1.58	1	
99-2924	313	2	7.06	4.1	G	sm		sm	2.31	1	
99-2924	331	1	7.08	1.9	G	sm		sm	1.75	1	
99-2924	287	3	7.1	6	G	br		sm/smdg	1.38	1	
99-2924	315	2	7.14	3.6	G	cordm		sm/smdg	1.65	1	
99-2924	294	3	7.15	4.8	G	cordm		eroded	1.5	1	
99-2924	286	4	7.18	9.2	G	sm		brn	1.68	1	base fragment
99-2924	285	4	7.18	5.4	G	ind lin st	sm over	sm/smdg	2.21	1	
99-2924	259	7	7.2	31.5	G	ind lin st	ovrst	sm	1.52	1	
99-2924	323	2	7.22	4	G	cordm		sm	1.9	1	
99-2924	306	3	7.28	8.6	G	curv comp st	ind scroll	sm/smdg	1.48	1	
99-2924	289	3	7.3	9.8	G	ind lin st		sm/smdg	1.08	1	
99-2924	348	4	7.3	11.5	G	coarse		sm	1.36	1	
99-2924	291	3	7.32	7.7	G	comp st	ind	brn/smdg	1.92	1	
99-2924	273	2	7.34	3.6	G	ind lin st		sm	2.1	1	
99-2924	264	5	7.35	18	G	scr		sm	2.12	1	
99-2924	342	2	7.35	3.9	G	coarse		redfilmed	1.72	1	
99-2924	355	2	7.38	3.7	G	coarse		sm/smdg	1.48	1	
99-2924	347	2	7.4	2.2	G	sm		sm	1.32	1	

99-2924	301	3	7.42	6.4	G	ind lin st	sm over	sm	1.52	1	
99-2924	265	5	7.42	8.6	S	sm		sm	2.54	1	
99-2924	283	3	7.44	6.5	G	sm		sm	1.6	1	base fragment
99-2924	277	4	7.52	12.3	G	cordm		brn/smdg	1.5	1	carinated shoulder
99-2924	284	3	7.58	5.8	G	curv comp st	ind	sm	1.5	1	
99-2924	356	4	7.6	12.2	G	ind lin st		sm/smdg	1.58	1	
99-2924	266	5	7.6	17.6	grit	comp st	ind	brn	1.3	1	
99-2924	338	3	7.65	5.9	G	curv comp st	ind	sm	1.2	1	
99-2924	296	3	7.68	6.3	G	ind lin st		sm	1.7	1	
99-2924	322	2	7.68	3.6	G	sm		sm	1.4	1	
99-2924	312	2	7.72	4.2	G	cordm		sm	2.73	1	
99-2924	352	2	7.78	2.9	G	ind st		sm	1.4	1	
99-2924	278	2	7.84	4.8	G	ind st	sm over	sm	1.25	1	
99-2924	304	3	7.87	6.4	G	ind st		sm/smdg	1.06	1	
99-2924	256	6	7.9	24.3	G	ind lin st		coarse	1.85	1	carinated shoulder
99-2924	274	3	7.94	7.9	G	coarse		sm	1.24	1	
99-2924	349	2	8.02	5.3	G	ind st		sm/smdg	2.01	1	
99-2924	295	3	8.04	4.4	G	sm		sm	1.45	1	
99-2924	297	4	8.08	10.8	G	curv comp st	ind	sm	1	1	wide grooves
99-2924	290	3	8.22	10.2	G	comp st	ind	brn/smdg	0.85	1	
99-2924	337	1	8.22	2.2	G	coarse		brn	1.42	1	
99-2924	262	4	8.28	9.9	G	smpl st	ovrst	sm	0.95	1	comp design made with a smpl paddle?
99-2924	293	4	8.3	13.1	G	comp st	ind	sm	0.98	1	
99-2924	268	3	8.3	8.2	G	comp st	ind	brn/smdg	1.25	1	
99-2924	346	2	8.3	2.4	G	ind lin st		brn/smdg	2.05	1	
99-2924	261	4	8.38	14.8	G	sm		brn	1.45	1	
99-2924	329	2	8.4	3.4	G	coarse		coarse	1.7	1	
99-2924	299	3	8.4	7.9	G	coarse		sm	1.64	1	
99-2924	281	2	8.4	4.5	G	ind st		sm/smdg	1.17	1	
99-2924	314	2	8.45	4	G	coarse		sm	2.7	1	
99-2924	326	3	8.52	7	G	curv comp st	ind	brn	1.48	1	
99-2924	341	3	8.62	5.8	grit	ind lin st		sm	0.81	1	carinated shoulder
99-2924	344	3	8.72	6.7	G	cordm		sm	1.85	1	
99-2924	309	3	8.74	5.3	G	cordm		sm	1.74	1	
99-2924	271	3	9	6.3	G	sm		sm	1.2	1	base fragment
99-2924	325	2	9.42	5.4	G	curv comp st	ind	sm	1.6	1	
99-2924	308	2	9.81	4.3	G	coarse		coarse	1.7	1	
99-2924	270	4	10.12	12.1	G	coarse		sm/smdg	2	1	base fragment
99-2924	260	6	10.38	34.8	G	ind lin st		coarse	2.15	1	
99-2924	340	2	10.5	4.5	G	coarse		sm	1.08	1	
99-2924	351	2	10.62	3.5	G	sm		sm	2.12	1	
99-2927	257	2	5.8	2	G	cordm		brn/smdg	0.9	1	
99-2927	258	2	6.52	2.9	G	sm		sm	1.62	1	
99-2927	261	2	6.68	3.6	G	ind st		sm	2.3	1	
99-2927	262	2	7.58	3.1	G	ind lin st		eroded	1.5	1	
99-2927	256	3	8.8	2.8	G	ind lin st		sm	1.47	1	
99-2927	259	1	8.8	2.3	G	ind st		sm	1.1	1	
99-2927	260	1	10.6	2	G	sm		sm	1.2	1	
99-2930	252	3	6.28	2.8	G	ind st		sm/smdg	1.3	1	
99-2934	265	4	5.99	4.3	grit	ind lin st		sm	0.73	1	
99-2934	260	2	7.31	3.6	grit	ind lin st		eroded	0.62	1	
99-2934	257	4	7.49	10.1	grit	ind lin st		sm	1.24	1	
99-2934	259	2	7.56	2.5	G	eroded		sm	0.96	1	
99-2934	261	2	8.27	3.2	G	eroded		sm	0.92	1	
99-2934	262	2	8.84	4	G	ind lin st	sm over	sm/smdg	1.17	1	
99-2934	258	4	9.64	10.3	G	ind st		scr	1.4	1	
99-2934	263	2	12.06	2.4	G	sm		sm/smdg	1.14	1	
99-2938	254	4	0	11.2	G	cordm		eroded	1.27	1	
99-2938	252	2	6.62	2	grit	ind st		sm	0.56	1	
99-2938	253	1	8.73	1.7	G	coarse		sm	1.32	1	
99-2938	256	3	9.15	12	G	coarse		sm	1.15	1	
99-2938	255	3	9.52	10.7	G	coarse		coarse	1.66	1	
99-2939	261	2	0	2.6	G	eroded		sm	1.06	1	
99-2939	265	3	6.16	7.7	G	ind lin st		sm/smdg	1	1	carinated shoulder
99-2939	259	3	6.75	3.4	G	ind st		sm/smdg	1.17	1	
99-2939	263	1	7.22	1.9	G	ind st		sm/smdg	1.02	1	
99-2939	266	3	7.38	7.1	G	ind lin st		sm	1.18	1	
99-2939	257	6	7.44	28.5	G	smpl st		sm	1.12	1	same vessel complex motif w/ smpl stamping; photograph
99-2939	260	3	7.52	7	G	comp st	ind	sm/smdg	1.32	1	
99-2939	262	2	7.92	3.3	G	ind lin st		sm	0.94	1	
99-2939	267	3	8.29	9	G	cordm		sm	1.4	1	
99-2939	256	5	8.54	26.4	G	coarse		sm	2.82	1	same vessel complex motif w/ smpl stamping; photograph
99-2939	255	8	8.58	52	G	smpl st		sm	2.59	1	same vessel complex motif w/ smpl stamping; photograph
99-2939	264	2	10.22	4.1	G	sm		sm	1.28	1	
99-2939	258	5	10.24	23.2	G	smpl st		sm	2.4	1	same vessel complex motif w/ smpl stamping; photograph
99-2939	253	6	10.4	24.8	G	smpl st		brn	1.46	1	same vessel complex motif w/ smpl stamping; photograph
99-2939	254	7	11.32	66.7	G	smpl st		sm	3.12	1	same vessel complex motif w/ smpl stamping; photograph
99-2944	255	2	0	2.4	G	eroded		sm/smdg	1.06	1	
99-2944	254	2	0	3.3	G	eroded		sm/smdg	0.8	1	
99-2944	253	2	6.32	3.1	G	cordm		sm	1.32	1	
99-2944	252	5	6.84	13.7	G	ind lin st		sm	1.55	1	
99-2944	251	1	7.88	1.8	G	cordm		sm	0.96	1	
99-2946	252	3	8.12	6.3	G	sm		sm	1.78	1	
99-2948	262	3	6.24	2.6	G	ind lin st		sm/smdg	1.95	1	
99-2948	256	2	7.14	5	G	ind lin st	sm over	sm/smdg	1.82	1	
99-2948	260	2	7.8	3.8	G	sm		sm	1.28	1	
99-2948	261	1	8.12	2.7	G	coarse		sm	1.12	1	
99-2948	263	1	9.33	2.9	G	ind lin st		sm	0.98	1	
99-2948	257	2	9.4	7.4	G	ind st	sm over	sm	1.48	1	
99-2948	259	2	9.42	4.4	G	sm		sm	1.18	1	
99-2948	258	2	9.42	6	G	ind lin st		sm	1.84	1	wide grooves
99-2950	261	7	6.5	24.6	G	ind lin st		sm/smdg	1.45	1	carinated shoulder
99-2950	260	5	6.9	14.8	G	smpl st	ovrst	coarse	1.98	1	comp design made with a smpl paddle?
99-2950	257	3	7.07	4	G	ind lin st		coarse	1.2	1	
99-2950	259	4	7.1	10.9	S	sm		sm	3.6	1	
99-2950	262	6	7.72	19.8	grit	ind lin st		sm/smdg	1.4	1	
99-2950	256	3	8.08	5.8	G	cordm		brn/smdg	1.52	1	
99-2950	264	2	8.55	2.7	G	ind st		sm/smdg	1.4	1	
99-2950	265	1	8.72	2	G	eroded		sm	1.2	1	
99-2950	254	3	8.74	6.6	G	comp st	ind	brn/smdg	1.42	1	
99-2950	255	4	9.28	9.7	G	curv comp st	ind scroll	sm	0.92	1	
99-2950	263	2	9.42	4.1	G	ind st		sm/smdg	1.5	1	
99-2950	258	5	9.62	13.8	G	smpl st	ovrst	brn/smdg	2.3	1	comp design made with a smpl paddle?
99-2952	254	2	6.72	5.1	G	ind lin st		sm	1.5	1	
99-2952	255	2	7.08	3.4	G	cordm		sm	1	1	
99-2953	252	2	0	1.8	G	coarse		eroded	1.28	1	
99-2953	254	2	6.4	2.1	G	sm		sm	1.2	1	

99-2953	251	2	6.7	2.8	G	ind st		sm	1.72	1	
99-2953	253	2	9.38	3.2	G	br		sm/smdg	1.14	1	
99-2954	267	2	0	2.3	G	sm		eroded	1.28	1	
99-2954	266	1	6.34	1.5	G	ind lin st		sm/smdg	1.18	1	
99-2954	271	3	6.48	3.9	G	ind st		sm	0.98	1	
99-2954	270	1	6.54	1.2	S	eroded		eroded		1	
99-2954	269	2	6.62	2.6	G	sm		coarse	1.8	1	
99-2954	265	2	6.64	2.5	grit	ind lin st		sm	0.75	1	
99-2954	262	3	6.98	4.6	G	ind st		sm	1.42	1	
99-2954	260	2	7.5	3	G	sm		sm	0.92	1	
99-2954	275	2	7.6	2.9	G	eroded		eroded	1.5	1	
99-2954	268	2	8.02	4.5	G	coarse		sm	2.1	1	
99-2954	261	2	8.35	4.3	G	ind lin st		sm	1.62	1	
99-2954	2750	1	8.5	2.4	G	ind lin st		sm/smdg	1.32	1	
99-2954	274	4	8.5	7.8	G	cordm		sm	1.38	1	
99-2954	273	2	8.56	4.1	G	ind st		eroded	1.12	1	
99-2954	272	1	8.58	2.4	G	ind lin st		sm	1.95	1	
99-2954	259	4	8.62	6.9	G	sm		sm	1.75	1	
99-2954	257	1	9.21	2.5	G	sm		eroded	1.31	1	
99-2954	258	3	9.44	7.5	G	cordm		sm/smdg	1.32	1	
99-2954	263	3	11.14	8.2	G	cordm		sm	1.62	1	
99-2956	252	3	6.46	5.6	G	ind lin st		sm/smdg	1.92	1	sooted
99-2956	254	2	7.88	2.6	G	cordm		sm/smdg	1.25	1	
99-2956	255	2	9.02	5.4	G	cordm		sm/smdg	1.5	1	
99-2956	253	2	9.42	3.8	G	cordm		sm/smdg	1.08	1	
99-2958	252	2	6.32	2.8	G	ind st	sm over	sm	1.08	1	
99-2958	254	2	6.82	2.9	G	sm		sm/smdg	1.52	1	
99-2958	256	2	7.34	5.6	G	ind lin st	sm over	sm	1.45	1	
99-2958	258	2	8.88	8	G	ind lin st		eroded	1.44	1	
99-2958	253	2	8.9	5.4	G	sm		sm	1.58	1	
99-2958	257	3	8.92	6	G	sm		sm	2.3	1	
99-2958	255	2	12.82	7	G	sm		sm/smdg	1.76	1	
99-2961	254	1	0	0.9	G	eroded		sm	1.08	1	
99-2961	252	2	7.2	3.1	G	ind lin st		sm/smdg	1.6	1	
99-2961	253	1	9.92	2	G	sm		sm	1.14	1	
99-2962	1	6	7.44	22.1	G	ind lin st		sm/smdg	1.2	1	
99-2965	2	9	6.97	44.7	grit	curv comp st	conc circles	sm	1.12	1	
99-2967	255	2	7.36	3.2	G	ind st	sm over	sm	1.13	1	
99-2967	256	2	7.37	5	G	ind lin st		sm	0.86	1	
99-2967	257	2	7.56	2.8	G	coarse		sm/smdg	0.75	1	
99-2967	254	3	7.68	7.3	G	coarse		sm	0.98	1	
99-2967	253	4	10.03	10.1	G	ind lin st		coarse	1.37	1	
99-2968	257	3	0	8.6	G	eroded		sm	0.9	1	
99-2968	259	2	0	3.6	G	eroded		coarse	1.18	1	
99-2968	256	2	0	2.8	G	eroded		eroded	1.76	1	
99-2968	258	2	5.86	4.4	G	ind lin st		sm/smdg	0.64	1	
99-2968	255	3	6.44	6.5	G	ind lin st		sm	1.43	1	
99-2968	263	3	6.84	6	G	ind st	sm over	brn/smdg	1.05	1	
99-2968	261	4	6.87	8.4	G	ind lin st	sm over	sm	1.18	1	
99-2968	268	1	7.06	2.7	G	ind lin st	sm over	eroded	1.59	1	
99-2968	265	2	7.24	3.4	G	ind st	sm over	sm	0.92	1	
99-2968	267	2	7.45	3.3	G	coarse		sm/smdg	0.86	1	
99-2968	262	3	7.9	7.6	G	coarse		brn/smdg	1.79	1	
99-2968	254	4	8.54	16.3	G	sm		sm	1.29	1	
99-2968	266	2	9.02	6.1	G	ind st	sm over	brn/smdg	1.44	1	
99-2968	260	2	9.43	2.9	G	ind st		sm	1.7	1	
99-29680	5	4	9.63	13.8	G	curv comp st	ind	sm	1.21	1	
99-2973	251	4	6.8	9.4	G	coarse		sm	1.26	1	
99-2976	252	2	7.28	3.4	G	ind st		redfilmed	1.75	1	
99-2978	261	1	0	1.7	G	eroded		sm	0.84	1	
99-2978	263	2	0	2.3	G	eroded		eroded	1.66	1	
99-2978	260	2	0	2	G	eroded		sm	1	1	
99-2978	259	1	0	1.4	G	eroded		sm	0.98	1	
99-2978	254	1	5.38	1.7	grit	ind lin st		sm	0.91	1	
99-2978	265	1	6.06	1.5	G	cordm		sm	0.82	1	
99-2978	266	3	6.18	5.8	G	coarse		sm	1.84	1	
99-2978	262	2	6.82	2.9	G	cordm		sm	1.5	1	
99-2978	256	2	7.25	3.5	G	ind st		sm	1.17	1	
99-2978	268	3	8.1	7.9	G	eroded		sm	1.6	1	base fragment
99-2978	255	2	8.28	6.1	G	ind lin st		sm	1.07	1	
99-2978	253	2	8.87	5.3	G	ind lin st		sm	1.48	1	
99-2978	264	2	9.42	1.9	G	brn		sm	1.7	1	
99-2978	267	2	9.44	6.5	G	ind lin st		sm/smdg	1.62	1	
99-2978	257	2	9.98	3.6	G	sm		sm	1.97	1	
99-2978	258	1	10.92	3.4	G	ind st		sm	1.68	1	
99-2983	253	1	6.22	1.8	G	ind st		sm	1.3	1	
99-2983	258	2	6.67	2.9	G	ind lin st		sm	1.67	1	
99-2983	257	2	6.82	2.5	G	coarse		sm	1.34	1	
99-2983	255	1	6.82	1.6	G	ind st		redfilmed	1.15	1	
99-2983	259	1	6.82	1.8	G	br		sm	1.18	1	
99-2983	252	3	7.04	3.8	grit	ind lin st		sm	1.02	1	
99-2983	254	2	7.52	1.7	G	sm		sm	1.45	1	
99-2983	256	2	7.58	4.3	G	coarse		sm	0.98	1	
99-2984	252	2	7.18	4.2	G	ind lin st		sm/smdg	0.88	1	
99-2984	255	2	7.75	3.8	G	ind lin st		sm	1.6	1	
99-2984	253	2	7.88	2.3	G	coarse		sm	1.82	1	
99-2984	254	2	8	3.1	G	ind st		sm	1.4	1	
99-2988	255	2	0	2.4	G	eroded		eroded	1.7	1	
99-2988	254	2	0	2.8	G	eroded		sm	2.1	1	
99-299	251	3	14.24	14.4	G	ind st		brn	2.4	1	
99-2991	252	3	5.62	4.2	G	ind lin st		sm/smdg	1.08	1	
99-2995	253	1	6.14	1.5	G	ind st		sm	1.3	1	
99-2995	254	3	7.08	7.1	G	ind lin st		sm	2.3	1	
99-2995	255	3	7.8	6.1	G	cordm		sm	1.2	1	
99-2995	256	2	8.06	3.7	G	ind lin st		sm	1.25	1	
99-2996	251	2	7.12	3.3	G	coarse		sm	1.72	1	
99-2996	252	2	7.25	4.9	G	ind lin st		sm	1.44	1	
99-2998	258	2	0	2	G	eroded		sm	1.26	1	
99-2998	254	2	6.77	3.3	G	ind lin st		sm	0.87	1	
99-2998	255	2	7.33	2.5	G	ind st		sm	1.15	1	
99-2998	257	2	7.64	2.4	G	coarse		sm	1.4	1	
99-2998	253	1	7.92	1.9	G	ind lin st		sm	1.32	1	
99-2998	262	2	8.72	4.4	G	cordm		sm	1.34	1	
99-2999	252	6	8.18	25.1	G	smpl st		sm/smdg	1.6	1	comp design made with a smpl paddle?
99-3	254	1	7.09	2.2	G	sm		sm	1.5	1	
99-3	253	2	7.1	3	G	sm		sm	1.28	1	
99-3	252	3	7.54	7.2	G	sm		sm/smdg	1.6	1	
99-3	251	2	8.22	5.9	G	sm		sm	1.5	1	
99-3002	263	2	0	1.9	S	eroded		eroded		1	
99-3002	260	2	4.72	1.9	G	sm		sm	0.67	1	
99-3002	257	2	6.6	2.1	G	sm		eroded	1.55	1	
99-3002	264	2	6.78	3.8	G	ind lin st		sm/smdg	1.98	1	
99-3002	265	3	7.06	5.4	G	sm		sm	1.5	1	
99-3002	253	1	7.1	1.6	G	eroded		eroded	1.22	1	
99-3002	258	2	7.3	2.1	G	ind st		sm/smdg	1.04	1	
99-3002	259	1	7.4	1.6	G	cordm		sm	1.6	1	
99-3002	254	2	7.82	4.4	G	ind lin st		sm	1.07	1	
99-3002	261	1	8.3	2.3	G	rgh		sm	0.89	1	
99-3002	262	2	8.32	3.7	G	ind st	sm over	sm	2.1	1	
99-3002	255	3	10.42	10.7	G	ind lin st		sm	1.4	1	
99-3005	253	5	6.72	18.9	grit	curv comp st	ind	sm/smdg	1.07	1	
99-3005	254	3	8.16	8.8	G	cordm		sm	1.18	1	
99-3009	284	2	6.4	3.6	grit	ind lin st		brn/smdg	1.92	1	wide grooves
99-3009	282	3	6.62	6.8	G	coarse		sm	1.42	1	
99-3009	285	2	7.86	7	G	cordm		eroded	1.12	1	
99-3009	283	3	7.94	6.8	G	ind lin st		sm/smdg	2.34	1	
99-3010	253	2	8.75	2.8	G	ind lin st		sm	1.46	1	

99-3011	254	1	7.9	1.4	G	eroded		eroded	0.9	1	
99-3011	253	1	9.28	2.1	G	cordm		sm	1.2	1	
99-3014	252	1	8.02	1.8	S	eroded		eroded		1	
99-3015	254	3	7.45	5.6	G	ind lin st		sm	2.01	1	
99-3016	264	2	0	1.6	G	ind lin st		eroded	0.8	1	
99-3016	259	2	5.42	3.9	G	cordm	sm over	sm	1.35	1	
99-3016	256	3	7.07	6.2	G	ind lin st		sm/smdg	2.12	1	
99-3016	255	3	7.08	5.1	G	cordm		sm	1.6	1	
99-3016	260	2	7.12	3.4	G	ind st	sm over	sm/smdg	0.92	1	
99-3016	261	2	7.41	3.5	G	ind lin st		sm	1.3	1	
99-3016	257	2	7.48	4.5	grit	curv comp st	ind	brn/smdg	0.85	1	
99-3016	253	4	7.74	9.3	G	curv comp st	ind	coarse	1.42	1	
99-3016	262	1	7.92	3.1	G	ind st		sm	1.32	1	
99-3016	252	7	8.22	19.4	G	cordm	ovrst	sm	1.79	1	
99-3016	258	2	8.5	4.7	G	ind st		sm	1.84	1	
99-3016	267	3	8.52	6	G	ind lin st		sm/smdg	1.58	1	
99-3016	254	3	8.56	7.3	G	coarse		sm	1.75	1	
99-3016	263	2	10.52	2.7	G	coarse		sm	1.72	1	
99-3019	278	2	0	1	G	eroded		sm	1.42	1	
99-3019	277	2	0	1.7	G	eroded		sm/smdg	1.62	1	
99-3019	261	2	0	1.6	G	eroded		eroded	0.9	1	
99-3019	269	3	0	3.1	G	eroded		sm	0.65	1	
99-3019	270	2	0	1.1	G	eroded		eroded	1.44	1	
99-3019	276	1	5.81	1.8	G	ind lin st		sm/smdg	1.3	1	
99-3019	282	2	6.07	2.1	G	ind lin st		sm/smdg	1.57	1	
99-3019	264	2	6.09	2.5	G	sm		sm	1.6	1	
99-3019	273	2	6.42	2.3	G	sm		sm	1.38	1	
99-3019	260	3	6.44	5.4	G	ind lin st		sm	1.18	1	
99-3019	272	2	6.52	1.6	G	sm		sm	1.25	1	
99-3019	259	3	7.02	5.3	G	ind lin st		brn/smdg	0.98	1	
99-3019	263	2	7.12	3.6	G	coarse		coarse	1.06	1	
99-3019	254	3	7.18	4.8	G	sm		sm	1.06	1	
99-3019	267	2	7.56	3.7	G	coarse		sm	1.3	1	
99-3019	255	3	7.68	5.5	G	cordm		sm	1.12	1	
99-3019	257	2	7.92	3	G	sm		sm/smdg	1.08	1	
99-3019	275	2	8.2	3.4	G	sm		sm	1.1	1	
99-3019	265	2	8.3	3.1	G	eroded		eroded	0.97	1	
99-3019	266	1	8.7	2.4	G	cordm		sm	1.25	1	
99-3019	274	2	8.74	3.7	G	coarse		sm	2.2	1	
99-3019	287	1	9.1	2.3	G	cordm		sm	0.75	1	
99-3019	271	2	9.4	2.8	G	ind st		sm	0.94	1	
99-3019	262	3	9.4	8.7	G	ind st		sm	1.6	1	
99-3019	268	2	9.7	3.6	G	ind st	sm over	eroded	1.52	1	
99-3019	279	1	9.99	2.2	G	cordm		sm	0.85	1	
99-3019	256	3	10.09	4.1	G	eroded		sm	1.72	1	
99-3019	280	1	11.46	2.1	G	eroded		sm	1.3	1	
99-3021	285	2	0	2.8	G	sm		eroded	1.3	1	
99-3021	253	1	5.88	1.5	grit	ind lin st		eroded	1.08	1	
99-3021	286	2	5.92	3.8	G	ind lin st		sm	1.7	1	
99-3021	308	2	5.96	4.1	G	ind lin st		sm	1.4	1	
99-3021	290	3	6	5.3	grit	eroded		brn	0.98	1	
99-3021	313	4	6.01	11.4	G	comp st	ind	sm/smdg	0.85	1	
99-3021	268	2	6.1	1.6	G	ind lin st		sm/smdg	1.2	1	
99-3021	258	1	6.12	1.7	G	sm		sm	1.2	1	
99-3021	299	3	6.24	3.8	G	ind lin st		sm/smdg	1.85	1	
99-3021	279	2	6.25	3.4	G	coarse		sm	1.1	1	
99-3021	309	5	6.3	14.4	G	coarse		coarse	2.35	1	
99-3021	300	3	6.5	6.2	G	curv comp st	ind	sm/smdg	1.35	1	
99-3021	260	2	6.5	2.6	G	coarse		sm	0.9	1	
99-3021	294	2	6.58	2.9	G	ind lin st		sm/smdg	0.97	1	
99-3021	274	2	6.75	2.5	G	ind lin st		eroded	1.5	1	
99-3021	288	3	6.75	4.2	G	ind st		sm	1.35	1	
99-3021	298	3	6.78	3.5	G	ind st		sm	1.75	1	
99-3021	257	2	6.78	1.7	G	eroded		sm/smdg	0.98	1	
99-3021	314	5	6.79	12.1	G	cordm		sm	1.6	1	
99-3021	275	2	6.82	2.7	G	ind st		sm	1.35	1	
99-3021	311	3	7.08	4.8	G	smpl st	ovrst	sm/smdg	1.4	1	comp design made with a smpl paddle?
99-3021	278	2	7.1	4	G	ind st		sm/smdg	1.9	1	
99-3021	276	2	7.11	3	grit	ind lin st		sm	0.98	1	
99-3021	291	4	7.12	8.9	G	ind lin st		sm	1.21	1	
99-3021	265	2	7.18	2.5	G	coarse		sm	2.08	1	
99-3021	277	2	7.3	4.5	G	sm		sm	1.05	1	
99-3021	302	3	7.32	8.1	G	curv comp st	ind	sm	0.98	1	
99-3021	280	2	7.32	3.8	G	cordm		sm	2.08	1	
99-3021	272	2	7.35	1.9	S	sm		sm	2.14	1	
99-3021	301	2	7.4	3	S	sm		sm	2.54	1	
99-3021	271	2	7.48	2.6	G	ind lin st		sm/smdg	0.98	1	
99-3021	262	2	7.48	2.4	G	eroded		sm	2.1	1	
99-3021	303	4	7.52	10.1	G	cordm		brn/smdg	1.42	1	
99-3021	307	4	7.6	7.8	G	comp st	ind	brn	1.9	1	
99-3021	261	2	7.62	3.9	G	ind lin st		sm	1.45	1	
99-3021	304	4	7.68	11.3	G	comp st	ind	sm	1.5	1	
99-3021	254	2	7.72	2.3	G	ind lin st		sm	1.52	1	
99-3021	281	2	7.82	5	G	ind lin st		sm	1.85	1	
99-3021	282	2	7.85	4.3	G	cordm		sm	0.98	1	
99-3021	289	2	7.89	4.5	G	sm		sm	1.64	1	
99-3021	266	2	7.9	2.3	G	ind lin st		sm	0.98	1	
99-3021	316	9	7.92	61.9	G	ind lin st		sm	1.8	1	wide grooves
99-3021	273	2	8	3.2	G	sm		sm	1.7	1	
99-3021	270	2	8.18	3.8	G	ind st		sm	1.32	1	
99-3021	283	3	8.2	4.4	G	ind st		eroded	1.7	1	
99-3021	305	4	8.22	8.3	grit	ind lin st		sm	0.78	1	
99-3021	287	2	8.22	3.6	grit	ind lin st		sm	1.08	1	
99-3021	317	4	8.25	9.4	G	curv comp st	ind	brn	1.65	1	
99-3021	256	2	8.35	2.6	G	ind st		eroded	1.8	1	
99-3021	267	2	8.35	5.6	grit	comp st	ind	sm	1.52	1	
99-3021	306	4	8.45	11.8	G	cordm		sm	0.98	1	
99-3021	255	1	8.58	2.4	G	ind st		sm/smdg	2.18	1	
99-3021	292	2	8.81	5.1	G	ind st	sm over	brn	2.31	1	
99-3021	295	3	8.92	6.5	G	ind st		sm	1.82	1	
99-3021	297	4	8.99	14.4	G	curv comp st	ind	sm	2.1	1	
99-3021	310	3	9.38	7.5	G	ind st		sm/smdg	1.68	1	
99-3021	264	1	9.42	2.5	G	sm		sm	1.5	1	
99-3021	293	2	9.48	4.2	G	coarse		coarse	1.82	1	
99-3021	263	2	9.7	3.1	G	ind st		sm/smdg	1.7	1	
99-3021	296	3	10.4	8.9	G	ind st		sm	2.08	1	
99-3021	284	2	11	5.4	G	coarse		sm	1.92	1	
99-3021	312	3	11.3	6	G	sm		sm/smdg	1.32	1	
99-3025	254	3	7.72	7.5	G	ind lin st		sm	1.8	1	
99-3025	256	1	9.54	1.5	G	eroded		sm	1.38	1	
99-3025	255	1	11.97	2.3	G	sm		sm	0.88	1	
99-3027	256	1	5.5	1.7	G	ind lin st		sm	1.96	1	
99-3027	259	1	5.6	1.8	G	sm		sm	1.68	1	
99-3027	257	2	5.92	2.4	G	ind st		sm	2.54	1	
99-3027	254	2	6.18	3	G	ind st		sm	1.08	1	
99-3027	258	2	7.5	2.7	G	ind lin st		coarse	1.6	1	
99-3027	252	6	8.42	38.7	G	cordm		brn/smdg	1.35	1	
99-3027	253	3	9.64	7.2	G	cordm		sm	2.28	1	
99-3028	252	1	0	1.4	G	eroded		sm	1.15	1	
99-3028	253	2	5.68	2.2	G	cordm		sm	1.32	1	
99-3028	255	2	7.62	3.4	G	sm		sm	1.08	1	
99-3028	254	2	8.38	3	G	ind st		redfilmed	0.65	1	
99-3039	252	2	0	3.3	G	eroded		brn/smdg	1.98	1	
99-3040	251	5	7.52	11.6	G	cordm		sm	1.48	1	
99-3040	255	2	8.08	1.5	S	sm		sm	2.03	1	
99-3040	253	2	8.5	4.6	S	sm		sm	2.2	1	
99-3040	254	1	8.56	2.2	G	sm		sm/smdg	1.08	1	

99-3045	263	4	6.32	8.9	G	smpl st	ovrst	sm/smdg	1.47	1	comp design made with a smpl paddle?
99-3045	265	3	6.38	4.4	grit	sm		sm	0.5	1	
99-3045	259	5	6.88	11.7	G	ind lin st		sm/smdg	1.7	1	
99-3045	264	3	6.98	4.8	G	coarse		sm	1.6	1	
99-3045	255	2	6.98	2.6	G	sm		sm/smdg	1.7	1	
99-3045	262	6	7.05	24.1	G	curv comp st	ind scroll	sm/smdg	1.45	1	
99-3045	256	5	7.06	11.4	G	cordm	ovrst	sm/smdg	1.55	1	
99-3045	266	2	7.42	2.8	S	sm		sm	1.89	1	
99-3045	253	2	7.48	2.8	G	cordm		brn/smdg	1.02	1	
99-3045	257	4	8.02	12.4	G	ind lin st	sm over	sm	1.62	1	
99-3045	254	3	8.62	8.5	G	cordm	sm over	sm/smdg	1.4	1	
99-3045	258	4	8.64	15.4	G	cordm	ovrst	sm/smdg	1.38	1	
99-3045	260	3	8.65	7.6	G	comp st	ind	sm	2.44	1	
99-3045	261	2	9.82	4.9	G	ind lin st		sm/smdg	1.25	1	
99-3047	253	2	6.14	1.9	G	ind st	sm over	sm/smdg	0.96	1	
99-3048	252	3	8.7	9.1	G	ind lin st	ovrst	sm	1.86	1	
99-3048	251	3	8.99	7.5	G	ind lin st	sm over	sm	0.74	1	
99-3051	7	3	7.44	5.7	G	sm		sm	2.2	1	
99-3052	254	4	6.68	8.3	G	ind lin st		sm	2.13	1	
99-3052	253	4	7.38	11.1	G	scr		sm/smdg	0.95	1	
99-3052	2520	5	7.58	14	G	scr		sm	2.4	1	
99-3052	255	3	7.68	4.3	G	ind lin st		sm	1.5	1	
99-3052	256	2	8.04	3.2	G	ind st		sm	1.22	1	
99-3052	252	3	8.7	5.1	G	ind st		sm/smdg	2.04	1	carinated shoulder
99-3053	267	2	5.25	3.9	G	ind st	sm over	sm/smdg	1.65	1	
99-3053	265	3	5.52	6	G	ind lin st		sm/smdg	1.6	1	
99-3053	266	4	5.85	7.1	G	ind lin st		sm/smdg	1.62	1	
99-3053	268	3	6.15	4	G	scr		sm	1.58	1	
99-3053	261	3	6.62	5.4	G	curv comp st	ind	sm/smdg	1.65	1	
99-3053	260	4	6.74	7.9	G	scr		sm	2.32	1	
99-3053	254	6	6.98	14.9	G	scr		sm/smdg	1.9	1	
99-3053	253	7	7.06	35.9	S	sm		sm	2.5	1	
99-3053	262	2	7.1	3.9	G	cordm		brn/smdg	1.85	1	
99-3053	269	2	7.18	3.6	G	cordm		sm/smdg	1.62	1	
99-3053	259	3	7.38	5.6	grit	ind lin st		sm/smdg	0.9	1	
99-3053	264	4	7.7	9.3	G	ind lin st		coarse	2.21	1	
99-3053	252	3	7.85	6.9	S	sm		sm	2.12	1	
99-3053	263	2	7.88	3.1	G	sm		sm	1.8	1	
99-3053	256	6	8.1	43.3	G	cordm		brn/smdg	1.9	1	
99-3053	257	5	8.2	16	G	sm		sm	1.68	1	
99-3053	258	5	8.3	16.7	G	cordm		sm	1.62	1	
99-3053	255	6	9.18	30.7	G	comp st	ind	sm	1.8	1	
99-3057	252	2	8.32	2.3	G	ind lin st		sm	1.36	1	
99-3060	252	2	6.94	3.5	G	ind lin st		brn/smdg	0.94	1	
99-3062	254	2	6.92	2.4	G	ind lin st		sm	1.46	1	
99-3062	253	3	9.3	4.7	G	ind st		brn	1.25	1	
99-3063	253	2	4.68	2.9	G	coarse		sm	1.12	1	
99-3063	252	3	7.92	5.2	S	sm		sm	2.42	1	
99-3064	253	3	5.7	4.7	S	sm		sm	2.3	1	
99-3064	252	3	6.6	4.7	G	ind st	sm over	sm/smdg	1.38	1	
99-3067	1	1	0	1.3	G	coarse		sm	1.72	1	
99-3068	265	2	0	2.3	G	eroded		sm	1.18	1	
99-3068	256	2	5.28	2.2	grit	ind lin st		sm	0.68	1	
99-3068	255	2	5.48	2.5	G	ind lin st		sm	1.78	1	
99-3068	263	2	5.74	3.3	G	ind st		sm	0.74	1	
99-3068	268	2	6.02	2.2	G	ind lin st		sm	1.28	1	
99-3068	262	1	6.14	2.1	G	cordm		sm	1.08	1	
99-3068	261	2	6.32	2.6	G	ind lin st		eroded	1.3	1	
99-3068	266	2	6.4	2.2	G	cordm		sm	1.28	1	
99-3068	271	1	6.42	2.4	G	coarse		sm	1.1	1	
99-3068	269	2	7.38	2.8	G	curv comp st	ind scroll	sm	1.28	1	
99-3068	270	2	7.4	2.2	G	comp st	ind	sm	1.5	1	
99-3068	264	2	7.5	2.9	G	ind st		sm	1.2	1	
99-3068	258	2	7.89	3.5	G	ind st		sm	2.15	1	
99-3068	274	2	7.99	3.7	G	ind st		sm	0.97	1	
99-3068	267	2	8.1	3	G	sm		sm	1.54	1	
99-3068	273	2	8.37	3.5	G	eroded		sm	1.01	1	
99-3068	272	3	8.62	5.1	G	cordm		sm	1.43	1	
99-3068	260	2	8.66	3.1	G	eroded		sm	1.45	1	
99-3068	254	1	8.9	2.2	G	eroded		sm	1.08	1	
99-3068	259	2	9.66	4.4	G	curv comp st	ind	sm/smdg	0.96	1	
99-3068	257	2	11.12	2.8	G	eroded		sm	0.98	1	
99-3071	252	1	0	1.2	G	eroded		sm	1.9	1	
99-3071	251	2	7.34	2.6	G	coarse		sm	1.25	1	
99-3073	258	1	0	1.4	G	eroded		sm	1.32	1	
99-3073	252	4	6.32	10.5	G	coarse		sm/smdg	1.44	1	
99-3073	257	2	6.54	2.5	G	ind lin st		sm	1.42	1	
99-3073	256	1	7.22	2.5	G	sm		sm	0.74	1	
99-3073	255	1	8.04	2.5	G	ind lin st		sm/smdg	1.23	1	
99-3073	253	2	8.74	6.1	G	cordm		sm	1.06	1	
99-3073	254	2	11.52	5.7	G	eroded		sm	1.04	1	
99-3074	261	1	0	1.9	G	eroded		sm	1.26	1	
99-3074	268	3	6.45	3.9	G	comp st	ind	sm/smdg	1.65	1	
99-3074	257	2	6.6	2.4	G	ind lin st		sm/smdg	0.78	1	
99-3074	266	3	6.84	4.8	G	ind st	sm over	sm	1.06	1	
99-3074	265	2	7.18	2.1	G	cordm		sm	1.08	1	
99-3074	267	2	7.23	3.1	G	coarse		sm	1.72	1	
99-3074	263	2	7.29	4	G	ind lin st		sm	1.25	1	
99-3074	258	2	7.38	2.8	G	sm		sm	1.44	1	
99-3074	259	2	7.42	2.8	G	ind st	sm over	sm	1.6	1	
99-3074	269	2	7.45	3.2	G	ind st		sm/smdg	1.07	1	
99-3074	264	2	7.8	2.9	G	cordm		sm	1.02	1	
99-3074	256	2	8.34	5.4	G	sm		sm	1.28	1	
99-3074	271	2	8.64	3.1	G	sm		sm/smdg	1.18	1	
99-3074	272	2	9	3.8	G	ind st		sm/smdg	1.48	1	
99-3074	262	2	9.24	3.7	G	ind lin st		sm	1.63	1	
99-3074	255	2	9.7	5.8	G	ind st		sm/smdg	1.4	1	
99-3075	252	2	6.92	2.5	G	ind st		sm/smdg	1.4	1	
99-3076	252	1	10.4	2	G	eroded		sm	1.58	1	
99-3078	256	1	0	1.8	G	eroded		sm	1.34	1	
99-3078	253	2	6.52	3.2	G	ind st	sm over	sm/smdg	1.28	1	
99-3078	255	2	8.3	3.8	G	ind lin st		sm	1	1	
99-3078	257	3	8.68	7.2	grit	ind st	sm over	sm	1.12	1	
99-3078	254	2	8.92	5.6	G	cordm		sm	1.7	1	
99-3079	3	1	9.28	2	G	eroded		sm	1.18	1	
99-3080	255	2	8.21	2.7	G	ind st		sm/smdg	1.82	1	
99-3109	252	1	14.8	2.1	G	sm		sm	2.1	1	
99-3110	256	1	0	2.7	G	eroded		sm/smdg	1.18	1	
99-3110	257	2	8.7	2.7	G	eroded		sm	1.65	1	
99-3112	255	2	6.86	3	G	ind st		sm	1.12	1	
99-3112	256	1	7.3	1.3	G	coarse		sm	1.28	1	
99-3112	254	2	7.48	3.1	G	cordm		sm	1.15	1	
99-3112	253	2	7.54	3.4	G	ind lin st		sm	1.72	1	
99-3113	262	1	0	2.3	G	eroded		sm/smdg	1.86	1	
99-3113	255	2	0	2	G	eroded		sm	1.2	1	
99-3113	263	2	0	1.3	G	eroded		sm	1.14	1	
99-3113	266	2	0	1.2	grit	eroded		sm	0.77	1	
99-3113	254	2	4.9	2.1	G	sm		sm	0.82	1	
99-3113	278	1	5.74	1.9	G	sm		sm	0.75	1	
99-3113	274	2	5.8	1.4	S	sm		sm/smdg		1	
99-3113	264	2	5.9	2.7	G	ind st	sm over	sm	1.42	1	
99-3113	280	2	6.08	1.8	G	sm		sm	1.06	1	
99-3113	259	2	6.25	3.7	G	ind st	sm over	eroded	1.82	1	
99-3113	265	2	6.36	1.9	G	ind lin st		sm	1.66	1	
99-3113	252	3	6.74	5.7	G	ind st	sm over	sm/smdg	1.8	1	
99-3113	279	2	6.92	3.2	G	ind lin st		sm	0.6	1	
99-3113	257	2	6.98	3	G	ind st		sm	1.18	1	

99-3113	271	2	7.08	2.8	G	cordm		sm	0.94	1	
99-3113	260	2	7.14	1.5	G	ind lin st		sm	1.28	1	
99-3113	277	1	7.15	2.1	G	eroded		sm	1.32	1	
99-3113	267	2	7.29	2.6	G	ind lin st		sm	1.8	1	
99-3113	282	1	7.48	1.9	G	ind lin st		sm	1.65	1	
99-3113	251	2	7.78	2.6	G	ind st	sm over	sm	0.87	1	
99-3113	272	2	7.9	5.1	G	cordm		sm/smdg	1.52	1	
99-3113	258	1	8.23	1.4	G	cordm		sm	1.4	1	
99-3113	253	2	8.26	2	G	eroded		eroded	2.67	1	
99-3113	261	1	8.29	1.7	G	eroded		sm/smdg	1.3	1	
99-3113	269	2	8.8	4.4	G	cordm		sm/smdg	1.44	1	
99-3113	281	3	8.98	7.4	grit	ind lin st		sm	0.83	1	
99-3113	275	2	9.52	5	G	sm		coarse	1.15	1	
99-3113	273	2	9.52	2.7	G	ind st		sm	1.62	1	
99-3113	268	3	11.9	4.7	G	sm		sm	1.4	1	base fragment
99-3113	270	3	12.6	8	G	sm		sm	1.28	1	base fragment
99-3113	256	2	13.3	5	G	sm		sm/smdg	1.8	1	base fragment
99-3115	256	2	6.96	2.4	G	ind st		sm/smdg	1.24	1	
99-3115	255	1	8.38	2.3	G	sm		sm	1.3	1	
99-3116	4	2	9.44	4	G	ind st	sm over	sm	2.4	1	
99-3117	252	3	0	2.6	G	coarse		eroded	1.38	1	
99-3117	256	1	0	1.5	G	eroded		sm	1.22	1	
99-3117	255	2	5.04	1.9	G	sm		brn/smdg	0.92	1	
99-3117	253	1	6.1	1.7	grit	comp st	ind	sm	0.67	1	
99-3117	251	2	6.42	3.1	G	ind lin st		sm	1.22	1	
99-3119	255	2	0	1.2	G	eroded		sm	1.62	1	
99-3119	256	1	6.5	1.5	G	sm		sm	1.4	1	
99-3119	252	3	6.6	5.5	G	curv comp st	ind	sm	1.3	1	
99-3119	254	1	6.85	1.4	G	ind lin st		sm	1.3	1	
99-3119	251	3	9.92	7	grit	curv comp st	ind	sm	0.86	1	
99-3119	253	2	11.1	5.8	grit	sm		sm	0.9	1	base fragment
99-316	297	2	9.77	0	G	cordm		sm	1.75	1	
99-3237	283	2	0	1.4	G	ind st		eroded	1.44	1	
99-3237	267	4	0	7.4	G	sm		eroded	1.52	1	
99-3237	284	2	5.78	3	G	sm		brn/smdg	1.42	1	
99-3237	295	5	6.28	10.1	S	sm		sm	0	1	
99-3237	273	3	6.3	3.1	S	sm		sm	0	1	
99-3237	292	3	6.4	9.6	S	sm		sm	0	1	
99-3237	274	3	6.57	3.7	S	sm		sm	0	1	
99-3237	286	3	6.6	4.6	S	sm		sm	0	1	
99-3237	265	2	6.8	2	S	sm		sm	0	1	
99-3237	256	2	6.82	3.7	G	sm		sm/smdg	1.75	1	
99-3237	270	4	6.84	8.6	S	sm		sm	0	1	
99-3237	272	4	7.04	6.3	S	sm		sm	0	1	
99-3237	293	6	7.13	16.9	G	sm		sm/smdg	1.2	1	
99-3237	289	4	7.25	12.4	G	ind st		coarse	1.8	1	
99-3237	275	2	7.38	3.7	G	sm		sm	1.68	1	
99-3237	282	2	7.38	2.6	S	sm		sm	0	1	
99-3237	287	2	7.4	3	S	sm		sm	0	1	
99-3237	268	4	7.5	7.9	S	sm		sm	0	1	
99-3237	285	3	7.7	3.3	S	sm		sm	0	1	
99-3237	296	9	7.8	59.8	S	sm		sm	0	1	
99-3237	276	2	7.9	3	G	sm		sm/smdg	1.2	1	
99-3237	277	2	8.08	2.7	S	sm		sm	0	1	
99-3237	297	6	8.28	22.7	S	sm		sm	0	1	
99-3237	264	2	8.64	3.1	G	sm		sm	1.34	1	
99-3237	294	9	8.9	100	G	br		sm	2	1	
99-3237	304	4	8.9	11.6	G	ind st	col st	sm	1.72	1	
99-3237	298	5	9.16	23.1	G	sm		brn/smdg	1.14	1	
99-3238	254	2	7.26	2.3	G	scr		brn	1.4	1	
99-3238	253	2	9.06	3.5	G	sm		eroded	1.7	1	
99-3241	269	2	0	2.7	G	coarse		eroded	2.04	1	
99-3241	273	2	0	2.4	G	rgh	sm over	eroded	1.07	1	
99-3241	275	2	5.76	2.9	G	sm		brn/smdg	1.52	1	
99-3241	292	6	5.78	16	S	sm		sm	0	1	
99-3241	280	2	5.9	6	G	rgh	sm over	brn/smdg	1.6	1	
99-3241	277	4	6.08	10.9	G	rgh		brn/smdg	1.98	1	
99-3241	271	1	6.2	2.5	G	rgh	sm over	brn/smdg	0.94	1	
99-3241	289	6	6.48	23	G	rgh	sm over	brn/smdg	1.46	1	
99-3241	288	9	6.5	46.6	G	rgh	sm over	brn/smdg	1.88	1	
99-3241	286	3	6.58	5.5	G	cordm		sm	1.25	1	
99-3241	279	3	6.78	5.7	G	sm		sm	1.96	1	
99-3241	281	4	6.8	12.2	G	rgh	sm over	brn/smdg	1.13	1	
99-3241	260	4	7.04	10	G	sm		brn/smdg	1.45	1	
99-3241	284	5	7.3	16.5	G	rgh	sm over	brn/smdg	1.6	1	
99-3241	274	3	7.84	8.8	S	sm		sm	0	1	
99-3241	291	10	8.38	64.7	G	br		sm	1.68	1	
99-3241	287	6	8.62	12.9	S	sm		sm	0	1	
99-3241	283	3	8.87	16.5	G	rgh		sm	2.06	1	
99-3241	263	2	9	2.8	G	sm		sm	0.78	1	
99-3241	278	3	9.02	7.5	G	sm		eroded	1.5	1	
99-3241	300	15	9.06	115.6	G	ind st	col st	sm	1.18	1	
99-3241	293	7	9.12	39.4	S	sm		sm	0	1	
99-3241	294	6	10.1	35.4	G	sm		sm	1.3	1	
99-3245	297	2	0	3.3	G	eroded		sm	3.08	1	
99-3245	298	2	0	3	G	eroded		sm	1.99	1	
99-3245	310	3	0	5.4	S	sm		eroded		1	
99-3245	318	2	0	2	S	eroded		eroded		1	
99-3245	344	2	0	1.9	S	eroded		eroded		1	
99-3245	346	2	0	2.4	G	ind lin st		eroded	1.5	1	
99-3245	331	2	5.69	1.8	S	sm		sm		1	
99-3245	323	2	5.74	1.6	S	sm		scr		1	
99-3245	314	2	5.84	2.5	S	sm		sm		1	
99-3245	329	2	5.95	3.4	S	sm		sm		1	
99-3245	270	3	5.97	8.6	G	coarse		sm/smdg	2.31	1	
99-3245	307	3	5.97	4.9	S	scr		sm		1	
99-3245	332	2	6.01	2.9	S	sm		eroded		1	
99-3245	337	2	6.01	2.3	S	sm		sm		1	
99-3245	340	1	6.09	1.4	S	eroded		eroded		1	
99-3245	308	3	6.09	3.9	S	scr		sm/smdg		1	
99-3245	319	2	6.15	2	S	scr		eroded		1	
99-3245	324	2	6.19	2.1	S	sm		sm/smdg		1	
99-3245	352	6	6.2	16.6	G	ind st	sm over	sm	2.41	1	
99-3245	339	2	6.23	2.8	S	scr		eroded		1	
99-3245	326	2	6.26	2.8	S	sm		sm		1	
99-3245	315	1	6.35	1.8	S	sm		sm		1	
99-3245	320	2	6.39	2.2	S	sm		sm		1	
99-3245	294	2	6.39	4.4	grit	ind lin st		sm/smdg	1.75	1	
99-3245	328	2	6.43	2.3	S	sm		sm		1	
99-3245	309	3	6.53	4.7	S	sm		sm		1	
99-3245	312	3	6.57	3.7	S	sm		sm		1	
99-3245	342	2	6.6	1.8	S	eroded		eroded		1	
99-3245	338	2	6.83	1.8	S	sm		sm		1	
99-3245	271	4	6.87	15.9	G	ind lin st	ovrst	sm	1.79	1	
99-3245	286	2	6.97	4.6	G	coarse		sm	1.28	1	
99-3245	341	2	7.01	2	S	eroded		eroded		1	
99-3245	311	3	7.03	4.1	S	sm		sm		1	
99-3245	275	4	7.35	11.5	G	coarse		brn	1.26	1	
99-3245	316	2	7.46	2.8	S	eroded		sm		1	
99-3245	304	4	7.58	13	S	sm		sm		1	
99-3245	334	3	7.75	7	S	sm		scr		1	
99-3245	282	3	7.82	6.6	G	sm		brn	1.48	1	
99-3245	281	3	8	6.9	G	sm		brn/smdg	2.43	1	
99-3245	327	3	8.04	7.7	S	sm		sm		1	
99-3245	300	2	8.04	3	G	ind st		sm	1.7	1	
99-3245	276	3	8.25	8	G	ind lin st		sm/smdg	1.49	1	
99-3245	306	6	8.32	11.8	S	sm		sm		1	
99-3245	325	2	8.44	4.4	S	sm		sm		1	

99-3245	317	2	8.79	2.9	S	sm		eroded		1	
99-3245	313	3	8.91	4.5	S	sm		sm		1	
99-3245	335	3	9.04	9.7	S	sm		eroded		1	
99-3245	280	3	9.15	7.9	G	coarse		sm/smdg	2.72	1	
99-3245	333	2	9.2	4.1	S	sm		sm		1	
99-3245	273	4	9.22	26.7	G	coarse		coarse	2.69	1	
99-3245	303	7	9.24	36.6	S	sm		sm		1	
99-3245	258	9	9.25	159.1	S	sm		sm		1	
99-3245	322	2	9.35	1.9	S	eroded		eroded		1	
99-3245	292	2	9.36	4	G	scr		eroded	1.74	1	
99-3245	336	2	9.39	3.9	S	sm		sm		1	
99-3245	296	2	9.4	3.1	G	coarse		sm/smdg	1.86	1	
99-3245	288	2	9.48	4.1	G	ind lin st	sm over	sm	1.61	1	
99-3245	290	2	9.49	4.9	G	coarse		sm	1.33	1	
99-3245	289	2	9.57	4.1	G	comp st	ind	sm	2.61	1	
99-3245	283	3	9.68	7	G	ind lin st	sm over	sm/smdg	2.04	1	
99-3245	274	7	9.96	44.8	G	smpl st	ind sm over	coarse	2.02	1	comp design made from smpl paddle?
99-3245	278	3	10.01	11	G	coarse		coarse	2.61	1	
99-3245	293	2	10.08	3.8	G	sm		sm/smdg	1.69	1	
99-3245	272	6	10.16	43.5	G	smpl st		sm/smdg	1.61	1	comp design made from smpl paddle?
99-3245	301	1	10.18	2.6	G	coarse		coarse	1.91	1	
99-3245	285	2	10.28	5.3	G	sm		coarse/ smdg	2.23	1	
99-3245	305	3	10.39	7.1	S	sm		sm		1	
99-3245	277	3	10.43	11.2	G	coarse		coarse	1.48	1	
99-3245	279	3	10.44	12.4	G	coarse		coarse	2.25	1	
99-3245	299	1	10.65	2.9	G	coarse		sm/smdg	2.16	1	
99-3245	321	3	10.7	4.5	S	sm		eroded		1	
99-3245	295	1	10.9	3.5	G	coarse		sm	1.62	1	
99-3245	291	2	10.98	4.1	G	ind lin st		sm/smdg	2.16	1	
99-3245	287	2	11.39	5	G	coarse		coarse/ smdg	2.37	1	
99-3245	284	2	12.15	4.7	G	coarse		coarse/ smdg	2.49	1	
99-3245	354	14	13.48	389.8	S	sm		sm		1	
99-3254	282	2	0	2.5	S	sm		eroded		1	
99-3254	323	3	4.62	3.3	G	brn		sm	1.46	1	
99-3254	262	2	4.95	2.1	S	scr		eroded		1	
99-3254	316	2	5.55	3.1	G	scr		sm	1.56	1	
99-3254	317	2	5.58	2.3	S	eroded		eroded		1	
99-3254	306	3	5.66	3	S	sm		sm		1	
99-3254	324	2	5.67	2.7	S	sm		sm/smdg		1	
99-3254	325	1	5.74	2.2	G	coarse		brn	1.54	1	
99-3254	263	2	5.75	1.6	S	sm		sm		1	
99-3254	298	2	5.77	2.4	S	eroded		eroded/ smdg		1	
99-3254	319	3	5.93	3.5	S	sm		sm		1	
99-3254	295	3	5.94	3.8	G	coarse		sm	2.12	1	
99-3254	289	1	5.98	1	S	sm		sm/smdg		1	
99-3254	322	3	6.01	3.7	S	scr		eroded/ smdg		1	
99-3254	264	2	6.02	1.9	S	sm		sm/smdg		1	
99-3254	279	2	6.06	3	G	coarse		sm	1.89	1	
99-3254	281	2	6.1	2	S	eroded		eroded		1	
99-3254	277	1	6.12	1.5	S	redfilmed		eroded/ smdg		1	
99-3254	271	2	6.12	2.2	S	sm		sm		1	
99-3254	310	2	6.3	2.5	S	eroded		eroded		1	
99-3254	259	1	6.37	1.3	S	eroded		eroded/ smdg		1	
99-3254	338	2	6.4	2.4	S	sm		sm/smdg		1	
99-3254	343	2	6.42	3	G	coarse		sm	1.4	1	
99-3254	283	2	6.42	1.9	S	sm		sm		1	
99-3254	255	2	6.45	1.5	S	sm		sm/smdg		1	
99-3254	340	3	6.45	5	S	eroded		sm		1	
99-3254	313	2	6.5	3	S	sm		sm		1	
99-3254	302	2	6.51	3.6	S	eroded		sm		1	
99-3254	321	3	6.53	4	S	sm		sm		1	
99-3254	280	2	6.58	2.4	S	sm		sm/smdg		1	
99-3254	314	3	6.6	7.1	G	sm		sm	1.71	1	
99-3254	326	1	6.64	2.3	G	ind st	sm over	sm	1.57	1	
99-3254	297	2	6.85	2.1	S	sm		sm		1	
99-3254	355	4	6.86	12.8	S	eroded		sm		1	
99-3254	267	2	6.87	2.1	S	sm		sm/smdg		1	
99-3254	266	2	7.05	1.8	S	sm		sm		1	
99-3254	332	3	7.06	7	G	sm		brn/smdg	1.64	1	
99-3254	275	2	7.09	2	S	eroded		eroded		1	
99-3254	330	3	7.24	6.5	S	eroded		eroded		1	
99-3254	346	2	7.36	2.2	S	scr		sm		1	
99-3254	336	4	7.38	10.4	G	coarse		sm	2.44	1	
99-3254	345	2	7.44	2.5	G	ind st	sm over	sm	1.55	1	
99-3254	291	1	7.47	1.4	S	sm		eroded		1	
99-3254	303	2	7.57	4.1	G	ind lin st	ovrst	sm/smdg	1.29	1	
99-3254	276	2	7.6	1.9	S	sm		eroded		1	
99-3254	334	2	7.63	6.9	G	coarse		sm/smdg	1.71	1	
99-3254	320	2	7.64	3.5	S	sm		sm		1	
99-3254	299	2	7.82	3.1	S	sm		sm		1	
99-3254	311	2	7.82	3.7	S	sm		sm		1	
99-3254	341	2	7.88	3.5	grit	ind st	sm over	sm	1.02	1	
99-3254	274	2	8.03	2.3	S	sm		sm		1	
99-3254	329	3	8.05	6.4	S	sm		sm		1	
99-3254	308	2	8.12	2.6	S	sm		sm		1	
99-3254	351	4	8.16	17.2	G	sm		sm	1.82	1	base fragment
99-3254	304	3	8.2	4	S	eroded		eroded		1	
99-3254	344	1	8.24	3.4	G	sm		sm	1.18	1	
99-3254	335	2	8.81	5.4	G	ind st		brn/smdg	1.79	1	
99-3254	350	3	8.91	7.3	G	coarse		coarse/ smdg	1.6	1	
99-3254	331	3	8.92	11.2	G	coarse		sm	2.88	1	
99-3254	318	3	9.04	5	G	scr		sm	1.42	1	
99-3254	305	2	9.51	4	G	coarse		coarse/ smdg	1.67	1	
99-3254	327	2	9.57	4.7	G	sm		brn/smdg	1.96	1	
99-3254	300	2	9.6	5	G	sm		sm/smdg	2.4	1	
99-3254	349	3	10.08	10.5	G	coarse		coarse	2.02	1	
99-3254	301	2	10.09	5.6	G	coarse		coarse/ smdg	2.07	1	
99-3254	339	2	10.32	6.8	G	ind st		coarse	1.69	1	
99-3254	337	2	10.83	7.6	G	coarse		sm/smdg	1.84	1	
99-3254	342	2	11.58	4.6	G	coarse		sm/smdg	1.48	1	
99-3254	315	1	13.03	3.1	G	sm		coarse/ smdg	1.73	1	
99-3255	254	2	6.47	2.1	G	ind st		brn/smdg	1.62	1	
99-3255	255	4	8.08	13	G	rgh		brn/smdg	1.74	1	
99-3256	253	1	5.79	1.4	S	eroded		eroded		1	
99-3256	259	3	6.23	4.5	S	eroded		eroded		1	
99-3256	261	4	6.52	8.8	S	scr		sm		1	
99-3256	258	2	6.66	3.4	S	sm		sm		1	sooted
99-3256	260	4	6.67	6.5	S	eroded		eroded		1	
99-3256	252	2	7.7	2	S	sm		sm		1	
99-3256	255	2	8.08	3.2	G	ind st		sm	1.02	1	
99-3256	262	3	12.06	10.6	G	coarse		sm/smdg	2.18	1	
99-3257	253	4	7.6	7.1	S/CR	scr		sm	1.67	1	
99-335	252	2	7.5	3.3	G	cordm		sm/smdg	1.72	1	
99-3417	303	3	7.34	5.9	G	cordm	sm over	sm	2.02	1	
99-3459	321	2	5.08	3.6	grit	scr		brn	0.54	1	
99-3459	315	4	5.55	7.8	G	coarse		sm	1.21	1	

99-3459	289	2	5.58	4.2	G	coarse		sm	1.54	1	
99-3459	258	3	6.84	13.6	G	ind lin st		brn	2.14	1	
99-3459	298	2	7.11	4.6	G	ind lin st	sm over	sm	1.58	1	
99-3459	264	5	7.22	20.6	G	ind lin st	sm over	sm	1.27	1	
99-3459	307	4	7.74	8.3	G	ind lin st		sm	1.17	1	
99-3459	285	2	8.04	3.4	G	coarse		sm	1.04	1	
99-3459	261	4	8.12	9.6	G	cordm		brn/smdg	1.67	1	
99-3459	274	3	8.17	6.2	G	coarse		sm	1.97	1	
99-3459	260	1	8.32	3.1	G	cordm		brn/smdg	1.3	1	
99-3459	291	2	8.4	5.2	G	coarse		brn	2.27	1	
99-3459	259	2	11.52	8.3	G	sm		brn/smdg	2	1	
99-3528	1	8	8.24	27.5	S	eroded		sm	3.2	1	
99-36	263	3	8.73	6.8	G	curv comp st	ind	sm	1.41	1	
99-3659	267	3	4.84	3.5	G	sm		brn	1.2	1	
99-3659	257	2	5.61	3	G	brn		brn	0.94	1	
99-3659	271	3	6.05	3.2	G	sm		brn	1.22	1	
99-3659	258	2	6.58	1.9	S	sm		sm	1.61	1	
99-3659	260	5	7.05	6.2	S	sm		sm	1.97	1	
99-3659	270	2	7.27	3.9	G	ind st		sm	1.56	1	
99-3659	256	3	7.67	6.3	G	coarse		sm/smdg	1.28	1	
99-3662	257	2	4.91	1.9	S	sm		sm	1.15	1	
99-3662	262	4	8.38	11.8	S	sm		sm	1.7	1	
99-37	255	3	8.41	5.1	G	coarse		sm	1.64	1	
99-37	254	5	8.85	15.2	G	coarse		sm	1.02	1	
99-3736	251	2	6.62	2	G	sm		sm	0.76	1	
99-3739	251	3	6.8	6	G	cordm		sm	1.6	1	
99-3739	252	1	8.65	2.1	G	ind st		sm	1.62	1	
99-3740	258	3	7.06	4.7	G	cordm		sm/smdg	1.25	1	
99-3740	257	2	7.72	2.7	G	sm		sm	1.28	1	
99-3740	2570	2	9.12	3.8	G	ind lin st		eroded	0.98	1	
99-3740	252	1	9.48	2.1	G	ind lin st		sm	2.32	1	
99-3745	255	2	6.92	1.9	G	sm		eroded	0.93	1	
99-3745	254	3	8.57	9.9	G	cordm		sm	1.26	1	
99-3745	252	4	8.58	17.6	G	cordm		sm	1.4	1	
99-3745	253	5	10.42	25.5	G	curv comp st	ind	sm	1.2	1	
99-3746	257	1	0	1.1	G	eroded		sm	0.97	1	
99-3746	255	2	5.44	3	G	ind lin st		sm	1.08	1	
99-3746	253	3	6.8	2.5	G	ind lin st		eroded	1.15	1	
99-3746	254	2	8.3	2	G	ind st		sm	1.08	1	
99-3746	256	2	9.48	2	G	sm		sm	1.46	1	
99-3749	253	2	0	1.9	G	eroded		sm	1.86	1	
99-3749	254	2	6.95	2.9	G	ind lin st		sm	2.1	1	
99-3760	252	1	10.18	2.9	G	ind lin st		sm/smdg	1.2	1	
99-3763	251	1	0	2.1	G	eroded		eroded	1.32	1	
99-3764	256	2	0	5.4	G	eroded		sm	1.55	1	
99-3764	265	3	0	3.5	G	eroded		eroded	0.61	1	
99-3764	266	2	6.02	3.8	G	ind st		sm/smdg	1.34	1	
99-3764	257	2	7.28	3.1	G	ind st		sm	0.73	1	
99-3764	260	2	7.85	6	grit	ind lin st		sm/smdg	0.66	1	
99-3764	264	2	8.26	3.7	G	cordm		sm	0.56	1	
99-3764	262	2	8.74	5.3	G	ind lin st		sm	1	1	
99-3764	258	2	9.4	5.6	G	sm		eroded	1.66	1	
99-3764	259	1	10.16	4	G	curv comp st	ind scroll	sm/smdg	1.2	1	
99-3771	255	2	7.62	4.2	G	ind st		scr	1.54	1	
99-3771	253	3	7.79	10.7	G	coarse		sm	1.1	1	
99-3771	256	4	7.8	7.4	grit	ind lin st		sm	0.84	1	
99-3771	258	3	7.98	4.8	grit	ind lin st		sm	1.38	1	
99-3775	257	2	5.5	3.7	G	coarse		sm	1.16	1	
99-3775	259	2	6.18	5.2	G	coarse		sm	1.99	1	
99-3775	256	2	7.28	2.8	G	ind st		sm/smdg	1.82	1	
99-3775	255	2	8.13	3.7	G	ind st	sm over	sm	0.9	1	
99-3781	5	2	6.6	3.2	grit	ind lin st		sm	1.1	1	
99-3781	6	3	8.75	6.5	grit	ind lin st		sm	1.12	1	
99-3782	255	1	7.44	1.6	G	coarse		sm	1.18	1	
99-3782	252	2	7.45	4.1	G	ind lin st		sm	0.98	1	
99-3782	253	2	8.22	5.6	G	sm		brn/smdg	1.33	1	
99-3782	254	1	8.61	2.2	G	coarse		sm	1.73	1	
99-3785	252	3	6.38	6.2	G	ind st	sm over	sm/smdg	1.61	1	
99-3785	254	2	7.71	2.7	G	sm		sm	1.68	1	
99-3785	255	2	8.21	3.4	G	ind lin st		sm	0.8	1	
99-3785	253	2	8.4	3.3	G	sm		sm	1.29	1	
99-3801	258	3	7.06	3.9	G	ind lin st		sm	1.79	1	
99-3801	262	2	7.6	3.3	G	ind st		sm/smdg	1.39	1	
99-3801	265	1	8	1.7	G	ind lin st		sm	1.4	1	
99-3801	263	2	8	3.7	G	sm		sm	1.62	1	
99-3801	253	6	8.59	22.5	G	cordm		sm	0.92	1	
99-3801	255	2	8.6	3.3	G	cordm		sm	1.73	1	
99-3801	254	4	8.61	12.5	G	cordm		sm	1.13	1	
99-3801	257	3	8.66	11.2	G	ind lin st		sm	1.29	1	
99-3801	256	3	8.95	6.9	G	ind lin st		sm	1.1	1	
99-3801	266	2	10.6	3.2	G	ind st		sm	1.75	1	
99-3806	254	2	6.03	2.3	G	coarse		sm	1.6	1	
99-3806	253	1	9.05	2	G	eroded		sm	1.35	1	
99-3807	254	2	0	2.2	G	sm		eroded	1.24	1	
99-3807	256	1	0	0.7	G	eroded		eroded	1.68	1	
99-3807	253	2	8.22	2.7	G	ind st		sm	0.87	1	
99-3807	257	4	9.35	8.4	G	cordm		sm	1.63	1	
99-3808	260	3	7.58	6.3	G	ind lin st		sm	1.2	1	
99-3808	255	3	7.73	8.1	G	cordm		sm	1.13	1	
99-3808	258	2	7.8	3.7	G	ind st		sm	0.8	1	
99-3808	254	3	7.81	9.9	G	cordm		sm/smdg	1.36	1	
99-3808	259	2	7.83	4.9	G	ind st		sm	1.05	1	
99-3808	256	2	8.41	5	G	cordm		sm/smdg	1.52	1	
99-3808	263	2	8.57	3.1	G	cordm		sm/smdg	1.21	1	
99-3808	257	2	8.6	5.1	G	cordm		sm/smdg	1.16	1	
99-3808	261	1	8.86	2.5	G	eroded		sm	1.18	1	
99-3808	262	2	9.3	2.8	G	ind st		sm	1.2	1	
99-3834	291	2	0	2	G	eroded		sm	1.08	1	
99-3834	277	1	0	1.4	G	eroded		sm	1.18	1	
99-3834	299	2	0	1.8	G	scr		sm	1.48	1	
99-3834	279	2	0	2.3	G	sm		eroded	1.73	1	
99-3834	278	2	0	2.1	G	eroded		eroded	1.4	1	
99-3834	276	1	0	2	G	eroded		sm	1.46	1	
99-3834	318	1	0	1.9	G	eroded		eroded	1.62	1	
99-3834	368	2	0	2	G	eroded		eroded	1.32	1	
99-3834	321	2	0	3	G	cordm		eroded	1.44	1	
99-3834	322	2	0	2.4	G	eroded		eroded	1	1	
99-3834	333	3	0	2.7	S	eroded		eroded		1	
99-3834	370	2	0	1.7	G	eroded		eroded	1.22	1	
99-3834	353	1	0	1.1	G	eroded		sm	1.83	1	
99-3834	355	2	0	2.2	G	ind st		eroded	1.57	1	
99-3834	363	2	0	3.1	G	eroded		sm/smdg	1.58	1	
99-3834	365	1	0	1.8	G	sm		eroded	1.98	1	
99-3834	340	2	0	2.8	G	eroded		eroded	1.46	1	
99-3834	344	2	4.68	1.3	S	sm		sm		1	
99-3834	275	2	5.3	2.3	G	ind lin st		sm/smdg	2.08	1	
99-3834	350	2	5.32	2.4	grit	sm		sm	0.65	1	
99-3834	334	2	5.73	2.8	S	eroded		eroded		1	
99-3834	281	2	5.79	2.6	G	sm		sm	1.22	1	
99-3834	264	2	5.9	2.9	G	ind lin st		sm/smdg	1.62	1	wide grooves
99-3834	313	2	5.96	2.2	G	ind lin st		sm/smdg	1.35	1	
99-3834	310	2	6.07	3.7	G	sm		sm	1.25	1	
99-3834	327	3	6.1	3.2	G	sm		sm	1.28	1	
99-3834	288	1	6.15	1.7	S/CR	ind st		sm/smdg	1.26	1	
99-3834	341	2	6.22	1.9	G	eroded		sm	1.42	1	
99-3834	315	1	6.38	1.9	G	ind lin st		sm	1.18	1	
99-3834	286	2	6.4	3.5	G	coarse		eroded	1.34	1	
99-3834	273	2	6.42	2.6	G	sm		sm	2.08	1	

99-3834	339	2	6.54	3.5	grit	comp st	ind	sm	0.72	1	
99-3834	292	2	6.55	3.6	grit	sm		sm	0.78	1	
99-3834	267	3	6.58	4.8	G	sm		sm	1.42	1	
99-3834	314	2	6.58	3.1	G	ind lin st		sm	1.01	1	
99-3834	274	2	6.6	1.9	G	ind st	sm over	sm	0.94	1	
99-3834	306	2	6.62	2.8	G	ind st	sm over	sm	1.7	1	
99-3834	326	3	6.64	6.8	G	curv comp st	ind	sm	1.07	1	
99-3834	309	2	6.7	2.2	grit	ind st		sm	1.08	1	
99-3834	303	2	6.72	2.1	G	sm		sm	1.56	1	
99-3834	345	2	6.73	2.8	G	ind st	sm over	sm	1.34	1	
99-3834	270	2	6.75	2.7	G	sm		sm	1.25	1	
99-3834	323	1	6.89	2.1	G	cordm		sm	1.28	1	
99-3834	329	2	6.92	3.7	G	ind lin st		sm	2.1	1	
99-3834	302	3	6.96	4.6	G	cordm		sm	1.41	1	thick cord
99-3834	290	1	7.02	1.9	G	ind lin st	sm over	sm	1.42	1	
99-3834	271	2	7.06	3.3	G	sm		sm	1.02	1	
99-3834	308	1	7.12	1.8	G	ind st		sm	1.42	1	
99-3834	272	2	7.15	3.4	G	scr		sm	1.6	1	
99-3834	268	2	7.18	4.3	G	comp st	ind	sm/smdg	1.06	1	
99-3834	352	2	7.18	4.2	grit	ind lin st		sm	1.32	1	
99-3834	295	3	7.21	7	grit	curv comp st	ind	sm/smdg	1.07	1	
99-3834	311	2	7.23	3.2	G	coarse		eroded	2.18	1	
99-3834	298	3	7.36	6	G	coarse		sm	1.32	1	
99-3834	324	2	7.38	3.1	G	curv comp st	ind sm over	eroded	1.68	1	
99-3834	285	2	7.42	3.2	G	ind lin st		sm/smdg	1.28	1	
99-3834	346	1	7.44	2.4	G	cordm	sm over	sm	1.04	1	
99-3834	332	2	7.52	3.1	G	ind lin st		sm	0.85	1	
99-3834	316	3	7.58	4.6	G	eroded		eroded	1.5	1	
99-3834	338	2	7.6	4.3	G	sm		sm	1.44	1	
99-3834	287	2	7.62	3.3	G	ind st	sm over	sm	1.34	1	
99-3834	319	2	7.63	3.3	G	ind st		sm	1.26	1	
99-3834	284	2	7.64	3.2	G	cordm		sm	1.21	1	
99-3834	354	1	7.68	2.5	G	ind st	sm over	sm	1.84	1	
99-3834	317	2	7.78	4.2	G	ind st	sm over	sm/smdg	1.09	1	
99-3834	320	2	7.82	3.2	G	ind st		sm	0.97	1	
99-3834	335	2	7.89	4.6	G	ind lin st		sm/smdg	1.3	1	
99-3834	351	2	7.9	3	G	coarse		coarse	1.3	1	
99-3834	328	2	7.94	3.8	G	ind lin st		sm	1.64	1	
99-3834	305	3	8.06	2.8	G	sm		eroded	1.2	1	
99-3834	266	2	8.08	4.3	G	curv comp st	ind sm over	sm	1.3	1	
99-3834	301	2	8.1	3.1	G	cordm		sm	1.6	1	
99-3834	283	2	8.22	5	G	cordm		sm	1.41	1	
99-3834	337	2	8.26	2.7	G	eroded		sm	1.62	1	
99-3834	269	2	8.38	2.9	S	eroded		eroded		1	
99-3834	366	3	8.42	7.4	G	ind lin st		sm	1.75	1	wide grooves
99-3834	349	1	8.46	1.6	G	cordm		sm	1.48	1	
99-3834	280	3	8.48	7.5	G	ind lin st	sm over	sm/smdg	1.42	1	
99-3834	330	2	8.5	3.4	grit	ind lin st		sm	1.15	1	
99-3834	348	2	8.52	4.9	G	ind lin st		sm	1.88	1	
99-3834	304	1	8.54	2.6	G	coarse		sm	1.65	1	
99-3834	294	3	8.62	8.6	G	sm		sm	1.7	1	
99-3834	347	2	8.62	4.6	G	ind st	sm over	sm	1.42	1	
99-3834	300	2	8.74	4.4	G	coarse		sm	1.05	1	
99-3834	296	3	8.78	8.3	G	rectilin comp st	conc sqs	sm	1.21	1	
99-3834	293	4	9.12	15.8	G	curv comp st	ind	eroded	2.58	1	
99-3834	325	1	9.22	2.4	G	ind st		sm	1.68	1	
99-3834	297	2	9.48	4.9	G	ind st		sm	1.8	1	
99-3834	282	2	9.5	4.2	G	ind st	sm over	sm	0.98	1	
99-3834	307	2	9.56	4.2	G	cordm		sm	1.34	1	
99-3834	265	1	9.6	2.8	G	cordm	sm over	sm	1.64	1	
99-3834	289	3	10.08	4.5	G	scr		sm/smdg	1.54	1	
99-3834	312	2	10.12	2.9	G	sm		sm/smdg	1.52	1	
99-3834	331	3	10.72	5.9	G	curv comp st	ind	sm	1.25	1	
99-3834	336	2	11.28	6.7	G	scr		sm/smdg	1.13	1	base fragment
99-3835	263	3	0	2	G	sm		eroded	1.64	1	
99-3835	264	2	0	2.7	G	eroded		sm	1.76	1	
99-3835	265	3	0	4.4	G	eroded		eroded	2.06	1	
99-3835	261	2	2.8	2.8	G	coarse		sm	1.72	1	
99-3835	257	3	4.9	4.3	G	ind lin st		sm/smdg	1.5	1	
99-3835	259	3	6.16	7.1	G	sm		sm	1.6	1	
99-3835	260	2	7.28	3.1	G	sm		sm	1.08	1	
99-3835	258	2	7.35	3	G	cordm		sm	2.21	1	
99-3835	999	6	9.22	25.3	G	ind lin st		sm	1.28	1	
99-3835	262	2	9.9	3.5	G	ind st		sm/smdg	1.68	1	
99-3836	259	1	0	1.3	G	eroded		eroded	1.78	1	
99-3836	260	3	8.9	9.2	G	comp st	ind	sm	1.42	1	
99-3836	256	3	9.32	13.9	G	sm		sm/smdg	1.38	1	
99-3840	252	2	5.6	2.2	G	cordm		sm	1.3	1	
99-3840	251	3	9.53	7.2	G	cordm		sm	1.3	1	
99-3842	255	2	6.9	3.7	G	comp st	ind	sm	1.23	1	
99-3842	254	1	11.08	2.7	G	sm		sm	1.26	1	
99-3852	309	2	0	2	G	sm		eroded	1.24	1	
99-3852	279	2	0	2.6	G	sm		eroded	0.78	1	
99-3852	321	2	0	2.9	grit	eroded		eroded	1.48	1	
99-3852	322	2	0	2.1	G	eroded		sm	1.3	1	
99-3852	328	2	0	1.9	S	eroded		eroded	0	1	
99-3852	329	2	0	2.7	G	ind lin st		eroded	1.25	1	
99-3852	332	2	0	1.5	G	eroded		sm	1.1	1	
99-3852	333	1	0	1.7	G	eroded		sm	1.62	1	
99-3852	314	2	4.21	1.1	S	eroded		eroded	0	1	
99-3852	312	2	5.01	2.4	grit	ind st		sm	1.1	1	
99-3852	311	3	5.12	2	S	eroded		eroded	0	1	
99-3852	282	2	5.4	2.4	G	coarse		brn/smdg	1.87	1	
99-3852	286	2	5.78	3.6	S	sm		sm	0	1	
99-3852	277	2	5.85	3.6	G	ind lin st		sm	1.18	1	
99-3852	281	2	6	2.8	G	sm		sm	1.44	1	
99-3852	308	2	6.08	2.1	S	sm		sm	0	1	
99-3852	331	2	6.2	1.9	G	ind st		sm	1.32	1	
99-3852	325	2	6.2	2.8	G	sm		brn/smdg	1.88	1	
99-3852	296	2	6.24	4.7	G	ind lin st		sm	1.5	1	
99-3852	280	2	6.25	4.1	G	ind lin st		sm	1.42	1	
99-3852	302	2	6.38	3.6	G	curv comp st	ind	sm	1.2	1	
99-3852	270	3	6.38	4.8	grit	sm		sm	1.2	1	
99-3852	267	2	6.58	3.3	grit	ind st		sm	0.78	1	
99-3852	317	2	6.68	2.2	G	ind lin st		eroded	1.08	1	
99-3852	284	3	6.77	5.5	G	ind st	sm over	sm	2.54	1	
99-3852	287	3	6.8	8.7	G	comp st	ind	sm/smdg	1.7	1	
99-3852	261	3	6.84	8.9	G	coarse		sm	1.2	1	
99-3852	272	2	6.84	3	G	sm		sm	1.12	1	
99-3852	288	2	6.84	3.1	G	ind st		sm/smdg	2.08	1	
99-3852	307	3	6.94	5.3	G	cordm		sm	0.98	1	
99-3852	275	2	7.02	3.2	G	coarse		sm	1.96	1	
99-3852	297	2	7.04	3.5	G	cordm		sm	1.75	1	
99-3852	262	2	7.2	2.5	G	sm		sm	1.74	1	
99-3852	326	1	7.25	1.9	grit	ind lin st		sm/smdg	1.1	1	
99-3852	301	2	7.3	3.4	G	ind lin st		sm/smdg	1.45	1	
99-3852	278	2	7.35	3.3	G	sm		sm	1.45	1	
99-3852	283	2	7.55	5.1	G	ind lin st		sm	1.72	1	
99-3852	264	2	7.62	4.6	G	ind st	sm over	sm	1.71	1	
99-3852	294	3	7.64	9.6	G	ind lin st		sm	1.3	1	
99-3852	319	2	7.7	3.5	G	coarse		sm	1.3	1	
99-3852	318	2	7.75	2.6	G	ind lin st		sm	1.6	1	
99-3852	292	3	7.88	7.6	G	ind lin st		sm/smdg	1.68	1	
99-3852	269	3	8.1	6.8	G	ind lin st		brn/smdg	2.08	1	
99-3852	285	2	8.12	2.9	G	sm		sm	1.68	1	
99-3852	304	3	8.18	7.6	G	comp st	ind	sm/smdg	1.58	1	
99-3852	290	2	8.18	5.7	G	incs	ind	brn/smdg	1.75	1	

99-3852	316	2	8.18	3.5	G	ind lin st		sm	1.34	1	
99-3852	298	3	8.32	5.4	G	cordm		sm/smdg	2.22	1	
99-3852	295	2	8.35	4.2	G	cordm		sm	1.88	1	
99-3852	306	3	8.42	5.7	G	sm		eroded	1.4	1	
99-3852	299	2	8.48	4	G	ind lin st		sm/smdg	1.65	1	
99-3852	276	2	8.5	5.2	G	sm		sm	1.38	1	
99-3852	289	3	8.52	6.9	G	curv comp st	ind	sm/smdg	1.74	1	
99-3852	273	1	8.54	2.1	G	sm		sm/smdg	2.02	1	
99-3852	323	1	8.7	2.3	G	ind st		sm	1.85	1	
99-3852	268	2	8.72	4.2	G	ind lin st		sm	0.98	1	
99-3852	300	2	9.18	5	G	ind lin st		sm/smdg	1.36	1	
99-3852	327	2	9.2	3.1	G	sm		sm	1.45	1	
99-3852	274	2	9.32	4.6	G	sm		sm	1.86	1	
99-3852	265	4	9.45	13.2	G	ind st		sm	1.36	1	
99-3852	291	3	9.5	7.1	G	cordm		sm	1.1	1	
99-3852	334	1	9.75	1.9	G	ind lin st		sm	1.6	1	
99-3852	293	4	9.92	15.2	G	ind lin st		sm	1.4	1	
99-3852	266	2	9.98	3.6	G	coarse		sm	1	1	
99-3852	315	2	10.01	3.5	G	ind st		sm	0.88	1	
99-3852	303	3	10.06	11.4	G	curv comp st	ind	sm	1.18	1	
99-3852	263	3	10.58	5.9	G	ind st		brn/smdg	1.46	1	
99-3852	271	3	11.4	5.7	G	sm		sm	1.32	1	
99-3853	253	2	7.18	4.5	G	ind st		sm	0.98	1	
99-3853	254	2	7.74	3	G	cordm		sm	1.68	1	
99-3881	258	1	6.3	1.6	G	eroded		brn/smdg	1.69	1	
99-3881	259	2	8	4.2	G	ind st		eroded	1.4	1	
99-3888	266	2	5.44	2.3	G	eroded		eroded	1.72	1	
99-3888	262	2	6.4	3.8	G	ind lin st		brn/smdg	1.1	1	
99-3888	268	2	7.27	4.9	G	cordm		sm	1.27	1	
99-3888	258	2	7.44	4.7	G	cordm		sm	1.35	1	
99-3888	272	2	7.5	4.6	G	ind lin st		sm	1.27	1	
99-3888	260	2	7.58	4.6	G	ind st		sm	1.2	1	
99-3888	267	3	7.8	5.9	G	ind lin st		sm	1.7	1	
99-3888	264	2	7.8	2.8	G	ind st		sm	1.07	1	
99-3888	265	2	7.92	3.3	G	ind st		sm	1.6	1	
99-3888	270	3	8.13	4.7	G	ind lin st		coarse	1.72	1	
99-3888	263	2	8.2	2.6	G	sm		sm	1.28	1	
99-3888	259	2	8.58	3.8	G	ind st		coarse	1.5	1	
99-3888	269	2	8.89	4.1	G	ind lin st		sm	1.42	1	
99-3888	261	2	9.05	6.5	G	ind lin st		sm	1.29	1	
99-3888	271	6	9.5	25.8	G	coarse		sm	1.62	1	
99-3889	252	3	8.78	10.8	G	comp st	ind	sm	1.15	1	
99-3890	257	2	0	2.3	G	eroded		eroded	1.52	1	
99-3890	259	2	0	1.6	G	curv comp st	ind	eroded	1.38	1	
99-3890	256	1	0	2.2	G	eroded		sm	1.7	1	
99-3890	258	3	6.42	6.7	G	sm		sm	1.5	1	
99-3890	253	2	7.44	3	G	ind st		sm/smdg	1.65	1	
99-3890	254	2	7.5	3.1	G	ind st		sm/smdg	0.85	1	
99-3890	255	2	8.01	5.2	G	curv comp st	ind	sm/smdg	1.3	1	
99-3892	296	2	0	1.7	S	eroded		sm		1	
99-3892	314	2	0	3.4	G	eroded		sm/smdg	1.7	1	
99-3892	279	2	4.97	2.4	G	sm		sm	1.1	1	
99-3892	299	2	4.98	2	G	eroded		sm	0.92	1	
99-3892	305	2	5.12	1.6	G	eroded		sm	1.62	1	
99-3892	298	2	5.45	2.3	grit	ind lin st		sm	0.75	1	
99-3892	292	3	5.76	2.9	G	ind lin st		sm/smdg	1	1	
99-3892	277	2	6.02	4.3	G	sm		sm	1.28	1	
99-3892	313	3	6.12	3.2	G	ind st	sm over	sm	1.18	1	
99-3892	303	2	6.17	2.7	G	eroded		sm	1.18	1	
99-3892	287	2	6.3	2.3	grit	ind lin st		sm	1.02	1	
99-3892	282	2	6.4	2.4	G	coarse		coarse	1.25	1	
99-3892	268	2	6.46	2.6	G	cordm		sm	1.8	1	
99-3892	269	2	6.7	2.8	G	ind lin st		brn/smdg	0.89	1	
99-3892	265	2	6.74	3.8	G	cordm		sm	1.24	1	
99-3892	281	3	6.8	6.3	G	ind lin st		sm/smdg	1.74	1	
99-3892	293	2	6.9	2.4	G	ind lin st		sm/smdg	0.94	1	
99-3892	312	1	6.92	1.7	G	ind lin st		eroded	1.4	1	
99-3892	301	2	6.94	4.7	G	coarse		sm	1.44	1	
99-3892	266	1	6.96	2.1	G	cordm		sm	1.12	1	
99-3892	300	2	6.98	2.8	G	coarse		sm	1.48	1	
99-3892	283	2	7.01	3	G	sm		sm	1.4	1	
99-3892	285	2	7.02	2.2	G	sm		sm	1.5	1	
99-3892	278	1	7.1	1.8	G	sm		sm	1.58	1	
99-3892	280	2	7.17	2.5	grit	scr		sm	1.28	1	
99-3892	263	4	7.18	13.6	G	cordm	ovrst	brn/smdg	1.22	1	
99-3892	267	2	7.21	2.9	G	cordm		sm	1.97	1	
99-3892	306	1	7.4	1.7	G	ind lin st		sm	0.89	1	
99-3892	275	3	7.4	5.2	G	coarse		sm	1.62	1	
99-3892	307	2	7.5	2.5	G	sm		sm	1.6	1	
99-3892	311	2	7.62	3.4	G	ind lin st		sm/smdg	1.23	1	
99-3892	262	4	7.62	14.3	G	curv comp st	ind	sm	1.25	1	
99-3892	308	2	7.82	4.5	G	coarse		sm	1	1	
99-3892	290	3	7.84	6.4	G	ind lin st		sm	1.65	1	
99-3892	264	3	8.06	7	G	cordm		sm	1.32	1	
99-3892	289	3	8.06	5.2	G	ind lin st		sm	1.46	1	
99-3892	274	2	8.24	2.7	G	ind st		sm/smdg	1.64	1	
99-3892	270	3	8.34	10.7	G	brn		sm	1.28	1	base fragment
99-3892	271	3	8.48	7.3	G	sm		sm	1.78	1	
99-3892	319	2	8.5	2.6	G	eroded		sm	1.02	1	
99-3892	291	3	8.6	7.4	G	ind lin st		sm	0.8	1	
99-3892	302	2	8.64	3.1	G	coarse		sm/smdg	1.32	1	
99-3892	295	2	8.68	4.7	G	ind lin st		sm/smdg	1.12	1	
99-3892	272	1	8.7	2.6	G	sm		sm/smdg	1.42	1	
99-3892	276	3	9	5.6	G	coarse		sm	0.98	1	
99-3892	288	2	9.08	2.6	G	ind lin st		sm	1.3	1	
99-3892	286	2	9.1	4.3	G	ind st		sm/smdg	1.08	1	
99-3892	297	2	9.92	5.5	G	smpl st	ovrst	sm	1.62	1	comp design made with a smpl paddle?
99-3892	294	2	10.54	10.3	G	ind lin st		sm	2.01	1	
99-3892	273	2	12.3	4.4	G	sm		sm/smdg	1.12	1	
99-3895	282	2	0	2.9	G	eroded		sm	1.4	1	
99-3895	284	1	0	1.3	G	coarse		eroded	1.12	1	
99-3895	285	2	5.15	2.3	G	eroded		sm	1.7	1	
99-3895	273	2	5.67	2.6	G	coarse		sm/smdg	0.8	1	
99-3895	271	2	5.9	4	G	coarse		brn/smdg	2	1	
99-3895	278	2	6.48	2.2	G	sm		sm	1.4	1	
99-3895	275	2	7.4	2.7	G	ind lin st		sm	1.7	1	
99-3895	279	2	7.42	2.9	G	scr		sm	1.44	1	
99-3895	267	2	7.5	3.7	G	cordm		sm	1.42	1	
99-3895	268	4	7.64	10.7	G	sm		sm	1.13	1	
99-3895	261	4	7.66	9.3	G	comp st	ind	sm	1.2	1	
99-3895	265	2	7.8	3.2	G	cordm		sm	2.34	1	
99-3895	266	2	8.05	3.7	G	cordm		sm	2.08	1	
99-3895	274	2	8.18	3.6	G	sm		sm	1	1	
99-3895	276	2	8.38	4	G	coarse		sm	1.08	1	
99-3895	272	3	8.4	5.9	G	coarse		sm/smdg	1.9	1	
99-3895	270	2	8.6	3.8	G	ind st		sm	1.2	1	
99-3895	264	1	9.1	2.5	G	cordm		sm	1.38	1	
99-3895	262	3	9.12	6.3	G	cordm		sm	1.82	1	
99-3895	269	3	9.32	9.1	G	ind st		sm	1.12	1	
99-3895	277	1	10.7	2.2	G	sm		sm	1.38	1	
99-3898	255	5	6.72	10.4	G	ind lin st		brn/smdg	0.87	1	
99-3908	253	2	5.35	1.8	G	ind st		sm	1.95	1	
99-3908	252	2	5.92	3.8	G	cordm		sm/smdg	1.37	1	
99-3908	254	3	7.57	6.9	G	coarse		redfilmed	1.15	1	
99-3916	1	3	5.6	5.7	grit	curv comp st	ind	sm	0.59	1	Qualla paste
99-3993	251	2	0	1	G	eroded		brn	1.2	1	
99-4040	253	1	0	1.9	G	eroded		brn		1	

99-4040	254	3	0	2.9	G	eroded		sm		1	
99-4040	261	2	0	2.7	G	eroded		sm		1	
99-4040	264	2	0	2.2	G	eroded		sm		1	
99-4040	257	2	6.44	2.4	G	coarse		sm		1	
99-4040	251	3	7.11	6	G	coarse		sm		1	
99-4040	262	1	7.14	1.6	G	sm		sm		1	
99-4040	256	1	7.27	1.6	G	sm		sm/smdg		1	
99-4040	263	3	7.36	8.6	G	coarse		sm		1	
99-4040	259	3	7.4	7.2	G	sm		brn/smdg		1	
99-4040	255	2	7.78	4.3	G	sm		sm		1	
99-4040	266	6	8.11	25.3	G	sm		eroded		1	
99-4040	258	6	8.19	17.11	G	ind lin st		sm		1	
99-4040	252	4	8.25	13.7	G	coarse		sm		1	
99-4040	265	3	8.4	3.9	G	sm		sm		1	
99-4040	267	9	8.41	76.4	G	coarse		sm		1	
99-4041	1	8	7.12	34.7	G	scr		sm	1.05	1	
99-41	12	2	8.54	2.5	G	coarse		sm	1.72	1	
99-415	272	2	6.84	0	G	ind lin st		sm	1.41	1	
99-415	283	2	7.21	0	G	ind lin st		sm/smdg	1.7	1	
99-415	270	2	7.46	0	G	scr		sm	1.13	1	
99-415	278	2	7.64	0	G	eroded		sm/smdg	1.22	1	
99-415	277	2	7.77	0	G	sm		sm	0.75	1	
99-415	281	2	8.94	0	G	ind lin st		sm	1.31	1	
99-415	274	1	9.27	0	G	ind st		sm	1.01	1	
99-415	276	3	9.62	0	G	coarse		sm	1.21	1	
99-4225	252	2	0	2.4	G	sm		eroded	1.32	1	
99-4225	251	2	7.68	4.7	G	ind st	sm over	sm	1.84	1	
99-4225	253	2	9.85	2.8	G	ind lin st		sm	1.65	1	
99-4226	252	6	7.4	35.2	G	curv comp st	ind scroll	sm/smdg	0.92	1	
99-4226	253	2	9.22	2	G	curv comp st	ind scroll	eroded	1.6	1	
99-4228	257	2	6.48	2.2	G	coarse		sm	1.62	1	
99-4228	255	2	6.95	1.9	grit	ind lin st		sm	1.24	1	
99-4228	256	2	7.12	4	G	ind lin st		eroded	1.25	1	
99-4228	260	4	7.7	10.2	G	ind lin st		sm	1.02	1	
99-4228	261	2	7.83	3.9	G	sm		sm	1.08	1	
99-4228	258	2	8.3	4	G	ind lin st		sm/smdg	1.22	1	
99-4228	254	1	8.35	2.2	G	eroded		sm	1.42	1	
99-4228	259	3	8.38	13.5	grit	ind lin st		sm	1.2	1	
99-4228	253	4	10.02	15	G	curv comp st	ind scroll ovrst	eroded	0.92	1	
99-4230	256	2	6.96	5.1	G	ind lin st		sm	1.8	1	
99-4230	255	2	7.92	4.7	G	ind lin st		sm	1.68	1	
99-4230	253	2	8.3	3.8	G	cordm		sm/smdg	1.9	1	
99-4230	254	2	9.92	4.1	G	ind lin st		sm/smdg	1.75	1	
99-4231	277	2	0	2	G	curv comp st	ind	eroded	1.1	1	
99-4231	254	1	4.52	1.3	G	sm		sm/smdg	1.07	1	
99-4231	270	2	6.08	3.7	grit	ind lin st		sm	0.67	1	
99-4231	261	2	6.48	2	G	ind lin st		sm	0.5	1	
99-4231	275	2	6.82	2.8	G	ind lin st		sm/smdg	1.65	1	
99-4231	268	1	6.85	2.3	G	ind lin st		sm	1.2	1	
99-4231	269	3	6.9	4.9	G	ind st	sm over	sm	1.3	1	
99-4231	280	2	6.96	4.7	G	scr		sm	2.01	1	
99-4231	267	2	7	2.6	G	sm		sm	1.3	1	
99-4231	260	1	7	2	G	ind st		sm	1.05	1	
99-4231	271	2	7.02	2.5	G	br		sm	0.54	1	
99-4231	253	4	7.3	13.2	G	cordm		sm	1.28	1	
99-4231	273	3	7.3	3.9	G	cordm		sm	0.8	1	
99-4231	264	2	7.64	4.5	G	scr		sm	0.95	1	
99-4231	256	2	7.72	1.9	G	punc	round	sm	0.7	1	
99-4231	258	2	7.82	3.7	G	sm		sm	2.4	1	
99-4231	263	2	7.82	2.4	G	cordm		sm	1.2	1	
99-4231	276	1	8.18	1.8	G	eroded		sm	1.6	1	
99-4231	255	2	8.18	2.9	G	eroded		sm	1.7	1	
99-4231	278	3	8.4	6.8	G	cordm	ovrst	sm	2.1	1	
99-4231	257	2	8.44	2.5	G	ind st		sm	1.7	1	
99-4231	266	2	8.7	2.2	G	sm		sm	1.8	1	
99-4231	259	2	8.82	4.1	G	ind lin st		sm	1.02	1	
99-4231	274	2	8.98	4.2	G	sm		sm	1.5	1	
99-4231	279	4	9.15	9	G	ind lin st		sm	1.05	1	
99-4231	262	1	9.4	2.3	G	ind st		redfilmed	2.07	1	
99-4231	272	2	10	6.1	G	eroded		sm	1.5	1	
99-4231	265	3	10.08	7.9	G	ind lin st		sm	1.7	1	
99-4244	252	3	7.13	3.6	G	ind lin st		sm	1.57	1	
99-4244	251	2	7.75	1.7	G	cordm		sm	1.95	1	
99-4245	7	2	4.97	2.5	G	coarse		sm	1.08	1	
99-4245	6	2	7.33	2.9	G	cordm		sm	0.91	1	
99-4247	254	1	7.07	2.3	grit	ind st		sm	0.41	1	sooted
99-4247	253	4	7.56	9.8	G	ind lin st		sm	0.86	1	
99-4247	252	5	10.73	16.6	G	ind lin st		sm	1.26	1	
99-44	252	2	6	2	G	rgh		sm	1.59	1	corn cob
99-44	253	1	6.91	1.7	G	curv comp st	ind	sm	0.92	1	
99-44	254	1	7.57	2.6	G	sm		sm	1.17	1	
99-4487	1	2	9.05	4.2	G	sm		sm	1.84	1	
99-4488	252	4	6.98	13.3	G	curv comp st	ind	sm	1.43	1	
99-4568	133	5	7.34	13.9	G	ind lin st		sm	1.26	1	
99-4568	129	1	7.42	2	G	sm		sm	1.14	1	
99-4568	128	1	7.44	2	G	sm		sm	1.4	1	
99-4572	412	2	5.63	3	G	sm		sm	1.15	1	
99-4572	420	2	6.44	1.8	G	cordm		sm	1.57	1	
99-4572	434	3	6.93	5.7	G	cordm		sm	1.5	1	
99-4572	419	2	9.39	2.4	G	sm		sm	1.29	1	
99-4575	9	2	8.22	4.6	G	ind lin st		sm	1.93	1	
99-4579	7	2	6.47	4.2	G	ind lin st		brn/smdg	1.01	1	
99-4579	8	2	7.86	3.2	G	sm		sm	1.4	1	
99-4579	6	2	8.18	3.3	G	ind lin st		sm	1.68	1	
99-4579	9	1	8.44	2.5	G	sm		sm	1.47	1	
99-4581	328	2	6.44	3.6	G	ind lin st		sm	1.21	1	
99-4581	302	2	6.52	2.5	G	ind st		sm	1.07	1	
99-4581	329	2	6.72	3.2	G	ind st		redfilmed	1.45	1	
99-4581	337	1	6.83	1.9	G	sm		sm	2.11	1	
99-4581	324	2	7.03	4.4	G	cordm		sm	1.05	1	
99-4581	318	3	7.17	4.9	G	ind lin st		sm	1.13	1	
99-4581	313	2	7.33	5.2	G	ind lin st		brn/smdg	0.89	1	
99-4581	333	2	7.48	3.2	G	ind lin st		sm	0.9	1	
99-4581	317	2	7.52	3.5	G	ind lin st		sm	0.99	1	
99-4581	309	2	7.74	5	G	ind lin st		sm	1.17	1	
99-4581	321	2	7.76	7.2	G	eroded		sm	1.76	1	
99-4581	322	1	7.79	2.2	G	ind st		sm	1.12	1	
99-4581	305	1	7.86	2.5	G	sm		sm	1.21	1	
99-4581	336	2	7.89	4.5	grit	ind lin st		sm/smdg	1.08	1	
99-4581	330	2	7.98	3.3	G	ind st		sm	0.95	1	
99-4581	341	2	7.98	3.3	G	sm		sm	0.81	1	
99-4581	343	3	8.21	7.3	G	ind st		sm	1.1	1	
99-4581	338	3	8.21	7.7	G	ind lin st		sm/smdg	1	1	
99-4581	314	3	8.22	4.3	G	sm		sm	1.44	1	
99-4581	303	2	8.22	4.4	G	ind st		brn	1.37	1	
99-4581	320	3	8.31	6.6	G	ind st		sm	1.53	1	
99-4581	311	3	8.32	7	G	sm		sm	1.1	1	
99-4581	298	2	8.4	4.2	G	ind lin st		sm	0.97	1	
99-4581	331	2	8.46	3.3	G	ind st		sm	1.02	1	
99-4581	319	2	8.62	4.1	G	cordm		sm	0.82	1	
99-4581	312	3	8.62	5.4	G	ind lin st		sm	2.4	1	
99-4581	346	4	8.64	15	G	cordm		sm	1.5	1	
99-4581	332	3	8.72	4.9	G	ind lin st		sm	1.4	1	
99-4581	323	2	8.96	3.9	G	ind lin st		sm	1.89	1	
99-4581	304	2	9.17	3	G	sm		sm	1.46	1	
99-4581	335	3	9.68	10.7	G	sm		sm	2.03	1	
99-4581	326	3	9.74	8.7	G	curv comp st	ind	sm/smdg	1.49	1	

99-4581	339	1	9.76	2.6	G	eroded		sm	1.06	1	
99-4581	327	2	9.86	3.5	G	ind st		sm	1.7	1	
99-4581	315	4	9.95	20.8	G	curv comp st	ind	sm	0.94	1	
99-4581	342	3	10.33	5.5	G	ind lin st		sm	1.7	1	
99-4581	334	3	10.58	7.1	G	ind lin st		coarse	2.4	1	
99-4581	325	3	14.42	8.3	G	cordm		sm	2.13	1	
99-4582	281	2	9.53	6.3	G	cordm	sm over	sm	0.67	1	
99-4582	275	2	10	4	G	ind lin st		sm	1.13	1	
99-474	262	2	7.1	0	G	scr		sm	1.47	1	
99-4749	252	3	4.37	4	G	ind lin st		brn/smdg	0.91	1	
99-493	254	2	6.6	4	G	sm		sm	1.21	1	
99-493	253	3	7.51	6.7	G	coarse		sm	1.82	1	
99-50	257	2	6.85	4	G	cordm	sm over	brn/smdg	1.78	1	
99-50	256	2	7.43	4.2	G	ind st		sm	0.75	1	
99-50	255	2	8.01	6.1	grit	ind lin st		sm	1.13	1	
99-5047	251	2	7.44	2.5	G	ind lin st		sm	1.67	1	
99-5048	250	2	7.75	3.7	G	ind st		brn/smdg	1.94	1	
99-5048	251	4	8.23	14.2	G	ind st		brn	1.55	1	
99-5048	252	3	8.49	6.3	G	coarse		brn/smdg	1.53	1	
99-545	251	2	5.3	2.6	G	sm		sm	1.86	1	
99-5560	252	2	7.23	0	G	sm		sm	1.94	1	
99-5571	253	2	8.5	0	G	cordm	sm over	sm	1.17	1	
99-5605	3	2	7.24	3.8	G	sm		eroded	1.9	1	sooted
99-5605	4	3	7.84	6.9	G	sm		sm	2.11	1	
99-5853	252	2	7.69	2.8	G	coarse		sm	1.34	1	
99-5861	2	2	6.47	0	G	sm		sm	1.05	1	
99-5900	1	3	9.01	11.8	G	cordm		sm	2.31	1	
99-591	254	2	4.7	2.3	G	sm		sm/smdg	1.8	1	
99-6	273	2	8.49	3.2	G	sm		sm	1.01	1	
99-607	251	3	5.1	2.8	G	coarse		sm	1.68	1	
99-6321	2	3	8.72	0	G	ind lin st		sm/smdg	1.12	1	
99-6343	1	4	8.07	9	G	sm		sm	2	1	
99-6355	251	8	7.15	45	S	eroded		eroded		1	
99-6382	252	3	6.37	0	S	sm		sm	2.03	1	
99-6382	251	2	9.73	0	G	coarse		sm	1.23	1	
99-6390	252	2	5.27	1.7	S	eroded		eroded/ smdg		1	
99-6390	254	3	5.83	6.2	G	scr		sm/smdg	1.64	1	
99-6390	253	2	6.24	3.2	grit	cordm	sm over	sm	0.82	1	
99-6391	3	5	6.73	14.1	G	comp st	ind	sm	1.02	1	
99-6391	2	3	8.3	8.6	G	ind st	sm over	sm	1.54	1	
99-6418	252	3	7.11	9.1	G	ind lin st		sm/smdg	1.27	1	
99-6418	253	1	7.63	2.1	G	ind lin st		sm	1.33	1	
99-6418	254	2	8.57	4.6	G	sm		sm	2.2	1	
99-6418	255	2	8.59	3.8	G	ind st	col st	sm/smdg	1.37	1	
99-6418	256	3	8.7	9.6	G	ind st	col st	sm/smdg	0.89	1	
99-6462	252	3	6.59	6.4	G	sm		sm	2.14	1	
99-67	251	3	7.24	8.2	G	sm		sm	2.18	1	
99-67	252	1	8.5	2.5	G	ind lin st		sm	1.18	1	
99-73	257	2	5.7	2.1	G	coarse		sm	1.2	1	
99-73	256	2	6.22	3	G	sm		sm	1.4	1	
99-73	252	3	7.56	8.4	G	coarse		sm	1.74	1	
99-809	306	2	4.79	1.7	S	sm		sm		1	
99-809	271	1	5.76	2.3	grit	sm		sm	0.62	1	
99-809	282	2	5.89	4.5	G	brn		sm	2.07	1	
99-809	284	1	6.03	1.7	G	coarse		brn/smdg	1.45	1	
99-809	296	3	6.32	6.3	grit	coarse		brn	0.73	1	
99-809	265	2	6.33	3	G	coarse		brn	1.79	1	
99-809	273	2	6.46	4.9	G	sm		brn	1.1	1	
99-809	293	4	6.48	8.8	S	sm		eroded		1	
99-809	300	3	6.55	7.1	G	sm		brn/smdg	1.88	1	
99-809	304	4	6.67	17.7	G	coarse		brn	0.93	1	
99-809	299	2	6.69	2.7	G	sm		brn/smdg	1.69	1	
99-809	314	2	6.69	3.2	G	sm		brn	0.86	1	
99-809	262	6	6.71	21.4	S	scr		scr		1	
99-809	276	3	6.72	5	grit	sm		brn	0.97	1	
99-809	307	2	6.73	3.1	S	sm		sm		1	
99-809	268	1	6.76	1.6	G	sm		brn/smdg	0.9	1	
99-809	258	5	6.8	12.5	S	sm		sm		1	
99-809	283	3	6.84	6.2	S	sm		eroded		1	
99-809	286	2	6.92	3.5	G	scr		brn	2.08	1	
99-809	256	7	7	15.7	S	eroded		eroded		1	
99-809	303	4	7.01	9.2	S	sm		sm		1	
99-809	290	2	7.1	3.6	G	sm		eroded	1.17	1	
99-809	295	2	7.15	3	S	scr		eroded		1	
99-809	261	5	7.2	19.1	G	coarse		brn	1.66	1	
99-809	280	2	7.21	3.3	S	scr		sm		1	
99-809	279	2	7.27	2.9	S	sm		sm		1	
99-809	310	3	7.29	4.7	S	sm		sm		1	
99-809	257	6	7.35	23.6	S	sm		sm		1	
99-809	260	5	7.4	16.3	S	sm		sm		1	
99-809	263	5	7.44	15.6	S	scr		eroded		1	
99-809	313	2	7.58	2.7	G	sm		brn/smdg	2.75	1	
99-809	302	5	7.59	23.4	G	scr		sm	1.73	1	
99-809	272	1	7.64	1.8	S	sm		sm		1	
99-809	288	3	7.67	6.7	G	ind lin st	sm over	coarse	1.73	1	
99-809	289	1	7.7	1.4	S	sm		eroded		1	
99-809	269	2	7.76	2.6	S	scr		brn		1	
99-809	298	2	7.76	3.7	S	sm		sm		1	
99-809	308	1	7.79	1.2	S	sm		eroded		1	
99-809	253	1	7.82	2.3	G	ind st		brn	1.9	1	
99-809	292	2	7.85	5	G	coarse		eroded	1.44	1	
99-809	275	2	7.88	7.6	G	ind st		brn	2.93	1	
99-809	294	4	8	11.3	G	sm		coarse	2.01	1	
99-809	264	5	8	20.7	S	eroded		scr		1	
99-809	309	4	8.08	14	S	scr		eroded		1	
99-809	267	1	8.44	1.9	grit	sm		sm	0.43	1	
99-809	312	2	8.64	2.9	S	scr		eroded		1	
99-809	281	2	8.7	3	G	coarse		brn	1.75	1	
99-809	254	2	8.71	3.4	S	scr		eroded		1	
99-809	291	4	8.76	11.8	S	sm		sm		1	
99-809	316	3	8.81	11.1	G	sm		coarse	1.25	1	
99-809	305	2	8.85	4.1	G	coarse		brn/smdg	2.3	1	
99-809	259	6	9.05	26.4	G	brn		brn	2.59	1	
99-809	266	1	9.07	1.1	S	sm		sm		1	
99-809	277	1	9.16	2.3	S	sm		eroded		1	
99-809	297	4	9.2	10.1	S	scr		sm		1	
99-809	285	1	9.35	1.8	S	sm		sm		1	
99-809	301	1	9.82	1.9	S	sm		sm		1	
99-809	315	3	11.91	14.1	G	coarse		coarse	1.82	1	
99-81	255	2	0	1.9	G	eroded		eroded	1.42	1	
99-81	252	3	5.7	5	grit	ind lin st		sm	0.92	1	
99-81	254	2	6.7	2.6	G	ind lin st		sm	1.54	1	
99-81	253	2	7.68	4.2	G	ind lin st		sm	1.94	1	
99-817	252	2	8.76	2.6	S	sm		sm		1	
99-819	268	2	0	1.5	G	sm		sm	1.1	1	
99-819	2610	1	7	2.2	G	sm		sm	1.82	1	
99-819	260	1	7.1	2.6	G	sm		sm	2.1	1	
99-819	256	3	7.14	8.6	G	coarse		sm	1.45	1	
99-819	255	3	7.68	5	G	sm		sm/smdg	1.5	1	
99-819	251	2	7.89	3.4	G	sm		sm	2.92	1	
99-819	253	2	8	3	G	sm		sm/smdg	1.35	1	
99-819	261	1	8.02	2	G	sm		sm/smdg	1.36	1	
99-819	254	1	8.06	2.3	G	sm		sm	1.5	1	
99-819	259	3	8.12	6.3	G	sm		sm/smdg	1.54	1	
99-819	265	4	8.26	8.9	G	coarse		sm/smdg	1.48	1	
99-819	263	4	8.3	14.2	G	coarse		sm/smdg	1.68	1	
99-819	257	2	8.52	5.8	G	sm		sm/smdg	1.18	1	

99-819	266	2	8.64	3.8	G	sm		sm/smdg	1.22	1	
99-819	262	4	8.68	11.3	G	coarse		sm	1.64	1	
99-819	264	3	11.22	9	G	sm		sm	1.48	1	
99-821	251	3	7.1	4.9	S	sm		sm	0	1	sooted
99-824	251	7	8.22	35.2	G	curv comp st	ind	scr	1.62	1	
99-824	253	3	8.46	7.5	G	curv comp st	ind scroll	coarse	1.65	1	
99-8282	283	2	0	2	G	eroded		brn	1.4	1	
99-8282	296	2	0	1	G	eroded		sm	2.4	1	
99-8282	279	2	0	2	G	sm		eroded	1.26	1	
99-8282	346	2	0	2.6	G	ind lin st		sm	1.66	1	
99-8282	313	2	0	2.6	G	eroded		eroded	1.81	1	
99-8282	306	2	0	2.3	G	eroded		sm	1.4	1	
99-8282	322	2	0	2.6	G	eroded		eroded	1.04	1	
99-8282	302	2	0	3.2	G	coarse		eroded	1.59	1	
99-8282	326	2	0	2	G	eroded		brn/smdg	1.78	1	
99-8282	325	2	0	2.7	G	ind lin st		eroded	1.76	1	
99-8282	324	2	0	2	G	eroded		sm/smdg	1.18	1	
99-8282	319	3	5.54	3.1	G	ind lin st		brn	1.32	1	
99-8282	263	2	5.64	2.7	G	sm		sm	1.34	1	
99-8282	316	2	5.7	2.8	G	coarse		brn/smdg	1.1	1	
99-8282	310	2	5.76	2.8	G	ind lin st		sm	0.66	1	
99-8282	265	3	5.82	5.2	G	coarse		sm	1.62	1	
99-8282	311	3	5.86	4	G	ind lin st		brn/smdg	1.2	1	
99-8282	272	2	6.06	2.8	grit	sm		brn	1.62	1	
99-8282	259	5	6.07	20.1	G	ind lin st		sm	2	1	
99-8282	293	3	6.21	5.2	G	comp st	ind	brn/smdg	1.7	1	
99-8282	285	2	6.3	2.8	G	ind lin st		brn	1.38	1	
99-8282	289	2	6.36	4.3	G	ind st	sm over	brn	0.96	1	
99-8282	314	2	6.4	3.9	G	ind lin st		sm	1.2	1	
99-8282	297	2	6.43	2.1	G	ind lin st		sm	1.25	1	
99-8282	298	2	6.5	2.2	G	coarse		sm	1.12	1	
99-8282	292	2	6.5	2.8	G	comp st	ind	brn	1.06	1	
99-8282	271	2	6.79	3	G	coarse		sm	0.85	1	
99-8282	281	4	6.8	8.2	grit	br		brn	1.06	1	
99-8282	308	2	6.84	3.7	G	curv comp st	ind scroll	brn	1.38	1	
99-8282	341	3	6.92	6.4	G	ind lin st		sm	1.02	1	
99-8282	318	2	6.92	3.5	G	ind st	sm over	brn/smdg	1.52	1	
99-8282	275	2	7	2	S	sm		sm		1	
99-8282	260	2	7.08	4.9	G	sm		sm	1.32	1	
99-8282	300	2	7.08	3.5	G	ind lin st		sm	1.24	1	
99-8282	270	3	7.08	5.2	G	coarse		sm	1.4	1	
99-8282	317	1	7.08	2.4	G	ind st		sm	1.94	1	
99-8282	330	4	7.22	10.1	grit	ind lin st		sm	0.97	1	wide grooves
99-8282	327	4	7.24	12.3	G	cordm		sm	3.2	1	
99-8282	291	2	7.32	2.9	grit	ind st		sm	0.47	1	
99-8282	344	2	7.34	2.2	grit	ind lin st		brn/smdg	0.57	1	
99-8282	282	4	7.38	12.1	grit	br		brn	1.68	1	
99-8282	278	2	7.4	2.9	G	coarse		brn/smdg	1.2	1	
99-8282	309	2	7.44	4.1	G	curv comp st	ind scroll	eroded	1.06	1	
99-8282	337	4	7.48	8	G	ind lin st	sm over	sm	1.16	1	
99-8282	273	2	7.5	5.3	G	ind st	sm over	sm	1.3	1	
99-8282	304	3	7.54	5.2	G	ind lin st		sm	2.04	1	
99-8282	343	2	7.64	4.5	G	ind lin st		sm/smdg	0.94	1	
99-8282	340	3	7.64	5.6	G	cordm		sm	0.85	1	
99-8282	258	6	7.7	29.9	G	cordm		sm	1.06	1	
99-8282	338	3	7.7	7.5	G	cordm		sm	1.5	1	
99-8282	342	2	7.75	3.9	G	comp st	ind	sm	0.82	1	
99-8282	287	2	7.78	4.4	G	ind st		brn	1.5	1	
99-8282	336	3	7.92	7.9	G	cordm		sm	0.8	1	
99-8282	331	2	7.94	4.3	G	cordm		sm	1.52	1	
99-8282	339	3	7.96	7.6	G	cordm		sm	0.93	1	
99-8282	294	2	8	6.4	G	scr		brn/smdg	0.96	1	
99-8282	264	4	8.08	7.5	G	ind st	sm over	sm	1.38	1	
99-8282	295	2	8.12	3	G	ind lin st		sm	1.12	1	
99-8282	276	2	8.18	4.1	G	coarse		brn/smdg	1.08	1	
99-8282	301	3	8.24	4.8	G	ind st		sm	1.1	1	
99-8282	307	3	8.25	5.3	G	ind st		brn/smdg	1.8	1	
99-8282	3310	4	8.28	10.2	G	ind lin st	ovrst	sm/smdg	1.18	1	
99-8282	257	6	8.34	25.4	grit	sm		brn/smdg	0.98	1	
99-8282	323	2	8.38	2.9	G	ind lin st		sm/smdg	1.4	1	
99-8282	328	4	8.4	17.2	G	ind lin st	ovrst	sm	1.5	1	
99-8282	303	5	8.5	17	G	ind lin st		sm	1.1	1	
99-8282	261	2	8.54	2.8	G	sm		sm	1.94	1	
99-8282	329	5	8.56	18.6	G	curv comp st	ind ovrst	sm	1.6	1	
99-8282	335	2	8.78	2.9	G	sm		sm	1.25	1	
99-8282	332	2	8.8	6.5	G	ind lin st		sm	0.92	1	
99-8282	288	2	8.8	5.5	G	cordm	sm over	sm	1.38	1	
99-8282	305	2	8.86	3.4	G	eroded		sm	1.1	1	
99-8282	2610	4	8.96	11.7	G	sm		eroded	1.3	1	
99-8282	312	2	9.04	2.9	G	ind st		eroded	1.12	1	
99-8282	290	3	9.07	5.8	G	sm		brn/smdg	2.08	1	
99-8282	262	2	9.12	5.5	G	sm		sm	1.4	1	
99-8282	266	4	9.15	12.7	G	scr		sm	0.9	1	
99-8282	333	4	9.28	11.4	G	ind lin st		brn/smdg	1.18	1	
99-8282	299	2	9.45	3.8	G	scr		sm	1.6	1	
99-8282	315	2	9.52	2.6	G	ind lin st		sm	1.07	1	
99-8282	321	2	9.59	3.6	G	ind st		sm/smdg	2.44	1	
99-8282	277	1	10.23	3.7	G	coarse		sm	1.69	1	
99-8282	286	2	10.62	5.8	G	ind st		sm	1.22	1	
99-8283	260	2	0	1.8	G	sm		sm	1.12	1	
99-8283	255	1	7.78	2.2	G	incs	ind	sm	0.8	1	
99-8283	254	1	8.08	2.3	G	sm		sm	1.14	1	
99-8283	257	2	8.7	3.4	G	cordm		sm	0.82	1	
99-8287	257	2	0	1.1	G	eroded		eroded	1.02	1	
99-8287	259	2	7.14	1.8	G	sm		sm	1.3	1	
99-8287	256	1	7.3	1.6	G	cordm		sm	1.72	1	
99-8287	254	2	7.34	2.4	G	eroded		coarse	0.78	1	
99-8287	261	2	7.54	2.1	G	eroded		sm/smdg	1.38	1	
99-8287	253	1	7.78	1.8	G	coarse		sm/smdg	1.64	1	
99-8287	258	1	7.9	1.9	G	cordm		sm	1.07	1	
99-8287	255	2	8.28	3.5	G	cordm		sm/smdg	0.78	1	
99-8287	252	2	9.22	1.6	G	sm		sm	1.42	1	
99-8287	260	1	9.24	2.2	G	sm		sm	1.21	1	
99-8288	251	3	6.08	6	grit	ind lin st		sm	0.88	1	
99-8289	251	4	7.62	12.2	G	ind lin st		sm	1.5	1	
99-829	265	4	5	6.8	G	coarse		sm	1.91	1	
99-829	279	5	5.85	13.1	G	sm		sm	1.71	1	
99-829	264	2	5.89	3.9	G	brn		sm	1.5	1	
99-829	268	2	6.14	2.9	G	sm		sm	0.94	1	
99-829	263	3	6.46	4.5	G	brn		sm	1.61	1	
99-829	255	1	6.61	1.9	G	sm		sm	2.38	1	
99-829	277	2	6.69	2.8	S	sm		sm		1	
99-829	266	3	7.12	6.2	G	coarse		sm	1.81	1	
99-829	259	3	7.12	4.2	S	sm		sm		1	
99-829	267	2	7.3	2.4	S	sm		sm		1	
99-829	271	4	7.71	9.8	S	scr		eroded	0	1	
99-829	257	2	7.72	4.3	grit	sm		sm	0.71	1	
99-829	274	3	8.05	8.7	G	sm		brn/smdg	1.59	1	compact paste
99-829	258	1	8.08	1.8	S	sm		scr		1	
99-829	275	3	8.17	5.7	S	sm		scr		1	
99-829	261	2	8.19	5.8	G	sm		brn	1.12	1	
99-829	256	4	8.51	7.1	S	sm		sm		1	
99-829	254	3	8.69	4.9	S	sm		eroded		1	
99-829	262	2	9.42	2.8	S	sm		sm		1	
99-829	272	8	10.27	67.9	G	coarse		sm	2.43	1	
99-8292	5	3	7.28	5.8	G	sm		brn/smdg	1.8	1	
99-8292	4	2	10.14	4.4	G	cordm		eroded	1.2	1	
99-8293	272	3	6.06	4.9	G	sm		sm	1.5	1	

99-8293	265	4	6.08	7.5	grit	ind lin st		brn	0.67	1	
99-8293	260	1	6.52	2.3	G	sm		sm	1.1	1	
99-8293	264	2	6.7	2	G	sm		sm	1.7	1	
99-8293	268	2	6.82	2.3	G	cordm		sm	1.1	1	
99-8293	266	3	7.22	4.2	G	ind lin st		sm	2.1	1	
99-8293	257	3	7.28	9.2	G	ind lin st		sm	1.4	1	
99-8293	274	2	7.3	3.1	G	eroded		sm	1.5	1	
99-8293	267	3	7.89	10.7	G	cordm		sm	1.98	1	
99-8293	270	1	7.98	2	G	ind st		sm	1.4	1	
99-8293	277	2	8.1	1.7	G	sm		sm	1.07	1	
99-8293	262	3	8.5	8.9	G	cordm		sm	1.3	1	
99-8293	276	2	8.6	2.7	G	sm		sm	1.3	1	
99-8293	263	2	8.62	4.9	G	sm		sm	1.3	1	
99-8293	269	2	8.8	1.7	G	ind lin st		sm/smdg	1.3	1	
99-8293	275	3	9	6.8	G	sm		sm	0.5	1	
99-8293	271	2	9.04	3.8	G	ind st	sm over	sm	1.85	1	
99-8293	259	2	9.08	2.7	G	eroded		sm	2.1	1	
99-8293	258	1	9.2	2.3	G	cordm		sm	1.92	1	
99-8293	261	2	9.24	4.5	G	sm		sm	0.7	1	
99-8293	273	3	9.74	9.6	G	cordm		sm	1.1	1	
99-8296	252	2	7.18	3.5	G	sm		sm	1.87	1	
99-8297	254	2	6.64	3.5	G	ind lin st		sm	2.5	1	
99-8297	257	1	7.92	2	G	cordm		redfilmed	0.75	1	
99-8297	256	3	8.5	9.2	G	ind lin st		sm	1.54	1	
99-8297	252	1	10.41	2.6	G	ind st		sm	1.2	1	
99-8299	252	3	6.58	3.1	G	ind lin st		sm/smdg	1.44	1	
99-8312	253	2	5.52	2.1	G	ind lin st		sm/smdg	1.24	1	
99-8312	254	2	5.86	2.9	G	sm		sm	0.68	1	
99-8312	261	2	6.22	2.3	G	sm		sm	1.48	1	
99-8312	260	2	7.14	2.5	G	cordm		sm	1.34	1	
99-8312	259	2	7.4	3.5	G	sm		sm	1.89	1	
99-8312	256	2	7.62	3	G	sm		sm	1.76	1	
99-8312	258	2	8.46	2.8	G	sm		sm/smdg	1.14	1	
99-8312	257	2	8.6	3.5	G	sm		sm	1.78	1	
99-8313	3	2	0	2	G	ind st		eroded	1.62	1	
99-8319	252	1	7.09	2.2	grit	ind lin st		sm	1.14	1	
99-8319	251	1	7.67	3.5	grit	ind lin st		sm	0.75	1	
99-8319	254	3	8.19	6.3	G	ind lin st		coarse	1.42	1	wide grooves
99-8325	253	2	5.96	2.4	G	ind lin st		sm	1.46	1	
99-8325	252	2	8.15	3.2	G	cordm		sm/smdg	1.8	1	
99-8326	12	1	6.78	1.8	G	coarse		sm	1.14	1	
99-8326	6	1	7.42	2.3	G	ind lin st		eroded	1.42	1	
99-8326	11	2	8.2	6.4	G	curv comp st	ind	sm	1.1	1	
99-8326	10	2	8.36	4.7	G	ind st		sm/smdg	1.2	1	
99-8326	5	3	8.54	5.9	G	ind lin st		sm	1.4	1	
99-8326	9	2	9.12	5.2	G	ind lin st		brn/smdg	1.1	1	
99-8326	8	2	9.46	6.4	G	cordm		sm	1.9	1	
99-8326	7	3	10.98	6.7	G	sm		sm	1.82	1	
99-839	280	1	0	1.5	G	eroded		sm/smdg	1.84	1	
99-839	268	4	4.7	8.4	G	sm		sm	1.08	1	
99-839	2710	3	5.1	3.9	G	sm		sm	2.07	1	
99-839	256	1	7.12	2.5	G	sm		sm	1.72	1	
99-839	254	2	7.2	3.8	G	sm		sm	1.88	1	
99-839	272	4	7.22	9	G	coarse		redfilmed	1.98	1	
99-839	260	2	7.6	2.7	G	sm		sm/smdg	1.46	1	
99-839	267	3	7.62	10.6	G	sm		sm	1.84	1	
99-839	264	4	7.68	12.3	G	sm		sm/smdg	1.8	1	
99-839	263	2	7.74	3.2	G	sm		sm	1.07	1	
99-839	269	1	7.88	2.3	G	sm		sm	1.87	1	
99-839	2760	1	7.88	1.6	G	sm		sm/smdg	1.3	1	
99-839	259	4	7.98	6.4	G	sm		sm	1.28	1	
99-839	229	2	7.99	3.3	G	sm		sm	1.42	1	
99-839	255	1	8	1.8	G	ind lin st		sm	1.7	1	
99-839	258	1	8.04	3	G	sm		sm	2.01	1	
99-839	281	1	8.22	1.6	G	sm		sm	2.24	1	
99-839	262	1	8.3	1.5	G	sm		sm	1.47	1	
99-839	282	2	8.34	2.4	G	sm		sm	1.13	1	
99-839	271	3	8.38	9.1	G	coarse		brn/smdg	1.72	1	
99-839	273	3	8.42	10.5	G	sm		sm	2.26	1	
99-839	251	2	8.42	2.6	G	sm		sm	1.5	1	
99-839	261	2	8.44	3.9	G	sm		sm	1.06	1	
99-839	275	3	8.48	10.2	G	coarse		sm/smdg	1.25	1	
99-839	265	4	8.5	13	G	sm		sm	0	1	
99-839	266	2	8.9	5	G	sm		sm	1.88	1	
99-839	257	1	8.96	2.6	S	sm		sm	0	1	
99-839	276	2	9.32	5.4	G	sm		sm	1.32	1	
99-839	278	2	9.82	2.5	S	sm		sm	0	1	
99-839	253	2	10.06	1.6	G	sm		sm/smdg	3.8	1	
99-839	252	4	10.32	12.2	S	sm		sm	1.66	1	
99-842	261	1	6.02	1.5	G	sm		sm	1.24	1	
99-842	258	2	6.68	4.5	G	coarse		sm/smdg	0.88	1	
99-842	260	2	6.9	2	G	sm		sm	2.01	1	
99-842	263	3	6.9	4.1	S	sm		sm	0	1	
99-842	255	3	7.18	5.8	S	sm		sm	0	1	
99-842	256	2	7.18	3.5	G	cordm		sm	1.73	1	
99-842	253	3	7.48	7.8	G	sm		sm/smdg	1.12	1	sooted
99-842	267	2	7.82	4.1	G	sm		sm	1.87	1	
99-842	257	2	7.92	3.5	G	sm		sm/smdg	1.98	1	
99-842	262	2	8.42	2.8	G	sm		sm/smdg	1.32	1	
99-842	251	8	8.42	49.1	S	sm		scr	1.98	1	
99-842	254	3	8.56	8.8	G	sm		sm/smdg	1.54	1	
99-842	252	3	8.86	9	G	ind st	sm over	sm	1.45	1	
99-842	259	2	9.12	4.5	G	sm		sm	1.35	1	
99-843	253	2	8.02	2.2	G	sm		sm/smdg	1.06	1	
99-843	254	2	8.18	4.6	G	sm		sm/smdg	1.52	1	
99-843	255	2	8.34	2.6	S	sm		sm	0	1	
99-851	253	1	7.2	2	G	ind lin st		sm	1.48	1	
99-8591	1	3	5.66	4	G	ind lin st		sm	1.68	1	
99-8594	252	2	7.12	3.1	G	ind lin st		sm	0.95	1	
99-8594	254	1	7.78	2	G	ind st		sm	0.9	1	
99-8594	255	1	8.95	2	G	ind st		sm	1.41	1	
99-8594	225	3	12.25	10	grit	sm		sm	1.06	1	base fragment
99-8596	257	2	5.48	2.3	G	sm		sm/smdg	0.85	1	
99-8596	256	2	6.7	2	G	ind st		sm/smdg	1.18	1	
99-8596	255	2	7.74	3.7	G	ind lin st		sm/smdg	1.2	1	
99-8596	254	2	8.9	3.2	G	cordm		sm	1.5	1	
99-8598	252	2	6.52	1.9	G	ind st		sm	1.02	1	
99-8598	257	3	7.16	5.1	G	comp st	ind	sm	1.28	1	
99-8598	255	2	7.29	4.9	G	sm		sm	1.08	1	
99-8598	258	5	7.6	16.9	G	ind lin st		sm	1.79	1	
99-8598	259	3	7.74	5.8	G	ind lin st		sm	1.1	1	
99-8598	261	7	8.12	26.7	G	smpl st	ovrst	eroded	1.14	1	comp design made with a smpl paddle?
99-8598	260	2	8.3	4.8	G	ind lin st		sm/smdg	0.79	1	
99-8598	253	2	8.35	4.7	G	cordm		sm	0.65	1	
99-8598	254	2	8.38	3.5	G	ind st		sm/smdg	1.1	1	
99-8598	256	4	8.92	10.6	G	ind lin st		brn/smdg	1.62	1	
99-8599	263	2	0	1.8	G	eroded		eroded	1.2	1	
99-8599	260	2	6.4	2.3	G	sm		redfilmed	2.04	1	
99-8599	264	2	6.54	2.2	G	ind st		sm	0.89	1	
99-8599	259	3	6.62	6.3	G	ind st	sm over	sm/smdg	1.1	1	
99-8599	262	2	7.34	4.1	G	ind st		sm	1.4	1	
99-8599	256	3	7.58	4	G	cordm		sm	1.42	1	
99-8599	257	2	7.78	3.1	grit	curv comp st	ind	sm	1.48	1	
99-8599	261	2	12.92	5.1	grit	sm		sm/smdg	1.28	1	
99-8600	263	3	6.18	4.2	G	sm		sm	1.09	1	
99-8600	262	2	6.4	3.2	grit	ind lin st		sm	1.02	1	
99-8600	261	2	6.48	2.6	G	ind st		sm/smdg	1.04	1	

99-8600	254	2	6.5	2.3	grit	ind lin st		sm	0.86	1	wide grooves
99-8600	255	4	6.62	8	G	ind lin st		sm	1.52	1	
99-8600	253	3	7.88	8.2	G	incs	ind vertical lines	brn/smdg	1.74	1	carinated shoulder
99-8600	256	2	8.08	4.2	G	cordm		sm	1.42	1	
99-8600	260	2	8.5	4.5	G	ind st	sm over	sm	1.06	1	
99-8600	258	3	9.48	7.5	G	ind lin st		sm	1.35	1	
99-8600	259	3	14.18	9.9	G	sm		sm	1.86	1	
99-8603	251	3	7.88	5.4	G	ind lin st		sm	1.62	1	
99-8605	255	2	7.56	3.2	G	eroded		sm/smdg	1.57	1	
99-8605	254	2	10.82	5.9	G	sm		sm	1.88	1	
99-8607	253	2	7.09	2.7	G	comp st	ind	sm	1.15	1	
99-8608	251	2	8.22	2	G	ind st		sm	2.1	1	
99-8612	253	1	4.58	1.8	S	eroded		eroded		1	
99-8612	251	2	5.15	5.2	S	eroded		sm		1	
99-8614	8	3	5.22	6.9	grit	brn		eroded	0.52	1	carinated shoulder
99-8614	3	3	7.12	4.7	G	comp st	ind	brn/smdg	0.67	1	
99-8614	4	4	7.52	10.3	G	cordm		sm	1.72	1	
99-8614	2	3	7.75	7.1	G	ind lin st		sm/smdg	1.32	1	
99-8614	6	2	8.5	5.1	G	ind lin st		sm/smdg	0.92	1	
99-8614	5	3	9.41	8.5	G	sm		sm	1.25	1	
99-8614	7	2	9.8	4.4	G	brn		brn/smdg	1.28	1	
99-8615	258	2	0	3.7	G	eroded		sm	1.64	1	
99-8615	263	2	0	1.1	G	ind lin st		sm	0.99	1	
99-8615	262	3	0	4.5	G	eroded		eroded	1.42	1	
99-8615	265	3	5.86	7.3	G	ind lin st		sm	1.1	1	
99-8615	268	1	6.06	2.2	G	ind st	sm over	sm/smdg	0.94	1	
99-8615	269	3	6.3	4.1	G	ind lin st		sm/smdg	1.64	1	
99-8615	271	3	7.07	4.4	G	ind lin st		sm	1.2	1	
99-8615	257	3	7.28	9.7	G	coarse		sm/smdg	1.79	1	
99-8615	266	2	7.38	4.5	G	ind lin st		sm	1.5	1	
99-8615	264	4	7.4	10.1	G	comp st	ind	sm/smdg	1.12	1	
99-8615	256	3	7.44	5.2	G	ind lin st	sm over	sm	2.74	1	
99-8615	261	2	8.32	4.1	G	ind lin st		sm/smdg	1.22	1	
99-8615	259	2	9.56	5.9	G	cordm		sm	1.18	1	
99-8615	267	2	9.58	4.4	G	ind st	sm over	sm	1.58	1	
99-8615	260	2	10	4.7	G	sm		sm/smdg	1.66	1	
99-8615	255	4	11.92	7.2	G	ind lin st	sm over	sm	1.6	1	
99-8615	270	4	13.66	26.4	G	cordm		coarse	2	1	
99-8615	254	3	14.74	5.7	G	sm		sm	1.72	1	
99-8616	252	2	6.7	4.1	G	ind st	sm over	sm	2.05	1	
99-8616	253	2	7.18	2.2	G	ind st		sm	1.8	1	
99-8617	251	4	6.72	10.2	G	sm		brn/smdg	1.8	1	
99-862	254	3	9.32	7.5	grit	ind lin st		brn	1.68	1	
99-8620	1	2	7.61	2.8	G	cordm		sm	1.12	1	
99-8623	5	3	6.28	2.5	G	sm		sm/smdg	0.78	1	
99-8623	6	2	7.04	2	G	ind st		sm	0.79	1	
99-8624	8	2	6.25	3.9	G	cordm		sm	1.38	1	
99-8624	17	2	6.25	1.9	G	ind lin st		sm	1.4	1	
99-8624	10	3	6.94	8.5	G	cordm	ovrst	sm	1.1	1	
99-8624	20	3	7.42	5.1	G	ind lin st		sm/smdg	1.48	1	
99-8624	13	2	7.44	2.4	G	ind st		sm/smdg	2.06	1	
99-8624	16	2	7.6	3.3	G	ind lin st		sm	1.12	1	
99-8624	11	2	7.68	3.5	G	coarse		sm	1.25	1	
99-8624	15	1	7.7	1.6	G	coarse		sm	1.58	1	
99-8624	7	2	7.9	2.6	G	ind st		sm	2.38	1	
99-8624	18	2	8	2.8	G	ind lin st		sm	1.25	1	
99-8624	14	1	8.08	1.8	G	ind st		sm	1.4	1	
99-8624	19	2	8.48	3	G	ind st		sm	1.25	1	
99-8624	9	2	9.58	3.9	G	sm		sm	1.85	1	
99-8625	7	3	7.48	6.6	G	ind lin st		sm/smdg	1.75	1	
99-8625	8	4	8.64	13.5	G	eroded		sm/smdg	1.12	1	
99-8625	4	2	8.81	4.4	G	sm		sm	1.52	1	
99-8625	5	2	10.58	8.1	G	coarse		sm/smdg	1.62	1	

99-8626	252	2	6.2	2.1	G	ind lin st		eroded	1.6	1	
99-8626	253	1	8.28	2.1	G	sm		sm	1.6	1	
99-8626	251	2	9.32	3.5	G	sm		sm	1.6	1	
99-8626	254	2	11.9	3.6	G	ind lin st		sm	1.8	1	
99-8627	256	2	6.25	2.1	G	sm		sm/smdg	1.38	1	
99-8627	255	2	6.74	2.7	G	ind st		sm	1.1	1	
99-8628	2	4	7.68	14.9	G	smpl st	ovrst	sm	0.98	1	comp design made with a smpl paddle?
99-8629	273	1	0	1.3	G	sm		eroded	1.4	1	
99-8629	289	1	0	1.1	G	coarse		eroded	1.67	1	
99-8629	287	2	0	3.8	G	sm		eroded	1.96	1	
99-8629	260	1	0	1.5	grit	eroded		sm	0.7	1	
99-8629	280	2	0	2.8	G	ind lin st		eroded	1.48	1	
99-8629	284	3	5.44	3	G	ind lin st		brn/smdg	1.12	1	
99-8629	293	2	5.5	2.1	G	sm		sm	0.69	1	
99-8629	285	1	5.5	1.7	G	sm		sm	1.1	1	
99-8629	276	2	5.86	3.9	G	curv comp st	ind	sm	1.42	1	
99-8629	278	3	5.89	3.3	grit	sm		sm	1.42	1	
99-8629	271	2	6.06	3.1	G	ind lin st		sm	1.28	1	
99-8629	268	1	6.3	1.4	G	eroded		sm	2.2	1	
99-8629	269	1	6.38	1.8	G	curv comp st	ind	sm	1.58	1	
99-8629	295	3	6.4	3.9	G	coarse		sm	1.6	1	
99-8629	283	1	6.42	1.8	G	ind lin st		sm/smdg	1.42	1	
99-8629	290	2	6.6	2.3	G	cordm		sm/smdg	1.45	1	
99-8629	298	2	6.6	2.5	G	ind lin st		sm	1.2	1	
99-8629	256	2	6.64	2.4	G	ind lin st		sm	2.08	1	
99-8629	296	1	6.88	1.6	G	ind st		sm	2.1	1	
99-8629	255	2	6.96	4.4	G	ind lin st		sm/smdg	1.34	1	
99-8629	261	2	6.99	3.5	G	cordm		redfilmed	1.8	1	
99-8629	263	2	7.1	2.2	G	ind st		sm	1.58	1	
99-8629	274	2	7.12	2.6	G	sm		sm	0.98	1	
99-8629	258	2	7.35	2.9	G	sm		brn	1.1	1	
99-8629	277	2	7.38	5.3	G	ind lin st		sm	1.84	1	
99-8629	265	2	7.52	2.8	G	ind lin st		sm	2.3	1	
99-8629	272	2	7.52	2.4	G	coarse		sm	1.38	1	
99-8629	297	2	7.58	3.2	G	ind st		sm	1.52	1	
99-8629	294	2	7.68	2.8	G	sm		sm	1.32	1	
99-8629	300	1	7.7	2.2	G	ind lin st		sm	1.14	1	
99-8629	292	2	7.92	3.9	G	sm		sm	1.5	1	
99-8629	266	2	8	3	G	ind lin st		brn	1.18	1	
99-8629	267	1	8.12	2.1	G	ind lin st		sm	0.99	1	
99-8629	286	2	8.3	3.5	G	ind lin st		sm	1.9	1	
99-8629	262	3	8.4	4.5	G	ind st		sm	1.75	1	
99-8629	279	1	8.4	2.2	G	ind st		sm/smdg	1.24	1	
99-8629	301	2	8.4	3.7	G	ind lin st		sm	1.6	1	
99-8629	299	2	8.52	2.6	G	ind st		sm	1.23	1	
99-8629	254	1	8.52	2	G	sm		sm	1.28	1	
99-8629	259	2	8.54	5	G	cordm		sm	1.35	1	
99-8629	264	1	8.72	2	G	eroded		sm	2.17	1	
99-8629	291	2	8.74	4	grit	ind lin st		sm	1.3	1	
99-8629	282	1	9.12	2.2	G	sm		sm	1.38	1	
99-8629	257	1	10	2.5	G	ind st		sm	1.4	1	
99-8629	2870	3	11.78	8.4	G	ind lin st		coarse	1.4	1	
99-8630	256	2	6.35	1.5	G	sm		sm	1.08	1	
99-8630	257	2	6.75	2.4	G	ind st		sm	1.19	1	
99-8630	258	1	6.97	1	G	sm		sm	1.15	1	
99-8630	254	1	7.87	2.2	G	ind st		sm	2.54	1	
99-8631	7	2	0	3.5	G	eroded		sm	1.15	1	
99-8631	8	2	6.55	3.3	G	ind lin st		sm/smdg	1.3	1	
99-8631	9	1	6.92	1.3	G	eroded		sm	1.5	1	
99-8631	11	2	7.06	4.9	G	curv comp st	ind	sm/smdg	1.32	1	
99-8631	10	2	8.26	3.2	G	ind lin st		eroded	1.02	1	
99-8631	5	2	8.5	3.5	G	ind st		sm	1.4	1	
99-8631	6	2	8.5	5.2	G	cordm		sm	1.75	1	

99-8631	3	3	8.63	9.4	grit	ind lin st		sm	0.89	1
99-8631	4	1	9.1	2.5	G	ind st		sm	1.45	1
99-8631	12	3	9.15	4.9	G	ind st		sm	1.99	1
99-8632	257	1	0	2	G	eroded		eroded	1.04	1
99-8632	255	2	7.38	3.8	G	sm		sm	1.18	1
99-8632	256	2	7.54	3.7	G	ind st		sm	1.02	1
99-8633	257	2	4.62	1.4	G	br		sm/smdg	1.08	1
99-8633	261	3	4.89	4	grit	ind lin st		brn/smdg	0.62	1
99-8633	258	2	5.2	2.3	G	sm		sm	0.92	1
99-8633	256	2	6.72	2.1	G	ind st	sm over	sm/smdg	1.42	1
99-8633	254	2	6.74	2.2	G	ind lin st		sm	1.12	1
99-8633	253	2	7.06	3.9	G	ind lin st		sm	1.25	1
99-8633	263	2	7.08	4.2	G	cordm		sm	0.92	1
99-8633	255	4	7.65	9.4	G	coarse		sm	1.15	1
99-8633	260	2	7.78	2.4	G	cordm		sm	1.15	1
99-8633	262	1	7.93	2	G	sm		sm/smdg	1.4	1
99-8633	259	2	9.08	3.8	G	ind st	sm over	sm	1.3	1
99-8636	256	2	0	2.1	G	ind st		eroded	0.91	1
99-8636	258	2	6.02	2.9	grit	ind lin st		sm	1.07	1
99-8636	261	3	6.14	5.2	grit	sm		sm	0.68	1
99-8636	259	2	6.33	3.9	G	ind lin st		sm	1.16	1
99-8636	257	2	6.5	2.4	G	ind lin st		sm/smdg	2.25	1
99-8636	253	5	8	10.9	G	ind lin st		sm	1.21	1
99-8636	260	1	8.16	2.5	G	ind lin st		sm	0.93	1
99-8636	255	2	8.57	5.1	G	ind st		sm	1.69	1
99-8636	254	1	10.6	2.3	G	sm		sm	1.84	1
99-8637	253	3	7.85	6.4	G	curv comp st	ind	sm	1.93	1
99-8638	253	2	7.55	6	G	ind st	sm over	sm	1.61	1
99-8638	251	3	8.57	8.6	G	ind lin st		sm	1.41	1
99-8638	252	3	11.35	7.2	G	ind lin st		sm	1.42	1
99-8639	259	2	0	3.3	G	eroded		sm/smdg	1.68	1
99-8639	268	3	0	4.6	G	eroded		sm	1.25	1
99-8639	261	1	6.2	1.7	G	sm		sm	1.5	1
99-8639	264	2	6.2	3.2	G	ind st		sm/smdg	0.79	1
99-8639	257	2	6.28	3	G	ind st		sm	1.03	1
99-8639	258	2	6.74	2.2	G	sm		sm	1.5	1
99-8639	267	1	7	2.1	G	ind st		sm/smdg	1.3	1
99-8639	266	1	7.12	2.2	G	sm		sm	0.88	1
99-8639	263	2	7.18	4.6	G	cordm		sm	1.44	1
99-8639	255	2	7.34	3.5	G	cordm		sm/smdg	1.06	1
99-8639	262	1	7.46	2.4	G	sm		sm	0.82	1
99-8639	260	2	8.62	3	G	ind st		sm	1.62	1
99-864	5	1	6.08	1.3	G	eroded		sm	1.6	1
99-864	8	2	8.64	4.1	G	ind lin st		brn/smdg	1.54	1
99-8640	255	2	7.62	2.6	G	ind st		sm	0.68	1
99-8640	256	3	7.7	8.7	G	ind st		brn/smdg	1.08	1
99-8641	251	3	6.78	5.7	G	ind lin st		sm/smdg	1.25	1
99-8641	253	2	7.48	2.7	G	ind lin st		sm	1.71	1
99-8641	254	1	7.52	2	G	ind st		sm	0.97	1
99-8641	252	1	7.9	3.3	G	coarse		sm	1.3	1
99-8642	255	3	5.86	2.7	G	ind st		sm	1.18	1
99-8642	254	2	6.54	3.1	G	ind lin st		brn	1.02	1
99-8642	253	3	6.6	4.1	G	ind lin st		sm	1.1	1
99-8642	256	3	6.92	3.9	G	ind lin st		brn	1.1	1
99-8642	257	2	7.8	4.6	G	ind st		sm	0.84	1
99-8642	252	3	8.68	7.9	G	cordm		sm/smdg	1.52	1
99-8645	254	3	6.1	5.9	grit	ind lin st	sm over	sm	0.92	1
99-8645	253	3	7.65	6.2	G	coarse		sm	1.04	1
99-8650	255	2	6.52	3.5	G	scr		redfilmed	2.05	1
99-8650	254	1	6.7	2.1	G	sm		sm	0.62	1
99-8650	260	2	7.25	3.6	G	cordm		sm	1.52	1
99-8650	257	2	7.3	4	G	ind lin st		sm/smdg	0.94	1
99-8650	259	1	7.35	2.5	G	ind lin st		sm	1.2	1
99-8650	253	3	7.44	7.6	G	ind lin st		sm	2.12	1
99-8650	252	2	7.6	3.1	G	sm		sm/smdg	1.6	1
99-8650	256	2	8.21	3.7	G	sm		sm	0.75	1
99-8650	258	2	8.6	3.1	G	cordm		sm	1.62	1
99-8651	5	3	7.38	10.4	G	ind lin st	sm over	sm	2.31	1
99-8651	2	4	8.24	12.5	S/CR	cordm		sm	1.44	1
99-8651	1	2	8.52	5.7	S	scr		sm		1
99-8651	4	2	10.02	5.1	grit	ind st		brn/smdg	0.66	1
99-8653	253	2	8	2.6	G	ind lin st		sm/smdg	1.21	1
99-8653	254	2	8.28	3.1	G	ind st		sm/smdg	1.84	1
99-8655	257	2	5.02	1.3	grit	eroded		sm	0.9	1
99-8655	270	3	5.88	3.3	grit	ind lin st		sm	1.04	1
99-8655	278	2	6.1	2.8	G	ind lin st		sm	0.98	1
99-8655	275	2	6.22	3.7	G	ind st		sm	1.4	1
99-8655	264	2	6.52	2.9	G	sm		sm	1.68	1
99-8655	276	3	6.58	4.5	G	cordm		sm	1.9	1
99-8655	277	3	6.6	3.9	G	ind lin st		sm	1.2	1
99-8655	267	1	6.75	1.1	S	sm		sm		1
99-8655	271	2	6.8	2.6	G	ind st		eroded	1	1
99-8655	255	2	6.9	4	grit	sm		sm	1.62	1
99-8655	259	2	7	2.7	G	sm		sm	2.18	1
99-8655	269	1	7	1.8	G	ind lin st		sm/smdg	2	1
99-8655	258	1	7.2	1.9	G	sm		sm/smdg	2.1	1
99-8655	261	2	7.3	3.4	G	ind lin st		sm	2.1	1
99-8655	262	3	7.64	5.7	G	ind lin st		sm	1.4	1
99-8655	273	2	7.99	2.4	G	sm		sm	1.44	1
99-8655	266	1	8.04	2.6	G	ind lin st		sm/smdg	1	1
99-8655	263	1	8.2	2	G	sm		sm	1.6	1
99-8655	274	2	8.35	3.1	G	cordm		sm/smdg	1.1	1
99-8655	265	1	8.55	1.9	G	ind st		sm	2.1	1
99-8655	272	1	8.78	2.5	G	sm		sm	2.01	1
99-8655	260	1	8.8	1.9	G	sm		sm/smdg	1.07	1
99-8655	256	2	9.15	3.8	G	sm		sm	1.36	1
99-8655	268	3	9.28	6.2	G	cordm		sm	2.2	1
99-8656	251	1	5.48	1.5	G	sm		sm	1.09	1
99-8656	258	2	6.22	2.5	G	ind st		sm	1.18	1
99-8656	259	1	7	1.9	G	ind lin st		sm	1.68	1
99-8656	257	3	7.96	5.5	G	cordm		sm	1.8	1
99-8656	253	3	8.38	7	G	curv comp st	ind	sm/smdg	1.1	1
99-8656	252	3	8.82	6.1	G	ind st	sm over	coarse	1.8	1
99-8656	254	3	9.22	12.4	G	curv comp st	ind	sm	1.2	1
99-8656	256	2	9.48	3.6	G	ind st		sm	1.3	1
99-8656	255	2	10.04	4	G	ind st		sm/smdg	1.8	1
99-8658	276	2	0	1.1	S	sm		sm		1
99-8658	278	2	0	2.3	G	eroded		sm	0.92	1
99-8658	280	2	0	1.9	G	ind lin st		sm	1.44	1
99-8658	289	2	0	2.5	G	sm		sm	1.38	1
99-8658	290	2	0	2.1	G	ind st		eroded	0.9	1
99-8658	292	2	0	2.6	G	eroded		eroded	1.28	1
99-8658	275	1	0	1.5	G	eroded		sm	1.32	1
99-8658	258	3	0	2.9	G	eroded		sm	0.7	1
99-8658	261	2	0	4.6	G	eroded		sm	1.66	1
99-8658	268	2	5.36	4.7	G	ind lin st		coarse	0.84	1
99-8658	260	2	5.52	3	G	ind lin st	sm over	brn	2.02	1
99-8658	281	3	5.58	4.4	G	sm		sm	1.35	1
99-8658	262	3	6.38	6.7	G	ind st	sm over	brn	1.45	1
99-8658	283	2	6.45	5.2	G	ind st	sm over	sm/smdg	1.22	1
99-8658	266	2	6.5	1.8	G	ind lin st		sm	0.81	1
99-8658	284	3	6.5	4.2	G	sm		sm	0.82	1
99-8658	293	2	6.52	2.5	G	ind lin st		sm	1.92	1
99-8658	295	1	6.7	2	G	coarse		sm/smdg	1.25	1
99-8658	263	3	7.14	9.5	grit	ind st		sm	0.62	1
99-8658	2750	3	7.36	6.8	grit	ind lin st		sm/smdg	0.57	1
99-8658	285	3	7.57	5	G	ind st		brn/smdg	1.9	1
99-8658	264	2	7.6	2.3	G	ind lin st		sm	1.51	1

99-8658	255	2	7.68	3.8	G	cordm		sm	1.45	1	
99-8658	286	2	7.8	5.6	G	ind lin st		sm/smdg	1.32	1	
99-8658	259	3	7.86	7.7	G	ind lin st		sm/smdg	1.12	1	
99-8658	282	3	7.98	10.5	G	cordm		sm	1.12	1	
99-8658	287	2	8	1.6	S	eroded		eroded		1	
99-8658	269	2	8.6	2.8	G	ind lin st		sm	1.32	1	
99-8658	257	3	8.62	4.6	G	cordm		sm	1.2	1	
99-8658	296	2	8.7	3.8	G	sm		sm	1.08	1	
99-8658	270	4	8.74	8.8	G	ind st		sm/smdg	0.98	1	
99-8658	273	3	8.89	4.9	G	ind st		sm/smdg	1.02	1	
99-8658	288	1	9	1.6	G	ind st		sm	1.59	1	
99-8658	256	1	9.04	2.3	G	cordm		sm	1.02	1	
99-8658	274	2	9.12	6.6	G	sm		sm	1.32	1	
99-8658	267	4	9.18	13.3	grit	ind lin st		sm	0.92	1	
99-8658	271	3	9.5	10.3	G	curv comp st	ind	coarse	1.99	1	
99-8658	254	2	9.52	2.4	G	eroded		sm/smdg	1.3	1	
99-866	277	2	5.3	2.5	G	ind lin st		sm	1.38	1	
99-866	274	2	5.62	2.4	G	curv comp st	ind	brn/smdg	1.01	1	
99-866	272	2	5.62	2.3	G	sm		brn/smdg	0.75	1	
99-866	263	2	5.67	2.4	grit	ind lin st		sm/smdg	0.98	1	
99-866	253	3	5.75	4.3	G	curv comp st	ind	brn	1.25	1	
99-866	265	2	5.75	3.2	G	ind st		sm/smdg	2.3	1	
99-866	261	3	5.89	6.9	grit	ind lin st		sm	2.55	1	
99-866	268	2	6.11	3	G	ind lin st		sm	0.99	1	
99-866	254	2	6.15	2.5	G	curv comp st	ind	sm	1.35	1	
99-866	270	2	6.18	2.2	G	ind lin st		sm	1.1	1	
99-866	273	2	6.18	3.2	G	ind lin st		sm	2.1	1	
99-866	271	3	6.2	7.7	G	ind lin st		sm	1.1	1	
99-866	259	3	6.45	4.3	grit	ind lin st		sm	1.85	1	
99-866	255	2	6.58	3.1	G	ind st		sm	1.92	1	
99-866	252	1	6.74	2.1	G	ind lin st		sm/smdg	1.02	1	
99-866	279	3	6.8	6.4	G	ind lin st		sm	0.79	1	
99-866	266	2	6.9	4.3	G	cordm		sm	0.67	1	
99-866	267	2	7.22	4.5	G	curv comp st	ind scroll	sm	1.33	1	
99-866	256	3	7.38	5.8	G	curv comp st	ind	sm	1.89	1	
99-866	260	3	7.4	6.2	grit	curv comp st	ind	sm	1.79	1	
99-866	276	2	7.5	4.4	G	ind lin st		sm	1.38	1	
99-866	264	1	7.63	2.3	G	ind st		sm	1.89	1	
99-866	275	2	7.7	3.5	G	cordm		sm	1.2	1	
99-866	278	2	7.82	3.8	G	sm		sm	1.07	1	
99-866	258	2	7.99	4	grit	ind lin st		sm	1.54	1	
99-866	269	3	8.41	6.7	G	ind st		sm	1.04	1	
99-866	262	3	8.52	7.4	grit	ind st	sm over	sm	0.79	1	
99-866	257	3	9.2	6.5	G	ind st		sm	1.9	1	
99-8662	9	1	0	1	G	sm		eroded	1.1	1	
99-8662	6	3	7.6	4.8	S	sm		sm	0	1	
99-8662	8	2	7.89	3.9	G	ind st		sm	1.2	1	
99-8662	7	1	8.2	1.9	G	ind lin st		sm	1.6	1	
99-8668	274	2	0	2.4	G	eroded		sm	1.52	1	
99-8668	276	2	0	2.1	G	sm		eroded	1.06	1	
99-8668	267	2	0	1.8	G	eroded		sm	1.32	1	
99-8668	262	2	6.4	3.4	G	ind lin st		sm/smdg	0.92	1	
99-8668	266	2	6.5	2.4	G	ind lin st		sm	0.98	1	
99-8668	260	2	6.52	2.2	G	sm		sm	0.68	1	
99-8668	264	2	6.84	4.1	G	coarse		sm	1.75	1	
99-8668	275	2	6.98	2.6	G	sm		eroded	1.42	1	
99-8668	265	2	7.32	4.3	G	coarse		sm	1.52	1	
99-8668	271	3	7.45	4.9	G	ind lin st		eroded	0.97	1	
99-8668	270	2	7.48	2.7	G	ind lin st		sm/smdg	1.08	1	
99-8668	272	2	7.5	3	grit	ind lin st		sm	1.12	1	
99-8668	269	2	7.7	3.6	G	ind lin st		sm	1.04	1	
99-8668	268	3	7.82	8.2	G	ind lin st		brn/smdg	2.04	1	
99-8668	277	2	7.85	3.8	G	ind lin st		sm	1.4	1	wide grooves
99-8668	263	2	8.08	3.1	G	sm		sm	1.44	1	
99-8668	261	3	8.32	7	G	ind lin st	sm over	sm/smdg	1.4	1	
99-8668	258	3	8.48	4.9	G	sm		sm/smdg	2.1	1	
99-8668	259	2	9.18	6.6	G	ind lin st		sm	1.38	1	
99-8668	273	2	11.85	4.1	G	sm		sm	2.02	1	
99-8669	257	2	6.32	3.1	G	ind st		sm	2.1	1	
99-8669	260	3	6.92	5.9	grit	curv comp st	ind	sm	0.78	1	
99-8669	259	2	7.32	4.3	G	ind lin st		sm/smdg	1.54	1	
99-8669	255	4	8.32	12.5	G	coarse		sm	1.06	1	
99-8669	254	2	8.99	4.4	G	cordm		sm	0.87	1	
99-8669	256	2	9.54	3.3	grit	sm		sm	1.08	1	
99-8671	1	4	7.52	15.1	G	curv comp st	ind	sm/smdg	2.4	1	
99-8673	1	17	8.64	268.7	G	curv comp st	ind ovrst	sm	2.21	1	
99-868	264	2	4.78	1.9	G	ind st		sm	0.6	1	
99-868	263	2	5.29	1.9	grit	ind lin st		sm	1.2	1	
99-868	257	3	5.72	5.9	grit	ind lin st		sm/smdg	0.57	1	
99-868	258	2	5.96	2.8	G	ind st		sm	1.07	1	
99-868	259	3	6.39	7.1	G	ind lin st		sm/smdg	0.89	1	
99-868	262	3	6.51	9.7	grit	curv comp st	ind scroll	brn/smdg	1.09	1	
99-868	254	2	6.55	3.2	G	coarse		brn	1.39	1	
99-868	256	2	6.65	4	grit	ind lin st		sm	1.13	1	
99-868	260	4	6.7	13.9	G	curv comp st	ind scroll	eroded	1.24	1	
99-868	261	4	6.8	11.4	G	curv comp st	ind scroll	brn/smdg	1.22	1	
99-868	253	2	7.65	4.3	grit	curv comp st	ind scroll	sm	1.51	1	
99-868	255	3	8.09	8.8	G	curv comp st	ind	brn	1.47	1	
99-8685	254	2	7.9	5.6	G	ind lin st		sm	1.54	1	
99-869	255	5	7.68	14.5	grit	curv comp st	ind	brn/smdg	1.74	1	
99-870	251	2	0	4.6	grit	sm		eroded	0.62	1	
99-8703	253	2	6.7	2.5	G	ind st		sm	1.78	1	
99-8707	255	2	0	2.2	G	eroded		sm	1.26	1	
99-8707	257	2	0	3.2	G	eroded		sm	1.28	1	
99-8707	259	1	0	1.2	S	eroded		eroded		1	
99-8707	253	2	6.3	2.7	G	comp st	ind	brn/smdg	1.18	1	
99-8707	258	1	8.3	1.9	G	sm		sm	1.4	1	
99-8711	252	3	6.81	5.9	G	ind st		sm	1.32	1	
99-8711	253	3	8.88	8.9	G	curv comp st	ind	sm	1.68	1	
99-8712	10	2	0	2.9	G	eroded		eroded	1.47	1	
99-8712	12	2	5.23	1.9	G	eroded		sm/smdg	0.87	1	
99-8712	13	4	6.42	12.7	G	eroded		sm	0.75	1	
99-8712	11	2	7.97	3.1	G	ind lin st		sm	1.15	1	
99-8716	265	2	7.32	2.2	G	sm		sm	1.3	1	
99-8720	1	7	8.38	36	grit	curv comp st	fig "9"	redfilmed	0.45	1	Qualla paste
99-8720	3	4	9.48	12.3	G	ind st		sm	1.4	1	
99-8720	2	3	10.22	6.7	G	ind lin st		sm	1.25	1	
99-8721	256	1	0	0.9	G	eroded		eroded	1.5	1	
99-8721	255	1	6.3	1.6	G	ind lin st		sm	1.4	1	
99-8721	257	2	6.4	2.7	grit	ind lin st		sm	0.6	1	
99-8785	254	2	10.02	5.4	G	sm		coarse	1.84	1	
99-8789	262	2	6.84	1.9	G	eroded		eroded	1.21	1	
99-8789	264	2	7.62	5.4	G	ind lin st		sm	0.88	1	
99-8789	259	2	8.08	4.1	G	ind lin st		sm/smdg	0.82	1	
99-8789	257	2	8.52	3.4	G	ind lin st		sm/smdg	1.26	1	
99-8790	8	1	6.62	2.3	G	ind st	sm over	sm/smdg	1.06	1	
99-8790	6	2	7.27	3.2	G	ind st		sm	0.75	1	
99-8790	9	4	7.72	10.3	grit	comp st	ind	sm	1.02	1	
99-8790	10	2	9.5	6.5	G	ind st		sm	0.64	1	base fragment
99-8791	255	2	6.52	6.5	G	ind st		coarse	1.37	1	
99-8791	254	2	8.65	8.7	G	ind lin st		sm	2.04	1	
99-8791	253	4	8.72	16.3	G	ind lin st		sm/smdg	1.48	1	
99-8797	251	2	8.9	5.4	G	ind st		sm/smdg	1.8	1	
99-8798	288	1	0	1.6	G	eroded		sm	1.87	1	
99-8798	292	1	0	1.3	G	sm		eroded	1.18	1	
99-8798	295	2	4.72	1.8	G	ind lin st		brn/smdg	0.98	1	
99-8798	265	2	6	3.8	G	ind st	sm over	sm	0.54	1	
99-8798	275	1	6.07	2	G	sm		sm	1.04	1	

99-8798	269	2	6.12	4.1	grit	ind st	sm over	sm	1.75	1	
99-8798	286	1	6.28	2.4	G	ind lin st		sm	1.3	1	
99-8798	289	2	6.3	2.2	G	coarse		sm	0.98	1	
99-8798	276	2	6.5	1.8	G	cordm		sm	1.5	1	
99-8798	267	2	6.6	3.9	G	coarse		sm	1.2	1	
99-8798	284	2	6.67	2.5	G	sm		sm	1.2	1	
99-8798	293	2	6.67	2.8	G	ind st		sm	0.85	1	
99-8798	294	2	6.75	3.3	G	sm		sm	0.75	1	
99-8798	270	2	6.84	2.7	grit	ind lin st		sm/smdg	0.7	1	
99-8798	285	1	6.9	2.6	G	ind st		sm	1	1	
99-8798	273	2	6.96	3.6	G	ind lin st		sm/smdg	0.87	1	
99-8798	274	2	7	3.1	G	ind st		brn/smdg	1.5	1	
99-8798	259	3	7.15	8.5	G	coarse		sm/smdg	1.2	1	
99-8798	260	3	7.18	6	G	ind lin st		sm	1.08	1	
99-8798	290	1	7.22	1.6	G	sm		sm/smdg	1.3	1	
99-8798	282	2	7.3	2.8	G	eroded		sm	0.75	1	
99-8798	258	3	7.3	6.8	G	cordm		sm	0.75	1	
99-8798	291	2	7.5	3.1	G	sm		sm	1.22	1	
99-8798	283	2	7.62	2.7	G	ind st		sm	0.97	1	
99-8798	264	3	7.68	8.1	G	curv comp st	ind	sm	1.15	1	
99-8798	287	1	7.81	2.2	G	sm		sm	1.38	1	
99-8798	262	3	8.24	7.6	G	cordm		sm	1.15	1	
99-8798	272	2	8.3	3.9	G	cordm		sm	1.82	1	
99-8798	261	3	8.32	7.2	G	sm		sm	1.64	1	
99-8798	271	2	8.44	2.4	G	ind lin st		sm	2.07	1	
99-8798	280	1	8.88	2.3	G	cordm		sm	0.92	1	
99-8798	281	1	8.96	2	G	eroded		sm	1.4	1	
99-8798	277	2	9.06	4.1	G	coarse		sm	2.01	1	
99-8798	266	2	9.38	5.5	G	ind st		sm	0.68	1	
99-8798	263	2	9.6	8.7	S/CR	ind st		sm	1.2	1	
99-8798	268	2	9.62	3.7	G	ind lin st		sm/smdg	1.38	1	
99-8799	11	2	0	2	S	sm		eroded		1	
99-8799	10	3	6.79	5.9	G	sm		sm	0.96	1	
99-8799	9	2	6.94	3	G	ind lin st		sm	0.88	1	
99-8799	6	4	7.92	13.6	G	cordm		sm	1.66	1	
99-8799	3	3	8.46	6.9	G	cordm		sm	1.54	1	
99-8799	4	4	8.62	15	G	cordm		sm	1.52	1	
99-8799	5	3	8.72	7.6	G	curv comp st	ind	sm	1.07	1	
99-8799	8	2	8.72	4.3	G	cordm		sm	1.9	1	
99-8799	7	3	9.38	10.2	G	cordm		sm	1.2	1	
99-8799	2	4	10.09	20.2	G	cordm		sm	1.15	1	
99-8816	13	3	7.3	9	G	cordm		sm	1.94	1	
99-8817	254	3	0	3	grit	eroded		brn/smdg	1.24	1	
99-8817	253	2	7.84	5.2	G	coarse		eroded	1.5	1	
99-8817	255	2	7.84	2.8	G	coarse		sm	1.28	1	
99-8817	251	2	8.38	2.9	G	eroded		sm	1.3	1	
99-8817	258	2	8.44	6.3	G	sm		sm/smdg	0.98	1	
99-8824	251	2	6.3	3.3	G	sm		sm	0.9	1	
99-8825	9	3	7.58	10	G	curv comp st	fig "9"	sm	1.3	1	
99-8825	11	2	7.66	3.9	G	ind st		sm	1.1	1	
99-8825	14	7	7.89	38.5	G	ind lin st		sm	1.38	1	
99-8825	15	8	7.96	51.7	G	scr		sm/smdg	1.92	1	
99-8825	8	3	8.52	7	G	curv comp st	ind	sm	1.56	1	
99-8825	12	2	8.56	4.6	G	cordm		sm	0.97	1	
99-8825	10	4	9.18	14.1	G	ind lin st		sm	1.78	1	
99-8825	13	6	11.84	34.3	G	curv comp st	ind ovrst	sm	1.74	1	
99-8826	262	2	5.7	3.2	G	coarse		sm	1.2	1	
99-8826	255	2	6.46	1	G	cordm		sm	1.25	1	
99-8826	264	2	6.92	2.9	G	sm		eroded	1.5	1	
99-8826	258	2	7.62	3.1	G	ind st		sm	1.82	1	
99-8826	263	3	7.65	6.1	G	cordm		sm	2.21	1	
99-8826	260	2	7.67	3.5	G	cordm		sm	1.45	1	
99-8826	261	3	7.7	4.4	G	ind st		sm	1.42	1	
99-8826	256	3	7.72	8.7	G	cordm		sm	1.57	1	
99-8826	253	4	7.92	14.2	G	cordm		sm	2.2	1	
99-8826	259	3	8.3	8.3	G	cordm		sm	1.6	1	
99-8826	257	2	8.94	2.7	G	sm		sm	1.32	1	
99-8826	254	2	9.68	5.8	G	cordm		sm	2.06	1	
99-8826	252	3	12.07	11.3	G	sm		sm	3	1	base fragment
99-8827	271	2	0	2.9	G	eroded		sm	1.42	1	
99-8827	272	2	0	1.8	G	eroded		eroded	1.54	1	
99-8827	273	3	0	4.7	G	eroded		sm	1.32	1	
99-8827	268	2	0	2.7	G	coarse		eroded	1.28	1	
99-8827	257	1	6.8	2.1	G	sm		sm	1.54	1	
99-8827	274	1	7.08	1.5	G	sm		sm	1.7	1	
99-8827	258	2	7.12	3.1	G	ind st		sm	1.58	1	
99-8827	259	3	7.18	2	G	ind st		sm/smdg	1.4	1	
99-8827	261	2	7.27	2.7	G	coarse		sm	0.99	1	
99-8827	264	2	7.38	2.9	G	cordm		sm	1.1	1	
99-8827	265	1	7.6	1.9	G	ind lin st		sm	1.08	1	
99-8827	255	3	7.74	4.1	G	ind st		sm	1.12	1	
99-8827	267	2	7.75	2.4	G	sm		sm	1.12	1	
99-8827	269	3	7.79	5.3	S	ind lin st		sm	1.5	1	
99-8827	270	1	7.82	2	G	sm		sm/smdg	1.12	1	
99-8827	266	3	7.96	7.4	S	ind lin st		sm		1	
99-8827	262	2	8.08	3.4	G	coarse		sm/smdg	1.15	1	
99-8827	256	1	8.52	2.9	G	ind st		sm	1.42	1	
99-8827	260	3	8.82	5.9	G	sm		eroded	1.46	1	
99-8827	263	2	9.02	5.1	G	cordm		sm	1.82	1	
99-8827	275	1	9.3	1.4	G	ind lin st		sm	1.02	1	
99-8828	34	3	0	4.6	G	ind st		eroded	1.02	1	
99-8828	27	3	5.7	5.7	grit	ind lin st		sm	1.01	1	
99-8828	30	2	6.25	2.8	G	ind lin st		sm	0.84	1	
99-8828	35	2	6.3	2	G	cordm		sm	1.02	1	
99-8828	29	2	6.34	4.1	G	incs	ind	brn	0.84	1	
99-8828	15	2	6.62	3.4	G	sm		sm	1.1	1	
99-8828	16	3	6.66	4.9	G	ind st		sm/smdg	0.98	1	
99-8828	23	2	6.75	3.5	G	ind st	sm over	sm	1.19	1	
99-8828	22	2	6.78	2.3	G	sm		sm	1.36	1	
99-8828	20	2	6.82	5.1	G	coarse		sm/smdg	0.62	1	
99-8828	32	2	7.38	3.9	G	ind lin st		sm	1.28	1	
99-8828	25	2	7.48	2.7	G	cordm		sm	1.3	1	
99-8828	33	3	7.82	5.4	G	ind lin st		brn/smdg	0.76	1	
99-8828	28	3	7.89	9.3	G	comp st	ind	sm	1.19	1	
99-8828	36	3	7.98	4.5	G	curv comp st	ind	sm	1.27	1	
99-8828	19	3	8.12	7.3	G	sm		sm	1.08	1	
99-8828	13	2	8.13	4.1	G	ind st		coarse	1.02	1	
99-8828	37	7	8.3	37.4	G	cordm	ovrst	sm	1.62	1	
99-8828	24	2	8.35	4.6	G	cordm		sm	1.6	1	
99-8828	14	3	8.38	6.2	G	sm		sm	1.56	1	
99-8828	26	4	8.7	9.6	G	comp st	ind	sm/smdg	1.61	1	
99-8828	31	1	8.85	2.1	G	ind lin st		sm	1.14	1	
99-8828	17	2	9.72	6	G	ind st		sm	1.38	1	
99-8828	18	3	11.48	10.4	G	ind st		sm	1.28	1	
99-8832	265	2	0	2.5	G	eroded		sm	0.78	1	
99-8832	262	2	5.6	3.1	G	coarse		sm/smdg	0.5	1	
99-8832	263	1	5.9	2	G	sm		sm	1.51	1	
99-8832	259	2	7.08	3.7	G	ind lin st		sm	0.44	1	
99-8832	258	2	7.2	3.7	G	ind lin st		sm	1.44	1	
99-8832	261	2	7.86	4.3	G	sm		sm/smdg	0.87	1	
99-8832	269	2	8.76	3.1	G	sm		eroded	2.46	1	
99-8832	260	2	8.98	5.1	G	sm		sm	1.22	1	
99-8832	267	1	10.28	3.9	G	ind lin st		sm	0.63	1	
99-8833	5	4	6.82	9.9	G	ind st		brn	1.38	1	
99-8833	6	3	7.84	6.6	G	cordm		sm	0.8	1	
99-8833	3	2	8.42	5.9	G	cordm		sm	0.92	1	
99-8838	253	2	7.48	4.6	G	ind lin st		sm/smdg	1.42	1	
99-8838	251	2	9.68	7.2	grit	cordm		sm	0.85	1	base fragment

99-8839	254	2	0	2.3	G	cordm		eroded	1.4	1	
99-8839	257	2	6.51	2.2	G	ind lin st		sm	1.3	1	
99-8839	264	2	6.8	1.8	G	sm		sm	2.4	1	
99-8839	261	1	7.15	1.9	G	ind st	sm over	sm	0.8	1	
99-8839	255	3	7.28	7.8	grit	comp st	ind	sm	1.12	1	
99-8839	256	3	7.3	5.9	G	ind lin st		sm	1.28	1	
99-8839	258	1	7.54	1.9	G	cordm		sm/smdg	1.38	1	
99-8839	263	1	8.26	2.6	grit	sm		sm	1.4	1	
99-8839	262	2	8.28	2.8	G	ind st		sm/smdg	1.52	1	
99-8839	259	3	9	6.8	G	coarse		sm	1.2	1	
99-8839	260	1	10.06	1.8	G	sm		sm	1.45	1	
99-8840	5	1	6.08	1.2	G	sm		sm	1.28	1	
99-8840	2	3	6.38	4.9	G	ind lin st		sm	1.4	1	
99-8840	4	1	7.62	2.4	G	sm		sm	1.67	1	
99-8840	1	3	7.96	5.8	G	cordm		sm	1.38	1	
99-8844	255	2	8.1	3.1	G	sm		sm/smdg	1.08	1	
99-8844	254	2	13.24	6.4	G	coarse		sm	1.5	1	
99-8846	323	2	0	2.3	G	eroded		brn/smdg	1.25	1	
99-8846	324	2	0	1.8	G	eroded		sm	0.78	1	
99-8846	313	2	0	2.6	G	ind lin st		eroded	0.89	1	
99-8846	326	2	0	1.8	G	ind lin st		eroded	1.18	1	
99-8846	319	2	0	2.8	G	brn		eroded	1.56	1	
99-8846	322	2	0	2.8	G	ind st	sm over	eroded	1.15	1	
99-8846	327	1	0	1.3	G	eroded		eroded	1.12	1	
99-8846	315	2	0	2.6	G	eroded		eroded	1.9	1	
99-8846	307	2	0	2.7	G	eroded		sm	1.42	1	
99-8846	309	2	0	3.8	G	eroded		sm	1.8	1	
99-8846	310	3	0	3.8	grit	sm		eroded	0.7	1	
99-8846	297	4	5.28	9.8	G	ind lin st		brn/smdg	1.25	1	
99-8846	300	2	5.34	2.8	G	ind lin st		sm	0.84	1	
99-8846	274	3	5.4	4	G	cordm	sm over	brn/smdg	1.21	1	
99-8846	317	2	6.02	1.8	G	coarse		sm	0.92	1	
99-8846	282	2	6.06	1.9	G	sm		sm	1.98	1	
99-8846	268	2	6.08	3.9	G	coarse		sm	1.44	1	
99-8846	272	2	6.13	2.5	G	ind st		sm	1.15	1	
99-8846	304	2	6.3	2.8	G	ind lin st		sm	1.12	1	
99-8846	277	2	6.3	5.1	grit	sm		sm	0.71	1	
99-8846	283	2	6.38	2.5	G	ind st		sm/smdg	0.92	1	
99-8846	278	3	6.58	5.6	G	scr		sm/smdg	1.25	1	
99-8846	306	2	6.6	3.4	grit	ind lin st		sm	0.68	1	
99-8846	316	3	6.76	4.1	G	ind st		sm	1.4	1	
99-8846	289	4	6.82	16	G	cordm		brn/smdg	0.97	1	
99-8846	275	3	6.89	6.8	G	sm		sm/smdg	1.03	1	
99-8846	271	4	6.9	8.8	G	sm		sm	1.4	1	
99-8846	291	2	6.98	2.9	G	cordm		sm	1.22	1	
99-8846	276	4	7.02	9.6	G	coarse		sm	1.42	1	
99-8846	303	3	7.02	6.3	G	ind lin st		sm	2	1	
99-8846	273	3	7.18	7.2	G	ind st		sm	1	1	
99-8846	264	4	7.24	9.7	G	coarse		sm	1.28	1	
99-8846	296	2	7.3	2.8	G	coarse		sm/smdg	1.76	1	
99-8846	285	3	7.42	5.6	G	sm		sm	1.6	1	
99-8846	301	3	7.42	5.6	G	ind lin st		sm	1.25	1	
99-8846	266	3	7.44	4.8	G	comp st	ind	sm	1.02	1	
99-8846	265	3	7.44	7.5	G	ind st	sm over	sm	0.62	1	
99-8846	284	2	7.5	2.9	G	ind st	sm over	sm	0.9	1	
99-8846	321	2	7.62	4.3	grit	ind st		eroded	0.76	1	
99-8846	267	3	7.69	9.7	G	ind st	sm over	sm	1.48	1	
99-8846	294	2	7.75	2.2	G	cordm		sm	0.99	1	
99-8846	314	2	7.79	3.6	G	ind lin st		coarse	1.08	1	
99-8846	320	2	7.8	3.1	G	ind lin st		eroded	0.97	1	
99-8846	311	2	7.8	3.2	G	ind lin st		sm	1	1	
99-8846	281	2	7.82	3.8	G	ind lin st		sm	1.58	1	
99-8846	280	2	7.89	2.4	G	ind st		sm	1.38	1	
99-8846	328	3	7.89	5.6	G	ind lin st		brn	1.66	1	wide grooves
99-8846	298	3	7.95	6	G	ind lin st		sm	1.48	1	
99-8846	305	2	8.04	3	G	ind lin st		brn/smdg	0.79	1	
99-8846	286	1	8.15	1.7	G	sm		sm	1.92	1	
99-8846	299	2	8.34	3.3	G	coarse		sm	1.4	1	
99-8846	287	2	8.54	2.7	G	ind st		sm	0.8	1	
99-8846	269	2	8.54	4.9	G	sm		sm	1.01	1	
99-8846	318	2	8.62	2.8	G	coarse		sm	1.58	1	
99-8846	325	2	8.66	4.1	G	curv comp st	ind	brn/smdg	1.48	1	
99-8846	293	1	8.68	2.9	G	cordm		eroded	1.22	1	
99-8846	292	1	8.82	2.4	G	cordm		sm	1.44	1	
99-8846	288	3	8.87	4.1	G	coarse		sm	1.87	1	
99-8846	262	8	8.96	39.5	G	curv comp st	ind scroll ovrst	sm	1.56	1	
99-8846	279	3	9.12	6.7	G	sm		sm	1.34	1	
99-8846	290	2	9.96	4.6	G	cordm		sm	0.94	1	
99-8846	270	2	10.04	6.4	G	ind lin st		sm	1.76	1	
99-8846	263	4	10.38	11.8	G	comp st	ind	sm	1.85	1	
99-8846	308	3	10.6	8.4	G	cordm	sm over	sm	1.18	1	
99-8846	302	5	10.62	18.7	G	cordm		sm	1.18	1	
99-8846	312	1	11.6	2.4	G	eroded		eroded	1.48	1	
99-8847	253	2	0	2	G	ind lin st		eroded	1.52	1	
99-8847	254	2	6.65	3.4	G	ind st		sm	1.05	1	
99-8847	256	2	6.71	2.3	G	eroded		sm	1.15	1	
99-8847	252	3	6.84	4.6	grit	ind lin st		sm	0.82	1	
99-8847	255	3	7.43	5.9	G	ind lin st	sm over	sm	1.23	1	
99-8855	269	2	0	2.7	G	eroded		eroded	0.98	1	
99-8855	267	2	0	2.4	G	eroded		sm	1.6	1	
99-8855	272	2	6.32	2.4	G	ind lin st		sm	1.2	1	
99-8855	263	3	6.33	4.9	G	sm		sm	1.48	1	
99-8855	259	2	6.96	3.1	G	cordm		sm	1.56	1	
99-8855	265	2	7.06	4.2	grit	ind st	sm over	sm	1.08	1	
99-8855	270	2	7.25	3.4	grit	ind lin st		sm	1.66	1	
99-8855	271	2	7.58	2.6	G	brn		brn/smdg	0.88	1	
99-8855	256	2	7.6	2.7	G	ind lin st		sm	1.7	1	
99-8855	260	2	7.6	3.2	G	cordm		sm	1.29	1	
99-8855	266	2	7.72	4.7	G	ind lin st	sm over	sm	1.54	1	
99-8855	268	1	7.92	2.1	G	ind st		sm	1.27	1	
99-8855	257	1	8.3	1.9	G	cordm		coarse	0.86	1	
99-8855	258	3	8.68	7.3	G	cordm		sm	1.38	1	
99-8856	11	2	0	3.5	G	eroded		sm	1.75	1	
99-8856	8	4	6	7.7	G	ind st	sm over	eroded	1.26	1	
99-8856	10	4	6.62	13.9	G	sm		eroded	1.7	1	
99-8856	9	3	7.34	7.2	G	sm		sm	0.91	1	
99-8857	257	2	6.29	3.3	G	sm		sm	1.32	1	
99-8857	260	1	7.7	1.5	G	sm		sm	1.26	1	
99-8857	258	2	8.18	4.5	G	cordm		sm	1.04	1	
99-8857	259	1	8.31	1.8	G	sm		sm	1.5	1	
99-8857	255	2	9.35	6.5	G	ind st		sm/smdg	1.26	1	
99-8857	256	1	10.2	2.5	G	cordm		sm	1.94	1	
99-8858	253	2	4.58	2.4	S	sm		sm		1	
99-8858	257	3	5.86	4.2	G	curv comp st	ind	sm	1.87	1	
99-8858	262	2	6.3	2.8	S	sm		sm		1	
99-8858	254	2	6.32	2	G	ind lin st		sm/smdg	0.98	1	
99-8858	261	1	6.84	1.6	G	ind lin st		sm	1.12	1	
99-8858	255	1	7.1	1.5	G	eroded		eroded	2.07	1	
99-8858	260	2	7.45	4.4	G	curv comp st	ind	brn/smdg	1.6	1	
99-8858	258	1	7.72	1.9	G	ind st		sm	2.4	1	
99-8858	259	2	8.22	1.7	G	ind lin st		eroded	1.5	1	
99-8858	256	3	8.6	7.4	G	ind lin st		sm	1	1	
99-8858	263	3	9.08	11.2	G	ind st		sm/smdg	1.67	1	
99-8859	269	1	5.6	1.7	G	ind st	sm over	sm/smdg	1.65	1	
99-8859	271	2	7.34	3.1	G	curv comp st	ind	redfilmed	0.75	1	
99-8859	268	1	7.38	1.8	grit	sm		redfilmed	0.58	1	
99-8859	267	2	7.38	3.9	G	ind lin st		sm	1.3	1	

99-8859	258	3	7.48	6.7	G	ind lin st		sm	1.8	1
99-8859	263	3	7.5	5	G	ind lin st		sm	1.5	1
99-8859	262	1	7.54	2.6	G	sm		sm/smdg	1.4	1
99-8859	255	2	7.54	4.3	G	coarse		sm	1.44	1
99-8859	260	1	7.64	2.3	G	sm		sm	1.7	1
99-8859	261	2	7.7	3.6	G	sm		sm/smdg	1.3	1
99-8859	257	3	7.7	5.1	G	sm		sm	1.7	1
99-8859	266	2	7.74	2.3	G	coarse		sm	1.2	1
99-8859	256	3	7.82	6.2	G	sm		sm	2.07	1
99-8859	270	2	7.9	3.4	G	ind st		sm/smdg	1.52	1
99-8859	264	2	8.28	3.6	G	sm		sm	1.4	1
99-8859	265	2	8.38	4.4	G	cordm		sm	1.2	1
99-8859	275	2	8.75	3.9	G	ind st		sm	1.07	1
99-8859	259	2	9.28	5.6	G	ind lin st		sm	1.3	1
99-8859	274	1	9.4	2.3	G	sm		sm	1.75	1
99-8859	272	1	9.78	2.1	G	ind st		sm	1.15	1
99-8859	273	1	10.46	2.7	G	sm		sm	1.5	1
99-8860	4	2	5.32	2.9	G	cordm		sm/smdg	1.01	1
99-8860	3	1	7.04	1.6	G	sm		sm	1.12	1
99-8860	5	2	8.22	3.7	G	ind lin st		sm	1.5	1
99-8860	2	2	8.24	4.3	G	cordm		sm	1.64	1
99-8860	6	2	8.62	5.6	G	ind lin st		sm	1.9	1
99-8860	7	3	9.72	9	G	ind lin st		sm	1.44	1
99-8860	1	3	10.42	8	G	ind lin st		sm	2.12	1
99-8862	254	2	6.35	2.2	G	ind st		sm	1.2	1
99-8862	252	3	6.52	5.4	G	ind st		sm	1.55	1
99-8862	263	2	6.56	3.4	G	coarse		sm/smdg	1.5	1
99-8862	264	4	7.84	14.9	G	ind st		sm	0.7	1
99-8862	261	2	7.9	5	G	ind lin st		sm/smdg	1.14	1
99-8867	1	2	7.35	2.5	G	ind st	sm over	sm	1.39	1
99-8867	2	3	8.67	1.8	G	ind lin st		sm/smdg	1.8	1
99-8868	255	1	6.42	1.9	G	ind lin st		sm	1.76	1
99-8868	254	3	9.92	6.6	G	coarse		sm/smdg	1.76	1
99-8870	252	2	6.36	3.3	G	cordm		sm	1.32	1
99-8870	253	1	7.8	1.7	G	ind st		sm	1.44	1
99-8873	257	1	6.87	1.6	G	ind lin st		sm	0.98	1
99-8873	253	1	8.2	3	G	coarse		sm	1.22	1
99-8876	265	2	0	1.8	G	eroded		sm	1.38	1
99-8876	264	2	0	3.4	G	ind lin st	sm over	eroded	1.18	1
99-8876	263	2	0	2.2	G	eroded		sm	1.2	1
99-8876	262	2	0	2.4	G	ind lin st		eroded	1.21	1
99-8876	259	2	6.32	5.4	G	ind lin st		sm	1.42	1
99-8876	260	2	6.72	2.3	G	cordm		sm	0.96	1
99-8876	255	4	7.06	13.1	grit	comp st	ind	sm	1	1
99-8876	270	5	8.2	18.7	G	ind lin st		sm	1.8	1
99-8876	254	2	8.28	5	G	cordm		sm/smdg	1.15	1
99-8876	257	4	8.3	12.5	grit	curv comp st	fig "9"	brn	1.28	1
99-8876	272	3	8.4	6.5	G	cordm		sm	1.4	1
99-8876	258	2	9.44	6.7	grit	ind lin st		sm/smdg	0.67	1
99-8876	267	3	9.6	8.4	G	cordm		sm	1.54	1
99-8876	266	2	9.6	5.4	G	sm		sm/smdg	1.6	1
99-8876	269	2	9.84	3.1	G	cordm		sm	1.16	1
99-8876	261	4	14.02	21.2	G	ind st	sm over	sm	0.78	1
99-8877	253	2	5.36	2	S	eroded		eroded		1
99-8877	254	2	5.94	3	G	coarse		sm/smdg	0.78	1
99-8879	253	1	0	1.2	G	eroded		sm	1.89	1
99-8879	255	2	0	3.4	G	ind lin st		eroded	1	1
99-8879	256	2	6.67	1.8	G	sm		sm	1	1
99-8879	254	3	6.8	3.2	G	ind st		sm	1.52	1
99-8879	252	2	7.07	4.8	G	ind st		sm	1.68	1
99-8881	258	2	0	1.9	G	cordm		eroded	1.44	1
99-8881	259	2	6.74	3.8	G	ind st		sm	1.62	1
99-8881	256	2	8.58	3.3	G	coarse		sm	1.22	1
99-8885	255	4	7.64	7.1	G	ind lin st	sm over	sm	1.5	1

99-8890	254	2	0	2.6	G	ind st		eroded	1.8	1
99-8891	252	2	6.78	3	G	ind lin st		sm	0.97	1
99-8891	253	2	7.2	3.5	G	ind lin st		sm	1.3	1
99-8893	254	3	6	5.8	G	brn		sm	0.98	1
99-8893	257	2	6.54	1.8	G	ind lin st		sm	1.34	1
99-8893	256	3	7.6	5.5	G	ind lin st	sm over	sm	1.02	1
99-8893	253	3	8.02	7.4	G	sm		sm	1.12	1
99-8893	255	2	9.3	6.4	G	ind lin st		sm	1.32	1
99-8894	270	2	5.22	2	G	sm		sm	1.18	1
99-8894	269	2	5.8	4.5	G	sm		sm	1.98	1
99-8894	264	3	6.42	8.2	G	curv comp st	ind	sm	1.68	1
99-8894	271	2	6.61	4.2	G	fn punc		brn/smdg	1	1
99-8894	268	3	6.84	8	G	curv comp st	ind	sm	1.3	1
99-8894	273	3	7.32	4.6	G	ind st		sm/smdg	1.38	1
99-8894	262	3	7.38	10.3	G	comp st	ind	sm	1.6	1
99-8894	272	2	8.32	5.9	G	cordm		sm	1.72	1
99-8894	274	2	8.4	4.4	G	eroded		sm/smdg	1.18	1
99-8894	267	2	8.68	4.2	G	ind st		brn/smdg	1.08	1
99-8894	276	1	8.89	3.2	G	ind st		sm/smdg	1.48	1
99-8894	275	2	9.16	5.7	G	coarse		coarse	1.45	1
99-8894	263	3	9.54	10.4	G	curv comp st	ind	coarse	1.48	1
99-8894	265	3	11.24	8.7	G	ind st		sm	1.04	1
99-8895	278	2	4.92	1.7	G	ind st		sm	0.77	1
99-8895	270	2	5.54	3.1	G	sm		sm	0.9	1
99-8895	265	2	5.88	3.7	G	sm		sm	1.85	1
99-8895	277	3	6.18	4.6	G	ind lin st		sm	0.96	1
99-8895	272	2	6.19	2.3	G	ind st		sm	0.98	1
99-8895	276	2	6.19	2.5	G	ind st		sm/smdg	1.52	1
99-8895	266	2	6.38	4.3	G	ind lin st		sm	1.46	1
99-8895	256	1	6.42	1.8	G	coarse		sm	1.5	1
99-8895	280	2	6.82	5.7	G	curv comp st	ind	sm	1.96	1
99-8895	283	2	6.94	3.1	G	ind lin st		sm	0.98	1
99-8895	281	2	7.01	2.9	G	ind lin st		sm	1.09	1
99-8895	267	2	7.25	2.8	G	sm		sm	1.42	1
99-8895	268	3	7.28	6.9	G	coarse		coarse	1.13	1
99-8895	227	2	7.5	3	G	coarse		sm	1.2	1
99-8895	274	2	7.7	2.2	G	cordm		sm	1.36	1
99-8895	275	2	7.9	2.9	G	cordm		sm	1.8	1
99-8895	269	2	7.91	3.1	G	ind st		sm/smdg	1.71	1
99-8895	260	2	8.1	3.3	G	coarse		sm	2.01	1
99-8895	273	1	8.46	2.2	G	cordm		sm	1.74	1
99-8895	271	2	8.56	4.6	G	ind lin st		sm	1.99	1
99-8895	264	1	8.8	1.8	G	sm		sm/smdg	1.32	1
99-8895	263	1	9.01	1.9	G	ind st		sm	2.31	1
99-8895	262	2	9.06	4.3	G	sm		sm	1.13	1
99-8895	261	2	9.15	4.5	G	sm		sm	2	1
99-8895	259	2	9.56	4.9	G	ind st		sm	1.32	1
99-8895	258	3	9.58	10.5	G	ind st		coarse	0.88	1
99-8895	279	2	9.66	6.1	G	cordm		sm	1.22	1
99-8895	255	4	11.2	21	G	ind st		sm	2.36	1
99-8899	255	2	4.82	1.5	G	sm		sm	0.75	1
99-8899	256	2	6.84	3.6	G	sm		sm	1.07	1
99-890	7	1	0	1.7	G	eroded		eroded	1.88	1
99-890	8	2	6.28	4.1	grit	ind st		sm	0.75	1
99-8900	264	2	5.48	2.5	G	ind st		sm	1.02	1
99-8900	263	2	5.84	2.1	G	ind st		sm	1.2	1
99-8900	265	2	6.5	2.1	G	ind st		sm	1.31	1
99-8900	260	2	6.93	3.5	G	incs	ind	sm	1.35	1
99-8900	261	2	6.98	3.8	G	ind lin st		sm	0.99	1
99-8900	258	1	7.66	1.8	G	ind st		sm	1.02	1
99-8900	266	1	7.72	2.2	G	ind lin st		sm	0.97	1
99-8900	257	1	8	1.6	G	sm		coarse	1.62	1
99-8900	262	2	8.7	4.6	G	sm		sm	0.87	1
99-8900	259	2	8.9	3	G	eroded		sm	1.51	1

99-8901	254	1	0	1	S	sm		eroded	2.21	1	
99-8901	255	2	5.9	3.9	G	sm		brn	1.2	1	
99-8901	259	2	6.16	2.5	G	sm		sm	1.64	1	
99-8901	253	3	6.44	9.1	grit	ind lin st		sm	1.28	1	
99-8901	257	2	7	3.2	G	cordm		sm	1.2	1	
99-8901	256	2	7.36	3.8	G	rgh		sm	1.23	1	
99-8901	258	3	7.79	6.3	grit	ind lin st		sm	2.39	1	
99-8901	252	3	8.82	7	G	ind st		sm/smdg	1.26	1	
99-8920	252	3	6.02	5.7	G	ind st		sm	0.82	1	
99-8922	255	1	7.01	7	G	ind st		sm	1.32	1	
99-8922	257	2	8.78	3.7	G	eroded		sm	2	1	
99-8922	256	2	10.92	4.2	G	ind st		eroded	1.62	1	
99-8923	21	2	6.5	2.5	G	sm		sm	0.73	1	
99-8923	14	5	6.52	12.5	G	ind lin st		sm	0.84	1	
99-8923	18	2	6.85	2.2	G	sm		sm	1.01	1	
99-8923	17	4	6.94	12.7	G	ind st		sm	0.65	1	
99-8923	20	1	7.16	1.8	G	coarse		sm/smdg	1.2	1	
99-8923	16	1	8.93	1.8	G	sm		sm	1.12	1	
99-8924	255	1	9.43	2.8	G	coarse		sm	1.65	1	
99-8925	4	1	6.09	2.1	grit	ind lin st		sm	0.48	1	
99-8925	3	2	7.51	4.1	G	cordm		sm	1.2	1	
99-8925	1	4	9.48	18.9	G	rgh		sm	1.27	1	corn cob
99-8925	2	3	11.39	9.4	G	cordm	sm over	sm	1.18	1	
99-893	257	2	6.32	1.8	G	ind lin st		brn/smdg	0.98	1	
99-893	253	2	7.18	2.1	G	ind lin st		sm	1.38	1	
99-893	252	2	8.28	2.9	G	scr		sm	1.15	1	
99-893	266	2	8.58	1.6	grit	ind lin st		sm	0.78	1	
99-893	255	2	9.01	7.4	grit	ind lin st		brn/smdg	1.2	1	
99-893	254	3	12.68	8.5	G	ind lin st		coarse	1.75	1	
99-893	251	4	14.52	13.9	G	eroded		coarse	1.86	1	
99-8931	254	2	6.28	2.9	G	sm		sm	1.06	1	
99-8931	260	1	7.55	7.6	G	sm		sm	1.1	1	
99-8931	257	2	8.06	3.1	G	ind st		brn	1.33	1	
99-8932	256	3	0	3.5	S	eroded		eroded		1	
99-8932	255	2	8.76	4	G	coarse		eroded	1.48	1	
99-8932	254	2	9.7	3.5	G	ind lin st		sm/smdg	1.56	1	
99-8938	264	2	5.57	5.1	G	sm		sm	2.14	1	
99-8938	263	2	6.65	2.2	G	sm		sm	1.86	1	
99-8938	260	2	6.72	3.1	G	curv comp st	ind	sm	1.8	1	
99-8938	262	2	7.47	4.8	G	cordm		sm	1.31	1	
99-8938	259	2	7.88	3.8	G	ind st		sm	1.07	1	
99-8938	261	4	8.18	11.1	G	sm		sm	1.7	1	
99-8938	265	2	8.4	2.9	G	ind lin st		sm	1.34	1	
99-8938	266	3	9.14	8.8	G	ind st		sm	2.5	1	
99-894	252	2	6.25	3	grit	ind lin st		brn/smdg	1.12	1	
99-894	257	2	7.44	3	G	ind st		sm	1.15	1	
99-894	259	1	7.84	1.7	G	eroded		eroded	1.45	1	
99-894	255	2	8.42	2.6	G	ind lin st		sm	2.02	1	
99-894	256	2	8.48	2.8	G	ind lin st		brn/smdg	1.42	1	
99-894	258	3	8.96	4.6	grit	sm		sm	1.01	1	
99-894	253	2	9.96	4.7	G	ind lin st		brn	0.92	1	
99-894	254	3	12.12	8.9	G	ind lin st	ovrst	sm	2.72	1	
99-8940	255	2	6.56	2.9	G	ind st		sm	1.48	1	
99-8940	254	1	7.74	1.5	S	eroded		eroded	1.63	1	
99-8942	12	3	7.48	5.5	G	coarse		sm	1.57	1	
99-8952	254	2	0	1.6	G	eroded		eroded	1.1	1	
99-8952	253	3	0	7.5	G	sm		eroded	1.22	1	
99-8953	251	2	6.66	4.1	G	ind lin st		brn	0.96	1	
99-8953	253	3	6.93	2.3	G	ind lin st		brn	1.05	1	
99-8953	252	1	7.86	3.6	G	cordm		sm	1.17	1	
99-8953	254	2	9.72	4	G	eroded		eroded	1.14	1	
99-8954	253	4	4.78	4.7	S	eroded		eroded		1	
99-8954	254	3	5.28	3.4	S	eroded		eroded		1	
99-8956	251	2	6.24	2.4	G	comp st	ind	sm	1.48	1	

99-8963	11	2	6.5	4	G	ind lin st		sm	1.2	1	
99-8963	10	2	6.81	2.5	G	sm		sm	1.43	1	
99-8964	260	3	6.05	5.1	G	sm		sm	1.01	1	
99-8964	258	4	6.05	8.7	G	ind lin st		sm	1.45	1	
99-8964	259	3	6.19	5.6	G	ind st		sm	1.23	1	
99-8964	251	4	6.26	7.9	G	coarse		brn/smdg	1.37	1	
99-8964	261	3	6.32	4	G	ind lin st		sm	1.35	1	
99-8964	265	2	6.84	2.7	G	scr		sm/smdg	1.17	1	
99-8964	254	3	7.33	8.6	G	curv comp st	ind	sm	1.66	1	
99-8964	253	4	7.91	15.7	G	coarse		sm	1.96	1	
99-8964	257	3	8.04	6.1	G	cordm		sm	1.25	1	
99-8964	252	4	8.26	10.1	G	ind lin st		sm	1.06	1	
99-8964	263	1	8.37	2.2	G	sm		sm	1.19	1	
99-8964	256	2	8.84	3	G	sm		eroded	1.63	1	
99-8964	255	2	9.34	4.7	G	ind lin st		sm	1.67	1	
99-8964	262	2	9.76	5.4	G	cordm		sm	1.31	1	
99-8964	264	2	10.12	4.5	G	sm		sm	2.36	1	
99-8965	254	1	0	1.1	G	eroded		eroded	1.8	1	
99-8966	255	2	7.74	4.4	G	cordm		sm	1.14	1	
99-8967	1	4	8.39	15.7	G	smpl st	ovrst	sm	1.43	1	comp design made with a smpl paddle?
99-898	254	2	7.92	3.7	G	ind lin st		sm/smdg	1.68	1	
99-898	255	2	9.18	6.5	G	curv comp st	ind	sm	0.88	1	
99-8983	290	1	0	1.4	G	cordm		eroded	0.89	1	
99-8983	291	1	5.42	1.5	G	ind st		sm	1.3	1	
99-8983	280	2	5.82	3.1	G	ind lin st		brn/smdg	0.7	1	
99-8983	2690	4	5.84	12.3	G	sm		sm	0.67	1	
99-8983	270	3	6.33	7.3	G	coarse		sm	1.16	1	
99-8983	271	2	6.38	3.3	G	sm		sm	1.18	1	
99-8983	285	2	6.62	3.2	G	ind lin st		sm	1.6	1	
99-8983	287	1	6.68	2	G	ind st		sm	0.88	1	
99-8983	281	2	6.72	3.9	G	ind st		sm	1.9	1	
99-8983	289	2	6.73	2.1	G	ind st		sm	0.69	1	
99-8983	278	3	6.96	4.7	G	coarse		sm	1.32	1	
99-8983	282	2	6.98	3	G	cordm		sm	1.25	1	
99-8983	273	3	7.06	6.5	G	ind lin st		brn	1.12	1	
99-8983	277	2	7.1	5.8	G	sm		sm	1.2	1	
99-8983	268	3	7.22	7.3	G	ind lin st	sm over	sm/smdg	1.35	1	
99-8983	274	2	7.28	4.2	G	ind lin st		sm/smdg	1.15	1	
99-8983	288	2	7.3	1.8	S	sm		sm	1.3	1	
99-8983	266	3	7.5	5.4	G	cordm		sm	1.35	1	
99-8983	256	9	7.5	49	G	ind lin st		sm	1.4	1	wide grooves
99-8983	259	6	7.58	22	G	ind lin st		sm	1.08	1	
99-8983	257	5	7.75	27.1	G	ind lin st		sm	1.53	1	
99-8983	284	1	8.1	2.3	G	ind lin st		sm/smdg	1.26	1	
99-8983	276	2	8.15	5.7	G	ind lin st		sm	1.58	1	
99-8983	279	3	8.18	4.8	G	ind lin st		brn/smdg	1.1	1	
99-8983	275	3	8.19	6.8	G	coarse		sm	1.53	1	
99-8983	261	4	8.35	11.4	G	ind lin st		sm	0.85	1	
99-8983	263	3	8.38	5.7	G	cordm		sm/smdg	1.84	1	
99-8983	260	5	8.48	18.4	G	cordm		sm	1.6	1	
99-8983	265	2	8.5	6.1	G	cordm		sm	1.27	1	
99-8983	269	2	8.71	5.9	G	ind lin st		sm/smdg	0.92	1	
99-8983	267	3	8.72	5.1	G	ind lin st		sm	1.03	1	
99-8983	272	2	8.86	5.7	G	cordm		sm	1.82	1	
99-8983	262	3	9.18	9.3	G	sm		brn/smdg	1.02	1	
99-8983	286	1	9.64	3.8	G	sm		sm	1.18	1	
99-8983	258	6	10.25	20.8	G	coarse		sm	1.65	1	
99-8983	283	1	11.98	3.1	G	sm		sm	0.9	1	
99-9	257	2	0	1.9	S	scr		eroded	0	1	
99-9	256	2	4.07	1.2	S	sm		sm	0	1	
99-9	251	2	5	1.4	S	sm		sm	0	1	
99-9	252	3	5.9	4.9	S	sm		sm	0	1	
99-9	258	1	7.26	2.5	G	sm		sm	1.28	1	

99-9	259	3	7.46	5.1	G	ind lin st		sm	1.58	1	
99-9	255	4	9.7	11.6	G	coarse		sm	1.56	1	
99-902	253	1	5.76	1.6	grit	sm		sm	0.71	1	
99-902	254	2	7.22	4.1	G	cordm	sm over	brn	0.96	1	
99-902	252	6	8.72	48.3	G	coarse		coarse		1	
99-9021	251	3	5.97	6	G	sm		sm	2.65	1	
99-9021	260	1	6.85	2	G	ind lin st		sm	1.43	1	
99-9021	256	2	6.86	2.7	G	ind lin st		sm	1.54	1	
99-9021	253	4	7.28	8.3	G	scr		sm	1.35	1	
99-9021	254	3	7.42	3.7	G	coarse		sm	1.77	1	
99-9021	255	2	7.86	3.7	G	ind st		sm	1.66	1	
99-9021	258	1	8.11	2	G	cordm		sm/smdg	1.6	1	
99-9021	252	3	8.21	7.6	G	ind st		sm	1.17	1	
99-9021	259	1	8.31	2	G	sm		sm	1.53	1	
99-9021	257	2	9.56	3.9	G	sm		brn/smdg	1.94	1	
99-9022	253	3	6.36	6.2	G	ind st		sm	1.51	1	
99-9022	254	2	6.85	3.4	G	ind lin st		sm	2.03	1	
99-9023	2	2	5.87	3.9	G	ind lin st		sm	0.99	1	
99-9023	4	3	6.76	8.2	G	ind lin st		sm	1.77	1	
99-9023	3	5	7.68	21.8	G	curv comp st	ind	sm	2.21	1	
99-9023	5	4	8.74	14.4	G	cordm		sm	2.3	1	
99-9023	1	2	8.84	4	G	sm		sm/smdg	1.01	1	
99-9024	257	2	7.34	2.5	G	ind st		sm	1.36	1	
99-9024	256	3	7.67	5.9	G	sm		sm	1.14	1	
99-9024	254	2	7.7	4	G	sm		sm	1.54	1	
99-9024	253	5	7.99	14.2	G	ind lin st		sm/smdg	1.5	1	
99-9024	255	3	9.02	6.8	G	ind lin st		sm	1.07	1	
99-903	5	2	7.84	2.7	G	sm		sm	1.45	1	
99-9057	259	2	5.98	2.7	G	ind lin st		eroded	1.32	1	
99-9057	258	1	8.75	2	G	eroded		sm	1.12	1	
99-9057	261	3	9.32	6.1	G	ind st		sm	1.73	1	
99-9058	254	2	5.66	2.9	G	sm		sm	1.36	1	
99-9058	255	1	6.32	2.6	G	sm		sm	1.43	1	
99-9058	256	2	6.7	2	G	coarse		redfilmed	1.31	1	
99-9058	257	1	7.97	2.6	G	cordm		sm	1.18	1	
99-906	258	2	7.5	4.8	G	sm		sm	0.64	1	
99-906	257	2	7.95	3.2	G	sm		sm	1.43	1	
99-907	254	3	6.29	3.4	G	sm		sm	2.04	1	
99-907	252	5	6.72	13.9	G	comp st	ind	sm	1.31	1	
99-907	251	1	6.77	1.7	G	sm		sm	1.32	1	
99-907	253	4	6.81	11.1	G	curv comp st	ind	sm	1.47	1	
99-907	255	2	8.43	2.9	G	sm		sm	1.29	1	
99-908	12	2	6.97	5.5	G	ind lin st		sm	1.72	1	
99-908	10	3	7.03	6.2	S/CR	sm		sm	0.69	1	
99-908	11	3	7.41	6.6	G	smpl st	ovrst	sm	1.7	1	complex motif with a smpl stamp
99-908	13	3	8.77	12	G	coarse		sm	1.76	1	
99-9089	261	2	0	1.8	G	cordm		eroded	1	1	
99-9089	270	2	6.67	2.4	G	sm		sm	1.12	1	
99-9089	262	2	6.92	4.1	G	ind lin st		sm	1.52	1	
99-9089	283	3	7.02	4.4	G	ind lin st		sm	1.55	1	
99-9089	272	4	7.18	12.5	G	ind lin st		brn/smdg	1.82	1	
99-9089	276	4	7.26	12.2	G	ind lin st		sm	2.01	1	
99-9089	284	2	7.54	2.2	G	sm		sm	1.53	1	
99-9089	285	2	7.57	3.4	G	cordm		sm	0.79	1	
99-9089	263	2	7.59	4.1	G	cordm		sm	1.65	1	
99-9089	275	2	7.61	2.8	G	cordm		sm	1.28	1	
99-9089	280	2	7.7	6.8	G	ind lin st		sm	1.42	1	
99-9089	269	2	7.71	3.9	G	ind lin st		sm/smdg	1.79	1	
99-9089	265	1	7.74	1.4	G	ind lin st		sm	0.97	1	
99-9089	266	3	7.8	7.7	G	scr		sm	2.4	1	
99-9089	260	1	7.87	1.8	G	ind lin st		sm	1.8	1	
99-9089	268	3	8.05	8.2	G	cordm		sm	1.55	1	
99-9089	277	3	8.06	5.5	G	cordm		sm	1.72	1	

99-9089	264	2	8.16	4.6	G	curv comp st	ind	sm	1.47	1	
99-9089	278	3	8.34	10.1	G	ind lin st		sm	2.12	1	
99-9089	267	2	8.36	4.6	G	ind st	sm over	brn	1.45	1	
99-9089	274	3	8.44	12.2	G	cordm		sm	2.03	1	
99-9089	271	2	10.11	5.4	G	sm		sm	1.2	1	
99-9089	273	2	10.26	5.5	G	ind st		sm	1.27	1	
99-909	252	5	6.89	16.3	G	ind lin st		sm/smdg	1.21	1	
99-909	251	4	7.26	7.9	G	ind lin st		sm	1.26	1	
99-9090	255	2	8.64	3.2	G	sm		sm	2.12	1	
99-9095	260	1	0	1.9	G	eroded		sm	1.03	1	
99-9095	259	3	7.3	6.5	G	ind lin st		sm	1.21	1	
99-9095	258	2	7.44	3.7	G	ind lin st		sm/smdg	1.14	1	
99-9095	257	2	7.68	4.5	G	ind st		sm	1.83	1	
99-9108	253	1	7.32	2.3	G	sm		sm	0.94	1	
99-9108	252	2	7.43	2.4	G	sm		sm	1.69	1	
99-9108	255	4	9.15	11.4	G	sm		eroded	1.55	1	
99-9108	254	2	9.25	5.3	G	coarse		sm	1.1	1	
99-9109	253	3	0	3.6	G	ind st		eroded	1.25	1	
99-9109	252	1	6.2	2.1	G	ind lin st		sm	1.27	1	
99-911	251	2	0	2.4	S	eroded		eroded		1	
99-9110	256	4	6.18	11.8	G	curv comp st	ind scroll	sm	0.91	1	
99-9110	261	4	6.5	11.4	G	curv comp st	ind scroll	sm	1.27	1	
99-9110	252	3	6.67	4.1	grit	curv comp st	ind	sm	0.7	1	Qualla paste
99-9110	260	5	6.77	10.7	G	ind lin st	sm over	sm	0.89	1	
99-9110	253	3	7.03	7.2	G	ind lin st		sm	0.73	1	
99-9110	254	5	7.23	16.2	G	curv comp st	ind scroll	coarse	1.82	1	photo
99-9110	262	4	7.31	8.6	G	ind lin st		sm	1.47	1	
99-9110	255	2	7.44	3.6	G	incs	ind par hrz lines	sm	1.3	1	
99-9110	257	3	7.52	4.2	S	sm		sm	1.63	1	
99-9110	259	2	7.75	2.1	S	sm		sm	1.56	1	
99-9110	258	2	8.06	4.3	G	curv comp st	ind	sm	1.87	1	
99-9111	262	2	0	2.3	G	eroded		eroded	0.86	1	
99-9111	265	2	3.35	2	grit	ind lin st		redfilmed	0.87	1	Qualla paste
99-9111	266	3	7.88	5.4	G	cordm		sm	2.04	1	
99-9111	264	3	8.75	6.2	G	ind lin st		sm	1.37	1	
99-9111	267	2	9.03	3.8	G	ind st		sm/smdg	1.09	1	
99-9111	263	3	9.36	9.3	G	sm		sm	1.57	1	
99-9112	279	1	0	1.5	G	eroded		eroded	1.5	1	
99-9112	275	1	5.82	1.9	G	sm		sm	1.88	1	
99-9112	268	3	6.02	5	G	ind lin st		sm/smdg	1.5	1	
99-9112	264	3	6.03	5.6	grit	ind lin st		redfilmed	0.64	1	Qualla paste
99-9112	278	1	6.06	2.1	G	ind lin st		sm	1.46	1	
99-9112	281	1	6.12	1.3	G	ind st		sm	0.93	1	
99-9112	269	3	6.61	5.1	G	ind st		sm	1.65	1	
99-9112	282	2	6.63	5.2	G	sm		sm	1.49	1	
99-9112	272	3	6.7	3.9	G	ind st		sm	1.55	1	
99-9112	262	4	6.83	12.9	G	curv comp st	fig "p"	sm/smdg	1.24	1	
99-9112	267	2	6.87	4.4	G	ind st		sm	1.16	1	
99-9112	274	1	7.11	2.1	S	sm		sm	1.43	1	
99-9112	280	2	7.28	2	G	coarse		sm	1.61	1	
99-9112	273	1	8.26	2	G	ind st		sm	1.56	1	
99-9112	266	2	8.38	5	G	cordm		sm	2.06	1	
99-9112	265	2	8.38	3.7	G	ind lin st		sm	1.35	1	
99-9112	263	3	9.03	5.9	G	cordm		sm	1.96	1	
99-9112	276	1	9.46	2.2	G	sm		sm	1.08	1	
99-9146	4	2	7.24	2.9	G	ind lin st		coarse	2.21	1	
99-9146	1	5	7.79	19.5	G	ind lin st	sm over	coarse	2.25	1	
99-9146	2	3	8.43	6.6	G	curv comp st	ind	coarse	1.73	1	
99-9148	251	3	7.94	5.8	grit	ind lin st		brn/smdg	1.13	1	
99-9149	3	2	6.52	6.7	grit	cordm		sm	0.69	1	
99-9149	2	2	7.08	2.5	grit	ind st	sm over	sm	0.98	1	
99-9149	1	3	11.17	5.2	G	ind lin st		sm	1.67	1	
99-915	7	2	6.01	1.4	S	rgh		sm	1.26	1	corn cob

99-915	251	3	7.67	7.8	G	cordm		sm	2.23	1	
99-9151	259	2	5.88	2.5	G	ind lin st		sm	1.42	1	
99-9151	257	2	6.1	2.6	G	ind st		brn	1.28	1	
99-9151	258	1	7.38	2.4	G	coarse		coarse	1.16	1	
99-9151	256	3	7.59	5.4	G	cordm		coarse	1.78	1	
99-9151	260	2	8.02	4.7	G	cordm		sm	1.82	1	
99-9151	255	4	9.95	15.5	G	coarse		sm/smdg	2.58	1	
99-9152	1	6	8.68	24	G	ind lin st	sm over	sm	2.54	1	base fragment
99-9156	253	2	6.39	3.8	G	ind lin st	sm over	sm	1.69	1	
99-9156	252	2	7.08	2.6	G	sm		sm	1.97	1	
99-9156	258	5	7.15	16.8	G	ind lin st		sm/smdg	2.44	1	
99-9156	256	3	7.54	9	G	comp st	ind	sm/smdg	2.24	1	
99-9156	255	4	7.59	8.1	G	ind lin st		coarse	3.3	1	
99-9156	257	5	7.76	20.6	grit	curv comp st	ind	brn/smdg	0.98	1	
99-9156	254	2	7.96	3.9	G	ind lin st		sm	1.29	1	
99-9157	261	2	0	3.3	grit	ind lin st	sm over	eroded	0.76	1	
99-9157	257	2	6.24	3.1	grit	ind lin st		brn/smdg	0.72	1	
99-9157	264	2	6.72	2.5	G	ind st		brn/smdg	1.36	1	
99-9157	258	4	6.94	10.3	grit	ind lin st		sm	0.66	1	
99-9157	262	2	7.28	6.3	G	ind st		sm	1.1	1	
99-9157	259	2	7.38	4.1	G	ind st		sm	1.86	1	
99-9157	260	2	7.84	3.7	G	coarse		sm	1.98	1	
99-9157	263	2	10.24	5.1	G	coarse		scr	1.8	1	
99-9158	8	1	6	2	G	ind st		eroded	0.8	1	
99-9158	6	2	6.48	4.1	grit	ind lin st		sm	1.1	1	
99-9158	5	2	7.48	5.1	G	curv comp st	ind sm over	sm	1.34	1	
99-9158	10	2	7.92	6.7	G	ind lin st	sm over	sm/smdg	0.92	1	
99-9158	4	3	8.62	6.5	G	ind st		sm/smdg	1.6	1	
99-9158	7	1	9.58	3	grit	coarse		sm	0.87	1	
99-9159	5	2	6.54	2	S	eroded		eroded		1	
99-9159	3	3	8.18	8.1	G	scr		sm	1.78	1	
99-9159	4	2	8.19	5.1	G	ind lin st	sm over	brn/smdg	1.24	1	
99-9163	2	2	0	3.8	G	eroded		sm	2.39	1	
99-9163	1	3	6.03	7.5	G	coarse		sm	1.54	1	
99-9168	257	2	4.88	1.9	G	ind st		brn/smdg	1.38	1	
99-9168	259	2	6.34	2.5	G	ind lin st		eroded	1.5	1	
99-9168	258	2	7.32	3.3	grit	br		sm/smdg	0.7	1	
99-9169	12	3	0	2.5	G	ind st		eroded	1.32	1	
99-9169	8	3	5.88	2.8	G	ind lin st		sm	2.94	1	
99-9169	14	3	6.38	3.5	G	ind st	sm over	sm	1.5	1	
99-9169	10	2	6.64	4.1	G	ind st	sm over	sm	1.76	1	
99-9169	7	3	8.08	7.3	G	cordm		redfilmed	1.08	1	
99-9169	13	2	8.16	3	G	ind lin st		sm	1.3	1	
99-9169	5	5	8.36	16.4	G	curv comp st	ind	sm	1.8	1	
99-9169	11	3	8.62	4.5	G	ind st		brn/smdg	1.54	1	
99-9169	9	4	8.7	8.5	G	coarse		eroded	1.62	1	
99-9169	15	9	8.76	75.9	G	curv comp st	conc circles	sm	2.32	1	
99-9169	3	4	9.42	19.3	G	ind lin st		brn	1.72	1	
99-917	265	1	7.03	2.2	G	sm		sm	1.22	1	
99-9170	268	2	0	3.3	G	eroded		sm	1.94	1	
99-9170	274	2	0	2.2	G	eroded		eroded	1.4	1	
99-9170	261	2	5.42	2.1	G	coarse		brn/smdg	1.14	1	
99-9170	258	2	5.92	2.5	grit	sm		sm	1.03	1	
99-9170	287	2	6	3.1	grit	ind st		sm/smdg	0.44	1	
99-9170	284	2	6.02	2.9	G	cordm		sm/smdg	1.34	1	
99-9170	267	2	6.12	2.4	grit	sm		sm	1.1	1	
99-9170	260	2	6.15	3.9	grit	sm		brn/smdg	0.94	1	
99-9170	270	4	6.2	15.8	G	cordm		eroded	2.06	1	
99-9170	269	2	6.28	3.1	G	ind st		eroded	1.88	1	
99-9170	259	1	6.28	1.8	G	cordm		eroded	1.37	1	
99-9170	256	2	6.3	2.9	G	sm		brn	1.12	1	
99-9170	282	3	6.34	7.7	G	sm		brn/smdg	2.12	1	
99-9170	271	4	6.42	7.5	G	ind lin st		brn/smdg	1.18	1	
99-9170	278	2	6.55	2.7	G	ind st	sm over	brn/smdg	0.98	1	
99-9170	285	2	6.82	4.7	G	coarse		coarse	1.56	1	
99-9170	276	2	6.84	3.7	G	coarse		sm/smdg	1.4	1	
99-9170	275	2	7.04	4.3	grit	sm		sm	0.88	1	
99-9170	279	2	7.48	3.5	G	ind lin st		sm	1.04	1	
99-9170	263	2	7.54	4.6	G	ind lin st		brn/smdg	1.19	1	
99-9170	286	2	7.71	5.1	G	sm		eroded	1.38	1	
99-9170	281	2	7.9	5.1	G	ind st		sm	2.14	1	
99-9170	262	3	8.04	7.3	G	sm		sm	2.43	1	
99-9170	2720	2	8.22	6.1	G	ind lin st	sm over	eroded	1.65	1	
99-9170	283	2	8.24	4.8	G	ind lin st		sm	1.56	1	
99-9170	280	3	8.48	7.2	G	ind lin st		sm	2.48	1	
99-9170	257	2	8.58	2.7	G	rgh		sm	1.74	1	corn cob
99-9170	264	2	9.12	6	G	ind lin st	sm over	sm/smdg	2.08	1	
99-9170	266	2	9.24	3.8	G	sm		sm	1.74	1	
99-9170	273	3	9.28	12.2	G	coarse		brn	1	1	
99-9170	265	1	9.9	3	G	sm		sm	1.32	1	
99-9170	272	3	13.6	9.1	G	sm		sm	1.6	1	
99-9171	2	3	6.62	9.3	G	curv comp st	ind	sm	2.46	1	
99-9171	1	2	7.4	3.5	G	coarse		sm	2.42	1	
99-9171	4	4	8.45	17.2	G	ind lin st	sm over	brn	2.06	1	
99-9171	3	4	9.14	19.3	G	ind lin st	sm over	sm	2.32	1	
99-9171	5	3	9.36	5.4	G	sm		brn	1.12	1	
99-9171	7	6	10.98	42	G	comp st	ind sm over	brn	1.56	1	
99-9173	1	5	7.18	15.1	G	sm		sm	1.69	1	base fragment
99-9174	251	2	8.5	2.8	S	scr		scr		1	
99-918	251	3	5.95	3.3	S	sm		sm		1	
99-9185	253	2	4.88	4.3	G	coarse		sm	1.06	1	
99-9185	254	2	5.87	3.5	G	ind st	sm over	sm/smdg	1.38	1	
99-9185	256	2	5.9	3.8	G	scr		scr	1.38	1	
99-9185	255	3	7.21	7.5	G	ind st	sm over	brn/smdg	1.66	1	
99-9185	252	2	7.56	5.8	G	curv comp st	fig "9"	brn/smdg	1.14	1	
99-9185	257	2	8.27	4.1	G	ind st	sm over	sm	1.64	1	
99-9185	251	2	10	5.7	G	sm		sm	2.63	1	
99-9188	252	2	6.36	2.7	G	sm		eroded	1.86	1	
99-9188	251	4	6.92	8.4	G	brn		sm	2.9	1	
99-9192	6	2	6.44	3.3	G	coarse		sm/smdg	2.46	1	
99-9192	13	5	6.83	6.4	G	ind lin st	sm over	sm	1.2	1	carinated shoulder
99-9192	15	3	6.84	4.9	G	ind lin st		eroded	1.92	1	
99-9192	5	5	6.96	19.5	grit	curv comp st	ind	sm	1.5	1	
99-9192	9	3	7.28	7.5	grit	curv comp st	ind	brn	0.76	1	
99-9192	3	3	7.28	8.3	grit	curv comp st	ind	sm/smdg	1	1	
99-9192	2	5	7.54	22	grit	curv comp st	ind	sm	0.6	1	
99-9192	12	7	7.61	30.6	grit	curv comp st	ind	sm	0.79	1	
99-9192	10	9	7.69	71.5	grit	curv comp st	fig "9"	sm	1.44	1	same vessel as 99-9192-2, 99-9192-11
99-9192	8	2	7.72	2.4	grit	ind st		eroded	0.66	1	
99-9192	7	1	7.88	3.1	G	ind st		sm	2.58	1	
99-9192	4	3	8.4	5.5	G	coarse		sm	2.36	1	
99-9193	253	2	5.98	2.7	G	eroded		eroded	1.57	1	
99-9195	255	3	8.09	7	G	cordm		sm	1.29	1	
99-9195	256	2	8.41	2.8	G	ind st	sm over	brn	1.6	1	
99-9197	251	2	11.39	4.2	G	coarse		sm	1.71	1	
99-9198	2	3	6.51	5.9	G	curv comp st	ind sm over	sm/smdg	2.73	1	
99-9198	1	4	6.78	15.3	G	ind lin st	sm over	sm/smdg	1.93	1	
99-9200	251	2	7.43	5.4	G	ind lin st		sm	2.82	1	
99-9204	253	1	5.89	1.4	G	ind st		sm	1.79	1	
99-9204	252	2	6.9	2.3	G	cordm		sm	1.64	1	
99-9204	254	1	7.62	2.2	G	coarse		sm	1.73	1	
99-9204	251	2	8.4	3.6	G	sm		sm	2.31	1	
99-9208	251	2	5.38	2.8	G	ind st	sm over	brn/smdg	1.15	1	
99-9209	254	3	5.69	7.8	G	coarse		brn	1.96	1	
99-9209	253	2	9.75	6.8	G	ind st		sm	1.91	1	
99-921	251	2	0	0.8	S	eroded		eroded		1	
99-9212	8	2	5.88	2	G	scr		sm/smdg	1.38	1	

99-9212	5	3	6.44	5.2	G	ind lin st	sm over	brn/smdg	2.08	1	
99-9212	7	2	6.58	2.6	G	brn		brn	1.78	1	
99-9212	4	4	6.94	13.8	G	coarse		coarse	1.96	1	
99-9212	9	2	7.04	3.8	G	coarse		sm	1.52	1	
99-9212	6	3	7.68	6.3	G	coarse		coarse	2.1	1	
99-9212	3	5	11.52	29	G	cordm	sm over	coarse	2.96	1	
99-9217	254	2	7.59	5.1	G	ind lin st	sm over	sm	1.54	1	
99-9219	255	7	6.55	26.3	G	comp st	ind sm over	brn	1.38	1	
99-9219	254	3	7.39	7.7	G	ind lin st		sm/smdg	0.96	1	
99-9220	257	3	0	3.1	G	eroded		eroded	1.01	1	
99-9220	256	2	0	2.9	G	scr		eroded	1.68	1	
99-9220	260	2	7.44	2.6	G	coarse		sm	1.52	1	
99-9220	255	2	7.5	3.1	grit	ind lin st		sm/smdg	0.7	1	
99-9220	258	1	8.51	3.1	G	sm		sm	2	1	
99-9220	254	4	8.58	17.3	G	ind lin st	sm over	brn	2.52	1	
99-9220	261	4	9.08	16.1	G	ind lin st	sm over	sm	2.88	1	
99-9220	259	5	10.07	18.9	G	sm		sm	2.5	1	
99-936	260	2	6.59	2.1	S	sm		sm	1.54	1	
99-936	266	4	7	9.5	G	ind lin st		sm	1.9	1	
99-936	262	3	7.08	4	G	curv comp st	ind	sm	1.37	1	
99-936	263	2	7.09	2.9	G	comp st	ind	sm	1.67	1	
99-936	261	2	7.15	2	G	ind st		sm	1.17	1	
99-936	265	2	7.45	3.3	G	sm		brn	0.61	1	
99-936	259	2	8.89	2.7	G	ind lin st		sm	0.97	1	
99-941	274	2	6.55	2.8	G	sm		brn	1.16	1	
99-941	270	2	6.93	2.5	G	ind lin st		sm	1.66	1	
99-941	269	2	7.21	3.4	G	sm		sm	1.57	1	
99-941	273	4	7.49	13.6	G	curv comp st	ind	sm	1.3	1	
99-941	266	3	7.5	5.6	G	coarse		sm	1.89	1	
99-941	275	2	7.53	2.5	G	sm		sm	0.87	1	
99-941	277	3	7.74	6.3	G	sm		sm	0.57	1	
99-941	278	5	7.77	14.9	G	ind lin st		sm	1.44	1	
99-941	265	3	7.93	4.8	G	ind lin st		sm	1.54	1	
99-941	271	2	8.04	4.5	G	ind lin st		sm	1.7	1	
99-958	263	2	0	3.6	G	eroded		sm	2.1	1	
99-958	274	4	5	9.8	S	sm		sm	1.78	1	
99-958	280	2	5.3	3.4	G	curv comp st	ind	sm	0.64	1	
99-958	265	2	5.48	3.3	G	coarse		brn	1.5	1	
99-958	276	4	5.7	8.3	G	sm		sm	1.1	1	
99-958	281	2	5.92	2.2	S	sm		sm	1.1	1	
99-958	286	5	6.3	11.7	S	scr		sm	1.84	1	
99-958	282	3	6.44	3.8	S	sm		sm	1.9	1	
99-958	287	6	6.47	16	S	rgh		sm	1.67	1	corn cob
99-958	268	3	6.78	5.9	G	curv comp st	ind	brn	1.68	1	
99-958	285	5	7.04	10.1	G	sm		sm	1.58	1	
99-958	257	3	7.18	8.1	G	ind st		sm	2.28	1	
99-958	264	1	7.28	2.3	G	ind lin st		sm	1.38	1	
99-958	262	3	7.32	6.7	S	scr		sm	2.01	1	
99-958	260	4	7.35	12.6	G	curv comp st	ind	sm	2.1	1	
99-958	266	3	7.52	7.3	G	ind st		sm	1.46	1	
99-958	275	4	7.64	5.7	G	curv comp st	ind	sm	1.27	1	
99-958	273	3	7.78	10.1	G	coarse		sm	2.12	1	
99-958	290	5	7.8	21.4	grit	curv comp st	ind	brn	0.8	1	
99-958	270	4	7.8	9.9	grit	sm		sm	0.98	1	
99-958	277	2	7.88	3.2	G	ind lin st		sm/smdg	0.85	1	
99-958	272	2	7.92	2.4	S	sm		sm	1.2	1	
99-958	279	3	8.08	7.2	G	coarse		sm	1.07	1	
99-958	278	3	8.18	6.4	G	curv comp st	ind	brn	1.48	1	carinated shoulder
99-958	283	4	8.32	8.9	G	scr		sm	1.2	1	
99-958	258	3	8.58	5.6	G	sm		sm	1.4	1	
99-958	289	6	8.64	18.5	S	scr		scr	1.87	1	
99-958	259	4	8.75	9.1	G	curv comp st	ind scroll	brn/smdg	1.48	1	
99-958	267	3	9.04	6.3	G	ind lin st		sm	1.18	1	
99-958	269	3	9.3	7.8	G	coarse		sm/smdg	1.24	1	
99-959	16	4	4.84	5.4	G	coarse		brn/smdg	1.25	1	
99-959	13	3	6.94	7.6	G	curv comp st	ind	brn	2.01	1	
99-959	15	3	7.06	6.5	G	curv comp st	ind	sm	1.32	1	
99-959	17	2	7.34	3.5	G	ind lin st		brn/smdg	0.94	1	
99-959	14	3	8.36	11.5	G	ind lin st	sm over	sm	1.85	1	
99-963	77	3	6.95	4.4	G	ind lin st		sm	1.39	1	
99-963	81	3	7.1	4.1	G	ind st		sm/smdg	1.15	1	
99-963	82	1	8.13	1.9	G	sm		sm	0.79	1	
99-963	80	3	8.25	4.4	S	scr		sm	1.67	1	
99-963	79	2	8.79	4.8	G	coarse		sm	0.73	1	
99-963	83	3	8.8	8.6	G	cordm		sm/smdg	0.94	1	
99-963	78	2	9.32	2.4	G	sm		sm	1.37	1	
99-978	4	5	6.93	19.8	G	curv comp st	ind	sm	1.91	1	
99-978	5	2	8.13	4.4	G	coarse		sm	1.28	1	
99-9949	1	10	8.11	0	G	smpl st	ovrst	sm	1.47	1	complex motif with a smpl stamp

Appendix C

Data Recorded for Rim Sherds in the Ceramics Sample

KEY

appl:	applied	lin:	linear
bev:	beveled	N:	no
brn:	burnished	ntch:	notched
comp:	complicated	outw:	outward
cordm:	cordmarked	par:	parallel
CR:	crushed rock	pnch:	pinched
curv:	curvilinear	punc:	punctated
dir:	direct	rd:	rounded
exc:	excurvate	rimstr:	rimstrip
ext:	exterior	rstr:	restricted
F:	false	S:	shell
fil:	fillet	sm:	smoothed
fl:	flattened	smdg:	smudged
fold:	folded	smpl:	simple
frag:	fragment	st:	stamped
G:	gravel	sty:	stylus
h ev:	highly everted	T:	true
hmsp:	hemispherical	th:	thickened
hrz:	horizontal	undern:	underneath
inc:	incurvate	unmod:	unmodified
ind:	indeterminate	up:	upper
int:	interior	vrt:	vertical
inw:	inward	Y:	yes

Provenience Code	Specimen Number	Unique Rim	Vessel Form	Temper Material	Exterior Surface Treatment	Motif	Interior Surface Treatment	Rimstrip Present	Method of Attachment	Rim Inclination	Rim Curvature	Lip Shape	Rim Form	Basic Rimstrip Embellishment	Maximum Sherd Length (mm)	Maximum Sherd Height (mm)	Rimstrip Width (mm)	Estimated Orifice Diameter (cm)	Percent of Rim	Temper Particle Size (mm)	Weight (g)	Thickness at Lip (mm)	Thickness at Neck (mm)	Thickness at Shoulders (mm)	Thickness at Corona (mm)	Thickness below Corona (mm)	Coronal Thickness (mm)	Frequency
00-236	252	T	ind	G	sm		brn/smdg	Y	appl	ind	exc	rd	th	pnch	25	20	15.6	0	0	1.01	4.8	5.2	0	0	10.58	6.3	4.2	1
00-236	253	T	exc rim jar	G	coarse		sm	Y	appl	outw	exc	rd	th	sty ntch	36	34	18.49	0	0	1.71	12.61	6.47	7.06	0	14.26	7.06	7.2	1
00-248	251	T	exc rim jar	G	coarse		sm	Y	fold	outw	exc	rd	fold	pnch	56.14	22.82	19.6	0	0	1.68	35.4	8.36	7.4	0	16.8w	8	8.8	1
00-255	281	T	ind	G	sm		sm	ind	ind	ind	ind	rd	ind	ind	18	16	0	0	0	1	2.6	5.85	0	0	0	0	0	1
00-263	259	T	rstr orifice hmsp bowl	G	brn		brn	N		inw	inc	rd	unmod		29	32	0	0	0	1.24	8	5.19	0	6.67	0	0	0	1
00-265	263	T	ind	G	sm		sm	Y	appl	ind	ind	bev (int)	th	sty ntch	37	20	17.56	0	0	1.83	8.7	5.82	0	0	14.68	7.32	7.36	1
00-334	408	T	ind	G	sm		brn/smdg	Y	appl	ind	ind	rd	th	sm	43	16	13.62	0	0	1.21	8.3	6.03	0	0	13.43	6.45	6.98	1
00-334	411	T	smpl hmsp bowl	G	sm		sm	Y	ind	vrt	inc	rd	th	sm	22	20	20.38	0	0	1.54	5.3	5.48	0	0	15.02	9.87	5.15	1
00-334	406	T	exc rim jar	G	sm		sm	Y	appl	vrt	exc	rd	th	sm up/ pnch undern	32	28	20.7	0	0	1.66	12.3	6.27	0	0	14.71	7.12	7.59	1
00-334	410	F	rimstr frag	G	sm		eroded	Y	appl	ind	ind	ind	th	sty ntch	15	13	0	0	0	1.07	1.3	0	0	0	0	0	0	1
00-334	412	F	exc rim jar	G	sm		sm	Y	ind	outw	exc	rd	th	sty ntch	78	36	18.05	38	5	1.22	37.9	6.02	7.82	0	14.55	9.72	4.83	1
00-334	407	F	rimstr frag	G	sm		eroded	Y	ind	ind	ind	ind	th	sty ntch	24	12	0	0	0	2.15	3	0	0	0	0	0	0	1
00-334	405	T	ind	G	sm		sm/smdg	Y	appl	vrt	ind	rd	th	sty ntch	20	18	15.5	0	0	1.4	3.4	5.12	0	0	12.45	5.11	7.34	1
00-357	267	T	exc rim jar	G	sm		sm	Y	appl	outw	exc	rd	th	sm	70	38	14.66	36	6	1.44	28.6	7.13	12.87	0	13.81	7.78	6.03	1
00-363	150	F	rimstr frag	G	sm		sm	Y	ind	ind	ind	ind	ind	ind	16	12	0	0	0	1.34	1.8	0	0	0	0	0	0	1
00-363	143	T	ind	G	sm		sm	Y	ind	ind	ind	fl	th	pnch	36	24	24.3	0	0	0.83	8.6	6.45	0	0	13.53	5.85	7.7	1
00-363	153	T	exc rim jar	G	cordm		sm	Y	appl	outw	exc	rd	th	sty ntch	60	40	19.16	0	0	1.55	29.6	6.1	0	0	15.07	6.65	8.42	1
00-363	144	T	ind	G	sm		sm	Y	ind	ind	ind	rd	th	sty ntch	19	15	15.92	0	0	1.86	3.1	5.25	0	0	11.51	5.28	6.23	1
00-363	145	T	ind	G	sm		sm	Y	appl	ind	ind	rd	th	sm	32.5	17.5	16.65	0	0	1.66	6.4	7.05	0	0	14.61	6.45	8.16	1
00-363	141	T	ind	grit	ind lin st		brn	Y	appl	ind	ind	fl	th	sm	26	33	19.6	0	0	1.14	9	5.91	0	0	15.63	8.45	7.18	1
00-363	142	T	ind	G	sm		sm/smdg	Y	ind	ind	ind	rd	th	sm	27	14	14.7	0	0	1.04	3.5	5.68	0	0	11.3	4.73	6.57	1
00-363	152	T	exc rim jar	G	sm		sm	Y	appl	vrt	inc	rd	th	sm	93	75	20.6	28	9	2.03	97.7	7.2	0	0	18.53	10.88	7.65	1
00-363	148[1]	F	rimstr frag	G	sm		sm	Y	appl	ind	ind	ind	th	sty ntch	33	20	0	0	0	1.41	9.2	0	0	0	0	0	0	1
00-363	149	T	ind	G	eroded		sm	Y	appl	vrt	exc	bev (int)	th	sty ntch	28	33	17.81	0	0	0.95	9.1	4.68	0	0	13.44	6.62	6.82	1
00-381	329	T	ind	G	sm		sm	N		outw	ind	rd	unmod		34	18	0	0	0	3.27	4.7	5.94	0	0	0	0	0	1
00-381	332	T	exc rim jar	G	sm		sm/smdg	Y	appl	vrt	exc	rd	th	pnch	46	37	20.5	0	0	0.96	24.8	6.35	7.25	0	14.25	7.25	7	1
00-381	327	T	ind	G	sm		sm	Y	fold	ind	exc	rd	fold/fl	pnch	16	17	0	0	0	1.4	1.7	3.72	0	0	0	0	0	1
00-381	326	T	ind	G	sm		sm	Y	fold	ind	ind	bev (int)	fold/fl	pnch	16	14	14.6	0	0	0.72	2.2	5.26	0	0	0	0	1.66	1
00-381	323	T	exc rim jar	G	sm		sm	Y	appl	vrt	exc	rd	th	pnch	40	23	15.04	0	0	1.03	11.2	6.71	5.72	0	11.71	5.33	6.38	1
00-381	328	F	rimstr frag	G	sm		sm	Y	appl	ind	ind	ind	th	pnch	45	17	17.7	0	0	2.53	6.3	0	0	0	0	0	5.73	1
00-381	331	T	ind	G	sm		sm	Y	ind	vrt	exc	rd	th	sty ntch	23	20	12.16	0	0	1.45	3	4.88	0	0	10.58	7.23	3.35	1
00-381	325	F	rimstr frag	G	sm		eroded	Y	appl	ind	ind	ind	th	sty ntch	20	10	11.61	0	0	1.52	1.3	0	0	0	0	0	6.19	1
00-381	324	T	ind	G	sm		sm	Y	ind	vrt	exc	rd	th	sty ntch	20	18	11.72	0	0	1.88	3.9	4.8	0	0	10.63	6.13	4.5	1
00-381	330	F	rimstr frag	G	sm		eroded	Y	appl	ind	ind	ind	th	sty ntch	24	22	22.45	0	0	1.99	5.1	0	0	0	0	0	7.08	1
00-401	337	T	ind	G	sm		sm	Y	ind	ind	ind	rd	th	ind	21.93	18.6	0	0	0	1.47	3.8	6.6	0	0	0	0	0	1
00-401	339	F	rimstr frag	G	sm		sm	Y	ind	ind	ind	ind	th	sty ntch	17	14	0	0	0	1.57	1.6	0	0	0	0	0	0	1
00-401	338	T	ind	S	sm		sm	Y	appl (fil)	outw	exc	rd	th	punc	17	18	0	0	0	1.43	1.9	3.8	0	0	0	0	0	1
00-401	336	T	exc rim jar	G	cordm		sm	Y	appl	vrt	exc	rd	th	sty ntch	65	30	10.59	26	9	1.85	27.3	5.1	5.64	0	10.32	5.64	4.68	1

99-1	616	T	cazuela	grit	incised	lines & semicircles	brn/smdg	N		inw	dir	rd	unmod		30	33	0	0	0	0.67	6.9	4.36	0	0	0	0	0	1
99-10	321	T	ind	G	brn		sm	ind	ind	ind	ind	rd	rolled	ind	19.26	12.56	0	0	0	1.55	3.5	0	0	0	0	0	0	1
99-10	322	T	exc rim jar	G	coarse		coarse	Y	appl	outw	exc	fl	th/fl	sty ntch	62.43	45.42	31.7	35	5	1.75	30.9	5.08	12.24	0	12.14	8.1	4.4	1
99-10037	255	T	rstr orifice hmsp bowl	G	sm		sm/smdg	Y	ind	inw	inc	bev (int)	th/fl	punc	20.82	15.67	0	0	0	1.86	2.6	4.6	0	0	0	0	1.4	1
99-10039	265	T	exc rim jar	S	eroded		eroded	Y	fold	outw	exc	rd	fold	pnch	36.28	31.82	17.06	0	0	3.84	6.4	5.45	0	0	11.75	6.64	5.11	1
99-10056	255	T	ind	G	eroded		sm	ind	ind	outw	exc	rd	ind	ind	42.37	16.04	0	0	0	1.46	4.9	5.24	0	0	0	0	0	1
99-10061	1[2]	T	small jar	G	ind st	sm over	sm	N		vrt	exc	fl	unmod		26	25	0	0	0	1.3	5.7	5.36	4.95	0	0	0	0	1
99-10083	2	T	pnch rim jar	G	sm		brn	Y	ind	outw	h ev	rd	th/fl	pnch	58.7	26.39	22.47	0	0	1.94	19.8	4.62	0	0	11.22	8.3	2.92	1
99-10092	257	F	ind	G	sm		sm/smdg	ind	ind	outw	exc	rd	ind	ind	20.46	19.17	0	0	0	1.42	3.8	7.13	0	0	0	0	0	1
99-10092	258	F	pnch rim jar	G	sm		sm	Y	ind	outw	h ev	rd	th/fl	pnch	21.78	18.47	0	0	0	1.42	3.5	8.23	0	0	0	0	0	1
99-10093	15	T	pnch rim jar	G	sm		sm	Y	ind	outw	h ev	rd	th/fl	pnch	33.02	13.48	10.44	0	0	1.56	6.8	4.93	0	0	10.45	9.03	1.42	1
99-1036	7	T	pnch rim jar	G	sm		sm	Y	appl	outw	h ev	ind	th/fl	pnch	42	22	18.04	0	0	0.93	8.4	5.82	0	0	11.03	7.96	3.07	1
99-1039	272	T	exc rim jar	S	sm		sm	Y	ind	vrt	exc	rd	th	sty ntch	29	28	20	0	0	0.8	6.3	5.5	0	0	10.72	7.3	3.42	1
99-1044	313	T	smpl hmsp bowl	G	brn		brn	N		vrt	inc	fl	unmod		43.36	40.96	0	22	6	1.91	15.1	5.43	0	0	0	0	0	1
99-1044	309	F	rimstr frag	S	sm		sm	Y	ind	ind	ind	ind	th	ind	30.89	13.51	11.91	0	0	0.5	4.6	0	0	0	0	0	0	1
99-1044	310	F	rimstr frag	grit	sm		sm/smdg	Y	appl	ind	ind	ind	th	pnch	24.79	20.19	15.36	0	0	0.8	6.4	0	0	0	15.42	10.44	4.98	1
99-1044	312	T	exc rim jar	G	coarse		sm	Y	appl	outw	exc	rd	th	sty ntch	45.92	57.38	19.91	0	0	2.08	30.1	5.57	7.68	0	13.54	7.52	6.02	1
99-1044	307	T	ind	S	sm		sm	Y	appl	outw	exc	rd	th	sty ntch	39.92	17.22	17.22	0	0	0.75	6.8	5.61	0	0	0	0	7.73	1
99-1045	262	T	exc rim jar	S	sm		sm	Y	appl	outw	exc	rd	L-shaped	pnch	56.28	36.36	11.94	16	7	1.77	14.1	4.73	5.69	0	9	5.58	3.42	1
99-1045	261	T	rstr orifice hmsp bowl	S	sm		sm	Y	appl	vrt	inc	bev (int)	th	punc	29.81	17.65	11.27	0	0	2.1	3.3	4.18	0	0	8.99	5.66	3.33	1
99-1045	259	F	rimstr frag	G	sm		sm	Y	ind	ind	ind	ind	th	sty ntch	18.23	13	0	0	0	0	0	0	0	0	9.12	4.2	4.92	1
99-1062	282	T	rstr orifice hmsp bowl	G	cordm		sm	ind	ind	inw	inc	fl	ind	ind	44.39	37.28	0	0	0	3.05	9.9	0	0	6.44	0	0	0	1
99-1062	276	F	exc rim jar	S	sm		sm	Y	ind	outw	exc	ind	th	ind	43.54	22.45	0	0	0	2.88	9.29	0	0	0	0	0	0	1
99-1062	279	T	exc rim jar	G	coarse		sm	Y	appl	outw	exc	rd	th/fl	pnch	32.48	37.16	18.11	0	0	1.87	11.9	6.12	0	0	9.78	6.97	2.81	1
99-1062	281	T	rstr orifice hmsp bowl	G	sm		sm	Y	fold	inw	inc	rd	fold	sm	22.96	13.32	13.32	11	5	2.79	1.8	4.52	0	0	0	0	4	1
99-1062	284	T	exc rim jar	S	sm		sm	Y	appl	outw	exc	fl	th	sty ntch	42.83	40.54	19.65	0	0	3.05	13.3	6.24	0	0	14.96	7.98	6.98	1
99-1064	252	T	ind	grit	sm		sm/smdg	ind	ind	ind	ind	fl	ind	punc	15.33	13.36	0	0	0	0.66	1.7	5.84	0	0	0	0	0	1
99-10676	262	T	exc rim jar	G	sm		sm	Y	appl	outw	exc	rd	th	pnch	38	22	20.67	0	0	1.62	8.9	3.96	0	0	12.41	5.64	6.77	1
99-1073	283	T	ind	S	sm		sm	Y	appl	outw	exc	rd	th	sty ntch	44.1	21.91	21.91	0	0	0.7	7.7	5.4	0	0	12.28	5.27	7.01	1
99-1078	332	T	ind	G	sm		eroded	N		ind	exc	rd	rolled		39	24	0	0	0	1.5	11.58	14.8	0	0	0	0	0	1
99-1078	336	T	ind	G	eroded		brn/smdg	Y	ind	ind	ind	rd	th	ind	22	22	0	0	0	1.72	4.91	7.32	0	0	0	0	0	1
99-1078	330	T	ind	G	sm		sm/smdg	Y	appl	outw	exc	bev (int)	th	sty ntch	39	17	0	0	0	1.5	8	5.79	0	0	0	0	0	1
99-1078	329	T	exc rim jar	S	sm		sm	Y	fold	outw	exc	fl	fold	sty ntch	83	46	12.8	40	7	2.5	30.39	4.59	5.92	0	10.06	5.9	4.16	1
99-1078	381	F	rimstr frag	G	sm		sm	Y	ind	ind	ind	ind	th	sty ntch	27	11	0	0	0	1.36	1.62	0	0	0	0	0	0	1
99-1078	335	T	exc rim jar	G	sm		sm	Y	appl	outw	exc	fl	th	sty ntch	37	32	16.89	0	0	1.54	9.87	5.5	0	0	12.02	6.4	5.62	1
99-1078	333	T	ind	G	sm		sm	Y	fold	vrt	exc	rd	fold	sty ntch	46	12.8	12.8	0	0	1.4	7.34	5.32	0	0	10.42	6.3	4.12	1
99-1078	334	T	ind	S	Sm		Sm	Y	fold	vrt	exc	fl	fold	sty ntch	30	27.5	23.8	0	0	2.48	4.72	3.95	0	0	8.36	6.72	1.64	1
99-1090	264[3]	F	exc rim jar	G	cordm		brn	Y	fold	outw	exc	rd	fold	sty ntch	76.73	38.73	15.31	0	0	1.03	28.4	4.21	5.83	0	9.73	6.23	3.5	1
99-1091	260[4]	T	exc rim jar	G	cordm		brn	Y	fold	outw	exc	rd	fold	sty ntch	104.09	59.13	17.05	32	11	2.22	51.8	6.22	5.79	0	8.97	6.1	2.87	1
99-1099	259[5]	F	exc rim jar	G	cordm		brn	Y	fold	outw	exc	rd	fold	sty ntch	65.6	37.82	13.96	0	0	2.51	20.2	4.59	6.53	0	9.1	6.67	2.73	1
99-11	252	T	ind	S	sm		sm	Y	ind	outw	exc	rd	th	ind	21.04	23.44	16.28	0	0	1.45	2.4	4.58	0	0	9.52	6.44	3.08	1
99-11	253	F	rimstr frag	S	sm		sm	Y	appl	outw	exc	fl	th	ind	32.03	19.25	19.25	0	0	2.29	2.5	0	0	0	0	0	4.37	1
99-11	251	T	exc rim jar	S	sm		sm	Y	appl	outw	exc	rd	th	pnch	54.27	27.5	16.3	35	5	2.47	8.6	4.47	4.93	0	10.54	4.69	5.85	1
99-11	254	T	ind	S	sm		sm	Y	fold	vrt	inc	rd	fold	pnch	20.57	21.96	11.03	0	0	1.59	3	5.14	0	0	8.41	5.76	2.75	1
99-11087	23	T	ind	G	sm		sm	Y	ind	vrt	exc	bev (int)	th	sm	34	21	21	0	0	1.93	7.4	5.92	0	0	0	0	4.07	1
99-11094	11	T	pnch rim jar	G	curv comp st	wavy lines	sm	Y	fold	outw	h ev	rd	fold/fl	pnch	140	90	15.5	35	12	2.66	115.6	5.22	8.39	0	9.69	7.5	2.19	1

99-11094	12	T	pnch rim jar	G	coarse		brn	Y	appl	outw	h ev	rd	th/fl	pnch	71	46	21.5	0	0	2.98	43.4	5.68	13.43	0	13.88	10.55	3.33	1
99-11094	13	T	exc rim jar	S	sm		sm	Y	appl (fil)	vrt	exc	rd	th/fl	pnch	125	70	17	37	10	3.17	61.9	6.8	6.8	0	9.37	7.29	2.08	1
99-11388	251[6]	T	ind	G	sm		sm	Y	ind	ind	ind	rd	th	sty ntch	2	2	14.62	0	0	1.7	4.6	5.7	0	0	11.3	5.67	5.63	1
99-11418	261	T	cazuela	G	incised	line-filled triangles	sm	N		inw	inc	rd	unmod		18	22	0	0	0	1.08	3.6	8.09	0	0	0	0	0	1
99-11418	262	T	ind	G	sm		sm	ind	ind	outw	exc	rd	ind	ind	14	12	0	0	0	2.46	1.4	4.6	0	0	0	0	0	1
99-11429	1761	F	rimstr frag	G	sm		sm	Y	appl	vrt	exc	fl	th	sty ntch	29	17	13.59	0	0	1.84	6.4	4.29	0	0	14.84	6.69	8.15	1
99-11430	467	F	rimstr frag	G	sm		sm	Y	ind	ind	ind	ind	th/fl	pnch	22	17	17.05	0	0	1.07	2.8	0	0	0	0	0	1.15	1
99-11441	428	T	ind	G	sm		sm	Y	fold	outw	exc	rd	fold/fl	pnch	22	24	16.34	0	0	1.77	3.7	4.68	0	0	8.21	6.1	2.11	1
99-11452	278	T	ind	G	sm		sm	Y	ind	outw	exc	bev (int)	th	pnch	38	28	17.81	0	0	1.26	7.7	5.11	0	0	9.57	7.31	2.26	1
99-11461	1	T	pnch rim jar	G	sm		sm	Y	ind	outw	h ev	rd	th/fl	pnch	39	12	12.6	0	0	1.25	5.5	7.01	0	0	0	0	0.78	1
99-11619	497	T	ind	grit	sm		sm	Y	ind	outw	exc	rd	th	ind	14	15	0	0	0	0.59	1.6	4.57	0	0	0	0	0	1
99-11629	162	F	ind	S	sm		sm	N		ind	ind	fl	unmod		20.67	27.89	0	0	0	1.38	3.3	5.4	0	0	0	0	0	1
99-11629	165	T	ind	S	sm/smdg		sm	ind	ind	outw	ind	fl	ind	ind	32.67	22.49	0	0	0	1.38	3.7	5.2	0	0	0	0	0	1
99-11629	170	F	ind	S	sm		sm	ind	ind	ind	ind	rd	ind	ind	60.28	22.32	0	0	0	2.34	6.7	5.44	0	0	0	0	0	1
99-11629	164	T	ind	S	sm		sm	ind	ind	ind	ind	fl	ind	ind	38.2	24.1	0	0	0	1.82	7	6.13	0	0	0	0	0	1
99-11629	163	T	ind	S	sm		sm	ind	ind	ind	ind	fl	ind	ind	25.56	21.18	0	0	0	2	3.2	6.1	0	0	0	0	0	1
99-11629	161	F	ind	S	sm/smdg		sm	ind	ind	ind	ind	rd	ind	ind	12.98	23.42	0	0	0	1.54	2	5.48	0	0	0	0	0	1
99-11629	168	T	ind	S	sm		sm	Y	ind	outw	exc	fl	th	pnch	32.8	21.79	19.12	0	0	1.99	5.9	5.7	0	0	14.83	8.75	6.08	1
99-11629	169	T	rstr orifice hmsp bowl	G	sm		brn/smdg	Y	ind	inw	exc	rd	th	sty ntch	26.62	32	15.14	0	0	1.45	9	6.21	0	0	10.68	6.3	4.38	1
99-1295	254	T	exc rim jar	G	coarse		brn	Y	ind	outw	exc	bev (int)	th	sty ntch	32	30	14.6	0	0	1.84	11.1	4.6	6.62	0	11.14	6.7	4.44	1
99-13	256	T	ind	G	sm		sm	Y	ind	vrt	exc	rd	th	ind	25	26	19.21	0	0	2.64	5.3	6.48	0	0	0	0	0	1
99-1657	14	T	exc rim jar	S	sm		sm	Y	fold	vrt	exc	fl	fold	sty ntch	47	44	21.24	0	0	2.8	10.28	4.18	6.92	0	9.4	6.6	2.8	1
99-1657	13	T	smpl hmsp bowl	S	sm		sm	Y	appl (fil)	vrt	inc	rd	th/fl	sty ntch	68	33	33	0	0	3.8	15.56	4.7	0	0	8.74	6.4	2.34	1
99-1657	12	T	exc rim jar	S	sm		sm	Y	fold	vrt	exc	fl	fold/fl	sty ntch	45	59	20.89	0	0	2.38	20.4	4.86	7.9	0	9.7	6.8	1.9	1
99-2171	290	T	exc rim jar	G	sm		sm	N		vrt	exc	rd	unmod		62	52	0	0	0	2	28.6	6.35	7.33	0	0	0	0	1
99-2171	294	T	ind	G	incised	ind par diagonal lines	sm	N		vrt	exc	fl	unmod		18	25	0	0	0	1.25	3	6.38	0	0	0	0	0	1
99-2171	291	T	ind	G	sm		sm	ind	ind	ind	exc	rd	ind	ind	53	17	0	0	0	2.19	8.2	6.13	0	0	0	0	0	1
99-2171	292	T	pnch rim jar	G	sm		sm	Y	appl	outw	exc	rd	th/fl	pnch	29	20	17.03	0	0	1.88	6.1	7.45	0	0	7.99	6.54	1.45	1
99-2180	255	T	cazuela	G	incised	ind par vrt lines	brn	N		inw	inc	rd	unmod		25	17	0	0	0	3.18	2.8	5.57	0	0	0	0	0	1
99-2180	254	T	cazuela	G	incised	ind par vrt lines	sm	N		inw	dir	rd	unmod		23	20	0	0	0	1.2	4	5.65	0	0	0	0	0	1
99-2180	253	T	cazuela	G	incised	ind par hrz lines	brn/smdg	N		inw	exc	rd	unmod		16	29	0	0	0	1.4	3.6	5.35	0	0	0	0	0	1
99-2184	259	T	cazuela	G	incised	nested half squares	brn/smdg	N		inw	exc	rd	unmod		22	36	0	0	0	2.34	6.5	6.31	0	0	0	0	0	1
99-2184	258	T	ind	G	incised	line-filled triangles	sm	N		vrt	exc	rd	unmod		52	26	0	0	0	1.04	9.1	6.46	0	0	0	0	0	1
99-2188	253	T	cazuela	G	incised	ind par vrt lines	brn	N		inw	exc	rd	unmod		25	26	0	0	0	1.84	4.7	5.69	0	0	0	0	0	1
99-2202	262	T	cazuela	G	incised	ind par hrz lines	sm/smdg	N		inw	dir	rd	unmod		26.5	35.5	0	0	0	0.98	7.1	5.96	0	0	0	0	0	1
99-2202	253	T	cazuela	G	incised	ind par vrt lines	brn	N		inw	exc	rd	unmod		25	27	0	0	0	1.18	6.4	6.19	0	0	0	0	0	1
99-2202	255	T	ind	G	ind lin st		sm	ind	ind	ind	ind	rd	ind	ind	23	18	0	0	0	2.14	2.9	5.61	0	0	0	0	0	1
99-2202	254	T	pnch rim jar	G	sm		sm	Y	ind	outw	h ev	rd	th/fl	pnch	18.93	21	21.93	0	0	1.53	4.2	5.47	7.39	0	9.39	7.2	2.19	1
99-282	331	T	pnch rim jar	G	sm		sm	Y	ind	outw	h ev	ind	th/fl	pnch	26	23	15	0	0	1.15	4.49	0	0	0	7.98	6	1.98	1
99-2842	4	T	rstr orifice hmsp bowl	G	cordm		brn/smdg	Y	fold	inw	Inc	rd	th/fl	pnch	152	93	12.78	28	15	1.34	184.2	5.22	0	9.29	8.56	7.41	1.15	1

99-2870	253	T	smpl hmsp bowl	G	sm		sm/smdg	N		vrt	Inc	rd	unmod		42	29	0	0	0	1.79	10.6	6.81	0	0	0	0	0	1
99-2883	254	T	ind	G	sm		sm	Y	fold	ind	exc	rd	fold/fl	pnch	25.9	22.1	14.9	0	0	1.3	4.2	5.18	0	0	9.4	6.6	2.8	1
99-2885	262	T	pnch rim jar	grit	sm		sm	Y	ind	outw	exc	bev (int)	th/fl	pnch	33.62	20.78	20.78	0	0	1.1	6.6	5.58	0	0	0	0	4.5	1
99-2890	256	T	ind	G	sm		sm	Y	ind	outw	exc	ind	th	ind	19.79	13.22	0	0	0	1.43	2.7	0	0	0	0	0	0	1
99-2895	33	T	ind	grit	sm		sm	Y	ind	vrt	exc	rd	th	pnch	24.4	18.1	18.1	0	0	1.15	4	4.4	0	0	0	0	6.24	1
99-2895	32	T	rstr orifice hmsp bowl	G	sm		sm	Y	ind	inw	Inc	rd	th/fl	sm	33.08	16.67	11.82	0	0	1.23	3.6	8.98	0	0	0	0	0	1
99-2899	270	F	rimstr frag	G	sm		sm	Y	ind	ind	ind	ind	ind	ind	16.52	16.89	0	0	0	1.38	2.2	0	0	0	0	0	0	1
99-2899	271	T	exc rim jar	G	sm		sm/smdg	Y	ind	outw	exc	ind	th/fl	pnch	20.28	24.12	19.5	0	0	1.5	6.3	0	0	0	10.02	7.28	2.74	1
99-2910	255	F	rimstr frag	G	sm		sm	Y	appl	ind	ind	ind	ind	ind	20	18.2	18.2	0	0	1.57	1.8	0	0	0	0	0	0	1
99-2923	349	T	cazuela	G	incised	line-filled triangles	brn	N		inw	dir	bev (int)	unmod		20.06	21	0	0	0	0.92	2.3	3.72	0	0	0	0	0	1
99-2923	347	T	smpl hmsp bowl	G	ind lin st		sm	N		outw	dir	bev (int)	unmod		33.68	24.54	0	0	0	1.22	5.4	5.74	0	0	0	0	0	1
99-2923	344	F	rimstr frag	G	eroded		eroded	Y	ind	ind	ind	ind	th	ind	25.18	13.78	0	0	0	1.38	4.5	0	0	0	0	0	0	1
99-2923	346	F	rimstr frag	G	sm		eroded	Y	ind	ind	ind	ind	th	ind	17.66	17.82	0	0	0	1.1	1.9	0	0	0	0	0	0	1
99-2923	348	T	ind	G	eroded		coarse	Y	appl	ind	ind	rd	th	ind	30.84	23.38	0	0	0	1.7	5.1	4.6	0	0	0	0	0	1
99-2923	351	T	pnch rim jar	G	sm		sm	Y	ind	outw	exc	fl	th/fl	pnch	30.42	12.06	12.06	0	0	1.87	4.5	5.38	0	0	0	0	2.25	1
99-2923	352	F	rimstr frag	G	sm		eroded	Y	ind	ind	ind	ind	th/fl	pnch	22.08	20.82	0	0	0	1.38	4	0	0	0	0	0	0	1
99-2923	343	F	rimstr frag	G	sm		sm	Y	ind	ind	ind	ind	th	sm	12.86	16.24	0	0	0	2.96	2.2	0	0	0	0	0	0	1
99-2923	350	F	pnch rim jar	G	sm		eroded	Y	appl	outw	h ev	rd	th/fl	sm	30.62	15.58	16.02	0	0	1.94	2.2	5.16	0	0	0	0	2.42	1
99-2923	353	T	ind	G	coarse		sm	Y	fold	ind	dir	rd	fold/fl	sm	22.4	17.98	0	0	0	1.68	3.8	7.58	0	0	0	0	0	1
99-2923	342	F	rimstr frag	G	sm		sm	Y	appl	ind	ind	ind	th	sm up/ pnch undern	27.78	18.24	18.24	0	0	0.74	4	0	0	0	0	0	12.14	1
99-2924	374	T	smpl hmsp bowl	G	cordm		sm	N		vrt	inc	rd	unmod		32	28	0	0	0	1.3	5.8	5.5	0	0	0	0	0	1
99-2924	372	T	cazuela	G	incised	ind par diagonal lines	sm	N		inw	inc	rd	unmod		22	12	0	0	0	1.8	2.1	4.2	0	0	0	0	0	1
99-2924	368[7]	T	small jar	G	ind lin st		sm	N		vrt	exc	rd	unmod		30	33	0	0	0	1.7	7.7	4	5.01	0	0	0	0	1
99-2924	361	T	cazuela	G	sm		sm	N		inw	dir	bev (int)	unmod		20	19	0	0	0	1.4	3.8	5.62	0	8.72	0	0	0	1
99-2924	366	T	ind	G	sm		sm	ind	ind	ind	exc	rd	ind	ind	16	9	0	0	0	1.34	1.2	4.48	0	0	0	0	0	1
99-2924	365	T	ind	G	sm		sm	ind	ind	ind	ind	rd	ind	ind	26	8	0	0	0	1.1	1.6	4.7	0	0	0	0	0	1
99-2924	364	T	ind	G	ind lin st		sm	Y	ind	outw	exc	rd	ind	ind	23	12	0	0	0	0.87	1.9	4.07	0	0	0	0	0	1
99-2924	360	T	ind	G	sm		sm	ind	ind	outw	exc	bev (int)	ind	ind	18	16	0	0	0	0.97	2	3.98	0	0	0	0	0	1
99-2924	358	F	rimstr frag	G	sm		sm	Y	ind	ind	ind	ind	th	pnch	22	13	0	0	0	1.1	2.6	0	0	0	0	0	0	1
99-2924	359	T	pnch rim jar	grit	sm		sm	Y	ind	vrt	h ev	bev (int)	th/fl	pnch	55	23.8	22.02	0	0	0.54	14.9	4.9	0	0	0	0	2.04	1
99-2924	362	T	pnch rim jar	G	sm		sm	Y	appl	outw	exc	bev (int)	th/fl	pnch	49	21	21	0	0	1.3	12.4	7.18	0	0	13.6	7.9	5.7	1
99-2924	363	T	exc rim jar	G	sm		sm/smdg	Y	ind	outw	exc	rd	th/fl	pnch	39	24	24.2	0	0	1.07	8.6	5.5	0	0	9.28	7.8	6.48	1
99-2924	379	T	ind	grit	sm		brn/smdg	Y	fold	outw	exc	rd	fold/fl	pnch	18	19	0	0	0	0.75	2.5	5.72	0	0	0	0	0	1
99-2924	378	T	pnch rim jar	G	sm		brn/smdg	Y	ind	outw	exc	bev (int)	th/fl	pnch	36	24	24	0	0	1.67	7.5	5.06	7.9	0	9.34	7.04	2.3	1
99-2924	377	T	exc rim jar	G	sm		bunished	Y	appl	outw	exc	bev (int)	th	pnch	48	31	21.6	0	0	1.22	14.8	5.25	0	0	11.98	7.01	4.97	1
99-2924	376	T	pnch rim jar	G	sm		sm/smdg	Y	ind	outw	h ev	rd	th/fl	pnch	41	21	21	0	0	1.52	10.2	5.38	9.14	0	12.62	10.15	2.47	1
99-2924	375	T	exc rim jar	G	sm		brn	Y	appl	vrt	exc	bev (int)	th	pnch	46	22	22	0	0	1.98	16.6	5.54	0	0	17.3	10.28	7.02	1
99-2924	3740	T	exc rim jar	G	sm		brn	Y	ind	outw	exc	rd	th/fl	pnch	22	23	23.4	0	0	1.38	3.9	5.5	0	0	9.58	7.5	2.08	1
99-2924	380	T	rstr orifice hmsp bowl	G	sm		brn	Y	fold	inw	inc	rd	fold	punc	24	24	13.28	0	0	2.2	5	5.9	0	0	8.9	5.8	3.1	1
99-2924	369[8]	T	exc rim jar	G	sm		brn	Y	appl	outw	exc	rd	th	sty ntch	37	35	19.62	0	0	1.08	14.4	4.56	8.12	0	13.3	7.9	5.4	1
99-2934	266	F	ind	G	sm		sm	Y	ind	outw	exc	rd	th	pnch	21.26	12.95	0	0	0	1.02	4.3	0	0	0	0	0	0	1
99-2934	267	T	rstr orifice hmsp bowl	G	ind lin st		sm	Y	fold	inw	inc	ind	fold/fl	sm	23.08	15.42	0	0	0	0.78	2.2	0	0	0	0	0	0	1

99-2939	268[9]	F	shoulderstrip frag	G	sm		sm	Y	appl	ind	ind	ind	ind	incised up/pnch undern	27.28	16.66	0	0	0	1.28	6.6	0	0	0	15.64	7.88	7.76	1
99-2939	271[10]	F	pnch rim jar	G	ind lin st		brn	Y	ind	outw	h ev	rd	th/fl	pnch	130.2	47.74	22.4	38	15	1.52	73.3	6.5	7.33	0	9.7	7.38	2.32	1
99-2939	269[11]	T	pnch rim jar	G	ind lin st		sm	Y	appl	outw	h ev	rd	th/fl	pnch	75.05	33.54	17.44	0	0	1.44	25.8	0	9.92	0	11.06	8.06	3	1
99-2946	253	T	rstr orifice hmsp bowl	G	sm		sm	N		inw	inc	rd	unmod		63	36	0	18	12	1.48	18.1	5.18	0	7.9	0	0	0	1
99-2948	261	T	exc rim jar	grit	sm		sm	Y	appl	outw	exc	rd	th/fl	pnch	66.1	23.75	23.75	28	7	1.8	19.9	6.15	0	0	11.21	6.92	4.29	1
99-2950	267[12]	T	jar with lug handle	G	sm		brn	N		vrt	exc	fl	unmod		45	43	0	0	0	1.79	25.3	5.2	8.9	0	0	0	0	1
99-2950	268	T	ind	G	sm		sm	ind	ind	vrt	ind	rd	ind	ind	25	23	0	0	0	3.1	4.2	5.78	0	0	0	0	0	1
99-2950	269	T	pnch rim jar	G	coarse		sm	Y	fold	vrt	h ev	bev (int)	fold/fl	pnch	39	19	19	0	0	1.79	8.2	5.22	0	0	0	0	2.3	1
99-2954	277	T	cazuela	G	incised	line-filled triangles	sm	N		inw	inc	rd	unmod		42	29	0	0	0	1.87	13.9	6.38	0	8.68	0	0	0	1
99-2954	278	T	ind	G	ind lin st		sm	Y	ind	outw	exc	ind	th	ind	25.4	19.84	0	0	0	0	3.4	0.88	0	0	0	0	0	1
99-2956	257	T	ind	G	sm		brn	ind	ind	ind	ind	rd	ind	ind	18	13	0	0	0	1.48	1.9	5.8	0	0	0	0	0	1
99-2956	259	F	rimstr frag	G	sm		sm	Y	ind	ind	ind	ind	th	pnch	17	10	0	0	0	1.4	1.7	0	0	0	0	0	0	1
99-2956	258	F	rimstr frag	S	sm		sm	Y	appl (fil)	ind	ind	ind	th	pnch	26	23	0	0	0	3.3	5.5	0	0	0	10.02	6.02	4	1
99-2973	252	T	ind	G	sm		sm	ind	ind	outw	exc	rd	ind	ind	36	16	0	0	0	1.23	5.1	5.35	0	0	0	0	0	1
99-3005	255[13]	T	exc rim jar	grit	sm		sm	Y	appl	outw	exc	rd	th/fl	pnch	39.84	25.3	22.42	0	0	1.6	9.8	5.28	0	0	9.98	5.78	4.2	1
99-3009	286[14]	T	small jar	G	sm		sm	Y	ind	vrt	exc	rd	th	sty ntch	13.26	13.12	12.29	0	0	1.48	2.7	3.86	0	0	0	0	7.04	1
99-3016	266	T	rstr orifice hmsp bowl	G	sm		sm	Y	fold	inw	inc	rd	fold/fl	punc	15	13	11.7	0	0	1.4	1.7	5.1	0	0	0	0	1.3	1
99-3019	258	T	smpl hmsp bowl	G	sm		sm	N		vrt	inc	rd	unmod	pnch	29	29	0	0	0	1.54	6	5.6	0	0	0	0	0	1
99-3021	326	T	ind	grit	sm		sm	N		ind	inc	rd	unmod		30	19	0	0	0	0.85	5.3	5.45	0	0	0	0	0	1
99-3021	323	T	ind	G	sm		sm	ind	ind	ind	ind	rd	ind	ind	25	9	0	0	0	0.88	2	5.3	0	0	0	0	0	1
99-3021	324	T	ind	G	sm		sm	ind	ind	ind	ind	rd	ind	ind	37	14	0	0	0	0.97	4.6	6.25	0	0	0	0	0	1
99-3021	328	T	exc rim jar	G	sm		sm	Y	ind	outw	exc	bev (int)	th/fl	pnch	23	27	18.85	0	0	2.1	6	5.21	0	0	9.42	6.28	3.14	1
99-3021	325	T	pnch rim jar	G	sm		brn	Y	appl	vrt	h ev	rd	th/fl	pnch	68	26.9	23.25	34	6	1.24	22.3	5.4	0	0	11.5	7.3	4.2	1
99-3021	329	T	exc rim jar	G	sm		sm	Y	ind	vrt	exc	bev (int)	th/fl	pnch	49	25	17.8	0	0	1.48	14.2	5.05	0	0	10.98	8.9	2.08	1
99-3021	327	T	ind	G	sm		sm	Y	fold	outw	exc	bev (int)	th	sm	27	19	15.8	0	0	1.15	3.9	4.4	0	0	0	0	0	1
99-3027	260	T	exc rim jar	G	scraped		sm	Y	appl	vrt	exc	rd	th	sm up/ pnch undern	110	100	22.7	32	10	2.6	168.7	8.1	9.7	9.3	18.5	9.5	9	1
99-3051	8	T	ind	G	sm		brn	Y	ind	outw	exc	rd	th	ind	17	20	0	0	0	0.92	4.2	5.5	0	0	0	0	0	1
99-3052	258	T	ind	G	sm		sm/smdg	ind	ind	ind	ind	rd	ind	ind	12	14	0	0	0	2.18	1.4	5.6	0	0	0	0	0	1
99-3052	257	T	exc rim jar	G	sm		sm	Y	ind	outw	exc	rd	th/fl	pnch	32	21	17.3	0	0	1.18	6.4	4.7	7.7	0	10.48	7.3	3.18	1
99-3053	272[15]	T	small jar	grit	cordm		brn/smdg	N		vrt	exc	rd	unmod		36	26	0	16	7	0.88	8.2	4.42	5.9	0	0	0	0	1
99-3053	271	T	exc rim jar	S	sm		sm	Y	appl (fil)	outw	exc	rd	th	pnch	35	25	11.4	0	0	2.1	8.8	5.2	0	0	11.08	7.3	3.78	1
99-3053	273	T	pnch rim jar	G	sm		sm	Y	ind	outw	exc	bev (ext)	th/fl	pnch	32	17	17.5	0	0	1.3	5	4.32	0	0	0	0	2.04	1
99-3053	270	T	pnch rim jar	G	sm		sm	Y	ind	vrt	exc	bev (int)	th/fl	pnch	30	22	12.8	0	0	1.75	4.6	0	0	0	0	0	1.47	1
99-3053	274	T	pnch rim jar	G	sm		sm	Y	appl	outw	exc	bev (int)	th/fl	pnch	45	19	18.9	0	0	1.5	6.8	4.57	0	0	0	0	1.5	1
99-3068	275	T	rstr orifice hmsp bowl	G	ind st	sm over	sm	ind	ind	inw	inc	bev (int)	ind	punc	18.9	20	0	0	0	1.28	2.7	3.62	0	0	0	0	0	1
99-3074	276	T	smpl hmsp bowl	G	sm		sm	N		vrt	inc	fl	unmod		11.2	12.14	0	0	0	1.08	2.6	6.9	0	0	0	0	0	1
99-3074	277	T	ind	G	sm		sm	ind	ind	ind	ind	rd	ind	ind	18.6	12.3	0	0	0	0.84	1.5	5.24	0	0	0	0	0	1
99-3113	284	T	ind	G	sm		sm	Y	ind	outw	exc	rd	th	ind	21.5	16	0	0	0	1.88	2.7	5.06	0	0	0	0	0	1
99-3113	285	T	ind	G	sm		sm	ind	ind	ind	ind	fl	ind	ind	18	13	0	0	0	1.04	22	7.18	0	0	0	0	0	1
99-3115	257	T	ind	G	sm		sm	Y	ind	ind	ind	rd	th/fl	pnch	25.5	17.92	17.92	0	0	1.09	3.4	6.38	0	0	0	0	3.55	1

99-3237	307	T	smpl hmsp bowl	S	sm		sm	N		vrt	inc	fl	unmod		29	33	0	0	0	1.82	5.2	8.4	0	0	0	0	0	1
99-3237	309	T	pnch rim jar	G	coarse		brn/smdg	Y	fold	outw	h ev	rd	fold/fl	pnch	130	46.9	12.62	34	12	1.36	97.2	9.46	9.12	0	9.25	8.75	0.5	1
99-3237	308	T	exc rim jar	G	sm		sm	Y	appl	vrt	exc	bev (int)	th	pnch	105	53	13.38	34	9	1.6	65.4	6	7.9	0	15.62	7.02	8.6	1
99-3237	306[16]	T	exc rim jar	G	sm		brn/smdg	Y	ind	outw	exc	bev (int)	th	sty ntch	33	22	11.3	0	0	1.5	5.5	4.7	5.62	0	8.9	5.64	3.26	1
99-3237	305[17]	F	exc rim jar	G	sm		brn/smdg	Y	ind	outw	exc	bev (int)	th	sty ntch	22	26	9.5	0	0	1.2	5.4	4.8	6.3	0	8.82	6.4	2.42	1
99-3241	302[18]	T	exc rim jar	G	sm		sm	Y	appl	outw	exc	rd	th	sty ntch	87	58	13	38	6	1.65	60.3	6.21	7.7	0	11.96	7.9	4.06	1
99-3241	301	T	exc rim jar	grit	sm		brn/smdg	Y	ind	outw	exc	bev (int)	th	sty ntch	38	28	11.75	0	0	1.07	9.9	6.02	6.2	0	9.55	6.6	2.95	1
99-3241	290	T	exc rim jar	G	ind st		brn/smdg	Y	appl	outw	exc	bev (int)	th	sty ntch	95	106	11.48	16	12	1.4	96.6	5.98	5.57	6.2	8.9	5.6	3.3	1
99-3245	347	T	ind	S	sm		sm	ind	ind	outw	exc	fl	ind	ind	40.72	17.32	0	0	0	1.7	4	6.1	0	0	0	0	0	1
99-3245	348	T	ind	S	sm		sm	Y	ind	ind	ind	fl	th	ind	23.32	19.52	0	0	0	1.27	2.9	5.41	0	0	0	0	0	1
99-3245	349	T	ind	G	sm		sm	ind	ind	ind	ind	rd	ind	ind	24.93	28.2	0	0	0	1.08	4.2	4.65	0	0	0	0	0	1
99-3245	351	T	ind	S	sm		sm	ind	ind	outw	exc	fl	ind	ind	44.6	22.67	0	0	0	2.1	6.7	6.4	0	0	0	0	0	1
99-3245	360	T	exc rim jar	G	coarse		sm	Y	ind	outw	exc	rd	th	pnch	83.58	54.78	21.24	32	7	2.42	54.3	7.66	10.23	0	13.12	8.79	4.33	1
99-3245	354	T	exc rim jar	S	sm		sm	Y	ind	outw	exc	fl	th	pnch	40.28	31.3	18	0	0	2.28	8.1	7	0	0	15.44	7.5	7.94	1
99-3245	356	T	rstr orifice hmsp bowl	G	sm		brn/smdg	Y	fold	inw	inc	rd	th	punc	36.82	29.34	13.1	22	5	2.18	9.14	5.99	0	0	12.55	6.52	6.03	1
99-3245	353	T	rstr orifice hmsp bowl	G	sm		brn/smdg	Y	fold	inw	inc	rd	th	punc	39.63	29.1	11.9	0	0	1.32	11	5.81	0	0	11.42	5.92	5.5	1
99-3245	358	T	rstr orifice hmsp bowl	G	sm		brn/smdg	Y	ind	inw	inc	rd	th/fl	sm	19.5	16.48	0	0	0	1.12	3.1	6.38	0	0	0	0	0	1
99-3245	355	T	exc rim jar	S	sm		sm	Y	appl	outw	exc	rd	th	sty ntch	36.99	35.04	12.52	0	0	1.76	7.8	4.33	6.28	0	13.82	6.42	7.4	1
99-3245	357	F	rimstr frag	S	sm		sm	Y	ind	outw	exc	ind	th	sty ntch	47.74	23.57	0	0	0	1.89	8.9	0	0	0	13.18	6.58	6.6	1
99-3245	361	T	exc rim jar	S	eroded		sm	Y	appl	vrt	exc	rd	th	sty ntch	107.5	42.5	10.37	36	9	3.21	46.1	5.73	7.16	0	12.23	6.41	5.82	1
99-3254	362	T	ind	S	sm		sm	ind	ind	ind	ind	rd	ind	ind	17.72	20.74	0	0	0	1.73	1.4	5	0	0	0	0	0	1
99-3254	363	T	ind	S	sm		sm	ind	ind	ind	ind	fl	ind	ind	25.6	16.4	0	0	0	1.44	2	6.28	0	0	0	0	0	1
99-3254	364	F	rimstr frag	G	eroded		sm/smdg	Y	ind	ind	ind	ind	th	pnch	26.1	13	0	0	0	2.04	4.2	0	0	0	0	0	6.77	1
99-3254	365[19]	F	exc rim jar	G	sm		brn/smdg	Y	ind	outw	exc	rd	th	sty ntch	35.71	25.27	10.67	26	17	1.38	8.4	5.04	6.28	0	9.46	6	3.46	1
99-3255	256[20]	T	exc rim jar	G	sm		brn/smdg	Y	ind	outw	exc	rd	th	sty ntch	42.26	25	10.83	26	17	1.36	11.4	4.4	6.23	0	10.18	6.01	4.17	1
99-3256	264	T	ind	S	sm		sm	ind	ind	ind	ind	rd	ind	ind	32.6	24.5	0	0	0	2.06	3.7	5.68	0	0	0	0	0	1
99-3459	328	T	pnch rim jar	G	sm		sm	Y	ind	outw	h ev	rd	th/fl	pnch	54.52	19.76	0	0	0	1.25	11.4	6.38	0	0	0	0	0	1
99-3459	329	T	ind	grit	brn/smdg		brn/smdg	Y	appl	outw	exc	rd	th	sty ntch	37.26	13.12	12.9	16	6	0.82	5.4	3.79	0	0	10.23	4.51	5.72	1
99-36	264	T	ind	G	sm		sm	Y	ind	ind	exc	rd	th	sty ntch	20	13	13	0	0	1.44	2.3	6.12	0	0	0	0	3.11	1
99-3764	270[21]	T	cazuela	G	incised	ind par hrz lines	sm	N		inw	Inc	rd	unmod		22.08	17.42	0	0	0	0.5	2.8	3.49	0	6.49	0	0	0	1
99-3764	27	T	pnch rim jar	G	sm		brn/smdg	Y	appl	outw	h ev	bev (int)	th/fl	pnch	29.42	22.46	0	0	0	1.15	5.7	4.43	0	0	0	0	0	1
99-3764	222	T	ind	G	sm		brn	Y	ind	outw	exc	ind	th	pnch	23.36	18.53	0	0	0	1.42	2.8	0	0	0	0	0	0	1
99-3801	270	T	pnch rim jar	G	sm		sm	Y	ind	outw	exc	rd	th/fl	pnch	41	21	20.92	0	0	1.71	8.4	5.9	0	0	9.22	6.7	2.52	1
99-3834	361	T	ind	G	brushed		sm/smdg	N		outw	dir	bev (ext)	unmod		19.3	21.2	0	0	0	1.4	2.9	4.38	0	0	0	0	0	1
99-3834	371	T	cazuela	G	incised	ind	eroded	N		inw	inc	ind	unmod		19.22	23.8	0	0	0	1.96	2.9	4.6	0	0	0	0	0	1
99-3834	369	F	rimstr frag	G	eroded		eroded	Y	ind	outw	exc	ind	th	ind	18.9	12	0	0	0	1.56	3.1	0	0	0	0	0	0	1
99-3834	360	T	ind	G	sm		brn/smdg	ind	ind	outw	exc	rd	ind	ind	21.5	16.3	0	0	0	1.25	2.8	7.18	0	0	0	0	0	1
99-3834	359	T	rstr orifice hmsp bowl	G	eroded		sm	ind	ind	inw	inc	rd	ind	ind	27	13.1	0	0	0	1.21	2	0	0	0	0	0	0	1
99-3834	367	T	exc rim jar	G	sm		sm/smdg	Y	appl	outw	exc	rd	th	ind	24.5	25.8	21.1	0	0	1.21	7	6.21	8.38	0	13.1	7.62	5.48	1
99-3834	362	F	rimstr frag	G	sm		sm	Y	appl	ind	ind	ind	th/fl	pnch	24.4	18	15.7	0	0	1.2	3.6	0	0	0	0	0	2.9	1
99-3834	364	T	ind	G	sm		sm	Y	ind	outw	exc	rd	th/fl	pnch	25.6	18.32	15.38	0	0	2.9	5.2	6.96	0	0	11.42	6.38	5.04	1
99-3835	266	T	ind	G	sm		sm	Y	appl	outw	exc	bev (int)	th	sty ntch	19.5	15.42	0	0	0	1.35	2.7	4.62	0	0	0	0	0	1
99-3852	337	T	ind	G	eroded		sm	Y	ind	outw	exc	rd	th	ind	12.5	23.4	0	0	0	0.86	3.9	6.22	0	0	0	0	0	1
99-3852	341	T	ind	G	sm		sm	ind	ind	outw	exc	rd	ind	ind	22	15.1	0	0	0	1.2	2.3	6.43	0	0	0	0	0	1
99-3852	340	T	rstr orifice hmsp bowl	G	sm		sm	Y	ind	inw	dir	rd	th/fl	pnch	24	24.8	20.8	0	0	1.92	5	4.47	0	0	0	0	2.97	1

99-3852	339	T	rstr orifice hmsp bowl	G	sm		sm	Y	ind	vrt	exc	rd	th/fl	pnch	46.3	25.8	25.8	34	5	1.57	13.7	5.9	8.99	0	0	0	2.17	1
99-3852	338	T	pnch rim jar	G	ind lin st		sm	Y	appl	outw	h ev	rd	th/fl	pnch	34.7	23.28	14.72	0	0	1.15	9	10.94	0	0	8.3	6.8	1.5	1
99-3852	342	T	ind	G	sm		sm	Y	fold	ind	ind	rd	fold/fl	sm	26.9	14.7	11.4	0	0	1.12	4.2	8.6	0	0	0	0	2.92	1
99-3852	310	T	ind	G	coarse		coarse	Y	ind	ind	ind	rd	th/fl	sm	22	30	16.74	0	0	1.25	4.83	5.7	0	0	9	6.26	2.74	1
99-3888	276	T	pnch rim jar	G	sm		sm	Y	ind	outw	h ev	rd	th/fl	pnch	42.7	20.2	20.2	0	0	1.12	8.4	5.7	7.38	0	0	0	2.08	1
99-3888	273	F	rimstr frag	G	sm		sm	Y	ind	ind	ind	ind	th	pnch	25.4	28.7	28.7	0	0	1.78	8.7	0	0	0	14.32	7.08	7.24	1
99-3888	275	T	pnch rim jar	G	ind st	sm over	sm	Y	ind	outw	exc	bev (int)	th/fl	pnch	30.3	28.2	21.15	0	0	1.73	6.9	4.35	0	0	9.74	6.08	3.66	1
99-3888	274	T	ind	G	sm		sm	Y	ind	outw	exc	rd	th	pnch	24.9	21.62	0	0	0	1.32	4.1	5.5	0	0	0	0	0	1
99-3892	284[22]	T	smpl hmsp bowl	G	coarse		sm	N		vrt	inc	fl	unmod		23	27	0	0	0	0	3.1	3.64	0	4.72	0	0	0	1
99-3892	320	T	exc rim jar	G	sm		sm	Y	appl	outw	exc	bev (int)	th/fl	pnch	34.5	19.75	13.2	0	0	1.6	6.5	5.9	0	0	8.32	4.99	3.33	1
99-4040	269	T	rstr orifice hmsp bowl	G	sm		sm/smdg	Y	appl	vrt	inc	fl	th	punc	7	5	19.86	30	7	2.07	33	4.9	0	0	11.16	7.39	3.77	1
99-4232	251	F	rimstr frag	G	brn		brn	Y	ind	outw	exc	ind	th	pnch	25.8	21.1	0	0	0	0.87	6.3	0	0	0	0	0	6.74	1
99-4245	11	T	ind	G	eroded		brn	ind	ind	ind	ind	rd	ind	ind	20	22	0	0	0	1.75	2.1	0	0	0	0	0	0	1
99-4245	8	F	rimstr frag	G	sm		brn/smdg	Y	ind	outw	h ev	ind	th/fl	pnch	21.44	16.51	16.51	0	0	1.86	3.3	0	0	0	8.44	6.57	1.87	1
99-4248	1	T	ind	G	sm		sm/smdg	Y	fold	outw	exc	rd	fold/fl	sm	60	24	22.01	0	0	1.65	17	8.71	8.64	0	0	0	1.05	1
99-4568	142	T	smpl hmsp bowl	G	brn		brn/smdg	N		vrt	Inc	fl	unmod		16	20	0	0	0	1.27	2.6	8.47	0	0	0	0	0	1
99-4581	354	T	ind	G	sm		sm	Y	ind	outw	exc	rd	th/fl	pnch	29.8	20	21.84	0	0	0.98	6.7	8.51	0	0	0	0	1.51	1
99-4581	351	T	ind	G	ind lin st		sm	Y	fold	outw	exc	rd	fold/fl	sm	14	16	7.68	0	0	1.55	1.6	5.66	0	0	0	0	1	1
99-492	253	T	exc rim jar	G	cordm		sm	ind	ind	outw	exc	rd	ind	ind	50	50	0	0	0	1.62	10.97	7.11	0	0	0	0	0	1
99-50	258	T	rstr orifice hmsp bowl	G	sm		sm	N		inw	Inc	rd	unmod		17	22	0	0	0	1.25	3.3	5.6	0	7.03	0	0	0	1
99-5048	255	T	ind	G	sm		sm	Y	ind	ind	ind	rd	th	sty ntch	17	16	10.63	0	0	1.97	2.3	5.04	0	0	10.1	7.1	3	1
99-559	2	T	cazuela	G	sm		brn/smdg	N		inw	dir	rd	unmod		73.76	38.68	0	0	0	1.84	22.7	3.98	0	6.16	0	0	0	1
99-5605	5	T	exc rim jar	G	sm		sm	Y	ind	vrt	exc	fl	th	pnch	40.3	21.33	10.96	0	0	1.97	10.3	5.9	0	0	11.52	6.92	4.6	1
99-6369	3	T	ind	G	sm		sm/smdg	Y	ind	outw	exc	fl	th	sty ntch	22.64	15.26	13.44	0	0	1.25	4.1	5.6	0	0	11.84	7.24	4.6	1
99-6391	4	T	exc rim jar	G	coarse		brn/smdg	Y	ind	outw	exc	bev (int)	th	sty ntch	43.95	31.36	12.78	0	0	1.36	15.3	3.98	15.08	0	15.02	7.65	8.37	1
99-687	253	F	rimstr frag	G	sm		eroded	Y	appl	ind	ind	ind	th	sty ntch	68.82	13.52	13.52	0	0	1.3	6	0	0	0	0	0	6.32	1
99-788	261	F	rimstr frag	G	sm		sm	Y	ind	ind	ind	ind	th	pnch	20.6	12.05	0	0	0	0.9	1.7	0	0	0	0	0	0	1
99-809	324	T	ind	S	sm		sm	ind	ind	ind	ind	fl	ind	ind	24.53	17.74	0	0	0	1.8	1.9	5.93	0	0	0	0	0	1
99-809	323[23]	T	rstr orifice hmsp bowl	S	sm		sm	Y	appl	inw	Inc	fl	th	sty ntch	46.76	29.93	18	24	5	1.95	14.5	7.4	0	0	14.47	8.59	5.88	1
99-809	322[24]	T	rstr orifice hmsp bowl	G	sm		brn	Y	appl	vrt	exc	fl	th	sty ntch	43.28	24.38	14.97	26	5	2.45	13.7	7.04	0	0	15	10.13	4.87	1
99-8282	347	T	exc rim jar	G	brn/smdg		brn/smdg	N		outw	exc	ind	unmod		33.74	31.99	0	0	0	1.12	11	0	0	0	0	0	0	1
99-8282	354	T	rstr orifice hmsp bowl	G	cordm		sm	N		inw	inc	bev (ext)	unmod		38.4	30.8	0	0	0	1.57	6.3	4.45	0	0	0	0	0	1
99-8282	355	T	small jar	grit	punc (reed)		sm	N		vrt	exc	rd	unmod		37	47.3	0	11	8	0.54	17.5	4.72	0	0	0	0	0	1
99-8282	356	T	rstr orifice hmsp bowl	G	ind st	sm over	sm	N		inw	exc	rd	unmod		50.4	53.26	0	0	0	1.26	26.5	7.65	0	6.92	0	0	0	1
99-8282	349	T	ind	G	sm		sm	Y	ind	ind	ind	rd	th	ind	25	11.42	0	0	0	1.38	3.8	5.12	0	0	0	0	0	1
99-8282	351	T	ind	G	sm		sm	Y	ind	outw	exc	ind	th	ind	48.4	30.78	22.3	0	0	1.18	15.8	0	0	0	0	0	0	1
99-8282	348	T	pnch rim jar	G	sm		sm	Y	ind	outw	exc	rd	th	pnch	22.08	19.14	0	0	0	1.18	4	6.45	0	0	12	7.68	4.39	1
99-8282	350	T	pnch rim jar	G	sm		sm	Y	appl	outw	exc	rd	th	pnch	35.28	25.21	24.12	0	0	1.01	6.9	6.64	0	0	0	0	0	1
99-8282	353	F	ind	G	sm		sm	Y	ind	outw	exc	rd	th	pnch	28.96	12.3	0	0	0	1.62	4.7	6.13	0	0	0	0	0	1
99-8282	284	F	rimstr frag	G	sm		eroded	Y	ind	ind	ind	ind	th/fl	pnch	26.9	22.1	0	0	0	1.2	3.3	0	0	0	0	0	0	1
99-8282	331	T	pnch rim jar	G	sm		eroded	Y	ind	outw	h ev	rd	th/fl	pnch	25.52	21.36	15.88	0	0	0.84	4.5	5.84	0	0	0	0	1.16	1
99-8282	352	T	ind	G	coarse		sm	Y	ind	outw	exc	ind	th/fl	sm	30.11	22.44	20.28	0	0	1.74	7.2	0	0	0	0	0	2.18	1
99-829	273[25]	T	exc rim jar	G	sm		brn/smdg	Y	appl	outw	exc	rd	th/fl	pnch	53.14	37.7	14.8	27	6	2.03	18.8	5.15	0	0	12.34	8.39	3.95	1

99-829	276	T	exc rim jar	G	coarse		brn	Y	fold	outw	exc	rd	fold	pnch	155.3	114.2	15.94	28	20	2.44	209.7	5.9	7.56	6.79	10.96	7.2	3.76	1
99-829	275	T	rstr orifice hmsp bowl	G	sm		brn	Y	ind	vrt	exc	rd	th	punc	38.3	17.67	10.17	0	0	1.38	6.5	7.1	0	0	8.4	5.46	2.94	1
99-839	284	T	ind	G	sm		sm	Y	ind	ind	ind	fl	th	sty ntch	28.9	15.12	15.12	0	0	1.03	2.7	5.44	0	0	10.9	5.6	5.3	1
99-842	268[26]	T	jar with strap handle	S	sm		sm	N		outw	exc	rd	unmod		80	68	0	21	12	1.21	88.6	7.13	7.4	0	0	0	0	1
99-845	275[27]	T	rstr orifice hmsp bowl	G	sm		sm	Y	ind	ind	ind	rd	th	punc	30.8	15.94	15.94	0	0	2	4.2	7.37	0	0	0	0	0	1
99-85	253	T	smpl hmsp bowl	G	sm		sm	ind	ind	inw	inc	bev (int)	ind	ind	11.2	12.24	0	0	0	0.78	1.5	3.86	0	0	0	0	0	1
99-8596	258	T	ind	G	sm		sm	Y	ind	outw	exc	rd	th	ind	12.27	15	0	0	0	1.48	2.1	5.5	0	0	0	0	0	1
99-8596	259	T	ind	G	sm		sm/smdg	Y	ind	outw	exc	rd	th/fl	pnch	13.3	16.5	0	0	0	1.18	2.7	5.52	0	0	0	0	0	1
99-8598	264[28]	T	exc rim jar	grit	ind lin st	overstamp	sm/smdg	N		outw	exc	fl	unmod		31.48	23.68	0	15	5	1.13	5.5	3.9	6.15	0	0	0	0	1
99-8598	263	T	cazuela	G	incised	line-filled triangles	brn/smdg	N		inw	dir	rd	unmod		22.1	25.4	0	0	0	1.1	6	5.86	0	8.1	0	0	0	1
99-8598	262	T	ind	G	sm		sm	N		ind	exc	rd	unmod		38.35	22.9	0	0	0	1.19	6.7	8	0	0	0	0	0	1
99-8599	265	T	ind	G	ind lin st		sm/smdg	ind	ind	outw	exc	rd	ind	ind	25	27.5	0	0	0	1.25	5.28	5.78	0	0	0	0	0	1
99-8599	266	T	ind	grit	ind lin st		sm/smdg	ind	ind	outw	exc	rd	th	ind	22.6	22	0	0	0	1.74	4.6	8.9	0	0	0	0	0	1
99-8600	257	T	ind	G	sm		brn	Y	ind	ind	exc	bev (int)	th/fl	pnch	24	18	0	0	0	1.54	4.9	4.8	0	0	0	0	0	1
99-8607	254	T	ind	grit	sm		red-filmed	ind	ind	ind	exc	rd	ind	ind	13	12	0	0	0	0.7	1.6	6	0	0	0	0	0	1
99-8614	9	T	pnch rim jar	G	sm		sm	Y	appl	outw	exc	bev (int)	th/fl	pnch	22.5	21.12	21.12	0	0	1.4	5.4	5.15	0	0	0	0	2.37	1
99-862	255	F	pipe bowl frag	grit	sm		sm	N		outw	exc	rd	unmod		22	15	0	4	20	1.6	2.82	0	0	0	0	0	0	1
99-8625	3	T	rstr orifice hmsp bowl	grit	ind lin st		brn/smdg	N		inw	Inc	fl	unmod	punc	34	30	0	0	0	0.88	7	5.02	0	0	0	0	0	1
99-8642	258	T	exc rim jar	G	ind lin st		sm/smdg	N		outw	exc	rd	unmod		27	27	0	0	0	1.49	6	4.5	5.94	0	0	0	0	1
99-8658	300	F	rimstr frag	G	coarse		sm	Y	ind	outw	exc	ind	th	ind	23.6	12.7	0	0	0	0.84	2	0	0	0	0	0	0	1
99-8658	298	T	ind	G	sm		sm	Y	ind	outw	exc	fl	th	ind	37	26	0	0	0	1.24	8.3	6.38	0	0	0	0	0	1
99-8658	299	F	rimstr frag	G	sm		sm	Y	appl	ind	ind	ind	th/fl	pnch	20.3	19.9	0	0	0	1.25	3.1	0	0	0	0	0	2.68	1
99-8658	297	T	pnch rim jar	G	sm		sm	Y	appl	outw	exc	rd	th/fl	pnch	25	22	15	0	0	1.18	5.7	6.7	8.08	0	0	0	2.54	1
99-8658	302	F	rimstr frag	G	cordm		sm	Y	appl	outw	exc	ind	th/fl	pnch	28	29	0	0	0	1.38	7.5	0	0	0	11.02	8.22	2.8	1
99-8658	303	T	pnch rim jar	G	sm		sm	Y	ind	outw	exc	rd	th/fl	pnch	30	23.58	23.58	0	0	1.3	6.2	5.62	7.78	0	0	0	2.58	1
99-8658	301	F	rimstr frag	G	coarse		sm/smdg	Y	ind	outw	exc	ind	th	pnch	13	21	0	0	0	1.22	1.8	0	0	0	0	0	0	1
99-866	285	T	exc rim jar	grit	sm		sm	N		outw	exc	rd	rolled		43	27	0	0	0	1.79	16.2	8.64	0	0	0	0	0	1
99-8669	262	T	ind	G	ind st		sm	Y	ind	outw	exc	rd	th	ind	21	19	0	0	0	1.25	2.42	7.42	0	0	0	0	0	1
99-8681	25	T	ind	G	sm		sm	Y	appl	outw	exc	fl	th	sty ntch	19.92	20.81	12.06	0	0	1.86	3.8	5.34	0	0	0	0	6.34	1
99-8707	2	T	exc rim jar	G	sm		sm	Y	appl	outw	exc	rd	th/fl	pnch	32.3	21.9	21.9	0	0	1.02	7.8	5.28	0	0	10.58	8.78	1.8	1
99-8707	261	T	pnch rim jar	G	sm		sm	Y	appl	outw	h ev	rd	th/fl	pnch	25.12	14.89	14.89	0	0	1.18	3.1	8.15	0	0	0	0	2.38	1
99-8712	15	T	ind	G	sm		sm	ind	ind	ind	ind	rd	ind	ind	15.42	10.94	0	0	0	0.72	1.2	4.72	0	0	0	0	0	1
99-8825	16	T	ind	G	coarse		sm	ind	ind	outw	exc	rd	ind	ind	38	19.5	0	22	6	1.57	6.1	7.04	0	0	0	0	0	1
99-8827	277	T	ind	G	sm		sm	ind	ind	outw	exc	rd	ind	ind	13.15	16.92	0	0	0	1.48	2.2	4.96	0	0	0	0	0	1
99-8827	278	F	rimstr frag	G	sm		sm	Y	appl	ind	ind	ind	th/fl	pnch	28.9	28.72	28.72	0	0	1.28	5.8	0	0	0	6.82	5.32	1.5	1
99-8828	38	T	pnch rim jar	G	sm		sm	Y	appl	outw	h ev	rd	th/fl	pnch	41.9	32.3	10.06	0	0	1.44	14.8	6.5	8.15	0	10.68	7.78	2.9	1
99-8833	7	T	ind	G	sm		sm	Y	ind	outw	exc	bev (int)	th/fl	pnch	22.7	19.42	0	0	0	0.7	4.3	4.94	0	0	0	0	0	1
99-8852	255	T	ind	G	coarse		brn	Y	ind	ind	ind	rd	th	sty ntch	19.45	20.52	20.52	0	0	1.55	3.9	6.06	0	0	0	0	7.06	1
99-8853	251	F	rimstr frag	G	coarse		sm/smdg	Y	ind	ind	exc	ind	th	pnch	17.48	16.96	0	0	0	1.26	2.7	0	0	0	0	0	0	1
99-8855	273	T	ind	G	sm		sm	ind	ind	outw	exc	rd	ind	ind	26	12.3	0	0	0	1.51	2.9	6.12	0	0	0	0	0	1
99-8855	274	T	ind	G	coarse		sm	ind	ind	outw	exc	rd	ind	ind	23.6	15	0	0	0	1.94	2.4	4.8	0	0	0	0	0	1
99-8855	275	T	ind	G	sm		sm	ind	ind	outw	exc	rd	ind	ind	18.4	16.38	0	0	0	2.14	2.5	5.52	0	0	0	0	0	1
99-8855	278[29]	T	pnch rim jar	G	sm		sm	Y	appl	outw	exc	bev (int)	th/fl	pnch	43	21.9	21.9	18	7	1.64	10.7	5.34	7.08	0	10.15	5.4	4.75	1
99-8855	277[30]	F	pnch rim jar	G	sm		sm	Y	fold	outw	exc	rd	fold/fl	pnch	46	24.4	20.2	0	0	1.25	11.6	6.26	8.24	0	9.15	7.3	1.85	1
99-8862	265	T	ind	G	sm		sm	Y	ind	ind	ind	rd	th	ind	32.38	12.8	0	0	0	0.72	5.7	9.08	0	0	0	0	0	1

99-8862	266	T	pnch rim jar	G	ind lin st		sm/smdg	Y	appl	outw	exc	rd	th/fl	pnch	67.89	32.08	14.75	34	6	1.11	23.9	10.12	8.75	0	10.98	8.22	2.76	1
99-8873	258	T	ind	grit	sm		sm	ind	ind	ind	ind	rd	ind	ind	22.24	9.3	0	0	0	0.6	1.3	5.08	0	0	0	0	0	1
99-8876	271	T	pnch rim jar	G	sm		sm	Y	ind	outw	exc	ind	th/fl	pnch	21.1	19	0	0	0	0	2.9	0	0	0	0	0	0	1
99-8877	257	T	pnch rim jar	grit	sm		sm	Y	ind	outw	exc	rd	th/fl	pnch	30.07	12.12	0	0	0	0.9	4	4.68	0	0	0	0	1.21	1
99-8890	261	T	ind	G	eroded		sm	ind	ind	ind	exc	ind	ind	ind	18.15	15.2	0	0	0	0.9	2.1	0	0	0	0	0	0	1
99-8890	260	T	ind	G	sm		sm	ind	ind	ind	ind	rd	ind	ind	23.72	15.7	0	0	0	1.17	2.9	5.86	0	0	0	0	0	1
99-8893	258[31]	T	pnch rim jar	G	sm		sm	Y	appl	outw	exc	rd	th/fl	sm	35.7	30.5	24.5	0	0	1.7	10	4.72	0	0	8.68	6.9	1.78	1
99-8894	278	T	rstr orifice hmsp bowl	G	ind st	sm over	sm	Y	fold	inw	inc	ind	fold/fl	ind	25.1	21.8	0	0	0	1	5.1	0	0	0	0	0	0	1
99-8894	277	T	pnch rim jar	G	sm		sm	Y	appl	outw	h ev	rd	th/fl	pnch	31.2	14.9	14.9	0	0	1.5	4.6	5.08	0	0	0	0	2.94	1
99-8895	287	T	ind	grit	sm		brn/smdg	Y	ind	outw	exc	rd	th	ind	23.3	13.4	0	0	0	0.74	3.5	6.34	0	0	0	0	0	1
99-8899	257	F	rimstr frag	G	sm		sm/smdg	Y	ind	ind	ind	ind	th/fl	pnch	39	21	0	0	0	1.8	8.7	0	0	0	10.31	8.35	2.16	1
99-890	10	T	ind	grit	ind lin st		sm	ind	ind	outw	exc	ind	ind	ind	31	28	0	0	0	1.68	8	4.82	0	0	0	0	0	1
99-8900	268	F	rimstr frag	G	sm		sm	Y	ind	ind	ind	ind	th	pnch	23	16	0	0	0	1.4	3.5	0	0	0	0	0	0	1
99-8900	267	F	rimstr frag	G	sm		sm	Y	ind	ind	ind	ind	ind	punc	17	16	0	0	0	0.97	1.7	0	0	0	0	0	0	1
99-8949	11	T	pnch rim jar	G	sm		sm	Y	ind	outw	exc	ind	th	pnch	17.16	17.52	0	0	0	0.67	2.7	0	0	0	0	0	0	1
99-8983	297	T	pnch rim jar	G	ind st		brn	Y	appl	vrt	h ev	rd	th/fl	pnch	47	42	21.08	0	0	1.62	22.3	5.14	11.62	0	11.52	7.48	4.04	1
99-8983	293	T	ind	G	sm		sm	Y	ind	ind	ind	rd	ind	pnch	46	18	0	0	0	1.78	8.4	5.4	0	0	0	0	0	1
99-8983	294	T	pnch rim jar	G	ind lin st		sm/smdg	Y	ind	outw	exc	rd	th/fl	pnch	32	33	15.5	0	0	1.7	10.3	0	0	0	0	0	0	1
99-8983	295	F	rimstr frag	G	sm		sm/smdg	Y	ind	ind	ind	ind	th/fl	pnch	35	21	0	0	0	1.12	6	0	0	0	0	0	0	1
99-8983	296	T	pnch rim jar	G	sm		brn/smdg	Y	appl	outw	h ev	rd	th/fl	pnch	33	27	24	0	0	1.05	9	5.48	8.22	0	7.62	6.51	1.11	1
99-9023	6[32]	T	small jar	G	sm		sm	N		vrt	exc	bev (int)	unmod		28.5	26.6	0	0	0	0.87	7.7	3.83	7.01	0	0	0	0	1
99-905	2590	F	rimstr frag	G	sm		eroded	Y	ind	ind	ind	ind	th	sty ntch	12.04	12.6	12.6	0	0	1.43	2.5	0	0	0	0	0	9.64	1
99-905	259	F	rimstr frag	G	sm		eroded	Y	appl	ind	ind	bev (ext)	th	sty ntch	17	17.62	17.62	0	0	0	2.5	0	0	0	0	0	7.2	1
99-9057	262	T	ind	G	sm		sm	ind	ind	ind	ind	rd	ind	ind	15	11	0	0	0	1.7	1.3	6.07	0	0	0	0	0	1
99-9058	261	T	ind	G	sm		sm	ind	ind	ind	ind	fl	ind	ind	16	9.9	0	0	0	1.39	1.3	5.83	0	0	0	0	0	1
99-9058	260	T	pnch rim jar	G	cordm		sm	Y	appl	outw	exc	bev (int)	th/fl	pnch	25	27	15.22	0	0	2.05	5.8	4.68	0	0	8.99	6.54	2.45	1
99-906	259	T	ind	G	sm		sm/smdg	Y	ind	vrt	ind	rd	th	ind	16	19.2	0	0	0	2.16	3.6	5.06	0	0	0	0	0	1
99-9089	288	T	ind	G	ind st		sm	N		vrt	exc	rd	unmod		33	30	0	0	0	2.38	9.2	6.68	0	0	0	0	0	1
99-9089	287	T	pnch rim jar	G	sm		sm	Y	ind	outw	h ev	rd	th/fl	pnch	43	23	23.2	0	0	1.18	12	6.32	8.94	0	10.28	8.7	1.58	1
99-9109	255	F	rimstr frag	G	sm		sm	Y	appl	ind	ind	ind	th/fl	pnch	26	19.5	0	0	0	1.67	4.2	0	0	0	0	0	0	1
99-9148	252	T	rstr orifice hmsp bowl	grit	sm		sm	N		inw	Inc	bev (int)	unmod		20.25	23.84	0	0	0	0.25	3.2	3.04	0	0	0	0	0	1
99-9149	4	T	rstr orifice hmsp bowl	G	sm		sm/smdg	Y	ind	vrt	exc	rd	th/fl	pnch	28.08	18.82	11.23	0	0	2.58	6.1	8.89	0	0	10.83	9.09	1.74	1
99-9151	261	T	pnch rim jar	G	ind st	sm over	sm	Y	fold	outw	h ev	rd	fold/fl	pnch	36.8	32.16	16.76	0	0	1.83	11.8	4.21	5.53	0	8.24	5.66	2.58	1
99-9156	262	F	ind	G	sm		eroded	Y	appl	outw	exc	fl	th	ind	39.09	19.77	0	0	0	2.13	3.8	5.19	0	0	0	0	0	1
99-9156	263	T	pnch rim jar	G	ind lin st	overstamp	brn	Y	fold	outw	exc	rd	fold/fl	pnch	70.45	45.67	18.82	0	0	2.02	31.9	5.03	9.61	0	10.08	7.32	2.76	1
99-9156	261	T	pnch rim jar	G	coarse		brn/smdg	Y	ind	outw	exc	rd	th/fl	pnch	27.5	24	0	0	0	1.24	5.3	5.32	0	0	0	0	0	1
99-9156	256	T	pnch rim jar	G	coarse		sm	Y	ind	outw	h ev	bev (int)	th/fl	pnch	67.9	19.46	0	30	7	2.11	14.9	4.7	9.94	0	0	0	0	1
99-9156	260	T	pnch rim jar	G	sm		brn/smdg	Y	ind	outw	exc	bev (int)	th/fl	pnch	41.42	13.27	0	0	0	2.15	4.9	3.9	0	0	0	0	0	1
99-9157	265	T	ind	G	ind st	sm over	brn/smdg	ind	ind	outw	exc	rd	ind	ind	19.86	12.16	0	0	0	2.07	2.6	5.99	0	0	0	0	0	1
99-9159	7	T	rstr orifice hmsp bowl	G	ind st	sm over	sm/smdg	N		inw	exc	rd	unmod		34.98	30.92	0	17	5	1.47	7.1	4.86	0	0	0	0	0	1
99-9159	6	T	exc rim jar	G	ind lin st		sm	Y	appl	vrt	exc	rd	th	pnch	32.81	34.89	16.18	0	0	1.56	14.5	6.94	0	0	14.51	7.43	7.08	1
99-9161	1[33]	T	pnch rim jar	G	brn		brn/smdg	Y	ind	outw	exc	rd	th/fl	pnch	41.06	23.17	0	16	5	1.96	11.9	7.44	0	0	0	0	0	1
99-9170	290	T	ind	G	sm		sm	Y	ind	outw	h ev	rd	th/fl	ind	20.27	14.49	0	0	0	1.71	2.6	5.65	0	0	0	0	0	1
99-9170	289	T	ind	G	sm		sm	ind	ind	ind	exc	rd	ind	ind	25.4	12.4	0	0	0	2.17	3.5	7	0	0	0	0	0	1
99-9170	288	T	ind	G	sm		sm	Y	ind	outw	exc	rd	th	pnch	29.69	13.02	0	0	0	1.6	5.9	7.03	0	0	0	0	0	1
99-9171	9	T	smpl hmsp bowl	G	comp st	ind over-stamp	brn/smdg	Y	appl	outw	inc	rd	th/fl	pnch	108.7	61.37	12.18	24	12	2.3	86.6	7.14	0	0	11.06	8.38	2.68	1

99-9171	8	T	rstr orifice hmsp bowl	G	sm		sm	Y	appl	vrt	exc	rd	th	sm	34.8	38.22	19.46	0	0	3.48	16	9.69	0	0	13.2	9.28	3.92	1
99-9192	14	T	pnch rim jar	grit	sm		sm	Y	ind	outw	h ev	rd	th/fl	pnch	34.22	28.05	22.05	0	0	0.83	9.2	5.98	0	0	11.1	7.08	4.02	1
99-9204	255	T	ind	G	sm		brn/smdg	ind	ind	ind	ind	rd	ind	ind	21.44	14.82	0	0	0	1.61	2.9	6.73	0	0	0	0	0	1
99-9220	264	F	exc rim jar	G	sm		brn/smdg	Y	ind	outw	exc	rd	th	pnch	15.06	21.24	18.48	0	0	1.62	4	5.9	12.37	0	12.37	6.04	6.33	1
99-9220	263	T	exc rim jar	G	sm		sm	Y	ind	outw	exc	rd	th	pnch	91.49	33.78	22.14	32	6	1.42	36.3	7.54	0	0	13.92	7.84	6.08	1
99-9220	262	T	exc rim jar	G	sm		brn/smdg	Y	fold	outw	exc	rd	fold	pnch	52.38	20	0	0	0	1.4	16.5	6.06	0	0	11.92	5.59	5.53	1
99-935	278[34]	T	rstr orifice hmsp bowl	G	sm		sm	Y	ind	ind	ind	rd	th	punc	24.26	17.12	17.12	0	0	1.33	2	0	0	0	0	0	0	1
99-958	296	T	exc rim jar	G	coarse		sm	Y	appl	outw	exc	rd	th	sty ntch	58	37	16.12	0	0	1.78	23.1	5.12	0	0	12.42	7.98	4.44	1
99-958	292	T	ind	G	sm		sm	Y	ind	ind	ind	rd	th	pnch	18	18	18	0	0	0.79	3.2	6.58	0	0	0	0	3.98	1
99-958	295	T	exc rim jar	G	scraped		sm	Y	appl	outw	exc	rd	th	sty ntch	41	34	15.8	0	0	1.5	21.3	6.8	0	0	15.78	8.54	7.24	1
99-958	293	T	ind	S/ CR	sm		sm	Y	ind	vrt	exc	fl	th	sty ntch	37	27	19.8	0	0	1.93	10.3	5.78	0	0	10.25	7.2	3.05	1
99-958	294	T	ind	G	ind st		sm	Y	appl	vrt	exc	fl	th	sty ntch	35	25	16.1	0	0	1.01	9.1	5.07	0	0	11.15	7.28	3.87	1

[1]Wide notch
[2]Small jar
[3]Fingernail notching? Same vessel as 259 and 260
[4]Fingernail notching? Same vessel as 259 and 264
[5]Fingernail notching? Same vessel as 260 and 264
[6]Wide notch
[7]Small jar
[8]Wide notch
[9]Strip attached to shoulder of cazuela
[10]Same vessel as 99-2939-269
[11]Same vessel as 99-2939-271
[12]Lug handle
[13]Good example of Qualla paste
[14]Small jar
[15]Small jar
[16]Same vessel as 305
[17]Same vessel as 306
[18]Wide notch
[19]Same vessel as 3255-256
[20]Same vessel as 3254-365
[21]Small cazuela
[22]Small bowl
[23]Wide notch
[24]Wide notch
[25]Sooted
[26]Strap handle
[27]Same vessel as 99-935-278
[28]Good example of Qualla paste
[29]Good for photograph
[30]Good for photograph
[31]Photograph cross section
[32]Small jar
[33]Small jar
[34]Same vessel as 99-845-275

Appendix D

Botanical Remains from Cherokee Contexts

Site 40Bt89

Feature	BCL Number	Plant Wt (g)	Wood Wt (g)	Common Name	Ct	Wt (g)
16, Zone A	99-910-1	5.01	0.43			
				acorn	3	0.00
				bark	117	1.23
				bean cf.	11	0.07
				bud	1	0.00
				cane	15	0.07
				cheno/am	1	0.00
				chenopod embryo cf.	1	0.00
				corn cupule	54	0.44
				corn cupule cf.	5	0.03
				corn glume	3	0.01
				corn kernel	1	0.05
				grape	1	0.00
				grass family	143	0.00
				hazelnut cf.	1	0.00
				hickory	12	0.09
				knotweed	1	0.00
				maypop cf.	1	0.00
				pine cone	675	2.47
				pine cone cf.	6	0.02
				pitch	7	0.02
				purslane	1	0.00
				sedge cf.	118	0.00
				St. John's wort cf.	15	0.00
				unidentifiable	16	0.05
				unidentifiable seed	16	0.03
				unidentified seed	2	0.00
18, Zone A	99-918-1	0.28	0.18			
				black walnut	3	0.02
				cane	1	0.00
				corn cupule cf.	1	0.00
				gall/seed head	1	0.00
				hickory	4	0.03
				pitch	4	0.02
				spurge/St. John's wort	1	0.00
				unidentifiable	1	0.01
				walnut family/peach	2	0.02
21, Zone A	99-1080-2	16.61	8.02			
				acorn cap cf.	1	0.01
				bark	6	0.07
				bean	18	0.40
				bean cf.	7	0.03
				black walnut	81	3.00
				black walnut/peach	41	1.13
				cane	103	1.59
				corn cupule	41	0.43
				corn cupule cf.	1	0.01

Feature	BCL No.	Plant Wt	Wood Wt	Common Name	Ct	Wt
				corn kernel	6	0.11
				cucurbit rind	5	0.01
				hickory	14	0.27
				pine cone	39	0.21
				pine cone cf.	1	0.00
				pitch	40	0.60
				unidentifiable	3	0.02
				unidentifiable seed	8	0.00
				walnut family	58	0.70
21, Zone A	99-1081-251	5.07	1.95			
				bark cf.	2	0.01
				bean	99	2.17
				bean cf.	23	0.13
				black walnut	17	0.29
				cane	5	0.03
				corn cupule	8	0.09
				corn cupule cf.	2	0.00
				corn glume	2	0.01
				corn kernel	6	0.09
				corn kernel cf.	1	0.00
				cucurbit rind	4	0.02
				cucurbit rind cf.	3	0.01
				grape cf.	1	0.00
				hickory	5	0.05
				pine cone	4	0.02
				pine cone cf.	1	0.00
				pitch	21	0.14
				purslane	2	0.00
				unidentifiable	12	0.04
				unidentifiable seed	4	0.00
				unidentified seed	2	0.00
				walnut family	2	0.02
21, Zone A	99-1085-1	0.42	0.23			
				black walnut	5	0.08
				cane	1	0.00
				corn cupule	3	0.02
				corn glume	1	0.00
				corn kernel	4	0.01
				hickory	5	0.03
				pitch	5	0.05
				unidentifiable seed coat	2	0.00
21 (no HF), Zone A	99-1642-1	1.67	1.28			
				acorn cf.	1	0.00
				bean	1	0.01
				bearsfoot cf.	3	0.00
				bud	1	0.00
				cane	1	0.00

Feature	BCL No.	Plant Wt	Wood Wt	Common Name	Ct	Wt
				corn cupule	6	0.02
				corn cupule cf.	1	0.00
				corn kernel	1	0.07
				cucurbit rind	1	0.00
				persimmon seed cf.	1	0.00
				pine cone	2	0.01
				pitch	13	0.28
				unidentifiable seed	1	0.00
23, Zone A	99-1070-2	17.10	5.85			
				acorn	2	0.00
				bean/persimmon/acorn meat	7	0.05
				bedstraw	25	0.02
				bedstraw cf.	1	0.00
				black walnut	16	0.41
				black walnut/peach	21	0.48
				blackberry/raspberry	2	0.00
				bud	1	0.00
				bur	5	0.00
				cane	31	0.21
				cane, partially carbonized	10	0.06
				cheno/am	1	0.00
				chenopod	9	0.00
				corn cupule	36	0.23
				corn cupule cf.	20	0.15
				corn glume	2	0.00
				corn kernel	3	0.04
				corn kernel cf.	3	0.01
				cucurbit rind	25	0.09
				elderberry cf.	1	0.00
				gall/seed head	3	0.00
				grass family	113	0.08
				hazelnut	2	0.02
				hickory	5	0.04
				little barley cf.	1	0.00
				maypop	2	0.01
				pine cone	1988	8.79
				pitch	24	0.29
				spore clump	1	0.00
				unidentifiable	30	0.14
				unidentifiable seed	45	0.01
				unidentified seed	20	0.00
				walnut family	16	0.12
				weedy legume	1	0.00
24, Zone A	99-821-252	2.67	0.98			
				bean/persimmon/acorn meat	1	0.00
				bedstraw cf.	1	0.00
				black walnut	55	0.97
				black walnut/peach	9	0.16
				bud	1	0.00
				cane	5	0.02
				corn cupule	1	0.00
				corn glume	1	0.00
				cucurbit rind	1	0.00
				gall/seed head	1	0.00
				grass family	1	0.00
				hazelnut	1	0.00
				hickory	23	0.17
				pitch	7	0.03
				unidentifiable	3	0.03
				unidentifiable seed	2	0.00
				unidentified seed	1	0.00
				walnut family	42	0.31
38, Zone A	99-1041-1	0.38	0.29			
				bedstraw	1	0.00
				black walnut	2	0.02
				cane	3	0.00
				chenopod	2	0.00
				corn cupule	5	0.00
				corn kernel	1	0.00
				cucurbit rind	3	0.01
				hickory	4	0.04
				pitch	1	0.01
				unidentifiable	1	0.00
				unidentifiable seed fragment	2	0.00
				unidentified seed	3	0.00
				walnut family	2	0.01
44, Zone A	99-840-252	2.99	2.30			
				acorn	2	0.00
				bark	2	0.01
				black walnut	1	0.01
				corn cupule	1	0.00
				corn cupule cf.	1	0.00
				corn kernel	1	0.00
				hickory	2	0.02
				pine cone	1	0.00
				pitch	88	0.64
				walnut family	1	0.00
				wood, partially carbonized	1	0.01
44, Zone B	99-843-251	4.82	4.19			
				acorn	1	0.00
				bark	3	0.03
				bedstraw	4	0.00
				black walnut/peach	1	0.06
				cane	1	0.00
				corn cupule	1	0.00
				corn cupule cf.	2	0.00
				corn glume	1	0.00
				cucurbit rind	2	0.00
				gall	2	0.01
				gall/seed head	2	0.02
				hazelnut cf.	1	0.00
				persimmon/bean cf.	1	0.01
				pine cone	3	0.01
				pitch	90	0.48
				unidentifiable	5	0.02
				unidentifiable seed	2	0.00
				unidentified seed	1	0.00
				walnut family	4	0.02
45, Zone A	99-1037-1	0.01	0.01			
				pitch	1	0.00
				walnut family cf.	1	0.00
45, Zone B	99-1043-3	0.17	0.12			
				acorn	1	0.00
				cucurbit rind	1	0.00
				hickory	4	0.03
				pitch	2	0.01
				walnut family	1	0.01
48, Zone B	99-1099-258	76.07	47.32			
				acorn	1	0.00
				acorn shell/meat	1	0.01
				bark	12	0.07
				black walnut	1	0.01
				blueberry cf.	1	0.00

Feature	BCL No.	Plant Wt	Wood Wt	Common Name	Ct	Wt
				cane	17	0.08
				chenopod cf.	1	0.00
				corn cupule	3	0.03
				corn glume	1	0.00
				corn kernel	2	0.01
				corn kernel cf.	5	0.02
				cucurbit rind	3	0.01
				gall/seed head	2	0.01
				grass family	1	0.00
				hickory	38	0.80
				insect	1	0.00
				persimmon/bean cf.	1	0.00
				pine cone	1	0.00
				pitch	2018	26.10
				plum/cherry cf.	1	0.00
				spurge family	1	0.00
				sumpweed cf.	1	0.00
				unidentified seed	1	0.00
				unidentifiable	33	0.17
				unidentified—seed?	6	0.00
				wood, partially carbonized	0	1.44
50, Zone A	99-1049-4	4.80	3.08			
				acorn cf.	1	0.00
				bean cf.	3	0.01
				black walnut	15	0.38
				black walnut/peach	16	0.20
				cane	1	0.00
				corn cupule	9	0.05
				corn cupule cf.	1	0.00
				corn kernel	1	0.01
				corn kernel cf.	1	0.00
				cucurbit rind	10	0.12
				grape	1	0.00
				grass family	1	0.00
				hazelnut	2	0.00
				hickory	17	0.15
				maypop	2	0.00
				pitch	14	0.11
				smartweed	1	0.00
				tobacco/blueberry?	1	0.00
				unidentifiable	2	0.01
				unidentifiable seed	3	0.00
				unidentifiable seed fragment	3	0.00
				unidentified seed	0	0.00
				walnut family	16	0.18
				wood, partially carbonized	1	0.50
55, Zone A	99-817-4	13.06	11.63			
				acorn	1	0.00
				bark	1	0.02
				bedstraw cf.	1	0.00
				black walnut	6	0.07
				black walnut cf.	4	0.03
				blackberry/raspberry	2	0.00
				cane	1	0.00
				corn cupule	21	0.41
				corn cupule cf.	2	0.01
				corn kernel	14	0.11
				corn kernel cf.	11	0.07
				cucurbit rind	4	0.01
				gall	1	0.01
				hickory	18	0.22
				knotweed	1	0.00
				pitch	55	0.43
				purslane	1	0.00
				sumpweed cf.	1	0.00
				unidentifiable	6	0.05
				unidentifiable seed	6	0.00
55, Zone A	99-825-252	0.95	0.56			
				acorn	1	0.00
				acorn cf.	1	0.00
				bark	1	0.00
				black walnut	5	0.18
				bud	1	0.00
				cane	11	0.03
				corn cupule	2	0.01
				corn cupule cf.	1	0.00
				corn kernel	1	0.00
				cucurbit rind	2	0.00
				grass family	1	0.00
				hickory	5	0.04
				pitch	10	0.07
				spurge	1	0.00
				unidentifiable	8	0.00
				unidentifiable seed	4	0.00
				unidentified seed	7	0.00
				walnut family	4	0.03
				wood, partially carbonized	5	0.03

Site 40Bt90

Feature	BCL No.	Plant Wt	Wood Wt	Common Name	Ct	Wt
455, Zone A	00-259-1	0.34	0.21			
				black walnut	4	0.04
				corn cupule	2	0.00
				cucurbit rind	1	0.00
				false Solomon's seal cf.	1	0.00
				hickory	6	0.03
				honeylocust cf.	2	0.00
				pitch	4	0.03
				unidentifiable seed	3	0.00
				walnut family	5	0.03
702, Zone C	99-3804-5	4.23	0.55			
				acorn cf.	1	0.00
				bark	3	0.04
				black walnut	30	2.48
				cane	3	0.08
				corn glume	1	0.00
				hickory	77	0.79
				little barley cf.	1	0.00
				pine cone	1	0.00
				pitch	1	0.00
				unidentifiable	6	0.02
				unidentifiable seed	1	0.00
				unidentifiable, uncarbonized	2	0.09
				unidentified	1	0.00
				walnut family	24	0.27
705, Zone A	99-3027-1	40.38	24.46			
				acorn	4	0.01
				acorn cf.	2	0.00
				acorn meat cf.	2	0.00
				bark	7	0.52
				bedstraw	1	0.00
				black walnut	18	0.33

Feature	BCL No.	Plant Wt	Wood Wt	Common Name	Ct	Wt
				blackberry/raspberry	1	0.00
				bud	1	0.00
				cheno/am	2	0.00
				chenopod cf.	5	0.00
				corn cupule	80	0.77
				corn cupule cf.	5	0.00
				corn glume	17	0.03
				corn kernel	1	0.00
				corn kernel cf.	16	0.15
				cucurbit rind	2	0.00
				gall	4	0.00
				gall/seed head	1	0.01
				grass family	4	0.00
				hickory	42	0.41
				maypop	1	0.00
				persimmon seed coat cf.	1	0.00
				pine cone	3	0.00
				pitch	1561	13.33
				unidentifiable	41	0.17
				unidentifiable seed	2	0.00
				unidentified seed	2	0.00
				unidentified seed, 5-lobed	1	0.00
				walnut family	12	0.05
				wax myrtle cf.	1	0.00
				wood, partially carbonized		0.15
705, Zone B	99-3052-1	82.59	58.18			
				acorn	27	0.06
				acorn cap cf.	1	0.00
				acorn meat cf.	1	0.00
				bark	11	0.05
				bean	1	0.00
				black walnut	1	0.02
				bud	2	0.00
				cane	13	0.13
				corn cupule	11	0.21
				corn cupule cf.	11	0.04
				corn glume	1	0.00
				corn kernel	12	0.10
				corn kernel cf.	2	0.01
				cucurbit rind	2	0.00
				false Solomon's seal cf.	1	0.00
				gall	29	0.05
				gall/seed head	2	0.00
				hazelnut	2	0.01
				hickory	16	0.21
				monocot stem	1	0.00
				pine cone	11	0.08
				pitch	1735	16.08
				unidentifiable	21	0.12
				unidentifiable seed	10	0.00
				unidentified seed, 5-lobed	1	0.00
				walnut family	2	0.02
				wood, partially carbonized		7.27
706, Zone A	99-3787-1	17.87	17.36			
				bark	2	0.01
				pine cone	47	0.06
				pitch	62	0.36
				unidentifiable	7	0.08
				unidentifiable seed	1	0.00
936, Zone A	99-3238-1	3.02	1.42			
				acorn	1	0.00
				bean	2	0.02
				bean cf.	2	0.01
				bearsfoot	1	0.00
				black walnut/peach	6	0.14
				blackberry/raspberry	1	0.00
				cheno/am	1	0.00
				chenopod	2	0.00
				corn cupule	30	0.20
				corn cupule cf.	1	0.00
				corn glume	4	0.02
				corn kernel	149	0.67
				corn kernel cf.	42	0.18
				gall/seed head	4	0.01
				grass family	5	0.00
				hickory	2	0.02
				maypop cf.	1	0.00
				mustard cf.	1	0.00
				persimmon seed coat cf.	4	0.00
				persimmon/bean cf.	1	0.00
				pine cone/bark	5	0.02
				pitch	24	0.20
				purslane	1	0.00
				stem	2	0.00
				unidentifiable	21	0.09
				unidentifiable seed	3	0.00
				walnut family	3	0.03
936, Zone A	99-3240-251	1.43	0.94			
				acorn	1	0.00
				bean cf.	2	0.00
				bean/persimmon cf.	1	0.01
				bedstraw cf.	1	0.00
				blackberry/raspberry	1	0.00
				cane	6	0.03
				corn cupule	13	0.11
				corn cupule cf.	6	0.02
				corn kernel	16	0.25
				cucurbit rind cf.	1	0.00
				grass family	30	0.00
				hickory	5	0.03
				pine cone	3	0.01
				pitch	7	0.03
				stem	1	0.00
				unidentifiable	1	0.00
				unidentifiable seed	1	0.00
1019, Zone A	99-3256-1	7.83	5.43			
				bark	7	0.06
				bean	1	0.05
				bean cf.	1	0.00
				bedstraw	19	0.01
				black walnut	1	0.00
				bud/achene?	1	0.00
				cane	2	0.01
				catkin	1	0.00
				corn cupule	35	0.39
				corn cupule cf.	14	0.07
				corn glume	4	0.02
				corn glume cf.	1	0.00
				corn kernel	25	0.35
				corn kernel cf.	5	0.02
				cucurbit rind	2	0.00
				gall	2	0.00
				grass family	1	0.00
				hickory	6	0.08

Feature	BCL No.	Plant Wt	Wood Wt	Common Name	Ct	Wt
				little barley cf.	12	0.01
				maypop	2	0.01
				maypop cf.	1	0.00
				node	1	0.00
				pine cone	8	0.01
				pitch	46	1.18
				thorn	1	0.00
				unidentifiable	11	0.06
				unidentifiable seed	11	0.00
				unidentified seed	10	0.00
				wood, partially carbonized	0	0.07
1019, Zone A	99-3258-253	8.21	6.11			
				acorn	11	0.01
				acorn cf.	1	0.00
				acorn meat cf.	11	0.06
				bark	2	0.03
				black walnut/peach	1	0.03
				blackberry/raspberry	1	0.00
				bud	1	0.00
				cane	106	1.16
				cane cf.	1	0.00
				corn cupule	5	0.08
				corn cupule cf.	1	0.00
				corn glume	1	0.00
				corn kernel	1	0.01
				corn kernel cf.	7	0.03
				gall/seed head	1	0.01
				grass family	1	0.00
				hickory	9	0.08
				knotweed	1	0.00
				morning-glory	1	0.00
				node	1	0.01
				pine cone	178	0.39
				pine cone cf.	1	0.00
				pine seed cf.	1	0.01
				pitch	19	0.15
				plum/cherry cf.	5	0.00
				purslane	6	0.00
				unidentifiable	5	0.03
				unidentifiable seed	1	0.00
				unidentifiable seed fragment	12	0.00
				unidentified seed	2	0.00
				walnut family	2	0.02
1020, Zone A	99-3660-1	6.37	5.35			
				acorn	1	0.00
				amaranth	1	0.00
				bearsfoot cf.	2	0.00
				bedstraw	18	0.01
				blueberry	2	0.00
				cane	2	0.01
				chenopod cf.	1	0.00
				corn cupule	2	0.00
				corn cupule cf.	1	0.00
				corn glume	1	0.00
				corn glume cf.	1	0.01
				corn kernel	3	0.03
				cucurbit rind	4	0.01
				hickory	9	0.08
				little barley	45	0.01
				monocot nodes/stems	7	0.01
				persimmon seed cf.	4	0.00
				pine cone	2	0.01
				pitch	107	0.78
				unidentifiable	8	0.04
				unidentifiable seed	33	0.02
				unidentified seed	24	0.00
1996, Zone A	99-8878-1	10.11	7.32			
				acorn	3	0.00
				acorn cf.	1	0.00
				bark	10	0.04
				bedstraw	1	0.00
				black walnut	4	0.07
				bud	2	0.00
				cane	21	0.19
				corn cob	1	0.24
				corn cupule	135	1.34
				corn cupule cf.	14	0.03
				corn glume	55	0.21
				corn kernel	47	0.38
				corn kernel cf.	7	0.04
				cucurbit rind	10	0.00
				gall	2	0.00
				grass family	2	0.00
				hazelnut	1	0.00
				hickory	12	0.05
				hickory cf.	7	0.00
				maypop	1	0.00
				pine cone	9	0.00
				pitch	20	0.12
				unidentifiable	28	0.08
				unidentifiable seed	1	0.00
				unidentified seed	1	0.00
PM 2117	99-5560-5	0.12	0.03			
				acorn	1	0.00
				hickory	3	0.04
				pitch	7	0.04
				walnut family	1	0.01

Site 40Bt91

Feature	BCL No.	Plant Wt	Wood Wt	Common Name	Ct	Wt
94, Zone A	99-2685-1	0.01	0.00			
				hickory	2	0.01
				pitch	1	0.00
390, Zone A	99-892-2	0.69	0.56			
				acorn	2	0.00
				bark	1	0.03
				bark/pine cone	2	0.01
				black walnut	1	0.00
				bud	1	0.00
				cane	2	0.01
				corn cupule	3	0.02
				corn glume	1	0.00
				hickory	1	0.00
				pitch	4	0.03
				unidentifiable	2	0.01
				walnut family	3	0.02
390, Zone A	99-893-3	1.14	0.98			
				acorn meat cf.	3	0.00
				bark	2	0.00
				bedstraw cf.	1	0.00
				black walnut	2	0.01
				bud	3	0.00

Feature	BCL No.	Plant Wt	Wood Wt	Common Name	Ct	Wt
				hickory	8	0.05
				pine cone	1	0.00
				pitch	11	0.09
				unidentifiable	2	0.00
				unidentified	4	0.01
392, Zone A	99-867-2	0.85	0.70			
				acorn	2	0.00
				acorn cf.	1	0.00
				bark	6	0.00
				black walnut	1	0.01
				bud	1	0.00
				cane	2	0.01
				catkin	1	0.00
				corn cupule	3	0.01
				corn kernel	1	0.00
				false Solomon's seal	3	0.00
				hickory	6	0.01
				pine cone	1	0.02
				pitch	10	0.04
				unidentifiable	1	0.00
				unidentifiable seed	20	0.02
				walnut family	1	0.03
394, Zone A	99-851-1	0.09	0.05			
				acorn meat/persimmon seed cf.	1	0.00
				bark	1	0.03
				pine cone	1	0.00
				pitch	1	0.01
394, Zone C	99-852-1	0.00	0.00			
				unidentifiable	1	0.00
394, Zone A	99-857-1	0.08	0.02			
				bark/wood	1	0.03
				hickory	1	0.02
				pine cone	3	0.01
				unidentifiable	1	0.00
394, Zone C	99-862-2	0.05	0.04			
				acorn meat/persimmon seed cf.	2	0.01
				bark	1	0.00
				hickory	1	0.00
				pine cone	3	0.00
497, Zone B	99-2204-251	39.89	36.23			
				acorn	1	0.00
				bark	11	0.08
				bean	2	0.17
				bean cf.	1	0.00
				bean/legume	3	0.00
				black walnut/peach	1	0.01
				cane	1	0.02
				corn cupule	2	0.04
				corn embryo	3	0.02
				corn kernel	4	0.03
				corn kernel cf.	10	0.05
				gall	1	0.00
				grape	1	0.00
				hackberry cf.	1	0.00
				pine cone	3	0.02
				pitch	243	3.10
				unidentifiable	29	0.12
				unidentifiable seed	1	0.00
497, Zone B	99-2206-5	41.36	36.22			
				acorn	3	0.00
				acorn cap	1	0.00
				bark	7	0.03
				bark/fiber	1	0.00
				bedstraw cf.	1	0.00
				black walnut	9	0.26
				bud	2	0.01
				cane	2	0.02
				corn cupule	1	0.01
				corn cupule cf.	1	0.00
				corn embryo	1	0.00
				corn kernel	25	0.11
				corn kernel cf.	10	0.04
				gall	8	0.02
				hackberry cf.	3	0.00
				hickory	19	0.10
				hickory cf.	1	0.01
				persimmon seed cf.	1	0.00
				pine cone	13	0.04
				pitch	460	2.82
				stem/catkin	1	0.01
				unidentifiable	18	0.06
				walnut family	3	0.02
				wood, partially carbonized	0	1.60

Appendix E

Faunal Remains from Cherokee Contexts

KEY

bl:	black	perm:	permanent
calc:	calcined	R:	right
decid:	deciduous	rsr:	rays, spines, ribs
ind:	indeterminate	U:	unfused
L:	left	UID:	unidentifiable
n:	nearly	Y:	yes

Feature	Taxon	Element	Portion	Side	Count	Weight (g)	Fusion	Modification
Site 40Bt89								
21	*Odocoileus virginianus*	decid. premolar	complete		1	0.46		none
	Odocoileus virginianus	decid. premolar	lower		1	0.46		none
	Odocoileus virginianus	maxilla	fragment	L	1	2.46	U	none
	Odocoileus virginianus	metatarsal	fragment	R	1	2.54	U	burn-black
	Odocoileus virginianus	metatarsal	proximal	R	1	2.54	U	burn-black
	Rodentia	carpal	complete		1	0.03		burn-calc
	Rodentia	ulna	proximal		1	0.01		burn-calc
	Rodentia	vertebra, caudal	complete		1	0.01		burn-calc
	large mammal	acetabulum	fragment	R	11	7.33	U	none
	large mammal	femur	condyle		2	4.15		burn-black
	large mammal	femur	condyle		2	4.15		carnivore
	large mammal	femur	epiphysis		2	4.15		burn-black
	large mammal	femur	epiphysis		2	4.15		carnivore
	large mammal	femur	lateral		2	4.15		burn-black
	large mammal	femur	lateral		2	4.15		carnivore
	large mammal	ind bone	diaphysis		1	24.54	U	none
	large mammal	UID	diaphysis		6	5.46	U	burn-black
	large mammal	UID	segment		6	5.46	U	burn-black
	ind mammal	UID	fragment		2	1.42		none
	ind mammal	UID	fragment		4	0.40		burn-calc/bl
	ind mammal	UID	fragment		2	2.05	U	none
	bivalve	shell/mollusk	fragment		1	2.92		none
	UID	UID	fragment		17	2.00		burn-black
	UID	UID	fragment		3	0.29		burn-calc/bl
	UID	UID	fragment		19	2.15		burn-calc
	UID	UID	fragment		25	1.41		none
	UID	UID	fragment		5	0.99		burn-calc
	UID	UID	ind		121	2.33		burn-calc
	UID	UID	ind		114	1.40		burn-calc/bl
23	ind mammal	UID	fragment		15	2.33	U	none
	ind mammal	UID	fragment		1	0.76	U	none
	UID	UID	fragment		2	0.61	U	burn-calc
38	large mammal	illium	fragment		1	6.61	U	none
44	ind mammal	UID	fragment		1	0.47	U	burn-calc/bl
	ind mammal	UID	fragment		2	3.17	U	none
48	ind mammal	UID	fragment		1	0.51	U	burn-calc
	ind mammal	UID	fragment		1	0.38	U	none
	ind mammal	UID	fragment		18	7.24	U	none
	Meleagris gallopavo	tarsometatarsus	diaphysis		1	1.22	U	none
	Meleagris gallopavo	tarsometatarsus	distal		1	1.22	U	none
	Meleagris gallopavo	tarsometatarsus	fragment		1	1.22	U	none
	Meleagris gallopavo	tibiotarsus	diaphysis	L	1	3.59	U	none
	Meleagris gallopavo	tibiotarsus	distal	L	1	3.59	U	none
	ind bird	1st phalange	complete		2	0.55	Y	none
	ind bird	1st phalange	complete		1	0.37	Y	none
	ind bird	2nd phalange	complete		1	0.25	Y	none
	ind bird	3rd phalange	complete		1	0.18	Y	none
48 cont.								
	ind bird	claw	complete		1	0.12	Y	none
	ind bird	UID	fragment		4	1.35	U	none
	Anuran	humerus	fragment		1	0.04	U	none
	Anuran	humerus	proximal		1	0.04	U	none
	Anuran	ind cranial	complete		1	0.04	Y	none
	Anuran	tibio-fibula	n complete		2	0.23	Y	none
	Bufo	femur	complete	L	1	0.16	Y	none
	Bufo	illium	complete	L	1	0.04	U	none
	Bufo	illium	complete	L	1	0.14	Y	none
	Bufo	illium	n complete	R	1	0.08	U	none
	Bufo	scapula	complete	R	1	0.13	Y	none
	UID	UID	fragment	R	7	5.51	U	burn-calc
50	*Odocoileus virginianus*	astragalus	complete	R	1	6.45		none
	Castor canadensis	perm molar	complete		1	1.48		none
	ind mammal	UID	fragment		1	1.26	U	none
	ind mammal	UID	fragment		1	0.15	U	burn-calc
	UID	UID	fragment		22	0.62	U	burn-calc/bl
55	*Odocoileus virginianus*	femur	diaphysis	L	1	33.34	N	none
	Odocoileus virginianus	femur	distal	L	1	33.34	N	none
	Odocoileus virginianus	radius	diaphysis	L	1	25.92	Y	none
	Odocoileus virginianus	radius	distal	L	1	25.92	Y	none
	Odocoileus virginianus	tibia	diaphysis	R	1	18.09	N	none
	Odocoileus virginianus	tibia	proximal	R	1	18.09	N	none
	ind mammal	UID	fragment		2	0.57	U	none
	UID	UID	fragment		8	1.82	U	none

Feature	Taxon	Element	Portion	Side	Count	Weight (g)	Fusion	Modification
Site 40Bt90								
118	Canidae	carpal	complete	L	1	1.59		none
	Urocyon cinereoargenteus	perm molar	complete	L	1	0.37		burn-black
	Urocyon cinereoargenteus	perm molar	lower	L	1	0.37		burn-black
	Sciurus carolinensis	femur	diaphysis	R	1	0.28	Y	none
	Sciurus carolinensis	femur	distal	R	1	0.28	Y	none
	Sciurus carolinensis	sacrum	n complete		1	0.23	N	none
	Sciurus carolinensis	sacrum	proximal		1	0.23	N	none
	Sciuridae	perm molar	complete		1	0.01		none
	small mammal	ind cranial	fragment		1	0.04	U	none
	large mammal	phalange	distal		1	0.37	U	burn-calc
	large mammal	phalange	fragment		1	0.37	U	burn-calc
	ind mammal	ind tooth	fragment		2	0.58	U	burn-black
	ind mammal	mandible	fragment		7	3.15	U	burn-black
	ind mammal	UID	diaphysis		1	0.92		none
	ind mammal	UID	diaphysis		2	0.50		burn-calc
	ind mammal	UID	diaphysis		5	4.37		none
	ind mammal	UID	diaphysis		2	0.44		burn-black

Provenience	Taxon	Element	Portion	Side	Count	Weight	Fusion	Modification
118 cont.								
	ind mammal	UID	diaphysis		1	0.26	U	none
	ind mammal	UID	diaphysis		1	0.47	U	none
	ind mammal	UID	fragment		1	0.92		none
	ind mammal	UID	fragment		2	0.43		burn-calc
	ind mammal	UID	fragment		5	4.37		none
	ind mammal	UID	fragment		3	1.04		burn-calc
	ind mammal	UID	fragment		5	1.69		burn-black
	ind mammal	UID	fragment		1	0.56		burn-calc
	ind mammal	UID	fragment		7	2.08		none
	ind mammal	UID	fragment		2	0.44		burn-black
	ind mammal	UID	fragment		2	1.07		none
	ind mammal	UID	fragment		1	0.66		none
	ind mammal	UID	fragment		1	0.66		none
	ind mammal	UID	fragment		5	1.14		none
	ind mammal	UID	fragment		2	0.50		burn-calc
	ind mammal	UID	fragment		1	0.26	U	none
	ind mammal	UID	fragment		1	0.47	U	none
	ind bird	UID	diaphysis		2	0.24	U	none
	ind bird	UID	fragment		2	0.24	U	none
	Terrapenne carolina	epiplastron	fragment	L	1	1.17		burn-black
	Terrapenne carolina	epiplastron	lateral	L	1	1.17		burn-black
	Testudines	carapace	fragment		1	0.28	U	burn-calc
	Testudines	carapace/plastron	fragment		3	0.69		none
	Testudines	carapace/plastron	fragment		1	0.28		burn-black
	Testudines	carapace/plastron	fragment		2	0.30		burn-black
	Testudines	carapace/plastron	fragment		3	0.63		burn-black
	Testudines	carapace/plastron	fragment		1	0.11		burn-black
	Testudines	carapace/plastron	fragment		1	0.32		burn-calc
	Testudines	neural	fragment		1	0.07		none
	Colubridae	vertebra, dorsal	complete		1	0.01		burn-calc
	Viperidae	articular	complete	R	1	0.11		none
	Anuran	vertebra, ind	complete		1	0.06		none
	Anuran	humerus	diaphysis	L	1	0.07		none
	Anuran	humerus	proximal	L	1	0.07		none
	Anuran	inominate	acetabulum		1	0.03	U	burn-black
	Anuran	inominate	fragment		1	0.03	U	burn-black
	Bufo	urostyle	complete		1	0.03		none
	Rana	inominate	fragment	L	1	0.05		none
	Rana	inominate	proximal	L	1	0.05		none
	ind fish	pharyngeal	fragment		1	0.01		none
	ind fish	premaxilla	fragment		1	0.13		none
	ind fish	ptergyiophore	fragment		4	0.04		none
	ind fish	rsr	fragment		10	0.10		none
	ind fish	spine	fragment		2	0.02		none
	ind fish	UID	fragment		12	0.05		none
	ind fish	vertebra, abdominal	complete		1	0.01		burn-black
	gastropod	shell/mollusk	fragment		1	0.60		none
	mammal/bird	UID	diaphysis		1	0.28	U	none
	mammal/bird	UID	fragment		1	0.28	U	none
	UID	UID	fragment		4	0.14		burn-black
118 cont.								
	UID	UID	fragment		4	0.63		burn-calc
	UID	UID	fragment		8	0.14		burn-calc
	UID	UID	fragment		23	0.52		none
	UID	UID	fragment		9	1.04		none
	UID	UID	fragment		9	0.86		none
	UID	UID	fragment		1	0.16		none
	UID	UID	fragment		4	0.86		none
	UID	UID	fragment		9	0.74		burn-black
	UID	UID	fragment		4	1.19		burn-calc
	UID	UID	fragment		1	0.31		none
	UID	UID	fragment		5	0.59		none
	UID	UID	fragment		2	0.39	U	burn-calc/bl
	UID	UID	fragment		3	0.16	U	burn-calc
	UID	UID	fragment		4	0.12	U	none
	UID	UID	fragment		2	0.55	U	burn-calc
	UID	UID	fragment		1	0.06	U	burn-black
130	ind mammal	UID	diaphysis		1	0.85		none
	ind mammal	UID	fragment		2	1.12		none
	ind mammal	UID	fragment		1	0.53		none
	ind mammal	UID	fragment		2	0.52		none
	ind mammal	UID	fragment		1	0.85		none
	ind mammal	UID	fragment		1	0.38		none
	Catostomidae	ind cranial	complete	R	1	0.12		none
	Perciformes	operculum	fragment		1	0.03		none
	ind fish	scale	fragment		1	0.01		none
	gastropod	shell/mollusk	fragment		1	0.95		none
	UID	UID	fragment		4	5.18		burn-calc
	UID	UID	fragment		17	5.40		burn-calc
135	*Ursus americanus*	perm molar	complete		1	0.74		none
	Ursus americanus	perm molar	lower		1	0.74		none
	ind mollusc	shell/mollusk	fragment		2	3.19		none
	UID	UID	fragment		18	0.69		burn-calc
438	large mammal	UID	diaphysis		1	9.08		burn-black
702	*Odocoileus virginianus*	fibula	complete	L	1	0.80		none
	Odocoileus virginianus	fibula	distal	L	1	0.80		none
	Odocoileus virginianus	ind tooth	fragment		1	0.33		none
	Odocoileus virginianus	perm premolar	complete		1	1.16		none
	Odocoileus virginianus	perm premolar	upper		1	1.16		none
	Odocoileus virginianus	tibia	diaphysis	L	1	12.52	Y	none
	Odocoileus virginianus	tibia	distal	L	1	12.52	Y	none
	large mammal	UID	diaphysis		2	3.86		burn-black
	large mammal	UID	diaphysis		1	2.13		none
	large mammal	UID	fragment		2	3.86		burn-black
	large mammal	UID	fragment		1	2.13		none
	ind mammal	UID	diaphysis		3	1.34		none
	ind mammal	UID	diaphysis		2	2.54		none
	ind mammal	UID	fragment		24	6.67		burn-calc
	ind mammal	UID	fragment		3	1.34		none
	ind mammal	UID	fragment		2	2.54		none
	ind mammal	UID	fragment		19	7.27		burn-calc

702 cont.								
	ind mammal	UID	fragment		7	3.35		burn-calc
	Terrapenne carolina	peripheral	fragment		1	0.52		none
	Testudines	carapace	fragment		5	1.36		none
	Testudines	carapace/plastron	fragment		2	0.42		none
	Testudines	carapace/plastron	fragment		4	0.56		burn-calc/bl
	UID	UID	fragment		1	0.27		none
705	*Neotoma floridana*	tibia	diaphysis	R	1	0.08	N	none
	Neotoma floridana	tibia	proximal	R	1	0.08	N	none
	Odocoileus virginianus	1st phalange	complete		1	3.60		carnivore
	Odocoileus virginianus	1st phalange	n complete		1	2.90	Y	none
	Odocoileus virginianus	antler	proximal		1	11.61		tool
	Odocoileus virginianus	antler	segment		1	11.61		tool
	Odocoileus virginianus	astragalus	complete	L	1	10.63		none
	Odocoileus virginianus	calcaneus	n complete	L	1	10.10		carnivore
	Odocoileus virginianus	ind tooth	fragment		1	0.14		none
	Sciurus	radius	complete	L	1	0.14	Y	none
	Sciurus	scapula	n complete	R	1	0.11		none
	Sciurus carolinensis	premaxilla	fragment	L	1	0.23		none
	Urocyon cinereoargenteus	parietal	fragment		1	0.16		none
	Urocyon cinereoargenteus	parietal	fragment		1	0.25		none
	small mammal	UID	fragment		6	0.24		none
	large mammal	UID	diaphysis		1	9.51		none
	large mammal	UID	diaphysis		1	7.50		carnivore
	large mammal	UID	diaphysis		1	2.85		none
	large mammal	UID	fragment		1	9.51		none
	large mammal	UID	fragment		1	7.50		carnivore
	large mammal	UID	fragment		1	2.85		none
	ind mammal	UID	diaphysis		3	4.56		none
	ind mammal	UID	fragment		3	4.56		none
	ind mammal	UID	fragment		1	1.28		burn-black
	ind mammal	UID	fragment		11	5.75		none
	ind mammal	UID	fragment		2	0.43		none
	Tyto	UID	diaphysis		2	2.58		carnivore
	Tyto	UID	fragment		2	2.58		carnivore
	Tyto	UID	diaphysis		7	15.31		none
	Tyto	UID	fragment		7	15.31		none
	Tyto	UID	fragment		3	2.07		none
	Tyto	UID	fragment		4	3.81		none
	large bird	UID	diaphysis		2	2.39		none
	large bird	UID	diaphysis		1	1.94		carnivore
	large bird	UID	fragment		2	2.39		none
	large bird	UID	fragment		1	1.94		carnivore
	ind bird	quadrate	n complete	R	1	0.08		none
	ind bird	UID	diaphysis		1	0.92		none
	Sternotherus oderatus	costal	fragment		3	0.66		none
	Terrapenne carolina	peripheral	fragment		1	2.97		none
	Terrapenne carolina	peripheral	fragment	L	1	4.18		burn-black
	Emydidae	carapace	fragment		18	6.34		burn-black
	Emydidae	carapace	fragment		2	1.55		none
	Emydidae	costal	fragment		1	0.64		none
705 cont.								
	Testudines	carapace	fragment		4	1.07		none
	Testudines	carapace	fragment		1	0.54		none
	Testudines	carapace/plastron	fragment		1	0.32		burn-calc
	Testudines	carapace/plastron	fragment		2	0.79		none
	Testudines	carapace/plastron	fragment		4	0.63		none
	Testudines	costal	fragment		1	0.12		none
	Testudines	peripheral	fragment		1	0.30		burn-black
	Testudines	peripheral	fragment		2	1.80		burn-black
	Testudines	plastron	fragment		2	0.46		none
	Ambloplites rupestris	dentary	n complete	R	1	0.03		none
	UID	UID	fragment		1	0.69		none
	UID	UID	fragment		13	5.01		none
	UID	UID	fragment		1	0.10		none
	UID	UID	fragment		11	1.50		none
	UID	UID	fragment		7	0.48		none
	UID	UID	fragment		2	0.59		burn-calc
	UID	UID	fragment		6	0.48		none
	UID	UID	fragment		4	1.06		none
722	ind mammal	UID	fragment		1	0.20		burn-calc
1019	ind mammal	UID	fragment		12	7.11		none
	UID	UID	fragment		1	0.34		burn-calc
	UID	UID	fragment		7	1.46		none
1020	UID	UID	fragment		7	4.85		none
1508	*Canis latrans*	calcaneus	n complete	L	1	0.74		burn-black
	Canis latrans	ind bone	body		2	1.06		none
	Canis latrans	inominate	fragment	L	1	3.23		burn-black
	Canis latrans	inominate	segment	R	1	0.74		burn-black
	Canis latrans	rib	fragment		6	2.26		burn-black
	Canis latrans	rib	fragment		5	2.54		burn-black
	Canis latrans	tibia	body		7	5.69		none
	Cervus canadensis	mandible	articular process/ surface		4	22.02		none
	Odocoileus virginianus	fibula	proximal	L	1	0.79		none
	Odocoileus virginianus	illium	body		1	1.08		none
	Odocoileus virginianus	ind bone	body		2	6.78		none
	Odocoileus virginianus	ind bone	body		1	1.95		cut
	Odocoileus virginianus	ind bone	body		4	2.81		cut
	Odocoileus virginianus	ind bone	body		1	1.78		none
	Odocoileus virginianus	ind bone	ind		9	18.98		burn-black
	Odocoileus virginianus	ind tooth	fragment		6	1.04		none
	Odocoileus virginianus	inominate	fragment		3	10.14		burn-black
	Odocoileus virginianus	inominate	fragment		4	3.61		none
	Odocoileus virginianus	inominate	fragment		1	4.29		none
	Odocoileus virginianus	inominate	process		2	8.24		none
	Odocoileus virginianus	mandible	anterior		1	4.71		burn-black
	Odocoileus virginianus	mandible	anterior	R	1	3.34	N	burn-black
	Odocoileus virginianus	mandible	body		19	13.4		burn-black
	Odocoileus virginianus	mandible	body	L	1	8.24		none
	Odocoileus virginianus	mandible	fragment		5	4.91		burn-black
	Odocoileus virginianus	mandible	fragment		5	4.91		burn-black

1508 cont.							
	Odocoileus virginianus	mandible	fragment		5	4.91	burn-black
	Odocoileus virginianus	mandible	fragment		5	4.91	burn-black
	Odocoileus virginianus	mandible	fragment		1	1.86	none
	Odocoileus virginianus	nasal	n complete	R	1	0.34	none
	Odocoileus virginianus	tibia	distal		5	12.22	none
	Odocoileus virginianus	tibia	distal	L	16	59.47	none
	Odocoileus virginianus	tibia	distal	R	47	51.65	burn-black
	Odocoileus virginianus	vertebra, lumbar	spine		2	1.84	burn-black
	Odocoileus virginianus	vertebra, lumbar	spine		7	2.33	none
	Ondatra zibethica	inominate	fragment		1	0.39	burn-black
	Ursus americanus	mandible	facet	R	23	48.94	burn-black
	ind mammal	ind bone	body		2	3.54	none
	ind mammal	ind bone	body		10	6.58	none
	ind mammal	ind bone	ind		5	1.79	none
	ind mammal	ind bone	ind		59	19.73	burn-calc/bl
	ind mammal	ind bone	ind		2	2.03	cut
	ind mammal	ind bone	ind		1	0.18	burn-black
	ind mammal	ind bone	ind		3	1.44	none
	ind mammal	ind bone	ind		18	3.33	burn-calc/bl
	ind mammal	ind bone	ind		27	9.56	burn-calc/bl
	ind mammal	ind bone	ind		4	1.81	none
	ind mammal	ind bone	ind		17	8.82	none
	ind mammal	ind bone	ind		31	32.5	burn-calc/bl
	ind mammal	ind bone	ind		16	5.25	burn-calc/bl
	ind mammal	ind bone	ind		46	26.84	burn-calc/bl
	ind mammal	ind bone	ind		7	3.27	none
	ind mammal	ind bone	ind		1	0.85	burn-black
	ind mammal	ind bone	ind		1	1.72	none
	ind mammal	ind bone	ind		1	3.88	none
	ind mammal	ind bone	ind		8	0.99	burn-calc/bl
	ind mammal	ind bone	ind		1	1.00	burn-black
	ind mammal	ind bone	ind		5	4.67	burn-black
	Rana catesbeiana	humerus	n complete	R	1	0.06	none
	Rana catesbeiana	humerus	proximal	L	1	0.03	none
	Rana catesbeiana	ind bone	body		2	0.03	none
	Rana catesbeiana	inominate	fragment		1	0.22	burn-calc/bl
	Rana catesbeiana	inominate	n complete	R	1	0.06	none
	Rana catesbeiana	radio-ulna	proximal	R	1	0.05	none
	Rana catesbeiana	scapula	distal	L	1	0.03	none
	Rana catesbeiana	tibio-fibula	n complete	L	1	0.05	none
	ind fish	vertebra, ind	n complete		1	0.07	none
	UID	ind bone	ind		1	7.35	none
	UID	ind bone	ind		5	0.65	none
	UID	ind bone	ind		4	1.64	burn-black
	UID	ind bone	ind		1	6.15	none
	UID	ind bone	ind		25	6.91	burn-calc/bl
	UID	ind bone	ind		1	0.48	none
	UID	ind bone	ind		1	1.78	burn-calc
	UID	ind bone	ind		62	14.75	burn-calc/bl
	UID	ind bone	ind		20	3.76	burn-calc/bl

1508 cont.								
	UID	ind bone	ind		6	0.83		none
	UID	ind bone	ind		23	4.50		burn-black
	UID	ind bone	ind		5	1.00		none
	UID	ind bone	ind		1	0.23		burn-black
	UID	ind bone	ind		2	0.50		none
	UID	ind bone	ind		2	0.41		burn-black
	UID	ind bone	ind		18	2.90		burn-calc
	UID	ind bone	ind		4	0.60		none
	UID	ind bone	ind		17	4.49		none
	UID	ind bone	ind		3	4.49		none
	UID	ind bone	ind		1	0.23		none
	UID	ind bone	ind		3	0.31		none
	UID	ind bone	ind		5	0.65		none
	UID	ind bone	ind		5	0.65		none
	UID	ind bone	ind		1	1.40		burn-bl
	UID	ind bone	ind		1	0.19		none
	UID	ind bone	ind		1	0.29		none
	UID	ind bone	ind		5	0.65		none
	UID	UID	ind		1	8.69		none
	UID	UID	ind		1	6.26		none
2000	UID	UID	fragment		1	0.02	U	burn-calc
	UID	UID	fragment		72	2.66	U	none

Site 40Bt91

391	UID	UID	fragment		1	0.14		none
394	UID	UID	fragment		2	0.19		burn-calc
	UID	UID	fragment		1	0.07		burn-calc
	UID	UID	fragment		3	0.90		burn-calc
438	*Sus scrofa*	tarsal	complete	L	1	8.78		none
	ind mollusc	shell/mollusk	complete		10	1.50		none
	ind mollusc	shell/mollusk	complete		2	0.31		none
497	*Odocoileus virginianus*	perm molar	complete	R	1	2.72		none
	Odocoileus virginianus	radius	diaphysis	R	1	6.38	U	rodent
	Odocoileus virginianus	radius	diaphysis	R	1	6.38	U	carnivore
	Odocoileus virginianus	radius	distal	R	1	6.38	U	carnivore
	Odocoileus virginianus	radius	distal	R	1	6.38	U	rodent
	large mammal	rib	segment		6	3.59		none
	large mammal	vertebra, thoracic	n complete		1	8.19		none
	ind mammal	UID	fragment		3	1.50		none
	ind mammal	UID	fragment		3	3.34		none
	ind mammal	UID	fragment		2	2.23		none
	Meleagris gallopavo	carpometacarpus	complete	L	1	6.34		none
	ind bird	eggshell	fragment		10	0.28		none
	ind bird	eggshell	fragment		27	0.60		none
	ind bird	eggshell	fragment		16	0.21		none
	Testudines	carapace/plastron	fragment		1	0.35		none
	Crotalus horridus	articular	complete	R	1	0.10		none
	Colubridae	vertebra, dorsal	complete		1	0.21		burn-calc
	Colubridae	vertebra, dorsal	complete		2	0.48		burn-black

497 cont.							
	Colubridae	vertebra, dorsal	complete		2	0.59	burn-black
	Colubridae	vertebra, dorsal	complete		2	0.25	burn-calc
	Colubridae	vertebra, dorsal	complete		1	0.14	burn-black
	Colubridae	vertebra, dorsal	n complete		1	0.14	burn-calc
	Anuran	tibio-fibula	complete	L	1	0.26	none
	Anuran	tibio-fibula	complete	R	1	0.08	none
	Anuran	UID	diaphysis		1	0.01	none
	Bufo	urostyle	caudal		1	0.06	none
	Centrarchidae	cleithrum	n complete	R	1	0.03	none
	ind fish	rib	complete		3	0.17	none
	ind fish	rsr	fragment		21	0.26	none
	ind mollusc	shell/mollusk	fragment		3	0.77	none
	UID	UID	fragment		3	0.65	burn-calc
	UID	UID	fragment		2	0.46	none
	UID	UID	fragment		9	1.66	burn-calc
	UID	UID	fragment		13	2.33	burn-calc
	UID	UID	fragment		11	1.23	none
	UID	UID	fragment		10	1.28	burn-calc
	UID	UID	fragment		1	0.11	burn-calc
	UID	UID	fragment		2	0.37	burn-calc
	UID	UID	fragment		3	0.19	none
	UID	UID	fragment		5	0.05	none
	UID	UID	fragment		4	0.49	none
509	UID	1st phalange	fragment		6	0.92	burn-bl
	UID	UID	fragment		12	1.50	burn-calc

References Cited

Abler, Thomas S.
1992 Beavers and muskets: Iroquois military fortunes in the face of European colonization. In *War in the Tribal Zone: Expanding States and Indigenous Warfare*, edited by R. B. Ferguson and N. L. Whitehead, pp. 151–74. School of American Research Press, Santa Fe, New Mexico.

Adair, James
[1775] 1986 *A History of the North American Indians*. Promontory Press, New York.

Allen, John, Doreen Massey, and Allen Cochrane
1998 *Rethinking the Region*. Routledge, New York.

Adams, Jenny
2002 *Groundstone Analysis: A Technological Approach*. University of Utah Press, Salt Lake City.

Andrefsky, William, Jr.
2005 *Lithics: Macroscopic Approaches to Analysis*, 2nd ed. Cambridge University Press, Cambridge.

Baden, William W.
1983 *Tomotley: An Eighteenth Century Cherokee Village*. Report of Investigations 36. Department of Anthropology, University of Tennessee, Knoxville.

Barker, Eirlys M.
1993 "Much Blood and Treasure": South Carolina's Indian Traders, 1670–1755. PhD dissertation, Department of History, College of William and Mary, Virginia.
2001 Indian traders, Charles Town, and London's vital links to the interior of North America, 1717–1755. In *Money, Trade, and Power: The Evolution of Colonial South Carolina's Plantation Society,* edited by J. P. Greene, R. Brana-Shute, and R. J. Sparks, pp. 141–65. University of South Carolina Press, Columbia.

Barnwell, John
1719 *Census of Indians of South Carolina and Nearby, 1715. Records in the British Public Record Office Relating to South Carolina, 1663–1717*, vol. 7, pp. 233–39. Microfilm, Charleston County Public Library, Charleston, South Carolina.

Bartram, William
[1791] 1996 Travels through North and South Carolina, Georgia, east and west Florida, the Cherokee country, the extensive territories of the Muscogulges or Creek Confederacy, and the country of the Chactaws. In *Bartram: Travels and Other Writings*, edited by T. P. Slaughter, pp. 3–426. Literary Classics, New York.

Bass, Quentin R.
1977 Prehistoric Settlement and Subsistence Patterns in the Great Smoky Mountains. Master's thesis, Department of Anthropology, University of Tennessee, Knoxville.

Bates, James F.
1986 Aboriginal ceramic artifacts. In *Overhill Cherokee Archaeology at Chota-Tanasee*, edited by G. F. Schroedl, pp. 289–331. Report of Investigations 38. Department of Anthropology, University of Tennessee, Knoxville.

Bauxar, Joseph J.
1957a Yuchi ethnoarchaeology, Part I: Some Yuchi identifications reconsidered. *Ethnohistory* 4(3):279–301.
1957b Yuchi ethnoarchaeology: Parts II–V. *Ethnohistory* 4(4):369–464.

Baxter, Michael J.
1994 *Exploratory Multivariate Analysis in Archaeology*. Edinburgh University Press, Edinburgh.

Bech, Jens-Henrik
1988 Correspondence analysis and pottery chronology. In *Multivariate Archaeology: Numerical Approaches in Scandinavian Archaeology*, edited by Torsten Madsen, pp. 29–35. Aarhus University Press, Aarhus.

Beck, Robin A., Jr.
2010 Catawba coalescence and the shattering of the Carolina Piedmont, 1540–1675. In *Mapping the Mississippian Shatter Zone: The Colonial Indian Slave Trade and Regional Instability in the American South*, edited by R. Ethridge and S. M. Shuck-Hall, pp. 115–41. University of Nebraska Press, Lincoln.

Bell, Robert E.
1958 *Guide to the Identification of Certain American Indian Projectile Points*. Oklahoma Anthropological Society Memoir no. 2. Norman, Oklahoma.

Bennett, Joanne L.
1999 Thermal alteration of buried bone. *Journal of Archaeological Science* 26:1–8.

Bennett, Monte
1983 Glass trade beads from central New York. In *Proceedings of the 1982 Glass Trade Bead Conference*, edited by C. F. Hayes III, pp. 51–58. Research Records 16. Rochester Museum and Science Center, Rochester, New York.

Bentz, Charles, Jr., and Lance Greene
1991 *Archaeological Investigations at the Site 40BT47: A Multicomponent Site in the Eastern Ridge and Valley of East Tennessee*. Draft report submitted to the Tennessee Department of Transportation, Nashville.

Blakely, Robert L. (editor)
1988 *The King Site: Continuity and Contact in Sixteenth-Century Georgia*. University of Georgia Press, Athens.

Blanton, Richard E.
1994 *Houses and Households: A Comparative Study*. Plenum Press, New York.

Blew, Joseph O., and John W. Kulp
1964 *Service Records on Treated and Untreated Fence Posts*. U.S. Forest Services Research Note FPL-068. Forest Products Laboratory, Forest Service, USDA, Madison, Wisconsin.

Bogan, Arthur E.
1976 A Zooarchaeological Analysis of Vertebrate Remains from Chota-Tanasi, A Historic Cherokee Village in East Tennessee. Master's thesis, Department of Anthropology, University of Tennessee, Knoxville.
1980 A Comparison of Late Prehistoric Dallas and Overhill Cherokee Subsistence Strategies in the Little Tennessee River Valley. PhD dissertation, Department of Anthropology, University of Tennessee, Knoxville.
1982 Archaeological evidence for subsistence patterns in the Little Tennessee River Valley. *Tennessee Anthropologist* 7(1):38–50.

Bogan, Arthur E., Lori LaValley, and Gerald F. Schroedl
1986 Faunal remains. In *Overhill Cherokee Archaeology at Chota-Tanasee*, edited by G. F. Schroedl, pp. 469–514. Report of Investigations no. 38. Department of Anthropology, University of Tennessee, Knoxville.

Bonnefoy, Antoine
[1741] 1916 Journal. In *Travels in the American Colonies*, edited by N. D. Mereness, pp. 239–58. MacMillan Company, New York.

Bourdieu, Pierre
1977 *Outline of a Theory of Practice*. Cambridge University Press. New York.

Bowne, Eric E.
2005 *The Westo Indians: Slave Traders of the Early Colonial South*. University of Alabama Press, Tuscaloosa.
2006 "A bold and warlike people": The basis of Westo power. In *Light on the Path: The Anthropology and History of the Southeastern Indians*, edited by T. J. Pluckhahn and R. Ethridge, pp. 123–32. University of Alabama Press, Tuscaloosa.

Brain, Jeffrey P.
1970 *Archaeological Survey of the Lower Yazoo Basin, Mississippi, 1949–1955*. Research Paper 25. Peabody Museum of American Archaeology and Ethnology, Cambridge, Massachusetts.
1979 *Tunica Treasure*. Papers of the Peabody Museum of Archaeology and Ethnology no. 71. Harvard University, Cambridge, Massachusetts.

Braun, E. Lucy
1950 *Deciduous Forests of Eastern North America*. The Blakiston Company, Garden City, New Jersey.

Braund, Kathryn, E.
1993 *Deerskins and Duffels: The Creek Indian Trade with Anglo-America, 1686–1815*. University of Nebraska Press, Lincoln.

Breitburg, Emanuel
1991 Verification and reliability of NISP and MNI methods of quantifying taxonomic abundance: A view from historic site zooarchaeology. In *Beamers, Bobwhites, and Blue-Points: Tributes to the Career of Paul W. Parmalee*, edited by J. Purdue, W. E. Klippel, and B. W. Styles, pp. 154–62. Illinois State Museum Scientific Papers vol. 23. Illinois State Museum, Springfield.

Briceland, Alan V.
1987 *Westward from Virginia: The Exploration of the Virginia-Carolina Frontier, 1650–1710*. University Press of Virginia, Charlottesville.

Brown, Ian W.
1976 *Glass Beads from the Early 18th-Century Portland Site, Mississippi*. Manuscript on file, Gulf Coast Survey, Alabama Museum of Natural History, Tuscaloosa.
1979 Bells. In *Tunica Treasure*, edited by J. P. Brain, pp. 197–205. Papers of the Peabody Museum of Archaeology and Ethnology no. 71. Harvard University, Cambridge, Massachusetts.

Brown, M. Lee
1980 *Firearms in Colonial America*. Smithsonian Institution Press, Washington, D.C.

Burt, William H., and Richard P. Grossenheider
1980 *A Field Guide to the Mammals of North America*. Peterson Field Guide Series. Houghton Mifflin, Boston, Massachusetts.

Bushnell, Amy T.
1994 *Situado and Sabana: Spain's Support System for the Presidio and Mission Provinces of Florida*. Anthropological Papers no. 74. American Museum of Natural History, New York.

Bushnell, David I., Jr.
1907 Discoveries beyond the Appalachian Mountains in September, 1671. *American Anthropologist* 9(1):45–56.

Butler, William
2000 *Musical Handbells: A Comprehensive History of the Bells and Their Founders*. Phillimore & Co., Chichester, West Sussex.

Cambron, James W., and David C. Hulse
1964 *Handbook of Alabama Archaeology: Part I. Point Types*. Archaeological Research Association of Alabama, Huntsville, Alabama.

Cameron, Catherine M.
1991 Structure abandonment in villages. *Archaeological Method and Theory* 3:115–94.

Carmody, Stephen, and Kandace D. Hollenbach
2008 Plant remains from 31SW393. In *Archaeological Investigations of Sites 31SW393, 31SW451, 31SW459 and 31SW460 in the Great Smoky Mountains National Park, Swain County, North Carolina*, by Michael G. Angst, pp. 132–43. Report submitted to Eastern Band of Cherokee Indians Engineering, Survey, and Design Program. Archaeological Research Laboratory, University of Tennessee, Knoxville.

Carr, Lucien
1895 The food of certain American Indians and their methods of preparing it. *Proceedings of the American Antiquarian Society* 10:155–90.

Casselberry, Samuel E.
1974 Further refinement of formulae for determining population from floor area. *World Archaeology* 6:117–22.

Chapman, Carl H., and Leo O. Anderson
1955 The Campbell site: A Late Mississippi town site and cemetery in southeast Missouri. *Missouri Archaeologist* 17(2–3).

Chapman, Jefferson
1973 *The Icehouse Bottom Site, 40MR23*. Report of Investigations no. 13. University of Tennessee, Department of Anthropology, Knoxville.
1981 *The Bacon Bend and Iddins Sites: The Late Archaic Period in the Lower Little Tennessee River Valley*. Report of Investigations no. 31. Department of Anthropology, University of Tennessee, Knoxville; Publications in Anthropology no. 25. Tennessee Valley Authority, Knoxville.

Chapman, Jefferson, and Robert Newman
1979 Archaeological investigations at the Citico site. In *The 1978 Archaeological Investigations at the Citico Site (40Mr7)*, edited by J. Chapman. Report submitted to the Tennessee Valley Authority, Knoxville.

Chapman, Jefferson, and Andrea Brewer Shea
1981 The archaeobotanical record: Early Archaic period to contact in the lower Little Tennessee River Valley. *Tennessee Anthropologist* 6(1):61–84.

Chicken, George
[1715] 1894 Journal of the march of the Carolinians into the Cherokee Mountains, in the Yemassee Indian War, 1715–1716. In *Year Book. City of Charleston, South Carolina, 1984*, edited by L. Cheves, pp. 324–54.
[1725] 1916 Journal of the commissioner for Indian Affairs on his journey to the Cherokees and his proceedings there. In *Travels in the American Colonies*, edited by N. D. Mereness, pp. 95–174. MacMillan Company, New York.

Clowse, Converse D.
1971 *Economic Beginnings in Colonial South Carolina, 1670–1730*. University of South Carolina Press, Columbia.

Coe, Joffrey L.
1961 Cherokee archaeology. In *The Symposium on Cherokee and Iroquois Culture*, edited by W. N. Fenton and J. Gulick, pp. 51–61. Bureau of American Ethnology Bulletin 180. Smithsonian Institution Press, Washington, D.C.

Collins, Michael
1975 Lithic technology as a means of processual inference. In *Lithic Technology: Making and Using Stone Tools*, edited by Earl Swanson, pp. 14–34. Mouton Publishers, The Hague.

Conant, Roger, and Joseph T. Collins
1991 *A Field Guide to Reptiles and Amphibians of Eastern and Central North America*. Peterson Field Guide Series. Houghton Mifflin, Boston, Massachusetts.

Cook, Sherburne F.
1972 *Prehistoric Demography*. McCaleb Module in Anthropology 16. Addison-Wesley, Reading, Massachusetts.

Corkran, David H.
1962 *The Cherokee Frontier, 1740–1762*. University of Oklahoma Press, Norman.
1967 *The Creek Frontier, 1540–1783*. University of Oklahoma Press, Norman.

Cornett, B. Kenneth
1976 Excavations at Tallassee (40Bt8): An historic Cherokee village site in east Tennessee. *Tennessee Archaeologist* 31:11–19.

Cowan, C. Wesley
1994 The prehistoric use and distribution of maygrass in eastern North America: Cultural phytogeographical implications. In *The Nature and Status of Ethnobotany,* 2nd ed., edited by Richard I. Ford, pp. 289–300. Anthropological Papers, no. 67. Museum of Anthropology, University of Michigan, Ann Arbor.

Cowgill, George L.
1972 Models, methods, and techniques for seriation. In *Models in Archaeology*, edited by D. L. Clarke, pp. 381–424. Methuen, London.

Crane, Verner W.
1916 The Tennessee River as the road to Carolina: The beginnings of exploration and trade. *The Mississippi Valley Historical Review* 3(1):3–18.
[1929] 2004 *The Southern Frontier, 1670–1732*. University of Alabama Press, Tuscaloosa.

Cridlebaugh, Patricia
1981 *The Icehouse Bottom Site 1977 Excavations*. Report of Investigations no. 35. University of Tennessee, Department of Anthropology, Knoxville; Publications in Anthropology no. 34. Tennessee Valley Authority, Knoxville.

Crosby, Alfred W., Jr.
1972 *The Columbian Exchange*. Greenwood Press, Westport, Connecticut.

Cumming, William P.
1998 *The Southeast in Early Maps*, 3rd ed., revised and enlarged by L. DeVorsey, Jr. University of North Carolina Press, Chapel Hill.

Davis, R. P. Stephen, Jr.
1990 *Aboriginal Settlement Patterns in the Lower Tennessee River Valley*. Report of Investigations no. 50. University of Tennessee, Department of Anthropology, Knoxville.
2002 The cultural landscape of the North Carolina piedmont at contact. In *The Transformation of the Southeastern Indians, 1540–1760*, edited by R. Ethridge and C. Hudson, pp. 135–54. University Press of Mississippi, Jackson.

Deagan, Kathleen
1987 *Artifacts of the Spanish Colonies of Florida and the Caribbean, 1500–1800. Volume 1: Ceramics, Glassware, and Beads*. Smithsonian Institution Press, Washington, D.C.

DeBoer, Warren R.
1988 Subterranean storage and the organization of surplus: The view from eastern North America. *Southeastern Archaeology* 7:1–20.

Densmore, Francis
1974 *How Indians Use Wild Plants for Food, Medicine and Crafts*. Reprint, Dover Publications, New York. Originally published 1928, 44th Annual Report, Bureau of American Ethnology, pp. 279–397. Smithsonian Institution, Washington, D.C.

DePratter, Chester B., and Stanley A. South
1990 *Charlesfort: The 1989 Search Project*. Research Manuscript Series 210. South Carolina Institute of Archaeology and Anthropology, Columbia.

Dickens, Roy S., Jr.
1976 *Cherokee Prehistory: The Pisgah Phase in the Appalachian Summit*. University of Tennessee Press, Knoxville.
1979 The origins and development of Cherokee culture. In *The Cherokee Indian Nation: A Troubled History*, edited by D. H. King, pp. 3–32. University of Tennessee Press, Knoxville.
1985 The form, function, and formation of garbage-filled pits on southeastern aboriginal sites: An archaeobotanical analysis. In *Structure and Process in Southeastern Archaeology*, edited by R. S. Dickens, Jr., and H. T. Ward, pp. 34–59. University of Alabama Press, Tuscaloosa.
1986 An evolutionary-ecological interpretation of Cherokee cultural development. In *The Conference on Cherokee Prehistory*, compiled by D. G. Moore, pp. 81–94. Warren Wilson College, Swannanoa, North Carolina.

Dobyns, Henry F.
1983 *Their Number Become Thinned: Native American Population Dynamics in Eastern North America*. University of Tennessee Press, Knoxville.

Drooker, Penelope B.
2002 The Ohio Valley, 1550–1750: Patterns of sociopolitical coalescence and dispersal. In *The Transformation of the Southeastern Indians, 1540–1760*, edited by R. Ethridge and C. Hudson, pp. 115–34. University Press of Mississippi, Jackson.

Duff, Andrew I.
1996 Ceramic micro-seriation: Types or attributes? *American Antiquity* 61:89–101.

Duff, Meaghan N.
2001 Creating a plantation province: Proprietary land policies and early settlement patterns. In *Money, Trade, and Power: The Evolution of Colonial South Carolina's Plantation Society,* edited by J. P. Greene, R. Brana-Shute, and R. J. Sparks, pp. 1–25. University of South Carolina Press, Columbia.

Dunnel, Robert C.
1970 Seriation method and its evaluation. *American Antiquity* 35:305–19.

Dye, David H.
2002 Warfare in the protohistoric Southeast: 1500–1700. In *Between Contacts and Colonies: Archaeological Perspectives on the Protohistoric Southeast*, edited by C. B. Wesson and M. A. Rees, pp. 126–41. University of Alabama Press, Tuscaloosa.

Eastman, Jane,
1999 The Sara and Dan River Peoples: Siouan Communities in North Carolina's Interior Piedmont from A.D. 1000 to A.D. 1700. PhD dissertation, Department of Anthropology, University of North Carolina, Chapel Hill.

Egloff, Brian J.
1967 An Analysis of Ceramics from Historic Cherokee Towns. Master's thesis, Department of Anthropology, University of North Carolina, Chapel Hill.

Egloff, Keith
1980 *Colonial Plantation Hoes of Tidewater Virginia*. Research Report Series, no. 1. Virginia Department of Historic Resources, Richmond.

Emerson, Thomas E.
1997 *Cahokia and the Archaeology of Power*. University of Alabama Press, Tuscaloosa.

Esarey, Duane
2007 The 17th-Century Midwestern Slave Trade in Colonial Context. Paper presented at the 2007 Midwest Archaeological Conference, South Bend, Indiana.

Ethridge, Robbie
2006 Creating the shatterzone: Indian slave traders and the collapse of the southeastern chiefdoms. In *Light on the Path: The Anthropology and History of the Southeastern Indians*, edited by T. J. Pluckhahn and R. Ethridge, pp. 207–18. University of Alabama Press, Tuscaloosa.
2010 Introduction: Mapping the Mississippian shatter zone. In *Mapping the Mississippian Shatter Zone: The Colonial Indian Slave Trade and Regional Instability in the American South*, edited by R. Ethridge and S. M. Shuck-Hall, pp. 1–62. University of Nebraska Press, Lincoln.

Eveleigh, Samuel
1715 Letter to John Boone and Richard Berresford, 19 July 1715. In *Records in the British Public Record Office Relating to South Carolina, 1663–1717*, vol. 6, pp. 103–4. Microfilm, Charleston County Public Library, Charleston, South Carolina.

Faulkner, Charles H., and J. B. Graham
1966 *Westmoreland-Barber Site (40Mi11), Nickajack Reservoir, Season II*. Department of Anthropology, University of Tennessee, Knoxville.

Faulkner, Charles H., and Major C. R. McCollough
1973 *Introductory Report of the Normandy Reservoir Salvage Project: Environmental Setting, Typology, and Survey*. Normandy Archaeological Project, vol. 1, Report of Investigations no. 11. Department of Anthropology, University of Tennessee, Knoxville.

Fenstermaker, Gerald B.
1974 *Susquehanna Iroquois Colored Trade Bead Chart, 1575–1763*. Archaeological Research Booklet 1. Lancaster, Pennsylvania.
1978 *Tennessee Colored Bead Charts*. Archaeological Research Booklet 8. Lancaster, Pennsylvania.

Ferguson, R. Brian, and Neil L. Whitehead
1992 The violent edge of empire. In *War in the Tribal Zone: Expanding States and Indigenous Warfare*, edited by R. B. Ferguson and N. L. Whitehead, pp. 1–30. School of American Research Press, Santa Fe, New Mexico.

Fernald, Merritt Lyndon, and Alfred Charles Kinsey
1943 *Edible Wild Plants of Eastern North America*. Idlewild Press, Cornwall-on-Hudson, New York.

Fitch, Tobias
[1725] 1916 Journey to the Creeks. In *Travels in the American Colonies*, edited by N. D. Mereness, pp. 175–214. MacMillan Company, New York.

Fithian, Charles
1985 Firearms and their accoutrements in 17th century Chesapeake (Abstract). In *Proceedings of the 1984 Trade Gun Conference*, edited by C. F. Hayes III and J. P. Puype, p. 105. Research Records 18, Part II. Rochester Museum and Science Center, Rochester, New York.

Fleming, Victor K.
1976 Historic Aboriginal Occupation of the Guntersville Basin, Alabama. Master's thesis, Department of Anthropology, University of Alabama, Tuscaloosa.

Franklin, W. Neil
1932 *Virginia and the Cherokee Indian Trade, 1673–1752*. Publication no. 4. East Tennessee Historical Society, Knoxville.

Fritz, Gayle J., Virginia Drywater Whitekiller, and James W. McIntosh
2001 Ethnobotany of Ku-Nu-Che: Cherokee hickory nut soup. *Journal of Ethnobiology* 21(2):1–27.

Gallay, Alan
2002 *The Indian Slave Trade: The Rise of the English Empire in the American South, 1670–1717*. Yale University Press, New Haven, Connecticut.

Galloway, Patricia K.
1995 *Choctaw Genesis, 1500–1700*. University of Nebraska Press, Lincoln.
2002 Colonial period transformations in the Mississippi Valley: Disintegration, alliance, confederation, playoff. In *The Transformation of the Southeastern Indians, 1540–1760*, edited by R. Ethridge and C. Hudson, pp. 225–248. University Press of Mississippi, Jackson.

Gardner, Paul S.
1997 The ecological structure and behavioral implications of mast exploration strategies. In *People, Plants and Landscapes: Studies in Paleoethnobotany*, edited by Kristen J. Gremillion, pp. 161–78. University of Alabama Press, Tuscaloosa.

Gearing, Fred
1962 *Priests and Warriors: Structures for Cherokee Politics in the Eighteenth Century*. Memoir 93. American Anthropological Association, Washington, D.C.

Gibson, Susan G. (editor)
1980 *Burr's Hill: A 17th Century Wampanoag Burial Ground in Warren, Rhode Island*. Studies in Anthropology and Material Culture, vol. 2. Haffenreffer Museum of Anthropology, Brown University, Providence, Rhode Island.

Gilbert, William H., Jr.
1943 *The Eastern Cherokee*. Bureau of American Ethnology Bulletin 133. Smithsonian Institution, Washington, D.C.

Gilmore, Melvin R.
1932 Some Chippewa uses of plants. *Papers of the Michigan Academy of Science, Arts, and Letters* 17:119–43.

Gleeson, Paul (editor)
1969 *Archaeological Investigations in the Tellico Reservoir: Interim Report, 1969*. Report of Investigations 8. Department of Anthropology, University of Tennessee, Knoxville.

Good, Mary E.
1972 *Guebert Site: An Eighteenth Century Historic Kaskaskia Indian Village*. Memoirs no. 2. Central States Archaeological Societies, Inc., Wood River, Illinois.
1983 A comparison of glass beads from Upper Creek Indian towns in the Southeast and Oklahoma. In *Proceedings of the 1982 Glass Trade Bead Conference*, edited by C. F. Hayes III, pp. 159–66. Research Records 16. Rochester Museum and Science Center, Rochester, New York.

Grayson, Donald K.
1979 On the quantification of vertebrate archaeofaunas. In *Advances in Archaeological Method and Theory*, vol. 2, edited by M. B. Schiffer, pp. 200–238. Academic Press, New York.
1984 *Quantitative Zooarchaeology*. Academic Press, New York.

Greene, Jack P.
1989 Early South Carolina and the psychology of British colonization. In *Selling a New World: Two Colonial South Carolina Promotional Pamphlets*, edited by J. P. Greene, pp. 1–32. University of South Carolina Press, Columbia.

Gremillion, Kristen J.
1993 Adoption of Old World crops and processes of cultural change in the historic Southeast. *Southeastern Archaeology* 12(1):15–20.
1981 Why Hopewell cores and bladelets? *Ohio Archaeologist* 31:18–19.

Grubb, Thomas C.
1981 Why Hopewell cores and bladelets? *Ohio Archaeologist* 31:18–19.

Guthe, Alfred K., and E. Marian Bistline
1981 *Excavations at Tomotley, 1973–74, and the Tuskegee Area: Two Reports*. Report of Investigations 24. Department of Anthropology, University of Tennessee, Knoxville.

Haan, Richard L.
1981 The "Trade Do's Not Flourish as Formerly": The ecological origins of the Yamassee War of 1715. *Ethnohistory* 28:341–58.

Hahn, Steven C.
2002 The mother of necessity: Carolina, the Creek Indians, and the making of a new order in the American Southeast, 1670–1763. In *The Transformation of the Southeastern Indians, 1540–1760*, edited by R. Ethridge and C. Hudson, pp. 79–114. University Press of Mississippi, Jackson.

Hally, David J.
1986a The Cherokee archaeology of Georgia. In *The Conference on Cherokee Prehistory*, compiled by D. G. Moore, pp. 95–121. Warren Wilson College, Swannanoa, North Carolina.
1986b The identification of vessel function: A case study from northwest Georgia. *American Antiquity* 51:267–95.
1988 Archaeology and settlement plan of the King site. In *The King Site: Continuity and Contact in Sixteenth-Century Georgia*, edited by R. L. Blakely, pp. 3–16. University of Georgia Press, Athens.
1994 An overview of Lamar archaeology. In *Ocmulgee Archaeology, 1936–1986*, edited by D. J. Hally, pp. 144–74. University of Georgia Press, Athens.
2002 As caves beneath the ground: Making sense of aboriginal house form in the protohistoric and historic Southeast. In *Between Contact and Colonies: Archaeological Perspectives on the Protohistoric Southeast,* edited by C. B. Wesson and M. A. Rees, pp. 90–109. University of Alabama Press, Tuscaloosa.

Hamel, Paul B., and Mary U. Chiltoskey
1975 *Cherokee Plants and Their Uses—A 400 Year History*. Herald Publishing Company, Sylva, North Carolina.

Harmon, Michael A.
1986 *Eighteenth-Century Lower Cherokee Adaptation and Use of European Material Culture*. Volumes in Historical Archaeology 2. South Carolina Institute of Archaeology and Anthropology, Columbia.

Hassan, Fekri A.
1981 *Demographic Archaeology*. Academic Press, New York.

Hatch, James W.
1995 Lamar period upland farmsteads of the Oconee River Valley, Georgia. In *Mississippian Communities and Households*, edited by J. D. Rogers and B. D. Smith, pp. 135–55. University of Alabama Press, Tuscaloosa.

Hatley, M. Thomas
1995 *The Dividing Paths: Cherokees and South Carolinians Through the Era of Revolution*. Oxford University Press, Oxford.

Havard, V.
1896 Drink plants of the North American Indians. *Bulletin of the Torrey Botanical Club* 23(2):33–46.

Herbert, John
[1727] 1936 Journal. In *Journal of Colonel John Herbert Commissioner of Indian Affairs for the Province of South Carolina, October 17, 1727, to March 19, 1727/8*, edited by A. S. Salley, pp. 4–29. Historical Commission of South Carolina, Columbia.

Heye, George G., Frederick W. Hodge, and George H. Pepper
1918 *The Nacoochee Mound in Georgia*. Contributions from the Museum of the American Indian 4(3):1–103. Heye Foundation, New York.

Hicks, Charles
1826 Letter to John Ross, February 1, 1826. In *Traditions and History of the Cherokee Indians to 1776*, vol. VII, by J. H. Payne, pp. 1–4. Microfilm on file at the Davis Library, University of North Carolina, Chapel Hill.

Howard, A. Eric
1997 *An Intrasite Spatial Analysis of Surface Collections at Chattooga: A Lower Town Cherokee Village*. Report submitted to the United States Forest Service, Francis Marion, and Sumter National Forests, South Carolina.

Howell, Cameron
2005 Overhill Pottery from the Townsend Site. Paper presented at the Cherokee Ceramics Workshop, Research Laboratories of Archaeology, University of North Carolina, Chapel Hill.

Hudson, Charles
1976 *The Southeastern Indians*. University of Tennessee Press, Knoxville.
2002 Introduction. In *The Transformation of the Southeastern Indians, 1540–1760*, edited by R. Ethridge and C. Hudson, pp. xi–xxxix. University Press of Mississippi, Jackson.

Huey, Paul R.
1983 Glass trade beads from Fort Orange, Albany, New York c. A.D. 1624–1676. In *Proceedings of the 1982 Glass Trade Bead Conference*, edited by C. F. Hayes III, pp. 83–110. Research Records 16. Rochester Museum and Science Center, Rochester, New York.

Hughes, Pryce
1713 Letter to the Dutchess of Ormond, October 15, 1713. In *Five Pryce Hughes Autograph Letters, Proposing a Welsh Colony*. South Caroliniana Library, University of South Carolina, Columbia.

Jenkins, Ned J.
1981 *Gainesville Lake Ceramic Description and Chronology. Archaeological Investigations in the Gainesville Lake Area of the Tennessee-Tombigbee Waterway, Volume 2*. Report of Investigations 12. Office of Archaeological Research, University of Alabama, Moundville.

Jennings, Matthew H.
2010 Violence in a shattered world. In *Mapping the Mississippian Shatter Zone: The Colonial Indian Slave Trade and Regional Instability in the American South*, edited by R. Ethridge and S. M. Shuck-Hall, pp. 272–94. University of Nebraska Press, Lincoln.

Jeter, Marvin D.
2002 From prehistory through protohistory to ethnohistory in and near the northern lower Mississippi Valley. In *The Transformation of the Southeastern Indians, 1540–1760*, edited by R. Ethridge and C. Hudson, pp. 177–223. University Press of Mississippi, Jackson.

Johannessen, Sissel
1993 Food, dishes, and society in the Mississippi Valley. In *Foraging and Farming in the Eastern Woodlands*, edited by C. Margaret Scarry, pp. 182–205. University Press of Florida, Gainesville.

Johnson, Jay K.
1987 Cahokia core technology in Mississippi: The view from the South. *In The Organization of Core Technology*, edited by J. Johnson and C. Morrow, pp. 187–205. Westview Press, Boulder, Colorado.

Johnson, Nathaniel, Thomas Broughton, Robert Gibbs, George Smith, and Richard Beresford
1708 *Census. Records in the British Public Record Office Relating to South Carolina, 1663–1717*, vol. 2, pp. 203–9. Microfilm, Charleston County Public Library, Charleston, South Carolina.

Joyce, Arthur, and Sissel Johannessen
1993 Abandonment and the production of archaeological variability at domestic sites. In *Abandonment of Settlements and Regions: Ethnoarchaeological and Archaeological Approaches,* edited by C. M. Cameron and S. A. Tomka, pp. 138–56. Cambridge University Press, Cambridge.

Justice, Noel D.
1987 *Stone Age Spear and Arrow Points of the Midcontinental and Eastern United States*. Indiana University Press, Bloomington.

Karklins, Karlis
1985 Guide to the description and classification of glass beads. In *Glass Beads*, 2nd ed., pp. 85–118. Studies in Archaeology, Architecture, and History. Parks Canada, Ottawa.

Kauffman, Henry J.
[1972] 1994 *American Axes: A Survey of their Development and their Makers*. Olde Springfield Shoppe, Elverson, Pennsylvania.

Kavasch, Barrie
1977 *Native Harvests: Botanicals and Recipes of the American Indian*. American Indian Archaeological Institute, Washington, Connecticut.

Keel, Bennie C.
1976 *Cherokee Archaeology: A Study of the Appalachian Summit*. University of Tennessee Press, Knoxville.

Kelly, Arthur R., and Clemens de Baillou
1960 Excavations of the presumptive site of Estatoe. *Southern Indian Studies* 12:3–30.

Kelly, Arthur R., and Robert S. Neitzel
1961 *The Chauga Site in Oconee County, South Carolina*. Laboratory of Archaeology Report 3. University of Georgia, Athens.

Kelton, Paul
2002 The great southeastern smallpox epidemic, 1696–1700: The region's first major epidemic. In *The Transformation of the Southeastern Indians*, edited by R. Ethridge and C. Hudson, pp. 21–37. University Press of Mississippi, Jackson.

2010 Shattered and infected: Epidemics and the origins of the Yamasee War, 1696–1715. In *Mapping the Mississippian Shatter Zone: The Colonial Indian Slave Trade and Regional Instability in the American South*, edited by R. Ethridge and S. M. Shuck-Hall, pp. 312–32. University of Nebraska Press, Lincoln.

Kendall, David G.
1971 Seriation from abundance matrices. In *Mathematics in the Archaeological and Historical Sciences*, edited by F. R. Hodson, David G. Kendall, and P. Tautu, pp. 215–52. Edinburgh University Press, Edinburgh.

Kent, Barry C.
1983 The Susquehanna bead sequence. In *Proceedings of the 1982 Glass Trade Bead Conference*, edited by Charles F. Hayes III, pp. 75–82. Research Records 16. Rochester Museum and Science Center, Rochester, New York.

Kenyon, Ian T., and Thomas Kenyon
1983 Comments on seventeenth century glass trade beads from Ontario. In *Proceedings of the 1982 Glass Trade Bead Conference*, edited by C. F. Hayes III, pp. 59–74. Research Records 16. Rochester Museum and Science Center, Rochester, New York.

Kidd, Kenneth E., and Martha A. Kidd
1970 *A Classification for Glass Beads for the Use of Field Archaeologists*. Occasional Papers in Archaeology and History 1:45–89. Canadian Historic Sites, Ottawa.

Kimball, Larry
1992 *The Function of Hopewell Blades from the Southeast*. Research Notes no. 2. McClung Museum, Knoxville, Tennessee.

King, Duane H.
1977 Vessel morphology and eighteenth-century Overhill ceramics. *Journal of Cherokee Studies* 2:154–69.

Kintigh, Keith W., and Albert Ammerman
1982 Heuristic approaches to spatial analysis in archaeology. *American Antiquity* 47:41–63.

Klein, Richard G., and Kathyrn Cruz-Uribe
1984 *The Analysis of Animal Bones from Archaeological Sites*. University of Chicago Press, Chicago.

Klinck, Carl F.
1970 Biographical introduction. In *The Journal of Major John Norton, 1816*, edited by C. F. Klinck and J. J. Talman, pp. xiii–xcviii. The Champlain Society, Toronto.

Knight, Vernon James, Jr.
1975 Some observations concerning plant materials and aboriginal smoking in eastern North America. *Journal of Alabama Archaeology* 21(2):120–44.
1985 *Tukabatchee: Archaeological Investigations at an Historic Creek Town, Elmore County, Alabama, 1984*. Report of Investigations 45. Office of Archaeological Research, Alabama State Museum of Natural History, University of Alabama, Tuscaloosa.
1994 The formation of the Creeks. In *The Forgotten Centuries: Indians and European in the American South, 1521–1704*, edited by C. Hudson and C. C. Tesser, pp. 373–92. University of Georgia Press, Athens.

Koldehoff, Brad, and Joseph M. Galloy
2006 Late Woodland frontiers in the American bottom region. *Southeastern Archaeology* 25:275–300.

Kowalewski, Stephen A.
2006 Coalescent societies. In *Light on the Path: The Anthropology and History of the Southeastern Indians*, edited by T. J. Pluckhahn and R. Ethridge, pp. 94–122. University of Alabama Press, Tuscaloosa.

Krzyzewski, J. C., C. Ralph, and B. Spicer
1980 *Performance of Preservative-treated Fence Posts After 43 Years of Tests*. Eastern Forest Products Laboratory, Environment Canada. Report submitted to Forintek Canada Corp., Ottawa.

Kuhnlein, Harriet V., and Nancy J. Turner
1991 *Traditional Plant Foods of Canadian Indigenous Peoples: Nutrition, Botany and Use*. Gordon and Breach Science Publishers, Philadelphia.

Lacquement, Cameron H.
2004 How to Build a Mississippian House: A Study of Domestic Architecture in West-Central Alabama. Master's thesis, Department of Anthropology, University of Alabama, Tuscaloosa.

Lafferty, Robert H.
1981 *The Phipps Bend Archaeological Project*. Research Series no. 4. Office of Archaeological Research, University of Alabama, Tuscaloosa.

Law, Robin
1992 Warfare on the west African slave coast, 1650–1850. In *War in the Tribal Zone: Expanding States and Indigenous Warfare*, edited by R. B. Ferguson and N. L. Whitehead, pp. 103–26. School of American Research Press, Santa Fe, New Mexico.

Le Jau, Francis
[1708] 1956 Letter to the Secretary, April 22, 1708. In *The Carolina Chronicle of Dr. Francis Le Jau, 1706–1717*, edited by F. J. Klingberg, pp. 37–41. University of California Publications in History vol. 53. University of California Press, Berkeley.
[1713] 1956 Letter to the Secretary, August 10, 1713. In *The Carolina Chronicle of Dr. Francis Le Jau, 1706–1717*, edited by F. J. Klingberg, pp. 132–35. University of California Publications in History vol. 53. University of California Press, Berkeley.
[1715] 1956a Letter to the Secretary, October 3, 1715. In *The Carolina Chronicle of Dr. Francis Le Jau, 1706–1717*, edited by F. J. Klingberg, pp. 165–68. University of California Publications in History vol. 53. University of California Press, Berkeley.
[1715] 1956b Letter to the Secretary, November 28, 1715. In *The Carolina Chronicle of Dr. Francis Le Jau, 1706–1717*, edited by F. J. Klingberg, pp. 169–71. University of California Publications in History vol. 53. University of California Press, Berkeley.

Lengyel, Stacey N.
2004 Archaeomagnetic Research in the U.S. Midcontinent. PhD dissertation, Department of Anthropology, University of Arizona, Tucson.

Lewis, Thomas M. N., and Madeline D. Kneberg
1946 *Hiwassee Island: An Archaeological Account of Four Tennessee Indian Peoples*. University of Tennessee Press, Knoxville.

Lewis, Thomas M. N., Madeline D. Kneberg, and Lynne P. Sullivan
1995 *The Prehistory of the Chickamauga Basin*. University of Tennessee Press, Knoxville.

Lightfoot, Kent G., Antoinette Martinez, and Ann M. Schiff
1998 Daily practice and material culture in pluralistic social settings: An archaeological study of culture change and persistence from Fort Ross, California. *American Antiquity* 63:199–222.

Lyman, R. Lee
1994 *Vertebrate Taphonomy*. Cambridge University Press, Cambridge.

MacLean, J. D.
1926 *Service Tests on Treated and Untreated Fence Posts*, pp. 401–23. Proceedings of the American Wood-Preservers' Association.

Madsen, Torsten
1988 Multivariate statistics and archaeology. In *Multivariate Archaeology: Numerical Approaches in Scandinavian Archaeology*, edited by T. Madsen, pp. 7–27. Aarhus University Press, Aarhus.

Mainfort, Robert C., Jr.
2005 A K-means analysis of late period ceramic variation in the central Mississippi Valley. *Southeastern Archaeology* 24:59–69.

Marcoux, Jon B.
2008 Cherokee Households and Communities in the English Contact Period, A.D. 1670–1740. PhD dissertation, Department of Anthropology, University of North Carolina, Chapel Hill.
2010 *Pox, Empire, Shackles, and Hides: The Townsend Site, 1670–1715*. University of Alabama Press, Tuscaloosa.

Martin, Alexander C., and William D. Barkley
1961 *Seed Identification Manual*. University of California, Berkeley.

Martin, Joel W.
1994 Southeastern Indians and the English trade in skins and slaves. In *The Forgotten Centuries: Indians and Europeans in the American South, 1521–1704*, edited by C. Hudson and C. C. Tesser, pp. 304–24. University of Georgia Press, Athens.

Mathew, A. J., A. J. Woods, and C. Oliver
1997 Spots before the eyes: New comparison charts for visual percentage estimation in archaeological material. In *Recent Developments in Ceramic Petrology*, edited by A. Middleton and I. Freestone, pp. 211–263. Occasional Paper no. 81. British Museum, London.

McCutcheon, Patrick T.
1992 Burned archaeological bone. In *Deciphering a Shell Midden*, edited by Julie K. Stein, pp. 347–70. Academic Press, New York.

McDowell, William L., Jr. (editor)
1992 *Journals of the Commissioners of the Indian Trade, September 20, 1710–August 29, 1718*. South Carolina Department of Archives and History, Columbia.

McEwan, Bonnie G.
1993 *The Spanish Missions of La Florida*. University Press of Florida, Gainesville.

McGill, Robert, John W. Tukey, and Wayne A. Larsen
1978 Variations of box plots. *The American Statistician* 32:12–16.

McIntosh, Roderick J.
1974 Archaeology and mud wall decay in a West African village. *World Archaeology* 6:154–71.

McNutt, Charles H.
2005 Seriation: Classic problems and multivariate applications. *Southeastern Archaeology* 24:209–22.

Medsger, Oliver Perry
1972 *Edible Wild Plants*. Collier Books, New York.

Merrell, John H.
1989a *The Indians' New World: Catawbas and Their Neighbors from European Contact through the Era of Removal*. University of North Carolina Press, Chapel Hill.
1989b "Our Bond of Peace": Patterns of intercultural exchange in the Carolina piedmont, 1650–1750. In *Powhatan's Mantle: Indians in the Colonial Southeast,* edited by P. H. Wood, G. A. Waselkov, and M. T. Hatley, pp. 196–222. University of Nebraska Press, Lincoln.

Milner, George R.
1980 Epidemic disease in the postcontact Southeast: A reappraisal. *Midcontinental Journal of Archaeology* 5:39–56.

Milner, George, Scott Hammerstedt, and Kirk French
2010 Chert hoes as digging tools. *Antiquity* 84:103–13.

Moerman, Daniel E.
2004 *Native American Ethnobotany: Database of Foods, Drugs, Dyes and Fibers of Native American Peoples, Derived from Plants*. http://herb.umd.umich.edu/. Accessed March 20, 2007.

Mooney, James
1900 *Myths of the Cherokee*. Bureau of American Ethnology Annual Report 19:1–576. Smithsonian Institution, Washington, D.C.

Moore, Alexander
1988 Introduction. In *Nairne's Muskhogean Journals: The 1708 Expedition to the Mississippi River*, edited by A. Moore, pp. 1–31. University Press of Mississippi, Jackson.

Moore, Jerry D., and Janine Gasco
1990 Perishable structures and serial dwellings from coastal Chiapas. *Ancient Mesoamerica* 1:205–12.

Morey, Darcy, and Walter Klippel
1991 Canid scavenging and deer bone survivorship at an Archaic period site in Tennessee. *Archaeozoologia* 4(1):11–28.

Morris, Ernest
1959 *Tintinnabula: Small Bells*. Robert Hale, London.

Morrow, Carol A.
1987 Blades and Cobden chert: A technological argument for their role as markers of regional identification during the Hopewell period in Illinois. In *The Organization of Core Technology*, edited by J. Johnson and C. Morrow, pp. 119–49. Westview Press, Boulder, Colorado.

Muller, John
1997 *Mississippian Political Economy*. Plenum Press, New York.

Myer, William E.
1928 *Indian Trails of the Southeast*. Bureau of American Ethnology Annual Report 42. Smithsonian Institution, Washington, D.C.

Nairne, Thomas
[1708] 1988 Thomas Nairne's memorial to Charles Spencer, Earl of Sunderland. In *Nairne's Muskhogean Journals: The 1708 Expedition to the Mississippi River*, edited by A. Moore, pp. 73–79. University Press of Mississippi, Jackson.
[1710] 1989 A letter from South Carolina. In *Selling a New World: Two Colonial South Carolina Promotional Pamphlets*, edited by J. P. Greene, pp. 33–76. University of South Carolina Press, Columbia.

Nash, R. C.
2001 The organization of trade and finance in the Atlantic economy: Britain and South Carolina, 1670–1775. In *Money, Trade, and Power: The Evolution of Colonial South Carolina's Plantation Society,* edited by J. P. Greene, R. Brana-Shute, and R. J. Sparks, pp. 74–107. University of South Carolina Press, Columbia.

Neusius, Sarah W.
2007 Game procurement among temperate horticulturalists: The case for garden hunting by the Dolores Anasazi. In *Case Studies in Environmental Archaeology*, 2nd ed., edited by Elizabeth Reitz, C. Margaret Scarry, and Sylvia J. Scudder, pp. 297–314. Springer, New York.

Newman, Robert D.
1986 Euro-American artifacts. In *Overhill Cherokee Archaeology at Chota-Tanasee*, by Gerald F. Schroedl, pp. 415–68. Report of Investigations 38. Department of Anthropology, University of Tennessee, Knoxville.

Noël Hume, Ivor
1969 *A Guide to Artifacts of Colonial America*. Vintage Books, New York.

Norris, John
[1712] 1989 Profitable advice for rich and poor. *In Selling a New World: Two Colonial South Carolina Promotional Pamphlets*, edited by J. P. Greene, pp. 77–147. University of South Carolina Press, Columbia.

Norton, John
[1816] 1970 Journal. In *The Journal of Major John Norton, 1816*, edited by C. F. Klinck and J. J. Talman, pp. 1–370. The Champlain Society, Toronto.

Oatis, Steven J.
2004 *A Colonial Complex: South Carolina's Frontiers in the Era of the Yamasee War, 1680–1730*. University of Nebraska Press, Lincoln.

Odell, George
1994 The role of stone bladelets in Middle Woodland society. *American Antiquity* 59:102–20.
1998 Axe/adze. In *Archaeology of Prehistoric Native America: An Encyclopedia*, edited by Guy Gibbon. Garland Publishing, Inc., New York.

Orton, Clive, Paul Tyers, and Alan Vince
1993 *Pottery in Archaeology*. Cambridge University Press, Cambridge.

Page, Lawrence M., and Brooks M. Burr
1991 *A Field Guide to Freshwater Fishes: North America North of Mexico*. Peterson Field Guide Series. Houghton Mifflin, Boston, Massachusetts.

Palmer, Edward
1871 *Food Products of the North American Indians*. *Report of the Commission for 1870,* pp. 404–28. U.S. Department of Agriculture, Washington, D.C.

Pauketat, Timothy R.
1989 Monitoring Mississippian homestead occupation span and economy using ceramic refuse. *American Antiquity* 54:288–310.
2003 Resettled farmers and the making of a Mississippian polity. *American Antiquity* 68(1):39–66.

Payne, John H.
n.d. *Traditions and History of the Cherokee Indians to 1776*, vol. III. Microfilm on file at the Davis Library, University of North Carolina, Chapel Hill.

Pearsall, Deborah M.
2000 *Paleoethnobotany: A Handbook of Procedures*, 2nd ed. Academic Press, San Diego.

Pennington, Edgar L.
1931 The South Carolina Indian War of 1715, as seen by the clergymen. *South Carolina Historical and Genealogical Magazine* 32(4):251–69.

Perdue, Theda
1998 *Cherokee Women: Gender and Culture Change, 1700–1835*. University of Nebraska Press, Lincoln.

Perino, Gregory
1966 *The Banks Village Site, Crittenden County, Arkansas*. Memoir No. 4. Missouri Archaeological Society, Columbia.

Perttula, Timothy K.
2002 Social changes among the Caddo Indians in the sixteenth and seventeenth centuries. In *The Transformation of the Southeastern Indians, 1540–1760*, edited by R. Ethridge and C. Hudson, pp. 249–70. University Press of Mississippi, Jackson.

Peterson, Lee Allen
1977 *Edible Wild Plants of Eastern and Central North America*. Houghton Mifflin, New York.

Peterson, R. Tory
1980 *A Field Guide to the Birds: A Complete New Guide to All the Birds of Eastern and Central North America*. Peterson Field Guide Series. Houghton Mifflin, Boston, Massachusetts.

Phillips, Phillip, James A. Ford, and James B. Griffin
1951 *Archaeological Survey in the Lower Mississippi Alluvial Valley, 1940–1947*. Papers of the Peabody Museum of American Archaeology and Ethnology, vol. 25. Harvard University, Cambridge, Massachusetts.

Piker, Joshua
2004 *Okfuskee: A Creek Indian Town in Colonial America*. Harvard University Press, Cambridge.

Pluckhahn, Thomas J.
1996 Beads, pendants, and buttons from early historic Creek contexts at the Tarver sites, Georgia. *Beads* 8–9:45–66.
1997 *Archaeological Investigation of the Tarver (9Jo6) and Little Tarver (9Jo198) Sites, Jones County, Georgia*. Southeastern Archaeological Service, Inc. Report submitted to the Federal Emergency Management Agency.

Polhemus, Richard
1983 Tennessee bead seriation (Abstract). In *Proceedings of the 1982 Glass Trade Bead Conference*, edited by C. F. Hayes III, pp. 145. Research Records 16. Rochester Museum and Science Center, Rochester, New York.
1985 Beads from Santa Elena (1984 season). In *Excavation of the Casa Fuerte and Wells at Ft. San Felipe, 1984*, by S. A. South, pp. 145–55. Research Manuscript Series no. 196. South Carolina Institute of Archaeology and Anthropology, Columbia.
1987 *The Toqua Site:A Late Mississippian Dallas Village*. Report of Investigations no. 41. Department of Anthropology, University of Tennessee, Knoxville; Publications in Anthropology no. 44. Tennessee Valley Authority, Knoxville.

Powers, Stephen
1873–1874 Aboriginal botany. *Proceedings of the California Academy of Sciences* 5:373–79.

Price, F. G. Hilton
1908 *Old Base Metal Spoons with Illustrations and Marks*. Society of Antiquaries, London.

Purslow, D. F.
1976 *Results of Field Tests on the Natural Durability of Timber (1932–1975)*. Building Research Establishment Current Paper 6/76. Department of the Environment, London.

Puype, Jan P.
1985 Dutch and other flintlocks from seventeenth century Iroquois sites. In *Proceedings of the 1984 Trade Gun Conference,* edited by C. F. Hayes III and J. P. Puype, pp. 1–119. Research Records 18, Part I. Rochester Museum and Science Center, Rochester, New York.

Radford, Albert E., Harry E. Ahles, and C. Ritchie Bell
1964 *Manual of the Vascular Flora of the Carolinas*. University of North Carolina Press, Chapel Hill.

Ramsey, James G. M.
[1853] 1999 *The Annals of Tennessee to the End of the Eighteenth Century*. Overmountain Press, Johnson City, Tennessee.

Ramsey, William L.
2001 "All & Singular the Slaves": A demographic profile of slavery in colonial South Carolina. In *Money, Trade, and Power: The Evolution of Colonial South Carolina's Plantation Society,* edited by J. P. Greene, R. Brana-Shute, and R. J. Sparks, pp. 166–86. University of South Carolina Press, Columbia.
2003 "Something Cloudy in Their Looks": The origins of the Yamasee War reconsidered. *The Journal of American History* 90:44–75.

Reid, John P.
1976 *A Better Kind of Hatchet: Law, Trade, and Diplomacy in the Cherokee Nation during the Early Years of European Contact*. Pennsylvania State University Press, University Park.

Reitz, Elizabeth J., and C. Margaret Scarry
1985 *Reconstructing Historic Spanish Subsistence with an Example from Sixteenth Century Spanish Florida*. Special Publications Series 3. Society for Historical Archaeology, Glassboro, New Jersey.

Reitz, Elizabeth J., and Elizabeth S. Wing
1999 *Zooarchaeology*. Cambridge University Press, Cambridge.

Riggs, Brett H.
1989 Ethnohistorical and archaeological dimensions of early nineteenth-century Cherokee intrahousehold variation. In *Households and Communities*, edited by S. MacEachern, D. Archer, and R. Garvin, pp. 328–38. Archaeological Association of the University of Calgary, Proceedings of the Chacmool Conference 21, Calgary.
1999 Removal Period Cherokee Households in Southwestern North Carolina: Material Perspectives on Ethnicity and Cultural Differentiation. PhD dissertation, Department of Anthropology, University of Tennessee, Knoxville.
in press Chestowee reconsidered. In *"One of the Other Nations": Yuchi Indian Histories Before the Removal Era*, edited by J. B. Jackson. University of Nebraska Press, Lincoln.

Riggs, Brett H., and Christopher B. Rodning
2002 Cherokee ceramic traditions of southwestern North Carolina. *North Carolina Archaeology* 51:34–54.

Riggs, Brett H., M. Scott Shumate, and Patti Evans-Shumate
1997 *Archaeological Data Recovery at Site 31JK291, Jackson County, North Carolina*. Report submitted to the Eastern Band of Cherokee Indians, Office of Cultural Resources, Cherokee, North Carolina.

Rigney, Phyllis
2009 Usewear Analysis of Flake Tools from the Townsend Project (Sites 40BT89, 40BT90, 40BT91, and 40BT94), Blount County, Tennessee. Master's thesis, University of Tennessee, Knoxville.

Ringrose, Trevor
1993 Bone counts and statistics: A critique. *Journal of Archaeological Science* 20:121–57.

Roberts, Wayne D.
1987 Lithic artifacts. In *The Toqua Site: A Late Mississippian Dallas Village*, by Richard Polhemis, pp. 689–909. Report of Investigations no. 41. Department of Anthropology, University of Tennessee, Knoxville; Publications in Anthropology no. 44. Tennessee Valley Authority, Knoxville.

Rodd, Charles
[1715] 1928 Letter to a gentleman, May 8, 1715. In *Calendar of State Papers, Colonial Series, America and West Indies, August 1714–December 1715*, vol. 28, edited by C. Headlam, pp. 166–69. Public Record Office, London.

Rodning, Christopher B.
2002 Reconstructing the coalescence of Cherokee communities in southern Appalachia. In *The Transformation of the Southeastern Indians, 1540–1760*, edited by R. Ethridge and C. Hudson, pp. 155–76. University Press of Mississippi, Jackson.
2004 The Cherokee Town at Coweeta Creek. PhD dissertation, Department of Anthropology, University of North Carolina, Chapel Hill.
2007 Building and rebuilding Cherokee houses and townhouses in southwestern North Carolina. In *The Durable House: Architecture, Ancestors, and Origins*, edited by R. A. Beck, Jr., pp. 464–84. Occasional Paper 35. Center for Archaeological Investigations, Southern Illinois University, Carbondale.

Romenofsky, Ann F.
1987 *Vectors of Death*. University of New Mexico Press, Albuquerque.

Rothrock, Mary U.
1929 *Carolina Traders Among the Overhill Cherokees, 1690–1760*. Publication no. 1. East Tennessee Historical Society, Knoxville.

Rountree, Helen C.
2002 Trouble coming southward: Emanations through and from Virginia, 1607–1675. In *The Transformation of the Southeastern Indians, 1540–1760*, edited by R. Ethridge and C. Hudson, pp. 65–78. University Press of Mississippi, Jackson.

Rubertone, Patricia E.
2001 *Grave Undertakings: An Archaeology of Roger Williams and the Narragansett Indians*. Smithsonian Institution Press, Washington, D.C.

Rumrill, Donald A.
1991 The Mohawk glass trade bead chronology: ca. 1560–1785. *Beads* 3:5–46.

Russ, Kurt C., and Jefferson Chapman
1983 *Archaeological Investigations at the Eighteenth Century Overhill Cherokee Town of Mialoquo*. Report of Investigations 37. University of Tennessee, Department of Anthropology, Knoxville.

Scarry, C. Margaret
1993 Agricultural risk and the development of the Moundville chiefdom. In *Foraging and Farming in the Eastern Woodlands*, edited by C. Margaret Scarry, pp. 157–81. University Press of Florida, Gainesville.
2003 Patterns of wild plant utilization in the prehistoric Eastern Woodlands. In *People and Plants in Ancient Eastern North America*, edited by Paul E. Minnis, pp. 50–104. Smithsonian Books, Washington, D.C.

Scarry, John, F.
1995 Apalachee homesteads: The basal social and economic units of a Mississippian chiefdom. In *Mississippian Communities and Households*, edited by J. D. Rogers and B. D. Smith, pp. 201–23. University of Alabama Press, Tuscaloosa.

Schiffer, Michael B.
1972 Archaeological context and systemic context. *American Antiquity* 37:156–65.

Schopmeyer, C. S. (technical coordinator)
1974 *Seeds of Woody Plants in the United States*. Agriculture Handbook 450. U.S. Department of Agriculture, Forest Service, Washington, D.C.

Schroedl, Gerald F.
1986a *Overhill Cherokee Archaeology at Chota-Tanasee*. Report of Investigations 38. Department of Anthropology, University of Tennessee, Knoxville.
1986b Toward an explanation of Cherokee origins in east Tennessee. In *The Conference on Cherokee Prehistory*, compiled by D. G. Moore, pp. 122–38. Warren Wilson College, Swannanoa, North Carolina.
1989 Overhill Cherokee household and village patterns in the eighteenth century. In *Households and Communities*, edited by S. MacEachern, D. Archer, and R. Garvin, pp. 350–60. Archaeological Association of the University of Calgary, Proceedings of the Chacmool Conference 21, Calgary.
1994 *A Summary of Archaeological Studies Conducted at the Chattooga Site, Oconee County, South Carolina*. Report submitted to the United States Forest Service, Francis Marion and Sumter National Forests, South Carolina.
2000 Cherokee ethnohistory and archaeology from 1540 to 1838. In *Indians of the Greater Southeast: Historical Archaeology and Ethnohistory*, edited by B. G. McEwan, pp. 204–41. University Press of Florida, Gainesville.

Schroedl, Gerald F., and Emmanuel Breitburg
1986 Burials. In *Overhill Cherokee Archaeology at Chota-Tanasee*, edited by G. F. Schroedl, pp. 125–215. Report of Investigations 38. Department of Anthropology, University of Tennessee, Knoxville.

Setzler, Frank M., and Jessie D. Jennings
1941 *Peachtree Mound and Village Site, Cherokee County, North Carolina*. Bureau of American Ethnology Bulletin 131. Smithsonian Institution, Washington, D.C.

Shapiro, Gary
1984 Ceramic vessels, site permanence, and group size: A Mississippian example. *American Antiquity* 49:696–712.

Shennan, Stephen
1997 *Quantifying Archaeology*, 2nd ed. University of Iowa Press, Iowa City.

Shumate, M. Scott, Brett H. Riggs, and Larry R. Kimball
2005 *The Alarka Farmstead Site: The Archaeology of a Mid-Seventeenth-Century Cherokee Winter House/Summer House Complex, Swain County, North Carolina*. Report submitted to National Forests in North Carolina, Appalachian State University Laboratories of Archaeological Science, Boone.

Shumway, George
1985 English pattern trade rifles. In *Proceedings of the 1984 Trade Gun Conference,* edited by C. F. Hayes III and J. P. Puype, pp. 11–50. Research Records 18, Part II. Rochester Museum and Science Center, Rochester, New York.

Simmons, William S.
1970 *Cautantowwit's House: An Indian Burial Ground on the Island of Conanicut in Narragansett Bay*. Brown University Press, Providence, Rhode Island.

Sinclair, Anthony
2000 Constellations of knowledge: Human agency and material affordance in lithic technology. In *Agency in Archaeology*, edited by M. Dobres and J. E. Robb, pp. 196–212. Routledge, London.

Skowronek, Russell K.
1991 *Return to Peachtree: A Catalogue of Amateur Surface Collections from Cherokee and Clay Counties, North Carolina*. Report submitted to the North Carolina Department of Cultural Resources, Raleigh.

Smith, Betty A.
1979 Distribution of eighteenth-century Cherokee settlements. In *The Cherokee Indian Nation: A Troubled History*, edited by D. H. King, pp. 46–60. University of Tennessee Press, Knoxville.

Smith, Bruce D.
1995 The analysis of single-household Mississippian settlements. In *Mississippian Communities and Households*, edited by J. D. Rogers and B. D. Smith, pp. 224–49. University of Alabama Press, Tuscaloosa.

Smith, Bruce D., and C. Wesley Cowan
2003 Domesticated crop plants and the evolution of food production economies in eastern North America. In *People and Plants in Ancient Eastern North America*, edited by Paul E. Minnis, pp. 105–25. Smithsonian Books, Washington, D.C.

Smith, Marvin T.
1982 "Eye" beads in the Southeast. In *The Conference on Historic Site Archaeology Papers 1979*, vol. 14, pp. 116–27.
1983 Chronology from glass beads: The Spanish period in the Southeast, c. A.D. 1513–1670. In *Proceedings of the 1982 Glass Trade Bead Conference*, edited by C. F. Hayes III, pp. 147–58. Research Records 16. Rochester Museum and Science Center, Rochester, New York.
1987 *The Archaeology of Aboriginal Culture Change: Depopulation During the Early Historic Period*. University Press of Florida, Gainesville.
1991 Glass beads from Mount Pleasant. In *Ye Pleasant Mount: 1989 & 1990 Excavations*, edited by D. T. Elliot, pp. 120–26. Publication 11. LAMAR Institute, Watkinsville, Georgia.
1992 Glass beads from the council house at San Luis. *Florida Archaeology* 6:107–18.
2001 Glass beads from Charles Towne Landing (31Ch1a). In *Exploring 1670 Charles Towne (38Ch1a): Final Archaeology Report*, by M. J. Stoner and S. A. South, pp. 104–15. Research Manuscript Series no. 230. South Carolina Institute of Archaeology and Anthropology, Columbia.
2002a Aboriginal population movements in the postcontact Southeast. In *The Transformation of the Southeastern Indians, 1540–1760*, edited by R. Ethridge and C. Hudson, pp. 155–76. University Press of Mississippi, Jackson.
2002b Eighteenth-century glass beads in the French colonial trade. *Historical Archaeology* 36:55–61.
n.d. *European Artifacts from the Plum Grove Site, 40Wg17*. Manuscript on file, Department of Anthropology, Valdosta State University, Valdosta, Georgia.

Smith, Marvin T., and Mary E. Good
1982 *Early Sixteenth Century Glass Beads in the Spanish Colonial Trade*. Cottonlandia Museum Publications, Greenwood, Mississippi.

Smith, Marvin A., Mark Williams, Chester B. DePratter, Marshall Williams, and Mike Harmon
1988 *Archaeological Investigations at Tomassee (38OC186): A Lower Cherokee Town*. Research Manuscript Series 206. Institute of Archeology and Anthropology, University of South Carolina, Columbia.

Southworth, Scott, Art Schultz, and Danielle Denenny
2005 *Geologic Map of the Great Smoky Mountains National Park Region, Tennessee and North Carolina*. Open file report submitted to the National Park Service. http://pubs.usgs.gov/of/2005/1225/OF05_1225_report.pdf. Accessed July 12, 2008.

Steponaitis, Vincas P.
1983 *Ceramics, Chronology, and Community Patterns: An Archaeological Study at Moundville*. Academic Press, New York.

Stevenson, Marc G.
1982 Toward an understanding of site abandonment behavior: Evidence from historic mining camps in the southwest Yukon. *Journal of Anthropological Archaeology* 1:237–65.

Stewart, John
[1690] 1931 Letter to William Dunlop, April 27, 1690. *South Carolina Historical and Genealogical Magazine* 32(1):1–33.

Stone, Glenn Davis
1993 Agricultural abandonment: A comparative study of historical ecology. In *Abandonment of Settlements and Regions: Ethnoarchaeological and Archaeological Approaches,* edited by C. M. Cameron and S. A. Tomka, pp. 74–81. Cambridge University Press, Cambridge.

Stone, Lyle M.
1974 *Fort Michilimackinac, 1715–1781: An Archaeological Perspective on the Revolutionary Frontier.* Publications of the Museum Anthropological Series no. 2. Michigan State University, East Lansing.

Sullivan, Lynne P.
1989 Household, community, and society: An analysis of Mouse Creek settlements. In *Households and Communities*, edited by S. MacEachern, D. Archer, and R. Garvin, pp. 317–27. Archaeological Association of the University of Calgary, Proceedings of the Chacmool Conference 21, Calgary.
1995 Mississippian community and household organization in eastern Tennessee. In *Mississippian Communities and Households*, edited by J. D. Rogers and B. D. Smith, pp. 99–123. University of Alabama Press, Tuscaloosa.

Swanton, John R.
1930 The Kaskinampo Indians and their neighbors. *American Anthropologist* 32(3):405–18.
1946 *The Indians of the Southeastern United States*. Bureau of American Ethnology, Bulletin 137. Smithsonian Institution, Washington, D.C.
1998 *Early History of the Creek Indians and Their Neighbors*. University Press of Florida, Gainesville.

Sweat, Jeremy
2009 Lithic Resource Survey of the Upper Little River Drainage: Raw Material Availability and Use at the Townsed Sites. Master's thesis, University of Tennessee, Knoxville.

Talalay, Laurie, Donald R. Keller, and Patrick J. Munson
1984 Hickory nuts, walnuts, butternuts, and hazelnuts: Observations and experiments relevant to their aboriginal exploitation in eastern North America. In *Experiments and Observations on Aboriginal Wild Plant Food Utilization in Eastern North America*, edited by Patrick J. Munson, pp. 338–59. Prehistory Research Series 6(2). Indiana Historical Society, Indianapolis.

Thomas, Cyrus
1894 *Report on the Mound Explorations of the Bureau of Ethnology.* Bureau of Ethnology Annual Report 12:3–730. Smithsonian Institution, Washington, D.C.

Thornton, M., and J. Fee
2001 Rodent gnawing as a taphonomic agent: Implications for archaeology. In *People and Wildlife in North America: Essays in Honor of R. Dale Guthrie*, edited by S. C. Gerlach and M. S. Murray, pp. 300–306. BAR International Series 900, Oxford.

Timberlake, Henry
[1762] 2001 Memoirs. In *The Memoirs of Lieutenant Henry Timberlake*, edited by S. C. Williams, pp. 22–175. Mountain Press, Signal Mountain, Tennessee.

Tukey, John W.
1977 *Exploratory Data Analysis*. Addison-Wesley, Reading, Massachusetts.

Turbyfill, Charles O.
1927 *Work Done in Western North Carolina during the Summer of 1926*. Manuscript on file, Archives of the National Museum of the American Indian, Washington, D.C.

Turnbaugh, William A.
1984 *The Material Culture of RI 1000, a Mid-17th Century Burial Site in North Kingstown, Rhode Island*. University of Rhode Island Press, Kingston.

U.S. Department of Agriculture, Natural Resources Conservation Service
2004 *Plant Guide: Purple Passionflower*. National Plant Data Center. http://plants.usda.gov/plantguide/pdf/cs_pain6.pdf. Accessed December 2010.
2010 *The PLANTS Database*, Version 3.5. Data compiled from various sources by Mark W. Skinner. National Plant Data Center, Baton Rouge. http://plants.usda.gov. Accessed October 2008.

Ulmer, Mary, and Samuel E. Beck
1951 *Cherokee Cooklore: Preparing Cherokee Foods*. Museum of the Cherokee Indian, Mary and Goingback Chiltoskey, Cherokee, North Carolina.

Usner, Daniel, Jr.
1992 *Indians, Settlers, and Slaves in a Frontier Exchange Economy*. University of North Carolina Press, Chapel Hill.

VanDerwarker, Amber M., and Kandace R. Detwiler
2000 Plant and animal subsistence at the Coweeta Creek site, Macon County, North Carolina. *North Carolina Archaeology* 49:59–77.
2002 Gendered practice in Cherokee foodways: A spatial analysis of plant remains from the Coweeta Creek site. *Southeastern Archaeology* 21:21–28.

Varien, Mark D., and Barbara J. Mills
1997 Accumulation research: Problems and prospects. *Journal of Archaeological Method and Theory* 4:141–91.

Varien, Mark D., and James M. Potter
1997 Unpacking the discard equation: Simulating the accumulation of artifacts in the archaeological record. *American Antiquity* 62(2):194–213.

Varnod, Francis
[1721] 1971 A true and exact account of the number of names of all the towns belonging to the Cherrikee nation. In *The Ohio Valley in Colonial Days,* edited by B. Fernow, pp. 273–75. Burt Franklin, New York.

Vassar, Rena
1961 Some short remarkes on the Indian trade in the Charikees and in management thereof since the year 1717. *Ethnohistory* 8(4):401–23.

Velleman, Paul F., and David C. Hoaglin
1981 *Applications, Basics, and Computing of Exploratory Data Analysis*. Duxbury Press, North Scituate, Massachusetts.

Victoria and Albert Museum
1927 *A Picture Book of English Silver Spoons*. Victoria and Albert Museum, London.

Wagner, Gail E., and Jamie Civitello
2000 *Ancient Gardening in South Carolina, 10,000 B.C.–A.D. 1700*. http://www.cas.sc.edu/anth/gardening/ancientgardening.html#c. Accessed January 10, 2008.

Walker, Renee B.
1995 *Faunal Remains from the Chattooga Site (38Oc18), Oconee County, South Carolina*. Manuscript on file, Department of Anthropology, University of Tennessee, Knoxville.

Ward, H. Trawick
1985 Social implications of storage and disposal patterns. In *Structure and Process in Southeastern Archaeology*, edited by R. S. Dickens, Jr., and H. T. Ward, pp. 82–101. University of Alabama Press, Tuscaloosa.

Ward, H. Trawick, and R. P. Stephen Davis, Jr.
1991 The impact of Old World diseases on the native inhabitants of the North Carolina piedmont. *Archaeology of Eastern North America* 19:171–81.
1993 *Indian Communities on the North Carolina Piedmont, A.D. 1000 to 1700*. Monograph no. 2. Research Laboratories of Anthropology, University of North Carolina, Chapel Hill.
1999 *Time Before History: The Archaeology of North Carolina*. University of North Carolina Press, Chapel Hill.
2001 Tribes and traders: Contact and change on the North Carolina piedmont. In *Societies in Eclipse: Eastern North America at the Dawn of Civilization*, edited by D. Brose and R. Mainfort, pp. 125–42. Smithsonian Institution Press, Washington, D.C.

Warrick, Gary A.
1988 Estimating Ontario Iroquoian village duration. *Man in the Northeast* 36:21–60.

Waselkov, Gregory A.
1989 Seventeenth-century trade in the colonial Southeast. *Southeastern Archaeology* 8:117–33.
1990 Historic Creek architectural adaptations to the deerskin trade. In *Archaeological Excavations at the Early Historic Creek Indian Town of Fusihatchee (Phase 1, 1988–1989)*, by G. A. Waselkov, J. W. Cottier, and C. T. Sheldon, Jr., pp. 39–44. Report submitted to the National Science Foundation, Washington, D.C.
1993 Historic Creek Indian responses to European trade and the rise of political factions. In *Ethnohistory and Archaeology: Approaches to Postcontact Change in the Americas*, edited by J. D. Rogers and S. M. Wilson, pp. 123–31. Plenum Press, New York.
1994 The Macon trading house and early European-Indian contact in the colonial Southeast. In *Ocmulgee Archaeology, 1936–1986*, edited by D. J. Hally, pp. 190–96. University of Georgia Press, Athens.
1998 The eighteenth-century Anglo-Indian trade in southeastern North America. In *New Faces of the Fur Trade: Selected Papers from the Seventh North American Fur Trade Conference, Halifax, Nova Scotia, 1995*, edited by J. Fiske, S. Sleeper Smith, and W. Wicken, pp. 193–222. Michigan State University Press, East Lansing.

Watson, Patty Jo
1976 In pursuit of prehistoric subsistence: A comparative account of some contemporary flotation techniques. *Midcontinental Journal of Archaeology* 1(1):77–100.

Watson, Patty Jo, and Richard A. Yarnell
1966 Archaeological and paleoethnobotanical investigations in Salts Cave, Mammoth Cave National Park, Kentucky. *American Antiquity* 31(6):842–49.

Wells, Edward William, III
2006 Soapstone Vessel Chronology and Function in the Southern Appalachians of Eastern Tennessee. Master's thesis, University of Tennessee, Knoxville.

Wesson, Cameron B.
1999 Chiefly power and food storage in southeastern North America. *World Archaeology* 31:145–64.
2008 *Households and Hegemony: Early Creek Prestige Goods, Symbolic Capital, and Social Power*. University of Nebraska Press, Lincoln.

White, Theodore E.
1953 A method of calculating the dietary percentage of various food animals utilized by aboriginal peoples. *American Antiquity* 18:393–99.

Wilk, Richard R., and Robert M. Netting
1984 Households changing form and function. In *Households: Comparative and Historical Studies of the Domestic Group*, edited by R. McC. Netting, R. R. Wilk, and E. J. Arnould, pp. 1–28. University of California Press, Berkeley.

Wilk, Richard R., and William L. Rathje
1982 Household archaeology. *American Behavioral Scientist* 6:617–39.

Williams, Samuel C. (editor)
1928 *Early Travels in the Tennessee Country, 1540–1800*. Watauga Press, Johnson City, Tennessee.

Wilson, Gilbert Livingstone
1917 *Agriculture of the Hidatsa Indians: An Indian Interpretation*. Bulletin of the University of Minnesota, Studies in the Social Sciences, no. 9. University of Minnesota, Minneapolis. http://digital.library.upenn.edu/women/buffalo/garden/garden.html. Accessed January 10, 2008.

Wilson, Gregory D.
2005 Between Plaza and Palisade: Household and Community Organization at Early Moundville. PhD dissertation, Department of Anthropology, University of North Carolina, Chapel Hill.
2008 *The Archaeology of Everyday Life at Early Moundville*. University of Alabama Press, Tuscaloosa.

Wilson, Gregory D., and Christopher B. Rodning
2002 Boiling, baking, and pottery breaking: A functional analysis of ceramic vessels from Coweeta Creek. *Southeastern Archaeology* 21:29–35.

Wolf, Eric R.
1982 *Europe and the People without History*. University of California Press, Berkeley.

Wood, Peter H.
1989 The changing population of the colonial South: An overview by race and region, 1685–1790. In *Powhatan's Mantle: Indians in the Colonial Southeast,* edited by P. H. Wood, G. A. Waselkov, and M. T. Hatley, pp. 35–103. University of Nebraska Press, Lincoln.

Woodward, Henry
[1674] 1911 A faithful relation of my Westoe voyage. In *Narratives of Early Carolina, 1650–1708*, edited by A. S. Salley, Jr., pp. 125–34. Charles Scribner's Sons, New York.

Worth, John E.
1995 *The Struggle for the Georgia Coast: An Eighteenth-Century Spanish Retrospective on Guale and Mocama*. Anthropological Papers no. 75. American Museum of Natural History, New York.
2006 Bridging prehistory and history in the Southeast: Evaluating the utility of the acculturation concept. In *Light on the Path: The Anthropology and History of the Southeastern Indians*, edited by T. J. Pluckhahn and R. Ethridge, pp. 196–206. University of Alabama Press, Tuscaloosa.

Wray, Charles F.
1983 Seneca glass trade beads, c. A.D. 1550–1820. In *Proceedings of the 1982 Glass Trade Bead Conference*, edited by C. F. Hayes III, pp. 41–50. Research Records 16. Rochester Museum and Science Center, Rochester, New York.

Yanovsky, Elias
1936 *Food Plants of the North American Indians*. U.S. Department of Agriculture Miscellaneous Publication no. 237. Washington, D.C.

Yarnell, Richard A.
1982 Problems of interpretation of archaeological plant remains of the Eastern Woodlands. *Southeastern Archaeology* 1(1):1–7.
1993 The importance of native crops during the Late Archaic and Woodland periods. In *Foraging and Farming in the Eastern Woodlands*, edited by C. Margaret Scarry, pp. 13–26. University Press of Florida, Gainesville.

Yarnell, Richard A., and M. Jean Black
1985 Temporal trends indicated by a survey of Archaic and Woodland plant food remains from southeastern North America. *Southeastern Archaeology* 4(2):93–106.